WORLD
PHILOSOPHY

WORLD PHILOSOPHY

An Exploration in Words and Images

CONSULTANT EDITOR
David Appelbaum B.A., M.A., PH.D.

GENERAL EDITOR
Mel Thompson B.D., M.PHIL., PH.D., A.K.C.

'Philosophy, beginning in wonder, as Plato and Aristotle said, is able to fancy everything different from what it is. It sees the familiar as if it were strange, and the strange as if it were familiar. It can take things up and lay them down again. Its mind is full of air that plays round every subject. It rouses us from our native dogmatic slumber and breaks up our caked prejudices. Historically it has always been a sort of fecundation of four different human interests, science, poetry, religion and logic, by one another. It has sought by hard reasoning for results emotionally valuable. To have some contact with it, to catch its influence, is thus good for both literary and scientific students. By its poetry it appeals to literary minds; but its logic stiffens them up and remedies their softness. By its logic it appeals to the scientific; but softens them by its other aspects, and saves them from too dry a technicality. Both types of student ought to get from philosophy a livelier spirit, more air, more mental background.'

from *Some Problems of Philosophy* by William James, written in the final months before his death in 1910, and unfinished.

Philosophy opens up new perspectives. Perhaps the physical insignificance of human life and society, set in the context of the known universe, is easier to appreciate for those living in the village of Lauterbrunnen, tucked deep within its Alpine valley, dwarfed by the cliffs and surrounding peaks of the Bernese Oberland. But should that lead to existential despair, or to a sense of wonder?

ISBN 1-84333-613-8

A catalogue record for this book is available
from the British Library

First published in 2002 by

Vega
64 Brewery Road
London, N7 9NT

A member of **Chrysalis** Books plc

Visit our website at www.chrysalisbooks.co.uk

Printed and bound in China

Designed by Andrew Sutterby
Production by Susan Sutterby
Jacket Photograph by Adam Jones

CONTENTS

CONTRIBUTORS

CONSULTANT EDITOR

David Appelbaum

David Appelbaum is Professor of Philosophy at State University New York and editor of *Parabola* magazine.

His publications include *The Heart of Delay* (SUNY Press), in press; *The Vision of Hume* and *The Vision of Kant* (Element books, 1993, 1995); *The Stop* (SUNY Press, 1995); *Everyday Spirits* (SUNY Press, 1993) and *Real Philosophy* with Jacob Needleman, (Arkana, 1990).

GENERAL EDITOR

Mel Thompson

Mel Thompson is a freelance writer and editor. He is the author of over 25 titles, including *Ethics*, *Philosophy*, *The Philosophy of Religion*, *Eastern Philosophy*, *The Philosophy of Science* and *The Philosophy of Mind* in the 'Teach Yourself' series, and *Ethical Theory* and *Religion and Science* in Hodder & Stoughton's 'Access to Philosophy' series.

COPY EDITOR

The contributions have been edited, and embellished with additional biographical and background information, by **Nigel Rodgers**, an experienced writer and editor, with a special interest in Philosophy, History and the History of Art.

His own recent works include biographies of *Hitler* and *Churchill*, published by Hodder & Stoughton.

Martin Bentham

Having trained initially as a painter at Cheltenham College of Art, and taken an MA in Art Theory at Bath, Martin Bentham is currently doing research in Aesthetics at the University of Warwick.

His particular interest is in the work of the influential American art critic Clement Greenberg and his legacy. He is also preparing material for an introductory book on The Philosophy of Art for a UK educational publisher and is author of *Picasso* (Hodder & Stoughton, 2002).

Alexander Bird

Alexander Bird lectures in the philosophy of science and mathematics at the University of Edinburgh. He has been Visiting Professor at Dartmouth College, New Hampshire four times and has also lectured at Caen and Siena Universities.

His book *Philosophy of Science* was published in 1998 by UCL Press. His interests include the history of science, rowing and contemporary classical music.

Linda Edwards

Linda Edwards (née Smith) was formerly lecturer in Religious Education at King's College London. Since 1998 she has worked freelance as an Adlerian counsellor, writer and part-time lecturer in Theology and Religious Studies at Trinity College, Carmarthen, Wales.

She is the author of several well-known text books for schools and colleges including, co-authorship of *A Beginner's Guide to Ideas* (Lion Publishing, 1991), an extended edition of which was published in 1999 by Zondervan in the USA. Her latest book is *A Brief Guide to Beliefs: ideas, theologies, mysteries and movements* published by Westminster John Knox Press (2001).

Andrew Harrison

Andrew Harrison is Reader in the Philosophy of Art at the University of Bristol.

His publications include: *Making and thinking, a study of intelligent activities* (Harvester, Hassocks/ Hackett, 1978); *Philosophy and the Visual arts: seeing and abstracting* (ed.) Reidel (Dordrecht, 1987); *Philosophy and the arts: seeing and believing,* (Thoemmes Press, Bristol, 1997); 'Representation and conceptual change' in Vesey (ed.) *Philosophy and the Arts* , Royal Institute of Philosophy Lectures, 1973; 'A Minimal syntax for the pictorial' in Kemal and Gaskell (ed.) *The Language of Art History* (Cambridge University Press, 1991); 'Style', 'Genre' in Cooper (ed.) *A Companion to Aesthetics* (Blackwells, Oxford, 1992); 'Medium' in Kelly (ed.) *Encyclopaedia of Aesthetics* (Oxford University Press, 1998); 'Realism and representation: Pictures, models and theories' in *Visual Representation and Interpretations* Paton and Neilson (ed.) (Springer, London, 1999).

Eugene Heath

Eugene Heath is Associate Professor of Philosophy at the State University of New York at New Paltz.

The author of several essays on 18th-century British moral philosophy and political philosophy, he has recently published a text on business ethics, *Morality and the Market: Ethics and Virtue in the Conduct of Business* (McGraw-Hill, 2002).

Paul Helm

Paul Helm was Professor of the History and Philosophy of Religion, King's College London 1993-2000. He currently holds the J I Packer Chair of Philosophical Theology at Regent College, Vancouver.

Among his books are *Eternal God* (1988), *The Providence of God* (1993), *Belief Policies* (1994), *Faith and Understanding*, (Edinburgh University Press, 1997) and *Faith with Reason* (2000). He is the editor of *Faith and Reason* (OUP, 1999) and *Referring to God* (1999). His latest book, *John Calvin's Ideas*, is forthcoming (OUP).

Caroline Ogden

Following a career in the theatre, a First Class Honours degree in Philosophy, with Linguistics and Religious Studies, and an MA with Distinction in Sociolinguistics, Caroline Ogden is now a freelance writer with a special interest in Gaelic language and culture.

Author of *God: A Beginner's Guide* (Hodder & Stoughton, 1999), she is currently working on a study of themes in *The Lord of the Rings*.

John Peacock

John Peacock has taught Indian philosophy at the University of Warwick and contemporary French and German thought at the University of Manchester and Bolton Institute of Higher Education. At the time of writing for this project, he was also teaching Buddhist thought and Indian religions in the Theology and Religious Studies department of the University of Bristol.

He has published a number of journal articles on both Indian and contemporary western thought and is currently working on a book on Indian aesthetics entitled *Art and Freedom*.

Krishnamurthi Ravishankar

Krishnamurthi Ravishankar is an Associate Professor of Mathematics at State University New York, New Paltz.

He has made research contributions to the areas of Statistical Mechanics and Probability Theory. His interests outside of Mathematics include Philosophy of Science, Theories of Knowledge, and more recently, Connections between Science, Theories of Nature, Ecology, and Economic Development.

David Rothenberg

Philosopher and musician David Rothenberg is Associate Professor of Philosophy at the New Jersey Institute of Technology.

He is the author of *Sudden Music: Improvisation, Art, Nature* (Georgia, 2002), *Blue Cliff Record: Zen Echoes* (Codhill Press, 2001), *Hand's End: Technology and the Limits of Nature* (California, 1993), *Is It Painful to Think? Conversations with Arne Naess* (Minnesota, 1992), and many edited anthologies, including *The Book of Music and Nature* (Wesleyan, 2001), and *Parliament of Minds* (SUNY Press, 1999), interviews with leading philosophers in conjunction with the PBS series of the same name, of which he was a co-producer.

Martin Stone

Martin Stone is Lecturer in the Philosophy of Religion at King's College, London.

His publications include: 'Philosophy of Religion' in *Philosophy* (ed.) A.C.Grayling (Oxford, Oxford University Press, 1998), and is currently joint editor of a series of books for Routledge, including *Humanism and Early Modern Philosophy* and *The Proper Ambition of Science*.

Veronica Voiels

Veronica Voiels is Senior lecturer in Religious Studies and Religious Education at Manchester Metropolitan University, and is involved in courses for teachers at the Womens University of Bombay and the education depatment of the University of Delhi, in India.

She specializes in teaching about Hinduism and Buddhism in primary and secondary schools, and has been a principal examiner in World Religions at A level in Great Britain for many years.

She is author of a major school textbook, *Hinduism: a new approach* (Hodder & Stoughton, 1998), and has contributed various articles and chapters on social, moral and spiritual development in education.

Denis Walsh

D M Walsh is lecturer in Philosophy at the University of Edinburgh. He received a PhD in biology from McGill University, Montreal and a PhD in philosophy from King's College London.

His interests are philosophy of biology, philosophy of mind, philosophical logic and metaphysics. He is currently working on a project on the nature of teleological explanation in psychology and biology.

Ann Whiteside

Ann Whiteside is a former lecturer in fine art at a College of Further Education in Nottingham, with a special interest in eastern iconography, and is currently working as a freelance editor.

FOREWORD
PROFESSOR DAVID APPELBAUM

Philosophy is a riddle. Ask what it is and you will be answered by another question: why do you wish to know?

In an impatient age, we easily dismiss the reply as playful, mocking, obscure, or indirect. To question the question brings an unsettled feeling. It drives the questioner backward, toward a dark region. In this backward movement, there waits the fundamental experience, the datum, of philosophy. We meet an unknown 'something' that, looking back, riddles us. Philosophy is born.

Stumped by a question, a philosopher labours under a sense of wonder and awe. Socrates, the archetype philosopher of our Western tradition, often speaks of philosophy as a birth process. But the image he uses contains many surprises. We are not only the one who brings a new life into the world. We also are an attendant – a midwife – to the event. And we are that new life itself.

A new life is a new set of thoughts, attitudes, and responses to the world inside and around us. That philosophy brings new life, is attested to by countless individuals who, like Epictetus, Boethius, Gandhi, and the legendary King Chou of the I Ching, discover that prison (actual or existential) does not limit their thought. Philosophy sets the mind free to question the question. The only possible human freedom for philosophers follows from that.

The function of the midwife is to prepare the way and stay on hand for emergencies. The midwife has, as Socrates knew (since his mother was one), tools of the trade. Philosophy also has tools. They let us discard assumptions, faulty logic, bad data, and exaggerated attitudes about our own capacities. By continued use, we learn about the tools—and the process they facilitate.

Much of philosophical discipline involves acquaintance with argument, principle, terminology, and position – some of the tools.

Although there is a danger in mistaking the tool for the task, if we continue to practice, our relation to the riddle shifts. New respect for its unsolvability appears. We look less for a solution and more at how the process works on us. As we grow less prone to accept certainties and more tolerant of complexity, the on-going nature of new thought becomes more apparent. We become caught up in a search.

Different traditions distinguish between the philosopher and sage, or in the Buddhist tradition, the *bikkhu* and the *arhat*. The sage possesses all-inclusive wisdom. The sage knows what a human being is and the place of humanity in the universe. A sage has accomplished the task of becoming human and can respond, as Aristotle puts it, like unto the divine.

For the philosopher, it is otherwise. The philosopher practices wisdom but is not yet wise. Because, as Plato writes, the philosopher 'loves the sight of the truth,' philosophy is more like exercise, endless pursuit, and consistent exertion than attainment of a goal.

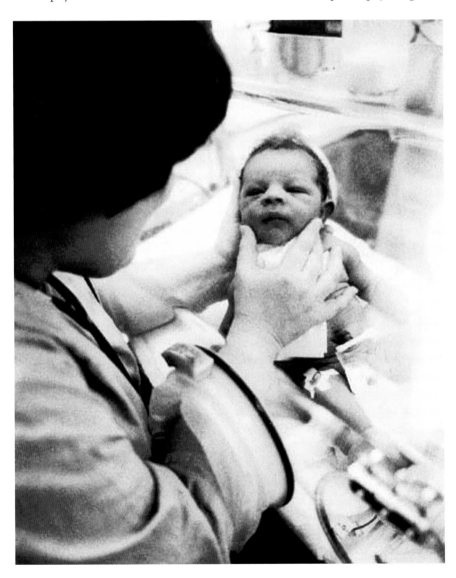

Philosophy is like a birth process, bringing about the new life of thoughts, attitudes and responses to the world around us.

There is but one ultimate goal and perspective.

To philosophize is to be on the way. Although we hunger for sagacity, one thing needs to be kept in mind. If the riddle is prematurely answered, its mysterious challenge ceases. Our human stature is diminished.

Philosophy as activity is one thing; philosophy as discourse, another. The second is the record or trace of the first, which is open-ended, fluid, and unresolved. Discourse is important in the same way tracks are. Both let us follow our prey, and in the case of philosophy, learn through the intelligence of thinkers before us.

Whether we discard or pursue their example, their approaches are guideposts. They show what to look for and how to proceed. With their maps, we are less likely to get lost in the unknown terrain we explore.

But we are good students of their texts only when we remember that ultimately we seek our own understanding.

By its nature, philosophical activity aims for the whole picture. Why things are, what they are, how they are, and that they are: these questions push beyond limit and boundary. This is the reason that philosophy is a global phenome-non. Even though the word philosophy comes from the Greek and means 'love of wisdom', it has its Eastern counterpart in the Sanskrit *darsana*. Practice and expression differ according to history and point of view. But just as different family members are bound by resemblance, so the different philosophies comprise a single family. This book reflects this overall unity, and presents philosophy as a world event.

A whole is made up of parts; there is diversity in unity. Since ancient times and in many traditions, philosophical discourse has been divided into areas. There are texts that ask, 'What is there?', 'What is real?' others ask, 'How can we know what is true?', and others, 'How can we live rightly in accordance with what there is?' That is, 'How can we care for our souls?'

These areas – metaphysics, epistemology or logic, and ethics – are interrelated, and have different weights in different systems of thought. The differences are important. They make up a great portion of the argument between various philosophical points of view. In world philosophy, it is especially important to respect variation.

Some schools of thought place ethics first, others, metaphysics, and still others, logic or epistemology. For instance, the Stoic would give priority to Arguna's question in the *Bhagavad Gita*: 'What makes a person commit evil against his own will as if impelled by force?'

But other schools believe that ethical concerns follow only from a correct view of reality, and that metaphysics comes first. Aristotle before and Immanuel Kant after, echo an ancient Buddhist text that asks, 'Is form permanent or transient?'

Still other schools argue that we cannot know what to do until we understand what really is. We first need confidence in our knowledge of reality. Do our minds import subjective biases into the picture of things, as Lao Tzu, the Sceptics, and David Hume suggest? This view gives top priority to logical or epistemological questions.

What does this prevalence of difference and variation imply? Here too the philosopher would step back and question the question. Is difference viewed as a failure to come to agreement and therefore proof that thought is relative to the thinker or school? Or is it an accomplishment of diversity and so evidence of a rich, abundant truth?

'In the beginning was the Word...' Humankind, faced with the wonder of nature, has always sought in it a sense of purpose or design – whether the Logos, or Dharma, or Tao, or Torah or Shari'ah.

Each major area of philosophy breaks down into more specialized disciplines. Questions of value include not only ethics but also philosophy of religion, philosophy of law and politics, and philosophy of art. Questions of reality include not only metaphysics but also philosophy of science. Questions of knowledge also include logic, philosophy of mind, philosophy of history, and philosophy of education.

To enter into the work of philosophy, whether as practice or as discourse, one must respect the elements of the discipline. There are four elements, and they have been evolving throughout the millennia. It is unnatural to think them fixed and defined for all times. They are: question, theme, argument, and term. Different thinkers (or even the same thinker at different points) will emphasize one or the other. Schools and traditions also will make different uses of the elements.

First, a **term** is a word or concept that emphatically needs to be clear. Terms like thought, cause, good, order, God, origin, and meaning are examples of words that different philosophers have tried to clarify. Just as notes are the medium of communication for music, words are the medium of philosophy. One's personal views often hinge on unexamined notions about what words mean.

The discipline of discovering what a word actually means, rather than what one believes it to mean, can dissipate the force of a private position. A greater sensitivity to the idea already contained in a word, opens thought to hidden relations and secret implications. Conversely, being dogmatic about a meaning that is strictly one's own, closes one to the conversation that is central to philosophy.

Second, there are **arguments**. Some well-known arguments include those for the existence of God and of the external world.

Others are the argument against scepticism and the argument that it is better to suffer than to do evil. An argument is a carefully designed series of thoughts, which arrives at a definite conclusion.

The study of argument goes back to ancient times, to Aristotle in the West, and to the classical Grammarians of Hindu thought. The study of argument, known as logic, comes from the Greek word *logos* – a concept central to the thought of Heraclitus and of the Stoics. For them, *logos* was the rational principle underlying all reality, akin to the *Tao* of classical Chinese thought, or the *Brahman* of the Indian Upanishads. Though our view of logic is more restricted, many positions can be undermined by sound logic. The rules of argument can point the way to a refinement that moves us closer to the doorway into philosophy.

Third, there are **themes**. Some themes that have organized this Foreword are those of search, practice (praxis), and global diversification. Other themes have been alluded to, for instance, the theme of insight, of clarity, and of the self. Themes are parts of philosophical discourse, the way melodies are of music. Melodies differ from strings of notes flung together, and a good musician discerns when sounds form a melody and not an ill-sounding cluster. A philosopher too discerns when a cluster of thoughts is a theme and not the ramblings of an unschooled mind.

Many themes come with a long tradition of reflection already behind them, like the theme of the origin of things or of the first principle. Other themes are recent discoveries like that of evolution or of other minds.

Last come the **questions**. Questions are the primary instruments of doing philosophical work. What a question is, is a good question. Surely, not every sentence that is followed by a question mark is a true question. A true quest involves setting out to cross an unknown terrain for the sake of some goal. Similarly, a true question is guided in this crossing by a love of the truth. The nature of the guide – truth, discernment, or knowledge – is a subject of the most provoking and fundamental question. 'What is truth?' as asked of a Socrates, Jesus, or Buddha, is the occasion for giving the core lesson of the teaching. Everything else follows from it.

'Philosophy … is something intermediate between theology and science.'

Bertrand Russell, *History of Western Philosophy*, 1946

Philosophy is a living thing; its concepts are nourished and grow, putting out fresh shoots in each new context. Approaching philosophy as though it were an organized filing system, with facts guaranteed to fit neatly into each other, can only lead to frustration. We do not think in structured propositions of uniform length, but in concepts that touch one another, interact and breed. We see one thing and are reminded of another; we may have an intuition long before we can articulate or justify it. Philosophy is organic, always changing and responding to its cultural environment. It is a fascinating jungle, through which one moves with caution.

HOW TO USE THIS BOOK

USING THE ILLUSTRATIONS

Philosophy is a matter of careful, logical thought; arguments are presented and analysed; evidence is assessed. Philosophy deals with words, ideas, concepts. It works through debate and argument. It seeks to define meaning and show what may reasonably be accepted as true. It may be discussed or written, but how can it be illustrated? How can a photograph or work of art contribute to a rational argument?

Much of the language used to describe intellectual understanding is related to the visual: we 'see the point' or gain 'enlightenment', we have a 'new perspective' on a problem or 'perceive' what someone is trying to say. That link between language and vision is not accidental. Hence the value of images, for an image may suggest more than a literal description of its subject matter.

Looking at an image involves far more than receiving a visual stimulus. Things are seen 'as' something, suggest a whole range of concepts, stir memory and evoke a response. An image may suggest something of its underlying reality.

Philosophy often takes what is familiar and explores it in ways that give us a new perspective. Visually, too, we need to be prepared to look again, to appreciate the significance of a fresh angle, or an unusual combination of images. To many people, the world is sadly ordinary, to the philosopher, the same world may be extraordinary, just as the artist or photographer tries to capture the essence of a subject by looking at it anew.

Concepts and intuitions are particularly embodied in works of art – music, architecture, the visual arts, drama. If it were not so, art would be meaningless. Illustration is therefore not alien to the world of philosophy, for although the process of philosophizing involves concepts and arguments, those concepts reflect and are reflected in images, visual or otherwise.

Philosophy takes place within a particular era and culture. The questions with which it deals, the concepts it uses, even the way in which it is transmitted, depends on that cultural matrix.

To know people well, you need to see them at home, in the environment that has formed them or which they themselves have helped to shape. You also need to get a feeling for the world in which they have grown up and the language that has shaped their thoughts. Similarly, the culture within which a particular argument or approach to philosophy has developed provides visual clues to the hopes and fears of its people and their view of the world and the place of humankind within it. Cultural artefacts can therefore be valuable as aids to interpreting the concerns and concepts that arose among and were important to the people of that time and place. So within this book we shall find images that give the context for the ideas that are presented.

Images do not explain, they evoke. What you see, depends to a large extent on your willingness to enter imaginatively into the world of the artist or the photographer. Above all, the visual medium is one which offers perspective. We see an object as familiar, because we perceive it in a familiar way. From a different angle, or at a different magnification, it might appear startlingly different. Reality is in the relationship of perceiver and perceived. There is no single, definitive, or objective way of looking. We see what we choose to see.

As you read philosophy, be prepared to have your perspectives challenged, for within the scope of world philosophy there are few assertions that have not been questioned by one thinker or another. Philosophy is not a two dimensional experience: concepts lie one behind another in a three dimensional pattern. As you move from idea to idea, thinker to thinker, back and forth across eras and cultures, your perspective on an issue may not simply be changed, but may become enriched and multifaceted.

BRANCHES OF PHILOSOPHY

The central questions of philosophy have been explored over and over again, each generation of philosophers contributing something new as they re-examine earlier traditions.

Hence, the usual way to approach philosophy is through the main subjects that it explores, for example The Philosophy of Science, The Philosophy of Art, or The Philosophy of Religion. But there are also fundamental questions about what we can know, how we gain knowledge, and how we can demonstrate that beliefs are true or false. These questions underlie all branches of philosophy, and are generally considered under the headings of metaphysics (general questions about the nature of reality) and epistemology (the theory of knowledge).

The range of questions and issues to be explored is set out on page 15.

HOW TO EXPLORE . . .

. . . a Branch of Philosophy

Each of the main branches of philosophy is presented within a single chapter of this book. Where appropriate there are sections on Eastern as well as Western thought. Each chapter outlines the key issues and introduces the contributions of the principal philosophers. Generally, material dealing with a particular topic is set out in chronological sequence, to show the development of the key questions through successive historical periods.

. . . a particular thinker

For each of the principal philosophers there is a general information box, giving brief biographical details, a note of his or her most important writings and contribution to philosophy.

But the great philosophers have important things to say about a wide variety of questions. Thus, for example, Aristotle contributes to the theory of knowledge, to ethics, to religion, to art, to science, to logic and to politics. These contributions are found in their relevant chapters, but they are listed in the cross reference boxes, as well as in the index. Thus one can see each philosopher's contribution to the ongoing debates within the different branches of philosophy.

. . . an historical period or culture

On pages 16 to 21, each of the historical periods and cultures is set out with a note of the key issues of concern at that time and a list of some of the major philosophers. At a glance, it is possible to be reminded of the scope of philosophy at that time, before choosing to follow up on relevant individual thinkers and the main questions with which they were concerned.

. . . a general overview

Page 15 gives an overview of the world of philosophy, with each of the principal areas of philosophy and the key questions to be considered within it.

FLEXIBILITY

This exploration of world philosophy has been designed for maximum flexibility of use. All thinkers and issues are cross referenced, enabling the reader to move within or across branches of philosophy and historical periods, to get either a broad overview of the whole world of philosophy, or a more detailed exploration of a particular thinker or approach. The wide variety of styles and illustrations reflects the rich diversity within philosophy itself.

This is not a book to read from cover to cover, it is one through which one can move from concept to concept, image to image, in creative interaction with the world's great thinkers.

THE WORLD OF PHILOSOPHY

Philosophy explores a whole range of questions, which may be arranged according to the subject matter into which they are probing. Each of the resulting divisions forms a branch of philosophy, and this book is arranged in chapters, each of which examines one of these major branches.

However, it soon becomes clear that these branches cannot operate in isolation from one another: a study of the fundamental nature of reality leads into questions about religion or science; political philosophy has implications for ethics, and vice versa; the philosophy of mind is linked to many other branches, as is the philosophy of language. These fascinating links between arguments and approaches may be explored through the many cross-references.

The branches of philosophy to be explored here are set out opposite, along with the key questions with which they are concerned:

There is a saying of Dr Johnson that 'He who is tired of London is tired of life' and the same could be said of New York or any other great city. It could also to be said of philosophy, for philosophy is the examination of the fundamental questions concerning our life in all its many aspects.

KNOWLEDGE AND REALITY

What can I know and how can I know it?
Of what can I be certain?
How can I justify my beliefs?
What are the fundamental principles of reality?
Does knowledge start with thought or with experience?

These are absolutely basic questions for philosophy, and many other issues relate back to them. They are generally considered under the headings of epistemology (the theory of knowledge) and metaphysics (the nature of reality).

ETHICS

What does it mean to say that something is right or wrong?
Are there absolute moral principles?
Should actions be judged according to their consequences?
Is it possible to define the word 'good'?
Are we motivated primarily by reason or by emotion?
Am I ever completely free to choose what to do?

THE PHILOSOPHY OF SCIENCE

What counts as science?
How are its claims justified?
What problems are raised by the modern scientific world view?
To what extent can reality be determined by our observation of it?
How does science make progress?

THE PHILOSOPHY OF MIND

What is the mind, and how is it related to the body?
How do I know other minds?
Can machines think?
Are there limits to the possibilities of artificial intelligence?
Is consciousness individual, or part of something cosmic?

THE PHILOSOPHY OF RELIGION

Does God exist?
Why do people suffer?
Are miracles possible?
What is the nature of religious experience?
Does human life have a goal?
How does religion relate to science?
Is religious faith reasonable?

LOGIC

How can we show the steps by which we move from premises to conclusions?
How do we know that an argument is sound?

THE PHILOSOPHY OF LANGUAGE

How do we understand the meaning of the words we use?
What is the function of language?
By what criteria do we assess the truth of statements?
Does language describe reality or create it?
Can a riddle, like a Zen koan, induce insight?

THE PHILOSOPHY OF EDUCATION

What is the purpose of education?
How is education related to culture and to politics?
Should education be centred on the individual, or organized for the benefit of society?
Which takes priority in education, personal experience or received tradition?

THE PHILOSOPHY OF ART

What is beauty?
How can we define 'art'?
What is the function of the artist?
How do we understand the creative process?
How does fiction relate to non-fiction?
How does art relate to religion in Eastern thought?

THE PHILOSOPHY OF HISTORY

Can we be certain about past events?
Is all history a matter of interpretation?
How should we understand the passing of time?
Can we ever be free from our history, as individuals or as a society?

THE PHILOSOPHY OF LAW AND POLITICS

What is justice?
What is the purpose of law?
Upon what principles should societies be established?
How should political power be exercised?
How should we understand individual rights and freedoms?

ERAS AND CULTURES

Although this particular book is arranged according to the subject matter of philosophy, it is equally possible to explore philosophy from the perspective of a particular era or culture.

Much Anglo-American and European philosophy, which is now global in terms of the world community of those who practice as academic philosophers, has its roots in Ancient Greece. The history of Western thought may be divided into Ancient Greece and Rome, The Medieval and Renaissance Period, The Modern Era, and The Twentieth Century. There are also

the distinctive contributions of Muslim and Jewish philosophers.

These are not in any way hard and fast divisions in philosophy, merely convenient ways of categorizing a vast body of work.

Another tradition of philosophy, covering many of the same areas of enquiry, but coming at them with rather different cultural and religious assumptions, stems from the Indian sub-continent, and includes the Hindu, Buddhist and Jain traditions of philosophy and religion that are now found world-wide.

A third source of philosophy is China, with its Confucian and Taoist traditions, later blending with Mahayana Buddhism to form the broad tradition of Far Eastern philosophy of the Chinese and Japanese cultures.

The following pages set out some of the principal thinkers who wrote from within each particular era or culture. They also give an indication of some of the key issues of concern to the philosophers of each time or culture.

Key themes:
Hindu thought displays a blending of many different strains of philosophy.

It is particularly concerned with religious issues, the nature of the self, the cause of human suffering and the place of the individual in the universe.

Buddhist and Jain philosophies approach the same issues, but reaching very different conclusions from those of mainstream Hindu philosophy.

Philosophy is particularly related to the overall aim of spiritual development and personal salvation.

INDIAN PHILOSOPHIES

Key thinkers and schools:

THE PHILOSOPHIES OF THE FAR EAST

Key thinkers:

Key themes:

A blending of Confucian, Taoist and Buddhist traditions provides a rich mixture of concepts.

It is particularly concerned with the nature of social tradition on the one hand, and the natural process of change on the other.

Philosophy is seen as very much 'this worldly' – giving sound advice for living the good life.

The 20th century saw the influence of Western thought, particularly that of Marx (through Mao Tse Tung) in China and in Japan, where there has been an exploration of how Eastern concepts might be expressed in Western terminology.

OTHER SOURCES OF PHILOSOPHY

There are, of course, other sources of philosophy that could have been included, for example African thought, or the ideas of the Native American peoples. There are also religions and cultures of historical interest, whose legacy in terms of philosophy, mythology and religion, is extensive. One might explore the philosophical implications of beliefs held in Ancient Egypt, or Mesopotamia. The whole world of ancient mythology is not irrelevant to the rise of philosophy, especially in terms of its implied theories of reality.

These have not been included, however. The reason for this, quite apart from the natural limitations on space within a single-volume work, is that they contribute less directly to mainstream philosophy as it is presently practised as an intellectual discipline.

On the other hand, it is to be hoped that those interested in these other sources of ideas will find that the discipline of philosophy, as explored here, will prove a valuable tool for examinining such beliefs, and a useful perspective for evaluating their relevance.

ANCIENT GREECE AND ROME

Key Thinkers:

Key themes:

This period has set the agenda for almost all subsequent Western philosophy.

Fundamental questions were raised in metaphysics, the theory of knowledge, and in the concepts of justice, goodness and the nature of the good life.

The Pre-Socratics questioned the nature of physical reality seeking some overall explanation, precursors of modern science.

Important steps were taken in mathematics and logic.

This period provided many of the concepts within which the emerging Christian religion was to express itself.

THE MEDIEVAL PERIOD AND THE RENAISSANCE

Key thinkers:

Key themes:

Christian doctrines, during the first centuries CE, were explored and explained using Greek concepts.

There were distinctive contributions during this period from both Jewish and Muslim philosophers.

With the rediscovery and translation of the writings of Aristotle in the 13th century, Aquinas uses them to take a systematic approach to philosophy of religion.

With the Renaissance, there is a resurgence of philosophy and humanist views.

Key thinking here paved the way for the rise of science, and a re-examination of the great authoritarian systems of Church and State.

THE 'MODERN' ERA

Key Thinkers:

Key themes:

The quest for certainty and questions about how we acquire knowledge (epistemology), form the background to a whole range of issues.

Empiricist philosophy accompanies the rise of modern science.

Great rationalist systems of thought are developed by Kant and Hegel.

There is an examination of the basis of political life, leading to the fundamental principles of modern democracy. Hegelian ideas influence the development of Marx' view of the process of social and political change.

The basis of religion is explored and its authority challenged.

Utilitarian and other ethical theories are developed.

THE TWENTIETH CENTURY

Note: Philsophers marked with a *, although writing mainly in the 19th century, are considered here, since their work was of seminal importance for 20th century philosophy.

Key themes:

The earlier part of the century was dominated by questions of linguistic philosophy. There followed a broadening of approaches to language, and developments in all spheres of philosophy, particularly applied ethics and the political philosophy.

This was also the century whose traumas highlighted religious dilemmas that had been raised by earlier thinkers.

The middle years of the century saw the rise of existentialism. There were important advances in the philosophy of science, in mathematics and in logic.

In the spheres of art and language (among others), there is a new self-consciousness, giving rise to modernism, followed by postmodernist developments.

The 20th century also saw the rise of global communication, and with it a blending of cultures and philosophies. We find Japanese philosophers using Western ideas, and Western philosophers dealing with the philosophies of Ancient India.

What can we know and **how** can we know it? These are the crucial questions that philosophers have been asking themselves ever since the time of the Ancient Greeks. *Epistemology* is the term used for the branch of philosophy concerned with knowledge. It asks three fundamental questions:

- **How can we know?**
- **How much can we know?**
- **How can we be certain that what we know is correct?**

Closely linked to Epistemology is *Metaphysics*, which is concerned with the final nature of what exists. This involves different kinds of questions:

- **What is reality as a whole?**
- **Is there a reality outside human experience (the suprasensible)?**
- **Can we establish absolute first principles as the foundation for all other types of knowledge?**

These very basic problems lie at the heart of any philosophical enquiry. For example, if we believe that we can know some basic things about the world, the study of science and philosophy becomes possible. But if we think that it is impossible to know anything for certain, all knowledge becomes *opinion* (which is personal and subjective) rather than *fact* (which is impersonal and objective). Philosophers have long been divided over questions about where knowledge comes from and how we arrive at it.

The first Greek philosophers were obsessed with the problem of the *One* and the *Many*. They saw that the world was constantly changing and therefore asked how we might possibly find any underlying, coherent order in it?

To find such an order means you have to find knowledge that is *certain*. The first Greeks, of the sixth and fifth centuries BCE, thought that philosophers should aim to discover the permanent, unchanging reality behind the changing appearances of the physical world. Their conclusions varied considerably:

- **Thales** claimed that the whole world

was made out of one fundamental substance: water. This was not an unreasonable conclusion to reach, considering how essential water is to all life forms.

- **Heraclitus** proclaimed that 'everything is flux', believing that the basic matter of the universe was fire, itself forever changing.
- **Parmenides**, on the other hand, argued that, if the world was formed from one unchanging substance, then change itself was impossible. He denied the concepts of time, variety and motion. The world, in his view, had to be made of one uniform continuous element, and this could not be *matter* (which itself would change by its very nature).

These early Greek philosophers asked questions that are fundamental to later philosophy and science. They are generally called 'Pre-Socratic' because they lived before the great philosopher **Socrates (c. 470-399BCE)**.

To sit thinking in the shade of an olive tree – the perfect image of what it would have been like to be a philosopher in ancient Greece? Not necessarily. Thales made his money from olives; Socrates was condemned to death; both Plato and Aristotle were highly political. The early thinkers were not remote from the concerns of their day.

PHILOSOPHERS AND BUSINESS

Early Greek philosophers could be highly practical men. Thales, tired of people mocking his poverty, noted that there was going to be a good olive harvest and bought up all the olive oil presses in his city. His fellow-citizens were then forced to rent the presses from him at very high rates, proving that philosophers, too, could be astute businessmen – when they wanted to be.

Plato (c.428-348BCE) was a pupil of Socrates, and most of what we know about Socrates comes from Plato's writings. Plato was much affected by Socrates' trial and death, his early works being partly defences of his master. These take the form of dialogues, usually with Socrates as the protagonist. They are the earliest complete writings to survive in Western philosophy.

Plato accepted Socrates' belief in a supra-sensible, imperishable world, and saw in philosophy the way of freeing the earthbound soul from its preconceptions and delusions.

'For just as doctors…believe that the body cannot benefit from any food offered it until the internal obstacles have been removed, so the purifier of the soul knows that his patient will not benefit from the application of knowledge until he is refuted.'

Plato thought that, as our senses are fundamentally unreliable and true knowledge has to come from somewhere, it must be pre-existent.

This led him to what is perhaps his most radical and fundamental beliefs: that the 'real world' consists of Ideal Forms, which can only be apprehended intellectually by those who follow the right philosophical path. All his thinking leads up to this supreme end but his thought also covered an enormous range of topics, from politics and education to mathematics.

In their day, Plato and Socrates were opposed by the disparate group of philosophers known as the Sophists. One of them, Gorgias, is famous for saying:

'Nothing exists, and if it did, no one could know it, and if they knew it, they could not communicate it.'

The Sophists (literal meaning 'wise ones') were seen as sceptics and subversives. Many Athenians considered Socrates himself a Sophist, an allegation Plato vehemently rejected. He condemned the Sophists for treating philosophy as a skill to be taught (they took fees from their pupils, unlike Socrates) rather than as a quest for truth.

For Plato, philosophy was not a game of intellectual curiosity nor, as it often is today, a highly technical subject, only discussed in a language far removed from that used by the average intelligent person. To Plato, philosophy was a way of life.

Through reasoning, alone, worthwhile knowledge is acquired and knowledge is the supreme virtue. The man or woman who is a real philosopher is so primarily because their soul is ruled by reason.

PLATO'S MAJOR WORKS

The Apology (Socrates' defence at his trial)
The Crito (Socrates' reasons for not trying to escape after he had been condemned)
The Phaedo (Socrates' last hours arguing for the immortality of the soul)
The Meno
The Symposium
Philebus
Timaeus
The Republic
Gorgias
Phaedrus
Theaetetus
Protagoras
The Sophist

The early dialogues seek to expound and defend Socrates' teachings. They are mainly concerned with politics and ethics. Later dialogues cover a much broader range of issues and represent the ideas of Plato himself, rather than Socrates. The most important of the dialogues, covering a range of issues, including the problem of knowledge, is *The Republic*.

Teaching in his house, called Academy (from which the general terms academy and academic are derived), he effectively established the first university.

SEE ALSO PLATO ON:

ETHICS PAGE 75

POLITICS PAGE 292

RELIGION PAGE 151

MIND PAGE 130

EDUCATION PAGE 231

PLATO'S THEORY OF FORMS

Plato's Theory of Forms has permeated not just most of Western philosophy but much of Western culture. He believed in:

1 A visible (changing, corruptible) world of the senses, the world of 'Appearances'.
2 An 'intelligible' world beyond the senses, which he considered the true, eternal Reality, discernible only by the intellect.

Plato described this 'real' world of Truth, Beauty and Justice as the world of the 'Forms'. He thought of the Forms as having a real existence, independent of either the workings of people's minds or of the natural world. There may be particular instances of beauty in the world but these things are only beautiful because they share, however imperfectly, in the universal Forms of Beauty.

Plato claimed that the person who concerns himself with beautiful things only has 'opinions' about them, but the person who is concerned about Beauty in itself, may come to possess 'true knowledge'. For example, two people may hold differing opinions about a work of art. Opinions often differ about objects in the natural world so it is impossible to have true (universal) knowledge about them.

Plato's Theory of Forms is central to his ideas partly because it classifies objects in the world and attempts to understand their nature. For example, the world 'dog', refers to a four-legged, furry, barking animal which is definitely not a 'cat'. But obviously not all dogs are the same size, colour or breed. But, according to Plato, all dogs share a kind of archetypal 'dogginess,' which we recognize whenever we see one. Just as there is a Form of Beauty or a Form of Justice, there is also a Form of Dog. The ideal Dog is created by God and is the only true, real Dog. All other particular dogs in this world are only instances of dog and belong only to the world of 'appearances'.

For Plato, the World is therefore divided into 'reality' and 'appearance' – the One and the Many.

Plato was also a mathematician, who saw mathematical harmonies beneath the chaos of the world of appearances. This led him to say that universal Forms were connected in a pattern discernible only by the mind, not the eye, and that the highest Form of all is the Form of the Good.

The quest for knowledge leads to discovering the Form of the Good, so philosophy makes you a better person. In *The Republic*, the Good is the greatest thing you can ever learn.

What is the fundamental essence of a dog? The artist may attempt to capture such an essence by constructing an image that is both clearly canine and also abstract. It represents a particular dog, and yet also explores the reality of any and every dog. But is the process of abstraction and definition a genuine attempt to get at what is 'real' about dogs, or to escape from it? To use Plato's terminology: which is more real, the particular or the Form?

PLATO'S ALLEGORY OF THE CAVE

Plato's Theory of Forms is illustrated by one of his most famous passages, the 'Allegory of the Cave' in *The Republic*, in which Socrates describes a deep cave, connected to the outer world only by a narrow passage. Inside it prisoners are sitting chained so tightly together that they cannot move even their heads, which are turned to the far wall. Behind them in the cave is a bright fire, separated from them by a rampart on which people pass to and fro, carrying objects on their heads. The prisoners can only see flickering shadows on the wall; they can hear only the echoes of these people's voices. They take these echoes and shadows as the sole reality.

If one prisoner were set free, he would at once turn and see the objects and the fire. If he were taken right outside the cave, he would at first be dazzled by the light of the sun. But then he would see things as they really are.

If he returned to the cave and attempted to explain to the other prisoners about that external reality, they could not begin to understand him. As Plato explains, through the mouth of Socrates:

'The prison house is the world of sight, the light of the fire is the sun, and you will not misapprehend me if you interpret the journey upwards to be the ascent of the soul into the intellectual world according to my poor belief.'

For Plato true knowledge meant leaving the world of the senses and searching by reason to find the Forms or universals in one's own mind. Grasping these Forms intellectually leads to true knowledge and ultimately, to grasping the Good. He believed that only the Forms could be 'known'. Mathematics could be 'understood', but the changing physical world of nature could never be truly 'known' and so was not a suitable subject for philosophical reflection.

'When the mind's eye is fixed on objects illuminated by truth and reality, it understands and knows them, and its possession of intelligence is evident; but when it is fixed on the twilight world of change and decay, it can only form opinions, its vision is confused and its opinions shifting, and it seems to lack intelligence.'

The Republic

Despite the near-mysticism of the Cave Allegory, Plato was essentially a rationalist in his approach to philosophical enquiry about knowledge and reality. To explain the similarities and resemblances among objects of the physical world, he developed a metaphysics of Forms. For Plato, true knowledge lies in recollecting what is potentially already in your mind and soul at birth ('anamnesis'), not perceiving new things.

'Our birth is but a sleep and a forgetting:
The Soul that rises with us, our life's Star,
Hath had elsewhere its setting
And cometh from afar...
From God who is our home.'

William Wordsworth (1770-1850)
Ode: Intimations of Immortality

According to Plato, most people are content with the reflections that we know from our sense experience, and think them the whole of reality. The people in this photograph are enjoying an illusion of reality on a cinema screen. But they know that what they are seeing requires a temporary suspension of disbelief, whereas Plato claimed that such restricted vision is all that most people know, or believe they can ever know.

KNOWLEDGE AND REALITY

Aristotle was born in about 384BCE at Stagira, a north Greek city. His father was the King of Macedonia's doctor but died when he was young. Aged 18, Aristotle went to Athens and became a pupil of Plato. He stayed at Plato's Academy for almost 20 years until Plato died. Aristotle then married and in 342BCE became tutor to Alexander the Great, then a young prince. No two men could have been less alike, however, and Alexander probably learnt little.

Aristotle returned to Athens where he founded a school in the Lyceum in 332 BCE, which soon rivalled Plato's Academy. When Alexander died in 323BCE there was such strong anti-Macedonian feeling in Athens that he had to flee, and died the following year.

Unlike Plato, Aristotle focused his interest on the natural world. He wrote on subjects such as zoology, astronomy, botany, ethics, politics, mathematics and philosophy. It is to his inexhaustible curiosity about the natural world and his organizing genius we owe the traditional division of the sciences and philosophy. Only a fifth of what he wrote has survived, mainly lecture notes. Because these lack the literary elegance which makes Plato one of the greatest of Greek writers, Aristotle can seem dull by comparison. From Aristotle's work we get the term 'metaphysics'. One theory about this is that an untitled book of Aristotle's was found among his other works. As it came after Physics it was called Meta-Physics (*meta* is Greek for after). Metaphysics is concerned with searching beyond the world of the senses to try and explain why the world is as it is, looking for the 'One' behind the 'Many'.

The most famous of his writings are: *The Analytics, Metaphysics, Physics, On the Soul, Nicomachean Ethics* and *Politics*.

ARISTOTLE

If Plato was the great visionary, Aristotle was the great systematizer and inquirer, inexhaustibly fascinated by every detail of both the natural and human worlds. Although only his lecture notes remain, they cover such a vast range of topics, all logically organized, that they became the cornerstone of Christian and Muslim medieval philosophy.

In his *Metaphysics* Aristotle, who was by far Plato's greatest pupil, attacked his master's central idea: the Theory of Forms. For Plato, the real world is that of ideal Forms in a higher realm understandable only by the intellect. For Aristotle, the real world is 'matter', the stuff that this world here and now is made of.

This at once led him to the problem of change. Plato had said that, as an acorn changes into an oak, it retains its nature by sharing in an ideal 'oakiness', but Aristotle rejected this. If an oak and acorn appear to be two completely different things, he wondered, is there any continuity between them? In the Physics, Aristotle dealt with this question of change. He came to believe that all material substances are, in fact, composite. A house consists of bricks, glass and mortar, but it is not just a pile of bricks, for it contains a structure – a 'houseness' that makes it a house, not a shed or a garage. He decided that all substances have two parts: material and structure – or 'matter' and 'form'.

Matter and form both belong to this world, not to a world beyond, as Plato believed. Form is the organizing principle, which turns matter into recognizable objects. This belief led Aristotle to say that the 'soul' is the form of the body.

Aristotle's favourite example of a particular 'form' is a human being. A human is a composite of form, psyche (translated 'soul') and matter (flesh and blood). Plato's psyche was an immaterial reality unhappily imprisoned in a body; but Aristotle's psyche is very different. In his treatise on the soul (*De Anima*) every living thing has psyche; it is this which makes it alive. The lowest things, like plants, have capacities only for nourishment and reproduction, animals have other capacities for sensation and movement, higher animals have levels of memory and humans have in addition the capacity to reason.

Objects change, and their change has a purpose or goal. Acorns turn into oaks; children turn into adults. According to Aristotle this change is *teleological* as it has an 'end' (*telos*) in view. Because all objects are composed of matter, they are all subject to change. Therefore they can never become perfect. Only God, who exists as 'form without matter', is perfect. Human beings can aspire to perfection by contemplating this pure form by means of pure thought.

ESSENTIAL DIFFERENCES BETWEEN PLATO AND ARISTOTLE

- Plato started with intellectual ideas.
- Aristotle started with observations of the natural world.
- Plato saw reality as essentially mathematical, arranged along theoretical lines, to be deduced intellectually.
- For Aristotle, understanding was based on perception, observation and investigation.
- Aristotle claimed that individual things make the primary realities. This is in contrast to Plato, who believed that sensible objects in this world are only shadowy reflections of the true reality. This can be described by giving an account of what these inadequate particulars reflect and imitate.

SEE ALSO ARISTOTLE ON:

ETHICS PAGE 76

RELIGION PAGE 152

LAW AND POLITICS PAGE 295

THE FIRST WESTERN PHILOSOPHERS

Thales, philosopher c.636-546BCE

Pythagoras, philosopher, mathematician, c.582-507BCE

Heraclitus, philosopher, 535-475BCE

Parmenides, philosopher (b.515BCE)

Sophocles, dramatist 496-406BCE

Euripedes, dramatist c.485-406BCE

Democritus, philosopher c.460-370BCE

Socrates c.470-399BCE

Plato c.428-348BCE

Aristotle, philosopher 384-322BCE

Some other significant people and events:

Persian Wars 499-449BCE

Parthenon built in Athens
447-432BCE

Peloponnesian War, Athens v Sparta
431–404BCE

Democracy restored in Athens
399BCE

King Philip 11 of Macedon 359-336BCE

Plato founds the Academy
c.387BCE

ATHENS AND SPARTA

Plato lived in Athens during the latter part of its golden age in the fifth and fourth centuries BCE. The city was a thriving, contentious, often turbulent democracy – in fact the world's first true democracy, despite many faults such as slavery.

Athens, bursting with new ideas and art, has with good reason been called the Cradle of Western civilization. But the state Plato admired was Sparta, Athens' complete opposite: a grimly autocratic, militaristic state, in some ways communistic, in other ways fascistic.

Sparta's citizens were trained never to think, only to fight, drilled only to obey orders. Sparta was a perfect example of a 'closed society', in contrast to Athens, a very open society. In Sparta, Plato's master Socrates could never have even opened his mouth, let alone begun to teach – a paradox Plato ignored.

'The master of those who know…'

Dante Alighieri (1265-1321) *Inferno* (referring to Aristotle)

'By nature, all men long to know. An indication is their delight in the senses. For these, quite apart from their utility, are intrinsically delightful, and that through the eyes more than the others.'

The opening lines of Aristotle, *The Metaphysics*

RENÉ DESCARTES

Born in March 1596 at La Haye, near Tours in France. He was educated at the famous Jesuit college of La Flèche where he received a traditional Scholastic (Aristotelian) schooling while at the same time studying some of the most recent advances in science.

In 1613 he went to Paris and made the acquaintance of the mathematician Mydorge. Descartes then became a soldier in Holland. On the 10 November 1619 he had a dream, which he interpreted as a revelation. He was convinced that "it was the Spirit of Truth that willed to open for him all the treasures of knowledge". This was to be the unfolding of a wonderful new science. In his own mind, Descartes was first and foremost a scientist, but he is remembered as a philosopher.

In 1629 he settled in Holland, and stayed there for 20 years. From his personal retreat he wrote, his most notable works *Le Monde* (1632) *Discourse on Method* (1637), *Meditations* (1641) *Principles of Philosophy* (1644). His work was intended for the educated public not just philosophers and he wrote in French, not Latin.

Descartes' writing was widely attacked by theologians and in 1649 he accepted an invitation from Queen Christina of Sweden to teach her philosophy. This decision was unfortunate, he was unhappy at court and the Swedish winter did not suit him. He died in Stockholm in 1650 of pneumonia. He is regarded as the first French philosopher and chief architect of the 17th-century intellectual revolution.

The rationalist movement in Epistemology developed during the 17th and 18th centuries. Descartes, Spinoza and Leibniz are key exponents of this approach. Rationalism holds three important principles:

1 The belief that a knowledge of what exists can be obtained by reason alone.
2 The belief that knowledge is a single system which can be deduced by logic.
3 The belief that everything that is can be explained in rational terms and that it fits together in a unified system.

The term Rationalist is sometimes used to describe those who accept a limited version of the above beliefs. So for example, the existentialist philosopher Sartre was called a Rationalist, but he believed only in a limited Rationalist view that everything was explicable in terms of one system.

DESCARTES' METHOD

Descartes' work marks the beginning of modern philosophy. He is part of the Enlightenment where there was a clean break with the philosophy of Aristotle and medieval scholasticism. It was a time when science was sceptical of religion and religion distrusted science. Descartes wanted to show that they could be reconciled. He set out to put knowledge to the test. His aim was to find a solid intellectual foundation or bedrock upon which to rebuild the entire structure of human understanding.

To do this he devised a method of doubting. He would have been familiar with this from his Jesuit education. His aim was to peel away everything that could possibly be doubted so that all that remained was what could not be doubted at all. He aspired to find knowledge. which was certain.

His method was:
● Only accept truths which are self-evident (as in mathematics, where for example, a straight line is self-evidently the shortest way between two points).
● Divide problems into smaller fragments to make it easier to solve them.
● Order your thoughts to start with the simple ones and work up to the more complicated.
● Check that you have taken everything into account in your thinking.

Descartes put all his own opinions to the test but he put religion and morality aside in a kind of 'temporary shelter' while the 'house' of his beliefs was being reconstructed.

But Descartes believed also that people were born with certain innate ideas. In this he is like Plato. For example, he would say that we have an idea of God, but we never encounter God with our senses. We have an idea of a perfect circle, but we never encounter one in the world; so we are born with certain ideas in us, which we can discover through reason.

COGITO ERGO SUM

He began his reconstruction by examining accepted beliefs systematically. His first subject was the senses, which he found could at times deceive – such as a straight stick which looks crooked in water. He said,

'It is prudent not to trust entirely anything that has once deceived.'

Yet there are some sensory experiences that only a madman would doubt. 'For example, that I am here seated by the fire wearing a dressing gown'. But then a further doubt comes: I could be dreaming, in which case the belief about the fire and the dressing gown might well be false. He followed this thought with questions:

If our senses can give us such faulty information, how can we know that we are not being deceived all the time?

If I dream I am awake while I am asleep how do I know that I am not dreaming all the time and that what I see and experience is an illusion?

But, he thought, if everything is an illusion, can parts of that illusion still be true?

'For whether I am awake or asleep, two and three together always make five, and the square can never have more than four sides, and it does not seem possible that truths so clear and apparent can be suspected of any falsity or uncertainty...'

This, at least, appears to be certain. But then Descartes introduces the famous device of a malignant demon,

'... who has employed all his energies in deceiving me. I shall consider the sky, earth, colours, shapes, sounds, and all external things are not more than the delusions of dreams...

SEE ALSO DESCARTES ON:

MIND PAGE 132

RELIGION PAGE 165

I shall consider myself as having no hands, no eyes...'

The First Meditation ends with universal doubt.

After casting doubt on the senses, science and mathematics, Descartes came to his famous conclusion that even if the demon can lie to him about everything, he cannot lie about the fact that Descartes himself exists and is thinking. Descartes concludes:

'I am, I exist, is necessarily, true as often as I put it forward or conceive of it in my mind.'

This argument is found in the *Discourse* in the form:

'I think, therefore I am.'

(*Je pense, donc je suis*, or in the Latin – *cogito ergo sum*)

Descartes has argued:

- No one can deceive me into thinking I exist if I do not exist.
- I cannot think that my existence is a false one, because if I think this, then I am really thinking, and my existence must therefore be a fact.

Through his method of doubting, Descartes had established the existence of the self. He then went on to establish the existence of God. He finally took on a central challenge in epistemology, which is to prove that an external world exists.

Descartes was a rationalist philosopher. He would have accepted that there were a priori truths that were not derived from experience and whilst some ideas were developed from experience, he was steadfast in his belief that certain ideas were innate.

His scientific model resembles the deductive model, where a hypothesis is advanced, and the results logically deduced from it are then compared with actual observations.

'The whole of philosophy is a tree whose roots are metaphysics, whose trunk is physics, and whose branches are the other sciences.'

KEY FIGURES OF THE ENLIGHTENMENT IN THE 17TH AND 18TH CENTURIES

René Descartes 1596-1650

John Locke 1632-1704

Bishop Berkeley 1685-1753

David Hume 1711-1776

Thomas Hobbes 1588-1679

Rembrandt 1606-1669 painter

Robert Boyle 1627-1692 chemist

Benedict Spinoza 1632-1677

Isaac Newton 1642-1727 scientist

Gottfried Leibniz 1646-1716

Jonathan Swift 1667-1745 satirist

William Hogarth 1697-1764 painter/satirist

Voltaire 1694-1778 philosopher/writer

Samuel Johnson 1709-1784, writer, lexicographer

Jean-Jacques Rousseau 1712-1778 philosopher, writer

Immanuel Kant 1724-1804

Wolfgang Amadeus Mozart 1756-1791, composer

Some other significant people and events:

Authorized Version of the Bible 1611

English Civil War 1642-1648

Louis XIV King of France 1643-1715

Glorious Revolution, England 1688

Wesley's preaching 1738-1791

Catherine the Great, Empress of Russia 1762-1796

James Cook reaches Australia 1770

American Revolution 1775-1783

French Revolution 1789-1799

LEIBNIZ

Leibniz was an amazing polymath. In mathematics, he devised a system of calculus in 1675 independently of Sir Isaac Newton. (Newton's own system of calculus had been invented in 1666, but was not published until after Leibniz's.) Law and politics were also subjects of enduring interest to Leibniz.

However, he published only one book on philosophy during his lifetime – the *Theodicy* in 1710, which concerned itself with natural theology. His numerous unpublished works include the *Monadology*, the *Discourse on Metaphysics*. He also wrote a chapter-by-chapter reply (*New Essays Concerning Human Understanding*) to Locke's *Essay Concerning Human Understanding*, which was still unpublished at the date of Locke's death in 1704.

Although a Rationalist philosopher, Leibniz vigorously criticized the positions of Descartes, Locke, Newton and Spinoza.

Leibniz came to believe that the world consists of countless conscious centres of spiritual energy, known as monads, organized in a hierarchy with God as the governing monad. Each monad represents an individual microcosm, which reflects the universe in varying degrees of perfection, developing independently of all other monads.

(In some ways Leibniz saw his monads as possessing physical energies also, so anticipating aspects of modern physics.)

Of relevance to both the Philosophy of Religion and the Philosophy of Mind, Leibniz' view here raises questions about whether or not one should accept evils, such as death and illness, as essential parts of a universal harmony.

GOTTFRIED LEIBNIZ (1646-1716)

The son of a professor of moral philosophy at Leipzig. During his life he was a sociable public figure who corresponded with almost everyone intellectually prominent. In 1673 Leibniz went to Paris. He remained there for three years and also visited Amsterdam and London, devoting his time to the study of mathematics, science and philosophy – all subjects in which he excelled.

In 1676 he was made librarian and privy councillor at the court of Hanover, north Germany. For the next 40 years until he died, he served Ernest Augustus, Duke of Brunswick-Luneburg, and George Louis, elector of Hanover, later George I King of Great Britain.

'… there is nothing in things except simple substances, and, in them, nothing but perception and appetite. Moreover, matter and motion are not so much substances or things as they are the phenomena of percipient beings...'

Leibniz

SPINOZA

Spinoza's philosophy is written in a complex, notoriously difficult language, but his message is one of startling, radical simplicity. Essentially, he believed that God is One and All is God.

He reached this – to contemporaries deeply shocking – deduction by following his reasoning with logical necessity from a few basic truths. Such truths were not conjectures but were true because they could not logically be denied. The aim of the philosopher is to state these truths.

Influenced by Jewish medieval philosophy, Hobbes and especially Descartes, Spinoza used Descartes' mathematical methods to overthrow Cartesian Dualism. Against Descartes he argued:

- The definition of substance makes it impossible for the mind and the body to be distinct substances.
- The definition of substance requires that only a single substance exists.
- So mind and body, God and the universe, are just two modes of the single infinite substance.

Spinoza agreed with Hobbes' negative view of popular religion, which he saw as mere superstition. But Spinoza took a more positive view of society, arguing in effect for religious and political freedom and against monarchs, which was radical even in Holland, the most liberal country of the age.

Spinoza's main interest, however, was moral philosophy. The chief goal of human life, he declared is the 'intellectual love of God' although this may not be possible for all.

Spinoza's pantheism (identification of God and the Universe) was attacked as mere atheism until long after his death, but from the late 18th century on, Romantic poets and writers revered him. Hegel, Nietzsche and Bertrand Russell were among later philosophers deeply influenced by him.

'The noblest and most lovable of the great philosophers.'

Bertrand Russell on Spinoza

BENEDICT SPINOZA
(1632-1677)

A Dutch Jewish rationalist born in Amsterdam to a distinguished Jewish family in exile from Portugal, he went to a Jewish School where he was instructed in Judaism and the work of Arab theologians. His father wanted him to be a Rabbi, but in his early twenties he was tutored by the non-Jewish Frances van den Engden, from whom he learned Latin, scholastic philosophy and the new philosophy of Descartes. He distanced himself from mainstream Judaism until, in 1656, he was excommunicated by the Jewish community as a heretic. He supported himself by grinding lenses and giving lessons on Cartesian philosophy. In 1673 his work *Tractatus Theologico-Politicus* was published anonymously and banned four years later because its advocacy of toleration threatened the current political and religious authorities. His masterpiece was the simply titled *Ethics*, only published posthumously, as there was a wild rumour that he was about to show there was no God. He died on February 21 1677 of a lung ailment associated with the glass dust from his lens grinding. There are accounts of his simplicity, authenticity, charm and courage.

Individual grains of sand, or parts of a beach? Are we individual monads, or do we share a single, universal substance? Patterns and structures raise issues about the one and the many.

In contrast to the Rationalists' views, the development of the British Empiricist school of philosophy in the 17th and 18th centuries argued that the experience of our senses is the chief source of our ideas and of knowledge itself.

Locke, Berkeley and Hume all reject the view that the human mind comes already equipped with a range of innate ideas or concepts that owe nothing to the world of experience.

These empiricists lived in an age when experimental science was developing as something distinct from pure mathematics and other academic disciplines. Experiment and observation formed the basis of the new science, and every claim to knowledge was limited by the possibility that further evidence might require it to be modified.

It is easy to see how empiricism flourished in this intellectual atmosphere. The empiricists were characteristically sceptical about the claims of all embracing unifying systems of philosophy and metaphysics.

'For whatever truth we come to the clear discovery of, from the knowledge and contemplation of our own ideas, will always be more certain to us than those which are conveyed to us by traditional revelation.'

John Locke, *An Essay Concerning Human Understanding*

LOCKE

Locke's *Essay Concerning Human Understanding* begins by viewing the role of the philosopher, whose task it is to clear the ground and remove 'some of the rubbish that lies in the way of knowledge'.

In Book I, Locke disagrees with both Plato and Descartes and points out that:
- Just because something is agreed universally, it is not necessarily true.
- Just become something is known universally, it is not necessarily innate in every human mind.

In Book II, Locke's starting point is that all knowledge comes through experience. He likened the mind to a blank sheet of paper on which our senses write. Locke wrote that

'All ideas come from sensation or reflection.'

Three terms have a particular meaning in Locke's thought:
- To him, an 'idea' is a 'mental image', a notion of experience. We perceive ideas, not the things themselves.
- 'Sensation' refers to perceiving through the senses.
- 'Reflection' comes after sensation. It is any mental activity such as thinking, feeling or doubting.

'Let us suppose the mind to be, as we say, white paper, void of all characters, without any ideas; how comes it to be furnished? Whence comes it by that vast store, which the busy and boundless fancy of man has painted on it with an almost endless variety? Whence has it all the materials of reason and knowledge? To this I answer in one word, from experience: in that all our knowledge is founded, and from that it ultimately derives itself.'

John Locke, *An Essay Concerning Human Understanding*

These views give rise to two fundamental questions for the theory of knowledge:
- How can we know for certain that all our knowledge comes through sensation and reflection?
- Is all our thinking derived from experience? For example does our knowledge of God or of mathematics really rely on our sensory perception?

SEE ALSO LOCKE ON:

RELIGION PAGE 166

LANGUAGE PAGE 206

EDUCATION PAGE 233

LAW AND POLITICS PAGE 310

JOHN LOCKE
(1632-1704)

The first British Empirical philosopher, he was educated at Westminster School and Christ Church College, Oxford, where he trained to be a doctor. His Puritan background explains his strong sense of moral duty. At University he associated with and was influenced by Robert Boyle. Boyle was the leading scientist of his day and was committed to empirical and experimental methods. Locke's life changed dramatically in 1666, however, when he met Lord Ashley, later Earl of Shaftesbury and an important political figure at the court of Charles II. Locke worked as Shaftesbury's physician and also became involved in politics. His political writing is just as important as his philosophy; his democratic ideas have been highly influential in Europe and America – the founding fathers of the American Revolution were indebted to Locke's ideas. In 1683, to avoid being implicated in a conspiracy, Locke fled to Holland, where he wrote most of his masterpiece *Essay Concerning Human Understanding*. After the "Glorious Revolution" of 1688, when William of Orange and Queen Mary replaced the Catholic James II, Hobbes returned to England, escorting Queen Mary from Holland in February 1689. His politics influenced his philosophy in his dislike of extreme solutions. His Protestant world-view encouraged his philosophical world-view of a self-conscious individual facing a Newtonian universe.

Locke published *An Essay Concerning Human Understanding* and *A Letter concerning Toleration* in 1689, and *Two Treatises of Government* in 1690. Locke's 'Essay' sets out to give an 'Account of the Ways, whereby our Understandings come to attain those Notions of Things we have'. While Locke was in France from 1674 to 1679, he had closely studied Descartes' work, although he rejected Descartes' doctrine of innate ideas. In later life he became a Commissioner of Trade, and he worked on fresh editions of the 'Essay' until his death in 1704.

'… words, seen or heard, recall to our thoughts those ideas only which to us they have been wont to be signs of, but cannot introduce any perfectly new and formerly unknown simple ideas.'

John Locke, *An Essay Concerning Human Understanding*

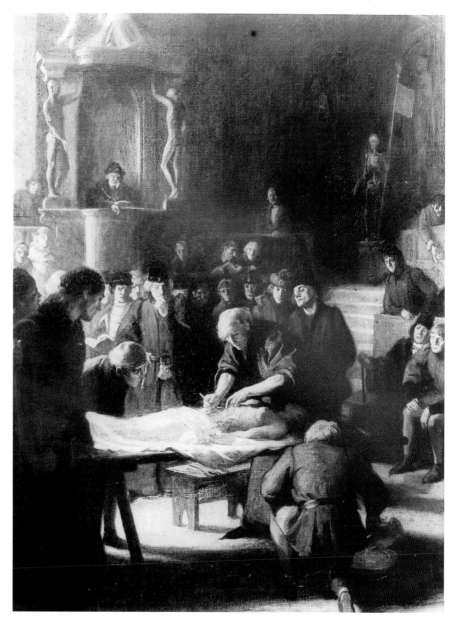

The process of dissection and analysis, in whatever form it takes, is basic to an understanding of the composition and workings of things. Empiricism is therefore fundamental to scientific knowledge; to understand, one must look carefully and then reflect on what one sees.

LOCKE'S THEORY OF KNOWLEDGE

Locke divided 'ideas' into simple and complex. The simple idea is 'in itself uncompounded'. We do not imagine it but receive it passively. A complex idea is made up of simple ideas and we imagine these actively. In other words, our minds are involved in putting together the various simple ideas that go to make up an object.

In considering physical objects, Locke gives these 'primary' and 'secondary' qualities. Primary qualities are objective and mathematical, such as size and shape. Secondary qualities are subjective and 'sensible', such as colour, smell and taste.

Locke accepted the scientific views of his time, which was that the universe itself was devoid of all these 'secondary qualities', in other words, it was devoid of colour, sound or taste. In effect, he is saying that without ears there would be no sound, without eyes no colour, and without noses no smell.

Locke continued his theory by saying that these properties we perceive must be held together in and by something. He concludes that they are held in material substance; therefore matter must exist. We perceive the idea, but cannot know the thing. The implications of Locke's ideas are that the natural world can never really be known fully. Consequently, science is based more on guesswork than knowledge.

Locke believed that there were three distinct kinds of knowledge:

Intuitive knowledge. Like Descartes Locke sees the fundamental basis of knowledge as intuition. This is the knowledge of ourselves and our existence.

Demonstrative (Deductive) knowledge - as in mathematical calculation where each step in the argument is demonstratively certain. Through this domain comes knowledge of God.

Sensitive knowledge, through which comes our knowledge of the external world of physical objects.

Intuitive knowledge is the only certainty, the second type, demonstrative knowledge is sure in the way a mathematical proof is sure. Knowledge from our senses is problematic – it is at best a good guess. He commented:

'All men are liable to error.'

Even so, Locke said that while final proof is one thing, ordinary common sense is another, and the knowledge from our senses is enough for the purposes of everyday life.

But Locke was concerned with morals as well as science. He held the view that without God morals would simply dwindle to a matter of taste, not one of duty. Although he drew a fine line between faith and scepticism, being one of the greatest exponents of religious toleration along with political liberty, Locke believed his philosophy led to knowledge of God. Given cause and effect, he argued that, if something exists, something must always have existed, and this something (God) is the cause of that which exists now.

This is a form of the cosmological argument, which we shall examine in the chapter on the Philosophy of Religion, page 160).

'Our business here is not to know all things, but those which concern our conduct.'

If all we know comes from the senses, then perhaps we need to regain the freshness of vision that we had in childhood, exploring sensation, without the clutter of concepts and values that define and constrict adult awareness.

Berkeley was a devout Christian, worried that the mechanical Newtonian science and philosophy of his time might lead people towards atheism.

He held strong views on what we perceived as the error of Materialism, which led him to advocate 'immaterialism'. He argued that only the 'contents' of our experience, as perceived in our own minds, can be said to exist. He therefore appeared to be denying the objective existence of matter.

Berkeley said that, strictly speaking, what we see are only 'signs' giving us clues to the objects we may perceive by touch. However, we learn to interpret these clues so effortlessly that we end up by confusing the experience of seeing something with the tangible thing itself.

'To be perceived is to exist.'
Berkeley

Put another way, for things to be perceived, there must be a perceiver. Therefore I have a notion of myself. I perceive the world as there, because I am here perceiving it.

But surly, things continue to exist whether I perceive them or not. Berkeley therefore argued that there must be an omnipresent Perceiver with a capital 'P'.

This gave him the notion that the apparent permanence of those things that we only know through our fleeting perceptions, is possible, because everything is an idea in the mind of God.

Berkeley thought his ideas were so true and so obvious that 'a man need only open his eyes to accept them'. His contemporaries, however, found them strange and incomprehensible.

If Locke championed the idea that matter is more important than mind, Berkeley argued that mind is more important than matter. Berkeley's idea of the subject as all-important perceiver is one that has stood the test of time and refuses to go away, even for those who do not share his Christian views.

Ronald Knox summed up Berkeley's philosophy in a famous limerick:

There was a young man who said, 'God,
I find it exceedingly odd
That this tree which I see
Should continue to be
When there's no one about in the Quad'.

To which the reply is:

'Dear Sir: Your astonishment's odd.
I am always about in the Quad:
And that's why the tree
Will continue to be
Since observed by
Yours faithfully,
God'

Clearly, this was Berkeley's way of overcoming the obvious criticism that he makes the world appear to depend on the mind, while common sense says that the world exists objectively. He argued that the existence of God gave the world that sense of reality that we naturally assume it to have.

BISHOP GEORGE BERKELEY (1685–1753)
Berkeley was a Protestant Irish philosopher, born in Kilkenny who became a fellow of Trinity College, Dublin. He wrote three of his most important books: *An Essay Towards a New Theory of Vision* (1709), *A Treatise Concerning the Principles of Human Knowledge* (1710) and *Three Dialogues Between Hylas and Philonous* (1713) by the time he was in his mid twenties. He went to America in 1728 aiming to found a new college there and also in Bermuda, but money was lacking for either. He mixed with the leading figures of his day back in Europe and became Bishop of Cloyne in 1734. The city of Berkeley in California and one of the colleges of Yale University are named after him.

'To me it is evident, for the reasons you allow of, that sensible things cannot exist otherwise than in a mind or spirit. Whence I conclude, not that they have no real existence distinct from being perceived by me, there must be some other mind wherein they exist. As sure, therefore, as the sensible world really exists, so sure is there an infinite omnipresent spirit, who contains and supports it.'
Berkeley

SEE ALSO BERKELEY ON:

RELIGION PAGE 166

If Bishop Berkeley went almost as far as abolishing matter, David Hume effectively abolished mind. He began by taking a scientific method and applying it to the mental world rather than the physical world. He was one of the great sceptics of philosophy. A sceptic says we cannot know anything for sure, and Hume criticized knowledge of the world, knowledge of the self and knowledge of God.

Hume's philosophical aim was to question reason as a first principle. Reason, he said, was just a human habit, like any other. In the *Treatise of Human Nature*, he argued that we cannot base our knowledge of the external world upon our sensory experience, we can but look at our psychological beliefs about that world:

'If we believe that fire warms or water refreshes, 'tis only because it costs us too much pain to think otherwise.'

He divides human understanding into:
Impressions: these we receive through our senses (primary), including 'our sensations, passions and emotions'.
Ideas: memories or 'faint images' of impressions, which we use together in thinking and reasoning. An idea is everything of which we are immediately aware.

Neither of these is grounded in reason as all ideas are ultimately derived from impressions. Our knowledge is therefore very limited. Hume is sceptical also about imagination. Our imagination may appear boundless but, in fact, it is only a combination of impressions we already have.

This statue of Hume in Edinburgh depicts him dressed as a philosopher of Ancient Greece.

He says:

'All this creative power of the mind amounts to no more than the faculty of transposing, augmenting, or diminishing the materials afforded us by the senses and experience.'

Hume agrees with Locke and Berkeley, saying that we can never really know what is going on outside ourselves. In his writings he often relied on psychological description rather than philosophical analysis, and he went on in his thinking to demolish the sacred belief in cause and effect, which had proved necessary both to science and to religion.

HUME'S PHILOSOPHY OF CAUSE AND EFFECT

Descartes and other rationalist philosophers believed that it is a logical, a priori truth that everything must have a sufficient cause, and that certain sorts of things either must be or cannot be the causes of other sorts of things. Hume put forward the negative thesis that what usually happens does not necessarily always happen.

'When we look about us towards external objects, and consider the operation of causes, we are never able in a single instance to discover any power or necessary connection, any quality, which binds the effect to the causes, and renders the one an infallible consequence of the other.'

David Hume *Dialogues Concerning Natural Religion*

In his view, causation was an idea, not an impression. If you see a rock shatter a mirror, what you see first is the rock and then the broken glass. We can never see the one actually cause the other; we assume it, because we see that the two things occur together. Hume argued that because these two things have always been seen to happen together in the past, it does not follow that they always will in the future. Hume propounds a psychological not a scientific explanation for cause and effect. At its best all we can see are conjoined events. There are no connections between things.

FOR HUME ON:
ETHICS SEE PAGE 88
RELIGION SEE PAGE 166
ART SEE PAGE 240

HUME'S VIEW OF THE SELF

Hume claimed that the 'Self' was an idea without real, fixed existence. Berkeley had said that there were no thoughts without a thinker; that to have perceptions you had to have a perceiver. But Hume said there were only thoughts and perceptions. He divorced the idea of thoughts and perceptions from the self. If I look inside myself, I find only thoughts and perceptions – so how then can I say that a self exists?

'I may venture to affirm of the rest of mankind, that they are nothing but a bundle or collection of different perceptions, which succeed each other with inconceivable rapidity, and are in perpetual flux and movement.'

Hume is saying that when I search for my own identity, when I ask myself, 'Am I the same person that I was yesterday?' all I ever find is a transitory perception, never any kind of permanent self. Then why do I believe that I am the same person I was yesterday? Hume believes it is because I have been influenced by the great similarity between today and yesterday and therefore I take it for granted that there is some sort of persistent 'I'.

'For my part, when I enter most intimately what I call myself, I always stumble on some particular perception or other, of heat or cold, light or shade, love or hatred, pain or pleasure. I never can catch myself at any time without a perception, and never can observe anything but the perception.'

Treatise of Human Nature

His argument about causality and his argument about the self have basic features in common. In both of them, he examines a concept which is taken for granted, something which supposedly describes something in the real world. He therefore looks for some particular experience or feature of the world, on which these concepts are based. And to everyone's amazement, when they look for an empirical basis of the concepts, they find that it does not exist. In other words, there is no particular thing that corresponds to 'cause' or to 'self'.

Hume's philosophy of the self is not without its problems. The hotly debated point is: why should I believe there is an 'I' in the first place? Hume acknowledged the problem in his philosophy of the self.

He believed that as long as he was talking about nothing but the mind and its workings, he would not encounter any intellectual difficulties. They would only arise if he moved outside his own mind to consider the nature and relationships of the world outside. But even so, he could not solve the problem of giving a satisfactory account of the mind itself.

On his view, it follows that if there is no self, then there is no soul and no immortality. Hume attacked both religion and science by his 'scientific method'. He attempted to demolish much of the basis of thought in his day:

● There is no genuine cause and effect.
● The principle of reason does not exist.
● There is no certainty in induction (deciding what is true and real from the evidence).

Science was built, it turned out, on faith, not on certainty. On the subject of religion he never declared himself an atheist although history has treated him as one.

The biographer James Boswell visited Hume just before his death to discover what he felt about facing the end of life. Hume was cheerful. He said that the philosopher 'persisted in disbelieving a future state even when he had death before his eyes'.

DAVID HUME
(1711-1776)

Historian, essaying and one of the greatest philosophers of the 18th century, Hume was born in Edinburgh and studied at the University there, before entering the law at his father's insistence. He hated this and, after a nervous breakdown, moved to France in 1734. There he began writing *A Treatise of Human Nature*, his most significant work, but one that was totally ignored when published in London in 1740.

He failed to get university posts in Edinburgh and Glasgow, mainly because of his notoriously sceptical attitude to religion, but such views did not prevent him from being one of the best-loved of men.

Hume did various things to make a living, most notably writing *A History of England* in the 1750s. He was better known in his lifetime as a historian than as a philosopher. His most controversially sceptical work, *Dialogues Concerning Natural Religion*, was written in his forties but not published until after his death. In his later years Hume formed part of the Scottish Enlightenment, along with Adam Smith and James Boswell, but his reputation as a philosopher was far greater on the Continent than in Britain.

'I have always considered him... as approaching as nearly to the idea of a perfectly wise and virtuous man as perhaps the nature of human frailty will permit.' Adam Smith on Hume

Kant was born in Königsberg (now Kalinidgrad) in East Prussia. He received a good education and eventually became a lecturer on numerous subjects at Königsberg University in 1755, being elected Professor of Logic and Metaphysics in 1770.

All commentaries on the life of Kant portray him as an extremely orderly, hyper-punctual man. Local people would set their watches by his daily walk through the town. He never travelled more than 50 miles from home and his outward life was one of legendary calm and predictability, but Kant's intellectual work rightly justified his own claim to have effected a "Copernican revolution" in philosophy.

It was said of him by A M Quinton that 'he came as near as anyone ever has to combining in himself the speculative originality of Plato with the encylopedic thoroughness of Aristotle'.

In 1781 Kant published his *Critique of Pure Reason* is which he set out an enlightened approach to human knowledge. He aimed at a systematic re-examining of key areas of philosophy:

Metaphysics: What can I know about the world?

Religion: What may I hope and believe?

Ethics: What should I do?

Anthropology: What is humankind?

Kant's major writings were:

Critique of Pure Reason (1781)

Prolegomena to any Future Metaphysics (1783)

Groundwork of the Metaphysic of Morals (1785)

Critique of Practical Reason (1788)

Critique of Judgement (1790)

Kant, generally regarded as the greatest philosopher of the 18th-century Enlightenment, was deeply concerned with whether there could be knowledge which is not derived from experience (in other words, a priori knowledge), but which is a condition of understanding experience (synthetic a priori knowledge).

Kant agreed with the Empiricists that there could not be innate ideas (anything known prior to any sensory experience) but he was not prepared to say that therefore all knowledge must be derived from experience. Kant opposed these two extreme views.

In contrast he believed that all knowledge is related to experience but that it cannot all be reduced to what we experience.

KANT AND METAPHYSICS

Kant opposed the rationalism of Descartes and Leibniz and the empiricism of Locke, Berkeley and Hume. He differed from both these views, in that he believed that all knowledge is related to experience, but that it cannot all be reduced to what we experience. This middle course between empiricism and rationalism he called '**transcendental idealism**'.

Kant was 13 years younger than Hume. In Kant's own words, it was Hume's account of causality, 'that first interrupted my dogmatic slumber and gave a completely different direction to my enquiries in the field of speculative philosophy' (from *Prolegomena*).

In his first *Critique* Kant aimed to examine whether metaphysics, which had been regarded in the Middle Ages as the 'queen of the sciences', could be restored to her throne. He took the view that the most important issues in philosophy had been reduced to endless controversy without any solutions. This seemed to be in contrast to the natural sciences, which seemed to be making considerable progress.

Kant greatly admired the progress of Newton in the scientific world and he hoped to make comparable progress in philosophy by attempting to examine the nature of reason itself.

The 'pure reason' in the title of his first *Critique*, means a priori reason, – that which can be known by the mind, prior to anything which is derived from sense experience.

Kant started his examination by:

Agreeing with the empiricists that there cannot be 'innate ideas in the sense of anything known prior to any sense experience'.

Disagreeing with the empiricists' view that all knowledge must be derived from experience.

As a result, his own position – transcendental idealism – was that we have knowledge only of 'appearances' (things as they appear to our minds through that which comes to us through sensation) and not of 'things as they are in themselves' independent of our perceiving them.

This, as we shall see, was crucial to his theory of knowledge.

A central question of Metaphysics was how the human mind could relate objects to one another, and to the perceiving mind, a priori – independently of the input of the senses.

One possible answer that can be given to this question was:

The mind employs a faculty which relates to objects directly or 'intuitively.'

SEE ALSO KANT ON:

ETHICS PAGE 89

RELIGION PAGE 168

LANGUAGE PAGE 212

ART PAGE 241

But equally, another posible answer to this question was:

The mind apprehends its objects indirectly, through the use of general concepts, which are not themselves the products of sense experience.

Philosophers from Plato onwards had usually held that the human mind has a direct insight into objects, apart from the information that is given through the senses. Kant rejected such claims as mystical.

In answer to the question 'How might the human mind relate objects a priori, independently of the input of the senses?' Kant came up with a solution that was to prove revolutionary. He argued that the way in which we perceive and reflect upon objects might itself have a kind of structure, a way of organising information, which in some way influences the way we experience things.

In other words, the mind plays an active rather than a passive role in experience. It does not merely record what is out there, it sorts, interprets and structures its experience in some way.

We tend to assume that the world, as we experience it, is set out before us rather like a building site or set of archæological remains. Objects exist in relation to one another in ways that we can measure. I assume that space 'exists' because I perceive the relationship between parts of these remains. I assume time 'exists', since there would once have been a thriving city in this, now silent place.

But do space and time actually exist? Are they out there to be discovered, or are they simply the way our mind handles experience? And if the latter is the case, then what does that say about those things that we tend to infer from experience, like the existence of selves or of God? Are these also in the mind, rather than 'out there' in the objective world? These are questions that lie at the heart of Kant's philosophy.

SENSE EXPERIENCE

Kant would say that no existing object could be presented to and understood by human beings 'as it is'. What is given in human understanding is always modified by the manner in which it is received. His central thesis is that the possibility of human knowledge presupposes the active participation of the human mind.

Only an original intuition, one that causes the very existence of the object, would be able to represent its objects as they are 'in themselves'.

So he concludes that some of the properties we observe in objects may be due to the nature of the observer not to the objects themselves. It is only through the understanding that sense experience comes to be ordered and classified into experience of the objective world.

Kant does not dismiss the importance of sense-experience but he does not believe that it accounts for all knowledge. So, for example, Kant holds to the view that some of our general concepts (e.g. that of a dog) are derived from the senses, but others (e.g. that of a supreme being) are generated 'spontaneously' by the human mind itself. This generation of concepts is therefore a priori and an authentic starting point for metaphysical enquiry.

In his Prolegomena (Section 40) Kant says:

'The root and peculiarity of metaphysics is the occupation of reason merely with itself and the supposed knowledge of objects arising immediately from this brooding over its own concepts, without requiring experience or indeed being able to reach that knowledge through experience.'

Kant rejected the traditional metaphysical view that the a priori origin of metaphysical concepts applies to objects, which are independent of sense-experience. In other words, he rejected the idea that we can have rational knowledge of that which is beyond, or transcends, the world of the senses. Kant says that such concepts are used transcendently in vain to gain access to 'hyper-physical' objects, such as God. Trying to apply pure concepts to non-sensible objects he sees as an illusion and a disaster to metaphysics.

Kant's alternative view is to retain an a priori element in knowledge, but to confine it to objects of sense-experience. What this means, in practice, is that the mind cannot know what is beyond sense experience, what it can know is how to handle and interpret that experience.

As we have noted, Kant held that any object given to the human mind is subject to the means by which it is received by the mind.

Thus, for example, Kant claimed two 'forms' of intuition: space and time; all objects of sense-experience are to be found in some area of space or in some period of time. Space and time are a priori forms because they are not taken from experience, but imposed upon it by the mind.

KANT AND THE CATEGORIES

Kant claimed to have discovered twelve a priori concepts (categories) that were not learned from experience, but were understood independently of sense experience and then applied to it.

Kant saw these concepts as essential. They were basic to anyone being able to analyse their experience, and without such conceptual equipment you could not make sense of the world.

Prominent among the categories is that of cause and effect, whose principle states that every change in an object of sense-experience is determined by its previous state in accordance with a rule. But this category, like all the others, can only be applied to sense experience.

Kant saw the futility of applying the categories, a priori concepts, to the transcendent. For example, the category of causality could be extended to conceive of an uncaused cause. Such an object cannot be met in sense-experience (which is subject to the principle that every change in an object is the outcome of its prior state and is itself a rule governing its transition to the next state). And there is something very unsatisfying to human reason in the supposition of an endless series of causes. For Kant, it may be useful to assume an uncaused cause, but its existence can never be proved or disproved.

This failure of transcendent metaphysics to achieve certainty, is essential for Kant, as it allows for the possibility of human freedom in the sense that the human will is considered as a non-sensible object.

'Human reason has this peculiar fate that in one species of its knowledge it is burdened by question which, as prescribed by the very nature of reason itself, it is not able to ignore, but which, as transcending all its powers, it is also not able to answer.'

Which makes it a hard life being a philosopher!

PHILOSOPHICAL CRITICS OF KANT

Philosophers were quick to oppose and circumvent Kant's conclusions about human understanding and its limitations:

Fichte objected to the whole idea of things-in-themselves, while Schopenhauer thought he could produce reason for believing that there was only one thing in itself, which was to be identified with the Will.

But it was Hegel who put forward the most radical view. He thought that reason could certainly do what Kant thought impossible.

Reason was able to lead to the idea of an identification of self and object.

Hegel's metaphysical system is huge and encyclopaedic, claiming to bring all phenomena within its terms of reference. He developed a form of absolute idealism, which was worked out in terms of a system of developing categories which resulted in Hegel's absolute notion that 'Spirit knows itself as Spirit'.

There were various Existentialists who

disagreed with Hegel. In particular, Kierkegaard objected to the view that existence precedes essence and he criticized Hegel for leaving out individuality. He thought Hegel's all comprehensive system for understanding reality left out the individual.

Marx made use of Hegelian terms but in his own way insisted that all reality and thought could be understood on a material and social basis.

Space and time are not the only significant categories used by the mind to interpret experience. Equally universal is the idea of causality. When something happens we ask for a cause. We examine data, looking for a reason for everything. Nothing happens by chance, because our minds are programmed to work in terms of cause and effect. As soon as we start asking 'Why?' and 'How?' we demonstrate this fundamental feature of our mental equipment. When faced with a road accident, or other disaster, we automatically assume there must be a cause, a reason, perhaps even a person to blame. Equally, when the traffic comes to a standstill on the highway, we assume that there must be a cause, for example an accident up ahead. In ordinary life, we cannot assume that things just are as they are. We see twisted wreckage and automatically ask how the accident happened; we examine evidence; we accept that a complex series of causes and factors can bring about an event.

In examining contemporary approaches to knowledge and reality, we need to look at three very different philosophical traditions:

- analytical philosophy.
- phenomenology and existentialism.
- postmodernism.

ANALYTICAL PHILOSOPHY

Analytical philosophy is the term used for the approach that sees the task of philosophy as that of the analysis of language and concepts. By seeking the simplest or most basic propositions, it attempts to set out as clearly as possible the criteria of truth and meaningfulness.

Inevitably, this approach has concentrated on language, since it is language that it analyses in order to examine claims to knowledge and reality. In the analytic tradition, what we know and what we can say are very closely linked, although the question remains about whether it is possible to have knowledge of a mystical or intuitive kind that cannot be expressed. One of the key thinkers in this tradition is Wittgenstein, and his early work sets the context for this aspect of the theory of knowledge.

Wittgenstein

There has been much debate about the background of the philosophical views of **Ludwig Wittgenstein (1889-1951)**. The influences of **Bertand Russell (1872-1970)**, **G E Moore (1873-1958)** are evident; he knew **Gottlob Frege (1848-1925)** and other German thinkers, and his earlier philosophy was deeply influenced by the phenomenology of **Edmund Husserl (1859-1938)**.

With Frege and Husserl, the focus of philosophy began to shift away from a study of epistemology and the problem of how knowledge is to be given secure foundations, to a study of the more basic problem of how knowledge is gained and given meaning in the first place.

Wittgenstein does not attempt to deny the possibility of metaphysics, the problem that epistemology had traditionally found itself unable to ignore. Rather, he sets out the limitation of the possibility of our speaking of metaphysics and he narrows down what kind of ontological claims (claims about the nature of being) can be made.

Wittgenstein wanted to reveal the bankruptcy of philosophical, metaphysical and ethical discussion. Such discussion, he claimed, is misled by the complicated and illogical nature of the language it uses. He accused metaphysicians of thinking that language gives a greater grasp on reality than is in fact logically and empirically possible.

The first phase of his thinking is presented in a slim, but very tightly argued book, known as *Tractatus*, which was written during the First World War, and published in 1922. In it Wittgenstein argued that language, which contains logic, marks the limit of human thought. In other words, what can be thought can be said. Hence, if metaphysics is the attempt to set out the nature of reality as it reveals itself to thought, the key to that, in Wittgenstein's view, lies in language.

Wittgenstein called his own philosophy 'useful nonsense' in that it acts as a ladder one climbs in order to see things as they really are. But in becoming aware of things as they really are, one must accept that the ladder, which helped the new understanding, must be thrown away.

The pictorial relationship of words to the simple underlying 'facts' of reality 'shows' itself and what shows itself cannot be said. In other words, philosophy, is trying to achieve the impossible by describing the indescribable in words.

At the end of the *Tractatus*, Wittgenstein, with impeccable logic, tells the reader to acknowledge that the model of language and 'facts', which he has presented, has little relevance to everyday living. But those things which are fundamentally important – morality and the good, aesthetics and the beautiful, theology and the nature of reality – may be shown and experienced but cannot accurately be spoken of. This is because you can never reach a point where the connection between the word and the 'fact' is inevitable.

The consequences of Wittgenstein's thought are startling if followed through. If 'facts' can only be shown and they must define their relationship to us afresh in each succeeding present moment, this means that there is no such thing as the human subject to think or entertain ideas. He says in *Tractatus* proposition 5.641:

> 'The philosophical self is not the human being, not the human body, or the human soul, with which psychology deals, but rather the metaphysical subject, the limit of the world – not a part of it.'

The very act of thinking becomes another 'fact' in existence within reality. The thinking fact carries with it the illusion of consciousness, as part of the characteristic of what it means to be a human.

Wittgenstein's philosophy challenged and tried to replace the whole Cartesian way of thinking, with its belief in the autonomy and sovereignty of the thinking, rational human subject, which still dominated philosophy at the time Wittgenstein wrote the *Tractatus*.

As a result of this first part of his philosophical career, Wittgenstein was convinced that philosophising had been reduced to meaningless, ultimately useless activity. So he retired from it and took up gardening and then teaching in rural Austria.

Logical Positivism

Logical Positivists were attracted to Wittgenstein's repudiation of metaphysics and philosophy. He had relied on the logical concept of tautologies (statements that are self-evidently true, for example, 'they arrived one after another in succession'). The philosophers of the Vienna Circle argued that the meaning of a proposition lay in how it could be verified or checked. Logical positivism maintained that for something to be meaningful, it had to be either self-evident or else verifiable by observation. As a result, they declared the language of aesthetics, ethics and metaphysics meaningless. At best, these propositions can be allowed to function as expressions of emotional attitudes, rather than statements of fact.

The task of philosophy under this system is now not to establish philosophical doctrines but to tease out meanings or focus attention on the lack of them.

However, in struggling to back up its own founding proposition that facts must be self-evident or verifiable, Logical Positivism struggled with the problem of being self-referentially incoherent – that it was itself a value system, which therefore must also be open to question!

Wittgenstein's *Tractatus*, in contrast to the Positivists, allows that there are con-cepts that cannot be verified, but can only be shown or experienced.

This is of the most fundamental value. While Wittgenstein severely limited the ability of 'God–talk', metaphysics and ethics, to grasp reality he regarded them highly. They are not seen as nonsense; rather, for Wittgenstein, our relation to the 'facts' of reality is a highly mystical and open-ended experience.

In discussions with the Vienna Circle, Wittgenstein realized that his first philosophy had not solved the basic problems of philosophy in the way he had hoped. It was this realization that persuaded him to take up philosophy again and led to his second philosophy, articulated in its most complete form in the *Philosophical Investigations* (published in 1953 after his death from cancer in 1951).

> **Logical Positivism** is the term used for the range of ideas typical of a group of philosophers, called the Vienna Circle, in the 1920s and 1930s. Influenced by the empirical tradition, and especially the work of David Hume, Logical Positivism was distinctive in its method for it attempted to develop empiricism with the help of further conceptual tools given by the logical and mathematical theory, especially that of Russell and Wittgenstein.

One comforting implication of Wittgenstein's argument in the *Tractatus* is that you will never experience your own death! Death is simply a way of describing the limit of experience. In this sense, one's own death is completely unknowable. Yet that does not stop people having intuitions about what it might be like to be dead, it simply means that they cannot justify those intuitions with reference to experience of any kind. Religious and moral beliefs belong to that class of ideas that go beyond experience, and therefore beyond the range of propositions analysed by the early work of Wittgenstein. They are known through mystical awareness, not through propositions backed up by experience.

Wittgenstein's later philosophy

In his later philosophy (some of which appeared in *Philosophical Investigations*), Wittgenstein showed the limitations of the philosophy of his *Tractatus*.

The meaning of language is no longer to be located solely by reference to the object it represented. Instead the meaning of a word depends on its location in a sentence and the use to which that sentence is normally put. A priori conceptions of what words actually mean are rejected.

Rather than asking for the meaning of a word, one should look at its use. Language is now seen as an essentially social instrument or a range of instruments, being always developed by society to serve an effectively unlimited variety of purposes. So there are no all-embracing criteria of assessment to which we can appeal. His critique of philosophers is that they have been inclined to look for simplicity and uniformity where none actually exists.

But is such philosophy about what we can know, or simply about what we can say? In a sense, the two have to go hand in hand. In examining the use to which we put language, we are also examining the experience of the world that gives rise to language.

The aim of Wittgenstein's philosophy is to bring out the misunderstandings that gave rise to philosophical problems in the first place. Any critique of philosophical problems is always internal to a particular language game; it is therefore difficult to escape the relative context of that culture and its way of approaching philosophical problems.

Both Wittgenstein and Heidegger (whose work we shall examine in the next section), although different in method, are equally sceptical about our ability to secure certain knowledge of reality.

FOR FURTHER INFORMATION ON:
WITTGENSTEIN, ESPECIALLY ON HIS THEORY OF LANGUAGE, SEE PAGE 207
FOR FREGE, SEE PAGE 208
FOR RUSSELL, SEE PAGE 208

'We must do away with all explanation, and description alone must take its place.'

Wittgenstein, *Philosophical Investigations*

'Logical investigation explores the nature of all things. It seeks to see to the bottom of things and is not meant to concern itself whether what actually happens is this or that. It takes its rise, not from an interest in the facts of nature, nor from a need to grasp causal connections; but from an urge to understand the basis, or essence, of everything empirical. Not, however, as if to this end we had to hunt out new facts; it is, rather, of the essence of our investigation that we do not seek to learn anything new by it. We want to understand something that is already in plain view. For this is what we seem in some sense not to understand.'

Wittgenstein, *Philosophical Investigations*

PHENOMENOLOGY AND EXISTENTIALISM

The approach to philosophy known as Phenomenology discarded preconceived notions in the theory of knowledge (epistemology) that presupposed an onlooker who asked for proof of an objective world. **Edmund Husserl (1859-1938)** set out a programme for the systematic investigation of consciousness. He insisted that existence can only be understood through *Dasein*, the basic mode of being in the world through participation and engagement. For him, consciousness is the fundamental, undeniable true state. Objects that are perceived relate to the state of mind of the perceiver, so that no distinction can be made between what is perceived and the perception of it.
Martin Heidegger (1889-1976) adopted Husserl's phenomenological method to examine the data of immediate experience. Heidegger was an

Heidegger sees us as being 'thrown' into life with a particular set of circumstances, and it is up to us what we make of them. They are the background facts of our lives, given and not chosen. Nevertheless, faced with the freedom of choice, we may not know what to do with our lives, and be tempted to fall back on the acceptance of fixed roles that fit in with our circumstances. Having been offered the freedom to choose how to live, we find it more comfortable to accept external restraints. For Heidegger, we are constantly in danger of accepting the limited roles that others give us, rather than striving to act out our own authentic existence.
We accept a social role. Our uniform tells us that we are authorized to give orders. The social rules under which we live require us to accept the authority of others. This may be necessary in the case of directing traffic, it can be dangerous if it pervades all aspects of life. Are we nothing more than the cyclist who has to ride on the right, or the person with a whistle who directs traffic?

Existential philosopher. He believed that human beings must be primarily concerned with the question of Being because they are naturally concerned with their own existence.

Heidegger turned Descartes' famous saying on its head. Instead of 'I think therefore I am', he preferred, 'I am, therefore I think.'

As the name suggests Existentialist philosophers have been concerned with the problems of human existence, not

the existence of objects or plants but solely human existence.

Phenomenology and existentialism do not so much solve earlier problems about knowledge and reality as take a radically different perspective on them. For phenomenology, the world you experience is just that – the world you experience. For existentialism, the focus of attention shifts radially towards the experience of being a thinking, choosing individual.

The literature on Postmodernity is endless and complex. There is a lot of disagreement over what it means to be 'Postmodern'.

The concept covers a wide range of developments in thought, art and society, all with philosophical and sociological implications.

Some modern philosophers argue that to talk of the Postmodern is essentially to talk about the heightening of factors already seen in the Enlightenment, rather than the conceptual dawn of a new age. Even so, it is hard to deny that a cultural shift of some kind now seems to be occurring in late-modern Western culture.

Three philosophers who have contributed to this shift in thinking are Jacques Lacan, Michel Foucault and Jacques Derrida.

As we know, Kant's rational philosophy was a response to the scepticism of David Hume's empirical writings. Hume had stated that there was no basis upon which we could move from our perceptions and experience of the world to say anything about reality, without the charge of it being mere opinion.

Postmodern thought represents the empirical scepticism of Hume taken to its absolute limits. Postmodernism questions the very foundations of the philosophical heritage of Socrates, Plato and Aristotle, for it challenges the coherence of language itself.

Because of this focus it is an epistemological problem – a problem of knowing – which has important implications for ontology, the branch of philosophy traditionally concerned with the study of being, of reality in its most fundamental form.

JACQUES LACAN (1901-1981)

Western culture has been heavily influenced by the idea that we are all autonomous individuals, and philosophers, including Descartes, have made much of this. The judicial systems and the laws within Great Britain or the United States of America assume that individuals normally have the freedom to choose how to act.

As a result of this belief we are responsible to others and society for our actions. Think what would happen to society, schools, businesses and other institutions if this belief in our autonomy were to vanish.

Lacan challenged this concept of autonomous human beings. He played a key role in developing Freudianism and psychoanalytical theory, but he was deeply influenced as a thinker by structuralism, which is fundamentally a belief about how language works.

Ferdinand de Saussure (1857-1913) was the father of structuralist thought. He looked at the world of language by referring to the signifiers (the words we use to talk) and the signified (the reality we describe in our talk). His argument was that the signifiers themselves represent particular ways of interpreting the thing in reality that they refer to. As such they cannot be seen as definitively describing that which is signified. He stated that:

'Language is a social construct upon which a community places an agreed network of given assumptions and meaning. Each individual term can be understood only by considering how it differs from other terms.'

This idea of difference conferring on language its meaning, is key to much postmodern writing.

Lacan used these ideas and argued that the human subject both knows and does not know itself because of the dynamic interplay of two factors:

Is there an author for what appears on the screen? With an intention? With a unique meaning? Or do the words themselves provide the meaning? Can this computer keyboard generate literature, or do we have to assume a creative input from an individual human source?

- Language constructs the human self.
- The way the ego (conscious self) judges and connects all this content, and so comes to conceive of itself as being a certain kind of person in relation to the world.

Lacan's thought about the human subject, when linked to a structuralist view of language, have enormous consequences for epistemology and metaphysics.

The point is that the signifier is always separated from the thing signified and has an existence in language apart from it. So words are never able to correspond absolutely with the world that is lived in. Signs, symbols, images of every type become understood in a symbolic and metaphorical way.

Lacan has challenged the following:

- **Descartes' idea of autonomy**, because the human individual is now seen as highly subjective. Self identity is unsta-

ble and fluctuating and can be never fully known.

- **The world of Science**, where language is always found in its present use and immediate context does not escape the charge of subjectivity.
- **Any view of language or thought** which supposes the ability of words to provide a transparent representation of an objective reality, is radically undermined by Lacan's theory.

In such a situation how free are we as individuals? And what does 'to be free' mean anyway?

Modernism, in many aspects of culture, particularly in fine art and literature, places emphasis on the self-conscious expression of the creative artist or writer. Things are produced in order to express a vision or intuition, the words or images are vehicles for a more profound intuition.

For Modernism, words primarily reflect the intention of the user. For

Postmodernism, language has more of a social and cultural role; it is a shared commodity.

Commenting on Postmodernism, Thomas Docherty (the editor of *Postmdernism: a Reader*) says:

'In its broad usage, this is a "family resemblance" term deployed in a variety of contexts (architecture, painting, music, poetry, fiction, etc.) for things which seem to be related – if at all – by a laid-back pluralism of styles and a vague desire to have done with the pretensions of high Modernist culture.'

Words can be transparent to meaning. They can also be a barrier, interposed between the individual and the world. They have their own life and shape what we can say or think. People may hide behind newspapers, which are not transparent, but which influence and shape our thinking.

MICHAEL FOUCAULT
(1926-1984)

Foucault was a French historian and philosopher who was influenced by structuralist thought but also critical of some aspects of it.

Foucault is more accurately described as a post-structuralist. His major thesis was called *Madness and Civilisation*, in which he was concerned with madness and reason as they related to the institutions of psychiatry.

When he was considering Descartes' 'I think, therefore I am' as a rationalist foundation for knowledge, Foucault doubted everything except his own sanity, the possibility of which he had rejected in his 'First Meditation'.

Foucault concentrated on what madness meant in contrast to reason, and arrived at the conclusion that Descartes' understanding of madness and reason, far from being universally objective, was dependent on a particular understanding of the terms derived from Descartes own historical situation.

This call to cultural and historical relativism can be seen in various strands of his writing:

- Foucault uses the term 'discursive practice'. This refers to the rule-governed set of statements, which give the basis by which any human community, at any point in time, shows what it believes to be 'knowledge'. He suspected that there was no possibility of any conception being truer than any other, outside of a particular 'discursive practice'.
- The effects of this evolving relativism, threatens to reduce discussion of reality to a relative status.
- In his later writings Foucault reflected on how particular organizations or bodies of knowledge – such as the scientific community – hold authority and power over people despite the fact that they still fail to escape the problems of subjectivism and relativism.

In the *Order of Things*, Foucault says:

> '*As the archaeology of our thought easily shows, man is an invention of recent date. And one perhaps nearing its end... Like a face drawn in the sand.*'

Foucault rejected the power that discourses and world-views have over us, as they put a limit on the possibilities of what we can be as human beings. But we are left wondering what would

We are bombarded with images and adverts; it is a normal part of urban life and of the media. To what extent are we defined by them?

happen if everyone took such an approach. Would there be anything left to guide our lives, or offer us new possibilities, except the desires that already exist within us?

The following comment was made by Joe Staines in *The Hutchinson Dictionary of Ideas*, 1994:

> *We can no longer make sense of the world because there is no cohesive world to make sense of, instead we occupy a state of what Jean Baudrillard has called 'hyper-reality', an unreal world of dreams and fantasy, of 'simulacra' — the world of TV, of the shopping mall, of video games, of Disneyland.*

JACQUES DERRIDA (B.1939)

Derrida was born to a Jewish family living in Algeria. He is a long time professor of philosophy at the Ecole Normale Supérieure in Paris. He has been attacked as a charlatan by some of the members of the philosophical community at Cambridge University — remarks occasioned by a proposal to offer Derrida an honorary degree in 1992. His work is highly controversial.

Derrida's ideas have been instrumental in forming a new school of criticism,

'deconstruction', so called because he has sought to desconstruct Western rationalist thought and metaphysics to show the incoherence of its foundations.

He set forth his theories in *Writing and Difference* (1967) and *On Grammatology* (1967) basing his ideas on a broad reading of the Western philosophical traditions. He focuses on Language and sets out to subvert narrative assumptions about the text of language by challenging the idea that text has an unchanging unified meaning.

In opposition to the theory of Saussure, Derrida challenged the primacy of spoken language and emphasized the written language's ability to alter speech and thought in creating rather than transmitting meaning. Derrida is attempting to show that language is constantly shifting.

He rejects also the whole Socratic method of questioning reality to reach a clearer understanding, and Aristotles' logic of identity which depends on asserting:

The Law of Identity; that 'whatever is, is'.
The Law of Contradiction: nothing can both be and not be.
The Law of the Excluded Middle: everything must either be or not be.

These are reduced by Derrida to incoherence. This is because any bases on which judgements might support and apply the logic of identity systematically come under deconstruction themselves.

Derrida calls for philosophy to abandon its desire to find the truth about things. Instead it should think of itself as just another literary genre, which is attempting to examine the practice of various genres and how they interrelate with others.

For Derrida this does not imply negative conclusion, because deconstruction of any text may bring about new and creative ways of reading the text. It could go either way. The important thing is that philosophy should be understood to be immanent, in other words, to be immediately present in all intellectual activity.

It is not surprising that Derrida's ideas have been met with such hostility. He does not play the philosophy game by the accepted rules.

KNOWLEDGE AND REALITY: SOME CONCLUDING COMMENTS ON WESTERN APPROACHES

We have seen that the task of philosophers is a difficult one, especially when they are trying to account for the assurance ordinary people seem to have in what they know about the world in which they live. The philosophical attempt to construct a theory of knowledge and reality that is adequate, has raised some of the most difficult theoretical problems known to humanity.

Bertrand Russell once suggested that the real problem with epistemology and metaphysics was that no one had ever succeeded in developing a theory that is both credible and consistent.

It is easy to see that some of the most logical and consistent theories appear to be unbelievable and that some of the more believable ones appear to contain serious inconsistencies. The task of philosophy in this area of enquiry is not yet finished.

One might be tempted to ask...

Am I writing what I think?

Or am I thinking what I write?

SEE ALSO DERRIDA ON:

HISTORY PAGE **279**

INDIA

Some of the most ancient philosophical approaches to knowledge and reality are to be found in the literature of the Indian subcontinent, with much of the earliest metaphysical speculation being found in a class of literature known as the *Upanishads*. The composition of many of these texts pre-dates the emergence of Greek thought in the fifth and sixth centuries BCE.

As with Western philosophy, most of the philosophical positions to be found in Indian thought were forged via a process of argument and counter-argument. This has given rise to systems of thought that are enormously varied and extremely complex. This means that nearly every metaphysical position found in Western thought can be found in its Indian counterpart.

India, despite the mystical image it has in the West, has a long tradition of reasoned argument and debate. This process of debate has produced, for example, instances of monism, dualism, pluralism, naive realism (that things are exactly as they appear to the perceiver), and materialism in Indian thought.

However, we must remember that in talking about 'Indian' or 'Eastern' thought we are always dealing with something extremely heterogeneous. This sometimes gets forgotten, especially when we casually talk about Hinduism, Jainism, Buddhism, or even, in China, Taoism and Confucianism. All of these names used for religions or philosophies can be seen as umbrella terms, which mask a multiplicity of differences and can easily become more misleading than clarifying.

THE FOUNDATION OF INDIAN THOUGHT: THE VEDAS AND THE UPANISHADS

The very earliest metaphysical speculations can be found in the *RigVeda* (Veda in the ancient form of Sanskrit used in the

composition of these texts literally means knowledge) which was composed c.1200-900 BCE.

For the most part the *Rig Veda*, and the three other Vedas (*Sama*, *Yajur*, and *Attharva Veda*) consist of a miscellaneous collection of poems or hymns dealing with aspects of daily life and Vedic ritual. However, among this disparate collection, there can be discerned some distinct metaphysical principles governing Vedic society.

In all, we can discern three major principles: *Rta*, *Satya*, and *Tapas*.

Rta (pronounced Rita) is eternal order in the cosmic sense and stands for the law of nature that imposes order on chaos and creates aesthetic forms of beauty (*Rupa*, *vapus*).

Rta is also the uniformity of nature and the ordered course of things. In the social sense *Rta* is the fundamental moral law and order governing the life and character of human beings and is responsible for creating ethical behaviour and goodness.

As such the moral law governing Vedic society is seen to be an essential part of *Rta*.

Both the natural law and the moral law are known as *Dharman*. In later Indian thought this becomes *Dharma*, a term which has immense importance in the history of Indian philosophy. Nearly every school of Indian thought sees itself as expounding its vision of the *Dharma*, or the way things are in reality.

Satya (Truth), the second major term used in the *Rig Veda*, possesses two aspects: firstly, it is an integral part of *Rta*; secondly it is *Sat* or eternal truth which is conceived as being the ultimate nature of reality, only accessible through an inner vision.

What is significant about this is that even at this early point in the development of Hindu thought, reality, the way things really are, can only be approached **by turning away from the sensory world**.

The final term is *Tapas* which has connotations of a spiritual fire which lifts human beings from an animal like existence to a spiritual plane. This spiritual power is found to become active by *Tapas* arousing *dhi*, which is the higher intellect.

BRAHMAN AND ATMAN

It is in the *Rig Veda* that we find one of the most famous hymns in this whole corpus of literature. This is the *Nasadiya* or 'Hymn of Creation' (Rig Veda X, 129). It is worth quoting a brief section of this so that we can begin to get the flavour of metaphysical speculation in the late Vedic period.

Who, really, knows? who can here declare it —
whence was it born and whence comes this creation?
The Devas (gods) are later than this world's production;
Then, who knows from where it came into being?

That from which this creation came into being,
whether it had formed it, or it had not,
He who surveys it in the highest region,
He, truly, knows it, or maybe He does not know!

This hymn has been interpreted as the forerunner of two distinct philosophical positions, namely, monism (there is one substance underlying the whole of reality) and monotheism (there is one God). It was the former that was to become enormously influential with the philosopher **Samkara**'s (pronounced: Shankara) interpretation of the Upanishads in the eighth century CE and the foundation of the school that became known as the **Vedanta** (the cream or end of the Veda).

In Samkara's reading of the Upanishads there is one substance, which is the substratum for the whole universe and this is known as *Brahman*.

Brahman takes two forms: **Nirguna Brahman** and **Saguna Brahman**. In its Nirguna form, Brahman is beyond time,

space and causality. However, without Nirguna Brahman time, space, and causality could not exist. It is claimed that it is the existence of Nirguna Brahman as an unchanging substratum that allows us to understand proximity in space, succession in time, and interdependence in the chain of causality.

In addition Nirguna Brahman is said to be devoid of any empirical attributes and hence no description of it is possible. Quite literally the only thing that can be said of it is 'Neti, Neti!', 'Not this, not this.'

Nirguna Brahman could be seen to be analogous to the unchanging white screen in the cinema without which one could not relate the disjointed images of the film. The necessary hypothesis of something like Nirguna Brahman is needed, so it is argued, for us to make sense of our world.

It should be obvious from the foregoing that no direct relationship can be established with Nirguna Brahman. Nirguna Brahman is not a God and it therefore cannot be worshipped, prayed to, or meditated upon.

Nevertheless Nirguna Brahman is the foundation of all relative existence and the intangible unity that pervades all. As such, Nirguna Brahman is seen to provide a metaphysical foundation for ethical behaviour.

In its Saguna Brahman form, Brahman is conditioned and has empirical attributes. Thus Saguna Brahman is Brahman known through *maya*, or the 'veil of illusion'. Creation, preservation, and destruction are all activities that take place in Saguna Brahman. In this form Brahman can be conceived as a personal God.

However, Nirguna and Saguna Brahman are not two separate entities they are one and the same thing seen in two different ways. *Maya* too has no independent existence, it is also inherent in the nature of Brahman.

Overall the *Upanishads* can be seen as a number of disparate attempts by early Indian thinkers to determine the essential nature of the universe, what we could conceive of as the first principle behind all existence.

SAMKARA

The founder of the Vedanta system of Hindu thought, Samkara is generally thought to have lived in the eighth century CE. Legends associate his conception with the Hindu god Siva and credit the young Samkara with being a master of all the sciences at a very early age. When he was very young it is said that he retired to the forest where he met the sage Govinda and became his chief disciple. Thereafter Samkara travelled all over India engaging in philosophical debate and triumphing over opponents of his Vedanta system.

One of the premises that these thinkers started from was that the essential nature of things did not reveal itself to sense perception, which took place in space and time. The real was conceived of as outside of space and time. Therefore, sense perception rather than giving us things as they are in themselves merely gives us appearances.

This is analogous to the Greek philosophers Parmenides and Plato, who asserted that the empirical world was simply a shadow of reality.

Likewise the Upanishadic thinkers declared that empirical knowledge is not true knowledge (*vidya*) but merely *avidya*, or ignorance. Moreover these thinkers radically discriminated between that which belonged to the essential nature of something and that which did not. The non-essential was declared to be non-self and was not to be taken into consideration.

The inference that they made, as a result of these deliberations, was that the universe (Brahman) was indentical with the individual self (*Atman*).

One of the earliest of the Upanishads, the *Brhadaranyaka*, speaks of the lone reality of Atman and the unreality of the universe outside of Atman. What this means is that, if Atman is the sole reality, and the knowing subject in us, then there can be no reality outside consciousness. Thus all forms of duality are declared to be *maya* (illusion). The philosophy of the Upanishads, both in the texts themselves, and in Samkara's inter-

pretation, is a thorough-going non-dualism (*Advaita*). Real knowledge (*vidya*) is said to be a consequence of the perception of this comprehensive form of non-dualism.

SAMKHYA-YOGA

The Samkhya school – 'Samkhya' in Sanskrit means 'right knowledge' as well as 'number' – is usually considered to be the oldest of the six 'orthodox' schools of Hinduism and can be described as propounding an atheistic realism and an uncompromising dualism.

For the Samkhya there are two 'reals', which are known as *Purusa* and *Prakrti* (pronounced: 'Purusha' and 'Prakriti').

The principle ontological claim of the Samkhya is that experience takes place via a knowing subject (Purusa) and known object (Prakrti).

Prakrti (usually translated as 'primordial nature'), which is the known object, is composed of a dynamic tension between three forces, which are known as the *gunas: sattva, rajas* and *tamas*.

The gunas are the three main constituents or strands of existence and form the material structure of the universe. Furthermore the universe and every object in the universe, so it is argued, evolves. The Samkhya have a complex theory of evolution, out of prakrti, which is composed of the three gunas.

Each guna represents a distinct type of energy. In the physical world *sattva* can

Are we in fact at one with the universe, and all forms of duality illusion? Is ultimate reality single or multiple?

be conceived of as what is pure and fine whilst *rajas* informs what is active, and finally *tamas* is seen to exemplify resistance and solidity.

Purusa is the unchanging principle of intelligence or pure consciousness, whilst all change or activity takes place in prakrti which is non-intelligent.

The Samkhya philosophers resorted to an analogy to describe the relationship between purusa and prakrti. Purusa was compared to a lame man who was seated on a blind man who could walk (prakrti).

Change in prakrti is said to take place not by any direct action or intervention by purusa but by the simple presence of purusa. If this initially appears difficult to understand then once again we can resort to an anology: A magnet (purusa) can cause iron filings (prakrti) to move simply by its presence without any direct intervention.

Purusa is also seen to be the unchanging principle of intelligence behind the universe. As such it is entirely distinct from the physical and mental universe, which remains entirely separate from it.

If purusa is the unchanging principle of intelligence, then prakrti is the ever-changing, unintelligent, uncaused cause of the physical and mental universe. Included within prakti are 'mind-stuff' (*antahkarana*), the senses and matter. Anything which can said to take a form will be found in prakrti. In addition, anything that is to be found within prakrti will be composed of the three gunas.

In Samkhya epistemology, three factors are said to be involved:

- **A knower,**
- **an object of knowledge,**
- **the process of knowing.**

For all forms of knowledge the sole knower is said to be purusa who alone is

FOR FURTHER INFORMATION ON THE HINDU CONCEPT OF ATMAN IN:

THE PHILOSOPHY OF MIND,

SEE PAGE 146

THE PHILOSOPHY OF RELIGION,

SEE PAGE 184

the true experiencer.

Samkhya thinkers give a complex account of the formation of knowledge as a process. Briefly this process takes the following form:

- The senses come into contact with an object and carry impressions to brain centres and organs.
- These organs in turn carry impressions to the mind (manas), which organizes the received impressions into some form of percept.
- The *ahamkara* (self-sense) then refers the percept to the intellect (*buddhi*), which then interprets the percept with the resultant formation of a concept.
- It is from the buddhi that the purusa then receives the concept and perception then follows.

It is worth noting that what we in the West would call 'mind' is composed of three factors: manas, ahamkara, and buddhi, all of which are entirely non-conscious and non-intelligent. As such 'mind' is simply an apparatus for the reception of impressions of the objective world. The only real knower, on such a view, is purusa.

Knowledge which has its origins in sense impressions is known as 'sense perception'. As well as this kind of knowledge, Samkhya acknowledges two other forms of knowledge, namely, inference (*anumana*), and revealed words or scriptures (*aptavakya*).

Inference is especially important for the Samkhya school, in that most of the fundamental conceptions of Samkhya are based on inferential reasoning. Samkhya thinkers state that there are seven kinds of relations, and the presence or absence of something can be inferred from these relations.

Inference itself is believed to be of three kinds:

- inference from an antecedent to a consequent – from a cause to an effect,
- inference from a consequent to an antecedent – from an effect to a cause, and
- that which is based on invariable connection established through empirical observation.

'Eternal among eternals, conscious among the conscious, the One among the many, he disposes over desires: he is the cause, he can be comprehended in theory (samkhya) as in spiritual exercise (yoga); knowing this God a man is from every fetter freed.'

from the *Svetasvatara Upanishad*

If the teachings of the Upanishads and the Samkhya school represent the growing complexity of Indian thought on metaphysical and epistemological issues, then early Buddhism represents an attempt to break with metaphysical questions entirely.

It is worth noting that the 'philosophy' of the Upanishads would probably have formed the primary intellectual background to the Buddha's teaching, and that much of what is encapsualted in those early teachings can be seen as a direct response to that background.

The term 'Buddha' is the title given to the historical person known as **Siddhartha Gautama (566–486BCE)**, which means 'the one who has woken up'. Though there is no explicit metaphysics to be found in early Buddhism, a good deal is to be found in an implicit form.

It could be argued that, although there may be no specific metaphysical aim underlying the Buddha's teaching, there is to be found a metaphysical view that is fundamental to what he has to say.

Whenever metaphysical views were put to the Buddha he generally avoided them simply replying that such questions are 'neither profitable nor conducive to the highest good.'

As an amplification of this belief he states that:

'Philosophy purifies none, peace alone does.'

Majjhimanikaya, 633

What he reiterates to his disciples again and again is that:

'Two things only do I teach my disciples — suffering and the cessation of suffering.'

The Buddha's teaching is traditionally summarized under the headings of the 'Four Noble Truths' (*arya satya*) and the 'Eightfold Path'. What should perhaps be made clear is that the Buddha is not a philosopher but a socio-ethical reformer and an existential thinker. This becomes entirely clear when we look at the substance of the Four Noble Truths and the Eightfold Path.

The Four Noble Truths are as follows:
- There is suffering (*duhkha*);
- There is a cause to suffering;
- There is a cessation to suffering;
- There is a path leading to the cessation of suffering.

Within this formulation we have both the diagnosis and cure to what the

Buddha perceives to be the most implacable scourge of existence, *duhkha*. This term has come to be almost universally translated as 'suffering'. No matter how widely accepted this practice is, however, it fails to do justice to the immense pervasiveness that Buddhist thinkers attribute to *duhkha*. This term more properly translates as 'the totality of all unsatisfactory experience'. As such, *duhkha* ranges from the most minor irritation to the utmost intensity of mental and physical anguish. Existence, for Buddhist thinkers – conditioned existence that is – is characterized by *duhkha*.

However, that is not the end to the story because, as the second of the Noble truths makes clear, *duhkha* has a cause. It is the idea that things have causes, and produce certain effects, that is central to the Buddhist world view and at the heart of its soteriology (doctrine of salvation).

Notice that the ending of suffering depends upon both ethical qualities and also a true understanding of the nature of the self. Within Buddhism, ethical wholeness is sometimes presented as a precondition of insight.

THE BUDDHA
566-486BCE

The Buddha was born sometime in the sixth century BCE. The most widely cited dates for the Buddha's life are 566-486 BCE. The very earliest Buddhist sources state that the Buddha was born Siddhartha Gautama in Kapilavastu, what is now a small town on the Indo-Nepalese border but was then a small state.

According to legends, he was born the son of a king and was destined to a life of luxury. However, while living in the palace and deliberately protected from all kinds of unpleasantness he rode out one day and encountered the existential facts of birth, old age and death. Shocked by his discovery he ran away to join a group of ascetics living in the forest.

For many years he practised severe yogic austerities with his companions until eventually he grew dissatisfied with the progress he was making and left to follow his own path.

Upon reaching the small village of Bodhgaya in the modern state of Bihar he seated himself under a tree (*ficus religiosa*) and resolved to remain there until either he reached enlightenment or death claimed him. Legend tells us that the legions of Mara (the god of death) assailed the Buddha, seeking to sway him from his chosen task.

Eventually, on the full moon in May, the figure once known as Siddhartha Gautama became a 'Buddha', a fully awakened or enlightened one. His ministry began in Sarnath near the ancient city of Benares where he taught what he had discovered to his former colleagues. The Buddha's ministry was to last for about 40 years and in this time he taught his message to young and old, irrespective of caste.

However, in this period the Buddha did not write anything down. What we now have preserved in the middle-Indian language of Pali are discourses that were remembered by his disciples and transmitted orally for approximately 400 years. Many of the discourses start with the formula "Thus have I heard..." The canon of the Buddha's teaching was not committed to writing until the first century BCE.

'Non-greed is a root of the wholesome; non-hate is a root of the wholesome; non-delusion is a root of the wholesome... When a noble disciple has thus understood the unwholesome and the root of the unwholesome, he entirely abandons the underlying tendency to lust, he abolishes the underlying tendency to aversion, he extirpates the underlying tendency to the view and conceit "I am", and by abandoning ignorance and arousing true knowledge he here and now makes an end of suffering.'

From the *Majjhima Nikaya*, in a translation by Bhikku Nanamoli and Bikkhu Bodhi

SEE ALSO THE BUDDHA ON:

ETHICS PAGE **80**

RELIGION PAGE **187**

EDUCATION PAGE **232**

IMPERMANENCE AND DEPENDENT ARISING

Implicit in the second and third of the Buddha's Noble Truths is the doctrine of 'interconnectedness' or 'dependent arising' – *pratiyasamutpada*. Within Buddhist thought the world of suffering existence, the world conditioned by *duhkha*, is known as *Samsara*, or cyclic existence. *Samsara* represents a state of eternal becoming in which all beings are entrapped.

What dependent arising tells us is that in the empirical world everything is impermanent. All things are conditional, relative, dependent, and subject to birth and death. The causal formula that underlies dependent arising is as follows:

'This is; that arises.'

This can simply be restated as,

'Depending on a cause; an effect arises.'

As a corollary to this it becomes evident that all thought is necessarily relative – every thought arises in accordance with the formula of dependent arising. Thought can be seen to be relative, because it is neither unreal (it appears to arise) nor real (it passes away).

Therefore from the Buddhist perspective, all objects of thought and the phenomenal world hang somewhere between reality and nothingness.

It is entirely with this in mind, that the Buddha named his doctrine the 'Middle Way' (*Madhyama pratipat*). As a middle way it was seen to be the 'middle' between the two extremes of eternalism and nihilism.

When the Buddha outlined the doctrine of dependent arising he did so in terms of twelve mutually conditioning links. The twelve links can be viewed as a graphic illustration of the Buddhist notion of Samsara.

The twelve links of dependent arising are as follows:
1. Ignorance (*avidya*)
2. Karmic formations (*samskara*)
3. Consciousness (*Vijnana*)
4. Psycho-physical organism (*nama-rupa*)
5. Six sense organs – five senses + mind (*sadayatana*)
6. Sense- object contact (*sparsa*)
7. Sense-experience (*vedana*)
8. Craving for sense-enjoyment (*trsna*)
9. Clinging to this enjoyment (*upadana*)
10. Will to become (to be born) (*bhava*)
11. Birth or rebirth (*jati*)
12. Old age and death (*jara-marana*)

Dependent arising describes the very structure of reality. In addition, what the formula of dependent arising depicts is a 'process' that occurs moment to moment. All phenomena are momentary, that is, that are in existence only so long as the conditions that sustain them remain.

The argument for this runs in the following manner:
- If we say that a thing arises dependent on its causes, this is actually to admit that it is momentary, for when we remove its causes the thing will cease to be.
- Also, that which is produced in this way is necessarily subject to death or extinction.
- Thus any thing that is subject to death and extinction is impermanent; being impermanent it is momentary.

If dependent arising illustrates the functioning of the world of becoming, which is characterized by *duhkha*, then that process is headed by ignorance. It is ignorance (*avidya*) that is said to be at the root of samsaric existence and it is only when this root cause is destroyed that Samsara ceases – this would be the attainment of Nirvana.

Once again the translation of the term *avidya* by 'ignorance' does not bring out the many resonances contained within it. *Avidya* is the very opposite of *vidya* or knowledge. However, *avidya*, rather than simply lack of knowledge – nescience or lack of knowledge is what is implied by the English word 'ignorance' – implies the positive misconception that the world seen through the lens of *avidya* is the way

the world is. The consequence of this is that individuals cling to this distorted view, believing that they have a true view of reality.

If, as the Buddha suggests, reality is characterized by a complex web of causal relationships, then if one brings about a cessation of the primary cause, this will inevitably bring about the cessation of the effects. Therefore, if 'ignorance' (*avidya*) is brought to an end then its effect, *Samsara*, with its attendant suffering (*duhkha*), will also be brought to an end.

The theory of karma is a direct consequence of the causal principle outlined above. Karma is simply a law of action – 'action' is literally what the Sanskrit means – and indicates that every action gives rise to a 'fruit' (*phala*) or effect.

If actions are conditioned by ignorance (*avidya*) then the consequences of such actions cannot be predicted. Yet the Buddhist view is that actions will inevitably give rise to results, if not in this lifetime, then perhaps in future lifetimes.One further corollary to the Buddha's teaching of dependent origination needs to be mentioned – the doctrine of 'No-self' (*anatman*).

What the doctrine of 'No-self' represents is a thorough-going critique of doctrines such as those represented in the Samkhya school and the literature of the Upanishads. As such this is a critique of the notion of the self as some kind of unchanging substance – *purusa* in Samkhya and *Atman/Brahman* in the Upanishads.

The self, as represented in these two traditions is essentially what we are, and it is ultimately free from the vicissitudes of suffering existence. It is the eternal within the individual. Instead of speaking of an essential self the Buddha spoke about five aggregates (*skandhas*), which give rise to the notion of the self.

These are:

form (*rupa*) which includes the body and the five senses;

feeling (*vedana*) which is the way in which we respond to stimuli in terms of seeing them as pleasant, unpleasant, or neutral;

perception (*samjna*) which on the Buddhist model is a classifying or sorting of experience whereby we come to recognize phenomena;

Volitional formations (*samskara*). In the recognition of phenonema desire, wishes, and habitual tendencies are provoked which become fossilized ways of dealing with the world;

finally, there is **consciousness** (*vijnana*) which is the basic sense of self-consciousness.

What we have here are five interdependent factors, which give rise to a nominal entity, which we call 'self'. Rather than there being any fixed, eternal principal within the individual, there is only this set of co-dependent factors. In Buddhist parlance the 'self' is a dependent arising just like any other phenomena.

Notice here that the teaching is not presented as fixed doctrine to be accepted, but as an invitation to examine this particular interpretation of experience here and now, to see whether it is effective. Like philosophy, but unlike most religions, Buddhist teaching is not dogmatic, but invites critical examination, with the possibility that it may lead to a personal understanding of its interpretation of reality.

Everything is subject to change, whether it is a human being, a physical object, an idea even. To acknowledge this and to resist the temptation to crave permanence, is the key to the Buddhist path to overcome suffering.

NYAYA-VAISESIKA

The Nyaya are what might be termed in Western philosophy 'naive realists'. They are realists in at least three possible senses. Firstly, they accept the reality of external objects that exist independently of any perception of them; secondly, they admit the existence of universals that are not merely linguistic, that is to say, some of the objects that exist independently of perception are universals; finally, their philosophical explanation are almost always an attempt to validate our common-sense views of the world.

Knowledge, for the Naiyayikas (the followers of the Nyaya), consists of a correct apprehension of objects, which exist independently of our cognition of them. Thus genuine knowledge is a kind of correct 'mirroring' of independent states of affairs.

In addition, all forms of knowledge will involve conceptualization and language (see the section on the Philosophy of Language). Language in this view is seen as a non-distorting medium by which we can understand the world as it is independently of our cognition of it.

Of particular interest in regard to the Nyaya-Vaisesika school of Hinduism are its theories concerned with the valid means of knowledge (pramanas). Rather than asking the question 'What is knowledge?' thinkers within the Nyaya concentrated their attention on the question of what was a valid way to gain knowledge.

These thinkers recognized four valid means by which we can know something:

i   perception (pratyaksa),
ii inference (anumana),
iii analogy (upamana),
iv credible testimony.

As a result of an interchange of views with Buddhist thinkers, the Nyaya came to espouse a trenchant form of realism in which reality was considered to be composed of seven categories (padarthas) and nine substances. In particular it is the seven categories that came to be conceived of as possessing ultimate reality.

The seven are as follows:

i   Substance (dravya),
ii   Quality (guna),
iii Action or motion (karma),
iv   Genus (samanya),
v   Species (visesa),
vi   Relation (samavaya),
vii Negation or absence (abhava).

What is represented here is a kind of common sense scientific outlook in that the universe is perceived to be both pluralistic and multiple.

Nyaya thinkers therefore did not attempt to reduce the seven catagories to one. However, it is substance that is seen to have independent existence, for all the other catagories depend upon it.

Nyaya thinkers therefore deduced nine forms of substance:

i   Self (atman),
ii   Mind (manas),
iii Earth,
iv   Fire,
v   Air,
vi   Water,
vii Ether,
viii Time (kala),
ix   Space (dik).

Once again, these substances are all viewed as possessing objective reality.

In the Nyaya-Sutra there can be found criticism of the position of Madhaymaka Buddhist thinkers, who claimed that thought and conceptualization are entirely subjective and only capable of giving us appearances. What the Nyaya attempt to do is vindicate the objectivity of the pramanas and valorize their capacity to know the real as it is.

To illustrate the four pramanas, let us take as an example the number of ways in which a black swan can be known. The first is fairly simple in that I have a direct perception of the bird in question. In the second case I stumble across some large swan-like foot impressions in some damp mud and perceive a few black feathers lying around from which I infer that there must have been a black swan recently present. In the third case someone describes to me what a black swan is like by describing it as a very large black bird that swims in water and is very similar to the white swans I see on the river. In the last case an eminent zoologist tells me he has seen a black swan in Australia. In all four cases the knowledge acquired refers to an objective reality.

MADHYAMAKA

Madhyamaka is one of the four principal schools of Mahayana Buddhism. 'Mahayana' means 'Great Vehicle'and is usually opposed to the 'Hinayana' or 'Little Vehicle' of Buddhism which is now represented by the school of Buddhism which is dominant in Sri Lanka, Burma, Thailand, Laos and Cambodia. This school is more correctly know as the 'Theravada' or 'Doctrine of the Elders'.

The origins of the Mahayana are both complex and obscure. We know, however, that this form of Buddhism gained dominance in China, Tibet, Korea, and Japan. It is **Nagarjuna**, and his disciple **Aryadeva** who are traditionally credited with founding the Madhyamaka school, sometime in the second century CE. In the history of Buddhist thought the Madhyamaka ('Middling School') can be seen to represent the growth of a more critical – some would claim more sceptical – approach to the possibility of knowledge.

One of the principal claims of Nagarjuna, and later Madhyamikas (followers of the Madhyamaka) is that all phenomena lack self-existence or essence (*svabhava*). In attacking this notion, Nagarjuna is particularly aiming his criticism at other Buddhists (Abhidharmists) who claimed that it is **dharmas**, or the ultimate elements of existence, that have 'self-existence'. In the Abhidharmist view conventional existents, such as tables, chairs, beds, dogs, and persons, all lack intrinsic existence. However, the dharmas, out of which these things are composed, **do** possess some kind of ultimate existence. Nagarjuna interprets this as the claim that the **dharmas** do not just

possess some kind of essence but that they have 'real' independent being.

To reiterate: this asserts that the **dharmas** exist independently and in their own right. Nagarjuna speaks of all **dharmas** as being 'empty' (**sunya**) and as a consequence he is claiming that all things lack intrinsic or inherent existence.

It ought to be made quite clear at this stage that Nagarjuna is not saying that tables, chairs, and persons do not exist but that the inherent existence of the chairs and tables does not exist.

Nagarjuna is not refuting the existence of the conventional world but is attacking the metaphysical claim that things, such as the *dharmas*, possess some kind of essence or independent existence. For something to exist 'inherently', from its own side, it would have to be independent of any cause or condition that would sustain it. It is this kind of existence that is being denied by Nagarjuna and his followers.

To what extent can this chair be said to have inherent existence? What it is depends on how we relate to it, and its existence is related to causes and conditions. Without tree, no wood; without wood, no chair. But unless we know it is something to sit on, it is not a chair. Both physically and conceptually, a 'chair' depends on many things.

SEE ALSO NAGARJUNA ON:

ART PAGE 272.

Nagarjuna's claim is that all things depend for their being on causes and conditions, and therefore that they are 'empty' (*sunya*) – that is, empty of inherent existence.

That a thing depends on causes and conditions for its existence is synonomous with it being empty of inherent existence.

When Nagarjuna, and his later followers claim that, on investigation, all things will be found to be empty, or that instead of the 'thing' they find emptiness, they are not claiming that they have found some kind of metaphysical absolute.

'Emptiness' (*sunyata*), it should be stressed, is not an Absolute, it is the actual absence of any absolute principal, and is simply the way things really exist, that is, with the absence of intrinsic identity.

Nagarjuna, in arguing in this way, believes that he is bringing back the 'middle' to the Buddha's 'Middle Way', interpreted here as a 'Middle way' between eternalism and nihilsim. Nagarjuna clearly believed he had avoided both extremes.

Yet, in the history of Indian thought, Nagarjuna has often been accused, both by fellow Buddhists and non-Buddhists, of being a nihilist. This issue has given rise to much debate, and was directly responsible for the emergence of the 'mind only' (*vijnanavada*) school of Buddhism. The Vijnanavadins claimed that all things lacked inherent existence apart from the 'mind' or 'consciousness' which perceived these things.

While it is not possible to assess the debates here, Nagarjuna at least thought that he had avoided extremes of nihilism in that he did not negate the empirical and conventional world but simply reoriented our understanding of how that world exists.

Saying that all things are 'empty' does not affirm anything about the way they exist, but simply negates the common way that we think they exist.

In the parlance of Buddhist logic, particularly in the Tibetan understanding of it, 'emptiness' is a 'non-affirming

negative' (**prasajyapratisedha**).

It is worth noting that Nagarjuna's philosophy, and the Madhyamaka school in general, was enormously influetial in the development of Chinese Ch'an and Japanese Zen Buddhism.

DOGEN AND THE METAPHYSICS OF TIME

The Japanese thinker **Dogen (1200-53)** in his major work the *Shobogenzo*, states that both the limitations of metaphysics and existential problems, can be directly related to a distorted understanding of time.

Dogen is particularly critical of the way time has been represented ontologically in the history of Buddhist thought. Time can be seen as a fundamental issue in Buddhist philosophy in that the Buddha's analysis of existence states that all the factors of our experience (Sanskrit: *dharmas*, Japanese: *ho*) are selfless (*anatman*; *muga*) and transitory (*anitya*; *mujo*) events which do not simply move in time, but are intrinsically temporal in nature.

Time is often viewed as a static substratum in which events move – a kind of 'container' picture of time. Based on this view, time is usually presented as a linear series of 'nows' in which the present is a present 'now', the past a former 'now', and the future a 'now' yet to arrive.

This linear conception of time, which surfaces in such seemingly innocuous phrases as 'time flies' and 'time passing us by', appears to be so self-evident that we very rarely question it. Dogen thinks that such a conception of time contains an implicit ontology, which, from the Buddhist viewpoint, is existentially destructive, impeding self-understanding and self-realization.

Dogen illustrates the conventional view of time by giving us the example of someone who lives in a valley, crosses a river, climbs a mountain and finally reaches a palace on the summit of the mountain.

With the attainment of the goal, he claims, the mountain and the river get relegated to things of the past, which are disconnected from the present moment. Man, in Dogen's view, is obsessively fixated at any particular time on the present and yet he continuously feels himself to be swept along by time and the rapid succession of now-points that characterize this view of time.

Rather than deny the reality of the present 'now' and the three tenses of time, Dogen attempts to reorient our understanding of these dimensions of our experience, by showing the ineluctable connection between time and the existence of self and world.

In order to achieve this Dogen speaks of Primordial Time or Time-Being (Uji). Time-Being is seen to be a fluid and dynamic process that is intimately connected with all forms of human activity.

It is Time-Being that Dogen believes underlies our conventional understanding of time, and as such is the disguised basis for that view. Conventional time is referred to as 'derivative time', which is time inauthentically derived from Time-Being.

In his reflections on time, Dogen is presenting us with a phenomenological view of its nature. It is phenomenological in that **each moment of our experience is intimately connected with every other moment.** Beings for Dogen are temporal events in that they are 'Be-ing'. However as temporal events their pasts are radically entangled with their presents and their future.

It could be said, on this view, that our past is our present, and that present which is replete with past experience, is also our future. Moreover, we are not temporally isolated as our temporality is entwined with all beings. Dogen's views on time are intimately connected to his soteriology in that he believes that enlightenment is possible now because the present is our past and our future.

The photo on the left shows the flow of people crossing a street. Since a camera captures only a brief moment of time, the faster the people move, the less they will appear on the image.

Take a very long exposure in a crowded street, and it will appear empty; the buildings will remain, but everything that moves will progressively fade into nothing. How then is movement, or the trace of movement, related to reality?

We tend to think of ourselves as fixed entities, moving from one event to another, and time as some kind of container, in which these events are sequenced.

In practice, according to Dogen, our very nature is flowing and moving – we carry our 'past' with us, taking it into our 'future'. We are a dynamic process.

FOR THE IMPLICATION OF THIS FOR THE PHILOSOPHY OF HISTORY, SEE PAGE 282

CHINA – TAOISM

Taoism, or more correctly tao chia (the school of the Way), is at least as old as Confucianism. The great flowering of philosophy in China occurred between the sixth and third centuries BCE, the period that saw the emergence of its two rival philosophical traditions: Taoism and Confucianism. The centre of interest for both was the right Way (*Tao*) for humanity and its place in both society and the natural world.

Taoism's two earliest and most important works are the *Tao te Ching* (The Way and its Power) and the *Chuang Tzu* (Master Chuang). The *Tao te Ching* is a celebration in poetic form of the Tao (Way). Although the *Tao te Ching* is essentially concerned with ethical and moral virtue, that ethical view is firmly based on the ontology of the Way.

In Taoism, that Way is to be conceived as fundamentally the way things actually are. The Taoist sage should live in accord with that Way.

To help us understand this vision of reality we can perhaps view it as the 'grain' of the world. Lao Tzu, the supposed author of the *Tao te Ching*, urged that the natural life is one that does not entail living 'against the grain'. The Way is conceived of as being the One, which is natural, spontaneous, nameless, and indescribable (See section on Taoist approaches to language).

Further, and here Taoism is at odds with Confucianism, the imposition of our own will and ideals upon the world invariably means going 'against the grain' and is a prime source of all human misery and unhappiness.

Lao Tzu urges us not to try to impose our wills upon a world that is entirely indifferent to us. To live in accord with the Way is to 'do nothing' (*wu wei*).

Rather than being a kind of oriental quietism, *wu wei* does not literally mean doing nothing; it means that one should do nothing that is not in accord with the *Tao*.

In the *Tao te Ching* it is the absence of struggle that denotes being at one with the world.

Chuang Tzu provides a wonderful illustration of this notion in the story of the butcher Ting:

'When this carver Ting was carving a bull for the king, every touch of his hand, every inclination of his shoulder, every step he trod, every pressure of the knee, while swiftly and lightly he wielded his carving knife, was as carefully timed as the movement of a dancer...'

'Wonderful', said the king, 'I could never have believed that the art of carving could reach such a point as this.' 'I am a lover of the Tao,' remarked Ting, putting away his knife, 'and I have succeeded in applying it to the art of carving.'

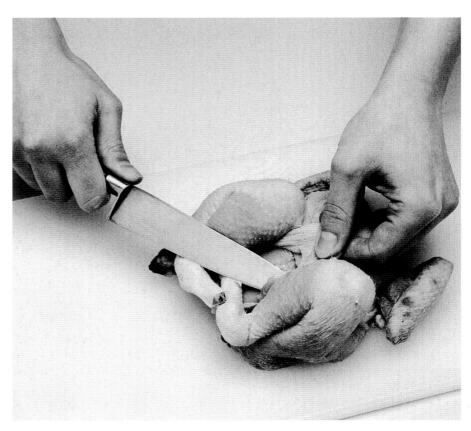

CHUANG TZU

Very little is known about the life of Chuang Tzu (Master Chuang) who is considered to be one of the founders, together with the legendary figure of Lao Tzu, of philosophical Taoism. It is said that he originated from Meng in the province of Honan and held a minor civil service post. He eventually abandoned this post in favour of a private life – this very act can be seen as antithetical to everything that Confucianism stood for. The only other information that we appear to have about Chuang Tzu is to be found in snippets to be gleaned from his work the *Book of Chuang Tzu*.

Practical Mysticism

In terms of knowledge, Taoism advocates purely practical knowledge and consequently deprecates all forms of knowledge acquired through books. But it is mystical as well as practical. The claim that there is a mystical dimension to our existence, which cannot possibly be put into words, is interwoven with wholly practical forms of wisdom as closely as yin is entwined with yang in the Tao symbol.

Theoretical knowledge – of the kind most books contain – is not real knowledge in that it admits of no degrees. We can make no sense of saying, for example, that I know that it is raining but not as well as Jane does. Whereas, in terms of practical knowledge it would be entirely sensible for me to say that I know how to swim but not as well as Jane does. In other words, practical knowledge does enable some people to be 'better' than others.

However, those who struggle do not really know the Tao. If too much effort is required for a task, this implies ignorance of the Tao. In contradistinction effortlessness constitutes a sign of real knowledge.

In effect, Taosism is the deprecation of all forms of theoretical or intellectual knowledge in favour of wholly other approaches – the polar opposite of the Western tradition in almost all its forms except, intringuingly, some aspects of Wittgenstein. From it, more obviously, spring Cha'n or Zen Buddhism.

'The highest form of goodness is like water.

Water knows how to benefit all things without striving with them.

It stays in places loathed by all men.

Therefore, it comes near the Tao.

In choosing your dwelling, know how to keep to the ground.

In cultivating your mind, know how to dive in the hidden deeps.

In dealing with others, know how to be gentle and kind.

In speaking, know how to keep your words.

In governing, know how to maintain order.

In transacting business, know how to be efficient.

In making a move, know how to choose the right moment.

If you do not strive with others, you will be free from blame.'

Tao te Ching, 8
from the translation by John C H Wu

'Those who know don't speak,
Those who speak don't know'.

Lao Tzu *Tao te Ching*

SEE ALSO TAOIST IDEAS IN:
ETHICS PAGE 82
RELIGION PAGE 194
ART PAGE 274
LANGUAGE PAGE 228

Ethics, or Moral Philosophy, is concerned with issues of right and wrong, with the criteria by which people assess human behaviour, and with the various codes and agreements through which they have sought to create a fair and just society.

It is the study of the moral choices that people make and the way in which they justify them. Underlying this is the basic question 'What does it mean to live a good life?'

'Ethics is the general enquiry into what is good.'
G E Moore

There are three basic ways to approach ethics:

1 Descriptive ethics simply describes patterns of behaviour. It does not attempt to say whether such actions are either right or wrong.

2 Normative ethics looks at the norms and values which influence moral choices, and examines why people call one action right and another wrong.

3 Meta-ethics is the study of ethical language. It asks if moral statements are meaningful and, if so, how they are to be understood and if they can be shown to be either true or false.

And of course, all three forms of ethics relate back to a basic understanding of life, for every choice a person makes reflects his or her fundamental beliefs and values.

Arguments about ethical issues may be based on:
- the anticipated results of action
- a rational view of what is 'natural'
- self-interest
- the needs of society
- religious belief
- pure practical reason
- self-identity and personal fulfilment

and ethical debates arise where these conflict with one another.

Everyone who acts on the basis of a personal choice, has some view of the future and of what he or she wishes to achieve. That view influences the values the person holds and provides the impetus for moral action. Part of the task for ethics, therefore, is to identify what it is we are hoping to achieve by the choices we make.

The questions we need to ask are:
- Am I free to make choices and act upon them?
- If so, how do I decide what I should do? What is right and what is wrong?
- Are there absolute rules that can be applied, or does everything depend on circumstances?
- Do I base my choice on the expected results of my action, or some general principle of what is right?
- Should moral issues be considered primarily in terms of their impact on individuals or on society as a whole?
- How do moral choices relate to a fundamental understanding of and beliefs about life?

Ethical theories fall into two general categories: those concerned with duty and rules (deontological theories), which focus on what is 'right', and those that consider the purpose or aim of behaviour (teleological theories), which focus on what is 'good', generally based on predicted results.

Ethics raises fundamental questions about life and its values. What do we think of as the 'good life'? What values do we need to promote in order that a 'good life' can be a possibility for ourselves and other people? Without some understanding or intuition about what is 'good', how can we decide what to do?

In this sense, ethics is an inescapable feature of human life. Being rational and autonomous implies the ability to make choices – and hence to an implicit ethics. On the other hand, to claim that we are neither, rational, free or autonomous also

has implications for ethics – for we cannot be responsible for those actions over which we have no control.

THE SCOPE OF APPLIED ETHICS

This chapter is primarily concerned with ethical theory. We shall be looking at what moral language means, at how we can justify calling one thing right and another wrong, and at some influential moral codes and arguments. But it is important to recognize that ethics is not merely a theoretical study; the application of these arguments to those areas of life where people are forced to make significant moral choices is of crucial importance.

Some of the current ethical issues are global. Environmental ethics, examines the guidelines that are used in assessing the way we treat the environment? It raises general questions: Is human need paramount? Does the natural environment itself have rights? What about other species? Animal issues form another important area of moral debate.

Sexuality is such a potent factor in human life, with such obvious and immediately experienced implications in interpersonal relationships, self-understanding and social acceptance, that it is not surprising that sexual issues have often appeared to dominate moral debate. Traditionally, sexual morality was concerned with what sexual acts were morally permissible and with whom they should be performed. Today, the debate is far broader, and includes the whole range of issues concerning sexual identity, self-expression and social conformity.

There are also ethical issues that are concerned with the professions: medical ethics, nursing ethics, media ethics, business ethics, warfare, scientific research and technology.

Practical questions in all these areas of applied ethics raise issues of a fundamental nature. Decisions made about genetic manipulation, or treatment of other species or the environment, are based on principles that are rooted in an understanding of the nature of human life, of its place in the universe and of what can be considered its 'good'.

Applied ethics is therefore central to the whole philosophical project, for it highlights the practical consequences of ideas about the nature of life and of human thought and language.

Ethics has been a feature of the philosophy of all eras and cultures – inevitably, since 'What should I do?' and 'What is life for?' are questions that follow on the fundamental human desire to understand the world.

For example, consider the rearing of animals in 'factory' conditions, rather than in a more natural environment. We might want to ask:

Can this be justified on the grounds of the additional food produced? To what extent should the satisfaction of human

need be necessarily accepted as the only valid 'good'? More generally, do animals have rights? How does our understanding of ourselves as a species relate to the rest of the animal realm?

Should there be limits on the use of animals in experiments? If so, who decides and on what basis? Should it depend on the potential human benefit? So, for example, is it morally right to inflict suffering on an animal in order to facilitate a cure for cancer, but not in order to test cosmetics?

What image do we have of 'the good life'? Is it something that everyone could achieve, or does it depend on some element of exclusivity? How does the image shape our ambitions and our values, and how do these – in turn – influence our actions? We may also want to consider whether the image of 'the good life', as it is presented by the media and through advertisements, influences the choices we make. Part of the technique of advertising is to sell an image, a dream perhaps, rather than just a product. Issues of right and wrong cannot be separated from the ideals and needs that motivate us, and 'ethics' concerns the ethos of our lives, as well as the moral significance of individual actions.

ETHICS

I cannot be blamed for failing to jump thirty feet into the air, because for me that is a physical impossibility. Neither can I be blamed for having hair, eyes or skin of a particular colour. We can only rightly be praised or blamed for those things over which we have some measure of control. Morality implies freedom.

But there is a basic problem to be considered: 'Are we free to choose what we do?' To what extent are human beings determined, either physically, psychologically, emotionally and socially?

The situations where we are either completely free or completely determined would seem to be (on a common-sense approach) rather limited. Mostly we are aware of having a certain amount of freedom within other given parameters. The nature of moral choice is what to do with those windows of opportunity with which we are presented.

Only physical?
One could analyse everything to the point of saying that every movement of your body takes place within a physical system that runs according to what we call 'the laws of nature'. You could say that everything you do is conditioned by those laws of physics, and you are not able to influence them in any way. If everything is in theory controlled by everything else, we have no freedom – only the illusion of autonomy.

You may reach into your pocket, take out a gun – and shoot someone. At every point your actions can be traced down the chain of physical causality, muscles contracting due to chemicals, which are released as a result of electrical activity within the brain. These physical processes explain every action. Are you then free? Could you argue that it wasn't you, but only your muscles, that fired the shot?

I may sense that I am free to choose what I do, but what about an animal? Is a cat free to choose whether to torture

Beneath the surface, is everything I do determined? Am I effectively a robot? Am I utterly at the mercy of my genes, or my environment, or my upbringing, or my place within a class struggle?
The experience of freedom (or lack of it) has implications for many other aspects of philosophy, including the nature of Mind, and the Philosophy of Science.
For example, if one believes that everything is absolutely determined, one could also go on to say that everything may be reduced to its constituent parts, and is nothing more than those parts. Are we simply the sum total of the cells that make up our bodies? If so, are our actions determined by the same kind of scientific laws that determine the operations of individual cells? Reductionism is the term for this 'nothing more than' approach.

or befriend a mouse? If I am drugged, or drunk, or stunned, or traumatized or brought up in a particular way, am I still free?

In law, a charge of murder may be reduced on the grounds of diminished responsibility. The key question here is whether we should always be in a position to claim diminished responsibility, because of those physical and psychological factors that determine action. Would any jury convict if it knew everything there is to know about the accused?

In consultation with an analyst, can we claim that anything we did was completely free from impulses beyond our conscious control. And if not, do we have sufficient freedom to accept moral praise or blame for what we do?

THE EXPERIENCE OF FREEDOM

What we experience as freedom may gradually be eroded the more our actions

are seen as predictable on the basis of physical, psychological or social influences. Does that mean that I am in fact not free to choose what to do? We have to ask, 'Can I experience myself as free, indeed, can I actually be free, even though science could theoretically explain the movement of every cell in my body and every thought in my mind?' In other words, can I be conditioned, but at the same time experience myself as free? This is a key question, and we shall see later how this was tackled by the philosopher Kant.

Society imposes restraints upon the actions of individuals, in the interests of the majority of citizens. Areas of agreed restraint are embodied in laws. But you have to be free to break a law for there to have been a need for the law in the first place. Legislation only arises in order to prevent something happening.

Is the photo on the right a suitable image for the life of an individual? Choices lead to yet more choices; one road branches into another. Some lead on; some loop back.
To travel by road requires the acceptance of a restricted number of options. Take a 'wrong' turning, and you may end up heading in a direction you did not originally choose. Yet choices and their consequences seem inevitable.
Without rules, traffic would quickly become snarled up and nobody would be able to move.
You might be physically able to break the rules, but you might be injured as a result, or society might impose some restriction on you by way of punishment.
You are free to disobey, but must be prepared to take the consequences.
Looking at the tangle of roads in life, one might ask 'How did I get here?' or 'Was I really free to choose this route?'

KARMA

In Hindu, Buddhist and Jain philosophy, one's present experience and action is influenced by actions performed in the past. The term karma literally means 'action', but it is commonly extended to refer to the consequences of actions for the person who performs them.

This idea is linked closely with the idea of the self. In Hindu and Jain thought, the self is eternal, and at death passes on from one life to another. The karma from one existence, which has not yet produced its results, is therefore carried forward into the next life.

Buddhist philosophy is rather different, in that there is no eternal 'soul' or self, but rather a constantly changing set of states. On the other hand, karma has a crucial role to play, in that the consequences of action continue to influence the future, even if there is no identity between what is conventionally considered the 'self' in the future as opposed to the 'self' in the present.

In these philosophies you are never free from the controlling influence of past actions. Yet that does not imply that everything is determined, since what you choose to do now will influence the future.

The conditions in which you find yourself now are determined by past karma, but what you choose to do now will influence your conditions in the future. Thus the human agent has a measure of creative input into the process of change.

For Indian philosophies, ethical seriousness implies freedom, but the idea of karma implies determinism. The balance these philosophies offer is one of creative action within an ever-changing set of conditions. Looked at simply from the standpoint of conditions, everything is determined. Looked at from the standpoint of the moral agent, there is choice and therefore some measure of freedom.

'What we are today comes from our thoughts of yesterday, and our present thoughts build our life of tomorrow: our life is the creation of our mind.

... If a man speaks or acts with an impure mind, suffering follows him as the wheel of the card follows the beast that draws the cart.

... If a man speaks and acts with a pure mind, joy follows him as his own shadow.'
The Buddha *Dhammapada* verses 1,2

This does not imply that one is somehow punished or rewarded according to some external set of values, rather that everything has its natural consequences, and everything is connected with everything else. We may not be entirely free, since many things influence us as causes and conditions, but we have a measure of choice, and are therefore able to be held responsible for the intentions that lie behind our actions.

FOR FURTHER

INFORMATION ON:

KARMA, SEE: PAGES **186** AND **190**

SEE ALSO

THE SECTIONS ON HINDU,

BUDDHIST AND JAIN ETHICS.

Although everyone knows the words good and bad, right and wrong, their precise meaning is far from straightforward. What, for example, do all 'good' things have in common? A good person; a good car; a good meal: there is no obvious common factor.

It is possible to use the terms simply with reference to a chosen goal or purpose: so you can talk about using the right tool for the job. But to say that something is good or right in itself, implies a value judgement, and sets that thing or action in the context of a general understanding of life. Ethical theories, such as Natural Law or Utilitarianism, are attempts to establish a framework within which it makes sense to speak of right and wrong.

Once we have a sense of the meaning and justification of these basic terms, others can be defined with respect to them. We can go on to speak of duty, moral obligation, authority and conscience. We can also get a sense of whether the terms right and wrong are being used in some absolute sense, or whether they are consciously being related to a particular society or situation.

There are three basic possibilities:

1 That everything depends on circumstances and therefore it makes no sense to say that anything is either right or wrong in itself (relativism).
2 That moral language simply expresses the feeling, wishes or suggestions of the speaker (emotivism and prescriptivism).
3 That right and wrong, good and bad, do have a meaning, and it makes sense to argue about the basis upon which they should be applied.

It is also possible to hold (option 3) that the terms have meaning, but that we cannot frame a rational argument to explain it. This view is termed intuitionism, a position associated particularly with the philosopher G E Moore (1873-1958). In his *Principia Ethica* (1903) he argued that the term 'good' could not be defined. Similarly, you cannot define the colour yellow but, once a number of yellow things have been pointed out, you know what 'yellow' means.

Thus we could say that we know intuitively when a particular action is good or bad. But equally, we could argue that what we know intuitively are the principles by which we then go on to assess individual actions. This latter view has the advantage of showing that we do not start from scratch every time we want to say that something is good, and we can state clearly the principles or values that we shall call 'good', and it is those values that we know intuitively.

'Everyone does in fact understand the question "Is this good?" When he thinks of it, his state of mind is different from what it would be, were he asked "Is this pleasant, or desired, or approved?" It has a distinct meaning for him, even though he may not recognise in what respect it is distinct.'

G E Moore *Principia Ethica*

G E MOORE
(1873-1958)

His influence on 20th century philosophy was immense because of the directness, even naivety of his views. In the field of language, he insisted that the philosopher's task was to analyse the meaning of statements, rather than simply argue about whether or not they were true, on the grounds that many apparent problems were mere confusion over the use of words. Such linguistic analysis became, through the work of Russell, Wittgenstein and others, vastly influential, at least in the English-speaking world. In the field of Ethics, his *Principia Ethica* (1903) offered a major critique of existing ethical theory, introducing not only his intuitionist approach, but also highlighting the 'naturalistic fallacy'.

NATURALISTIC FALLACY

G E Moore pointed out what Hume (see page 88) had already argued, namely that you cannot argue from an 'is' to an 'ought' – something which he termed the 'naturalistic fallacy'. It is this absolute divide between facts and values that dominates meta-ethics through much of the 20th century, as those who see no way of justifying value judgements factually, try to find some other function for moral language.

Thus, for example, protests about moral isses are not about what is actual, nor what is possible, nor what is legal, but what is 'right' or 'wrong'. If you want to argue your case as a protester, you have to do so on the basis of values you share with those to whom you are appealing. Just presenting facts is not enough; they alone cannot form a moral argument.

FOR FURTHER INFORMATION ON:

WITTGENSTEIN SEE PAGE 42, 207

In the early part of the 20th century, many influential thinkers took a view of language that restricted its meaning to the description of empirical facts. Notable among them were Wittgenstein and the philosophers of the Vienna Circle, whose work was publicised by A J Ayer's *Language Truth and Logic*.

A general term for this approach is Logical Positivism (see page 43).

Since these thinkers held that empirical verification was the sole criterion of meaning, moral statements were considered entirely meaningless. Hence, there were areas of life about which one simply could not make meaningful propositions.

The aim of this movement was to put language on a solid scientific basis, analysing it as facts and logical connections. But in so doing, it relegated all moral statements to the category of things that were not literally significant and about which Wittgenstein therefore believed we should remain silent.

But people continue to use moral language. If it is meaningless, what are they doing? There are two approaches to this:

EMOTIVISM

The approach taken by A J Ayer was that the person who said that something was right or wrong was simply expressing his or her personal likes or dislikes. If you approve of something, you call it good and right. Thus a moral statement has the same status as cheering for, say, a football team; when you cheer, you are not making factual claims about your team, you are simply indicating that you want them to win.

A major exponent of this approach was the American philosopher **C L Stevenson (1908-1979)**. He wrote *The Emotive Meaning of Ethical Terms* (1937) and *Persuasive Definitions* (1938), and further developed the theory in *Ethics and Language* (1944). His views roused some hostility. It was feared that the emotive approach might undermine moral standards by reducing them to a matter of personal preference.

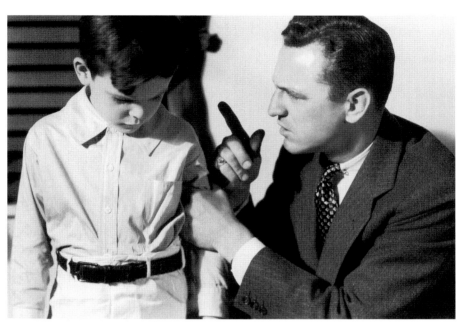

Telling a child to be good and keep quiet. We know that this really means, 'I would prefer it if you were quiet.' Therefore 'being good' is simply a way of expressing my preference for quietness. On another occasion it might be 'good' to speak up.

Therefore, it could be argued that the term 'good' has no meaning other than to express the preference of the person who uses it.

Education is generally held to be a vehicle for instilling values as well as imparting facts. Hence parents may choose schools reflecting their own religious or social views. In reality, even if rational arguments are presented, does not the ethos of the school and the personal standing of those who express certain views, play as important a part as logic in instilling shared values and moral views? And if this is the case, then the actual way in which moral education works has definite elements of both emotivism and prescriptivism.

'For in saying that a certain type of action is right or wrong, I am not making any factual statements, not even a statement about my own state of mind. I am merely expressing moral sentiments.'

PRESCRIPTIVISM

Associated particularly with the work of R M Hare, this approach suggests that when we use moral language, we are simply prescribing a course of action. To say that something is right, simply means that, in a similar situation, that is the thing that I would recommend you to do. It does not imply that there is any quality of 'rightness' or 'wrongness' that inheres in the action itself.

Within prescriptivism, there is no logical connection between the facts under consideration and the action that is prescribed. The only requirement that Hare makes is that, to be consistent, a person needs to be able to universalise that prescription, accepting it both for oneself and for everyone else in similar circumstances.

R M Hare (b.1919) established his moral theory with *The Language of Morals* (1952).

As we shall see later, several thinkers have attempted to establish an objective basis for ethical judgements. For example, Aquinas based his ethics on Natural Law, a rational interpretation of what he saw as the purpose for which each thing was created, while Kant based his argument on pure practical reason and the experience of moral obligation.

At the other extreme, there are those who hold that moral codes are useful human creations, which help people to live together, but which do not have any absolute or objective basis. There is no such thing as absolute right or wrong, only what we in this place and this time choose to call right or wrong. This tradition goes back to the Sophists of Ancient Greece, such as Protagoras. Plato places a similar argument (which he later demolishes) in the mouth of Thrasymachus (in *The Republic*) to the effect that justice is simply what is in the interests of the strongest.

The issue of whether moral claims can be absolute, or whether they are always relative to the society that adopts them, is a fundamental question of values. If there is no established aim and purpose in life, there can be no absolute moral principles.

Of course, these are the extremes, and few people wish to adopt them without qualification. Some (e.g. Fletcher, with his *Situation Ethics*) want people to be able to judge for themselves what is right in any given situation, but he still wants to set down the general principle upon which they make that judgement – in his case, doing whatever is most loving.

Others hold absolute values but recognise that no two individual situations are alike. Buddhism, for example, recognizing that everything arises in dependence upon the conditions that bring it about, calls actions 'skilful' or 'unskilful' depending on whether they help or harm spiritual progress. This sounds relativistic, but note that it leaves intact the values by which those actions are judged. Hence, it is fundamentally absolutist, although recognizing great variety in the way in which values are put into practice.

Is there any absolute obligation to help those who suffer? If so, on what is it based? On emotion? On reason? On enlightened self-interest? Does a troubled conscience indicate the presence of an absolute demand? Or is conscience simply the result of upbringing?

ETHICS

In looking at the issues of intention, conscience and social duty, there is a distinction between Hindu and Jain ethics. In the latter, actions – whatever the intentions of the person performing them – keep the 'soul' trapped within its material matrix, and therefore defer its ultimate goal of escape from the material world.

Jain thought is radically dualistic in this respect (see page 192). Hinduism accepts some measure of significance for intention, and Buddhism, at the other extreme, sees the intention of the agent as of primary significance (see page 81).

All three philosophies are concerned with personal salvation, and the moral status of an action is therefore judged according to the effect on the spiritual or moral state of the person who performs it.

Both the Jain and Buddhist traditions developed within circles of independent spiritual teachers, largely at odds with the Brahmin priesthood, and this may have led them to reject the more social considerations of mainstream Hinduism.

AHIMSA – THE KEY FEATURE OF JAIN ETHICS

Since killing has such negative consequences in Jain philosophy, monks and nuns take extreme measures to avoid it; hence the wearing of masks to prevent the accidental inhalation of small insects, and the traditional practice of sweeping the path to avoid treading on tiny creatures.

In a modern context, although these practices are continued, there is emphasis on a more general concern with the protection of the environment.

MODESTY OF MEANS

Jain ethics encourages the consumption of food simply for the sake of personal survival and health, not for pleasure. So a Jain will try to live in a way that does least damage to the Earth's resources, and consumes as little of its goods as possible.

THE FINAL ACT OF COURAGE

There is a tradition that those most spiritually advanced, as they come to the end of life, may decide voluntarily that they will prepare themselves for death by ceasing to take food.

This death by voluntary starvation does not amount to suicide, since it is only undertaken when death is in any case imminent. It is seen as a mark of great courage.

A 'Jain' is one who is victorious over the world, and clearly the act of recognizing the arrival of death and consciously embracing it is a supreme example of such a victory.

Notice, in the various Eastern views outlined here, the balance between the absolute and relative in ethics. For all these traditions there remains an absolute ethical ideal, but particularly in the Hindu and Sikh traditions that ideal is overlaid by the sense of the individual's purpose within society as a whole. The ethical relativity that results does not negate the ideal of non-violence, but is a recognition that – where that ideal is not possible – there is moral value expressed in courage and a sense of social duty.

THE SIKH VIEW OF COURAGE

The Sikh religion developed in spite of persecution at the hand of the Muslim rulers, involving forced conversion and martyrdom. Hence there developed a positive view of courage among Sikhs, expressed particularly by the acceptance of a sword as one of the five marks of becoming an adult member of the Sikh community.

The sword represents the absolute right of self-defence and also the obligation to defend all those who are innocent, especially those within the Sikh 'panth' or community.

In this case, rather as in the Hindu view of social ethics, the idea of social duty predominates over personal considerations. The individual is seen primarily as a representative of the community.

However, the sword (or kirpan) also expresses the obligation to fight against the five evil tendencies in human nature: lust; anger; greed; attachment to worldly things; pride. So moral courage has a personal as well as a social dimension.

For Sikhs, however, effort and courage are not enough, and the evil impulses can only be overcome through devotion and personal inspiration.

The study of the values and aims that underlie moral choice is sometimes termed axiological ethics.

FOR FURTHER INFORMATION ON JAIN ETHICS AND THEIR RELIGIOUS SIGNIFICANCE, SEE PAGE 192/3

Indian philosophy has generally combined some absolutist claims (particularly the principle of ahimsa, non-violence) with a recognition that people in different positions in life should accept different responsibilities and duties.

RECOGNIZING DIFFERENCES

Hindu philosophy recognizes that the moral quality of an action relates to the person performing it and the circumstances in which it is performed. Dharma is not reducible to a set of fixed and universalized norms of conduct.

The Sanskrit word that sums up the Hindu approach is *varnashramadharma* – Dharma related to one's varna (caste group) and also one's ashrama (stage in life).

There are 4 main caste groups:
Brahmin (priest)
Kshatriya (ruler/warrior)
Vaishya (merchant)
Shudra (worker)

Such distinctions probably originated in the racial divisions between conquering Aryans and the darker skinned native Dravidians in the second millennium BCE – the literal meaning of varna is 'colour' – and were given religious sanction through the myth of the division of the cosmic man (Purusha), where each caste group is made from an appropriate part of his body.

But not only is the concept of correct action related to caste, it also changes with one's path through life.

There are four ashramas, or stages in life, each with its own set of duties:
Brahmacarya (student)
Grihasta (householder)
Vanaprasta (retired)
Sannnyasa (ascetic who renounce worldly things).

Hindu philosophy recognizes that the appropriate Dharma for each person is related to both varna and ashrama. Society requires an appropriate balance, with all castes and stages of life working in harmony.

Hindu social ethics is therefore based on its ideas of the right ordering of society. The ethics of the individual are related to that overall aim. This combines ethical principles with the acceptance of diversity of action. It also relates the concept of karma (see above page 67) since, in Hindu teaching, one's place in society is influenced by one's action in past lives. In acting according to one's social norm, one is therefore also working through the results of one's own earlier karma.

There are parallels here with Plato's argument that justice requires that each of the three classes of people within the state act appropriately (see page 75).

A key issue in popular ethical debate is whether, if one abandons absolute and universal moral standards, the result will be chaos, as everyone feels entitled to adopt whatever moral norms he or she wishes. Hindu social ethics offers an alternative to such extreme positions, since everyone is expected to accept an appropriate, but not universal, set of standards. But those standards are not thought of as imposed arbitrarily, but as naturally suited to one's own interests and abilities.

Life thrusts people together with a complex set of relationships and social roles. Can people who differ be expected to have the same moral duty? Hindu ethics relate duty to social position and stage of life.

NON-VIOLENCE

Although Hindu social philosophy recognizes a great variety of social situations, each with its own appropriate duties, there are certainly fundamental or universalisable moral principles within Hindu thought. There is a distinction to me made between the social and the philosophical aspects of Hinduism. This is shown particularly in the key moral principle of *ahimsa* (non-violence). The deliberate taking of life is regarded as wrong, both because of the harm done to the victim, but also because (through the law of Karma) the act of killing is thought to have damaging consequences for the person who performs it.

From a philosophical and religious standpoint, ahimsa is the basic moral principle. On the other hand, from a social standpoint, Hindu culture needed to find an appropriate justification for warfare and political control that inevitably involved a measure of violence and the taking of life.

How are the ideal and the socially and politically expedient to be reconciled? This is a fundamental problem for all ethics, and is highlighted by this 'dual track' approach taken by Hindu philosophy.

Within the teachings of M K Gandhi, the general principle of *ahimsa* is coupled with another term *satyagraha* (truth-force), which Gandhi coined to express his policy of a very positive resistance to evil, seeing to set right what is wrong, without however resorting to violence or force of a physical nature.

Thus, social change can be effected by deep personal commitment to non-violence. At the same time, by espousing the principle of non-violence, the person taking action does not thereby generate negative karma.

In the *Gita*, the god Krishna is said to describe the ethically good person as one who lives…

'…without hatred of any creature, friendly and compassionate, without possessiveness or self-pride.'

UNSELFISH DUTY

One answer to the dilemma of how to reconcile the ideal with the socially expedient, set out in the *Bhagavad Gita* (usually referred to simply as the *Gita*), is that one should do one's duty – even if this involves the taking of life – but one should be personally detached in terms of the results of such action. In other words, the criterion of moral praise or blame is not the action in itself, but one's intention in carrying it out.

This is related to basic Hindu metaphysics, in that all intentional action produces results (see karma), but disinterested action avoids the negative consequences of this. More generally, however, it is related to the idea of conscience. Conscience arises where social action conflicts with absolute personal principles or feelings.

IS THIS ACTION MINE?

In the *Gita* there is also the idea that we are mistaken in thinking that we own our actions, failing to recognize that, at a deeper level, things happen through us that are independent of our choice. We may not be the autonomous agents we suppose:

'Our identity as agents of our deeds and our destiny is in fact a fiction promulgated in the moment antecedent to an action by the thought, "This is my act." But the Bhagavad Gita says: "While all kinds of work are done by the modes of nature, he whose soul is bewildered by the self-sense thinks, 'I am the doer.'" The self-concept, an invention of the ego, credits itself with events which in fact arise independently of choice.'

D Appelbaum *Real Philosophy*

Socrates was particularly concerned with the question 'What is justice?' There were many possible answers to his question.

In *Theatetus* 167, Plato put into the mouth of Protagoras (a Sophist) this view:

> '*Whatever in any city is regarded as just and admirable is just and admirable in that city for so long as it is thought to be so.*'

Thrasymachus (in Plato's *Republic*) was very candid about his view of right:

> '*What I say is that "just" and "right" means nothing but what is in the interest of the stronger party.*'

Thrasymachus is out for power and pleasure – he is a kind of 'natural man' devoid of any social restraints. But in order to get what he wants, he has to assume a civilized, decent social manner, and know how to play the social game to his own advantage.

In the *Gorgias* three people – Gorgias, Polus and Callicles – debate with Socrates what is a person's supreme good. The suggestions put forward is that the supreme good is the freedom to have one's own way (a freedom secured politically by being skilled in rhetoric, as taught by the Sophists, and so able to sway others), or the power to get your own way, or the power simply to satisfy all your desires.

Socrates challenges all these, pointing out that what you think is to your good may actually harm you, and that human desires can never be fully satisfied.

In the *Gorgias*, the dialogue ends with Socrates' argument that whatever good a person wants has to be specified in terms of the life in which that good can be enjoyed. If nothing is specified, if you are free to do whatever you want without any restraint or guidance, you are likely to suffer confusion and a permanent lack of satisfaction. The pursuit of one's own desires without any sense of limit, put forward in the dialogue by Callicles, is self-defeating.

Crucially, Socrates held that nobody does wrong willingly, since what is right is also what is in one's own best interest. For Socrates, to do wrong is therefore an intellectual rather than simply a moral error. It is to fail to understand the nature of one's own 'good'.

SOCRATES
(c.470-399BCE)

The first philosopher in the West to have worked out his own moral philosophy. His method of doing so, which became known as the 'Socratic method', was to persist in questioning the meaning of words in such a way as to expose ignorance and arrive at a clearer understanding of the reality to which the words referred. Socrates' basic questions were about definitions. You needed to say what something was before you could say anything else about it. Socrates, by challenging his interlocutors on various points, worked towards valid definitions of terms.

His views are known to us through the work of his disciple Plato, whose writings take the form of dialogues in which Socrates generally plays a central role.

Villains are often portrayed as hungry for the power that will enable them to control all around them. In other words, they seek to be in a position to determine what they will consider to be justice. An accusation sometimes made against the very powerful or wealthy is that they are 'above the law' - exactly the view that Thrasymachus would have held.

When do political and military decisions become crimes against humanity? When does a leader become a villain? In the photograph above, Milosovic, the former Serbian leader, stands trial in 2002 for his part in atrocities committed during the Balkan conflicts.

Should he be held responsible for whatever actions were committed by those he ruled? Are those who inspire hatred, guilty of the hatred they inspire?

Key features of Socrates' moral philosophy (which comes to us through Plato's dialogues, and which therefore represent Plato's particular view of Socrates) are:

- That virtue is knowledge: to know what is right is to do what it right.
- That doing wrong is therefore the result of ignorance. Nobody deliberately chooses to do what he or she knows is not in his or her best interest.
- That all virtues are fundamentally the same, since they all arise through knowledge of what is good and just.

PLATO'S REPUBLIC

In the dialogues of his middle and later period, Plato increasingly used the figure of Socrates as a mouthpiece for his own views. He also goes beyond the 'Socratic method', seeking to develop answers, rather than simply exposing ignorance. In particular we have the development of his theory of Forms – with a distinction between appearance and underlying reality (see page 24). In the *Republic*, Plato examines the nature of justice within a state, and then, by analogy, applies it to the individual.

In considering and rejecting the views of justice offered by Thrasymachus and others, Plato includes the story of the Ring of Gyges. In this, Gyges finds a ring which, when turned on his finger, has the power to make him invisible. He recognises the power that this offers him and, with impunity, seduces his queen and kills the king. The story presents human good behaviour being only the result of social restraint based on fear and self-interest.

This is countered by Plato in two ways: by showing that reason, rather than will or appetite, should rule, and by examining the Form of the Good in order to get an absolute standard of goodness, by which all else may be judged.

In book VII of the *Republic*, Plato uses the analogy of the cave to illustrate the philosopher's progress from the perception of the objects of sense experience to an understanding of the Form of the Good. See page 25 for an outline of this analogy.

'In the world of knowledge, the last thing to be perceived and only with great difficulty is the essential Form of Goodness. Once it is perceived, the conclusion must follow that, for all things, this is the cause of whatever is right and good... Without having had a vision of this Form no one can act with wisdom, either in his own life or in matters of state.'

'What advantage can there be in possessing everything except what is good, or in understanding everything else while of the good and desirable we know nothing?'

Republic book 23

After dismissing as inadequate the views of justice offered by Thrasymachus and others, Plato suggests that, in order to see what justice is for an individual, it is easiest to start to consider what it is in a state.

He describes three different classes of people in a state:

1 The guardians; philosophers who are able to rule.
2 The auxiliaries; the military, whose task it is to defend the state.
3 The workers, who produce what is needed.

He argues that true justice will only be achieved if the state is ruled by guardians, who are trained to rule and do not seek their own self-interest.

His conclusion is then applied to the individual. The three classes of people are equated with three aspects of the self – the rational side, the will (or emotions) and the appetites. Just as, within a state, stability and justice are only obtained once it is ruled by reason, so for the individual, reason must hold appetite in check, and will do so using the power of the will and emotions.

The *Republic* throws up a wealth of issues that could be discussed in the context of moral philosophy – including selective breeding and education (in order to equip those most able to rule), the raising of children communally rather than in families, compulsory abortion or infanticide of babies born to couples whose union has not been approved by the state.

It presents a society in which the individual is forced to take his place within an overall scheme dominated by an intellectual elite. Justice reflects the superiority of the intellect, and therefore the continuance of the status quo. People are considered just to the extent that their appetites and wills are under the control of reason, a reason that goes beyond the superficial objects of sense experience, and appreciates the world of eternal Forms.

FOR GENERAL

INFORMATION ON:

PLATO SEE PAGE 23

For Aristotle, reason is what distinguishes human beings from all other creatures. Reason gives direction and purpose to human action. We act with something in mind:

'Every craft and every investigation, and similarly every action and decision, seems to aim at some good; so the good has been well described as that at which everything aims.'

Opening line of Book 1 of the
Nicomachean Ethics

Aristotle then makes the crucial distinction between happiness and everything else we might desire. Whereas one might find honour, understanding, pleasure and so on good in themselves, they are also good because they give us happiness. On the other hand, happiness is chosen for itself alone, and it is what we see as making life worthwhile.

In other words, whereas you might choose other things for the sake of the happiness they bring, it would be hard to see how you might choose happiness for the sake of anything else. Happiness is therefore self-sufficient, and the goal of the ethical life, since it is fundamental to what we choose in life.

Plato had insisted that individual 'good' things participated in the ideal 'Form of the Good', and that to appreciate them one had first to have some understanding of that eternal Form. Aristotle rejects such a distinction:

'Good itself will be no more of a good by being eternal; for a white thing is no whiter if it lasts a long time than if it lasts a day.'

He roots ideas in the concrete, thus:

'...it is puzzling to know what the weaver or carpenter will gain for his own skills from knowing this Good Itself, or how anyone can be better at medicine or leadership from having gazed on the Idea Itself.'

Rather than contemplating the eternal realm, Aristotle argues that we can acquire virtues in the same way that we gain practical skills. We become a builder by building, and a musician by playing music. So also we become virtuous by doing those things that are deemed to be good.

Actions were to be judged by their ability to produce happiness, which included both the notions of doing what is right, and living the good life.

THE MEAN

In evaluating action, Aristotle sees vices in both excess and deficiency – hence virtue is in the mean between them. He cites as examples of the mean such things as generosity (between wastefulness and meanness) and bravery (between being rash and timid), and extends this even to social manners:

'In sources of pleasure in amusements let us call this intermediate person witty, and his condition wit; the excess is buffoonery and the person who has it a buffoon; and the deficient person is a sort of boor, the state boorishness.'

But he accepts that there are particular

actions to which the idea of a mean cannot apply:

'We cannot do them well or not well – for example by committing adultery with the right person at the right time in the right way. On the contrary, it is unreservedly true that to do any of them is to be in the wrong.'

Similarly, there can be no mean in matters of temperance or bravery.

The concept of the mean seems to function as a guide to practical wisdom, and therefore appears as subordinate to those of virtue and happiness.

In general, the thrust of Aristotle's ethics is that virtuous actions are those that a reasonable person would choose as likely to lead to happiness and well-being. So the concept of virtue is linked to those of goodness and happiness.

THE FINAL CAUSE

The concepts of happiness and finding a mean between excess and deficiency seem to provide criteria for deciding between courses of action, but underlying these are the more fundamental questions about the quality of life and its overall purpose.

Another key feature of Aristotle's thinking addresses this, and it has been particularly important for the subsequent development of ethics. This is his idea that everything has a purpose or end, for which it is designed – a 'final cause'. If we know something's 'final cause' we can know its overall place in the scheme of things, and therefore how it should behave or be treated. This was taken up particularly by Aquinas (see page 79), and is the basis of the Natural Law approach to ethics.

EPICUREANS AND STOICS

The ethics of Socrates, Plato and Aristotle are set against the backdrop of the Greek polis, the city-state. Individuals find their virtue and happiness as members of a particular society, each with a function to perform.

The philosophers who followed them faced a world in which the city-states were giving way to large empires, and their emphasis consequently shifted to consider what morality might mean for individuals in the context of the universe as a whole.

The Epicureans took the view that the universe itself is impersonal and the gods (if any) far off and uninterested in humanity. If it is to have values, humanity itself must create them. Morality therefore comprises seeking happiness, both for oneself and for others, and framing principles that would make this possible.

Like Aristotle, they saw the need for moderation, restraining natural impulses to achieve an overall balance of pleasure over pain. Unlike Aristotle, they sought happiness in private life, not by taking an active role in society.

Epicureanism is named after Epicurus (c.341-270BCE), and was promoted by the poet Lucretius (c.95-52BCE) in his poem *De Rerum Natura* (On the Nature of Things).

By contrast, the Stoics saw a purposeful design incarnate within the cosmos. The ethical way, therefore, was to live in your allocated place in that overall design. Life, for Stoics, should be natural, and the person who followed the divine purpose inherent in nature, would find happiness as a result.

'Do not seek to have events happen as you want them to, but instead want them to happen as they do happen, and your life will go well.'
from note 8

How do you see the universe? As impersonal, or as having an overall design and purpose? Your answer to that question will incline you towards either the Epicurean or Stoic approaches to ethics.

'You are foolish if you want your children and your wife and your friends to live for ever, since you are wanting things to be up to you that are not up to you, and things to be yours that are not yours.'
from note 14
Encheiridion – by Epictetus

Founded by Zeno (334-262BCE), the influence of Stoic thought continued into the Roman period, where its exponents include Seneca (1-65CE), Epictetus (50-130CE) and the Emperor Marcus Aurelius (121-180CE).

It might seem that Stoics gave virtue precedence over happiness, and Epicureans happiness over virtue, but that would overlook the fact that their differences in approach derived from very different views of the universe:

If the universe has a divine purpose, it is reasonable to believe that happiness will spring from alignment with that purpose – hence the Stoic approach.

If it is impersonal, values and morality are human creations, with the overall aim of achieving happiness – hence the Epicurean approach.

That distinction is fundamental for all ethics, and one that links it with metaphysics. Subsequent ethical theories tend to fall into one or other of these two camps. Naturally enough, Western religions tend to favour the first (e.g. Natural Law), since morality is then related directly to belief in a creator God. Secular bases for ethics (e.g. Utilitarianism) tend to opt for the second, making ethics independent of metaphysics.

FOR FURTHER INFORMATION ON:

THE EPICUREANS, SEE PAGE 152, 299

THE STOICS, SEE PAGE 152, 299

What do you do when you face a world in which old certainties are crumbling? Augustine, faced with the fall of Rome (the Goths sacked it in 410), wrote 'The City of God' where he looked for an eternal reality (like a Platonic Form) to give a permanent sense of purpose and security in the face of the impermanent physical world.

Augustine had for a while been a Manichaean, believing in a dualism of good and evil. In this view, physical life was inherently and irretrievably sinful, and the spirit should free itself from it. The ethical implications of this were that physical things did not matter – which led to extremes of hedonism or asceticism. With his rejection of Manichaeism, Augustine sought a single overall principle. He found this in Christianity. But he also took the Platonist view that present phenomena are but passing shadows compared with their eternal counterparts.

One of the central beliefs of theism is that evil is not a separate, independent force, since God, as the omnipotent creator, will originally have made everything as good. Therefore, even if something is corrupted, no creature is entirely bad; its vices are simply an absence of goodness.

'What is called evil in the universe is but the absence of good.'

Augustine recognized also that the supreme law of love should take precedence over particular rules and regulations. He coined the famous phrase:

'Love and do what you will.'

ST AUGUSTINE
(354-430)

Born in Hippo, North Africa, near Carthage, to a Christian mother and pagan father. He was initially attracted to the Manichaean religion, but later became influenced by Neoplatonist thought. While Professor of Rhetoric in Milan, he was converted to Christianity under the influence of St Ambrose. He returned to North Africa, becoming Bishop of Hippo in 395.
His best known works are *The Confessions* and *The City of God*.

This should not be interpreted as endorsing a total, unfettered freedom, but rather that, if the overall principle is established (in this case, love), one should do what follows naturally. This may be related to the general principle that Plato took from Socrates: action follows understanding. If you genuinely understand love as the supreme value, then you will automatically be led to do what love demands, without needing specific rules and regulations.

This approach to Christian ethics was echoed in the 20th century by Fletcher, in his book *Situation Ethics*. Set in context of 1960s quest for freedom from conventional morality, it argued that doing what was most loving should be the sole rule of Christian morality, taking precedence over obeying moral rules.

On the other hand, Augustine was acutely aware of human fallibility. He developed the Christian doctrine of Original Sin, by which all humanity is by its nature sinful from birth, due to Adam's Original Sin (of disobedience) in the Garden of Eden. Augustine's views on love should be seen strictly in terms of a possibility offered through the direct

intervention of God saving human sinners, not a natural feature of humankind.

With this view came the idea of pre-destination (some are pre-damned) and torment in hell for the damned – doctrines with hideous consequences for the fear of sinners facing eternal punishment in hell was used to justify the torture of those whose soul was thought to be in danger of hell, in the hope that a forced repentance would save them from worse punishments later.

'Just as you apply no compulsion to past events by having them in your memory, so God by his foreknowledge does not use compulsion in the case of future events. Just as you remember your past actions, though all that you remember were not actions of your own, so God has foreknowledge of his own actions, but is not the agent of all he foreknows… [God] has no responsibility for the future actions of men though he knows them beforehand.'

Augustine *De Libero Arbitrio*

FOR FURTHER INFORMATION ON:
AUGUSTINE, SEE PAGE 154
FOR AUGUSTINE AND HISTORY, SEE PAGE 280
FOR AUGUSTINE ON LAW/POLITICS, SEE PAGE 301

Aristotle had argued that everything had a 'final cause' which was the aim or purpose to which that thing tended. The final cause of a baby was the adult into which it aims to grow. He also saw human action as tending to the achievement of some aim, by which it could be judged.

Aquinas (1225-1274), a monk as well as a philosopher, wanted to reconcile Christian theology with Aristotle's philosophy, being excitedly rediscovered and taught in European universities in the 13th century. He wanted to explore the implication of saying that everything had a 'final cause', a purpose for which it had been created by God. By rationally examining the design of the universe, it should be possible to see the 'natural' purpose of everything, and so have an objective criterion for saying what is right or wrong, according to whether or not something fulfils (or seeks to fulfil) that purpose.

If purpose is inherent in people, things and events, then we can judge good or bad according to its fulfilment. But if we project a sense of purpose back onto them, then the natural law argument is circular – for we attempt to receive back from nature what we have just given it!

You could argue that it would be 'natural' to accept a 'survival of the fittest' morality, in which the weak were eliminated. But 'natural law' is not based on an observation of nature, but on a rational consideration of purposes within nature. And that consideration is based on the prior conviction that nature is the creation of God, or that it expresses a fundamental 'logos' or rational principle.

FOR FURTHER INFORMATION ON:

AQUINAS SEE PAGE **161**

KEY ISSUE: CONTRACEPTION

Roman Catholic teaching uses the principle of Natural Law to argue as follows:

The rational purpose of sex is the conception of children.

Sex is therefore good and right if such procreation is its aim, for it is 'natural'.

Any use of sex that deliberately avoids the fulfilment of its aim is therefore wrong.

Of course, not every act of sexual intercourse leads to conception. Failure of conception is 'natural'. But that does not change the argument, since what we are concerned with here is a rational interpretation of nature, rather than an observation of nature; hence the Catholic argument that, although it is accepted that not every sexual act will lead to conception, nevertheless, every sexual act should be open to the possibility of conception.

The 'natural law' approach had already been taken by the Stoics (see page 77) for whom happiness depended upon living in harmony with nature, which was itself governed by a rational principle, the 'logos' (word).

It is possible to say exactly what the purpose of an aircraft is, since it is obviously the product of human design. It is not at all clear, however, what the purpose of a flower might be. Does it have a purpose outside itself – to give pleasure to others, for example? Is its purpose simply to exist? The very idea of purpose is a feature of the way in which human beings think. We see something and are led to ask what its purpose is. And this assumption that everything has a purpose is not automatically given in experience. Or is it? If a purpose can be established objectively, then natural law provides a sound basis for ethics. If purpose is imposed on our experience, we would seem to be no further forward.

It is fundamental to Buddhist philosophy that all things arise in dependence upon conditions, are temporary, lack inherent existence and are interconnected. Moreover, the basic cause of suffering is said to be *tanha* (grasping or craving), and happiness is said to be possible only when this is overcome.

Buddhist ethics are based on these two things, which Buddhists see as closely connected: the recognition of the ever-changing and interconnected nature of life and a recognition of the futility of craving and acquisitiveness.

Buddhism is essentially concerned with the release of individuals from suffering, and its ethical approach is shaped by this. It is based on the intention of the person who acts, since (according to the principle of *karma*, see page 67) a person's motive for acting in a particular way determines the karmic significance of that event and so the consequences that will flow from it.

Actions are not described as good or bad, but as skilful and unskilful. This recognises that an action takes its significance from its context. What might be right if done by one person might be wrong if done by another. Therefore it sees moral significance in terms of agents and their intentions, not in terms of the acts themselves.

Unskilful actions are those that are said to lead to an increase in greed, hatred and ignorance. Skilful actions are those that lead to an increase in generosity, compassion and wisdom.

Fundamental to Buddhism is the concept of *anatta* (see page 56) – the idea that the self has no separate or permanent existence. It sees the idea of the separate self as the root cause of ignorance, and therefore of suffering. Overcoming this false notion of a separate self is said to lead to wisdom, and the ethical consequence of that is compassion for all sentient beings.

'If we think carefully about the interdependence of all earthly phenomena, our little local problems lose their gravity and naturally we begin to see things globally, in terms of humanity as a whole.

'In this context, the idea of "me" and "you" loses its priority. When we realise this fact, this thought spontaneously brings about a deep feeling of responsibility for the common good.'

Dalai Lama *Beyond Dogma*, Souvenir Press, 1996

Calmness, serenity, and dispassionate concern: these are the qualities suggested by Buddhist images. But note that they are all practical and ethical qualities, rather than metaphysical ideas. Buddhism does not promote speculation on metaphysical matters, but the cultivation of qualities leading to skilful action.

PRECEPTS AND PARAMITARS

Buddhist ethics are not expressed in terms of rules, primarily because actions are seen as relative to the motives of the person performing them and the circumstances in which they arise. But there are some universal precepts, which give general moral guidelines, and five of these are accepted by all Buddhists:

- Not taking life
- Not taking what is not given
- Not misusing the senses
- Not telling lies
- Not using intoxicants to dull the mind.

The corresponding positive qualities are to be promoted: compassion, generosity, contentment, truthfulness and mindfulness.

There are, of course, other precepts and very many specific rules within the monastic *vinaya* for those who join a monastic community. Some lay Buddhists take on extra precepts for a short period, perhaps as a mark of respect at a festival.

Mahayana Buddhism extends the concept of the Bodhisattva (an enlightened being who remains on Earth to help others), so that it becomes an ethical and religious ideal, based on compassion and expressed in terms of developing six qualities or *paramitars*.

They are:

- *Dana* (generosity)
- *Shila* (morality)
- *Kshanti* (patience)
- *Virya* (energy in pursuit of the good)
- *Dhyana* (meditation)
- *Prajna* (wisdom)

We therefore have an ethic based on the cultivation of qualities, rather than on any utilitarian conception of the results of action or any idea of social contract.

These do not prescribe any particular course of action, nor give rules by which the actions of others may be objectively assessed. They simply express a goal in terms of qualities indicative of enlightenment. How exactly these qualities should be put into practice is up to the individual.

With all Buddhist ethical systems, it is intention that determines moral significance. Thus unintentional killing or misappropriation of property would not be considered morally 'wrong' in the sense of unskilful. They are simply mistakes to be rectified. Only when an action is intentional can that intention be evaluated in terms of whether it helps or hinders the progress of that person towards enlightenment.

Another approach to Buddhist ethics resembles a Natural Law argument, or the natural action of Taoism:

> '...I believe that love and affection comprise the fundamental nature, the primordial quality, of human beings. When we show our love, our altruism, we cannot help but feel a certain satisfaction because we are acting in harmony with our own nature.'
>
> Dalai Lama

He does not deny the reality of human malice, but argues that it is not fundamental to, but a distortion of, humanity's true nature.

A PRACTICAL EXAMPLE: BUDDHISM AND ABORTION

Since its first precept is against taking life, Buddhism is in principle opposed to abortion. It holds that consciousness starts at the moment of conception and therefore that an embryo should be treated as a living being and treated with compassion. On the other hand, it accepts that there are exceptional circumstances, for example where the life of the mother is in danger or where a child is to be born with severe abnormalities.

In each case, Buddhist ethics considers two things:

- the advantages and disadvantages of the course of action
- the motivation behind the action

But Buddhism would not argue that there is a point at which an unborn child should start to be considered as an independent individual, mainly because it denies the reality of inherently existing, independent individuals.

Other areas of applied ethics to which Buddhism is particularly relevant, include environmental ethics and animal welfare. The Buddhist view of the interconnectedness of all life argues against any attempt to see human welfare as independent of that of other species or the environment.

Ahimsa (non harming) is a basic ethical quality flowing naturally from the recognition of the interconnectedness of things. Many Buddhists are vegetarians, and those that eat meat generally refrain from actually killing animals themselves. All consumption of food entails the destruction of life, but Buddhists are encouraged to keep this to a minimum. On the other hand, one's own life must also be protected. Therefore Buddhist ethics allows for an individual to do whatever is necessary to preserve his or her own life – and that would include eating meat if it were considered essential for health.

The principle of living in harmony with the natural design of the universe was expounded as a philosophy in China long before the time of Aquinas or even the Stoics. It is the principal feature of Taoism.

Tao means 'path' or 'way' and refers to the natural way things are, as governed by *ch'ang*, the eternal principle, or law. Taoism as philosophy is the attempt to understand the way in which things work together and change, and through such understanding, to live in a natural, balanced and harmonious way. This forms the basis of both its metaphysics and ethics. Taoism emphasizes the individual rather than society and culture, which it generally sees as artificial and imposed.

Religious Taoism, as it developed from the second century CE, placed more emphasis on the conservation of Ch'i (one's vital energy or breath), in its quest for long life and even immortality. This also had ethical implications, avoiding those things that were judged to sap one's Ch'i.

A correctly designed interior is one in which one's energies flow naturally, leading to a sense of personal harmony.

'The Tao is to the world what a great river or an ocean is to the streams and brooks.'

Tao te Ching, chapter 32

YIN AND YANG

Originally an independent philosophical school, but later integrated into Taoism, the yin-yang approach is to view all life in terms of balance. Yang is regarded as masculine and yin feminine. In the broadest sense, yang represents heat, activity and creativity; yin represents cool, passivity and reflection.

The terms Yin and Yang originally referred to the sunny and shady side of a mountain, with the implication that one cannot have one without the other. The flowing nature of the symbol, with a spot of black in the white area and vice versa, expresses the idea that each contains something of the other. Following the natural Tao requires a balance of these two aspects of life.

Comparing this with the Natural Law approach to ethics (see page 79), for Aquinas, following Aristotle, there is an attempt to understand the essential nature of each thing and thus its 'final cause' or purpose. Action is then judged by whether or not it conforms to that final purpose. By contrast, for Taoism, there is no single fixed entity, no defined final cause. Everything is in a state of flux, with yin and yang, as opposite but interpenetrating realities.

FENG SHUI

An appreciation of the Tao can be applied to many practical aspects of life. The design of artificial environments – gardens and houses, for example – can be made in such a way that they allow a natural flow of positive *ch'i* (energy). Feng Shui, of which the original meaning was wind and water (natural elements flowing and changing a landscape), is the art of translating an awareness of fundamental qualities and balance into practical design. In the broadest sense, Feng Shui is a basis for ethics, in that it is the attempt to create an environment that will give rise to a natural style of life.

FOR INFORMATION ON THE TAO TE CHING AND LAO TZU SEE PAGE **194**.

WU WEI (NATURAL ACTION)

The key ethical concept within Taoism is *wu wei*. The literal meaning of this is 'no action'. This does not mean inactivity, however, but actions undertaken in a way that does not violate the natural flow of the Tao.

It implies two things:
1 That in such action no effort is wasted
2 That in such action nothing is done that goes against nature

This contrasts with any action that imposes the will of the person performing it upon some external object against its natural course.

Wu wei is natural, not consciously premeditated action. Usually human beings look at a situation and imagine how it might be different. They therefore take action to realize their mental picture, doing violence to the actual situation in the process. By contrast, *wu wei* is action that is entirely spontaneous, being based on a perception of what actually exists, not on what might exist as a result of the action. It is therefore always appropriate.

However, Chuang Tzu argued also that one should only act when that action can be effective. So, although the nature of one's action should not be determined by anticipated consequences, its likely effectiveness is a useful indication of its naturalness.

This approach is contrary to any system of conformity to abstract ideas at the expense of natural inclinations. Once a person stops to consider if an action is right or wrong, the naturalness of *wu wei* is already lost. Thus *wu wei* is action taken without ethical consideration – it is, in a sense, 'no-ethics' as well as 'no-action'.

If ethical positions divide into two groups, those based on individuals and those based on the social needs and the implied contracts between members of society, then Taoism comes down firmly on the side of the individual. Chuang Tzu argued that one should not consider praise or blame when thinking of action, although that does not imply that one is free to act against the well-being of others. The key concept here is integri-

ty – what Chuang Tzu says in effect is that the weighing of external effects (a utilitarian approach) detracts from the prime requirement of any action, which is that it should express personal integrity. This is itself an expression of the naturalness of the Tao and its ethical expression in *wu wei*.

In politics, such a position generally leads to minimalism. A government should interfere with people's lives as little as possible.

Chuang Tzu also argued that nothing was good or bad in itself, but only according to the circumstances in which it was done, and that it is impossible to find any absolute moral stance, since everyone acts from a particular perspective. Any mediator who attempts to resolve a dispute will simply bring yet another point of view, or else side with one or other of the disputing parties.

CHUANG TZU
(369-286BCE)

The greatest Taoist philosopher, known particularly for his scepticism and moral relativity but also for his implicit monism. His relativism attempted to reduce the importance placed on conventional social norms, especially by those following a Confucian approach to life, and to emphasise the importance of individuality within the Taoist tradition.

However, such an approach did not ignore social consequences of action, for according to Chuang Tzu, action is to be considered both in terms of its naturalness and also its effectiveness.

His teachings are found in the first seven chapters of the book that is named after him, the *Chuang Tzu*.

See also the note on the life of Chuang Tzu on page 63.

'Tao does nothing,
But there is nothing it does not do.
If dukes and rulers could hold to this,
the myriad creatures would transform themselves.'

Tao te Ching, chapter 37

'The highest type of ruler is one of whose existence the people are barely aware.'

Tao te Ching, chapter 17

'Strive for the effortless.'

Tao te Ching, chapter 63

FOR FURTHER INFORMATION ON:
CHUANG TZU, SEE PAGE 194
FOR CHUANG TZU ON LANGUAGE
SEE PAGE 228

In contrast to both Taoist and Buddhist ethics, Confucian ethics is based on the good of society as a whole, and the personal qualities that should be cultivated for individuals to play their part within society.

There are two key terms used in the *Analects* that need to be appreciated here: Jen (humaneness) and Li (rites).

JEN (OR REN)

In several passages in the *Analects*, the Master (Confucius) is asked to give a definition of Jen (humaneness). Here are two such definitions:

'It is to love others.'
12.22

'Courtesy in private life, reverence in handling business, loyalty in relationships with others. They should not be set aside, even if one visits barbarian tribes.'
13.19

Confucius also said that one would have achieved humaneness if one was able to bring about the practice of five qualities in life:
- **courtesy;**
- **tolerance;**
- **faithfulness;**
- **diligence;**
- **kindness.**

These are therefore seen as the key virtues within a Confucian ethic.

Confucius considered that it was only by accepting a strict code of social etiquette that one could achieve humaneness. In this, he was following the literary and ethical traditions of the Chou Dynasty that he took as the basis of his teaching. Basically, it is ritual that balances and orders life:

The Master said: 'If one is courteous but does without ritual, then one dissipates one's energies; if one is cautious but does without ritual, then one becomes timid; if one is bold but does without ritual, then one becomes reckless; if one is forthright but does without ritual, then one becomes rude.'
8:2

In other words, a formal social structure is necessary in order to control generally positive qualities which, if left untamed, can become negative.

One could explore parallels here between the *Analects* and Aristotle's idea of the mean (see page 76).

In the *Analects*, the 'gentleman' is frequently contrasted with the 'small man' as a way of highlighting the qualities and virtues that make for humaneness. For example:

The Master said: 'The gentleman has universal sympathies and is not partisan. The small man is partisan and does not have universal sympathies.'
2.14

The Master said: 'The gentleman is calm and peaceful; the small man is always emotional.'
7.37

His approach to ethics is rational rather than emotional, social rather than individual. Personal virtues are cultivated and regulated through social custom so that society as a whole may benefit. In the concepts of jen and li, we have a genuine humanist ideal, and the detailed working out of social ethics in the Confucian tradition codifies what the true 'gentleman' would naturally try to follow.

THE CONFUCIAN GOLDEN RULE

In the *Analects*, Confucius gives the following summary of his teaching:

'Zigong asked: "Is there a single word such that one could practise it throughout life?" The Master said: "Reciprocity, perhaps? Do not inflict on others what you yourself would not wish done to you."' (15.24)

Mo Tzu (c.479-380BCE or possibly a century later) was a critic of Confucianism at a time of political unrest. He argued for universal love, the priority of reason over formalities and tradition, and became involved as a mediator in disputes. His followers are generally referred to as Mohists or Moists.

With his emphasis on tradition, on filial loyalty, and on the correct performance of rites, Confucius produced a vastly influential ethic which encouraged social hierarchy and formality in people's dealings with others.

Mo Tzu criticized this on the grounds that it encouraged particular concern for one's own family at the expense of a more universal feeling of goodwill. He believed that this sense of loyalty was the root of all evil, and wanted to see it replaced by a general affection (jianai) for all alike.

The fundamental principle Mo Tzu set down for his ethics was that one should avoid doing anything that had an adverse affect on others. He set out a form of the 'golden rule', that one should love others as oneself, and argued that in order to benefit society as a whole, it was essential that people should help one another without distinction.

On a practical level, Mo Tzu believed that those appointed as rulers should know and understand the common people. He believed in a frugal and simple lifestyle, and was particularly critical of the Confucian tendency to lavish resources on funeral rites. He was also opposed to war and aggression of any kind, although self-defence was permitted.

Mo Tzu wanted to set aside tradition and authority and to examine society and its ethics on the basis of reason alone. He seems to have had some belief in a deity, with a purpose and a will, which could

FOR INFORMATION ON THE CONFUCIAN PHILOSOPHY OF RELIGION SEE PAGE 196

FOR A CONFUCIAN VIEWS OF EDUCATION SEE PAGE 236

Consider the great mass of humanity; anonymous faces in a crowd. Is it possible to love everyone equally? If it is, then utilitarianism and contract-based ethics can be effective, since all will agree to do what is in the interests of the majority. On the other hand, a traditional Confucian approach recognizes a hierarchy of loyalty and affection.

be perceived in the order of the universe. He argued that all were equal in the eyes of heaven and should be loved equally.

The Confucians responded to this by saying that to have no special loyalty to father or sovereign was inhuman, for it was human nature to love those to whom one is nearest before developing love for strangers. Mencius (390-305BCE) said that the Mo Tzu's view outraged every human feeling.

Mo Tzu argued that people understand what is to their benefit and what to their harm. Therefore he held that the common good, and the agreement of all to work for that common good, should be the ruling principle of society.

Mo Tzu's ethic has many interesting parallels with Western ethics. At some points it comes close to the contract-based views of Locke and Rousseau (see pages 310, 312), or even to the more modern political view of Rawls (see page 329), where people attempt to frame laws without partisan self-interest. His near-utilitarianism (see page 87) lies in seeking the greatest good for the greatest number of people.

There are also obvious parallels with the Christian ethic of loving both your friends and your enemies.

'The greatest happiness to the greatest number.'

Francis Hutcheson

Jeremy Bentham (1748-1832) is generally regarded as the founder of Utilitarianism, that peculiarly British school which rejected religious and philosophical tradition, seeing the benefit and happiness of people as the aim of ethical action. Bentham argued for what we would call basic 'act utilitarianism'. That is, he examined every action in terms of its expected results. If those results led to an increase in human happiness, that action was to be considered good. The happiness of all concerned should be taken into account equally, and so – using Hutcheson's phrase – he sought that which would provide 'the greatest happiness to the greatest number.'

'Nature has places mankind under the governance of two sovereign masters, pain and pleasure. It is for them alone to point out what we ought to do, as well as to determine what we shall do.'

Jeremy Bentham

Bentham assumed that the tendency for human beings to seek happiness and to avoid pain was universal and as certain as a scientific law. He therefore presented the principle of 'utility', so that actions should be judged by the happiness or pain that they caused.

'The creed which accepts as the foundation of morals "utility" or the "greatest happiness principle" holds that actions are right in proportion as they tend to promote happiness; wrong as they tend to produce the reverse of happiness.' **J S Mill**

J S Mill (1806-1873) developed a form of 'rule utilitarianism' since he went beyond an assessment of the results of particular acts to consider general principles, whose acceptance would benefit society as a whole:

'In the golden rule of Jesus of Nazareth, we read the complete spirit of the ethics of utility. "To do as you would be done by," and "To love your neighbour as yourself," constitute the ideal perfection of utilitarian morality. As the means of making the nearest approach to this ideal, utility would enjoin, first, that laws and social arrangement should place the happiness or (as, speaking practically, it may be called) the interest of every individual as nearly as possible in harmony with the interest of the whole; and, secondly, that education and opinion, which have so vast a power over human character, should so use that power as to establish in the mind of every individual an indissoluble association between his own happiness and the good of the whole ...'

J S Mill *Utilitarianism*, chapter II

As an example, Mill cites the situation of someone who is tempted to lie in order to get some immediate benefit. He argues that the principle of telling the truth is of such great benefit to humankind as a whole, that it should not be set aside for some immediate advantage.

Should happiness be considered quantitatively or qualitatively? Mill argued that there were higher and lower pleasures and the former should be preferred to the latter, but notes that people often lapse in this, and set aside what is nobler for the sake of inferior pleasures.

Utilitarianism was further developed by Henry Sidgwick (1838-1900), who became the first secular Professor of Philosophy at Cambridge in 1883. His work on ethics influenced G E Moore. His principal work *The Methods of Ethics*, was first published in 1874.

Certainly, he does not accept some simply mathematical way of summing up happiness, nor can his type form of utilitarianism be thought of as simple hedonism.

Utilitarianism has been (and still is) immensely influential, but it has its critics. One possible objection is that it does not seem to allow for self-sacrifice. Mill anticipated and countered that suggestion:

'The utilitarian morality does recognize in human beings the power of sacrificing their own greatest good for the good of others. It only refuses to admit that the sacrifice is itself a good. A sacrifice which does not increase or tend to increase the sum total of happiness, it considers as wasted.'

Utilitarianism

There are at least two other major problems. One, as outlined by G E Moore (see page 68) is that, ultimately, Utilitarianism needs to be supported by a definition of what we mean by 'good' – a definition that Moore thinks impossible. Without it, there is no criterion for deciding between different forms of happiness.

But a significant question to ask of Utilitarian theories is 'Are they too stringent?' At what point can any action be justified? Is it possible to have a completely unambiguous assessment of consequences? The immediate results might be painful (as where a doctor causes pain in order to set a broken limb) in order to achieve a more general good.

But equally we cannot know all the results of what we do. For example, one might save a child from drowning, only to find that the child grows up to be a mass murderer. It is impossible to know such consequences at the time of making the decision to save the child, so how can we use them to validate the choice that is made? There will always be the possibility that a calculation of consequences may be spoiled by subsequent events.

Hence there is a tendency in Utilitarian arguments to settle for a principle of sufficient benefit. I may not be able to show that what I do is absolutely guaranteed to bring the greatest happiness to the greatest number, but is there a sufficient balance of happiness over unhappiness in those consequences I can foresee?

Another approach is to consider the preferences of all those who are concerned. Such 'preference utilitarian' arguments can be found in the work of R M Hare (see page 69) and Peter Singer (see page 100).

FOR FURTHER INFORMATION ON:

J S MILL, SEE PAGE 322

FOR FURTHER INFORMATION ON:

MACHIAVELLI SEE PAGE 304

AN ETHIC OF SOCIAL SURVIVAL?

Ethical theory asks fundamental questions about what is good or right. In practice, however, people often make choices between limited possibilities for a specific purpose, not as a result of contemplating absolute principles or universal consequences. Niccolo Machiavelli (1469-1527) in his book *The Prince* sets out principles that are aimed at maintaining the strength, authority and security of the state.

There is a fundamental distinction between two kinds of moral imperative: absolute and hypothetical. Machiavelli presents a set of hypothetical imperatives: in other words, they take the form 'If... then... ' And in his case, the 'if' refers to the maintenance of power and the authority of the state.

☐ *...taking everything into account, he (the prince) will find that some of the things that appear to be virtues will, if he practises them, ruin him, and some of the things that appear to be wicked will bring him security and prosperity.*☐

(*The Prince*, section XV)

His ethics are simply the principles that will achieve his already chosen end. They are pragmatic. They are not based on any particular moral qualities of the Prince, nor on his particular inclinations, but simply on his duty in terms of maintaining power. In this sense, for Machiavelli, the end always justifies the means.

In a terrorist attack, people's lives are lost or put at risk in the attempt to further some social or political cause. A narrowly 'act utilitarian' argument might attempt to justify such acts – a few people suffer in order to benefit many in the long term. The more general 'rule utilitarian' position might, however, lead one to say that the overall principle of the taking of innocent life to further a cause, would inevitably lead to more suffering than benefit. A democratic alternative to terrorism can also be justified on utilitarian grounds, in that in seeks to allow everyone's preferences to be taken into account.

What motivates us to act? **Thomas Hobbes (1588-1679)** argued that all voluntary actions are preceded by thought, planning out the action with some purpose, and that purpose depends on appetite or desire. Ethics therefore start with emotions.

'...whatsoever is the object of any man's appetite or desire, that is it which he for his part calleth good: and the object of his hate and aversion, evil; and of his contempt, vile and inconsiderable. For these words of good, evil, and contemptible, are ever used with relation to the person that useth them: there being nothing simply and absolutely so; nor any common rule of good and evil, to be taken from the nature of the objects themselves...'

Leviathan, chapter 6

If individuals determine what is good or bad, Hobbes saw that in a natural state, when normal social order collapses (as in war), each would live only for himself:

'Whatsoever therefore is consequent to a time of war, where every man is enemy to every man; the same is consequent to the time, wherein man lives without other security, than what their own strength, and their own invention shall furnish them withal. In such condition, there is no place for industry; because the fruit thereof is uncertain; and consequently no culture of the earth; no navigation, nor use of the commodities that may be imported by sea; no commodious building; no instruments of moving, and removing, such things as require much force; no knowledge of the face of the earth; no account of time; no arts; no letters; no society; and which is worst of all, continual fear, and danger of violent death; and the life of man, solitary, poor, nasty, brutish, and short.'

Leviathan

Hobbes argued that, in order to avoid such anarchy, good and bad should be agreed upon within a commonwealth. And that agreement between individuals should be the basis for laws and therefore morality. Goodness is created, it is not an inherent quality.

Hobbes wrote after the English Civil Wars. From the upheavals of his age, he saw what could happen with the breakdown of civil order, and therefore argued that agreeing to obey a sovereign ruler was the best way of achieving social stability.

Hobbes was far from the only philosopher to take emotion as the basis for ethics. **Shaftesbury (1671-1713)** used the term 'moral sense' to indicate that feeling rather than reason lay behind ethics, and **Francis Hutcheson (1694-1746)** also believed that morality was in fact based on emotion, and particularly on a natural feeling of benevolence towards others.

They were followed by **David Hume (1711-1776)** who, in his quest to create a 'science of man' and avoid metaphysical speculation, argued that morality was based on natural sympathy rather than reason. Notice that this springs from the important point made by Hume that you cannot derive an 'ought' from an 'is'. In other words, he was looking for some source for the moral impetus, other than a rational analysis of what we experience.

'Reason is, and ought only to be the slave of the passions, and can never pretend to any other office than to serve and obey them.'

Hume *A Treatise of Human Nature*

G E Moore argues that 'good' is self evident, rather than being known by reason. (See page 68.) He developed Hume's argument about the 'naturalistic fallacy'.

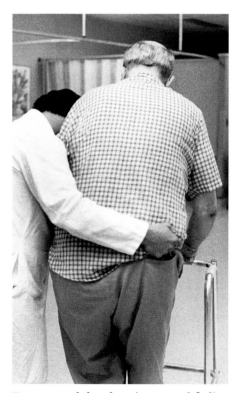

Hume argued that there is a natural feeling of benevolence and sympathy. We feel it when we see other people suffer, even if they are unknown to us and there is nothing we can do to help them.

We saw that the British Moralists (e.g. Locke and Hume) had argued for emotion as the basis of morality, whereas the Utilitarians (Bentham and Mill) considered the anticipated results of actions. We now turn to a totally different approach, one based on the idea that what counts is one's good intention, which can be assessed in terms of pure practical reason, without any reference to feelings or results.

The philosopher who made this dramatic switch was **Immanuel Kant**. He believed that he had found, with his 'categorical imperative', a logical and universal basis for morality. He is important for having effected a fundamental change in the way people thought of morality, by making it dependent upon the individual's will. In other words, acting morality could be seen as a creative activity, an expression of the individual's will and reason.

'Two things fill the mind with ever new and increasing admiration and awe the oftener and more steadily we reflect on them: the starry heavens above me and the moral law within me. '
Critique of Practical Reason

And Kant then makes the point that this awareness of the moral law within is directly associated with his consciousness of his own existence.

Kant is central to the European Enlightenment, that great attempt to go beyond authority and superstition and deal with the world on the basis of human reason. An early work, *The General History of Nature and Theory of the Heavens*

FOR FURTHER WORK ON CONTRACT-BASED ETHICS, SEE RAWLS PAGE **329**. FOR THE POLITICAL IMPLICATIONS OF CONTRACT SEE LOCKE AND ROUSSEAU PAGES **310** AND **312**.

(1755) was an attempt to use Newton's physical laws to explain the universe in a mechanistic way, without the need for Newton's idea of an external creator God.

Kant was partly influenced by Rousseau's emphasis on inner experience rather than what is known through the senses. This corresponded with his German Lutheran Pietist background, in which religion was based on inward personal experience.

But he was far more deeply disturbed by Hume's scepticism about what can be known from sensory experiences. The result of facing Hume's scepticism, which was expounded in the *Critique of Pure Reason*, was what Kant called his **Copernican Revolution**. It had been assumed that sense experience conformed to external reality, but – just as Copernicus found that his observations made sense once he had realized that the Earth moved round the Sun rather than the other way round – so Kant argued that we experience the world as we do simply because that is the way our senses function.

We do not know things as they are in themselves, called noumena, but only as they appear to us as phenomena. Space, time and causality are not 'out there' to be discovered, but are ways in which we organize our experience (see page 38).

His moral argument made a similar shift. He did not look at the world and ask if freedom and moral choice were possible. Instead, he started with the experience of moral choice, and then sought to find its implications. (i.e. We know we are free because we experience moral choice; we do not experience moral choice because we know that we are free.)

'There is no possibility of thinking of anything at all in the world, or even out of it, which can be regarded as good without qualification, except a good will.'
Groundwork for the Metaphysics of Morals

What Kant is really after is a sense of moral choice, the will to do something good, that is not tainted with considerations of rewards. After all, if something is to my advantage, what is specifically virtuous in doing it? For him, morality was a sign of true humanity and the means by which people could develop as human beings. It is action based on pure practical reason – acting not out of selfish gain but out of a genuine sense of what is of universal benefit. It is an action done for itself alone, not as a means of achieving something else.

'If the action is good only as a means to something else, the imperative is hypothetical; but if it is thought of as good in itself, and hence as necessary in a will which of itself conforms to reason as the principle of this will, the imperative is categorical.'
Groundwork of the Metaphysics of Morals

In making the Pure Practical Reason the basis for morality, Kant effectively dismisses the moral significance of acts done out of natural affection or inclination, or out of enlightened self-interest. All that counts is that one should do one's duty, rather than following one's desires. In other words, all that counts is having a 'good will'.

One could perhaps challenge Kant on this point, asking whether it is – in practice – ever possible to act from such a pure motive, or whether other factors, including one's natural inclinations, are always present in the process of moral decision making.

THE CATEGORICAL IMPERATIVE

Kant formulated the 'categorical imperative' as the principle of action. The first formulation of this is:

> '*Act only according to that maxim whereby you can at the same time will that it should become a universal law.*'

And the second:

> '*Always treat people as ends, never as means.*'

Kant believed that these principles would offer a way of knowing whether or not one's will was good and therefore one's action right, irrespective of the results of that action.

Kant's first formulation depends on the idea that something is only right if one can, without contradiction, will that it be applied universally.

He gave several examples of the application of this imperative. A person may be tempted to borrow money, promising to repay it, but knowing that he cannot do so. According to the imperative, although the immediate result would be beneficial to the borrower, in the long term, if applied universally, it would destroy the whole basis of making a promise. Hence, making a promise knowing that one cannot keep it, is wrong.

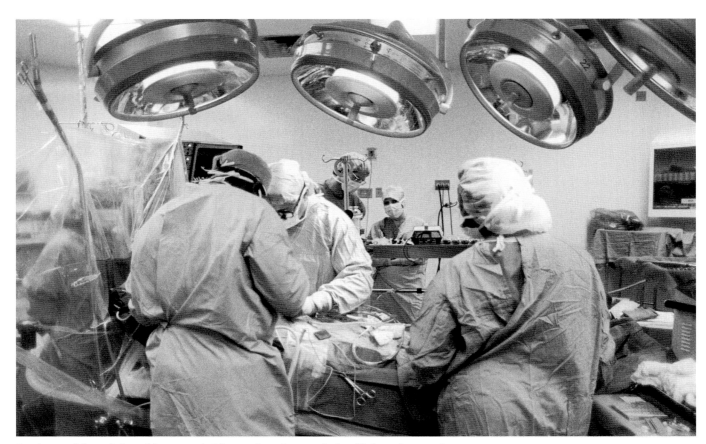

Kant's second formulation of the categorical imperative – that people should always be treated as ends never as means, is fundamental to what most people think of as morality, namely respect for individuals as individuals. This is particularly relevant to bioethics and the ethics of the nursing and medical professions. Here, respect for the individual rights of patients becomes paramount. So, for example, anyone taking part in a clinical trial should be told exactly what is being done, any risks involved, and the likely outcome. Without such safeguards, the people involved are being treated as means rather than as ends – and this remains a forceful ethical argument, even if the overall end being sought is extremely valuable, or if some benefit might be gained by not telling those taking part.

IMMANUEL KANT (1724-1804)

FOR GENERAL INFORMATION

SEE PAGE 38

FOR KANT ON: RELIGION PAGE 168

ART PAGE 241

MOVING BEYOND KANT

'Motives are causes experienced from within.' Schopenhauer

Kant had made the fundamental distinction between the world of objects known to the senses (phenomena) and the world of 'things in themselves' (noumena). All we know is limited to that world of experience, but he never doubted that there were actual separate noumenal entities, causing the phenomena.

This belief was challenged by **Arthur Schopenhauer (1788-1860)**. He argued that causality was limited to phenomena and that the idea of separate objects was a feature of the time and space that our senses impose on experience. Therefore the world beyond the senses cannot be divided up into separate things, but must be a single undifferentiated reality. Today, we might call such a reality 'field' or 'energy', but Schopenhauer called it 'will'.

This makes a vital difference to ethics. If the reality beyond our senses is not differentiated, then fundamentally we are all part of one and the same reality. Other people are not separate from ourselves, except at the superficial level of sensation. There is a single 'will' operative in all beings.

This led Schopenhauer to argue that we have a natural compassion towards others, and are naturally able to intuit the suffering of others and respond. By doing so, Schopenhauer gave compassion a firm basis in reality. Compassion is not unreasonable, nor is it simply one option chosen among many, but is a fundamental response to the most basic feature of reality.

Notice that for Schopenhauer (as for Kant) one can be at one and the same time phenomenally determined and noumenally free. In the act of moral choice one is freely exercising the will, while from the external point of view,

everything is considered in terms of space, time and causality and therefore appears to be determined.

What I experience as a motive, would (seen from the outside) appear as a cause. In other words, even if there are scientific reasons given for my behaving in a particular way (genes; hormones; age; social pressure), I still experience having to make a free choice about how to behave.

Another movement beyond Kant, but still owing much to his philosophy, is found in the work of **G W F Hegel (1770-1831)**. Hegel saw the whole of reality as a process of development, and the human spirit or mind as an essential feature of that process. The end of the development is the Absolute, when everything is in harmony with itself and the whole of reality. The process is one of developing self-awareness, and thus of the mind or spirit (the German term '*Geist*' has elements of both English words).

For Hegel, the process of change involved the reconciliation of opposites, in what is termed his dialectic.

Individuals are caught up in a continual process of change, and their choices and decisions are seen in the light of that wider purpose. It also means that every creative act takes place at a particular time, and reflects the influence of that time within the whole process: the '*Zeitgeist*' or spirit of the age.

The final point in the process is one in which the *Geist* comes to see that all the apparently contradictory things that have contributed to the process of dialectic –

and thus of change – are in fact parts of itself. At that point there is a single unified reality. At that point there is no need for further change.

Therefore, in terms of ethics, we should note that, following Hegel's ideas, all moral decisions take place in a particular context and time, as part of an ongoing process.

The implication of any such contextualization of ethics is that one cannot take a single decision or action, and ask if it is right or wrong without taking the context into account. For Hegel, everything is caught up in the process of change.

As we shall see overleaf, and again in the chapter on the philosophy of law and politics, much of the impact that Hegel's philosophy has had on ethics is due to the use of his idea of the dialectic by Karl Marx.

'The egoist feels himself surrounded by strange and hostile individuals, and all his hope is centred in his own good.

The good man lives in a world of friendly individuals, the well-being of any of whom he regards as his own.' Schopenhauer *The World as Will and Idea*

With Marx, the Hegelian dialectic is applied to the material and economic basis of society. People become caught up in the process of social and political change, and this provides the context for everything they do, including their moral choices.

They may also be dehumanized by the economic system in which they live:

'The worker becomes an ever cheaper commodity the more goods he creates. The devaluation of the human world increases in direct relation with the increase in value of the world of things. Labour does not only create goods; it also produces itself and the worker as a commodity...'
Economic and Philosophical Manuscripts

Marx's thought has many implications for ethics. As this quotation suggests, he saw capitalism as being against the second formulation of Kant's categorical imperative, since people are used as means rather than ends. He also saw action as evaluated in terms of the dialectic of class struggle. What is morally right is determined by the economic circumstances in which one finds oneself, all ethical choices are thus embodied in an historical and economic process.

Friedrich Nietzsche (1844-1900) was a most colourful, inventive and challenging writer. His work has importance particularly for the Philosophy of Religion and for Ethics. His best-known work is *Thus Spoke Zarathustra* (1883-5), but the ethical implications of his thought are more clearly found in *Beyond Good and Evil* (1886), *On the Genealogy of Morals* (1887) and in works that attack conventional religious morality, *Twilight of the Idols* and *The Antichrist* (1888).

'Man is a rope, fastened between animal and Superman — a rope over an abyss.' Zarathustra

Central to Nietzsche's moral thinking is the idea that 'God is dead', and that with the loss of God the traditional framework of self-understanding and morality is removed. However, he did not see this as a loss, but as an opportunity for a positive and life affirming attitude, with humankind taking responsibility for its own future:

'My Ego taught me a new pride, I teach it to men: No longer to bury the head in the sand of heavenly things, but to carry it freely, an earthly head which creates meaning for the earth.' Zarathustra

This positive attitude sees man as evolving towards something higher – the Ubermensch, or 'Superman', one who transcends himself:

'I teach you the Superman. Man is something that should be overcome. What have you done to overcome him?

'All creatures hitherto have created something beyond themselves: and do you want to be the ebb of this great tide, and return to the animals rather than overcome man?

'The Superman is the meaning of the earth. Let your will say: the Superman shall be the meaning of the earth.' Zarathustra

Thus, self-overcoming becomes his key ethical quality. He sees humanity as threatened by Christian and humanist compassion towards those who are weakest:

'The sickly constitute the greatest danger to man: not the evil, not the "predators". Those who are from the outset victims, downtrodden, broken — they are the ones, the weakest are the ones who most undermine life among men, who most dangerously poison and question our trust in life, in man.'
On the Genealogy of Morals

He distinguished between slave morality and master morality. He saw the former as typified by Christianity: it is

FOR FURTHER INFORMATION ON HEGEL AND MARX SEE PAGE 324

ALSO, FOR MARX ON:

RELIGION SEE PAGE 172

HISTORY SEE PAGE 284

Just as, for Aristotle, the Stoics or Aquinas, morality is grounded in the fundamental structure of reality, and 'goodness' comes from following what is deemed 'natural', so for Nietzsche, morality goes beyond traditional definitions of good and evil, and reflects the structure of evolution and development. Humanity is no longer seen as static, and morality should therefore take into account its direction of advance.

the morality of those who wish to band together to protect themselves, and therefore espouses meekness and co-operation. Master morality, by contrast, emphasizes dignity, nobility and the challenge of self-development.

Another important theme in Nietzsche's work is 'eternal recurrence'. By this, he means that one should be able to say 'Yes' to life, just as it is, and to accept it, even if it were to repeat itself over and over indefinitely. This he contrasts with the traditional religious hope for some other-worldly goal in an afterlife, the very idea of which deprived humankind of the incentive and ability to see the value of this present life.

In all this, Nietzsche challenged humankind to go beyond itself, to always be looking to achieve something more.

Unfortunately, the whole of Nietzsche's work has been tainted by its adoption by both Mussolini and Hitler as propaganda for their ideologies, especially for the Nazi doctrine of Aryan racial superiority and all the horrors to which that gave rise.

Nietzsche cannot be blamed for the later distortions of his work by people who did not begin to understand it. But there are extremely controversial elements in it, including his vitriolic attacks on Christianity and his insistence that the weak should not be allowed to impede the rise of the strong.

FOR FURTHER INFORMATION ON
NIETZSCHE'S VIEW OF RELIGION
SEE PAGE 174.
NIETZSCHE'S VIEW ON THE VALUE OF
HISTORY SEE PAGE 286

Richard Strauss's trumpet fanfares in the opening bars of 'Also Sprach Zarathustra' are linked in many people's minds with the launch of the Apollo space flights. Strauss was inspired by Nietzsche, and his music is therefore appropriate to accompany a moment of human development and inspiration – the quest to go further and be greater than previous generations. Nietzsche's philosophy is presented as a challenge to follow one's highest aspirations; to go beyond what has been done before; to move from man to 'over-man', to a higher form of humanity.

In matters of religion and ethics, the Danish philosopher **Soren Kierkegaard (1813-1855)** argued for the centrality of personal commitment. This approach developed into 'Existentialism', exemplified in secular philosophy by the work of Sartre and Camus, and in theology by Bultmann and Tillich.

'The only absolute either/or is the choice between good and evil.'

Kierkegaard, *Either/Or*

Kierkegaard argued that moral choice was a shaping process:

'... in making a choice it is not so much a question of choosing the right as of the energy, the earnestness, the pathos with which one chooses. Thereby the personality announces its inner infinity, and thereby, in turn, the personality is consolidated.'

Either/Or

In other words, the process of deciding between two options is an affirmation of what one considers to be good, and this shapes the personality. In this sense, one's existence comes prior to one's essence – a theme emphasized later by Sartre.

'Existence precedes essence.'

Sartre

A development of the existential approach to ethics taken by **Martin Heidegger (1889-1976)** recognized that we do not choose in a vacuum, but within a given set of circumstances and relationships. We are what we are by accident of birth, what Heidegger called 'thrown-ness' (*Geworfenheit*). We may

therefore act as though wearing masks determined by our various roles ('father', 'shop-keeper' and so on) and other people limit what we are able to be. Heidegger emphasized the need to get beyond such roles and strive for authentic existence, motivated always by the knowledge that our life is finite.

Like Kierkegaard, **Jean-Paul Sartre (1905-1980)** linked the act of choosing with an affirmation of value:

'... in creating the man that we want to be, there is not a single one of our acts which does not at the same time create an image of man as we think he ought to be. To choose to be this or that is to affirm at the same time the value of what we choose...'

Sartre

A fundamental feature of secular existentialism is the sense that, considered objectively, life does not achieve an end product. It is 'absurd'.

Albert Camus (1913-1960) illustrated this in his *Myth of Sisyphus* (1942). Sisyphus is condemned endlessly to push a boulder up a hill, only to find that it rolls down again. He knows that his efforts will never achieve a lasting result, but accepts this and settles happily to his absurd task.

It is fun to act out a role, or to appear in some ludicrous costume, but Heidegger points out that this is what we may well do for much of our lives – accepting a role that does not allow us authentic existence.

One might argue that it is safer, and sometimes therefore more comfortable, to act out a role than to live our own unique existence. It may also be easier to treat others according to the role they play for us, rather than seeing them as unique.

In terms of ethics, existentialism emphasizes:

- the centrality of person choice
- the shaping of the personality through moral choice
- the priority of existence over essence
- the recognition of the given limitations of life
- the ultimate absurdity of all human effort

Taken together, these argue against attempts to create objective moral criteria independent of the experienced reality of those who make moral choices.

FOR FURTHER INFORMATION ON KERKEGAARD AND EXISTENTIALISM SEE PAGE **171**.

Philosophy and ethics do not exist in a vacuum. Language, thoughts, moral assumptions and values are all produced within a particular society. Earlier in this chapter we looked at Eastern perspectives on ethics, and Hindu, Buddhist, Jain, Confucian and Taoist ideas were examined as philosophy, but those ideas clearly developed within particular religions and cultures.

So too, the impact of the three great Semitic religions – Judaism, Christianity and Islam – on the thinking of the West has been immense. Some philosophers (e.g. Augustine or Aquinas) worked consciously within a religious tradition. Others (e.g. J S Mill) compared their ethical theory with that given by religion. Still others (e.g. Nietzsche) reacted against religion, or were rejected by their religious group on account of their philosophy (e.g. Spinoza).

Thus, even where an ethical argument claims to be based on reason alone, the assumptions and values expressed within that argument may well be influenced by a religious view of life.

More directly, each of the religions sets out moral codes, and these have permeated the societies within which the religion has been practised. We shall therefore look briefly at the nature of those codes and the sources of moral authority associated with them.

JEWISH ETHICS

'Love your neighbour as yourself.' Leviticus 19.18

The starting point for Jewish ethics is the Torah: the Law, believed to be given by God to Moses and set down in the first five books of the Bible. Summarized in the Ten Commandments, it includes laws covering ethical, social and religious matters.

The function of Jewish ethics is the interpretation and re-application of the Torah.

Such interpretations were gathered (in about 200CE) as the Mishna, with further commentary (the Gemara) as attached.

These are printed together as the Talmud, a complex encyclopaedia of rules and traditions. Jewish ethics are therefore fundamentally deontological, in that they are about one's duty and obedience to externally given rules. It was famously summed up by Rabbi Hillel, in the first century BCE, in the single principle:

'What is hateful to you do not do to another.'

Jewish orthodoxy is a commitment to practice, to following the halakah, or path – and this applies to ethical as well as ritual matters. Faithfulness is the key virtue, seen primarily as loyalty both to the tradition but also to the Jewish community.

Jewish ethics is not utilitarian – it does not depend upon any assessment of results – rather it depends upon an authentic recognition of oneself as a member of a community which has a history and established moral principles, given by God. The principles are absolute, although their application may require the application of reason and conscience, especially as they are applied to situations very different from those of the era in which they were set down.

Also of ethical significance is the Jewish idea of the two impulses that are said to be within every individual – one good (displayed as reason and purposeful living) and the other bad (seen as desire and raw, undirected energy). The aim of one who is to behave in a morally acceptable way is to tame and channel the bad impulse in service of the good.

Of course, much Jewish ethics today is coloured, as is all Jewish thinking, by the horrors of the Holocaust. It is difficult to imagine how that could not totally dominate an ethical agenda – to suffer under such a regime gives an impetus to analyse the ills that brought it about, and also to recognize the absolute right to life and equality, which the Nazi regime refused to Jews and others.

Much Jewish thinking today reflects awareness of the suffering of Holocaust victims. What does morality, or even belief in God, mean in a world where such things can happen?

CHRISTIAN ETHICS

The moral teachings of Jesus and the early Church, as recorded in the New Testament, provide the basic authority for Christian ethics. However, in interpreting and applying them, it is necessary to see them within their cultural and theological context.

New Testament ethics may be described as 'eschatological' – to do with the last things before the Second Coming of Christ, which was imminently expected in the first decades of Christianity. The New Testament describes the belief that Jesus would soon return to earth, and that people therefore had only a very short time to mend their ways. Moral advice (for example in Paul's letters) was not given on the basis of an indefinite future and long-term benefits to society that might come from acting in a particular way, but the need to cut free from doomed social and personal structures that were soon to be judged. New Testament ethics are for an in-between age, where the old order has lost its value and the new is about to dawn. With the passage of time, emphasis on the immediacy of Christ's return diminished, but there continued to be a sense of an end-time, when Christ would return and people would be judged.

Jesus and his earliest followers were Jews, and much of what became Christian ethics was developed from that of the ancient religion of Israel, and so has close parallels with Judaism.

Many moral requirements in the New Testament, for example in the letters of Paul, were framed to meet the needs of particular situations. This creates problems for those attempting to derive general ethical principles from Christian teaching.

From the time of Augustine through until the Renaissance, Christian philosophers sought to show the compatibility of their own ideas, or those of antiquity, with Christian doctrine. We have seen this already in Augustine's interpretation of Neoplatonism and Aquinas' use of Aristotle.

The Christian concept of original sin, whereby it is believed that people inherit a natural tendency to sin, following the account of the original disobedience of Adam and Eve, leads to the teaching that it is only through God's power (grace) that people can be saved from the consequences of their sin.

Thus Reformation theologians (e.g.Luther) argued that, since mankind is fallen, human reason too is fundamentally sinful. Salvation comes only through God's unpredictable Grace, not by behaving rightly. The issue of debate within Christian ethics (as between Catholics and Lutherans, for example) is the extent to which the 'fall' renders null and void the validity of arguments presented by natural reason.

Whereas Aquinas saw God as a guarantor of world order, and therefore identified with the rational structures and purpose of the world (see page 79), for Luther, God always stands over against the world, judging it. As a consequence, Luther was prepared to allow the world's secular rulers near-autonomy, for the concepts and rules by which it operated were irrelevant to Christian salvation.

Against this secular autonomy, particularly from a Protestant point of view, is the emphasis on individual faith and commitment. This was expressed in Kierkegaard's emphasis on the inwardness of the either/or decision (see page 94).

The distinctive feature of Christian ethics, irrespective of the extent to which it accepts or rejects secular ethical arguments, is that it sees morality in terms of a human response to the activity of God, as seen in the person and work of Jesus, and as inspired by the Holy Spirit. Although it may choose to align itself with secular arguments, its fundamental moral stance is therefore independent of them, and the source of its morality is given in scriptures and in the authority of the Church.

'Love one another as I have loved you.' John 15.12

A key question, raised by the Christian teaching of the Fall, the nature of sin and grace, and the place of conscience, is how far humanity, on the basis of reason and will, can both frame and follow a moral path. Where Christian teaching takes a view of humanity unredeemed by God as inherently selfish, it sees secular ethics – however well intentioned – as impotent.

MUSLIM ETHICS

A Muslim is a person who 'submits' to the Allah, the source of life. Muslims therefore believe that every child is born a Muslim, since every child is born in a state of harmony with nature. Thus, a central theme of Islamic morality is that everything should be natural.

Muslims believe that the Prophet Muhammad received a revelation from God, and that the exact words of that revelation are contained in the Qur'an. The Qur'an therefore represents the final authority in Muslim ethics.

Muslims also take into account the example of Muhammad (called the Sunnah), the official accounts of which are contained in what are called Hadith, of which there are many collections.

The Shari'ah, or natural law of Islam, is therefore based on:
● the Qur'an
● the Sunnah of the Prophet (in the Hadith)
● the natural unity of all things in Allah.

Since moral situations arise that were not found in Muhammad's day, there are various ways of extending the literal interpretation of the Qur'an and Hadith. Scholars will sometimes use analogy, finding a parallel with a Qur'anic situation.

Where a gathering of Muslim scholars (the ulama) reaches agreement on a point of Islamic law, this is termed an Ijma.

Following the early experience of persecution, a key feature of Islamic morality is the requirement to defend the Ummah, or Muslim community. Morality is also aimed specifically at bringing peace and harmony throughout the Ummah, and the traditional greeting Salam means 'peace'.

Although ultimately Islam claims that

its moral principles simply restore what is natural to humankind, Muslims think it is right to impose the Shari'ah as law. This reflects the importance of the whole Muslim community – individuals within that community are required to 'surrender' to Allah, and so place themselves under the authority of his Ummah.

It is important to recognize a distinction between Muslim ethical theory and actual social practice in Muslim countries. As Islam spread, it adopted customs from among the people who joined the Ummah. Some of these have persisted, despite the Shari'ah being imposed on them, to a greater or lesser extent. Thus, although the principles of Islamic law are seen as universal, their application has varied in terms of its strictness from place to place. Essentially, for Islam, there is no division between secular and religious. Social and political structures are therefore required to confirm to religious moral rules.

Throughout the Qur'an there are references to the 'Day of Judgement' when Muslims believe that all their actions will be judged by Allah, and that they will receive reward or punishment. In this sense, every action is ultimately accountable.

In Islam, morality is less a matter of rational debate, than one of obedience. The function of reason and ethical debate is limited to the application to new situations of guidelines that are set down in the Qur'an or Hadith.

'None of you (truly) believes until he wishes for his brother what he wishes for himself.'

from An-Nawai's *Forty Hadith*

The unity of all Muslim people (the Ummah) is key for understanding Muslim ethics. Defending the Ummah against attack of any sort, whether physical, cultural or religious, is important for Muslims because the Ummah provides the context in which it is possible to 'submit' to Allah.

THE FEMINIST PERSPECTIVE

NO MORE DEAD MALES!

Such a slogan could be taken to suggest that there will be no more philosophy as we have known it over the last 3000 years. Or it could mean very different philosophies, emerging after millenia of male predominance.

Feminist ethics, and indeed the whole feminist critique of philosophy, stresses the way in which much of traditional thinking has been biased, often unconsciously, against women.

Not only have almost all philosophers been male, but their thinking and values have been shaped by their gender (sociocultural, rather than biological, differences between men and women). In *Emile* – to take a not atypical example – Rousseau considered women's minds to be merely practical, incapable of the speculative grasp required by science or philosophy. He saw women's place as one of obedience and fidelity to her husband and care for her children.

Aristotle, Spinoza, Kant and Nietzsche, among others, have been similarly dismissive of women as thinkers. Such views result not from rational debate, but from the unquestioned presuppositions of their societies and cultures, which colour all philosophy.

THE RIGHTS OF WOMEN

An examination of feminist ethics should start from *A Vindication of the Rights of Women* by **Mary Wollstonecraft (1759-97)**. This, published in 1792 at the height of the French Revolution and consciously echoing Tom Paine's *Rights of Man* of 1791, called for a social order freed from the chains of superstition and authority, in which everybody, irrespective of sex, class or creed, would enjoy the same rights. She did not, however, live long enough to elaborate on women's role in such a society.

Since then, feminist ethics has been more specifically concerned with whether or not there is a fundamental difference in the way in which women and men perceive and respond to ethical issues, with a critique of gender bias in existing thinking, and with a recognition of the ethical importance of issues relating to women. First, however, women had to win legal and political emancipation – from men.

The Utilitarian tradition of ethics, in considering the effect of an action on all those concerned, implied equality of the sexes. Jeremy Bentham pointed out that, in assessing happiness, each person's happiness should equal that of all others – a radical view in his day, when social position and power determined norms of behaviour.

From this Utilitarian perspective **J S Mill (1806-73)** referred to the position and rights of women within society, and argued for sexual equality. As a Member of Parliament he proposed that women should have the vote, and published *The Subjection of Women* in 1869, during the early years of the Suffragette movement. J S Mill is seen as a feminist, in that he denied the validity of making gender distinctions in either ethical or political thinking. The actual gaining of the vote, however, took another half century's sustained protest and a World War.

The feminist perspective on ethics covers two broad areas. The first, which we have been considering so far, is the recognition that utilitarian and other ethical arguments require that women and men be treated equally. This sets an agenda, based on the traditional inequality within Western society. It examines situations where decisions fail to take into account the concerns of women. Areas of applied ethics would include equal opportunities of self-expression and development in society and in work, and other spheres where the role of women has traditionally been seen as crucial, for example in family life and caring for the young, the old and the sick. It requires not simply equality of

'gender blindness' but a positive appreciation of the role of women as a basis for ethical views.

THE FEMALE VIEW

The other area – which needs to be explored for the first, and most obvious, approach to gender equality to make sense – is the exploration of the distinctively female view of life. In other words, it asks whether the concepts of justice or of individuality, for example, are shaped by a male environment, and therefore are automatically biased against women.

The chief distinction between men and women is that women alone are capable of having children. Consequently, the perception of the role of carer and bringer up of families has been seen as primarily a female one. The valuation of such archetypal and exclusively feminine activity thus gives a pretty good overall picture of the value placed on the raising of families within society. Too often, this has been relatively low – relative compared to careers in business, politics, or other aspects of public and commercial life, which women have been infiltrating with growing success in the last 50 years.

A key question was whether women could find fulfilment only within that particular role of child-bearing and raising. An intriguing question arises: is there a precise equality, ethically speaking, between a man who decides to have no children and a woman who does the same?

Is the value of caring for those who are young, old or sick, sufficiently recognised in society, for example? If not, does that indicate that the role of the carer is seen as primarily a female one, and undervalued just on that account?

Whether approaching such issues from a utilitarian or a rights-based view of ethics, there is a fundamental question to

be tackled: Is equality, in itself, an adequate goal from a feminist point of view, or is something more needed in order to remove the historical oppression of women within society?

World religions have a contribution to make in terms of the recognition of the rights of women. The difficulty here is in knowing what constitutes philosophy and what should be ascribed simply to prevailing social custom.

Thus, for example, Islamic law offers special protection to women, and recognition that their role in society is very different from that of men. But is that the result of a radical appreciation of women's needs and rights, or is it simply a rationalization of a male perspective on society? Similarly

Buddhist philosophy suggests equality between men and women in terms of spiritual development.

Of course, female philosophers need not be feminists, so for example Baroness Mary Warnock, in the areas of education and embryology (see page 100) or Iris Murdoch (see page 104) have contributed greatly in the area of ethics. The fact of being female may have contributed to the quality of their work, but their concerns have been within mainstream philosophy and ethics.

Gender does not necessarily influence the issues within which a philosopher may be concerned, and it would be utterly unfair to the many women who contribute to philosophy to see their work as defined by their gender.

What does this image suggest? A female in a male-dominated world, subject to male authority and the laws established by men? Yet is may also be taken as an image of proud defiance, exposing the bogus or superficial nature of that authority. It might even qualify for Gandhi's term *satyagraha* **(see page 73). Although highlighted historically by the Suffragette movement, there is a broadly based debate about gender bias in the values and assumptions about life that inform ethical debate.**

In recent years, professional groups around the world have become increasing concerned to draw up codes of ethics to define what is regarded as good practice and to give the public a clear idea of what service is being offered to them by professional practitioners. Sometimes such codes are given the backing of law, sometimes they form the basis of professional assessment.

Professional ethics has been given particular impetus by the rapid development of new techniques and the associated moral dilemmas presented in the medical and nursing professions, but it has quickly broadened to include the legal and other professions.

The impetus for ethical guidelines has come from within the professional bodies responsible for regulating and policing members of that profession. Ethical committees have responsibility for considering the norms of good practice, but also for assessing those situations where a person may be considered to have performed outside agreed professional guidelines.

So, for example, a doctor has both a legal and moral responsibility towards his patients. Quite apart from the outcome of any legal action taken against

THE HIPPOCRATIC OATH

From the 5th century BCE, the Hippocratic Oath is an example of professional ethics. In it, doctors are required to promise to... 'follow that system or regimen which, according to my ability and judgement, I consider for the benefit of my patients, and abstain from whatever is deleterious and mischievous. I will give no deadly medicine to anyone if asked, nor suggest any such counsel; and in like manner I will not give to a woman a pessary to produce abortion. With purity and with holiness I will pass my life and practise my Art.'

him for misconduct, he may be prevented from practising by fellow members of the profession. Such codes of practice are partly a response to a general concern about ethical issues in society, partly a response to threats of litigation from those who believe themselves the victims of unprofessional practice.

Professional ethics forms an interesting touchstone for applied ethics in general since, where the defining of professional responsibility is concerned, it is essential that ethical guidelines are both specific and practical.

'Ethics is practical, or it is not really ethical. If it is no good in practice, it is no good in theory either.'

Peter Singer

Peter Singer has been particularly involved in issues of human bioethics. His general approach to applied ethics is to foster an attitude of disinterestedness, and the resulting ability to give equal weight to the interests of each individual. This, he claims, is the basic requirement of any rational assessment of a situation, since to allow everyone to pursue unfettered self-interest at the expense of others is self-defeating.

The impact of utilitarian views in the field of applied ethics has been considerable. Anne Maclean in *The Elimination of Morality* (1993), criticized the whole

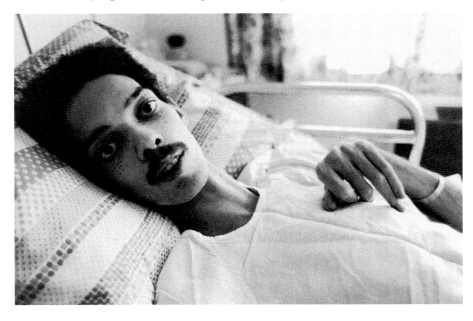

PETER SINGER
(B.1946)

A prominent figure in the world of applied ethics and has contributed to many areas, including bioethics, the treatment of animals and the distribution of resources. He is sometimes criticised for his strongly utilitarian approach to issues, and his tendency to dismiss what he sees as traditional Judeo-Christian morality. He has written and edited extensively, as well as holding academic posts and working with government agencies. His works include *Practical Ethics* (1979), *Applied Ethics* (1986), *A Companion to Ethics* (1991), *How Are We To Live* (1994) and *A Companion to Bioethics* (1998).

Bioethics is the term used for ethical issues arising as a result of the increasingly sophisticated application of biological science in areas of health care, fertility and genetic manipulation.

edifice of bioethics at that time on the grounds that those working in the field of applied ethics tend to assume that their particular utilitarian assessment was the only possible rational answer to ethical dilemmas. Her point is that philosophers should not try to impose a single rational answer on bioethical dilemmas, but simply assist with the rational examination of situations.

In spite of such criticisms, a broadly-based utilitarian approach has come to dominate the discussion of professional and applied ethics. This reflects the fact that, in most professions, decisions are taken about ends to be achieved by the action about which there may be ethical debate, so it is natural to start ethical debate by looking at the desirability or otherwise of those intended ends.

CLONING

The key point of ethical debate over cloning is not the possibility of exact human replication – which is hardly more than a caricature of what is happening – but rather the artificial creation of human organs for transplantation. Tissue cloning provides a realistic alternative to hunting for compatible tissue from live bodies.

Should one continue with a potential technique of immense potential benefit, if its development could one day lead to unacceptable results? The fact of cloning raises questions about human identity. Not simply is a clone part of myself; but more, is the tissue being grown artificially part of 'me'. If that tissue is subsequently destroyed, can I in some way claim damages, as though it were

BARONESS MARY WARNOCK
(B.1924)
A philosopher who has been involved with professional and ethical issues in the spheres of education and medicine. She chaired an enquiry into special educational needs in British schools in the 1970s, and later chaired the British government's 'Committee of Inquiry into Human Fertilisation and Embryology' (report published 1984). In terms of pure philosophy, she has written on ethics and the philosophy of mind.

the equivalent tissue in my body? If not, how do you specify what belongs to the self – it is simply a matter of physical location, of genetic make-up? Again, we have a whole range of ethical arguments that can be brought to bear on this issue, with utilitarian considerations being weighed against arguments about the absolute right of individuals over their own bodies.

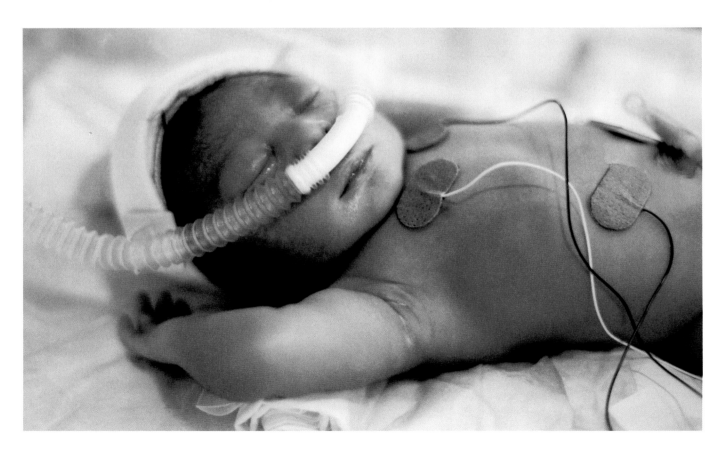

The medical and nursing professions are constantly being challenged by ethical issues, particularly those concerned with the use of techniques whose value to a patient may be questioned. Professionalism is not merely a matter of technical competence; it has an ethical dimension.

Can warfare ever be justified? If so, on what grounds, and within what limits?

BUSINESS ETHICS

Business ethics is another important area of development in applied ethics. It is concerned with the moral justification of various economic systems and the implications these have for those who work within them or are affected by them.

It may be studied at an international or national level, in terms of the principles that underlie economic activity.

It may also examine corporations, the way in which they operate, and the treatment of individuals within the business environment.

Discussions in business ethics may be based on utilitarian considerations, or on issues of contract, or on individual rights and responsibilities.

WARFARE

This debate has a long history, from Plato's recognition of the need for warriors to defend the city state, or the discussion in the Bhagavadgita about whether a Hindu prince should do his caste duty and kill an enemy, through medieval debates about what constitutes a 'just war', to modern agreements about how warfare should be conducted, such as the Geneva Convention.

Both the experience of the Vietnam War and the horrific implications of MAD (Mutually Assured Destruction) during the height of the Cold War arms race, may have encouraged a resurgence of interest in applied ethics.

MEDIA ETHICS

This is one of the newer branches of professional ethics, concerned with a whole range of issues such as:

- Freedom of speech and of expression
- The media and the Law and political influence
- Honesty and integrity in media coverage
- Objectivity
- Warfare and terrorism – special conditions and national interests
- Issues connected with sexual or racial bias or stereotyping
- The weighing of individual privacy against public interest.
- Censorship

Sexual ethics link to professional ethics at several points. For example, within media ethics there are the issues of the relationship between private sexuality and one's public role.

This is seen particularly clearly in terms of the sexuality of politicians and others who attract media attention. We need to ask if there is a norm of sexual behaviour required by society such that, even if private individuals are able to deviate from that norm with impunity, those holding public office are expected to conform. And, if so, is such a situation just?

Sexual ethics link with bioethics when it comes to issues such as whether it is right for a woman to use artificial methods of conception in order to have a family without having direct sexual or social contact with the male who will father the children.

Do we have a right to conceive children, and therefore a right to use whatever technical resources are available to make that possible?

What seems certain is that there will continue to be a demand for work in professional and applied ethics. It is one of the most obvious areas in which philosophy contributes to matters that are immediately relevant to the concerns of most people.

THE RETURN OF APPLIED ETHICS

Historically, most ethical thinkers have been concerned to apply their theories to practical questions about personal and social morality. On the other hand, in the first half of the 20th century much ethical thinking was influenced by questions arising out of Logical Positivism (see page 43). Its view questioned the meaningfulness of statements that did not simply report facts, and which led to an emphasis on meta-ethics – the study of the meaning of ethical statements – rather than the attempt to deal directly with moral issues.

Since the 1960s however, generally in response to social and political pressures, there has been a return to applied ethics. Hence, the range of topics illustrated on these pages now form an important part of any overall treatment of ethics.

In this chapter, however, we will be looking mostly at ethical theories, and applied ethics will be touched on only by way of illustration. There are two reasons for this:

1. To engage effectively in applied ethics, you need a grasp of fundamental ethical theory, in order to clarify the principles upon which you make ethical judgements.

2. To make an informed judgement in applied ethics, a great deal of factual data is generally required, in order for the actual situation and its implications to be clear.

Business decisions reflect values and perspectives, as well as economic realities. Business meetings may generate a whole range of human emotions and dilemmas that are beyond the scope of economics. Business can never be totally value-free, and therefore becomes a valid object of ethical scrutiny.

'All human beings are born free and equal in dignity and rights.'

Article 1 of the Universal Declaration of Human Rights

Today, both in the academic realm and in the wider world, there is a wide range of approaches to ethics, and its significance for many issues remains clear. Utilitarianism still dominates many ethical arguments, particularly in the sphere of applied ethics.

Approaches based on the concept of the rights of individuals remain very important, and link with political theory (see, for example the work of **Robert Nozik (1938-2002)** or **Ronald Dworkin (b.1931)**. Allied to this is the contract-based approach, again reflected in political thinking, this time by **John Rawls (b.1921)**, whose *A Theory of Justice* (1971), sees justice in terms of establishing fairness and leads him to be critical of utilitarian arguments that allow discrimination against minorities in the interest of a majority.

Virtue ethics, established in Ancient Greece but back in favour in recent years, looks at ethics in terms of the qualities and virtues of the good life. As presented by, for example, **Philippa Foot (b.1920)** this approach argued that morality should be concerned with traits that could be shown to be beneficial or otherwise to humankind, not dependent upon particular wishes or decisions.

There is also the approach that looks at ethics in terms of personal commitments. This is particularly associated with the work of **Bernard Williams (b.1929)**, who in *Ethics and the Limits of Philosophy* (1985) challenges as unrealistic theories that do not take into account the importance of an individual's personal aims in making moral choices.

Science continues to raise ethical questions, raising again problems associated with arguing from an 'is' to an 'ought', and therefore in trying to frame ethical theories and values on the basis of empirical evidence. One particularly difficult area here concerns the ethical implications of evolution. Following Darwin's theory of natural selection, the idea of the 'survival of the fittest', associated particularly with 'Social Darwinism' of **Herbert Spencer (1820-1903)**, who effectively suggested that those who were fittest should survive, as opposed to Darwin's claim, which was simply that those who were fittest did survive.

Nowadays, genetic theory raises this issue again, as in *The Selfish Gene* by Richard Dawkins. If there is absolutely no link between facts and values, then the selfish and competitive nature of genetic activity is irrelevant to ethics. On the other hand, any theory that links ethics with some fundamental reality of structure of the world (as, for example, Natural Law) needs to take this into account.

There is thus a lively and ongoing debate about the nature and justification of ethical statements, but somewhere in the midst all this there remains a fundamental quest for 'the good'.

Back in the 1960s, the philosopher and novelist **Iris Murdoch**, wrote a short book entitled *The Sovereignty of Good*. It was a time when many philosophers were arguing that moral judgements had no factual basis, but were simply expressing emotions, or suggesting a chosen course of action. On the other hand both psychology and sociology were throwing into the debate 'facts' that certainly had profound ethical implications. Freudian analysis of human motives made unselfish actions seem impossible, since the self was always motivated by its needs, especially sexual ones. Political and social activity reinforced a Hegelian or Marxist view that the individual was to be considered primarily as part of a larger social or political movement – his or her actions justified in terms of the ongoing process of history.

In contrast to all this, Iris Murdoch returned to Platonic ideas, seeing virtue as something that may be perceived to inform morally choices and thus provide an 'objective' basis for morality. She linked this with great works of literature and art in which the artist presents reality in such a way that it startles people out of their habitual, narrow preoccupations, and their natural inclination to do only what appears to offer an immediate purpose and reward.

When she comes to define what she means by 'good' she says:

This approach finds a natural resonance with all those situations where the sudden heroism of ordinary people speaks of a deep-seated sense of morality and purpose in life.

Whether it is the heroism of New York firemen and others, in the face of the horrors of the attack on the World Trade Centre, or the routine heroism of those who take the decision to work for the benefit of others, setting aside their own interest, there is a sense that such people, and such activities, touch something that is profoundly moral.

It may not be possible to define exactly when, and in what circumstances, it is right to do such things. Indeed, the very attempt to do so may seem to undermine their value.

Perhaps, G E Moore was right to claim that the 'good' cannot be defined, but simply known. Perhaps Iris Murdoch put her finger on it, by saying that the only genuine way to be good is to be good 'for nothing'. For such a 'nothing' goes beyond all superficial rewards and arguments, and touches the very core of what it is to be human.

'The Good has nothing to do with purpose, indeed it excludes the idea of purpose. "All is vanity" is the beginning and end of ethics. The only genuine way to be good is to be good "for nothing" in the midst of a scene where every "natural" thing, including one's own mind, is subject to chance, that is, to necessity...'

Iris Murdoch, *The Sovereignty of Good*

DAME IRIS MURDOCH
1919-1999
Known more as a prolific novelist than as a philosopher. In both sides of her work she was preoccupied with defining the nature of good and evil. Her most substantial book for exploring ethics and other philosophical issues is *Metaphysics as a Guide to Morals*.

A fireman works his way through the remains of the World Trade Centre in New York. Heroism and self-sacrifice are instinctively perceived as 'good'. It may be a difficult word to define, simply because (as G E Moore claimed) it cannot be reduced to anything more basic. Yet we know what it means, recognize it in the actions of others, and use it as the basis for our discussion of ethical issues. As Iris Murdoch pointed out, there is a goodness that rises about the ever-changing pattern of life's joys and sorrows. It is not a goodness that depends on results, but one that shows itself in acts of heroism, giving a profound sense of dignity human worth in the midst of life's fragility.

In the modern world it is commonly (but not unanimously) believed that science represents the special and remarkable achievement of modern civilization. At one time people, looking up at the night sky, wondered what the stars were, how far away they were, and how they came to be. Their answers were generally mythological or religious. But now scientists claim to know better. By analysing light emitted from stars they can tell exactly how far from the Earth they are, at what speed they are travelling, and what they are made of. Scientists also have theories about the origin of the universe and make plausible enough predictions about how it will change in the future.

Back on earth, evolutionary biologists with the help of palaeontologists explain how humanity came to be, while their colleagues are mapping the human genetic code. Such are the claims of scientists.

The material products of their achievements are much more easy to see and understand. Almost all societies have had some kind of technology. But the modern world is remarkable for the extent of its technology and for the fact that much of it stems from the discoveries of scientists.

The technological offspring of science may be good or bad, but either way they are important. Nuclear energy in both its peaceful and military forms derives from Einstein's theories on the nature of matter and energy. Genetically engineered crops may prove a blessing or curse, but it is astonishing that, thanks to an understanding of their genetic makeup we can now create new organisms in the laboratory unknown in nature.

Technology offers extraordinary opportunities but correspondingly large dangers. The science upon which it is based is extremely sophisticated – and beyond the power of most of us to understand, let alone judge. Science consumes vast sums of public money –

justified both by the utility of its products and also the intrinsic worth of the deep understanding of the world which it claims to give us. Science has superseded in our education system other systems of belief, such as religion. It is therefore no surprise that philosophers ask questions about science:

- Does it really give us the knowledge it claims to give?
- If so, how does it do so?
- Is there really 'scientific progress', or is it mostly a myth, substituting for old religious myths?
- Why do theories of science change?
- When should we believe a theory in the first place?

Science is not the only body of formally organized knowledge and doctrine. Historians give us knowledge of the past, but their work is for the most part more an art than a science. Theology is a systematic study but is no longer seen as a proper science. Then what is special about science? In what way are the claims of science different from beliefs held in other branches of study?

SCIENCE VERSUS PSEUDO-SCIENCE

One positive answer to this question was given by the British philosopher **Karl Popper (1902-1994)**. Assuming an almost Humean scepticism, Popper claimed that there is *a criterion of demarcation* which distinguishes science from non-science or *pseudo-science*.

The criterion is **falsifiability** – that is, **a claim is scientific if some possible observation could be made which would show it to be false.**

On this view, theology is unscientific, for no observations we could conceivably make would show that belief in God is false.

Popper did not condemn religious or similar beliefs for being unscientific; they were only bad if they claimed to be sci-

entific but were not.

Such theories are pseudo-scientific, and Popper regarded Marx's theory of history and Freud's psychoanalysis as particularly pseudo-scientific. Similarly, astrology is pseudo-scientific, since its predictions are so vague that they can seem to be confirmed by almost any occurrence.

But precisely what observations would falsify Darwin's theory of evolution by natural selection? It is not a theory whose predictions can be tested in a laboratory. Correspondingly, supporters of anti-evolution Creationism, the view that all species were created individually by God at the same time, claim that their opinions are equally scientific.

It may be that the distinction between science and non-science is not as important as the distinction between good science and bad science, between beliefs

SIR KARL POPPER
(1902-1994)

Karl Popper was born in Vienna in 1902. He trained as a science teacher and mingled with the Vienna Circle of philosophers, but he rejected their Positivism.

In 1934 he published his *Logic of Scientific Discovery,* which criticized inductivist philosophies of science and promoted **falsificationism**.

He also criticized Marxism and psychoanalysis for being pseudo-scientific. According to Popper they are presented as scientific, but they are constructed so as to be immune from any possible refutation. This makes them unscientific. Popper is also famed for his defence of liberal democracy against all forms of totalitarianism.

During the Second World War, he taught in New Zealand, where he wrote the book that made him famous, *The Open Society and its Enemies*, which was published in 1945. He spent the rest of his career at the London School of Economics.

The actual work done by scientists is largely concerned with the establishment of experiments and the testing of data. It is typically routine and methodical. In general, the Philosophy of Science is less concerned with that process than with the valid or invalid use of that data in framing theories.

properly founded on evidence and those based on prejudice or bad reasoning. In which case, the relevant question is:

What makes a scientific inference a good one?

FREUD AND MARX: FALLEN IDOLS?

Through much of the 20th century, many writers and thinkers regarded the psychological theories of Freud, and even more the economic and political theories of Marx, as almost infallible. Between them, they could be used to explain almost all of human life.

When historical or personal facts failed to fit these theories, those facts tended to be ignored, or distorted to fit the theories. Thus, for example, the Marxist prediction of the inevitable triumph of Communism survived many challenges, and interpreted any apparent failure of Communism as merely a step in the direction of its final triumph, a step that needed only to be accepted within and interpreted by Marxist theory.

There came a point, however, where the weight of evidence against an apparently 'scientific' theory, starts to throw

its value as science into question, even if it continues to be held as an article of belief or as an expression of home.

Finally, with the collapse of Communist power after 1989, it was clear that Marxist theory could no longer be maintained, and therefore – if it continued to be put forward – it should be seen as pseudo-scientific.

Popper's work, which we shall examine again later in this chapter, highlights the basic questions of what counts as valid science, and how scientific theories are to be judged.

Scientists carry out experiments and make observations. They do so in order to generate and gather evidence for or against theories or hypotheses.

- A *hypothesis* is a claim whose truth cannot be known directly through observation but only inferred from the evidence.
- A *theory* is a set of related hypotheses, which will typically be generalized and will help explain a range of phenomena.

For instance, Newton's theory of gravity explains, among other things, the orbits of the planets around the Sun. When it was observed that the orbit of Uranus did not precisely fit the theory, it was *hypothesized* that an unseen planet was affecting Uranus' orbit. (This was how the planet Neptune was later discovered, see page 117).

A hypothesis for which there is supporting evidence is said to be *confirmed* by that evidence.

The better confirmed a hypothesis is, the more justified a scientist is in believing it, although one would not be justified in believing a theory which was only weakly confirmed by a small amount of evidence. An important question therefore is:

- **When does evidence confirm a hypothesis?**

A related but distinct question is:

- **Under what circumstances does a well-confirmed hypothesis count as scientific knowledge?**

Both these questions have generated considerable and continuing philosophical discussion.

ENUMERATIVE INDUCTIVISM

The first and simplest account of confirmation is *enumerative induction* (sometimes called Baconian or Humean induction). According to naive enumerative inductivism, evidence takes the form of an observation of a regular conjunction of properties. Your evidence might be the fact that all ripe bananas you have eaten have tasted sweet. Or, at a more complicated level, your evidence might be that having tested a variety of pendulums of different lengths and measured the period of their swings, the period (in seconds) is always 2.01 x the square root of the length (in metres).

The inductivist account of confirmation is simple:

Observational evidence confirms hypotheses, working on the assumption that what has not been observed will be like what has already been observed. 'More of the same' is the motto of inductivism.

The weakest hypothesis to be confirmed by the evidence will say that the next observed thing will be like the previously observed thing: the next ripe banana will taste sweet, the period of the next pendulum will also be 2.01 x the square root of its length.

A more ambitious hypothesis confirmed by the same evidence says that all relevant things, whether past, present or future, whether observed or unobserved will be like the observed – all ripe bananas are sweet, the periods of all pendulums are equal to 2.01 x the square root of their lengths.

HUME'S PROBLEM OF INDUCTION

The Scottish philosopher David Hume believed that people do actually reason, on the whole, in accordance with naive enumerative induction.

He saw this as demonstrating the tendency of the human mind to habituate itself to the repeated occurrence of events.

BLACK RAVENS OR WHITE?

ENUMERATIVE INDUCTIVISM

A		all observed Fs are G
	confirms	the next F will be G
B		all observed Fs are G
	confirms	all Fs (observed and unobserved) are G

Inductivism regards scientific inference as a matter of projecting observed regularities into the future, or assuming things that have **not** been observed to exhibit the same regularities as found among things that **have** been observed. Imagine that 'F' and 'G' in the above are names of properties so 'F' might be 'raven' and 'G' might be 'black'. The observation of numerous Fs, which have all been found to be G (many ravens which have all been observed to be black), confirms both the hypothesis that the next F will be G (the next raven to be seen will be black) and the stronger hypothesis that all Fs are G (all ravens are black). The latter hypothesis is inherently less likely than the former, and so would require more confirmation before we could justifiably believe it. The *rule of induction* says that the degree of confirmation is dependent on the number of observed cases of Fs that are G.

He argued, however, that although enumerative induction might be natural, it still cannot lead to a justified belief in a hypothesis. If he is right, then no evidence can ever inductively confirm that hypothesis.

For, said Hume, in order for the rule of induction (see box on page 108) to yield a justified belief in a hypothesis, we must be justified in using that rule. (After all, there are other rules one could employ, for instance 'counter-induction', which says that if all observed Fs have been G, then expect the next F *not* to be G. Some gamblers argue in this way when they think that a run of heads in tossing a coin makes tails more likely on the next toss.)

Note that however much evidence we have, it does not logically guarantee that the next F will be G. However many ravens we have seen, all of which have been black, it is still conceivable that the next one will be white. So it cannot be logic which tells us to use the rule of induction.

If not logic, then perhaps experience tells us to use the rule. After all, as a matter of fact we do use induction all the time, and on the whole we get by pretty well – experience tells us that the rule of induction has worked for us in the past. So we should expect it to work well for us now. But here is Hume's catch. The argument from experience says that we should expect the rule to work in the future because it has worked in the past. That argument is itself inductive – it justifies our use of induction by using an inductive argument.

It therefore assumes what it sets out to justify. The argument from experience is a circular argument, and so Hume concluded that there is no justification for inductivism. We use it not because of genuine reason but **out of habit**.

Halley's comet. Halley predicted the appearance of the comet in 1759, on the basis of its previous appearances in 1531, 1607 and 1682 – an instance of inductive reasoning.

GOODMAN'S NEW RIDDLE OF INDUCTION

The American philosopher **Nelson Goodman (1906-)** created another puzzle which seems to undermine enumerative induction.

We can invent a new adjective *grue*, which is defined as follows:

X is grue = either X is green and observed before midnight on 31 December 2010

or X is blue and not observed before midnight on 31 December 2010

So an emerald observed today is grue, while a blue sapphire dug up for the first time in 2011 will also be grue. It follows from this definition that anything seen until today which is green can be counted as grue. So all observed emeralds are grue.

Now look at the box (on page 108) labelled 'enumerative inductivism'. Let us take the second formula (B) and put 'emerald' for 'F' and 'grue' for 'G'. That gives us: All observed emeralds are grue *confirms* that all emeralds are grue. We have seen that the first part is true. So now let's look at the hypothesis, which is confirmed: all emeralds are grue. This is

supposed to cover *all* emeralds, whether observed or not. So, in particular, an emerald that is first mined and seen in 2011, is grue.

Now look at the definition of 'grue'. It says that if something is grue, then if it has not been observed before midnight on 31 December 2010, then it is blue. So this emerald, first seen in 2011, should be blue.

So enumerative induction allows us, using the term 'grue', to infer that emeralds first seen after 2010 will be blue. Not only is this a strange conclusion, it is contradicted by employing enumerative induction using our normal word 'green', which tells us that the same emeralds are green. So it looks as if, depending on which vocabulary we use, we can use any evidence to confirm any hypothesis about the future, however bizarre. At the very least, in order to use enumerative induction, we must restrict our vocabulary to words like 'green', which seem well-behaved, and exclude ones like 'grue'. But how do we decide what to allow and what to exclude?

Furthermore, related problems arise even with well-behaved vocabulary. Let us say you are an ornithologist. You have observed many ducks, and they have all

been brown. So, using enumerative induction, you conclude that all ducks are brown. You have also made a study of arctic birds in general and observed that they are all white. So you conclude that all arctic birds are white. However, you have never seen an arctic duck. Should you conclude that arctic ducks are brown or that they are white?

HYPOTHETICO-DEDUCTIVISM

Enumerative induction gives the impression that the way to do science is to go about observing things, and then to infer that what is unobserved and in the future will be just like what has been observed in the past.

But enumerative induction cannot tell us about the nature of things which can never be observed, such as the interiors of atoms or stars. Since we cannot observe these at all, we cannot use enumerative induction to learn about them.

A more natural way to look at things is to suggest that a scientist first constructs a hypothesis, deduces observable consequences from it, and then checks whether these observable consequences are true. If they are, then those observations confirm the hypothesis.

Hopes are pinned, and fortunes made or lost on the basis of luck. Or is it luck? How do you predict whether red or black will come up next on the wheel? Do you assume red will come next because it has been red so often already? Or do you guess that it must be time to get a black instead? Science is concerned with prediction, and it is far from clear which way you should bet when it comes to observations.

LIGHT BENDS

An example of this in operation was the dramatic confirmation of Einstein's Theory of Relativity, which says that light should be bent by massive objects. Arthur Eddington deduced how the light from a star would be bent by the Sun. This allowed him to say where the star should be observed to be during a solar eclipse. In 1919 Eddington made the relevant observations, which closely agreed with the deductions from this theory (but not with those from Newton's theory). Thus Einstein's theory was spectacularly confirmed.

We know that light travels in straight lines; it is part of our everyday experience. We assume that light never bends, because we cannot imagine the Sun's rays travelling other than in straight lines as they illuminate and cast shadows on Earth; hence the remarkable nature of Einstein's claims, and their dramatic confirmation by Eddington.

THE PARADOX OF CONFIRMATION

Although hypothetico-deductivism is an improvement on enumerative induction, it still has its problems. One of these is known as the paradox of confirmation – or the raven paradox. Let our hypothesis be 'all ravens are black'. If we come across a raven, we deduce from the hypothesis that it should be black. And so if it is black, the hypothesis is confirmed. So far so good.

We next come across some white object in a tree. The hypothesis allows us to deduce something about this white object – that it is not a raven. So we investigate this white thing and find that it is a plastic bag, and so is certainly not a raven. The observable deduction from the hypothesis was found to be true.

By the pattern laid out in the box for hypothetico-deductivism, this too means that the hypothesis is confirmed. But it seems strange that the hypothesis 'all ravens are black' should be confirmed by a white bag, and indeed by any non-black thing which is not a raven.

Another way to see why this is a consequence of hypothetico-deductivism is to see that the hypothesis 'all ravens are black' is equivalent to 'all non-black things are non-ravens'.

There are two sorts of response to the raven paradox:

The first takes the conclusion to be an absurdity – for a white bag to confirm a hypothesis about ravens. Therefore the hypothetico-deductive model should be abandoned and we should look for a better account of confirmation.

The second response is to accept that the white bag does confirm the hypothesis, albeit to a very small degree. After all, it might be pointed out, on observing the white object it is still an open possibility that it will turn out to be a raven, thereby proving our hypothesis false. So it is some small success for the theory that on closer inspection it turns out to be a bag not a raven.

FALSIFICATIONISM

Some philosophers believe that Hume's problem shows that induction cannot be the rational basis of scientific knowledge and belief.

Either we must say that science is irrational, or we must show that something other than induction is the foundation of scientific reasoning.

Sir Karl Popper was one such philosopher. Believing that science is rational, he sought to develop a non-inductive account of science.

Since he rejected induction, Popper held that observing a black raven could never confirm the hypothesis that all ravens are black. But consider the person observing the white object in the tree. Imagine this time that the white object does turn out to be a raven. Now we know for sure that the hypothesis is false. So although we can never know that hypotheses are correct, we **can** know that they are mistaken.

This leads to Popper's characterization of the route by which science progresses, called *falsificationism*. This can be summed up as *conjecture and refutation*. First a scientist constructs a bold hypothesis – a conjecture.

Then he deduces observable consequences from it. So far this is similar to hypothetico-deductivism. But instead of seeking agreement between the predictions and what is observed, the falsificationist looks for sources of possible *disagreement*.

He tries his hardest to refute the theory. If he succeeds in finding a refutation – a disagreement between what the conjecture predicts and what is observed – then progress of some sort has been made. We know the conjecture is false, and now we construct a new one.

However long this process goes on, we do not get to know that a general theory is true. Even if a theory stubbornly resists every attempt to falsify it we still do not know it is true. Such a theory is said to be *well-corroborated*. But, insists Popper, corroboration should not be confused with confirmation. It is never a reason to believe a general theory or hypothesis.

Many scientists have found Popper's picture of science attractive. It describes the imaginative construction of conjectures and their rigorous testing. It tells us never to rule out the possibility that a seemingly quite successful theory might yet be falsified.

This strikes a chord with physicists who regard Newtonian physics as refuted by Einstein, although Newton's theories enjoyed more than two centuries of remarkable corroboration.

But other scientists dislike the idea that we can never know any theory to be true. Biologists and geneticists regard Darwinian evolution, supplemented by Mendelian genetics, as constituting a body of theory, which is sufficiently well-corroborated as to be regarded, in the main, as a body of knowledge.

Some would say that even if we do not know our theories to be true, we have reason to think that they are getting closer to the truth. The idea of 'nearness to the truth' is called

FALSIFICATIONISM

from the hypothesis *h* and certain known conditions *c*, the observable consequence *o* is deduced;

o is observed to be false

the hypothesis *h* is refuted (falsified) by *o*

Falsificationism can be contrasted with inductivism and hypothetico-deductivism.

Like hypothetico-deductivism, the approach based on falsificationism tells us to deduce observable consequences from our hypotheses. But unlike hypothetico-deductivism and inductivism it does not regard the truth of the observable consequences as confirming the hypothesis.

Instead, for the falsificationist, the only interesting outcome is the falsity of the observable consequence, since this tells us definitively that the hypothesis is false and may be rejected.

verisimilitude. Without induction, high degree of corroboration does not even show increasing *verisimilitude*.

This degree of scepticism seems incompatible with depicting science as rational. **How could science rationally aim at truth or verisimilitude if there is no way of actually achieving those things?**

Thus both inductivism and falsificationism lead to a questioning of any assumption that a scientific theory can offer certainty, for it is only ever as good as the evidence upon which it is based, and (if it is to be scientific) must always accept that it may eventually be shown to be inadequate.

ABDUCTIVISM

A rather different picture of scientific reasoning is provided by *abductivism*, which was first articulated by Charles Sanders Peirce.

Abductivism is also called *Inference to the Best Explanation*, which spells out the basic idea.

Scientists look for possible explanations of the phenomena they observe. When sufficient evidence has been gathered they may be in a position to infer that the best of the possible explanations is the actual, true explanation.

For example, palaeontologists have long wondered why the dinosaurs became extinct. There are three different possible explanations:

1. Dinosaurs lost out to mammals in a Darwinian struggle for existence,
2. Dust from an enormous volcanic eruption blotted out the sun, killing off their food sources,
3. A huge meteor collided with the Earth, creating a dust cloud, which - as in the eruption theory - killed off their food supply.

The unusual amounts of the element iridium found in geological strata associated with dinosaur extinctions favours the third explanation, for iridium is rare on Earth but common in meteors.

That sort of evidence may show one explanation to be much better than the others. According to abduction, that is a reason to believe it to be true.

Abductivism can incorporate enumerative induction. If all diamonds have been found to be harder than quartz, then perhaps the best explanation of this observed fact is that it is a law of nature that diamond is harder than quartz.

If that is true, all future and unobserved diamonds are harder than quartz. So enumerative induction is a special case of abduction, where the best explanation is some natural law.

While abduction can include enumerative induction, it also goes further. Very roughly, inferences using enumerative induction say only 'more of the same' – which means that a scientist will only be able to infer the existence of things like those things she has already seen – for example, more hard diamonds.

But much of science is concerned with making discoveries about things we have never seen – nor could ever see – like subatomic particles, or the Big Bang, or the movements of continents, or the extinction of the dinosaurs.

Abduction allows us to make inferences concerning these things since, although we may have never seen a certain thing or event, it may still be the best explanation of what we **do** see.

ABDUCTIVISM

- h, k, and l are competing hypotheses

- h is a much better explanation of the evidence e than k or l

- the hypothesis h is confirmed by e

Abductivism is also called 'inference to the best explanation'. According to abductivism, if there is sufficient evidence, we should look for the best putative explanation of that evidence. The best explanation will be the one most likely to be true.

The presence of iridium in the relevant geological strata, suggests that the dinosaurs became extinct due to dust thrown up by the impact of a huge meteor. Not only is this an example of abductivism, but such events are a constant reminder of the fragile and impermanent nature of life – a theme explored in other branches of philosophy. What does it mean, if life as we know it can be destroyed by a single impact? How does it change our view of things, or the values by which we live?

Whether abduction is rationally acceptable is constantly debated between realists and anti-realists and leads to the question:

● **What is the aim of science?**

We might think this obvious: science aims at truth, or at least at getting closer to the truth. This is a realist's answer. But the anti-realist argues that this cannot or should not be the aim of science. Instead, the purpose of a scientific theory is to be able to generate true predictions.

A theory can yield accurate predictions even if it is not true. Since our only way of evaluating a theory is through testing its predictions, **the most we can expect of a successful theory is that it will go on producing true predictions, not that it is itself true.**

THE COPERNICAN REVOLUTION

Debates like this have emerged several times in the history of science, notably in astronomy.

Between the second century CE and the 15th century, astronomy in Europe and Muslim countries was based on the theories of the Greek scientist Ptolemy of Alexandria. He placed the Earth at the centre of the Universe, with the Sun, planets and stars circulating around it.

Conscientious and accurate observations of the Universe as he saw it (with his naked eye, of course) enabled him to achieve a high degree of accuracy for this cosmology. The fit between theory and observation was impressively close, for long enabling detailed and successful predictions about eclipses to be made.

But it also meant positioning many awkward 'retrogressive' movements for the planets, which at times seemed to move backwards through the sky for no good reason. To explain these, complex epicycles were invented.

In 1543 the Polish cleric and astronomer Copernicus, perhaps influenced by Aristarchus of Samos (who flourished in the third century BCE), published a rival theory, which placed the Earth among the other planets rotating about the Sun, now radiant at the centre of the Universe.

Copernicus' system, which saw the planetary orbits as perfectly spherical, resolved many of the problems with Ptolemy's. But his theory, published only after his death in 1543, conflicted with Christian beliefs in human uniqueness, and made no sense in contemporary physics (i.e. before Newton's theory of gravity).

In a preface to Copernicus' book *On the Revolutions of the Spheres* the theologian Osiander ingeniously proposed that the new theory should be seen, not as stating the truth about the planets, but as seeking to provide an improved basis for computing their positions in the night sky as observed from the Earth. Osiander was proposing an *anti-realist* interpretation of Copernicus' work. The view that the purpose of a theory is only to produce accurate predictions is called *instrumentalism*.

The greatest observer of the heavens before the invention of the telescope by Galileo, was the Dane, **Tycho Brahe (1546-1601)**, who spent his life compiling highly detailed star tables based on his own observations. (He later bequeathed his tables to Johannes Kepler). While Tycho recognized the benefits of Copernicus' system, he thought a moving Earth an absurdity. In his system all the planets except the Earth rotate about the Sun – and the Sun rotates about the Earth.

This system and that of Copernicus are mathematically equivalent when seen from Earth. For that reason, they give the same observational predictions.

Are they then different theories or just the same theory presented in different ways? One's answer will depend on what view one takes of space.

ABSOLUTE OR RELATIVE?

In a debate, which took place a century after Tycho, Isaac Newton held that position in space is *absolute*, while the German philosopher and mathematician Leibniz argued that it is *relative*.

One way of looking at their difference in opinion is to ask whether the following supposition makes sense:

● Would things be in a new position if everything in the Universe were together moved one metre in the same direction?

According to the absolute view, there would be a difference – even though we could not observe that difference (because the observer's relation to observable things is unchanged).

The supporter of the relative view will say that there is no more to a thing's position than its relation to other things – so a change in position is a change relative to those other things. Hence a supposed change that is shared by everything, is no real change at all.

Thus, for the absolutist there is a real difference between Copernicus' system and Tycho's, while the relativist will deny any substantive contrast.

COPERNICUS AND TYCHO BRAHE

Ptolemy's system, which placed the Earth at the centre of the universe, held sway for more than 1,300 years.

In the 16th century, **Nicolas Copernicus (1473-1543)**, who found the Ptolemaic system simply did not agree with the observed facts of planetary movements, put forward a novel system with the Sun at the Universe's centre and the Earth and other planets rotating around the Sun, only the Moon moving around the Earth. But this was far too radical an idea for his contemporaries to accept, for it threatened to undermine the Christian (and Jewish and Muslim) view of the universe.

The astronomer Tycho Brahe (1546 - 1601) proposed a compromise system combining elements of both Ptolemy's and Copernicus' systems. According to Tycho, the Earth remains stationary at the centre of the universe, while the planets (other than the Moon) rotate about the Sun which itself moves around the Earth.

The two systems produce approximately equivalent observations of the heavens, although both in the end were wrong (the Earth and other planets move in elliptical, not spherical, orbits, as the great scientists of the 17th century discovered). They satisfy Popper's definition of real science, however, since they are capable of being falsified.

The whole episode shows that scientific theories can be revolutionary without being correct.

We take this modern view of the solar system for granted, and assume that, once scaled appropriately, reality is much as depicted by the artist. Yet in the 16th century, the shape of the solar system could only be known by deducation from the relative movements of the planets, which had the appearance of stars that moved against the backdrop of the fixed constellations – and it was far from obvious which interpretation best accounted for the observations.

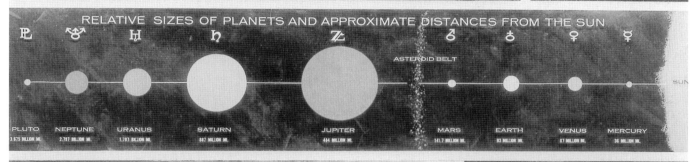

DALTON AND ATOMISM

Three centuries later, the British chemist **John Dalton (1766-1844)** sparked a similar debate, this time in chemistry. Chemists had noted that when gases react together, they do so always in fixed proportions. Hydrogen and oxygen gases react in the ratio 2:1 by volume – never 4:1 or 1.3:1. Further, as the Frenchman **Gay-Lussac (1778-1850)** noted, the ratios are always ratios of small whole numbers. This law of fixed proportions can be regarded as an experimental generalization. Dalton hypothesized that there is an underlying basis for the law. He suggested that gases like hydrogen and oxygen are made up of invisible particles – atoms, with a different sort of atom for each substance. When gases react, he said, the atoms combine to form clusters of the different kinds of atom, what we call 'molecules' and Dalton called 'compound atoms'.

If the molecules in a compound are always the same, and are composed of small numbers of elementary atoms, we would expect substances to react in fixed proportions, corresponding to the proportions of the component atoms in the molecules.

Dalton had proposed invisible atoms and unobservable modes of their combination as the best explanation of the experimental law.

Since the hypothesis could not be confirmed or refuted by observation, many of Dalton's contemporaries and successors rejected it is as pointless speculation. Like Sir Benjamin Brodie, they considered that chemical theories should confine themselves to articulating laws concerning quantities and operations, which could be observed or performed in the laboratory.

However, Dalton's atomic hypothesis became more widely accepted, because it could explain a new phenomenon, *isomerism*, discovered after his time. Isomers are distinct substances, which have different physical or chemical properties, but which share the same chemical formula and so are compounds of the same proportions of chemical elements. On the atomic hypothesis this is easily explained, since the same set of atoms might combine in different structures to form molecules with different properties. For instance they may form molecules which are mirror images of one another and so will bend light in different directions. The explanatory power of atomism ensured its success.

POSITIVISM AND EMPIRICISM

Sir Benjamin Brodie, in rejecting Dalton's atoms, was influenced by *Positivism*. Positivism has its roots in the empiricism of David Hume and was first expounded by the French philosophers Saint-Simon and Comte in the early 19th century. Positivists reject metaphysics and hypotheses concerning the unobservable – for them the whole point of science is

to establish correlations only among observable phenomena.

A very influential form of Positivism – Logical Positivism – was developed by the Vienna Circle group of philosophers in the 1920s. According to their principle of verification, the meaning of a sentence is the way in which it is verified. So, roughly, to ask what a sentence means is to ask how one might decide whether it is true. Since the Logical Positivists took the ground of all empirical knowledge to be experience and observation, often understood as the sensations of the observers, it follows that for them the meaning of any sentence is reducible to some claim about what one may observe or sense. So, in particular, any theoretical claim in science is really just about observations and sensations.

One version of this Positivism about meaning is Bridgman's *operationalism*. According to operationalism, any scientific statement is really a statement about various sorts of operations and measurements. A statement about electrons is not really about invisible particles but instead is about laboratory items such as vacuum tubes or bubble chambers.

NEWTON AND NEPTUNE

Newton's theory of gravity had allowed predictions of the motions of Uranus which were found by observation to be badly inaccurate. But this did not falsify Newton's theory, since it was possible to reject one of the auxiliary hypotheses, that no unobserved planets existed, and to replace it by another hypothesis, that an unseen planet was disturbing the orbit of Uranus. The replacement hypothesis was confirmed when Neptune was discovered by William Herschel in 1781. Faced with an apparent falsification, it may be wiser to keep the hypothesis under test and consider rejecting one of the auxiliary hypotheses.

The image on the left depicts the Voyager 2 approaching Neptune and its moon. Physical evidence replaces the hypothesis that Neptune must exist to account for the irregularity in the orbit of Uranus.

To many, it seems that the history of science is that of the steady accumulation of scientific knowledge. Once, many false theories were believed – that the Sun moves around the Earth, or that living creatures can grow out of dead matter. Now these theories have been replaced by true theories to which new discoveries and new knowledge are continuously being added.

The growth of scientific knowledge is a steady, if increasingly rapid, process. What explains this growth? Many scientists will tell you that it is the *scientific method*.

The idea behind scientific method is that it provides a framework for the testing and evaluation of hypotheses. But what this method might be is much debated. A theory of method is called a *methodology* and competing methodologies have been constructed around the various different accounts of scientific inference discussed earlier in this chapter. The iconoclastic Austrian-American philosopher of science, **Paul Feyerabend (1924–1994)**, rejected the very concept of scientific method.

LAKATOS AND THE METHODOLOGY OF SCIENTIFIC RESEARCH

The Hungarian-born philosopher **Imre Lakatos (1922–1974)** followed Popper in advocating falsificationism. But Lakatos realised that in practice scientists do not discard a theory immediately when faced with a single instance that appears to falsify the theory. This is for two reasons.

Firstly, there is no point in discarding a theory unless there is some better hypothesis to work on instead. A falsified hypothesis with an otherwise good track record may still be better than anything else we have been able to think of.

Secondly, hypotheses rarely yield observable conclusions directly. Rather, other hypotheses and beliefs, known as auxiliary hypotheses, need to be employed as well. For instance, we saw that Eddington was able to make predictions using Einstein's theory of relativity which were confirmed by his observations. But the theory of relativity did not lead to these conclusions alone, but only in conjunction with certain additional beliefs about the mass of the sun and the speed of light.

We can combine these insights. First, the development of what Lakatos calls a *scientific research programme* requires a theoretical hard core which remains constant, and a belt of auxiliary hypotheses which will change. The auxiliary belt may change because an auxiliary hypothesis is replaced by one which allows for more accurate prediction (thus avoiding falsification) or because new auxiliary hypotheses are added as the theoretical hard core is applied to new scientific problems.

Second, the rejection of a theory may be due to some competing theory. Theory A is to be preferred to theory B when A is *progressing* while B is *degenerating*. Think of Dalton's 'research programme' of atomism. When compared with Brodie's anti-atomistic alternative, the latter was degenerating where the former was progressing. Atomism could successfully explain new phenomena such as isomerism that its rival was unable to account for. Discarding a degenerating research programme can be seen as akin to the rejection of a falsified hypothesis in Popper's conception, only spread out over time.

The problem with Lakatos' picture is that while it is plausible as a description of scientific progress, it lacks plausibility as a methodology – a theory of method. This is because it is impossible to provide a rule, which tells us when a theory has been degenerating long enough for us to discard it in favour of a progressing rival. Perhaps the success of one and the failure of the other is a temporary matter, which would be reversed by future research.

KUHN AND SCIENTIFIC REVOLUTIONS

Lakatos' picture is of science as linearly progressive. That is, choices are made between theories and the better one chosen on each occasion. So, over time, the succession of theories contains ever greater quantities of knowledge.

By contrast, the account of scientific development put forward by **Thomas Kuhn (1922-1996)** is cyclical. The processes of scientific change repeat themselves in a way that prevents us from saying that later theories are better than earlier ones. The key element in understanding scientific activity is the idea of a *paradigm*.

Like Lakatos' theoretical hard-core, the paradigm includes the central theoretical commitments of a certain scientific field. But it also includes other features which guide the way scientists carry out research. Such features may include salient examples of the successful application of the core theory, which will stand as a model of scientific achievement for other scientists. Those examples along with other features of the paradigm will set the standards for what counts as good scientific practice.

Scientific activity governed by a paradigm is what Kuhn calls *normal science*. Normal science is a matter of puzzle-solving – applying the paradigm to new phenomena and accounting for previously inexplicable data. Just as someone tackling a crossword puzzle knows that there is a solution, and knows what counts as a satisfactory answer to the clues, a scientist operating within a paradigm believes the paradigm to have the resources to allow the puzzle to be solved, while it also provides the standards by which attempted solutions are judged. Scientific activity during normal science does not include high level theoretical examination of the core of the paradigm – that is taken for granted.

Not all puzzles are immediately solved – a puzzle that resists solution is called an *anomaly*. Normally, such a failure reflects not on the paradigm but on the abilities of the scientists who have tackled the puzzle. But if enough anomalies arise, which resist solution by the best scientists, then science enters a period of crisis, during which faith is lost in the existing paradigm. This allows radical proposals to be made for a change to the core theory of the paradigm, and a scientific revolution is underway. As a result of persuasion, propaganda and the changing careers of individual scientists, a new theory and a new paradigm will be adopted, ushering in a new phase of normal science, bringing the process of science, crisis – revolution – new paradigm – normal science, full circle.

Does the inception of a new paradigm constitute an advance in scientific knowledge? Is the new paradigm always better than the old one? Kuhn says that we are not in a position to compare the old and new paradigms, and so not in a position to say that one is better than the other. They are said to be incommensurable. Recall that paradigms supply the standards by which scientific activity such as puzzle solving is judged. Thus there are no standards outside of paradigms whose application to a decision between paradigms is agreed on by all.

'The real problem is that physics is a kind of metaphysics; physics describes "reality". But we do not know what 'reality' is. We know it only through physical description...'

Einstein, 1935, in a letter to Schrödinger.

'I seem to have been only a boy playing on the sea-shore... whilst the great ocean of truth lay all undiscovered before me.'

Isaac Newton (1642-1727)

FEYERABEND AND ANARCHISTIC SCIENCE

Paul Feyerabend (1924-1994), along with Kuhn, has suggested another reason why paradigms and the theories from different paradigms are incommensurable. The reason is that the meanings of key theoretical terms may change from one paradigm to the next.

So for instance to understand what 'mass' means to a scientist operating within Einstein's relativistic physics we must understand some at least of that particular physical theory. Similarly, what 'mass' meant before Einstein will depend on Newton's theories. Since the theories are different, the meanings are different too, and since the meanings are different we cannot directly compare statements made by scientists operating from the different paradigms.

The Newtonian says 'mass is always conserved' while the Einsteinian says 'mass is not always conserved'.

It looks as if they are contradicting one another. But if what they mean by 'mass' is different, it may be that they are just talking at cross-purposes.

The claim that changes in theory lead to changes in meaning and hence to incommensurability was exploited by Feyerabend to counter the common thought that science develops by building on and adding to the achievements of earlier scientists.

Feyerabend also argued in his *Against Method* that there is no method characteristic of science which explains its success and which demarcates it from other forms of enquiry and belief. There is no special feature of science which distinguishes particle physics from voodoo. The only rule of method which can be used in all enquiry in all circumstances is the anarchistic 'anything goes'.

Feyerabend took both incommensurability and the lack of a unique and special scientific method to lead to relativism. Relativism about science is the view that there is neither absolute truth nor absolute rationality, but rather, what is true and what is rational must be understood as relative to a given tradition.

Feyerabend's anarchism denied that what we regard as scientific rationality has any special status requiring us to accept the deliverances of science. Instead, it is up to people to decide democratically whether to accept them.

The two scientists depicted on this spread – Newton and Einstein – illustrate Kuhn's view of the paradigm shift that takes place from time to time in science. Einstein's theories of relativity showed that Newton's physics was valid only within a certain range of conditions. However useful Newtonian physics had been, with an awareness of Relativity, scientists had to revise their overall view of the physical laws governing the universe.

At the end of the 19th century the prevailing view of matter was comparitvely simple. Most stuff was made of particles, which could be thought of as like billiard balls but much smaller. These particles were subject to gravitational, electric and magnetic forces, and their motions were governed by Newton's laws.

Light, however, was different. Newton had thought that light also consisted of particles, but the Dutch physicist **Christian Huygens (1629-1695)** had argued that it behaves like a wave. One characteristic of waves, discovered by Thomas Young, is that they form diffraction patterns – most notably *interference fringes* when they pass through an apparatus consisting of a pair of narrow slits. When a wave passes through the slits and then hits some wall or screen, the result is a series of peaks and troughs, with the highest peak near the central point on the screen.

The clear distinction between wave-like and particle-like behaviour was upset in the early 20th century. The energy carried by a wave is dependent on its *amplitude* – the height of the wave. Thus the amount of energy delivered by a wave can be adjusted to any desired level, including as low as you like, by adjusting its amplitude.

THE FORCES OF LIGHT

Einstein discovered that, in the case of light waves, an unexpected phenomenon arose when the amplitude was reduces to very low levels. The energy delivered by a weak beam of light comes in discrete quantities, with a minimum quantity of energy (for a given wavelength of light). This minimum is known as a quantum and suggests that light is behaving in a manner akin to particles. The smallest packet or particle of light, which carries the quantum of energy, is called a *photon*.

What explains why light behaves sometimes like a wave and sometimes like a particle? Experiments devised to understand this lead to strange results.

THE DOUBLE-SLIT EXPERIMENT

When waves of any sort – light, sound or water – pass through a pair of narrow slits appropriately spaced, two sets of waves are produced which interfere with one another. When the peak of one meets a peak of the other, or troughs of each meet, the peaks and troughs reinforce one another. When a peak meets a trough, they cancel each other out. In the case of light, the result is a pattern of bright fringes with dark spaces in between.

Extraordinarily, particles like electrons, when fired at an appropriately spaced double slit, will also show these interference fringes, showing that they too have a wave-like character.

In the double-slit experiment, which shows that light is a wave, the energy of the light is reduced until there is only one photon in the apparatus at any one time. One slit is covered and the other kept open, alternating as each photon passes through.

After passing through, the photon hits the screen in a pinpoint of light. In time a pattern builds up, just as one would expect with particles – a smooth curve with at most two peaks and one trough showing that most photons are hitting the screen in the area directly opposite the slits, tailing off further from the slits.

If the experiment is repeated while keeping both slits open, since there is only one photon in the apparatus at any given time, we might expect the result to be the same. The photon must go through one slit; therefore whether the other is open or closed should make no difference. But in fact this is not what is observed. Instead we get the diffraction pattern characteristic of a wave.

Furthermore, precisely the same behaviour is shown by electrons. They can be fired through a double-slit apparatus one at a time, to hit a phosphorescent screen (which will light up, like a point on a television screen). If one slit is open at a time, the pattern built up is just that of a bright central area tailing off in brightness on either side. But if both slits are open then the pattern built up is a diffraction pattern even though only one electron is in the apparatus at any given moment.

So it seems as if the electron passes through *both* slits even though it lights up the screen in just one place, like an individual particle.

Imagine we were to try to find out whether the electron passes through both slits or just one, and if so which one, perhaps by placing some sort of electron detector near one slit. Now we find that the electron does pass through just one slit.

But if we look at the pattern we now get on the screen we see that the diffraction pattern has disappeared and we have the simple pattern for particles. It seems as if whenever we try to detect the photon or electron it behaves like a particle, but when undetected it behaves like light.

These discoveries of Einstein, Planck, de Broglie and Bohr require that we conceive of electrons and photons not just as continuous phenomena like waves, but also as discrete entities like particles. But thinking of them as mere particles makes it a mystery how the other slit has any influence on where the electron or photon hits the screen.

We are forced to think of both electrons and light as something akin to both waves and particles, but whose intrinsic nature is quite unlike anything we encounter in the everyday macroscopic world.

Furthermore, their behaviour seems to be strangely sensitive to our attempts to measure or detect them.

Notice that the mystery is one of how to *conceive* of what is *really* happening. The experimental results are not themselves contradictory and it is possible to come up with a mathematical theory that produces the right experimental predictions.

Recall positivism, which tells us that what is meaningful is that which can be interpreted in terms of observation or measurement. For the positivist there is no point in asking 'What is the electron really like?' As long as the mathematical theory is satisfactory, that is the most that can be said – there is

no 'fact' about what the electron is really like.

The Danish physicist Niels Bohr had these positivistic inclinations. In his 'Copenhagen Interpretation' of quantum mechanics he identified 'complementary' pairs of properties, which are such that examining one of the properties prevents measuring the other.

The wave and particle nature of matter illustrates this. If we try and observe the particle-like nature of an electron – for example by isolating its location through closing one slit or detecting it as it passes through – we forego the possibility of observing its wave-like nature.

'The whole of science is nothing more than a refinement of everyday thinking.'

Einstein

From Einstein's perspective that may indeed be so, but for most people Relativity and Quantum Theory are highly counter-intuitive, and require a suspension of what may be considered a commonsense view of reality.

Our view of the origins and nature of the universe are profoundly influenced by Relativity and Quantum Physics. For most people, the descriptions given by scientists have to be taken on trust, for physics has moved a great distance from the earlier and more easily understood world of Newton.

On page 121 we saw how, in Niels Bohr's Copenhagen Interpretation of quantum mechanics, there were 'complementary' pairs of properties, such that one could not measure both at the same time. The relationship between these complementary properties is governed by **Heisenberg's uncertainty principle**, which puts limits on the precision with which one can measure both of the complementary properties.

The realist will want to say that there is a fact of the matter as to the values of the properties in question, while on the positivistic Copenhagen Interpretation (see box opposite), there is no fact of the matter.

The very act of measurement affects the system, giving the entity the measured value.

For instance, a radioactive nucleus may decay emitting an electron. Let us ask then whether at a particular time, the nucleus has in fact emitted an electron? According to the Copenhagen Interpretation, if there is no act of measurement, both the possibility of the electron being emitted and the possibility of its not being emitted remain. It is only the act of measuring, for instance by a scientist using a Geiger counter, which makes one of these actual. This leads to a paradox known as the puzzle of Schrödinger's cat.

SCHRÖDINGER'S CAT

In the paradox of Schrödinger's Cat, we imagine an experiment in which a Geiger counter is set-up to detect the decay of an atomic nucleus. The Geiger counter and nucleus are set in a box, along with a domestic cat.

The Geiger counter is attached to a mechanism so that, if the Geiger counter is activated by an incoming electron, the mechanism will release a poisonous gas into the box. If decay is detected, then the cat in the box will be killed.

We would normally think that either the nucleus decays or it does not, and accordingly the cat will either be dead or alive. That is the common-sense view.

However, quantum physics seems, on the Copenhagen Interpretation, to tell us that there is no fact of the matter as to whether the nucleus decays, independently of our measuring the nuclear decay. Both possibilities, decay and non-decay, continue to exist until some measurement takes places, which pushes the nucleus into one state or the other.

But since the cat's life is causally linked to the state of the nucleus, it follows that until the scientist looks into the box, the possibilities of the cat's being dead and its being alive both continue to exist.

So, if the decay of the nucleus is not determinate, then the cat's death is not determinate. It would thus appear that only when the scientist opens the box does the fact of whether the cat is alive or dead become determinate. **But it seems extremely strange, to say the least, to think that the cat is neither alive nor dead until the scientist looks to see.**

There are a number of things one may want to say about Schrödinger's Cat. First you might think that the Geiger counter, box and cat are different from the nucleus and electron, since they are macroscopic things. But since quantum mechanics is a theory about the nature of all matter, it is not just the nucleus, which should be considered as a quantum system, but also the Geiger counter and the box and the cat.

Another view is that what is different about the scientist's measurement is that it is a mental act. Since the cat is a sentient creature it could be considered an observer like the scientist. Even so, we might replace the cat with a light bulb – surely, the light is either on or off, whether we look at it or not.

A different approach denies that the nucleus is in an indeterminate state of neither having decayed nor not decayed, but says that both states exist, but in different universes. Bohr himself took the results of Quantum Theory to require holism, the view that we cannot consider parts of the system in isolation from one another and in particular we cannot isolate the observer from the experiment – there is no subject-object dichotomy. This approach he associated with ideas to be found in Eastern thought.

Perhaps what Schrödinger's Cat illustrates most clearly – in the context of the philosophy of science – is not just the strange nature of Quantum Theory and the impossibility of measuring pairs of complementary qualities, but the more general issue of reality and the human imagination.

To say that the cat is neither dead nor alive, until we open the box, makes no sense in the ordinary way in which we perceive reality — we cannot imagine it being the case. But issues in physics and cosmology stretch the human imagination to embrace ideas that are counter-intuitive.

Cats do not fare well in thought experiments. For Schrödinger, one cannot tell if the cat is alive or dead. For the Zen master Nansen, as recorded in the Zen classic The Gateless Gate, a disputed cat is cut in two because none of the quarrelling monks are able to say a good word to save it!

NIELS BOHR
(1885-1962)

Niels Bohr studied physics at Copenhagen, Cambridge and Manchester. He devised the first quantum model of the atom. The positivist 'Copenhagen Interpretation' of quantum mechanics says that quantum systems are in an indeterminate state until an act of measurement forces the system into some determinate state. There is no hidden fact of the way the system really is.

Bohr likened this essential linking of subject and object to the interaction of Yin and Yang, whose symbol he incorporated in the design for his coat of arms, on which he included the motto "Contraries are Complementaries".

BERKELEY?

The view that it is the mind which makes things have a determinate state – in other words, that things are as they are because of our act of perceiving them – is reminiscent of Berkeley's idealism, for which see page 35.

The philosophy of biology has begun to attract widespread interest over the last two decades. It also has many attractions for philosophers.

Evolutionary biology has a robust, well confirmed theoretical underpinning; and has enjoyed enormous success in recent years from technological advances in the fields ranging from molecular and developmental genetics to the unification of ecology, morphology, taxonomy, physiology and ethology (behaviour) beneath a single, elegant theory.

The philosophical questions raised by evolutionary biology fall into three main areas:

- the structure of evolutionary theory and its place among the sciences,
- the ontological commitments of evolutionary biology,
- the extension of evolutionary theory beyond the traditional boundaries of biology.

RADICAL SIMPLICITY

The theory that underpins all evolutionary biology, **The Modern Synthesis Theory**, is startling in its simplicity. In a nutshell, it states that the diversity of biological form, the source of all marvellous adaptations organisms, is *heritable differences in fitness*.

Within a population there are variations in the capacity of individuals to survive and reproduce. This variation in so-called 'fitness' derives from the fact that individuals vary in their heritable traits.

Those individuals whose heritable traits make them better able to survive and reproduce have both more and *fitter* offspring. This is the (notorious) process of **natural selection**.

Over time, a population will come to comprise proportionately more individuals possessing these fitness-enhancing traits. The principal source of the variation on which selection acts is mutation

– random changes in the genetic information. Most mutations are neutral or harmful with respect to their effects on survival or reproduction. Occasionally, however, beneficial mutations occur.

Adaptation is the consequence of the gradual accumulation of beneficial variants and the elimination, through natural selection, of harmful ones.

The accumulation of gradual change over time can lead to enormous changes in populations. New species arise as a result of slow changes wrought by selection within a population.

THE NATURE OF SPECIES

Darwin's theory of natural selection tells us that new species evolve through the process of accumulating evolutionary changes. But what is a species? The traditional answer is that a species is a natural kind.

Natural kinds are thought of as the fundamental kinds of entities that make up the world; they carve nature at its joints. Natural kind concepts play an important explanatory and classificatory role in a natural science. Each kind is determined by essential properties. An essential property is a property that an object must have if it is to be a member of a given kind.

Darwin's theory presents a considerable challenge to the idea that species are natural kinds. If species evolve gradually from one form to another, there seems to be no determinate point where one species ends and another begins; there are no 'joints' in the biological order for natural selection to carve. But if species aren't natural kinds, what are they?

One suggestion is that *species fulfil the role in the theory of evolution that is played by individuals in other scientific theories*. Like individuals, but unlike kinds, species come into and go out of existence (through origin and extinction). They inhabit definite regions

of space-time. There are no laws of nature that specify the behaviours of particular species, as there are laws that specify the behaviours of kinds.

An alternative view – *pluralism* – is that *there is no real single species concept* and no need for one. Instead there are different concepts for different theoretical purposes. In some theoretical contexts, species play the role of kinds, in others, they play the role of individuals. According to pluralists, the very idea that there needs to be a single unified species concept is a throwback to an antiquated biology, one which sought to uncover the essences of species.

If species evolve gradually from one form to another, there seems to be no determinate point where one species ends and another begins; there are no 'joints' in the biological order for natural selection to carve.

FOR MORE ON THE ISSUE OF ESSENTIAL PROPERTIES AND NATURAL KINDS, WITHIN THE THEORY OF KNOWLEDGE, SEE PLATO ON THE FORMS, PAGE 24, AND ARISTOTLE, PAGE 27.

It has been supposed that a pervasive trend demonstrated by the history of science is the progressive reduction and unification of the various sciences.

As science progresses, the fundamental sciences, like physics, ought to subsume the less fundamental sciences, such as economics, sociology and psychology.

These so-called 'special sciences' are stop-gaps on the way to a complete and unified physics of all natural phenomena; as they mature, they are integrated into the more fundamental sciences.

The trend is toward the reduction of the laws and concepts of one science into the categories of lower sciences. Perhaps the most vivid example of subsumption is the unification of physics and chemistry.

Against this claim it is often pointed out that special sciences, rather than showing a trend toward unification, are actually proliferating like mad. There are now many sciences that did not exist

CHARLES DARWIN
1809-1882

Darwin's theory of natural selection, put forward in *The Origin of Species* (1859) provided a scientific basis for ideas about the development of living forms, by describing the mechanism by which changes in a species could come about.

Natural selection was controversial, since it did not require any external creator to account for the appearance of design within nature, and gave no special place for humankind within the natural order.

The Modern Synthesis Theory builds on the work of Darwin, but adds the idea of random genetic mutations as the means by which small variations come about, which are then open to the process of natural selection.

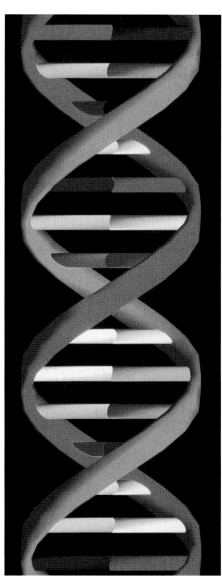

This represents a portion of a DNA molecule. A gene may be defined in strictly chemical terms, and yet its implications for life are enormous. The understanding and manipulation of genes presents the biological sciences with both an enormous source of information, but also, through resulting technologies, with the possibility of control and manipulation of the very building blocks of life.

The philosophy of biology therefore raises issues that are of immediate and personal relevance to human beings, since it presents a complex sequence of chemical units as the determining factor for many features of human life.

a century ago.

It is also claimed that neither the categories nor the laws of these special sciences can be wholly subsumed into more basic sciences.

The laws of economics, for example, explain the nature and behaviours of monetary transactions. A transaction may be realized in any number of physical ways; it may involve exchanging metal or paper, writing a cheque, swiping a magnetic strip on a card. These events have nothing in common except for being monetary transactions.

The laws of economics, but not the laws of more fundamental sciences, explain the law-like regularities in which these transactions participate.

Evolutionary biology, as a mature, successful special science, is a prime candidate for reduction, and we find that, to some extent at least, reduction has occurred.

For example, the concept of a gene began life as a functional category. A gene was defined in terms of an effect on morphology (the actual form of living things) or behaviour. Following the successes of molecular genetics, a gene now is defined as a certain portion of the DNA molecule.

The concept of a gene, it seems, has undergone a reduction from being a concept defined in terms of gross morphological function, to being a concept described in strictly chemical terms.

In addition, the Modern Synthesis Theory of evolution models evolutionary change as change in populations of genes. The issue of the reduction of evolutionary biology, then, hinges on the question whether all of evolutionary change can be explained in terms of selection acting upon genes.

This issue, which is commonly known as the 'units of selection debate', has therefore received a considerable amount of attention in recent years.

THE UNITS OF SELECTION

Richard Dawkins' 'Selfish Gene Hypothesis' notoriously proffers the view that *all natural selection takes place at the level of the genes*. Organisms are just strategies genes have devised for enhancing their own survival.

According to Dawkins we are 'lumbering robots', mere survival machines built by our genes. Other biologists maintain that while selection does, at least occasionally, act on genes, it also acts on higher levels of biological organization, typically individuals, sometimes even groups of individuals.

Gene selectionists, such as Dawkins, offer two sorts of arguments. The first identifies a distinctive function subserved by genes and genes alone: they are replicators. A replicator is an entity that makes copies of itself. In contrast, organisms are interactors. An interactor is an entity which interacts with the environment as a cohesive unit. It is the actions of interactors, which determine the differential survival and reproduction of replicators.

Gene selectionists argue that only replicators (genes) are sufficiently long-lived to be the beneficiaries of selection. So only genes are the units of selection.

The second argument claims a unique advantage for the selfish gene hypothesis: all evolutionary change in a population can be represented as changes in gene frequencies. Gene selection is therefore the theory that represents the most effective and efficient way of achieving this, with least expenditure of energy.

Opponents of selectionism argue that neither the replicator/interactor distinction, nor the appeal to descriptive adequacy, is at all relevant. The units of selection debate is not an issue about who benefits from selection, or how best to represent the effects of selection. It is an issue about the *causes* of evolutionary change; the crucial question accordingly, is 'What are the properties, or entities, on which selection acts?'

The concept of 'common fate' is pivotal in the determination of the units of selection. An organism faces the challenges of the environment as a discrete and inte-

RICHARD DAWKINS
B.1941

Following a brief period in the 1960s as Assistant Professor of Zoology at the University of California at Berkeley, Dawkins returned to Oxford to become Lecturer in Zoology and a Fellow of New College.

In 1995, he became Charles Simonyi Professor of the Public Understanding of Science.

The Selfish Gene, published in 1976, became an international bestseller, and established his reputation for communicating issues in science in a way that general readers could understand, and which conveyed both the excitement and wonder of science. He also points out the implications of science for humankind and its general understanding of itself and its place within the world.

grated unit. If the individual survives, then each of the genes, which make up that individual, survives. The genes in an individual share a common fate ineradicably linked to the well-being of the individual.

In these cases, selection occurs at the level of the individual, but the notion of common fate may also be extended to groups. Some aggregates of individuals may be structured in such a way that each of the individuals benefits *as a consequence* of the properties of (or structure of) the group. In these cases there is 'group selection'.

GROUP SELECTION AND ALTRUISM

Biologists have long puzzled over altruistic behaviour in nature: this confers a benefit on others at a cost to the originator of the behaviour. Often this altruism

Are we in fact survival mechanisms built by our genes? Does selection work at the genetic level, or at the level of individuals? Gene theory gives reasons for what, from our personal perspective, feels like a straightforward case of sexual attraction. Is it we who want to make love, or our genes which want to maximise their evolutionary chances?

is reciprocal; organisms help each other. This seems paradoxical in Dawkins' theory, for, if natural selection merely retains those traits that benefit individuals or their genes, how could altruism evolve?

This problem can be addressed by the application of game theory. Suppose two players in a game must decide whether to co-operate or not. If they co-operate they both receive a reasonable pay-off. If they both refuse to co-operate the pay-off is very poor. If one co-operates and the other defects, the defector does very well while the co-operator does exceedingly poorly. The best situation is to be a defector if your opponent co-operates. The worst outcome is to be co-operator if your opponent defects.

The 'dilemma' is that, for any state of the game, individuals could do better by defecting if they are already co-operating. The best short-term strategy is to defect. However, the best long-term strategy is to co-operate. Tit-for-tat, the strategy of co-operating (unless you have been the victim of defection) brings the highest long-term pay-off. Playing tit-for-tat is engaging in reciprocal altruism.

This demonstrates that altruism can indeed be favoured by selection. But how does it evolve? Gene selectionists claim that the game theoretic considerations demonstrate that altruism is a selfish gene's strategy for enhancing its long-term fitness.

However, group selectionists have recently countered that the mechanism by which reciprocal altruism evolves, fits the presumed model for group selection. It is the structure of the group (the pairwise relation between co-operator and defector or co-operator and co-operator), which determines the pay-offs to the individuals in the group.

Each individual in the group benefits from the structure of the co-operating groups. Yet, on each occasion, an individual forfeits a fitness pay-off by joining the group. Tit-for-tat is a strategy which is selected because it makes for groups whose structure benefits individuals. There is individual selection *against* altruism, as one would expect, but there is group selection *for* it.

How do you assess a business strategy? Can you trust those with whom you deal? They may be out for their own ends, but is that in itself something to be welcomed or regretted? At what point will he or she 'defect', rather than continue to co-operate?

If altruism is programmed in order to secure long-term benefits, what does that say about fundamental morality, or self-sacrifice? What does it say about the function of religion within human life? Is is just another strategy for survival and successful procreation of the species. Are we kind for the benefit of the long-term survival of our genes?

ADAPTATION AND TELEOLOGY

Adaptive explanations are commonplace in biology, and yet their scientific credentials have for some time been under question.

An 'adaptive explanation' appears to explain the presence of a trait by appealing to the *purposes* it serves in an organism. For example, biologists explained the presence of sonar in bats by demonstrating that it aids in navigation in the dark.

Adaptive, or functional explanations, are *teleological explanations* (explaining something by its goals). Further, in their normal biological usage, adaptive explanations seem to imply something about what a trait *ought* to be able to do. Any bat's sonar system which cannot help the bat fulfil its goal of navigating in the dark is malfunctioning; it isn't doing what it is supposed to do.

The apparent problem with this explanation involves this implicit appeal to goals or purposes. The contribution to a biological goal is an effect. So in explaining the presence of a trait, an adaptive explanation appeals to the *effects of which the trait is a cause*. **But one cannot explain the presence of an item in the world by appealing to its effects: effects do not in themselves explain their causes.**

Nor can one explain the presence of a trait by citing what *purposes* it subserves. The natural world does not have manifest purposes, so a natural science cannot appeal to purposes in its explanations.

Natural selection, it is said, gives a completely new understanding of the concepts of adaptation. To be an adaptation, according to some advocates of natural selection theory, is to be the consequence of natural selection in the past. So to explain the presence of a trait by citing what it is an adaptation for is merely to explain what that trait has done in the past, in virtue of which it was favoured by natural selection.

Adaptive explanations do not appeal to purposes; they merely appeal to the effects of selection in the past.

Detractors point out that natural selec-tion is not sufficient for adaptation. Many traits – for instance novel traits, which have not undergone selection for their specific effects – may still have those effects as functions. The upshot of this view is that one cannot recast adaptive explanations as explanations which advert to the historical causes of a trait.

Accepting the inadequacy of this reductive approach to biological teleology, leaves us with two choices. One alternative is to deny that adaptive explanations are teleological at all. We might insist that they merely explain a trait's *effects*. The other alternative is to accept that adaptive explanations really do appeal to the purposes of traits, or the goals of an organism, but to deny that there is anything non-natural about goals.

This latter strategy draws heavily upon the newly emerging disciplines of Artificial Life and Complex Systems Dynamics. These fields study the principles by which complex entities are organized. Complex systems may spontaneously organize themselves out of more simple components.

At extreme levels of complexity, these

Is it possible, given a complex situation that requires us to adapt, to find a completely novel solution to our problem? Are we controlled by our inherited traits, or inspired by our goals? How do we make a creative switch in order to direct and take control of our future, rather than just responding to our present situation? Creativity suggests purpose and self-direction on the part of the individual.

systems exhibit behaviour that can only be described as goal-directed. Organisms, of course, are among the most complex systems known. It is only natural that they should exhibit finely tuned goal-directed behaviour. The adaptations present in organisms assist in the attainment and maintenance of the biological goals of survival and reproduction. The source of adaptation, it may be argued, is not natural selection, but the sheer complexity of organisms.

SEE ALSO THE ISSUES CONNECTED WITH TELEOLOGICAL EXPLANATIONS IN THE PHILOSOPHY OF RELIGION, PAGE 167.

Evolutionary theory is increasingly finding applications beyond the traditional boundaries of biology proper.

EVOLUTIONARY ETHICS

Human societies are distinctive in being underwritten by ethical codes of conduct. The principles of evolutionary biology have recently been applied to the study of the origin and function of morality. A long-standing problem for ethical theories is explaining why persons do or should feel morally obliged to act in ways which benefit others, even at times to the detriment of themselves. Some moral theorists, 'psychological egoists', contend that persons do not, or could not, have irreducible desires for the well-being of others.

Evolutionary biologists have pointed out that such desires often ensure a society's cohesion, and cohesive societies benefit the individuals in them. They argue that psychological altruism may therefore be of evolutionary benefit to the individuals. Ethical codes may be the strategies employed by our genes for promoting our own long-term selfish interests: psychological altruism may be a strategy of the evolutionary egoist. Others, predictably, argue that if groups characterized by non-egoistic ethical codes are more successful, then group selection will tend to cause such groups to proliferate. There is no need to suppose that psychological altruism must be undergirded by evolutionary selfishness.

EVOLUTIONARY PSYCHOLOGY

A current trend in psychology is to interpret the nature of human behaviour and human rationality from the perspective of evolutionary theory. Rather than being a universal problem-solving apparatus, human rationality constitutes a specific set of adaptive responses to a specific set of challenges raised in our ancestral environments. For example, the nature of human reasoning with if-then conditionals, is best explained as an adaptive response to the need for making and monitoring social contracts. Construing if-then reasoning in this way helps to explain the systematic logical errors encountered in the use of conditionals. Evolutionary psychology is a nascent, but already very exciting field.

PHILOSOPHY OF MIND

Philosophers have recently turned to evolutionary principles to account for the nature of mentality. The defining feature of mental states – like beliefs, desires, perceptual states – is *intentionality*. Intentionality is the property that mental states have of being *about* extra-mental objects or states of affairs: mental phenomena are directed upon the world.

The nature of intentionality has long posed an enormous problem for philosophers wishing to represent mental phenomena as part of the natural world. Recently philosophers have noticed a connection between the concept of a biological function and that of intentionality. For instance it is the function of a moth's light detection apparatus to direct toward light, the function of the hunger response to bring about the state of affairs that an organism eats. Philosophers of mind have begun to characterize mental states, like beliefs and desires, in terms of biological functions. It is the function of the belief that beer is thirst-quenching to represent a particular state of affairs in the world: viz. that beer is thirst-quenching. It is the function of the desire for beer to bring about a certain state of affairs in the world: viz. that the subject ingests some beer. If evolutionary theory can offer an account of the nature of biological functions, then it holds out the promise of yielding a scientifically respectable account of the nature of mental phenomena.

Desires and beliefs – for example that beer is thirst-quenching – may be a mechanism the body has devised to get a needed drink.

Two Buddhist monks looked up at a flag waving in the wind.

One said,
'The flag is moving.'
The other said,
'The wind is moving.'
Hui-Neng said,
'The flag does not move.
The wind does not move.
It is the mind that moves.'

This classic Zen koan goes right to the heart of those problems grouped together as the philosophy of mind. We human beings are always trying to make sense of the world around us, yet we can never be sure what is actually out there, nor what is going on inside the workings of human thought.

Where exactly is this thought happening? We, with our general faith in science say, 'It's all happening inside the brain.' But where exactly is the mind in the brain? What are the attributes of this mind? How does it connect to the actions and perceptions of our body? Is it a material thing, or an imagined construction? Is there such a thing as consciousness? Or is it just a convenient umbrella term to cover actually disconnected processes going on in the body, which have nothing to do with one another but which we force together to make sense?

If the mind is just a convenient concept for stringing thoughts together, then can we build it outside the body? Can machines think? Could computers ever be called intelligent? Are human beings intelligent enough to realize if we meet an intelligent machine?

Is reason separable from emotion or from spirit or from what religion thinks of as the soul?

The philosophy of mind asks all these questions. It has been a burgeoning area in the 20th century, as science and tech-

nology have advanced and become abstract enough, with the help of highly simplified and schematised logic, to emulate complicated processes of thought.

Computer power still increases exponentially, and no one knows how far this will accelerate. Yet imitation of thought is one thing, understanding of thought is something else. Can machines be *aware* of what they are doing? Can they care whether they win or lose a game of chess?

The mind seems so precious and essential, but is equally elusive. Hui-Neng's koan offers no easy answer to a difficult question: like any successful philosophical statement, it puts no matter to rest but instead makes us think. Words like this *get the mind moving*. So perhaps the finest achievement of philosophy as a discipline is not to be afraid to confront the ambiguities of the idea of the mind itself.

Although philosophy of mind is a broad area, we will concentrate here mainly on the *question of consciousness*. Does it exist? Is it something separate from the brain? Can it ever be more than self-consciousness, so that we might know other minds? And can machines have it or only humans? And what about other animals, or the whole non-human world?

In ancient times, mind and soul were generally considered the same thing, but a thing very hard to catch and pin down. People were thinking, and this thinking made us different from all other earthly beings, but it was hard to work out exactly where all this thinking was happening.

The Greek word *psyche* did not at first refer to soul or mind, but, in Homeric times, was a kind of life force that left our bodies when we died and went straight to Hades (the Underworld). The verb *psychein* meant simply 'to breathe.'

But a few hundred years later, Plato tried to pin the word down, and it

became that part of the human self that turns away from the limits of the sensory world and starts thinking about the pure and eternal Forms inside us, of which the world we experience is but an impermanent, imperfect copy.

But could Plato find the mind? In the dialogue *Thaetetus*, he says that there is no special organ in the body that does the work of thought, but that

'the mind is its own instrument for contemplating the common terms that apply to everything.'

How does it work? Later in the same dialogue he speaks of the mind as being like a slab of wax. If you have a good, hard slab of wax, it takes good impressions from the senses and holds them accurately in memory for a long time. But you might have a soft chunk of wax for a mind, and then it could be easily impressionable, and take a lot in, but soon melt and shift the impressions around so that you won't be sure of anything for long.

This was one of the earliest *metaphors* that philosophy has come up with to make sense of the mind. There are those today who argue that all we can ever find to explain the mind are various metaphors, and since we are always thinking when using these metaphors, we can never get far away enough from our thought processes to have an objective view of what is going on. Hence, we are trapped inside the mind, and will never be able to know whether one metaphor of the mind is any better than any other. And so philosophy keeps moving on, from breath to idea.

INTROSPECTION

The *method* behind philosophy is key to its approach to the understanding of mind from the inside. Philosophy uses *introspection*, with an individual (the philosopher) thinking about a problem, coming up with categories, testing them out, musing rigorously about the way things might be.

Philosophers do not collect empirical data as scientists do, they do not look to a revealed faith for a system that explains the universe to which they are supposed to adhere with absolute religious belief. Nor do they follow their creative urges all the way and describe the world artistically as they might wish it to be. Philosophers sit down with a blank page in front of them and try to figure out, using only their own minds, the way the world is supposed to be.

It is a curious method indeed, but one that still does not stop trying to figure out the most ineffable aspects of our world. Take René Descartes, sitting by a warm woodstove late at night in a cold room, continually questioning himself, and wondering just what he can be sure of. Doubt, uncertainty and uneasiness plague his commitment to just about any 'fact' he cares to consider. Stripping away every impression, every detail learned, every sensation, every unclear opinion, leaves the lonely thinker only one certainty, only one unassailable fact to convince himself that he is really there:

Cogito ergo sum

'I think therefore I am' – the most famous line in the Western tradition of philosophy.

Is it obvious? Is it significant? What it offers is the primacy of the mind. Thinking comes first, and it is our awareness of thinking that convinces us that we have minds in the first place. Something is working inside us and there is no sign of any matter moving in the

Is it the flags that move, or is it the wind? And where is the thought that poses this question?

world around. So what is the mind moving? What is moving the mind? Compared to this problem the wind and flag issue is easy.

This is the toughest conundrum in the philosophy of mind, and it is known as the *mind/body problem*. How, if the human mind is this wonderful, powerful thing does it manifest itself in the external world? Is it the same thing as the brain? If so, why can we not just look at the brain and find little gears and wires working at all those wonderful things that the mind seems able to do? Today

this is what cognitive scientists are busy trying to do, but in Descartes' day science was nowhere near this advanced. In fact, science was natural philosophy, a branch of this largely introspective approach to knowledge that wants to progress simply by thinking about the problem at hand!

FOR FURTHER INFORMATION ON:

PLATO, SEE PAGES 23-25

DESCARTES, SEE PAGES 28-29

Descartes did not so much solve the mind/body problem as make it startlingly manifest. The world, he decided, was not made up of one substance, matter, but of two: matter and mind.

'I concluded that I was a substance whose whole essence or nature consists in thinking, and whose existence depends neither on location in space nor on any material thing. Thus the self, or rather the soul, by which I am what I am, is entirely distinct from the body, is indeed easier to know than the body, and would not cease to be what it is, even if there were no body.'

Descartes, *Discourse on Method*

Mind is only found inside human beings, and it is that part of our brain which tells the rest of the brain, and then the rest of the body, exactly what to do. Animals? No minds there. They worked just as machines, following instinct, responding to stimuli, doing just what they are supposed to do in any situation, with no real curiosity and uncertainty in their lives or ideas.

Cartesian Dualism was convenient and necessary for the mechanistic worldview to triumph. After Descartes, it was easy to separate idea from action, thought from consequence. The material world becomes dead, inert, malleable, while the human mind is the one place that is creative, valuable, active and central:

We see and touch bodies; we interpret gestures; we recognize people, sensing that we know them as persons; we understand their minds to a greater or lesser extent.

But brains and faces are part of the physical world. If a face is painted it takes on a particular character; the clown always appears to be happy; the child at the fairground may take on animal features. But does the mind change to fit the face, or the face change to fit the mind? If we look better, we may feel better; but we may be merely putting on a show.

It is clear therefore that physical attributes are not the same as mental ones. The smile is not the same as the happiness it expresses, for the smile may be painted on, but the happiness or unhappiness beneath it remains. But Cartesian dualism is haunted by the problem of how minds and bodies, if they are so radically distinct, are able to affect one another. Descartes' location of the point of interaction, in the pineal gland, was always something of a compromise between his conviction of separateness of mind and body and the inescapable fact of a causal linkage between them.

'Nothingness possesses no attributes or qualities. It follows that, wherever we find some attributes or qualities, there is necessarily something of substance to be found for them to belong to; and the more attributes we discover in the same thing or substance, the clearer is our knowledge of that substance. Now we find more attributes in our mind than in anything else, as is manifest from the fact that whatever enables us to know anything else cannot but lead us to a much surer knowledge of our own mind.'

So much for the Zen quest for emptiness. We can learn everything about the world because it is logical and organized as a machine. If it breaks, we can fix it, once we figure out the rules. And the search for the rules is the task of science, which over the coming centuries was quick to eclipse philosophy in importance because it got things done, revealing new information about the great machine and building new technologies that make us stronger and able to see even more.

Meanwhile, the mind remains a confusing place. For, if it is really separate from the body, how does it affect that body? In attempting to answer this question, Descartes was really the first cognitive scientist, because he cut open a brain to find out. He chose a place in the brain where the interaction was supposed to take place, the pineal gland, the organ right at the centre of the brain. This, he supposed, was the seat of the mind, the home of the soul itself.

It should be noted that in Descartes' time the mind and soul were still basically conflated. He used both terms for the same thing. The human faculty that uniquely could think, was also the place that could contemplate God and our place in the cosmos. It was one and the same place.

Today, we still wonder about the soul, but do not usually try to search for it scientifically. You could say, though, that the mind is the secular successor to the soul in our world today. Both scientists and philosophers admit to looking for it.

The separation of mind from body was very convenient for the development of philosophy, while at the same time initiating what some consider the death knell of the philosophy of mind at the beginning of the 20th century. The body was seen as a machine, whose functions could be studied empirically and mechanically. Over the next three centuries this became the main concern of science, where real progress seemed to come from observing, collecting data, and hypothesizing from this data . All this began to form a tradition far removed from the speculative schema of philosophy.

Meanwhile, philosophy, from Spinoza and Leibniz on through Kant to the various French and English traditions, could freely speculate on the 'faculties' within the human mind, and put forth conjectures for and against causality, both out there in the world and inside the invisible realms of our thought processes.

There were, of course, dissenters to Descartes. Benedict Spinoza was perhaps the most honorable, with his sense of a unifying spirit accessible to the trained human mind. This was a most noble goal for philosophy, an inquiry which, for him, aimed

'to acquire knowledge of the union of mind with the whole of nature.'

The world was, to Spinoza, made up of only one substance – God – right here on Earth, in everything, from stone to star to idea:

'The human mind is part of the infinite intellect of God. Thus when we say the human mind perceives this or that, we are saying nothing but that God… has this or that idea.'

This pantheism combined belief in a single God with a sense of a spiritual power inherent in all earthly things. Not surprisingly, he got into a lot of trouble for this idea and was excommunicated by his own co-religionists. Today the similarities between Spinozistic and Buddhist views of the mind have been much studied.

But it is only by retaining the mind/body separation that philosophers can be set free to muse upon such essential problems. Otherwise they would have to collect data methodically, as scientists have to do before they can make guesses as to how the world is.

By the 20th century, the separation of mind and body was being called into question. Psychology began to emerge as a science and claimed to be able to discover what goes on in the mind by opening up the head and looking at the brain itself. The mind clearly had a place in the body, and scientists were learning more and more about it each year. How could philosophical methods compete with the progress that seemed inherent in the empirical scientific method?

SEE ALSO DESCARTES:
CERTAINTY, PAGE 28
RELIGION, PAGE 164

EXAMINING OUR OWN THOUGHT PROCESSES

One man who straddled the line between philosophy and psychology very successfully was the American **William James (1842-1910)**. He defended *introspection* as a scientific method, namely, that individuals could examine the thought processes of their own minds and draw empirical conclusions from that activity.

It is, in a sense, an update of Descartes' method, and also a defence of the method of any philosopher, believing you can sit down and think, and then generalize about other minds and the human species as a whole.

James's most lasting metaphor for the mind is strikingly similar to some of today's most radical ideas: there is no single thing we can call Mind or Consciousness. Instead, we have a mind that assumes completely different forms when presented with different kinds of experience. Experience remains at the root of all meaning for James, but it is not discrete or precise experiences, but the whole 'booming, buzzing confusion' which is pulsing around us: Chaos, Activity, Plurality.

There is nothing simple or clear in this amazing surrounding world:

'Often we are ourselves struck at the strange differences in our successive views of the same thing... From one year to another we see things in new lights. What was unreal has grown real, and what was exciting is insipid. The friends we used to care the world for are shrunken to shadows; the women once so divine, the stars, the woods, and the waters, how now so dull and common!'

Do you know how this man is feeling? Of course: pleased, happy, optimistic – he is all of these things. Non-verbal communication is important, and the actor who posed for this photograph knows exactly what to do in order to convey the required emotions.

But do we know what that actor is actually feeling? For Gilbert Ryle (see opposite) to speak of the mind is to speak of the gestures that we see and their significance for us, not of some inner ghost to be revealed by the external physical machine.

But how can the feeling be the same as the gesture? What would this do to the acting profession?

His famous metaphor

'stream of consciousness'

later came to refer to an especially loose, free-wheeling style in literature, but a more accurate representation of James's view would be 'streams of consciousness.' There are many more streams than the ordinary waking state and unconscious. All other forms of human understanding ought to be seen as different forms of experience. Especially religion, whose real importance lay not in the location of God but in the spiritual experience of distinct individual people. This was an idea that upset many of the religiously orthodox.

Science could help us clarify the situation, but it too is limited, because it tries to be objective and does not want to delve deeply into human experience. The quest for the mind ought to take place beyond the confines of our existing, limited forms of language, in the heart of experience, and the inexhaustible richness of multiple human possibilities.

It is an informed, but mystical, and daringly optimistic view for someone caught between the purity of metaphysics and the practicality of scientific inquiry.

FOR FURTHER INFORMATION ON:

SPINOZA, SEE PAGE **31**

WILLIAM JAMES, SEE PAGE **175**.

THE GHOST IN THE MACHINE

Although James eloquently defended the primacy of experience in revealing the many facets of the mind, brain science evolved through the 20th century to find more specific processes of thinking visible in the brain itself. How could philosophy defend its role in figuring out the elusive mind if the tangible brain was giving up so many of its secrets?

Gilbert Ryle argued around mid-century that philosophy could do very well without Cartesian dualism, for which he came up with the derisory epithet

'the ghost in the machine.'

Just as there are no perpetual motion machines, and no unmoved movers out there in the real world, there is no magic called the human mind.

Square within the tradition of analytic philosophy, Ryle argues that the belief in such a fabulous 'ghost' amounts to a misuse of language, a mistake among categories. We have never been interested in the mind *per se*, he says, but only in what the mind can *do*. The real effects of our thoughts are all that matters about the thoughts themselves.

This does not imply that humans are pure machines that just respond to stimuli in automatic ways. That would be simple behaviourism. Human beings are complex and we do think things through. But all we know about these thoughts is how they are manifest in actions. Logic is discovered only as we succeed in doing things with it.

So Ryle is an observer too, but not in the introspective searching way of James. He says that we learn about ourselves the same way we learn about others: by taking stock of behaviour.

Ryle's position that the mind is revealed through everyone's actions is often called *logical behaviourism* (though Ryle himself rejected the term). It sticks to what can be known of the mind's work, while remaining vehemently opposed to any search for the special experiences, say the taste of tea or the intuitive grasp of the colour red, that might, in a mind-centred perspective, differ immensely between one person and another. No sense looking for the *feel* of consciousness, says Ryle. Look for evidence of mind by studying just what mind does, not what you wish it could be.

He wants our minds to be more practical than convoluted. Ryle writes of Boswell trying to understand Johnson's mind:

> *'His descriptions were, of course, incomplete, since there were notoriously some thoughts which Johnson kept carefully to himself and there must have been many daydreams and silent babblings which only Johnson could have recorded and only a James Joyce would wish him to have recorded.'*

The real work of people's minds is what we can observe of their actions, not the far-flung fancies of creative fiction. What a convenient and consistent reality it is!

According to Ryle's view, what matters is not how the mind feels but what it accomplishes. Ironically, this view, as much as it wants to bury dualism forever, served to promote the development of 'minds' built logically but not linked to brains – digital computers. If Ryle is right, then we may assess the possible intelligence of these beasts not on the basis of how they are put together, but on what they do. Largely, this is the approach philosophers of artificial intelligence have taken to ascertain whether or not machines can think.

GILBERT RYLE
(1900–1976)

Taught at Oxford for many years. He is best known for his characterization of much philosophy, particularly of the Continental schools, as "systematically misleading expressions." Faulty theorizing has led philosophers over the years to invent all sorts of strange, non-existent monsters such as Plato's Ideal Forms, Categorical Imperatives, and Universal Truths. Philosophy should, instead, concentrate on how minds are revealed through the ways we behave. There is no secret unconscious; our thoughts reveal themselves in what we do.

This position is known as logical behaviourism. Ryle's most important work was *The Concept of Mind* (1949) in which he denounces Cartesian dualism as an impossible split without that absurd "ghost in the machine"— a piquant metaphor that stands as one of the great philosophical images of the 20th century.

'To talk of a person's mind is not to talk of a repository that is permitted to house objects that something called "the physical world" is forbidden to house; it is to talk of the person's abilities, liabilities and inclinations to do and undergo certain sorts of things...'

Gilbert Ryle, *The Concept of Mind*

If it is not even a reasonable question to ask of people whether we can think or not, why bother asking it of machines? Let's just look at what they do!

The study of the possible intelligence of logical machines makes a wonderful test case for the debate between mind and brain. For if material things, made up entirely of logical processes, can do exactly what the brain can, is the mind material or immaterial? Is it understood, or merely imitated? This fascinating question is the battleground for hotly debated opinions in the applied philosophy of mind.

First, it should be noted that the astonishingly quick and powerful development of computers in the late 20th century is at last proof that philosophy can change the real world. Without the advances in logic and analytic philosophy made in Britain in the early part of the century, computers could never have appeared. It was Ludwig Wittgenstein who invented the truth table, a simple analytic tool useful in his early work but absolutely essential to the conceptual basis of early computer science.

THE TURING MACHINE

It was a former student of Wittgenstein, **Alan Turing**, who, a few years before Ryle, came up with the mental experiment that would make computers possible.

Why is the history of computing so important for the philosophy of mind? Because the computer is the machine that does not do physical work, but rather *mental* work. We look at it in operation, and we can hardly tell if it is working. You judge its health by what it does, not by knowing how it does it. If the computer solves conceptual problems, then this is logical behaviourism in action.

Computers are material structures built out of circuits that emulate logic, the

logic codified by analytic philosophers in the beginning of this century. Who ever heard of a machine built out of ideas? By building small devices, that produce the results of the human mind solving simple logical problems, and stacking these little things on top of one another, any problem that can be divided into step-by-step decisions, can be solved by reducing it to the sum of many, many parts.

So begins the role of quirky thought-experiments in the philosophy of mind in this century. From this point on, the field becomes full of intense discussions around abstract, often fuzzy models of Chinese-speaking rooms, philosophers wanting to turn themselves into bats and thermostats, and people imagining themselves to be machines and their machines to be like people. It is a journey full of curious examples and even more peculiar ways to discuss those examples.

Alan Turing's first great contribution to the philosophy of mind is his thought experiment, the Turing Machine, which demonstrates that simple logic could be used to solve very complicated problems.

Imagine an endless tape divided into tiny cells, like a strip of film. Each cell along the tape is the same, and one follows the other. Each cell can either be empty or full, and can only be one state or another, like '1' or '0'.

The tape slides through the machine, and the machine can only do three things: mark on a cell, erase a mark on a cell, or move the tape to the left or the right, one cell at a time. It can turn 1 to 0 or 0 to 1 and then move to the next space. That is all there is to it.

Turing proved that any problem that could be broken down into discrete steps of logical decision making could be emulated on such a machine. It's a simple idea, if hard to believe. Yet it is the theorem that proved digital computers were worth building in the first place.

The first application of this idea was the cracking of secret Nazi codes, using the so-called Enigma Machine, which was used by the British in the Second World War. The problem with cracking the code was that, although it was relatively easy to outline the procedures that would be necessary to test all possible scrambling inside a cypher, no human team could work as methodically and repetitively as a machine could. Hence, the appearance of a machine that could check all possibilities in a systematic way, enabled the theoretical possibility to become actual, and Turing's contribution was vital to the Allied victory.

Does this mean the machine was 'smarter' than the people who built it? Logic helps us understand problems because it breaks them down into simple parts. If thought moves logically, then logic helps us solve the problem. But often, human thought works in intuitive, indescribable, analogical and inexact ways. Our thought processes do not always become clearer when broken down into logical parts.

The record of analysis is not the same as the living processes. A human being doing the same task over and over again gets rapidly bored. The computer is happy to crunch one variation after another until all have been tried. It is the work-horse of logic, one that hardly needs to be fed. Pure mind, or poor shadow of mind? This is where philosophy of mind comes back to question the veracity of the thinking machine.

A MACHINE THAT UNDERSTANDS THOUGHT, OR A THINKING MACHINE?

Fine. We can break human thought into tiny little parts, and build a machine that understands each of those tiny little parts. A form of 'reverse engineering,' as when someone tries to figure out how a device works by taking it apart piece by piece.

But analysis is not the same as synthesis. You might be able to analyse the structure of a Shakespeare play and figure out why it succeeds, but that doesn't mean you will be able to write a play like that yourself.

Never mind. You don't need to know how a mind works to know it is there – you just have to be convinced that you have encountered a mind. Later we'll come to the 'other minds' program, but for now let's stay with the question that motivated the early computer enthusiasts:

Can a machine think?

If so, how would we know? Turing, that brilliant conceptualizer, had a simple approach to that question. It has become known as the *Turing Test*.

THE TURING TEST

How can you tell if a machine is intelligent? Ask it some questions, study its response, and see if you discern an intelligence somewhere inside the black box. Picture a person sitting at a terminal (A), typing in questions. This terminal is connected to two other machines, (B) and (C). At terminal (B) sits another person, typing in responses to the questions from person (A). (C) is not a person sitting at a terminal, but a computer, programmed to respond to the questions. If person (A) cannot tell the difference between person (B) and computer (C), then computer (C) is just as intelligent as person (B), and then earns the title of 'artificial intelligence.'

What is so brilliant about this test is that you don't need to *define* intelligence to test for it. It is purely pragmatic: one only needs to be convinced that the machine is intelligent for it to *be* intelligent. At a trivial level, this happened often during the early days of computer science; humans interacting with computers often treated them with awe, and imagined that they knew much more

FOR FURTHER INFORMATION ON:

WITTGENSTEIN, SEE PAGES **43, 207**

Response and communication are essential to our understanding of mind. The 'Stone Man' fascinates because he is clearly human, and yet does not respond. He appears to have no mind – to be no more than a statue. Then he moves, even if only slightly, and there is the weird sense of the inanimate having spontaneously taken on life. Intelligence is suggested by a variety of visual clues, not merely by the ability to answer questions.

than they actually did. Amazement breeds surprising trust.

Now computers are so integrated into modern life that they operate all around us, performing all kinds of valuable repetitive calculations and turning much of our real work into information that can be processed and transmitted easily around the world. Nowadays, we are less

easily fooled by programs that attempt to engage us in conversation and pretend to understand what we are saying. But the Turing Test has an ironic or comical side. We often expect so little response from other people that it is easy to be convinced that there is an intelligence talking to us from the mysterious black box.

DOES A COMPUTER CARE?

The more sophisticated the computer the more it is able to emulate, rather than just simulate, human thought processes. The more neuroscientists discover about the workings of the brain, the more images there are with which to guide attempts to mimic brain activity with machines.

Computer science and brain science have developed in tandem, which is why the challenge of the thinking machine is so important for the philosophy of mind.

Is the Turing Test passed every time a person is fooled into thinking a machine is intelligent? Is it passed every time a computer helps us solve a problem that would be insoluble without it? Most commentators do not think these criteria are enough. More get uneasy as chess-playing programs like IBM's *Deep Blue* become able to beat routinely the world's grand chess masters. In the next few years it is likely that a computer program will become the chess champion of the world.

A computer does not play the game in the same way a human being would. Because it can test out so many possible moves a second, it is able to use the trial-and-error approach that would be impossible for a human being, who is able to use (as yet?) unquantified intuitions and mental hunches. But the faster the machine, the less efficiency it needs. In the near future the super-speedy computer will easily win.

How does this affect people who struggle for years to master the game of chess? Well, we know already that machines can be stronger and faster than the human body. What is so special about the mind that we worry if a black box can beat us? The answer, of course, is that the ability of a machine to think, in any sense that rivals the abilities of the human mind, implies the mind will no longer be the special something that separates human beings from the rest of the world. It will be a humbling day.

But so far the computer does not care whether it wins or not. There may be something else, besides mind, which separates humanity from Turing machines.

The champion may have to concede defeat but such contests do not quash the endurance of philosophers. Plenty have stood up to defend the human mind against the threat that it may be reduced to a logic-processing pile of circuits and rules.

Computers will soon be able to play chess better than we can, but some people think that this makes chess utterly uninteresting. It becomes a game that can be played and won by a device that simply follows a prescribed set of rules, but without understanding their wider significance.

To understand this view, proposed by American philosopher **John Searle**, it is helpful to appreciate how actual digital computers are a bit different from Turing's imaginary tape machines.

John von Neumann first came up with the brilliant idea that computers could be conceived of as being composed of two parts, the central processing unit (CPU), the place where calculations take place, and the memory, where data and instructions are stored together. No tape need be constantly feeding in and out of the beast – the machine can contain its own programs and also store the results of those programs, in one way like the human brain, but in another way more efficient.

We (especially those of us in a literate culture) can only store so much in our heads before we need to write it down and store it externally on paper, film or tangible structures. The computer can keep all of its work safe in its head – until the hard drive crashes!

Not only might the computer have a mind, then, but it might have a mind that could fill up all of that ready shelf space of memory with useful information, and not stay waiting, as our brains are supposed to do for most of our lives, in a state of latency. Forget the lazy brain; put it all on disk instead. Compress it to save space, and then put in even more.

You can see why this line of thought soon makes computer systems sound a lot more efficient than human minds. **John Searle** disagreed with this concept, so he devised a thought experiment along the lines of the Turing Machine, but a bit more complicated, to take into account the now-familiar structure of von Neumann's compartmentalized computer. It's called Searle's *Chinese Room*.

Is it a suitable image for the mind?

THE CHINESE ROOM

Imagine a man inside a sealed room. English is his only language. He has a simple, specific, job to do. There is an input slot to this room, through which instructions are fed to him. There is an output slot from the room, where he can spew out results. Slips of paper come in and go out – *all written in Chinese.*

But he does not know any Chinese, so how can he follow instructions? Simple: he has got an instruction book, a manual with rules to follow that he can look up,

so as to know what to do with all the papers that come in. A question is submitted in Chinese, and he can decipher it just by looking up all the words. Then, when it is time to answer he can look up the right symbols in his instruction book and write the answer on the paper and feed it out through the slot.

Whoever is using this machine on the outside would think that the Room understands Chinese. But all that is going on inside is a person, whom Searle calls the 'demon,' manipulating symbols according to a vast book of rules.

The Room is the computer, the instruction book is the program, the pieces of

paper are the memory and the information coming in and going out, and the busy person is the CPU of the computer at work. He knows nothing, but acts like the grim Nazi bureaucrat who only 'follows orders'.

But this machine clearly passes the Turing Test; the user smiles and

announces, 'It speaks Chinese.' Yet the demon inside only knows how to follow the rules. That is all a computer does, and we should not be fooled by it. There is much more to the mind than this.

Or is there? Searle uses his Chinese Room to debunk the idea that computers could be intelligent. But he also uses it to cut consciousness down to size. Put simply, he says the mind and brain are the same, but neither should be reduced to the emulative successes of logic machines, for the mind contains a basic, irreducible subjective quality. Consciousness, instead, is a question of

JOHN SEARLE
(1932–)

Professor of philosophy at the University of California, Berkeley and a staunch defender of the idea that the workings of the mind are directly caused by the workings of the brain. So without the real, biological brain, there cannot be a mind. He is opposed to the claims of strong artificial intelligence, and his vision of the Chinese Room is one of the most enduring thought-experiments that proponents of artificial intelligence must repeatedly argue against.

His earlier work dealt with the intentionality behind speech acts. Any sentence spoken, has both a syntax and a semantics; we speak the logic of the words but also may use the identical words for many different purposes. This is something no computer program can conceive of. His most important books include The *Rediscovery of the Mind* (1992) and The *Construction of Social Reality* (1995).

biology. It is found in humans and also in certain animal brains. It is caused by neurological processes and is as much a part of the biological world as photosynthesis or digestion. You do not need to say that the mind is some special kind of biological organ to demonstrate that it is capable of thinking. Our life cycle permits thought, so our body must be able to contain it.

Interestingly, Searle had some trouble when he lectured in India on these matters. Several people in the audience told him that he could not possibly be correct, since the soul exists intact through many lifetimes. Some of them said they themselves had earlier been frogs or elephants. Searle did not take these Hindu believers in karma and reincarnation very seriously: 'Given what I know about how the world works, I could not regard their views as serious candidates for truth.'

SEE ALSO SEARLE ON:

LANGUAGE PAGE **218**

For Searle, machines cannot think, because only brains contain the stuff of thinking. We should therefore focus our efforts to understand consciousness on the workings of the brain. When we discover these workings, we will find processes that can never seriously be emulated by machines.

What is most distinctive about Searle's position, is that he believes that mind is entirely contained in the biology of the brain, but does not think that the empirical discovery of neural processes can be applied successfully outside the brain. Rejecting all dualism of mind and body, he does not think you can build a brain outside the body.

More commonly, people believe the mind is wholly contained in the brain, and because of this, when we figure out these mental processes, we can build better machines that will emulate successfully the processes of thought.

The first important critic of Searle is **Daniel Dennett**. Taking cues from recent developments in cognitive science, he believes that we not only must give up the idea of a mind separate from the body or separate from brain processes, but we must drop the notion that there is a single part of a brain – which he dubs 'the Cartesian Theatre' – putting it all together. The mind is simply the brain's many processes all firing together and between, and what we call 'thought' comes from their multifarious collaboration.

Dennet's language is both accessible and colourful:

'There are multiple channels in which specialist circuits try, in parallel pandemoniums, to do their various things.'

The brain has a 'von Neumann-esque character', like the computer, not as a 'hard-wired design feature', but because all the specialized neurons and specific functions in the brain form coalitions when things need to get done.

'Thousands of memes, mostly borne by language, but also by wordless images and other data structures, take up residence in an individual brain, shaping its tendencies and thereby turning it into a mind.'

So the problem of a unified mind is either made trivial or side-stepped, depending how committed you are to its insularity.

Dennett's mind, made up of many parallel decision-makers with no guiding light behind them, is all that is needed for thought to take place.

No wonder he is not fazed by Searle's Chinese Room. So the demon inside the room does not understand Chinese? No problem – he facilitates the process of Chinese understanding by looking up the characters in his book and processing instructions exactly how he is supposed to. The Chinese happens because instructions are performed correctly. It is unnecessary, even uninteresting, to ask if anyone knows how it is done. Consciousness does not require self-consciousness to get the job done.

Brain scientists cannot find a single 'mind' at the brain's core. Computers can solve all explicit problems by piling up one logic problem upon another until their linked chains reach into the billions. Consciousness happens only when it is needed. Otherwise it is not really there.

So do we need it or not? Why cannot philosophers and scientists sit down and agree on all this? Because their very methods can be at cross purposes.

It is in the interests of philosophy to hang on to some aspects of mental activity that cannot be explained away mechanically. Otherwise they will argue themselves out of a job! (There is a school of philosophy which argues that philosophy itself is unnecessary, but that is another story.)

Consider Searle's point of view once again. Mind and brain are not exactly the same, but the brain states cause mental states, and in turn mental states affect brain states. There are still thoughts we can identify, articulate, reflect upon, and talk about. But when they happen, something concrete is happening in the brain.

Dennett, as also suggested above, takes this approach to a more mechanically sophisticated level, by invoking the metaphor of the parallel computer, with many thought processes simultaneously firing, with the brain organizing, temporarily and only when it needs to, around specific tasks. If the Room needs to learn Chinese, it will learn Chinese. But when back home, it can switch to English and the Chinese part will no longer be there.

In computer lingo, this is an instance of a massively parallel brain emulating a serial brain, i.e., the many firing neurons temporarily specializing to be able, when needed, to do one thing at a time. Some philosophers feel that this is a timid approach, taking a portion of the latest cognitive science as inspiration and then retreating to earlier, out of date or 'folk psychology' approaches to how we think.

The husband and wife team of Paul and Patricia Churchland are often dubbed 'eliminativists' – extreme materialists, who favour rejecting normal psychological concepts in favour of neuroscientific ones.

They argue that the brain is really a huge, parallel distributed processing machine in action. It is an amazing organ, not because it is magically organic but because it is an example of *a computer from the future*: something so multifaceted and quick that at present we can only dream of approaching its processing speed.

But, as anyone who's bought a computer recently knows, the speed of processing doubles every year and a half, so it may only be a matter of time... Or, more cautiously, there is nothing to prevent us inventing a machine that will manage to compute as fast as the human brain some day, perhaps not so far in the future.

The Churchlands are suspicious of any philosopher who claims that the way to understand the brain is to consider how it does one thing at a time. It *is never doing one thing at a time*. Looking at it like that is a throwback to our ordinary ignorant intuitions – what they pejoratively call 'folk psychology', but what analytic philosophers earlier in this century praised as 'common sense'.

Science, on the other hand, is empirical, advancing, detailed, formidable, and has really found many of these parallel processes working in tandem, and even though it is against our intuitions, it is in this direction that the search for the mind must go.

The sun is not rising, but the Earth is moving, even though it does not look that way to us. Even if the mind stands still, it is never one single thing.

So for the Churchlands, whose writing is filled with dazzling visions of how science is offering philosophy wonderful future thinking machines and comprehensible brains, Dennett (see page 140) starts in the right direction,

but is limited by a covert behaviourism, whereby his conceptual framework still does not correspond to anything real happening in the brain. They think he is still half-looking for the ghost in the machine, or the elusive life force or soul in his vision.

The Churchlands, on the other hand, consider themselves *scientific realists*, who believe that – entirely and solely through empirical scientific methods – we will gradually learn exactly what is going on in the brain, and then we will know exactly what is going on in thought. Only with this consistent view, will mind and brain truly be one, and thought will safely construct reality rather than fantasy. Any other view, they say, derives eventually from mere belief.

As Paul Churchland writes at the conclusion of his famous book *The Engine of Reason, the Seat of the Soul*,

'You came to this book assuming that the basic units of human cognition are states such as thoughts, beliefs, perceptions, desires, and preferences... But you will leave understanding that the basic unit of cognition is the activation vector.'

These vectors refer to the complex ways neural networks combine to allow our

brain to recognize things, such as faces and tastes, out there in the world.

This, and related new terminology, may sound cold and far from our naive experience, but with time our perspective will shift toward the truth, as it has often shifted in paradigm-upsetting moments before.

Well, despite reason having an engine and the soul sitting down to take a break, Churchland in effect has denied the existence of both. He and his wife think it silly that some of us still imagine that a mind can have some reality outside the booming, buzzing, but potentially comprehensible array of firing neurons. They tut-tut if we still want to hold onto our quaint, naive, unprovable beliefs.

The philosopher need not resort to religion; his job is to ask questions. Has cognitive science *really* removed the need to ask hard, important but perhaps unscientific questions? You probably do not believe it has, if you're reading this book.

'That's what I love about philosophy. No one wins.' D T Suzuki

And the debate is far from over. You can say all you want about how consciousness works, and argue until the neurons come home. But what does consciousness *feel* like? Is this question worth asking?

Thomas Nagel certainly thought so, in his famous critique of the whole scientific enterprise of explaining consciousness. In 1974 he asked a most excellent question:

'What's it like to be a bat?'

We all imagine we know a thing or two about bats. They can see in the dark using echolocation, or a form of sonar. They flit through the sky silently like moths. Being mammals, they seem akin to us. Numerous vampire movies have taught us to be more than a bit afraid if one gets caught in our hair.

Yet we can mix as many facts about their lives, along with anecdotes and legend, but we still cannot feel what it is like to be one.

Assume that bats have some form of consciousness. They are somehow aware of what they experience and express. We can read all about them but we still cannot share that awareness. Information will never substitute for experience, and the experience of a mind is the essence of consciousness.

Thus something about consciousness always remains subjective, and hence ineffable to one mind trying to comprehend another.

I am not you. I will never know what it is like to be you. I will never be able to explain your consciousness from its inside. I will never be able to explain my own consciousness satisfactorily to you. There is some part of experience that cannot be shared, no matter how much we try to put down into words, data, or scientific evidence.

No objective cognitive science can capture experience. We'll never collectively know what it's like for a mind to be working. We can only abstract, generalize, thin out the specific in the name of a watered-down guess.

It is a simple challenge that comes right out of common sense. A compelling image of what can't be captured by the enveloping march of any science that seeks a singular answer to the question

'What does it mean to have a mind?'

Your mind is your own, whether you are another species or another person. I can never know if chocolate tastes the same to you as it does to me. It is your choice whether to revel in that fact or be crestfallen by it.

Naturally this challenge does not easily faze the empiricists. Dennett, for one, says we know plenty about bats, and we can easily imagine what it is like to be one, by taking all that wonderful scientific information and envisioning what it would be like to see by hearing and dance weightlessly through the sky. He is no enemy of the subjective, but would rather say: take the information and use it.

Much more interesting than simply posing difficult questions of 'what's it like...' is to use your own mind and place yourself in imaginary spatial and tactile situations. He would probably applaud virtual reality 'bat simulators', and he would also point out that literature and poetry can use the vast evocative powers of language to thrust us almost effortlessly, like magic, into the strange world of bat consciousness. Never underestimate human flexibility; we can use our many parallel brain processes to call forth 'batness' in innumerable forms.

Churchland, not surprisingly, dismisses the impossibility of grasping bat-consciousness as a mere remnant of folk psychology. He is more troubled by Nagel's claim that our inability to feel bat-mind means there is some non-physical aspect of that mind which our advanced understanding of the bat's activities will never grasp.

Churchland will defend forward-marching brainscience to the very end. The bat knows its own bodily states in ways no human will ever be able to. But this does not mean science will not be able to understand the bat in its own terms. What the two methods can know is the same knowledge, only grasped in different ways, like two human languages saying the same thing. 'Non-physical knowledge,' he says, 'is not a solution to anything, even where one's self-knowledge is concerned.'

Does Nagel merely want to protect some aspect of the mind as something unknowable, for either logical or romantic reasons? He and his kind have been derisively labelled 'mysterians' by those who want all conundra bared. You are just protecting part of your beliefs as a mystery, say the materialists. But don't be so afraid — give up your ghost, and then consciousness will not lose its allure but become the most fascinating part of experience that our knowledge can ever encompass. We can know

Sometimes it is the simplest of questions that proves the most difficult to answer. 'What is it like to be a bat?' sounds straightforward, but leads into a serious consideration of the relationship between the act of experiencing and the objective study of the means by which we experience. After all, we all know how a bat finds its way around, but what we cannot know is what it is like to find one's way around in that way. You may be able to see what the bat sees, you know that the bat sees it (since it is able to avoid the object in its path), but you cannot see it in the same way that the bat sees it. Can you ever stretch your imagination enough to experience what it might be like to be a bat? Can you get outside the very means by which you habitually experience everything?

ourselves, and bats, and all levels of possible consciousness. It is just that we will be knowing it in an entirely new way.

Immanuel Kant, perhaps, offered hope for this, two centuries ago:

'The consciousness of my existence is at the same time an immediate consciousness of the existence of other things outside me.'

But it would be foolish to call these 'brain watchers' go-ahead optimists, and the 'mysterians' reactionary dreamers. The problem may well remain a philosophical wall, which your own intuitions, not to be ignored, will keep you from crossing.

Taking your own experience seriously may convince you that you cannot cross this wall. Dream on, but you still will never become a bat. The bat and its being have something that you do not; in the end, your knowledge is always only human.

THOMAS NAGEL
(1937-)

An American analytic philosopher, Nagel has been particularly concerned with the relationship between objective information about the world and our subjective understanding of the world. He argues that we can never separate off our knowledge of the world from our own nature, either as individuals or members of a community. He opposed the reductionism, common in 20th century philosophy, which sought to reduce subjectivity to some more basic objective and scientifically verifiable level.

His approach to these issues is set out in *The View From Nowhere*, 1986.

What about views that strive for the best of both worlds? Is it possible to combine the rigor of science with a wish that consciousness still remain something special?

David Chalmers thinks so. He argues that if you want to take consciousness seriously, you cannot simply reduce it just to physical brain states. Consciousness is mysterious, although cognition is not.

You must still be a kind of dualist, although you might not want to be, and you may believe dualism is the root of much evil in the story of Western progress. But why not just give up the materialist dogma of contemporary science? Accept the progress of science, but accept that there is something more. This view, Chalmers maintains, 'takes the best of both worlds and the worst of neither.'

But Chalmers is no easy mysterian. Even if he is suspicious of attempts to explain consciousness, he believes that we need a theory of consciousness. He is an analytic philosopher, not an inward-looking mystic. We will need laws or rules for how the mystery meets tangibility.

He starts with the same problem that perplexed Gilbert Ryle, but he does not alarmedly dismiss all 'ghosts in the machine'. No reason at all, says Chalmers, that the material world cannot give rise to immaterial mysteries. Cognitive processes may not be equivalent to the confusions of consciousness, but they can give rise to them. We just do not know exactly how.

His approach offers no simple answers but wants to keep the book open. Consciousness might have to do with information, originally identified as a type of communication that must get the message through despite the influx of noise.

This idea was developed by telephone scientists in the 1940s, but is now a symbol for a pulsating, on-and-off vision of the fundamental pieces of the world, analogical, but not necessarily mental or physical. Gregory Bateson called information 'the difference that makes a difference.' As more and more information becomes easily accessible in our world, the more the world seems to be made up of the stuff.

What does it have to do with consciousness? A simple feedback system, an on-and-off device that responds to its environment is, in some rudimentary sense, self-aware. Forget the inner life of bats; Chalmers asks:

'What's it like to be a thermostat?'

It might not be so interesting, but this simplest of cybernetic systems can command cooling, heating, or no action at all. It is always, though, responding to the phenomena of the environment. The thermostat is not self-conscious, of course, but it can be said to have experience, and – in a rudimentary way – be conscious.

We do not build the consciousness into the thermostat, but it comes along as if for free.

This suggests that experience might lie everywhere in the world where there is possible change, and Chalmers does not want to deny this possibility. His is an open approach to philosophy; he is not afraid to say that he is not sure. So it is no surprise that he has no fundamental objections to artificial intelligence.

We do not know how to make machines conscious, but we do not know why our brains are conscious, either.

If consciousness just arises mysteriously from the brain, then it might come magically one day from the machine. We just don't know.

Material could give rise to the immaterial. He applauds the continued efforts of science to try to explain, but knows full well that what we understand will continue to give rise to mysteries.

It is in the end a hopeful, if woolly view. There will be no end to science, and no end to philosophy.

Chalmers' magic dualism seems compatible with the way many of us think about our own consciousness. It is simply there and we don't know why. We are not too interested in having anyone convince us otherwise.

DAVID CHALMERS
(1966–)

Originally from Australia, Chalmers is Professor of Philosophy and Associate Director of the Center for Consciousness Studies at the University of Arizona.

His work represents an alternative position between the pundits of artificial intelligence and the defenders of the human mind against the machine.

Chalmers does not easily fit on one side of the fence or the other: he believes that consciousness is something separate and unified apart from the brain, and therefore he remains a dualist in these materialist times.

While a defender of the unique mystery within consciousness, he also has nothing against the possibility that machines will one day be developed to the point at which they are able to think.

His work is composed of the search for a general philosophical theory of consciousness. His major publication is *The Conscious Mind* (1996).

There is another philosophical tradition that does not want to dismiss naive intuition or folk psychology, but to expand upon our own sensations and experiences and have us take them more seriously than the mainstream history of Western philosophy has done. This is the phemomenological tradition, identified on the continent with **Husserl** and **Heidegger**, and brought up-to-date into cognitive philosophy with the notion of *the embodied mind*.

We have already seen how mainstream philosophy is content to investigate thought as a free play of ideas, without needing to consider the material functions that make thinking possible. Cognitive science in the 20th century challenged this, since it became clear that it was increasingly possible to identify elements of consciousness with particular parts of the physical brain, thus showing a direct link between physical and mental. Mental activity might be very different from physical brain processes, but it was clear that it occurred as a result of, or alongside, specific forms of brain activity.

Thus it showed a way perhaps to bring mind and body together, through the successful systems of science, though also inspired by the logical achievements of philosophy. While denying dualism, it has promoted a kind of dualism. Whether or not it still requires mystery is up to you to decide.

Phenomenology offers a slightly different view. The body that matters is not the objective, material human body that works like a machine, whether simple or complex. Instead it is the lived body, in which no idea is separate from a movement, an experience, or an action. The French philosopher **Maurice Merleau-Ponty** used the word 'flesh' to refer to our primal felt experience. Flesh includes the mind, and reason is the 'flesh of the world'. Nothing ethereal or abstract here. As the world is lived, it is also idea.

Although phenomenology is often invoked as a more *felt* argument for why there is a subjectivity to consciousness, rather than seeing it as something solely material, it can also be shown to be compatible with cognitive science.

That is what **George Lakoff** and **Mark Johnson** try to do in their most recent work. They argue that we live by metaphors, and we have metaphors for the mind as much as for anything else. Metaphors are tested not by whether we like them or whether they seem to make logical sense, but by how we feel them and how well they explain embodied experience. In other words, how well they express our generally held ideas of the world that recognize that the mind is nothing without the body that contains and guides it.

The mind is what thinks, perceives, believes, reasons, imagines, and wills. But as soon as we try to go beyond this skeletal understanding of mind, as soon as we try to spell out what constitutes thinking, perceiving, and so on, metaphor enters.

These metaphors are by no means arbitrary; the better ones are those that can recognize and elucidate the fact that every thought has a felt material form. Philosophy must listen to science, but not kowtow to science. The two must evolve together in the parallel investigation of new information and the same old mysterious but real experiences.

Philosophical sophistication is necessary if we are to keep science honest.

And philosophy cannot simply spin out fanciful theories of mind without being aware of the heights science has reached.

Despite phenomenology's traditional association with a poetic mysticism, which tends to point out ways science has failed us, Lakoff and Johnson want the introspective analysis of our own experience, however wonderful and magical, to cohere with the march of empirical progress that the Churchlands have espoused.

FOR HEIDEGGER
SEE ALSO PAGES **44** (RE KNOWLEDGE)
AND **229** (RE LANGUAGE)
FOR HUSSERL AND FOR MERLEAU-PONTY
SEE ALSO PAGE **224** (RE LANGUAGE)

A SPIRITUAL MIND?

Even spiritual experience is embodied. What is most amazing about the soul is that we experience it in the body! This may sound unscientific, but neuroscientists have found a tiny place in the frontal lobe of the brain that they call 'the God spot'. This appears to be stimulated during religious experiences.

Locating such a module is the task of science, but figuring out what such a discovery has to do with the experience it represents is the task of philosophy. An 'embodied philosophy' will want to look deeply at the experience and how the experience is changed by awareness of the discovery.

So how, after all this philosophy, are we to react to such sobering information?

If the mind and body are truly so interconnected, it is only reasonable to expect that we should find such a place where particular forms of experience are embodied. If thought is more than logic, then the stimulation of this group of neurons should be able to produce experiences we cannot easily explain.

This way there can be magic in the material, and we could even build a model of these processes and have it produce spiritual experiences that could not be accounted for in terms of any external stimulus.

No wonder that the computer visionary **Ray Kurzweil**, the inventor of reading machines for the blind and cutting-edge music synthesizers, writes in his book *The Age of Spiritual Machines* that by the middle of the 21st century, we should not be surprised to find machines thinking faster than us, feeling more than us, and being more connected reverentially to the whole fabric of the universe than we can ever hope to be.

But you will still have to believe that all this simulated mental activity has a body, or else it will appear to be an immaterial mind with no material basis to bring it about.

THE ATMAN

In Hindu philosophy, the world may be seen as made up of one substance, Brahman, and this essential substance is manifest inside us as the Atman, or self. This is not meant to imply that a portion of the whole lies within each individual self, but rather than there is a fundamental identity between Brahman and Atman.

The *Chandogya Upanishad* says that the Atman is

'myself within the heart, smaller than a grain of rice or a barley corn ... this is myself within my heart, greater than the earth, greater than the atmosphere, greater than the sky, greater than all these worlds.'

It is not so much where thought comes from that is the concern of this philosophy, but the status of the self and its identity with the whole.

It has a quality and a reality that is also universal. Taking pride in this quality, individuals can experience themselves as one with the world.

Thus, in a well-known analogy, the student is invited to cut open a pomegranate to reveal its seeds. Cut open the seeds and you will find the seed of seeds. Cut again and again until everything is divided into its smallest parts and there is nothing but nothingness.

Tat twan asi

says the master:

"You are that."

Something is there, but it is nothingness; the self and the universe are one.

HUANG PO
(D.850)

Also known as J. Obaku, is the Zen philosopher who is most known for articulating the idea of a mind that pervades the whole world, something of a precursor to Spinoza's view of an immanent God who is everywhere on Earth. But Zen mind is different, far more elusive, indeed confounding all of our usual categories of thought. 'The mind,' wrote Huang Po, 'is not among those things that exists or does not exist. It is something that cannot be caught, cannot be known, but only be inhabited. Our senses cannot be trusted, but we can train ourselves to grasp the true ambiguity of the world through meditative leaps of insight.' This is why Zen so anticipates the deep ambiguities of contemporary cognitive science. But make no mistake, science has not encompassed Zen methods, and never will. See *The Zen Teachings of Huang Po*, translated by John Blofeld (1994).

Have we bent the word *mind* so out of shape that it means almost nothing at all? This might be the time to return to the Zen Buddhist understanding of the same word. **Huang Po** (see box on page 146) tells us to forget analysis in trying to find true mind – you'll only get there by intuition.

This may be a slap in the face to much Western philosophy, or it may be a recommendation for the felt, introspective, phenomenological approach as an alternative to opening up brains and pointing out places where they're hard at work on specific things. In any case, it does not say no, but yes. Sure, mind is ambiguous, but we love it because of that ambiguity:

The mind is not something that belongs to you, but it is a quality of the whole world. Consciousness is nothing individual, but true thought connects you to a firmament of the universe.

Is this an ancient argument for the universe being made up of information? I don't think so. In one way it seems compatible with Descartes, because it advises us not to look for the mind in any part of the material world. At the same time, it denies Descartes and says mind is everywhere, in all things as the one thing that unites them. Yet you can't see it, you can't touch it, you can't even think it even

though it's called mind. Eluding the pinpoint of logic, it is the most important thing in the world – but never expect to describe it.

In this sense the Zen view of mind could be a denunciation of the whole history of philosophy and science in the West. However, there is a glimmer of its effervescence on our own side of the world. Wittgenstein alluded to it in his most famous lines

'whereof one cannot speak, thereof one must remain silent.'

Mind is like the void in which there is no confusion or evil... Pure mind is the source of everything, it is formless without form. You must get away from the doctrines of existence and non-existence, for mind, like the sun, shines without intending to shine.

The sand garden in a temple in Kyoto, Japan. According to Huang Po, we can only understand the mind through intuition, not through analysis. Perhaps the calmness induced by a spiritually sensitive environment might help.

ZEN TRAINING

Zen meditation, not Zen literature, trains us to know mind. It is a very disciplined form of silence that does not take to being summarized in a philosophy book.

This is most definitely not a form of intuited phenomenology. Indeed, Huang Po says:

our bodies are the creations of our own minds.

Wait, doesn't this give philosophy the advantage, and not render it useless? Zen wants you to grab the dilemma, or the ox, by its horns.

The novice confronts the master, asking for help:
"My mind is not at peace. Please bring it peace."
The master says,
"Bring me your mind, and I will pacify it for you."
The young monk searches and searches, but returns with his hands empty:
"I have looked for my mind, and I cannot find it."
The master says,
"Then your mind is at peace."

Keep asking, keep looking, and you will not be able to return with your own mind. It's not there. To quote *The Blue Cliff Record*,

What's going on in your mind? Call it awareness, and it's already changed.

All that exists is Mind, with a capital M, a property of the universe.

...peace

The Buddhist view stresses impermanence, and it has its contemporary analogues as well, that announce that consciousness is nothing more than a fleeting sense of being in control.

Danish science writer **Tor Nørretranders** calls consciousness a kind of 'user illusion' in which we imagine that we need a steering wheel or something at the controls to guide the decisions our mind is making. But is such control, as Zen suggests, utter illusion?

The culture of consciousness can be seen as something of relatively recent invention, a by-product of the enlightenment that brought education to the masses and encouraged each and every one of us to think that we are special enough to have our own ideas. But perhaps these ideas matter more than the self that supposedly produces them.

There is very little information contained in consciousness, says Nørretranders, because information is 'otherness and unpredictability', that difference that still makes a difference. He cites the physicist **James Clerk Maxwell** scrutinizing his own inquiring mind and deciding that:

what is done by what is called myself is, I feel, done by something greater than myself in me.

Is this Maxwell's belief in divine inspiration, or a sense of humility, suggesting that discoveries and new scientific knowledge are part of a mind that is greater and more coherent than each of our tiny places within it?

Zen wants us to give up our individuality in the wake of a greater sort of consciousness.

That greater thing, *shin*, is often translated as mind, though it sometimes comes out as heart, and the canonical Heart Sutra has also been called 'the Sutra of the Great Wisdom Gone Beyond'.

If that's what mind is, we ought never to be able to catch it. It would then be something unlikely to be reduced to brain functioning and resistant to discovery outside precise spiritual experiences.

But if Zen is to survive in this empirical age, sooner or later it has to be linked with cognitive science as well. A new book by **James Austin**, *Zen and the Brain*, attempts to do just that.

He wants to find out exactly what happens to the brain itself in the midst of meditation. Are there physical changes once you've reached enlightenment? A Zen practitioner himself, he recognizes the contradictions inherent in such a quest, indeed inherent in the whole attempt of thinking through consciousness from the insight.

The process is like a Zen *koan*, a problem that you have to live through over many years of rigorous practice, which eludes the false specificity of words or any categories tossed forth arbitrary in any kind of discrete analysis.

No surprise, then, that we are unable to find the mind. It is not that we have been looking in the wrong place, but the fact that we have been looking. We should instead be feeling our way through, beginning with self-consciousness or self-awareness and gradually releasing ourselves into an awareness of the whole world as mind.

You can reach that place, though you cannot 'figure it out'. Is this what Eastern traditions are teaching us – to take ourselves less seriously, and be more humble in the face of the world? Then perhaps the mystery becomes something we can more easily join in, rather than work to beat down.

Some will find this view beguilingly appealing as the promise of the primacy of the mystical. Wittgenstein would nod his head in agreement to that. Others will find it frustratingly unphilosophical, being impossible to dispute rationally.

But the philosopher's Zen is an attempt to see Zen logic as another way of framing questions that linger unsolvable through the centuries. Our discipline is so famous already for having better questions than answers. Zen answers are still questions, better questions than those that begat them.

Neither flag nor wind is moving. Mind is moving. You may retreat into yourself, and emphasize the you that is thinking the relationships through. Or you may place the full force of mind out there in the world. Either way, you have satisfied nothing. You have just set yourself up for another hundred lifetimes of speculation.

Daibai asked Baso: 'What is Buddha?' Baso said: 'The mind is Buddha.' *The Gateless Gate*, 30

THE PHILOSOPHY OF RELIGION
ANCIENT AND MEDIEVAL

The subject we today call the 'philosophy of religion' has a long, distinguished history. A means of reflecting on the nature and existence of a 'God' or 'gods', it is as old as philosophy itself, being one of the sets of questions discussed from ancient Greek times onward.

In antiquity, philosophical discussion of theological matters was termed 'natural theology'. Natural theology is an attempt to understand and to answer the question: Is there or is there not evidence for the existence of a deity or deities in the world?

THE ANCIENT WORLD

The gods of the ancient world as described by **Homer (c.800BCE)** and other poets were anthropomorphic deities. That is, they had manifestly human personalities and their actions can be understood in terms of specific human characteristics: anger, joy, jealousy, affection, lust etc.

Before **Socrates (c.470-399BCE)**, philosophers addressed what we would identify as theological matters in varying ways. Unlike the poets, philosophers from **Thales of Miletus (sixth century BCE)** sought to uncover the *arche*, or 'origin', of the universe and the natural world in which they lived. This approach led them to adopt many different theological positions.

Xenophanes of Colophon (c.570-c.475BCE), for instance, held that there is:

> One god, greatest among gods and men, in no way similar to mortals either in body or thought.

Further, Xenophanes attacked the depiction of the gods by the poets, his special targets being the epic poems of Homer and Hesiod, which he thought portrayed the gods as absurdly anthropomorphic.

This led him to posit a god who is the cause of all things:

> Always he remains in the same place, moving not at all; nor is it fitting for him to be at different places at different times.

In contrast to Xenophanes, **Democritus of Abdera (c.460-370BCE)** provided a completely mechanistic explanation of the universe. This was opposed to the idea of a universe created in the image of its creator.

The views of **Parmenides of Elea (early fifth century BCE)** differ from those of both Xenophanes and Democritus. While he does not refer to his definition of the *arche*, all embracing 'being' (*ousia*) as divine, 'being' is still defined in quasi-divine terms: uncreated, imperishable, continuous, unchangeable and perfect. Parmenides' work *On Nature* is an invocation of 'the goddess', who guides him to the realm of being ('the way of truth').

For Parmenides the main question for natural theology is not:

'How can we describe the relationship of *arche*, unchanging being, to those things dependent upon it?'

But,

'Does anything beside "being" exist at all?'

Being a monist (a philosopher who holds that only one substance can exist) Parmenides' answer to this last question was an emphatic 'No!'.

Given the profound differences which separated philosophers' theological views from those of the general public in antiquity, it is unsurprising that their opinions were often caricatured or seen as monstrously impious and a threat to the public good. A good example of this can be found in the play *The Clouds*, by the Athenian comic writer **Aristophanes**, in which he depicted the Sophists as promoters of godless immorality.

Years later, Socrates, the chief butt of Aristophanes' satire, was put on trial by his fellow Athenians for being 'completely godless (*atheos*)'. It is important to understand, however, that the Greek term *atheos*, or godless, did not mean exactly the same as the modern term 'atheist'. *Atheos* meant not honouring the gods of the city, not a denial of all divine reality. Among other more political matters, Socrates was tried for his unorthodox religious views.

The popular view of the gods in ancient Greece was very different from that of the philosophers:

> 'The ways of the gods are involved and mysterious; they send us good and bad fortune in turn, and all is for the best.'
>
> from Euripides, *Helen*

ON THE **PRE-SOCRATIC THINKERS AND THE THEORY OF KNOWLEDGE**
SEE ALSO PAGE 22

PLATO

Plato (429-347BCE), like the Presocratics and his master Socrates, attacked the way in which poets had portrayed the gods.

In the *Euthyphro*, one of his early dialogues, which especially shows Socrates' influence, he ridicules sacrificial offerings to the gods.

In the *Republic*, he puts into the mouth of Adeimantus a persuasive attack on the gods, especially their immorality. Later in the book, the poets are censored, because, in their depictions of the gods, they give them magnified human weaknesses, making them rather like modern film or rock stars.

In the *Timaeus* (50d), Plato portrayed god as a divine craftsman or Demiurge who brings order to formlessness. The Demiurge is not an omnipotent creator, but a divine agent who moulds already created, chaotic matter into a rational, orderly form.

The rationality that the Demiurge gives the universe is mathematical; the four elements defined by Plato as the building blocks of the cosmos are geometrical figures: fire is pyramidical, earth cubical, air octahedral, and water icosahedral. Each of the geometrical figures is resoluble into right triangles, which allows the elements of air, fire and water to change into each other.

Plato appears to have made the earth cubical for theoretical reasons, but he was criticized by Aristotle in *De Caelo* on the grounds that his theory did not correspond to any observable facts. Whether Aristotle was entirely fair to Plato is open to debate, but he was certainly correct in noting a concern in the *Timaeus* to subordinate particular facts to the demands of general theory.

Plato discusses theological issues more straightforwardly in the tenth book of the *Laws*. There, his spokesman, the Athenian Stranger, addresses religious impiety, which, he argues, undermines the constitution of a city. At the end of the book, Plato imposes penalties, including the death penalty, on various classes of religious heterodoxy. (This is richly ironic given the fate of Socrates.)

Plato also claims that the gods are concerned about the welfare of humans, arguing that the gods' concern for humanity is part of their very intelligibility.

The most important characteristic of the gods, as identified by Plato, is their goodness, which is presented in three of his works: *Timaeus, Phaedrus* and *Republic*. With that established, he argues, in *Theaetetus* (1716b1-3), that we too should seek the likeness of god (*homoiosis theoi*).

'Even manufactured things — furniture, houses, clothes — suffer least from wear and tear when they are made well and in good condition. So this immunity to change from outside is characteristic of anything which, thanks to art or nature or both, is in a satisfactory state...

'But surely the state of the divine nature must be perfect in every way, and would therefore be the last thing to suffer transformations from any outside cause...

'Being as perfect as he can be, every god, it seems, remains simply and for ever in his own form.'

Plato, *The Republic*, book II

THE DIFFERENCE IN EMPHASIS BETWEEN PLATO AND ARISTOTLE, MENTIONED ABOVE, HAS SIGNIFICANCE ALSO FOR THEIR CONTRIBUTIONS TO EPISTEMOLOGY (THE THEORY OF KNOWLEDGE)

FOR FURTHER INFORMATION ON THIS SEE PAGES 23-27

ARISTOTLE AND LATER DEVELOPMENTS

Aristotle's philosophical theology has much in common with Plato's. His teleological approach (i.e. the view that all things have an end or purpose) to physics and cosmology is equally incompatible with the materialist views that Plato criticises in his *Laws*, x. (See Aristotle's *Physics* viii. 1; and *Metaphysics* I. 8, 988, b22-28 for his exposition of this.)

Aristotle also favoured demythologising theology (*Metaphysics* xii. 8, 1074, a38-b14; *Politics* i. 2, 1252, b26-27), while still leaving room for the gods of civic religion (*Metaphysics*, xii. 8).

The Aristotelian conception of divinity combines the idea of immanent power with the idea that god is a final cause, in the same way in which 'the object of desire and the object of thought' are final causes, since they 'move but are not moved.'

The upshot of these reflections is a conception of god as an impelling force within the universe, and also an object of desire, drawing humankind beyond it.

Aristotle also speaks of the Unmoved Mover as

'thought thinking itself'.

In his *Metaphysics*, he rejects the notion that god might think of something other than itself precisely because this would diminish god's power.

The power that Aristotle is concerned with here is the power of god, which has an effect in the world. We must conceive of god's thoughts about itself as bound up with god's immanence, in other words with god's presence within the world. It is by thinking of itself, that god knows and controls all things.

Notice that god is referred to here as 'it' rather than 'he'. The Unmoved Mover in Aristotle is not to be automatically identified with the personal God of theism – although, as we shall see later – Aquinas saw it as his task to express Christian

ideas of God in terms that had been developed by Aristotle.

Three philosophical schools came to prominence after the death of Aristotle in 322BCE. These were Stoicism, founded by **Zeno of Citium (335-263BCE)** in about 300BCE, Epicureanism, founded by **Epicurus (341-270BCE)** in 307BCE, and, much later, Neoplatonism, a movement that stemmed from a systematic re-reading of Plato's work.

THE STOICS

The god of the Stoics is an immortal and rational being, perfectly blessed, good and provident. The Stoics' god is not a personal deity as in Christianity, but a physical *substance*.

The Stoics held that these and other characteristics of god are self-evident in our preconceptions about divinity. This led one Stoic, **Diogenes of Babylon (c.240-152BCE)** to propose that god's existence was self-evident. It was a fact, which, he claimed, could be proved by thought alone. In this manner, Diogenes anticipated the famous 'ontological argument' of Anselm of Canterbury (see page 158).

The Stoics put forward other arguments for the existence of god. Prominent among these were 'arguments from design'. This argues that, because we can see elements of design in the world, it is reasonable to believe that the world has a designer.

This type of theistic argument is based on experience, and also relies on the use of analogy. It begins by stating that there is an analogy between a typical feature of nature and a typical feature of what is produced by human contrivance. From this analogy, it concludes that the causes of these features are probably similar.

In other words, if the universe manifests a certain order and harmony, then it must have been designed in a particular manner and for a particular purpose by a divine designer.

A number of Stoic arguments from design are recorded and discussed by the Roman statesman and philosopher **Cicero (106-43BCE)** in his *On the Nature of the Gods* (Book II, 34-35).

The Stoics assimilated into their theology the traditional gods of civic religion, although like the Presocratics, Plato and Aristotle, they tried to avoid anthropomorphism.

For the Stoics, god pervades the world by bringing reason (*logos*) or cause to formless matter; the traditional Greek gods represent the immanent, active presence of god in the universe. Divine causation, although rational, is not conceived in Aristotelian terms, for cause, according to the Stoics, is simply 'that because of which'.

Divine providence is also evident in this teleologically ordered world (in other words, in a world which is understood in terms of purposes and 'ends').

Another name for providence is 'fate', which for the Stoics did not mean the fate of popular superstition, but that of nature. Humans live virtuously by conforming to reason, which is to live in accordance with the divine causation and order of the natural world.

The Stoic sage therefore resigns himself to the fact that things in the world cannot be other than as they are. The wise thing to do is not to fight against it, but to accept a voluntary resignation to this cosmic order.

THE EPICUREANS

Epicureanism explicitly contested many Platonic and Stoic ideas. As part of its general disdain for teleology, it rejected both the notion of the divine craftsman and the notion of a rationally ordered nature to which we must align ourselves.

Epicurus, perhaps wisely, did not explicitly deny the existence of a divinity, he simply stated that worshippers ought not to expect divine help in any form: the gods are immortal and perfect and impossibly distant from this world full of '*savage beasts and wailing babies*', but they are '*talking together in a language resembling Greek.*' The chief characteristics of the gods

FOR FURTHER INFORMATION ON THE ETHICAL IMPLICATION OF STOIC AND EPICUREAN THOUGHT, SEE PAGE 77

are seen as blessedness and immortality.

Some modern commentators have maintained that, in virtue of these arguments, Epicurus was an atheist in the modern sense of the term, since for him the gods did not really exist, but were simply psychological projections of man's ethical ideas.

This is used to explain his famous argument, later immortalized by his most famous disciple, the Roman poet **Lucretius (c.95-52BCE)** in Book III of his philosophical poem *On the nature of things* (*De rerum natura*), that we have no grounds on which to fear death, since while we exist death is not present, and when death is present, we no longer exist. Thus, we have no reason to be concerned about death, since we shall never experience it.

It is clear that Epicurean theology is distinct from those of the Stoics, Plato and Aristotle. Its reliance upon a materialistic metaphysics and physics, derived from Democritus, appears to preclude a strong allegiance both to philosophical theology and to the beliefs of popular religion.

NEOPLATONISTS

The founding father and much the greatest of the Neoplatonists was **Plotinus (204-270CE)**, a native of Alexandria, Egypt, reputedly of black African descent, who wrote in Greek.

Plotinus' attitude to popular religion was generally dismissive (*Enneads* III. 5. 2-3). For him, god is the ineffable One, below whom are ranged divine Mind or Intellect (which is not just 'god' but divinity in its entirety — *Enneads* V. 5.3. 1-3) and Soul.

The One is the Alone, different from all below it; it exists by itself, in all beings. Mind, on the other hand, is complex; in thinking of itself (as in Aristotle), it thinks of the Platonic Forms and functions as the divine demiurge or craftsman. Soul has direct contact with the material world; it is in fact a World Soul.

The causal relationship of the One (also called 'the Good') to the rest of the universe, as in Aristotle, is one of attraction and longing. Mind exists in so far it as it contemplates the One; Soul exists in so far as it looks to the Platonic Forms in the Mind; nature, which is not really separate from the Soul, has produced the world by a sort of accident, due to its distance from the divine.

For Plotinus, virtuous human beings are engaged in a lifelong attempt to ascend towards the One, which he called 'the flight of the one to the One'.

He claimed to have had mystical experiences of the One several times. Plotinus' spirit can be seen in his last words recorded by his disciple **Porphyry (232-c.305CE)** in his *Life of Plotinus*.

'Seek to lead the god within you up to the divine in the universe.'

Is the world designed and purposeful, or a matter of chance? Is there a One to which we can ascend, or are the gods projections of our own desires? For these Greek thinkers, religion was closely linked to their overall view of the nature of reality.

The course of ancient philosophical speculation about divine matters was dramatically altered as early as the first century CE by the pagan world's contact with Judaism and subsequently Christianity. The intellectual directions of Judaism and Christianity were also shaped through coming into contact with pagan Greek thought.

In Judaism there is an energetic effort to present the claims of revelation in philosophically articulate ways. The new effort of speculation about divine matters can be seen in the work of thinkers like **Philo Judaeus of Alexandria (c.39BCE-c.45CE)**. Among Christian thinkers, the so-called 'Alexandrian fathers' **Clement (150-215CE)** and **Origen (185-284CE)**, sought not only to evaluate but to preserve those elements of pagan learning that could be used to defend and clarify the claims of revealed religion. The work of Clement and Origen led not only to philosophical explorations of the Christian Scriptures, but also to the development of a view within Christian circles that the 'best' philosophy was to be found in Scripture.

Despite the efforts of those like **Tertullian (160- 230CE)** who sought to excoriate all philosophy in the name of the Gospel, the intellectual project began by the Alexandrians reached fruition in the philosophically sophisticated work of the Cappaodcian fathers: **Basil of Caesarea (330-379CE)**, **Gregory of Nyssa (335-c.395CE)** and **Gregory of Nazianzus (330-389CE)**.

The most outstanding figure in Christian antiquity is **Augustine of Hippo (354-430CE)**. He developed a theoretical basis for Christian theology that assigned priority to the revealed truths of Christian doctrine as known through the Bible.

With respect to pagan philosophy, Augustine argued that revealed truth serves as a rule, which the Christian thinker uses to measure the veracity and strength of philosophical arguments.

Thus the Christian theologian begins by believing the claims of revealed truth and seeks, by the use of reason and with God's help, to acquire understanding of what he formerly merely believed.

Augustine argues, most famously in his *On Christian Doctrine*, that when philosophical reflection begins from revealed truth and seeks to understand it, this will strengthen and improve Christian doctrine. He thereby rejected the anti-intellectualism of Tertullian.

For Augustine, reason is created by God and is that by virtue of which human beings are like God. To repudiate reason would be to reject God's image in ourselves.

The world of late antiquity was to produce one more individual who made a noteworthy contribution to philosophical theology. This was **Boethius (480-524CE)**. He composed several short theological treatises, one of which — *On the Trinity* — brought Aristotelian logic to bear on an issue central to Christian belief: the Triune nature of the Godhead. In this way, the intellectual legacy of pagan antiquity came to influence the methods and procedures of philosophical theology.

> ### AUGUSTINE
> ### (354-430)
> Christian theologian, philosopher and Bishop; Augustine is best known for his autobiography, the *Confessions*, and the *City of God*, prompted by the sack of Rome in 410. More then any other Latin writer, his influence dominated the middle ages and the Reformation. His ideas remain a continuing resource for those concerned to work out and assess the relations between faith and reason.

While puritanical Christian and most Jewish and Islamic thinkers, sought to distance themselves from all ancient philosophers and pagan beliefs, other Christian thinkers attempted to understand the nature of their own beliefs by co-opting elements (especially logic and metaphysics) from ancient philosophy.

SEE ALSO AUGUSTINE ON:

HISTORY PAGE **280**

LAW AND POLITICS PAGE **300**

ETHICS PAGE **78**

' … if I could show you something superior to our minds you would confess that it was God, provided nothing existed that was higher still… If there is anything more excellent than wisdom, doubtless it, rather, is God. But if there is nothing more excellent, then truth itself is God. Where there is or is not such a higher thing, you cannot deny that God exists… '

Augustine, *De Libero Arbitrio*

THE MEDIEVAL WORLD

Through the thousand years from the sixth to the sixteenth century, the main concern of philosophers was considering questions about the existence and nature of God. To understand this world properly, we need to replace a Eurocentric image of the medieval past, with one of a Mediterranean basin interacting with a Latin West that stretched from Ireland to the lands of the middle Danube. It is important to emphasize this, for the Byzantine East as well as the rich and sophisticated religious and philosophical cultures of Judaism and Islam played almost as vital a role in shaping medieval philosophical theology as did thinkers in the Latin West.

All four cultures shared a common Hellenic (Greek) philosophical heritage, a heritage that they each used and revised in different ways to make sense of the claims of their respective traditions and even to dispute with the claims of rival faiths.

In the Byzantine world, philosophers often continued the intellectual legacy of the early church fathers, appropriating pagan philosophical learning in order to defend the truths of the Christian religion. Influenced by the Cappodocian fathers rather than by Augustine – whose writings in Latin were not well known to Greeks – thinkers like **Maximus the Confessor (c.580-662CE)** sought to clarify issues relating to the nature and personality of Christ, by drawing on Neoplatonic and Aristotelian logic and metaphysics. Later philosophers such as **Michael of Ephesus (12th century)** and **Eustratius of Nicaea (c.1050-c.1120)** wrote commentaries on Aristotle, which made his philosophy much more accessible to Christian theologians.

Up to the last days of the Byzantine Empire in 1453, its robust intellectual culture continued to produce philosophers of great sophistication. Of these the most prominent were the startlingly pagan Neoplatonist **Gemisthos Plethon (1355-1450)** and **Theodorus Gaza (c.1400-c.1473)**. Their disputes about the respective merits of Plato and Aristotle, deeply influenced the thought of such Italian Renaissance philosophers as **Marsilio Ficino** and **Pico della Mirandola**, who were themselves highly influential on later writers.

Sometimes the linking of reason and religion is seen in architecture. The dome, expressing circular perfection and unity, is a common feature in religious buildings of many periods. Similarly, medieval buildings reflect religious ideas. The medieval world is sometimes caricatured as unsophisticated, but that is far from the truth, for it brought together a rich array of religious and philosophical traditions combining the great monotheistic religions of Judaism, Christianity and Islam with a common Greek philosophical heritage.

ISLAMIC PHILOSOPHY

When Islamic philosophers and theologians discovered the intellectual world of the Byzantine Empire, the works of Plato and Aristotle were made available through translations from Greek into Arabic.

Among the prominent philosophers of the ninth and tenth centuries such as **al-Farabi (875-950)**, Plato and Neoplatonism proved to be the dominant influences. Al-Farabi's successor, **Ibn Sina (Avicenna, 980-1037)** can be said to have adapted certain elements of the former's Neoplatonism, by arguing that God alone is the One whose very nature is to exist. Everything else must have existence bestowed upon it by the One, through whom everything that is, comes to exist.

In this way, the distinction between essence and existence offered Ibn Sina a way of expressing the fundamental division in being: between the One, which exists of itself, and everything else which may or may not exist.

Aristotle had earlier defined contingency in terms of some things being able

The Muslim tradition that it is idolatrous to make visual representations of Allah, or human beings, led to the tradition of using geometrical shapes and calligraphy as artistic embellishments. Many buildings that express Islamic culture – as here in the Moorish architecture in Granada, Spain, present the most wonderful interplay of light and shade, of pure geometric form and delicacy. There is a sense that beauty in this most abstract of forms, is an aid to an appreciation of the absolute that is Allah. But alongside such secular architecture, the simplicity of Mosque and Synagogue contrasts with the prolific use of images in pre-Reformation Christian church buildings, since these were used primarily as teaching aids.

to be other than they are. Ibn Sina now found a yet deeper explanation of the concept: everything other than the One, source of all there is, might never have existed at all. By focusing on these matters, he was able to distinguish necessary from contingent being, as well as to limit necessary being to the One.

In this, he was offering a philosophical analogue to the Qur'an's insistence that all being comes from a single creator.

While al-Farabi and Ibn Sina based their work on a mixture of Neoplatonism and Aristotelianism, later thinkers such as **Ibn Rushd (Averroes) (1126-1198)** were motivated to argue for a more accurate reading of Aristotelian theology, even though his work is still indebted to Neoplatonism.

The efforts of Ibn Rushd to convince his contemporaries that Aristotle exhibited the paradigm of human reasoning, was eventually to lead to conflicts among Islamic thinkers concerning the place and relevance of pagan philosophy in understanding the truths of revealed religion. One of Ibn Rushd's sternest critics, **al-Ghazali (1058-1111)**, argued that the former's teaching offended the Qur'an, notably in its conclusions regarding the necessary emanation of the universe from the One, as well as its Neoplatonic insistence on the immortality of the soul – a position which excludes the idea of bodily resurrection.

IMMORTALITY

There is a common misconception that Islamic and Christian beliefs require the idea of the immortality of the soul. This is not the case. Both religions argue for bodily resurrection, in which the whole self dies, but is then brought to life, in bodily form, by God. This is believed to happen at the end of time, and is related to the concept of judgement. The idea that individuals are naturally immortal, as is implied by Plato's philosophy, does not require God as an agent to bestow or guarantee life beyond death.

In this way, Islamic philosophers realized some years before their Jewish and Christian counterparts that the use of pagan learning for the purposes of clarifying and defending the claims of revealed religion was far from easy.

JEWISH PHILOSOPHY

The main issue in medieval Jewish philosophy was also the struggle between faith and reason. The goal of the philosopher, it was claimed, was to reconcile two very different approaches to knowledge: philosophical speculation (iyyun) and the acceptance of the dogmas of Judaism (emunah). The different attempts of **Moses Maimonides (1135-1204)** and **Gersonides (1288-1344)** are the most noteworthy.

Maimonides' *Guide to the Perplexed* is the most important work of Jewish medieval philosophy. Written to an (imaginary) follower, it demonstrates the logic of God's absolute perfection, which can be discerned beneath the anthropomorphic language of the Jewish prophets.

It argues that Biblical accounts of creation, though unprovable, are more probable than Aristotle's rival belief in the eternity of matter.

Maimonides is well known for his defence of 'negative theology'. This view, which originates in Neoplatonism, argues that God is beyond human understanding, and consequently that human language cannot grasp any attribute of God's being.

For the negative theologian, to utter sentences like 'God is good', 'God is merciful' is meaningless since God's actual goodness and mercifulness are incomprehensible, being far beyond what those terms would mean if applied to human individuals.

For this reason, a negative theologian, like Maimonides, rejects any attempt to investigate the attributes of God systematically. As God is ineffable, His being can only be embraced by *mystical* knowledge.

One finds a similar view in negative

theologians of other religious traditions, like the Christian thinker **Pseudo-Dionysius (c.500)**, whose blend of Christian theology and Neoplatonic metaphysics was very influential in the middle ages.

Gersonides, however, eschews esoteric approaches, in favour of gradually leading ordinary people toward a more sophisticated level of philosophical understanding.

What emerges from the work of these gifted philosophers is an earnest attempt to reconcile traditional Jewish beliefs with Greek philosophy – be it Plato, Aristotle or Neoplatonism.

Perhaps more than with the earlier Arab thinkers, with the possible exception of Ibn Rushd, the work of Maimonides and Gersonides exhibits a greater willingness to embrace philosophy as the best means for articulating the claims of religious belief and traditions.

MOSES MAIMONIDES
(1135-1204)

Rabbi Moses ben Maimon (generally known as Moses Maimonides) is widely recognized as the greatest of the Jewish philosophers of the medieval period. He was also a jurist and a physician.

During his lifetime, he was best known for his codification of Jewish law in the *Mishna Torah*, which offered a rational, clear and hugely influential interpretation. He also wrote medical texts, and earned his living as a physician.

His philosophical works were influential in Christian circles, and were cited by Aquinas, Meister Eckhart and Duns Scotus. His best-known work is the *Guide for the Perplexed*, which is his attempt to resolve the different approaches of biblical material and the science and philosophy of his day, which had its roots in Greek thought.

In anticipation of later Biblical scholarship, he points out the poetic writing and legal rules in the scriptures are necessary because of the limited awareness of human beings. As a rationalist, but one who was writing from within a religious tradition, his work has been hugely influential.

THE PHILOSOPHY OF RELIGION: ANCIENT AND MEDIEVAL

Like their Byzantine, Judaic and Islamic counterparts, thinkers in the Latin West did not shun the issues raised by the confrontation of ancient philosophy with revealed religion. In many works, the conversion or ascent of philosophy to faith is the central theme, as can be witnessed in the *Journey of the Mind to God* of **Bonaventure (c.1217–1274)**.

For other medieval thinkers philosophy serves as an intellectual foundation to faith, grasped and expressed as theology. Many imitated **Boethius'** *Consolation of Philosophy*, in which the figure of philosophy reminds him of truths without which his faith cannot be restored. This model is also evident in the work of writers like **John Scotus Eriugena (c.810–c.877)** and **Alan of Lille (d.1203)** who present philosophical doctrines as allegories of the Christian faith.

Perhaps the most enduring medieval model of speculative reflection on divine matters was developed out of reflection upon the work of Augustine. **Anselm of Canterbury (1033–1109)**, in his *Proslogion*, uses the Augustinian phrase *fides quaerens intellectum* (faith seeking understanding). We need to understand this formula properly to appreciate what many medieval philosophers hoped to accomplish.

It is simply untrue that, even at the start of their philosophical investigations, the medievals already knew exactly what they believed. They have a genuine interest in philosophy for its own sake. We find them again and again posing the question: 'But what do I believe?' In this sense they were not asking about the religious formulae to which, as members of a community of faith, they had given assent; they knew the formulae well. What they wanted to know was what those formulae *meant*; so as *fideles*, or people of faith, they went in search of understanding.

We can clearly see this strategy at work in Anselm's ontological argument in *Proslogion* II and III. Put simply, an onto-

ANSELM
(1033–1109)
Philosopher, theologian and Benedictine monk, later becoming Archbishop of Canterbury. Anselm is famous not only for his ontological argument for the existence of God in the *Proslogion* but also for his work on truth and atonement in other works, such as the *Monologion* and *Cur Deus Homo?*

logical argument purports to prove, from an analysis of the concept of God, that God's existence cannot be rationally doubted by any individual who entertains that concept. It is thus a purely a priori argument; that is to say, it does not appeal to any facts of experience, but is concerned solely with the implications of thinking about concepts under certain descriptions – in this case the concept of God as the supreme being.

THE ONTOLOGICAL ARGUMENT

Anselm's argument begins by a consideration of what God is. His answer is that God is:

> 'something than which a greater cannot be thought of' (aliquid quo nihil maius cogitari possit).

Next, Anselm considers the view of someone who says that there is no God. Such a person, Anselm says, 'understands what he hears, and what he understands is in his intellect (in intellectu).'

From this Anselm concludes that God exists even in the intellect of one denying his existence.

This, however, does not provide us with a complete proof for the existence of God, as there appears to be nothing exceptional in the observation that God exists in the understanding (in intellectu). Surely, if we want God to 'exist' in any tangible sense of that term, we will want God's existence to have much the same 'reality' as other objects in the world. In this sense we will want God to exist not only in the understanding (in intellectu) but also in reality (in re).

Anselm, aware of this requirement, asks 'Does God exist in any other sense?' His answer is 'Yes'. Anselm's point can be summarised as follows:

Something can be thought of as existing both in the intellect and also in reality. But this is greater than that which exists in the intellect alone. Therefore, if God is 'something than which a greater cannot be thought' then He must exist both in the intellect and also in reality.

In other words, if to think of 'God' is to entertain the concept 'something than which a greater cannot be thought of', then it follows that God must exist.

The argument continues in Proslogion III and can be paraphrased as follows:

Suppose I understand that a certain person, Fred, exists. By Anselm's lights, Fred exists in my intellect, and if Fred exists outside my intellect, then Fred exists both in my intellect and outside it. But Fred is not such that he cannot be thought not to exist. In other words, I can perfectly well acknowledge Fred's existence, without supposing that there is no possibility of his not existing.

By the same token, Anselm assumes, even if we know that God exists both in re and in intellectu, it does not follow that there is no possibility of God not existing. If we think that God is such that there is no possibility of him not existing, we need to know more of him than that he exists both in the intellect and outside it.

The aim of Proslogion III is to show that we do in fact know this of God.

The obvious retort to this is to ask 'How do we know this of God?'

Anselm argues that it can be thought that there exists 'something that cannot be thought not to exist.' If this is so, such a thing would be greater than something which can be thought not to exist. Yet God is that 'than which no greater can be thought', therefore God cannot be thought not to exist.

Anselm thus claims to have shown that God 'exists' on the basis of analysing what it is to entertain the concept 'God', and then demonstrating what follows from this.

One of the earliest criticisms of the Proslogion arguments was put by the monk Gaunilo, a contemporary of Anselm. In his A Reply to the Foregoing by a Certain Writer on Behalf of the Fool, Gaunilo takes issue with Anselm's claims about existence.

For Gaunilo, if Anselm is correct, then it is not only God's existence that can be established by this argument. The point is illustrated by the famous 'Lost-Island' example. Gaunilo's point is that if Anselm's arguments were valid, we could prove the existence of a lost island that surpasses the attractions of all inhabited countries, for actual existence is an essential element in any understanding of such superiority.

To be fair to Anselm, however, one could say that he is not concerned with the idea of something that is in fact greater than anything else of the same kind. Rather, his point is that God is something than which a greater cannot be thought of; which is to say that whatever the concept 'God' refers to, cannot be surpassed in any respect whatsoever. Gaunilo, on the other hand, is concerned with something (an island) that is better than any other island.

A supporter of Gaunilo might accept this point and yet still try to preserve the locus of their complaint. What if, they might say, we construe it as holding that if Anselm's argument is successful, then it is possible to establish the existence not only of the island which is better than all other islands, but also the island than which no more perfect island can be thought of.

This last move has seduced many, but it perhaps falls short of refuting Anselm. For it crucially depends on the assumption that the concept 'an island than which no more perfect can be thought of' is coherent.

Here we run into difficulties, for no matter what description of an island is produced, it is always possible that human imagination can improve on it. For this reason, some conclude that Anselm's argument survives Gaunilo's attack.

Gaunilo aside, other lines of criticism surfaced in medieval discussions of Anselm's Proslogion arguments. Some philosophers, such as **William of Auxerre (d.1249)** and **Alexander of Hales (c.1185-1245)**, were prepared to accept the basic insights of Anselm's arguments, while others, **John Duns Scotus (c.1266-1308)** and **Nicholas of Cusa (1401-1464)**, thought the arguments were in need of further clarification and extension.

Of the major medieval thinkers only **Thomas Aquinas (1225-1274)** and **William of Ockham (c.1290-1349)** thought the proof in error.

What is interesting about Aquinas' criticisms of what the medievals referred to as the ratio Anselmi (literally, 'Anselm's proof'), is the contrast it invites with modern criticisms of the proof. Aquinas thought Anselm's arguments invalid not for the reason (as argued by Kant, for example) that they treated existence as a predicate, but that the Anselmian formula, expressing the concept of God as 'that which nothing greater can be conceived of', does not provide any insight into God's nature. For this reason, Aquinas contends, the formula cannot be self-evidently true.

Supporting the Argument

While Anselm's argument had its detractors, it also had its supporters. Perhaps the most willing advocate of the *ratio Anselmi* was **Bonaventure**. He quotes and states Anselm's argument at great length before pointing out that it is subject to doubt only if someone has an erroneous notion of God; that is, if one fails to realize that God is that than which nothing greater can be conceived.

Bonaventure's defence of the proof reflects an understanding of Anselm's argument that persisted throughout the medieval and early-modern periods. In accordance with the Platonic-Augustinian tradition he so cherished, Bonaventure saw in Anselm's argument a way of preserving an innate conception of the perfect, which can be nothing else but God's imprint on the soul, not in the sense that the soul is perfect, but in the sense that the soul or the mind receives the idea of the perfect through divine illumination.

According to this view, we might say the very concept of 'God' affirms the concrete existence of God Himself, for it is the presence in the mind of the idea or concept of God that necessarily implies God's existence. Bonaventure's defence of the *ratio Anselmi* bears some resemblance to Descartes' subsequent version of the ontological argument in his *Fifth Meditation*.

Other Latin authors, following Anselm's project of faith seeking understanding, clarified the relation between philosophy and theology by insisting that philosophy must be studied thoroughly before proceeding to theology.

An example of this can be found in the work of the Oxford philosopher and natural scientist **Roger Bacon**

(c.1220-1292), who argued that nothing could be known about God without the prior study of languages, mathematics, optics, experiential science and moral philosophy.

As we proceed through the 13th century we find various authors so fully appropriating the methods and procedures of Aristotelianism and Neoplatonism that much of their theology is parasitic upon them. Examples of such tendencies can be found in the work of **Albertus Magnus (1200-1280).**

The high point of scholastic speculation on God was in the last quarter of the 13th and in the first half of the 14th century, with the works of Aquinas, Scotus and Ockham. They illustrate the range and diversity of Christian theologians' engagement with the Aristotelian inheritance.

The work of Duns Scotus, for instance, exhibits a multitude of sources and influences which he used to construct an ingenious synthesis, which addressed questions that are explicitly theological, concerning our knowledge of the created order and of the divine will.

William of Ockham saw fit to repudiate some of the central features of an uncritical use of Aristotle by some of his forebears, but sought to use Aristotle's work to support his own theological views, especially concerning the compatibility of divine omniscience with human freedom. Like others who made use of Aristotle's logic, he aspired to be perceived as a faithful interpreter of Aristotle's texts.

THOMAS AQUINAS
(1225-1274)

Philosopher, theologian and Dominican friar. Aquinas is credited with making the works of Aristotle known and appreciated among medieval theologians. His best-known work is the massive *Summa theologiae*, which he wrote as textbook for students of theology. Other known works include his *Disputed Questions on Truth* and the *Summa Contra Gentiles*. Aquinas is also known as the 'Angelic Doctor' a title that preserves the deeply felt spirituality, which pervades his work.

Perhaps the most systematic attempt to fix the proper relations between pagan Aristotelian philosophy and Christian theology comes in the work of **Thomas Aquinas (1225-1274)**. For Aquinas, theology (*theologia*) employs, improves, and then perfects the best of ancient philosophy.

Aquinas extended great deference to pagan philosophers; he frequently cites Plato, Cicero and others, giving Aristotle the honorific title 'the philosopher', and then embarks upon a systematic commentary on Aristotle's work. But whenever he speaks in his own voice, Aquinas systematically transforms most of the Aristotelian doctrines he discusses, often in directions quite opposed to Aristotle's original intentions. Such a strategy can found in his famous arguments for the existence of God, which are to be found in his *Summa Theologiae*.

These arguments are known as the '**five ways**', being five separate arguments.

Of these the 'third way' is worth examining for it illustrates the last set of theistic arguments to have come out of the philosophy of religion's ancient and medieval past: 'cosmological arguments'.

A cosmological argument is an argument for a cause or reason for the cosmos. Many versions of this argument begin by reflecting upon the question

'Why is there something rather than nothing?'

From there, they seek to make explicit the view that the world is not just sufficient of itself but points to a greater reality beyond itself.

Aquinas denies that God's existence is self-evident to us in this life. The first step of the 'third way' argument for the existence of God, begins with the observation that we experience things that are capable of existence and non-existence, and are subject to generation and corruption. It is impossible, Aquinas thinks, that all things that exist are capable of existing and not existing, because for anything that can fail to exist there is a time when it does not exist. If therefore all things are capable of not existing, at some time nothing whatsoever existed, and hence, nothing would exist now. Since not all beings are capable of existing and not existing, there must be a necessary being.

Instead of ending the argument there, however, Aquinas adds a second step. He argues as follows:

- **Every necessary being has something else which is a cause of its necessity.**
- **One cannot regress to infinity with caused necessary beings.**
- **Therefore, there must be a necessary**

being that does not depend on anything else for its necessity, and that causes the necessity in everything else.
- **This is a being 'which all name God' (quod omnes dicunt Deum).**

This argument is based on the simple idea that there is a regress of causes. Although it employs the distinction between things which are contingent and those which are necessary, it is not content with the conclusion that there is something necessary; for it goes on to argue that there may be many necessary things, and reaches God only once it has established that there is something which has necessity through itself (*per se*).

Traditional lines of criticism to this have usually focused on the second stage of the argument. This part has been thought invalid because, while it can be argued that, if something has an antecedent cause, it depends upon something else, it does not follow that everything (other than God) needs or requires something else, or is dependent on something else in this way.

The weakness here, it is claimed, is that the argument makes God the one exception to the supposed need for everything to have something else to depend on. Why should God, rather than anything else, be the uncaused cause?

In defence of Aquinas, however, there is the view that we do not simply assume that things just happen, or that things are just there; we naturally attempt to account for things in terms of something else.

If the world is an object, it is certainly pertinent to ask of it the sort of causal questions that would be relevant to a discussion of its parts. If it began to exist, what brought it about? What keeps it from perishing, in the way that its parts perish? And what keeps its processes going? In the end someone might simply observe that the universe goes about its merry way because it is in its nature to continue to exist. But the universe cannot have the nature it has unless it continues to exist, so the fact that it continues to exist can hardly be explained **in terms of** its nature.

To appreciate the force of Aquinas' argument, don't think of causation in terms of a chain stretching back into the past, in which each thing is caused by the the previous one. Rather, think of a sequence of causes moving outwards in all directions, like ripples on water. Traced outwards, everything in the universe has some causal contribution to make. But what causes the whole? That is Aquinas' question: Unless the ripple is to continue even further, there has to be an 'uncaused cause'.

SEE ALSO **AQUINAS ON:**

ETHICS PAGE **79**

LAW AND POLITICS PAGE **302**

THE RENAISSANCE – ITS ROOTS AND ITS LEGACY

The philosophers of the Renaissance continued to discuss issues that had been debated in antiquity and the Middle Ages. What distinguished thinkers in this period from earlier philosophers was the very different resources they brought to bear on traditional topics.

Renaissance philosophy cannot be disassociated from the literary movement known as *humanism*. Based on the recovery and study of the texts and documents of antiquity, humanism became a robust cultural movement that influenced virtually all aspects of the intellectual life of the 15th, 16th and early 17th centuries.

In philosophy, this had the effect of making available the classic works of Plato, Aristotle, the Stoics, Epicurus and the Sceptics in their original language. These revolutionized the study of philosophy, and in turn this led to a recasting of the relationship between religious faith and philosophical reason.

Such recasting provides the backdrop to some of the more dramatic theological debates of the Renaissance. The dispute between **Pietro Pomponazzi (1462-1524)** and **Agostino Nifo (1473-1538)** concerning whether or not the immortality of the soul can be proved by reason, could not have taken place if there had not been a prior debate about to how to find the best means of interpreting Aristotle's work *On the Soul*.

Likewise the attempt of **Marsilio Ficino (1433-1499)** to construct a 'Platonic theology' compatible with the doctrines of Christianity cannot be understood apart from his producing the first Latin edition of the complete works of Plato and Plotinus.

Other Renaissance philosophers such as **Pico della Mirandola (1463-1494)** continued the tradition of earlier thinkers by arguing that the principles and axioms of pagan philosophy needed to be 'corrected' by the truths of Christian theology. Pico developed a syncretic philosophy, trying to reconcile pagan Hellenism, Christianity and even the Jewish Kabbalah. For this brave but heterodox attempt, he was briefly imprisoned by the Pope.

The need to preserve the doctrines of Christianity in the face of challenges by a reinvigorated study of pagan philosophy constantly stimulated philosophical speculation about theological matters in this period. In different ways this tendency can be observed in the work of very different thinkers like **Giles of Vitterbo (d.1532)** and **Erasmus of Rotterdam (1466-1536)**.

One of the legacies of Renaissance philosophy to thinkers in the 17th century, was a precise way of identifying the truths of philosophical claims, in an intellectual culture conditioned by theological commitments. In part, if not in whole, this legacy accounts for much of the stimulus to debating the relationship of faith to reason in modern times.

Leonardo da Vinci represents the great cultural and artistic movement of the Renaissance – a rebirth into Western culture of the humanist values of Ancient Greece, and a time of a new awareness of classical philosophy. Drawing on classic texts, the Renaissance philosophers set an agenda for later thought in the Philosophy of Religion, particularly in the relationship between faith and reason.

RENAISSANCE AND REFORMATION

'Human nature is so blind that it does not know its own powers, or rather diseases, and so proud as to imagine that it knows and can do everything.' Luther

The Renaissance and the Reformation fragmented the medieval synthesis of faith and reason, although that synthesis was already coming under internal strain, particularly in the *fideistic* (belief by faith alone) emphases of **William of Ockham**. The cry of both Renaissance and Reformation thinkers was *ad fontes* – back to the sources. For the Renaissance, these sources were classical Greek and Latin culture; for the Reformation, the primitive sources of Christian thought, the Bible. Each shared an interest in languages and in textual scholarship, as well as a suspicion of the scholasticism that had been prevalent in the Middle Ages.

Yet recent scholarship has stressed the elements of continuity between medieval scholasticism and the thinking of the leaders of the Renaissance as well as of the Protestant Reformers, despite the obvious ecclesiastical ruptures that the Reformation brought about.

So, in this period, 'philosophy' stressed the use of the intellect both in scientific discovery and the re-discovery of the ancient learning. Each of these developments had the effect, at least in the minds of many, of re-affirming the claims of the Christian faith. For among the ancient learning that was rediscovered, was the text of the Bible, and the renewed use of the original languages in its study. In the Protestant Reformation, the tensions between faith and reason, now more commonly seen as a set of controversies between tradition, revelation and reason, was renewed as the Reformers stressed the evangelical imperatives of the Bible.

Erasmus is typical of those learned Renaissance scholars who, while not anti-theological in their views, were untheological in temper. For them, faith was seen mainly in terms of moral precepts, which they were confident that men and women could follow.

Luther is dismissive of the supposed ability of human beings to save themselves spiritually. For Luther, the human will is not free but in bondage to sin. Human reason, when unaided by special divine grace, is powerless. Luther used the terminology and some of the arguments that he had learned as an Augustinian monk, in defence of his Protestantism. Although often crude and outspoken, he was by no means the rednecked anti-intellectual that he has often been painted.

In the other great Reformer, **John Calvin**, we see a more measured

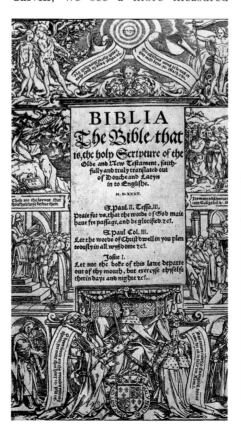

Title page of the Coverdale Bible

response. His recognition of natural theology, however minimalist, also indicates unbroken lines of continuity with the medieval thinkers.

At the end of this period, Thomas Hobbes may be said to anticipate those who questioned the rationality of the entire enterprise of religion, seeing it as the product of fear, or greed, or priest-craft. Such thinkers were forerunners of the Enlightenment.

THE PHILOSOPHY OF RELIGION: THE MODERN PERIOD

'Piety, great God! and religion are become a tissue of ridiculous mysteries.'

Spinoza

The religious issues characteristic of the Renaissance and Reformation, broadened even further in the period known as the Enlightenment, the 'Age of Reason'. The movement had its roots in René Descartes and John Locke and reached its most strident form in the Encyclopaedists, **D'Holbach, Diderot** and **D'Alembert**, compilers of the Encyclopédie (1751-1765), which included **Voltaire** and **Helvetius** among its contributors.

Though liberal social and political views were advanced, through writers such as Rousseau, one of the most bitter fruits of the Enlightenment was the arrogance and violence of the French Revolution.

While Renaissance and Reformation thinkers strove to get back to the biblical and classical sources, the Enlightenment was an attempt to make a clean break with the past, and to start afresh. What the medieval period, and the Reformation and Renaissance had in common was a fundamental belief that this was God's universe, his creation, and that we could gain knowledge of him, and of it, by reason and the senses, and also through divine revelation. In the Enlightenment there was a great change in intellectual temper from this theocentric perspective to a man-centred outlook, and from a reliance upon the past to scepticism about its worth.

The religious diversity engendered by the Reformation, and the political and military conflict that resulted, was a deep embarrassment. A distrust of the established religions arose because of their socially and politically divisive effects in Europe and elsewhere. Hence, there arose the idea that the claims of religion should be tested and constrained by autonomous human reason, and that its validity should turn on its personal and social usefulness. Great emphasis was placed upon method, and upon the sources of knowledge; on what we can know, and how we can know it.

Coupled with this was the belief that 'nature', including human nature, uncluttered by religious superstition and clerical domination, would provide all necessary guidance to happiness and personal fulfilment.

It soon became clear, however, that 'reason' meant different things to different people. And, just as the Renaissance and Reformation period was characterized by disputes about the nature of religious authority, with the Church, the Bible, tradition and reason vying with each other for supremacy, so the Enlightenment came to be characterized by disputes about the very nature of philosophy and the correct philosophical method.

These disputes were prompted by the quest for certainty, to combat the scepticism that the very existence of these competing claims to authority seemed to imply, and by the growing success and prestige of natural science.

Rome: a symbol, then and now, of the authority of the Church. That authority was challenged at the Reformation by the competing claims of biblical study and reason, but the thinkers of the Enlightenment went further, in making a rational assessment of religion in terms of its personal and social value as well as its beliefs .

> '*I recognise that it is not possible that my nature should be what it is, and indeed that I should have in myself the idea of God, if God did not veritably exist.*' Descartes

RENÉ DESCARTES
(1596-1650)

A scientist and mathematician; he is widely regarded as the founding father of modern philosophy. His method, and his emphasis on the primacy of epistemology (the theory of knowledge), has influenced and shaped three hundred years of philosophical reflection.

His philosophical publications include *Discourse on Method* (1637), *Meditations* (1641) and *Principles of Philosophy* (1644).

René Descartes (1596-1650), with his characteristic reliance on the clear and distinct ideas of reason, is a key influence on the Enlightenment and indeed on the whole of subsequent Western philosophy. In his *Discourse on Method* (1637) and *Meditations* (1641) he proposed a system of doubt, in order to place to one side all those beliefs which can be doubted, because they are not known clearly and distinctly by the eye of reason. Our knowledge must be based on what we can be indubitably sure of, by employing that reasoning which is itself indubitable.

Descartes is thus among the first, and is one of the most self conscious, 'foundationalists' – philosophers who claim that there is a class of foundational beliefs known without inference on which all our other knowledge claims must be appropriately based.

The reference to indubitable foundations, and in particular the appeal to the indubitability of his own existence, ('I think, therefore I am') was not, in Descartes' case, an expression of an anti-religious temper. Nevertheless his procedure had revolutionary implications for religion. God plays a crucial though subordinate epistemological role to that performed by the clear and distinct ideas of reason.

God is introduced by reason as the one who guarantees the reliability of our sensory awareness, and indeed the existence of a world beyond the certainty of one's own existence, for God would not deceive us.

The very fact of attempting to start from scratch gave Descartes' rationalism, and the outlook that it helped to cultivate, a modernist emphasis. For in theory at least, no inherited tradition was of any real epistemological value.

Descartes' dualism, his belief that the human person is comprised of two substances, a perishable body and an imperishable soul, has also been of considerable religious influence and is often believed to be the only viable alternative to a purely naturalistic account of the mind.

Descartes' appeal to reason was developed thoroughly by **G W Leibniz (1646-1716)** for whom the principle of sufficient reason was a keystone of his entire metaphysics, involving proofs of God's existence and the claim that this world, the world that God created, is (and must be) the best of all possible worlds. **B Spinoza (1632-1677)** developed a sophisticated form of pantheism. All these thinkers produced theological and philosophical systems by a variety of appeals to human reason in which any recourse to divine revelation was unnecessary, or was of secondary importance, as confirming and illustrating what reason alone could tell us.

SEE ALSO DESCARTES:

KNOWLEDGE, PAGES 28-28

MIND, PAGES 132-133

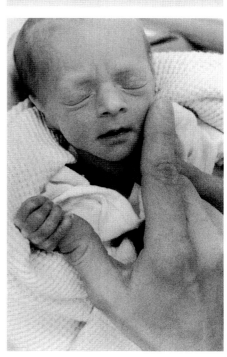

With what mixture of trust, fear or need do we first encounter the world, in those long-forgotten early days of life? What is a newborn baby learning as she grips a thumb with her tiny hand, or feels the brush of a finger upon her cheek? Later, she may grow to evaluate her awareness critically, to judge whether or not she is mistaken in what she sees of the world around her. She may even cast doubt on everything she experiences. But in those first hours of life, there was only the raw experience. With the developing of our critical faculties, do we need the idea of God to guarantee the reliability of our sensory awareness?

'Faith can never convince us of anything that contradicts our knowledge.'

Locke

John Locke (1632-1704) is the fountainhead of the other great philosophical tradition to flow from the 17th century and the subsequent 'Age of Reason'. Unlike the rationalists, Locke claimed that at birth the human mind was a 'tabula rasa', a clean sheet, and that all our knowledge is from simple ideas derived from the five senses.

Apart from his notable work in defence of (limited) religious toleration, the chief importance of Locke as far as the philosophy of religion is concerned is that he worked out a kind of philosophical apologia for 17th century Anglicanism. This involved the recognition of divine revelation, but of a type that is immune to what he called 'enthusiasm' – the claim to immediate inspiration that was characteristic of some of the more radical sects of the Commonwealth (Civil War) period.

While faith and reason have, as Locke put it, 'distinct provinces', the propositions of faith must show themselves to be in accord with reason. Locke appeals to miracles (considered as supernatural events, but historically verifiable) to validate the supernatural elements in religion.

DAVID HUME
(1711-1776)

Scottish philosopher, historian and man of letters, Hume was a leading figure of the Scottish Enlightenment. His cool, sceptical assessment of religion set the agenda for subsequent philosophy of religion. He published numerous philosophical works which include *A Treatise of Human Nature* (1739-1740), *An Inquiry Concerning Human Understanding* (1748) and *Dialogues Concerning Natural Religion* (posthumously published in 1779).

David Hume (1711-1776) developed a more radical and sceptical empiricism than Locke's. He argued that sensory 'impressions' cannot give us knowledge of the self, or of causation, or of the past. This radicalism expresses itself in Hume's rejection of (Locke's and others') appeal to miracles as the foundation of a religion, but also in his sharp critiques of the argument from design, and of religious language. In many ways Hume set the agenda for what, until recently, has formed the staple fare of the philosophy of religion, though the immediate influence of his ideas was not very great.

'Custom, then, is the great guide of human life.'

Hume

George Berkeley (1685-1753) was also more radical than Locke, but in a different way from Hume, holding that all our experience is of ideas which, insofar as they are reliable, are expressive of the mind of God.

Locke and Berkeley set the temper of

BLAISE PASCAL
(1623-1662)

French mathematician, physicist and theologian; his chief legacy is an apologetic work of the Christian religion which was aimed at the educated unbelievers of this day, published by the Jansenists as the *Penseés* in 1670.

---

much eighteenth century religious apologetics, of which **Joseph Butler (1692-1752)** and **William Paley (1743-1805)** are notable proponents. They laid stress on the assembling of evidence for Christianity by inductive, cumulative methods. But there were also significant reactions against the rationalism and empiricism of the age, notably by **Blaise Pascal (1623-1662)**, who in his famous Wager argument, in his *Pensés*, stresses not only the importance that the will plays in the forming of beliefs, but also that the value we place upon the ends of religion, also ought to determine our attitude to it. To believe in God, if he exists, is to gain, if he does not, then nothing is lost. On the other hand, not to believe in God, if he exists, spells doom, whilst, if he does not, nothing is lost. Therefore prudence (rather than reason) suggests that one should believe!

'Either God is, or He is not.' But which side shall we take? Reason can decide nothing here.

Pascal

FOR FURTHER INFORMATION ON:
LOCKE, SEE PAGES 34, 233, 310
ON HUME, SEE PAGES 36, 109
ON BERKELEY, SEE PAGE 35

JOHN LOCKE
(1632-1704)

Locke was the first of the great British empiricist philosophers. In his *Essay Concerning Human Understanding* (1690) he argued for religious knowledge, through both reason and revelation. In *The Reasonableness of Christianity* (1695), he defended revelation. He was also influential in political philosophy, with *The Two Treatises of Government* (1690) being his other major work.

As an intellectual movement, Deism was principally an English phenomenon. Though deistic tendencies recur throughout history, the roots of modern deism may be found in the work of **Lord Herbert of Cherbury (c.1583-1648)**. In Herbert, one finds an approach to religion that claims to be able to identify, through the diversity of theological approaches, a common core of rational religion, which can be discerned by those eyes that are not made dim by conventional religion.

The more immediate sources of deism as a movement were Locke's appeal to the reasonableness of religion, as well as the impact of Newtonian science. Locke's influence led to a dismissal of the Christian doctrines of the Trinity and the Incarnation, and so to the rise of Unitarianism both in the Church of England and in Dissent, and to the characteristic claim that Christianity is 'not mysterious'.

Newton's influence led to the stress of deism on the universe as a clockwork machine moving in accordance to fixed laws and by the impetus imparted to matter in the act of creation. Miracles were both impossible (because the laws were fixed) and unnecessary (because of the wisdom of the Creator who established them). Prominent deists included **Matthew Tindal (1655-1733)**, **Anthony Collins (1676-1729)** and **John Toland (1670-1722)**.

Deists were confident that they could, through reason and conscience, identify

> ### MATTHEW TINDAL
> #### (1655-1733)
> A Fellow of All Souls College, Oxford from 1678 until his death, Tindal is chiefly known for his *Christianity as Old as the Creation* (1730), one of the most important deist writings.

a natural religion, which was given to humanity by a well-meaning deity. It could, if uncorrupted by primitive and divisive religious ideas, sustain the human race through its many moral and spiritual vicissitudes

Perhaps the most sustained and sophisticated response to deism is found in the writings of the New England philosopher and theologian **Jonathan Edwards (1703-1758)**. Paradoxically, Edwards also was indebted to Locke, but used his work to formulate arguments against the deists and in support of the Puritan theology of his forebears. Against deism, Edwards stressed the immediacy of the divine relation to the universe. God does not act through fixed and immutable laws, but conserves the universe he has created by re-creating it moment by moment.

> ### JONATHAN EDWARDS
> #### (1703-1758))
> Edwards was an American Calvinist theologian and philosopher. Like other deists, he saw the laws of nature, established by God, as controlling everything. He therefore rejected the idea of an indeterministic freedom in his *The Freedom of the Will* (1754).

'Difficulties and incomprehensible mysteries are reasonably to be expected in a declaration from God.'
Jonathan Edwards

Deism as a religious movement was stopped dead in its tracks by the evangelical revival led by the Wesley brothers and George Whitefield, but its spectre lived on, conditioning the shape of the apologetic work of Christian writers such as Joseph Butler and William Paley until well into the nineteenth century.

> ### HERBERT OF CHERBURY
> #### (c.1583-1648)
> Philosopher, historian and diplomat, Herbert was a deist, though not in the direct line with later deist thought. He held a theory of God-given, innate ideas, which was attacked by John Locke with his *tabula rasa* argument (see page 166). His main works include *On the Truth* (1624), *De Causis Errorum* (1663) and *De Religione Gentilium* (1663).

In William Paley's most famous example of the design argument, he considers that, on finding a watch, one is led to assume – noting the way it is put together – that it is the product of an intelligent designer. Similarly, he sees elements of design within the world as proof of the existence of God.

'I have therefore found it necessary to deny knowledge, in order to make room for faith.'

Kant

In the work of **Immanuel Kant (1724-1804)** the man-centred thrust of the Enlightenment, and the view that religion is chiefly a moral matter, receives a definitive form. In his *Critique of Pure Reason* Kant argued against any form the claim that it is possible to have knowledge of God while in the *Critique of Practical Reason* he offers a proof of God's existence based upon the requirements of morality.

Kant's fundamental idea is that human knowledge is formed through a set of ideas which do not arise from our experience of reality, but which the human mind brings to reality a priori. Experience is filtered and structured by ideas that the human mind already possesses innately, particularly ideas of space and time and causality.

It is thus impossible ever to discover how things are in themselves, but only ever how they appear to us. We cannot know anything except that which appears within the categories of space and time.

Kant held that the traditional proofs of God's existence were flawed and so unpersuasive (though Kant was almost persuaded by the argument from design). God cannot reveal himself in history, because to claim to have knowledge of the God of metaphysics, the timeless and spaceless God of the classical metaphysical tradition (via an appeal to revelation, say), was an attempt by the human mind to go beyond the categories of space and time through which all knowledge was mediated. Such endeavours cannot result in an increase in knowledge, but in the generation of antinomies (paradoxes of thought).

Nevertheless, although God's existence could not be proved by the theoretical reason, it was necessary for it to be postulated by the practical reason. Morality demands the existence of God. So Kant's God had a purely moral role, functioning as the provider of the *summum bonum*, the highest good, which is the final goal of morality. In the hands of Kant, faith was no longer reliance upon the word of God, or trust in Christ, but no more than the recognition of all duties as divine commands.

The result was a purely moral religion,

> 'For the purely speculative use of reason, therefore, the Supreme Being remains, no doubt, an ideal only, but an ideal without a flaw, a concept which furnishes and crowns the whole of human knowledge, and the objective reality of which, though it cannot be proved, can neither be disproved in what way.'
>
> *Critique of Pure Reason*

Just as, in the theory of knowledge, Kant saw the mind shaping what we experience, rather than being conformed to it, there is a similar 'Copernican Revolution' in his philosophy of religion. In Kant's view, religion does not depend on external evidence or metaphysics, but is the expression of a moral seriousness and the goal of human life.

a religion requiring neither empirical nor metaphysical support, indeed a religion quite at odds with such support; a religion without revelation, a life of faith without any divinely-appointed means of grace. In his *Religion Within the Limits of Reason Alone* Kant in effect 'de-mythologises' key Christian ideas such as revelation, faith and prayer, redefining them in accordance with the tenets of his moral religion. Such a religion, in various forms, became characteristic of continental ('liberal') Protestantism until the First World War.

IMMANUEL KANT
(1724-1804)

A seminal figure of the Enlightenment period, Kant's 'Copernican Revolution' placed the autonomous human mind at the centre of metaphysics and ethics. Kant produced his most influential works late in life and the most important include the three Critiques: *Critique of Pure Reason* (1781), *Critique of Practical Reason* (1788) and *Critique of Judgement* (1790). His *Religion Within the Limits of Reason Alone* (1793) is an influential reconstruction of Christian theology.

FOR FURTHER INFORMATION ON KANT

ON KNOWLEDGE SEE PAGES **38-40**

ON ETHICS, PAGE **89**

ON AESTHETICS, PAGE **241**

ON POLITICS, PAGE **317**

Kant effectively blocked off any metaphysical basis for religion, and any access to God through revelation or religious experience. Religion thus came to be a matter either of personal moral fulfilment or of striving to build the Kingdom of God through social and political action, or a matter of sense or feeling. Religious ideas were not the result of reflection on and codification of what God has specially revealed in Scripture, but were to be constructed out of such feeling, the products of human sensibility.

F D E Schleiermacher (1768-1834) was, in effect, the intellectual founder of this approach to religion. He was influenced not only by his immersion in the thought of Kant but also by the pietism of his upbringing.

Schleiermacher's thought, expressed in On Religion: Speeches to its Cultured Despisers and The Christian Faith, is the source of one important strand of liberal Protestantism. His work not only directly affected the idea of religion and the nature of theology, but also the critical approach to the documents of the Old and New Testaments. These came to be seen not as God's revelation, but as the expression of the faith of Israel and of the early Christian church respectively.

> ## 'Religion's essence is neither thinking nor acting, but intuition and feeling.' Schleiermacher

In Schleiermacher's view, any account of God has to be one that has its source in human sensibility, either that of an individual or of a corporate body such as the Christian Church. The character of that sensibility, for Schleiermacher, was the 'feeling of absolute dependence', not so much an emotion but an awareness of contingency, and thus a recognition (though not an experience) of God as the source of that contingency.

Jesus is the paradigm of an individual with such feeling, one who possessed an immaculate God-consciousness. From such apparently slender resources, Schleiermacher attempts in The Christian Faith to formulate a Christian dogmatics of a new and distinctive kind.

This approach, which sees theology as a species of anthropology, has had a wide range of exponents until the present day, and notable among these is **Rudolf Otto (1869-1937)** who, in The Idea of the Holy, stressed religious experience as a non-rational irreducible core of all developed religions. This, the 'numinous', the 'mysterium tremendum et fascinans', is an awe-inspiring sense of what lies beyond oneself, and a corresponding sense of one's own insignificance. All religious language is an inadequate attempt to express this inexpressible sense of the beyond, though – in Otto's view – Christianity does the best job in attempting to conceptualize the core experience.

Feelings of absolute dependence, or the sense of something 'numinous' are at the root of many religious experiences. Schleiermacher and Otto feature them in writing about the nature of religious experience and therefore also of its content. They may be stimulated by occasions when human life is shown to be tiny and vulnerable in the face of nature as a whole.

Just as Schleiermacher may be said to have gone beyond Kant in his appeal to religious feeling, while nevertheless accepting Kant's basic philosophical outlook, so **G W F Hegel (1770–1831)** goes beyond Kant in seeing the entire course of history as the realization of God, or of the Absolute Idea.

In Hegel's thought, God does not stand apart from his creation, transcendent, but he is immanently at work in it, indeed he is to be identified with the totality of the many specific processes of human history in which he is realized. So the whole of history is seen as comprising the many finite forms in which the eternal Spirit comes to express itself, forms which will be reconciled and brought together at the end of history.

At any one stage in history, the past can be seen as what is necessary and sufficient to realize the character of the present. History follows natural laws, which are the expression of the one Absolute Mind. Hegel's philosophy is a form of idealism; history is the thought of one mind, it is that mind thinking itself, and its truth is to be found in history's own final coherence.

This coherence is divine reality. Anything less than this whole truth is a falsification, for only in the whole are apparent contradictions and incoherences to be reconciled.

The obscurity of Hegel's ideas cannot be denied, but they have nevertheless been immensely influential. Hegel himself reinterpreted Christianity, so that Jesus was seen as the concrete manifestation, in human form, of the Absolute Spirit. Jesus is thus an important landmark in this process of the Spirit becoming immanent (i.e. realized within the world), not the Son of God made flesh.

The idea of God being in process with his creation has been influential in the 20th century in the development of Process Theology by **A N Whitehead** in *Process and Reality* (1929) and **Charles Hartshorne** in numerous writings (for example *Man's Vision of God* and *The Logic of Theism* (1941)).

In Process Theology, God is seen to be in creative interaction with his creation, and to need this knowing and loving interaction for the full development of his own creative powers.

The pantheistic tendencies vividly at work in Hegel can be seen again in Process Theology; though, in its case, God is thought of as being contained in the wider universe. This is a version of panentheism (all things being within God) or even of panpsychism, which suggests that there is a spirit within everything, but which differs from panentheism in that it does not hold that all creation is divine.

There are many problems with this position from the standpoint of traditional Christian beliefs. It appears to make God depend upon the world, since his nature and power is developed through it. But also it appears to suggest that everything that happens is determined by its place in the on-going process.

Christian process theologians generally deny such deterministic implications, and have offered 'process' readings of Christology and of the Holy Spirit.

G W F HEGEL
(1770–1831)

A German idealist philosopher; many of his best known books arose out of his Berlin lectures and include *Philosophy of History* (1837), *Philosophy of Religion* (1832) and *Aesthetics* (1835–8).

FOR FURTHER INFORMATION ON:

HEGEL'S CRITICISM OF KANT,

SEE PAGE 41.

ALSO HEGEL ON:

ETHICS, PAGE 91

HISTORY, PAGE 324

Hegelian thought requires us to rise above the processes within which we are immersed, and gain a perspective on the whole of history. Is that ever possible? Perhaps it would be rather like this view down on the mountains and valleys of the Himalayas from Apollo 9. Are we sure what we are looking at? Is that perspective helpful? Things would look rather different if we were on the ground.

THE LEAP OF FAITH: KIERKEGAARD

'The works of God are such that only God can perform them'. Kierkegaard

In Hegel's philosophy of religion there is an overriding concern with system. Every event and act in history can only be understood in terms of every other, and each such act is an aspect of the realization of Pure Spirit. In such a system the significance of the individual person, or of the individual action, tends to get lost.

In the Danish thinker **Søren Kierkegaard (1813-1855)** there is a noteworthy reaction against this and in favour of the importance of the individual's decision for and commitment to the truth. For, in the Denmark of Kierkegaard's day, Hegelian idealism found religious expression in a merely nominal adherence to Christianity. Kierkegaard abhorred this, and referred to Hegelianism as 'the System' with disdain and distaste.

Whereas it is possible and indeed desirable for a Hegelian – and indeed for any investigation in the rationalist or empiricist tradition – to be detached about the truth, for Kierkegaard it is the truth for the individual that matters.

Kierkegaard wrote many of his earlier works under pseudonyms, and so it is not always easy to identify his own views. Sometimes he appears simply to be challenging an over-intellectualist view of faith, and emphasizing the aspect of voluntary, personal decision. At other times he seems to be discounting any evidential basis whatsoever for faith, claiming that it is a 'leap' which either has no evidence in its favour, or needs none.

Either way, Kierkegaard emphasized 'subjectivity', not as the elevation of personal idiosyncrasy or whimsical opinion, but as expressing the importance of the believing subject. The person, in order to be an authentic believer, must appropriate the faith for himself. No religion can be second-hand.

With his stress on the individual, Kierkegaard may be regarded as the founder of existentialism, and so as exerting influence over both secular existentialism, for example **Jean-Paul Sartre (1905-1980)** and **Albert Camus (1913-1960)** and crusaders against Christianity such as **Friedrich Nietzsche (1844-1900)**.

He is also of theological importance in the influence his writings exerted over the early **Karl Barth (1886-1968)** and a host of lesser 'existentialist' theologians. The call for personal, authentic, Christian commitment will always find an echo in some religious sensibilities, but it is quite another thing to sever Christian faith from any basis in history of metaphysics. For religious faith then becomes simply a set of private responses with no basis in fact. It is not obvious that Kierkegaard clears himself of this charge.

'For what a man knows he cannot seek, since he knows it; and what he does not know he cannot seek, since he does not even know for what to seek… Thus the Truth is not introduced into the individual from without, but was within him.' Kierkegaard on Socrates' philosophical method, from *Philosophical Fragments*, chapter 1

Imagine what it would be like if one had to gain a complete overview of the process of one's own life, and that of one's prospective partner, before entering into marriage. From that perspective, would anyone dare to make a commitment? Some actions require a 'leap of faith', to use Kierkegaard's term; they shape the process of our lives. An action may be reasonable, but not determined by reason. With hindsight, any action – even the commitment of marriage – may be seen as a mistake, but that does not invalidate the genuine authenticity of that act.

Kant argued that it was necessary to postulate God's existence in order to vindicate rational morality, for only by believing that God exists, as the *summum bonum* (the highest good) to reward virtue and to punish vice, can there be adequate support for the obligations of morality. It requires only a small step from postulating God's existence, the fruit (for Kant) of an eminently rational activity, to projecting his existence for less than fully rational considerations.

Why, given the confident Enlightenment critique of it, does religion nevertheless persist? One characteristic 19th-century answer is that religious, and specifically Christian, belief, has no rational ground but that it persists because of the presence in all of mankind, except for an enlightened elite, of irrational belief-forming mechanisms.

Ludwig Feuerbach (1804-1872) claimed that endemic moral failure, and the experience of evil in its various forms, led mankind to postulate one who, because of his sympathetic and benevolent character, will compensate for the suffering and moral failure of the present life in the world to come.

Karl Marx (1818-1883) took up Feuerbach's theme and gave it a characteristic twist. It is because of the social class system – economic exploitation by one class of another – that men and women seek relief from this vale of woe by smoking the opium of religion.

In the work of **Sigmund Freud (1856-1939)** the same explanatory mechanism was employed in his speculations about sexuality and parental authority; religion

This image of God may show him as a benign creator, but is belief in him a hindrance to personal emancipation? And is he no more than a projection, an attempt to find comfort and compensation for the ills of this world?

compensates for the need for a father figure by projecting a Father-God.

For all these thinkers, religion is an abnormal human condition; the return to normality lies, for Marx, in the social revolution in which the class oppression will disappear and with it the need for the compensatory fantasies of religion; for Freud, it lies in psychoanalysis.

At times, it appears that such theories of religious belief are being offered as empirical hypotheses. Marx seems to suggest conditions under which his hypothesis might be falsified. But it seems that at other times any attempt to rebut such claims, whether by evidence or by a priori reasoning, would simply provide additional evidence for its truth in the eyes of its proponents.

This criticism of both Marx and Freud by Karl Popper, in his contrast of genuine and pseudo-science, is set out on page 107.

LUDWIG FEUERBACH
(1804-1872)
German philosopher. His most celebrated work is *The Essence of Christianity* (1841), which was extremely influential, not least on Marx.

' …even love, in itself the deepest, truest human emotion, becomes by means of religiousness merely ostensible, illusory, since religious love gives itself to man only for God's sake, so that it is given only in appearance to man, but in reality to God.'

Feuerbach

Freud saw, in the meticulous observation of religious rites and duties, a form of activity similar to the compulsive behaviour of his neurotic patients. He therefore believed religion to be a 'universal obsessional neurosis', motivated by guilt.

'The abolition [of religion] as the illusory happiness of the people is required for their real happiness.'

Karl Marx

Such approaches to religion sharply distinguish between what appears on the surface of human life and what is allegedly happening in the depths. Men and women have religious beliefs and may give a variety of reasons for holding them. But below this surface of reasoning the religious (and other) beliefs are fomented by drives or needs, and the workings of this belief-forming mechanism are known only to theorists with the necessary insight.

So all reasoning in support of religion is in fact rationalization; it is the offering of artificially fabricated 'reasons' for something for which there are not, and could not be, good reasons.

Marx argued that, if religion survived through the longing of those who were oppressed, it would not need to be overthrown by arguing for atheism, but rather, by creating a social revolution that would enable people to take responsibility for their own welfare and remove the causes of oppression. In such an emancipated world, religion would no longer be needed, and would therefore wither.

'Religion is the sigh of the oppressed creature, the heart of a heartless world, the soul of the soulless environment. It is the opium of the people.'

Marx, from the *Introduction to the Critique of Hegel's Philosophy of Law*

KARL MARX
(1818-1883)
Marx was first and foremost a German economist, born into a family of Jewish rabbis. He wrote his *Communist Manifesto* in 1847 and his magnum opus, *Das Kapital*, in 1867.

FOR FURTHER INFORMATION ON:

MARX AND HIS POLITICAL THEORY
SEE PAGE 324

FOR MARX ON:

HISTORY, PAGE 284;

ETHICS, PAGE 92.

Kierkegaard is an example of an anti-philosopher, one who sought to challenge the dominant philosophical and religious system of his day, Hegelian idealism, and by implication all other philosophical and theological systems. He took an ethical stance against all such systems, rather in the way in which anarchists oppose the rule of law.

In this he was part of a wider philosophical and theological temper, which emerged in the late 19th century. Just as Kierkegaard attacked intellectual systems as such, so Friedrich Nietzsche was bitterly hostile and scornful of what he regarded as the negativity of Christian ethics. He did not so much argue his position – in this he was a consistent anti-philosopher – as repudiate it with the aid of wit, aphorism and biting sarcasm.

As he saw it, systems of ethics such as Christianity and utilitarianism (see page 86) have an egalitarian, levelling-down bias. Nietzsche saw the Christian ethic of renunciation as a sign of weakness and expresses an unwarranted distrust of human instinct. (It is an interesting question whether Nietzsche was repudiating Christian ethics as such, or rather the ethics of renunciation of the German philosopher **Arthur Schopenhauer (1788-1860)**.)

Nietzsche identified two approaches to life, which he called the Dionysian and the Apollonian. The first is marked by vitality, intoxication, rhythm and a sense of oneness with nature; the second by order, clarity, self-control and detachment. Both are necessary to life and art, but Nietzsche stressed the primary importance of the life-affirming Dionysian instincts (which he later came to see as including some Apollonian elements). It is life-denial, characteristic of the Apollonian approach, which gives rise to the need for metaphysics to provide solace amid life's contingencies.

Nietzsche saw the opportunity for a new era of Dionysians, strong-willed, joyous

'Ah, brothers, this God which I created was human work and human madness, like all gods!

'He was human, and only a poor piece of man and Ego: this phantom came to me from my own fire and ashes, that is the truth! It did not come to me from the "beyond"!'

Nietzsche, from *Thus Spake Zarathustra*

For some 'death of God' thinkers, God emptied himself to become man in Jesus, and died on the cross. The incarnation was taken to indicate that, for Christians, 'God' had ceased to exist as a transcendent reality, and that people should seek the reality that had been 'God', within humankind.

FRIEDRICH NIETZSCHE
(1844-1900)
German philosopher and philologist, who taught at the University of Basle, retiring in 1879. His writings have an aphoristic, poetic, ironic quality. Among his chief works are: *The Birth of Tragedy*; *Thus Spake Zarathustra*; *The Antichrist*; *Beyond Good and Evil*; *Daybreak: Thoughts on the Prejudices of Morality*; *Ecce Homo: How One Becomes What One Is*; *The Gay Science*; *Human, All Too Human: A Book for Free Spirits*; *On the Genealogy of Morals*; *The Will to Power*.

and powerful, to emerge: the Supermen.

In a passage entitled 'The Madman' in his *The Gay Science* the madman reports that God has been killed by humanity. Whatever the phrase 'the death of God' meant for Nietzsche it was seized upon in the 1960s by 'death of God' theologians and made to mean various things, including a view of the Incarnation in which God, in becoming man, died when Jesus was crucified. It also served as the basis for the proclamation of a kind of secular, religionless Christianity.

SEE ALSO NIETZSCHE ON:

ETHICS, PAGE 93

HISTORY, PAGE 287

> *'A rule of thinking which would absolutely prevent me from acknowledging certain kinds of truth if those kinds of truth were really there, would be an irrational rule.'*
>
> William James

WILLIAM JAMES (1842-1910)

An American psychologist and pragmatist philosopher, who taught at Harvard. His philosophy, in such works as *Pragmatism* (1907) and *A Pluralistic Universe* (1909) was mostly written for a wide public and has an accessible, attractive style. He is probably best known for *The Varieties of Religious Experience* (1902).

Writing in the 17th century, Blaise Pascal claimed that faith was not chiefly a matter of having a reasonable belief based on evidence. Even in the absence of evidence, the issues of faith were so important, that whether to 'believe' or not, was not a decision that could be shelved.

The idea that the will can play a significant role, both in coming to hold erroneous beliefs and in correcting them, ultimately goes back to Descartes.

A similar emphasis upon the will can be found in the American philosopher **William James (1842-1910)**. James argued that religious faith could never be simply a matter of evidence. For one thing, the evidence is never all in. But faith cannot be indefinitely postponed, for it is a practical matter.

In this claim, James was revealing his colours as a Pragmatist philosopher. For him, in general, the importance of philosophical disputes lies in the various alternative positions that they offer us.

> *'As a rule we disbelieve all facts and theories for which we have no use.'*

James was not saying that evidence is of no importance in religion; he was not a total irrationalist. In science, for example, he stressed that the possession of evidence was all that mattered.

But faith, at least faith of a certain kind, was a live option. By this James meant that it had presently operational consequences; it had 'cash value'. It was not a matter of dead controversy as is, say, the idea that mental illness is caused by the phases of the moon.

It was also a momentous option, for it concerned our whole view of life, and perhaps of life beyond the grave. Most importantly of all, perhaps, it was a forced option. For if we ignore the claims of faith, trying to be neutral or 'objective', then we are in effect taking the side of rejection.

James is a good example of someone whose religious views are 'fideistic', based primarily on faith, not reason. This does not mean that he rejects the use of reason or evidence, for he provides both arguments and evidence that the will is important in religion.

In *The Varieties of Religious Experience* (1902) James provided a significant treatment of religious awareness, claiming that religious experience offering a unique kind of cognition, which cannot be reduced to other modes of knowing.

SEE ALSO JAMES ON: MIND, PAGE 134

For a pragmatist philosopher, religion is a choice to be made about the whole of life, with immediate consequences. It is a live and relevant option for this life, not a matter of detached debate. It has consequences for the way we live.

'It is high time we philosophers took the Design Argument seriously. Whether the evidence of fine tuning points to multiple universes or to God, it does do some exciting pointing.'

John Leslie

Some proponents of Darwinian evolution claim, as did **Charles Darwin (1809-1882)** himself later in his life, that the idea of random natural selection excludes the possibility of divine design. They also claim that human rationality and sensibility, including of course religious sensibility, are merely the products of the processes of random mutation in environments that are sufficiently favourable. They survive even though they might fulfil no useful function.

The argument that the theory of evolution has usurped the idea of design, has intensified in the 20th century. By contrast, it has been held by some that the idea of 'fine tuning', that the laws of nature are such that even if they were only very slightly otherwise they could not support life, might now play the role of what, in the 18th century, **William Paley** referred to as the 'contrivances of nature', and so provide evidence for the existence of a designer, God.

'Fine tuning' does not imply that the universe had to exist in precisely the form that it does. Much less does it mean that the universe, this universe, could not have failed to exist.

If such a 'final' explanation of why the universe exists, and of the precise physical form that it takes, were to be possible from within science, then although God might exist he would have no role to perform. It would in principle be impossible to prove his existence by an appeal to the contingency of the universe. But it is hard to see, given that the universe might not have been, that it could carry the explanation of its existence within itself. Others argue that science and metaphysics converge in stressing that everything that begins to be, including the universe, must have a cause.

These debates between faith and scientific reason, often of an extremely speculative turn, can be said to be new phases of old debates about the perennial question: is the universe just there, or is there some explanation for its physical character, and for its very existence?

Could there be a scientific answer to these questions, an explanation that is in some sense internal to the character of the universe, or is it a mistake to expect any such answer? Or must there be (or might there be) an explanation in terms of the existence of God?

The fundamental philosophical issue in all of these debates is over naturalism, over whether everything that exists could be explained naturalistically. Can the human mind be explained naturalistically, reducing consciousness to brain processes? And can the universe be explained from within itself, or is it reasonable to look for an explanation in terms of some extra-natural agency?

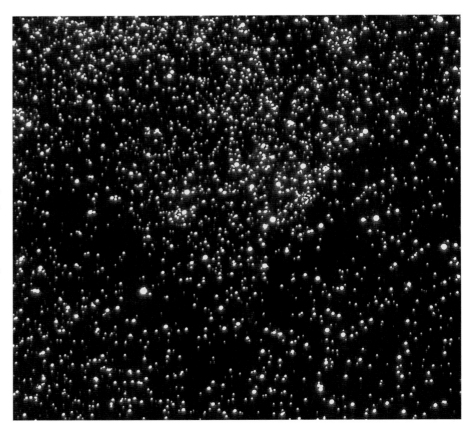

Ultimately, the quest of science is for an explanation of everything. What implications would the success of such a quest have for religious belief? Does the universe require an explanation beyond itself?

'To say that "God exists" is to make a metaphysical utterance which cannot be either true or false.'

A J Ayer

There is a close connection between human thought and the language we use to learn and express what we have learned. So philosophers have paid particular attention to issues about language when people attempt to speak and write about God.

Some understanding of the powers and limits of language is crucial to assessing what results we can expect from our reason. In religious language, sometimes the stress is placed on the non-literalness of theological language, or on the idea of divine transcendence, and this has led to a form of theological agnosticism.

This concern with language took a sharper turn in the 1930s and 1940s with the claim made by the **Logical Positivists** that all metaphysical language, including the language of religion and value, was cognitively meaningless. They claimed that the only truths are scientific truths, or those that are merely rules of language.

The claims that God exists, or that he is good (or that he does not exist, or is not good) say nothing that could be true or false, because such utterances cannot be verified by sense experience. Because such language is in principle scientifically uncheckable, it asserts nothing. And because it asserts nothing, there is nothing for reason to assess, or for faith to believe.

Many have argued that this claim rests upon a confusion between the truth of claim, and the evidence which we may (or may not) possess for its truth, and that in any case the verification principle is itself hardly a self-evident truth.

One important consequence of the stress (against the Positivists) on the centrality of truth-conditions (and not verifiability conditions) for meaning, and rejection of the view that all necessity is a matter of rules of language, has been a re-birth of theistic metaphysics. There has been a renewal of an interest in natural theology, in the divine attributes, and in God's relation to time, which has established important connections with pre-Kantian philosophical theology.

The Logical Positivist episode generated two other more unusual developments in religious language. One of these appeals to the cultural relativism, and especially the linguistic relativism of all our thought forms, including those of religion and theology. It nevertheless advocates the continued use of theological language for *non-cognitive* purposes. On this view, the fact that religious language is fictional is no great loss, for its value does not lie in its claim to be true, but like parables or other fictions, it provides a focus for our religious attention, moral motivation, or self-understanding.

A second development arising out of Logical Positivism appeals to certain ideas of **Ludwig Wittgenstein (1889-1951)**, particularly his account of the meaning of language in terms of language-games, or forms of life. These ideas have been used to develop what might be called an 'internalist' account of meaning and justification in religion. This would argue that it is a mistake, in principle, to attempt to understand religion in terms of concepts brought from outside – concepts of science or metaphysics, for example. Religion has its own criteria of meaning and truth, and these must be respected.

'When we first begin to believe anything, what we believe is not a single proposition, it is a whole system of propositions. (Light dawns gradually over the whole.)'

Wittgenstein *On Certainty*, 141

A J AYER
(1910-1989)
Wykeham Professor of Logic in the University of Oxford, from 1959 to 1978. Among his key publications are *Language, Truth and Logic* (1936); *Philosophical Essays* (1954); *The Problem of Knowledge* (1956).

SEE ALSO AYER ON:

LANGUAGE, PAGE 214

ETHICS, PAGE 69

FOR FURTHER INFORMATION ON WITTGENSTEIN, SEE PAGES 42-44, 215

AND ON LOGICAL POSITIVISM SEE PAGES 43, 214

The 17th century was the time of the greatest conflict between the claims of reason and revelation. But the 20th century has also been marked by a renewed interest in the idea of divine revelation and by fresh controversy. Theological liberalism, standing in the tradition of Immanuel Kant, thinks of revelation, if it had use for the idea at all, as arising from within the human consciousness, in the human sense of the divine, or the feeling of absolute dependence, or in commitment to certain ethical values.

Following the First World War, **Karl Barth (1886-1968)** and **Emil Brunner, (1889-1966)** the 'theologians of the Word', asserted (against the theological liberalism of their day) the primacy of divine revelation. God's word breaks into human consciousness from outside.

There is thus a sharp element of discontinuity, of fracture, between God's revelation and the normal operations of human reason. It is, Barth and Brunner (and many other imitators) claimed, the absolute duty of human reason to submit to God's revelation.

But it has seemed to many that such an understanding of revelation effectively insulates it from any critical scrutiny. How are we to know, from among the many claims to possess a revelation, which – if any – is the true one? And how are we to interpret it?

Other philosophers have approached the idea of revelation from what might be called a Lockean perspective, or even on the model to be found in much medieval discussion. On this view, the idea of a supernatural revelation builds upon natural theology. Given the reasonableness of believing that the universe is created by a powerful and good God, it is also reasonable (they claim) to suppose that such a God would wish to communicate to the human race more directly. And with regard to any purported revelation 'reason must judge' (as Locke put it) whether that revelation meets a set of reasonable internal and external criteria for being a revelation.

Problems remain. The problem of particularism: how is it that only some have the benefit of such a revelation? And how is it that a purported revelation such as the Bible is open to such a variety of interpretations? And there is the problem of pluralism. What is to be said of the fate of those who have not and who never will benefit from the teaching of such a revelation, or whose revelation is the Koran or the Book of Mormon?

KARL BARTH
(1886-1968)

Barth taught at Gottingen, Munster and Bonn, where he was dismissed in 1934 for opposing Hitler. He then held a Professorship at his native Basel for the rest of his career. His major work is the multi-volume *Church Dogmatics* (1936-61).

There has always been a concern, within the philosophy of religion, to strike a balance between the particular claims of religion and the more general understanding of human reason. For example, Aquinas sought to utilize Aristotle in service of Christian truths. But religion appeals to more than reason, and requires commitment and a distinctive view of life. Revelation makes demands. The preacher (here, Wesley) cannot simply present a range of philosophical options for reason to evaluate.

The problem of evil has come to be one of the most hotly debated topics in modern philosophy of religion, though the roots of the discussion go back to the debates of Hume, Leibniz and others in the 18th century and beyond. Contemporary interest, not surprising, in view of the horrors experienced during the last century, includes both the suffering inflicted by human beings on one another, or that which arises from natural calamities.

How can an all-powerful, all-loving God allow evil?

Surely if evil exists, this must be either because God is not all-powerful, or not all-loving, or both. Besides the obvious option of atheism, there have been three main lines of response to this challenge.

One has stressed the importance of human freedom. Moral evil, at least, is due, it is claimed, to the abuse of human freedom. Not even God could create free individuals and at the same time ensure that they only ever do what is right. For then they would not be free, but automata. God values freedom in his human creatures more than anything else, and is even prepared for some people to pay the price of the Holocaust to ensure it. In response, some have questioned the coherence of this idea of freedom, or whether it can reasonably account for the amount of evil, or whether possessing freedom could really be of greater value than the existence of a universe in which the Holocaust and other such evils were made impossible.

A second approach argues that God may allow evil for a greater good, and perhaps there are goods which only the existence of moral evil can make possible, goods such as compassion, mercy and patience. (If one thinks of human freedom itself as one of these goods, then this approach can be combined with the first). In the quote given at the top of this page, Augustine sees God's goodness even in his allowing evil. But is it not criminal to suppose that the Holocaust is

'God does well even in the permission of what is evil.'

Augustine

permitted for such reasons? But perhaps God, in permitting the Holocaust and other such evils, has reasons that we cannot think of, and perhaps could not think of. But if so, does this not suggest that the 'goodness' of God might bear little or no relation to goodness as we normally understand the term?

A third approach is to reject any attempt at justifying God's ways, or even

of offering a defence against the charge that God's existence is inconsistent with the existence of evil. Evil is intrinsic to our understanding of religion, and religion would be unintelligible if it did not include attitudes to the unexpected contingencies of life, including inexplicable evils. The appropriate religious response to evil is not to attempt to explain it, but – like Job – to submit to it.

There are many forms of evil that present a challenge to anyone claiming to believe in a loving God. The deliberate humiliation of human beings is one of them. Here, under the Nazis, Jews are forced to do crude, manual labour, scrubbing the streets, watched by a mocking crowd. Where is God when this happens? Is hatred and cruelty that price we have to pay for the freedom also to love?

'What the traditions severally regard as ultimates are different and therefore cannot all be truly ultimate'

John Hick

The idea that human reason and divine revelation might together provide a set of objective truths about God and the destiny of the human race, has raised problems about the many rival claims of the 'great religions'. The novelty attributed to the awareness of such diversity can, of course, be exaggerated. In their missionary and evangelistic endeavours, Christians and others have long been acutely aware of the existence of religions other than their own, and of the fact that these religions flourish at a deep level.

But exaggerated or not, the fact of a plurality of religions raises an epistemological issue. How can anyone be entitled to make claims for the objective truth of their religion and therefore for the objective reality of the God of that religion, given the many religions of the world?

Given that we know that there are numerous competing and incompatible religions, how can anyone be confident that one's own religion is the true one, since, no matter what reasons we might give for the truth of one's own religion, practitioners of other religions can do exactly the same?

It has been argued – for example by **John Hick (b.1922)** – that the great religions of the world have basically one message, to turn people from self-centredness to other-centredness, and that each of them are, at best, failing attempts to express the divine, the Real, which is beyond all human conceptuality.

So one cannot reasonably be confident of one's own religion to the exclusion of all others, but must allow that the great religions are equally valid, though perhaps not equally valuable, ways of approaching the ultimate divine reality that lies beyond all knowledge.

But such an approach, while apparently tolerant and irenic, in fact sets up an exclusivism of its own, and in so doing distorts the claims of the religions themselves. The adherent to some particular religion or other can surely support his or her position with good reasons, while all the time recognizing the possibility of being mistaken in so doing. In this endeavour, the pluralist is in a no more comfortable position than the exclusivist.

It is easy to appreciate beauty, whatever the religious tradition within which it is expressed. Here, for example, is the gateway to the tomb of the Emperor Akbar at Sikandra. Its inspiration is clearly Muslim, yet it can be appreciated by those of all religions or none. Equally, a Buddha image may be universally acknowledged as expressing serenity, and a medieval cathedral as the embodiment of the quest for the transcendent, with its sweeping gothic arches. It is not the reality of religious and cultural diversity that creates problems, but the fact that religions beliefs are expressed in the form of propositions which their followers assert to be true. Once that happens, there is scope for disagreement and incompatibility.

'If there is other evidence which makes it quite likely that there is a God all powerful and all good, who made the Earth and its inhabitants, then it becomes to some extent likely that he would intervene in human history to reveal things to them.' Richard Swinburne

One important strand running through the philosophy of religion, some would say the most important strand, concerns the issue of natural theology. Can the existence of God be proved from premises acceptable to any rational person?

Some have claimed that the development of positive natural theology is both possible and indispensably necessary in order for faith to be reasonable. Others have argued that natural theology is possible, but that it is not necessary for establishing the reasonableness of religious belief. Some, such as the *fideists*, have argued that it is neither possible nor necessary. And finally some, the religious sceptics, have argued that it is necessary but not possible.

A more fundamental point has also been made: that in discussion of the 'proofs' of God's existence, a standard of proof has been demanded greater than for the existence of anything else. Most people think that it is reasonable to believe that there is a past, but is there a convincing proof of this?

These debates have continued vigorously in the 20th century. Philosophical critics of the reasonableness of religious belief have usually started from the assumption that natural theology is necessary but not possible. A prominent instance of those who argue that natural theology is both necessary and possible is **Richard Swinburne (b.1934)**, who has revived and developed a form of the argument from design, combining it with an appeal to religious experience.

'There are many conditions and circumstances that call forth belief in God: guilt, gratitude, danger, a sense of God's presence, a sense that he speaks, perception of various parts of the universe.'

Alvin Plantinga

RICHARD SWINBURNE
(c.1934)

Nolloth Professor of the Philosophy of the Christian Religion at the University of Oxford since 1985, his key publications are *The Coherence of Theism* (1977); *The Existence of God* (1979); *Faith and Reason* (1981); *The Evolution of the Soul* (1986); and *The Christian God* (1994).

Alvin Plantinga (b.1932) has become an influential in arguing that natural theology is possible but not necessary to establish the rationality of religious belief, holding that a person is within his intellectual rights to have the proposition that God exists among the set of foundational beliefs that he possesses. Plantinga appeals to certain insights of the Reformer **John Calvin**, particularly to his idea that everyone possesses a *sensus divinitatis*.

But there are other patterns of rational belief; for example, a pattern that stresses the accumulation of pieces of evidence, as occurs in the solving of a crime or a crossword puzzle. Such positions offer a natural theology of a weaker kind, appealing to the accumulation of various types of evidence to justify and make religious belief reasonable, without claiming that the result ought to, or will, convince the sceptic.

ALVIN C PLANTINGA
(B.1932)

John A. O'Brien Professor of Philosophy at the University of Notre Dame, his most important books are *God and Other Minds* (1967); *The Nature of Necessity* (1974); *God, Freedom and Evil* (1974); *Warrant: The Current Debate* (1993); and *Warrant and Proper Function* (1993).

THE PHILOSOPHY OF RELIGION
PHILOSOPHY IN EASTERN RELIGIONS

HINDUISM

Hinduism is often described as a way of life rather than a religion, implying that it is a system of belief, moral principles and a practice of social and ethical and ritual behaviour, which characterizes and directs every aspect of life. Thus there is an underlying philosophy of life, which is expressed in personal attitudes and behaviour, social and family relationships in private and public spheres.

Within Hinduism, the common ground of religious philosophy gives coherence to the great variety and diversity of belief and practice. The religious teachings and insights which are formally expressed in sacred scriptures are regarded as the truths of philosophy, and so religion and philosophy are so intertwined that in India the study of philosophy implies the study of religious scripture.

BELIEF IN GOD OR GODS

The Hindu understanding of the nature of God is expressed in its Vedic scriptures and popular religious literature. In these texts, we can trace an evolving concept of God, which develops from fertility symbols in the Indus valley, to personification of the forces of nature in the Rig Veda, to creative forces or principles as expressed in the Hymn to Purusha.

The later Vedic hymns reveal a questioning about the origins of all creative forces, which is resolved in the emergence of the concept of Brahman in the Upanishads.

There are many hymns to Indra, who is the embodiment of the tremendous powers of nature in storms and thunder. Scholars have speculated about the similarities between Indra and the Nordic god Thor.

'I will extol the most heroic Indra who with his might forced earth and sky asunder... surpassing rivers and floods in his greatness.' Rig Veda x.89

Sometimes, stories of the gods and of creation are linked directly with the structure of Hindu society. Thus, in the famous 'Hymn to Purusha', or the Sacrifice of Primal Man, the gods divide up Purusha into parts, each of which represents one of the main Hindu caste groups:

The hymn then goes on to describe how his breath becomes the wind, the navel gives off the atmosphere; his head becomes the sky and his feet the earth.

The term 'Brahman' is rooted in the Sanskrit word meaning 'to give forth or bring forth' and is elevated into the idea of a life giving energy pervading the whole material universe.

This notion is given concrete expression in the OM symbol, and the three deities: Brahma, Vishnu and Shiva.

Brahma is the creative force of Brahman, **Vishnu**, the preserving maintaining and harmonizing aspect and **Shiva** the destructive and re-creative aspect.

These three aspects of Brahman can be understood either as different manifestations of the one ultimate truth or literally as three deities.

The notion that the manifestation of the ultimate source of life can take any form is expressed in the nine 'avatars' of Vishnu. As the preserving deity, he needed to maintain the order of the cosmos by intervening in earthly history and events, whenever the forces evil and chaos prevailed, by taking on an animal or human

And when they divided primal man Into how many parts did they divide him ?... The Brahman was his mouth. The arms made the prince, His thighs the common people And from his feet the serf was born.

form and descending to earth.

Krishna is one of the most popular avatars of Vishnu and is worshipped as a God in his own right. Stories about him are found in popular mythology as well as in the *Mahabharata* (the great epic of India), which reveals his unique qualities as a bringer of righteousness, and a teacher of a spiritual path to ultimate liberation.

The many forms and manifestations of God in human and animal form as well as in various natural phenomena such as rivers, trees and mountains give rise to a unique phenomenon in Hinduism: the paradox that God is both one and many. The images of the deities (called murtis) seen in temples and village shrines are recognized as containing the spiritual presence of the ultimate reality of Brahman, and can act as channels of divine energy to the devotee.

'You are man you are woman; you are youth and maiden too. You are an old man who totters along leaning on a stick. You are born with faces turned in all directions. You are the dark blue butterfly and the parrot with red eyes. You are the thunder cloud, the seasons and the oceans. You are without beginning and beyond all space and time. You are He from whom all worlds have origin.'

Svetasvatara Upanishad IV.3-4
(This and other quotations are from the translation of the Hindu scriptures by Dominic Goodall.)

The temple of Jagganath at Puri

THE NOTION OF SALVATION AND HUMAN DESTINY

In Hindu religious philosophy there are two possible destinies: re-incarnation or *moksha*. Moksha is the final goal of life in which the essential spiritual self or atman is released from the bondage of material existence and the seemingly endless cycle of rebirth (*samsara*) and attains a state of complete knowledge, freedom and bliss. Re-incarnation – or the transmigration of souls – is a process of continuous rebirth of the self (*atman* or soul) into a new and different physical form including animal, human and godly forms, according to deeds and moral character in the previous existence.

The fundamental question 'What happens to us after we die?' is directly confronted and answered in a variety of ways in Indian religious philosophy.

The early Vedic hymns suggest a destiny after death in a heaven or hell as a recompense for good or evil deeds. This notion was elaborated into a more sophisticated doctrine of reincarnation in the Upanishads.

The Brahmana texts refer to a fear of a renewed death, and many rituals are prescribed in order to escape it, whilst immortality is seen as the state beyond the possibility of renewed death.

The chief texts that set forth the doctrine of transmigration of souls, are found in the *Chandogya* and *Brihadaranyaka Upanishads*. In the latter, we are given an interpretation of the Hindu view of death in which all the physical elements of the body merge into the various aspects of the natural world, and all that remains is the energy of karma, which determines the nature and conditions of the next existence.

As the person's senses grow dim, his or her inner spiritual self gets stronger. With the loss of each of the senses, the Upanishad affirms that the dying person 'is becoming one'. Thus the essential self, soul or atman is released from the body and gathers strength and energy to itself in order to take on another form of existence.

It is described using the wonderful image of the caterpillar on a blade of grass:

'*As a caterpillar, drawing near to the end of a tip of a blade of grass, prepares its next step and draws [it]self up towards it, so does this self striking the body aside and dispelling ignorance (avidya) prepares its next step and draws [it]self up for its plunge into the Brahman world.*'

For many Hindus, their religion is expressed chiefly through the practice of *Bhakti*, or devotion. Here a family takes part in the Arti ceremony at a small shrine set up in the home.

And in the following verse, the imagery changes, and the process is likened to that of a goldsmith melting down a golden object to forge it into some new and more beautiful form.

In both images, the self enters into death, as part of a process of change and transformation, facing the unknown, as it looks forward to some new form of life.

However, the destiny of rebirth is not the final goal of life and repeated and renewed death can be seen as a curse. In the early Vedic hymns, the ultimate wish is to be in union with the Vedic gods (the state of *moksha*). The *Chandogya Upanishad* presents this alternative destiny of the 'way of the gods' or 'becoming one with Brahman', as the destiny of the forest dweller, as opposed to the destiny of the village dweller, which is to be born again.

In this, the notion that the spiritual life, seen in a rejection of worldly concerns, is presented as a more certain way of reaching *moksha*, for the forest dweller is prepared for such a move, but the village dweller, with more mundane concerns, is not.

This state of *moksha* is described in

> '*As streams flow and disappear in the ocean,*
> *Abandoning name and form ,*
> *So the wise, freed from name and form,*
> *Enter into that supreme divine spirit.*'
>
> Mundaka Upanishad

various ways in Indian religious philosophy. The more monistic scriptures describe it as a state of consciousness, knowledge and bliss, whereas the more theistic scriptures describe it as union with a personal god.

The inner self, or *atman*, is the reality of Brahman dwelling within the living being; so discovery of this true nature is self-realization and the final goal. Later Vedantic philosophy describes the goal of *moksha* as *sac'c'itananda*, i.e. being (*sat*), mind (*c'it*) and bliss (*ananda*).

Each human form of existence provides an opportunity to move towards the ultimate or final goal (*moksha*), when the essential self (*Atman*) can merge with the ultimate being (*Brahman*). This goal requires a strong and unequivocal

commitment and focus on spiritual development, through adopting one of the *yogas* or disciplines:

There are three *yogas*, or traditions of spiritual practice:

Karma yoga is the discipline of worldly action, with a clear sense of moral responsibility, selflessness, detachment and concern for the welfare of others.

Bhaki yoga is a way or surrendering selfish and worldly desires by focusing heart and mind fully on the worship and love of God. This implies that the saving grace of god will assist the devotee in his aspiration for union with god.

Jnana yoga is cultivating the mind to lead to insight and self realization, through meditation and contemplation of scriptures.

THE PROBLEM OF SUFFERING AND EVIL

In response to the questions 'Why does suffering exist in the world?' 'Why do some people suffer more than others?' and 'What is the source and nature of evil?' Hindu religious philosophy would answer in terms of *karma* and *samsara*:

KARMA

The meaning of karma is 'actions' or 'works' and refers to the law of cause and effect, which applies to all aspects of nature and existence. The consequences of thoughts, words and deeds determine the conditions of one's present and future life.

Every thought, word and deed will produce a positive or negative reaction, either in this life or in the next. Thus, the present conditions of one's life and even one's character, temperament and disposition towards goodness are determined by previous actions. The law of karma enables Hindus to understand suffering and good fortune in a person's life.

SAMSARA

Until complete purity of mind and full knowledge is realized then each living being is caught in the trap or curse of *samsara*, i.e. a seemingly endless cycle of birth, death and rebirth in the physical and material world.

'Those whose conduct on earth has given pleasure, can hope to enter a pleasant womb...'

Thus, those who have done good deeds in this life, hope to enter a womb that will see them born into conditions of happiness and comfort, not simply as recompense for what they have done here and now, but as a preparation for the next step on the route towards *moksha*.

DHARMA

The way to overcome any evil tendencies in human nature is to keep to the *dharma*, the prescribed moral duties, and seek *moksha* though one of the prescribed paths of *yoga*. Hindu religious philosophy clearly states that each living being is responsible for their own destiny according to the extent to which they live in accordance with dharma.

Dharma is a moral and religious law in which fundamental truths and righteousness are preserved. It is translated variously as 'duty', 'religious law' 'ethics', 'justice and rights'. In the early Vedas, it refers to correct performance of ritual, but in later scriptures – especially the *Dharma shastras* or the *Manu smriti* – it refers more generally to the obligation one has to ones position in society, that is, one's caste or class obligation, and duties appropriate to one's stage in life.

Dharma is also understood in a more universal way as *sanatana dharma*, which means the 'eternal principle' of goodness, honesty and purity in all personal, social and religious matters.

Why do some live in poverty, or suffer disease? Does the concept of *karma* give an adequate answer? What might Marx say about the hope for a better life in the future?

FOR FURTHER INFORMATION ON BOTH DHARMA AND KARMA, SEE THE SECTION ON HINDU ETHICS, PAGES 72 – 73

Buddhism is a religious tradition rich in cultural diversity, with a common ground of religious philosophy. Historically, it began in India 2500 years ago with the teachings of Siddharta Gotama, known as 'The Buddha' (i.e. the awakened or enlightened one). However Buddhists regard the teachings of Buddhism to be more important than the historical founder and many different schools of thought and scriptures developed as Buddhism spread from India in to South East Asia, the Far East, and Tibet.

The main forms of Buddhism are Theravada and Mahayana, although they can be better understood historically and geographically as Southern Buddhism (Theravada) in Sri Lanka, Burma, Cambodia, Laos and Thailand, Eastern Buddhism (Mahayana) as practised in China, Japan, Korea and Vietnam and Northern Buddhism (also Mahayana) in Tibet and Mongolia, Sikkim and Bhutan.

When Buddhism became established in other cultures, some of its teaching and practices were influenced by indigenous beliefs and cultural traditions. So there are some differences in their accepted scriptures, their conception of the Buddhist goal and of the nature of divine beings.

BUDDHA

The word 'buddha' simply means one who is awake and has the wisdom to know the *dhamma*, or basic truth of things. In one sense, anyone is a buddha who has achieved the goal of the Buddhist path. However, such a being is seen as having cosmic significance as 'one who has fully known the right way' and as such is extremely rare.

The focus of religious attention and commitment is therefore expressed in commitment to three 'refuges':
the **Buddha** (the enlightened one),
the **Dhamma** (teaching, and basic truth)

and the **Sangha** (community of the Buddha's disciples).

Mahayana Buddhists believe that many Buddhas have existed both before the historical Buddha and in other world systems. The three forms of the Buddha are:

1 the underlying Buddha nature within living beings,
2 the glorious and celestial manifestations of this Buddha nature,
3 its earthly manifestations.

There are also *Bodhisattvas*, who are thought of as beings who have already attained enlightenment, but are available for others to call upon to help them in their own path to enlightenment. In Far Eastern Buddhism the notion of the Bodhisattva shares some of the characteristics of the saving God of Western religions.

In the Pure Land Buddhism of China and Japan the principal Bodhisattva is Amida (Japan) or Amitabha (China). According to this Buddhist tradition the appeal to Amida at the moment of death, or concentration on Amida for ten moments, or faith in the efficacy of the

vow of commitment to Amida, are believed to cancel the karmic consequence of evil deeds and lead to re-birth in the Pure Land.

The *Lotus Sutra*, a most important scripture for Mahayana Buddhism, states repeatedly:

'There is only one way, not two or three, and that way is devotion to Amida.'

FOR FURTHER INFORMATION ON:
BUDDHA SEE PAGE 55
SEE ALSO BUDDHA ON:
THE NATURE OF REALITY, PAGES 54-55.
ETHICS, PAGES 80-81
EDUCATION, PAGE 232
IN ART, PAGES 272-273

THE NOTION OF SALVATION AND HUMAN DESTINY

In Buddhism, each living being determines its own fate, as every act of will in thoughts, words and deeds bears fruit in some future condition: good deeds produce good fortune; bad deeds, bad destiny. This is the law of *kamma* (or *karma* in Sanskrit), which is seen as a natural law inherent in life and all living beings.

So, rather than environment or genetics, its 'the law of *kamma*' which determines human destiny, creating the particular conditions of life into which living beings are born, including their material and social conditions, physical condition, mental capacity, character and temperament.

It is said that actions rooted in hatred tend to lead to rebirth in a hell realm, actions rooted in delusion lead to rebirth as an animal and actions rooted in greed, to rebirth as a ghost. Actions rooted in kindness and generosity lead to rebirth in the human or heavenly realm while development of meditative insight and wisdom leads to rebirth in the highest heavens. The various realms may be understood either literally, as places of material existence, or as psychological or mental states.

Buddhist cosmology consists of numerous world systems, which are interpreted both literally and symbolically. They are found within three realms: the realm of the senses, the fine material realm and the immaterial realm.

So, rather than salvation, the ultimate and final goal for all living beings is *nibbana*, freedom from the bondage of the law of karma. This final goal, which may take many lifetimes to attain, is described in the Theravada tradition as the cessation of suffering, without attachment, without craving.

The term 'Nibbana' is probably derived from a root meaning 'to extinguish' and this has sometimes led to the mistaken view that the Buddhist goal is non-existence. The extinguishing in 'nibbana' refers to the fires of greed hatred and delusion. Once these fires are extinguished, a person may be released into a state of full knowledge and bliss.

However, this can only be attained when there is a total letting go of attachment to views, feelings and the ego, for it is attachment, or craving, that creates more fuel for the fires that need to be extinguished.

THE THERAVADA PATH

In Theravada Buddhism, the *arahant* is one who has achieved the goal of Nibbana. Having destroyed the defilements of greed, hatred and delusion, such a person is free from future rebirths and has three unsurpassable qualities: vision, practice of the way, and deliverance.

> '**He is one with taints destroyed , who has lived the holy life done what has to be done, laid down the burden, reached the true goal, destroyed the fetters of being and is completely liberated through final knowledge**'
>
> *Majjhima Nikaya 1.51.*

The Suttas describe the various stages in the path to *nibbana*:

The first stage is preparatory, this-worldly, or mundane. In this, the follower embarks on the path and develops virtue, concentration and wisdom. Depending on emphasis, some are seen as 'faith followers' and others as 'dhamma followers'. For the latter, wisdom is seen as the dominant faculty to be cultivated.

At a certain level of maturity, followers can embark on the supramundane path. They may become 'stream enterers' who have entered the 'stream ' of the noble eight-fold path, which carries them irreversibly to Nibbana, the timeless unconditioned realm which the arahant finally enters at death, but which can also be fully experienced during life. A 'stream enterer' (who has unwavering confidence in the Buddha, Dhamma and Sangha, and unblemished morality) is free from adverse rebirths and will become an arahant within seven lives.

By deepening insight a 'stream enterer' may become a 'once returner', in other words, a person with only one life to go before final release.

The 'non-returner' is one who has destroyed sense-desire and ill-will, and

In the earliest phase of Buddhism, there were no Buddha images, but only symbols depicting the Buddha – as, for example, his footprints.

This may reflect the conviction that Buddhists should follow the Buddha's teaching (Dharma or Dhamma) without clinging to particular images of the Buddha. Later, with the development of a more devotional strand within the Buddhist tradition, a variety of images were developed, reflecting various aspects of the Buddha-nature, and expressing aspects of enlightenment.

who therefore need not be born again into the world of sense-desire, but only in one of the most refined heavens.

Finally, the arahant has destroyed all remaining fetters and attachments. With no more rebirths, the arahant is ready for the bliss of Nibbana.

THE MAHAYANA PATH

Whereas Theravada Buddhism stresses that human destiny is totally dependent in the individual's own volitional actions, in Mahayana it is possible to call upon the aid of *bodhisattvas* in the quest for enlightenment.

There are various levels of Bodhisattva:

The term can refer to an ordinary being who aspires to strive for buddhahood, and out of has compassion his taken the Bodhisattva vow to alleviate the suffering of others. In other words, to become a buddha for the sake of all sentient beings.

The term can also be used of a 'Celestial Bodhisattva', a 'Great Being' (*Maha-sattva*) or heavenly saviour-being who magically projects himself or herself into many worlds to help and teach beings.

Or, finally, it can refer to a fully perfected Bodhisattva, dwelling in the highest heaven in perfect omniscience.

One of the most important Bodhisattvas in Mahayana Buddhism is **Avalokiteshvara**, a Sanskrit name that means 'the lord who looks in all directions'. He is the embodiment of compassion. He is often depicted with a thousand arms and a thousand eyes, which expresses the idea that he is able to see all the suffering of humanity and respond instantly to all who call on his name.

He often has a child on his arm, and appears with feminine characterises. In China, he takes female form as **Kuan Yin**, the all-compassionate mother goddess. In Japan this female form is known as Kannon.

In Tibet, as Chenrezi, he is the protector of the land of the snows who becomes present in different individuals, to initiate or sustain buddha-teaching. Successive Dalai Lamas are regarded as incarnations of Avalokiteshvara.

In China and Japan, the Bodhisattva of Compassion is depicted in female form. Here, as the Chinese Kuan Yin.

THE PROBLEM OF SUFFERING AND EVIL

Buddhism claims to offer a coherent and convincing explanation of the nature and cause of suffering. It is contained in the 'law of *kamma*', which describes how past deeds determine present and future conditions.

A fundamental concept here is *dukkha*, which has been rather crudely translated as 'suffering' although it has wider implications than the English word. It is the first of the **Four Noble Truths**, which Buddhists see as a profound teaching, not easily understood without the preparation of moral and spiritual development.

The structure of this teaching is likened to the process by which a physician (the Buddha) cures a disease (suffering), and involved four stages:

1 The first truth is dukkha: the suffering to which all conditioned beings are subject.

Dukkha is the basic unsatisfactoriness of life, which is subject not just to physical and mental anguish – as expressed in the four sights (old age, disease, death and an ascetic) which were said to set Siddharta Gotama on his quest for enlightenment, but the impermanence and transitoriness of everything. Even happy or blissful states are said to include dukkha, since they are only temporary. In his first sermon, known as 'the turning of the Wheel of Dhamma' the Buddha expressed the first truth thus:

'Birth is dukkha (suffering), ageing is dukkha, sickness is dukkha, death is dukkha, sorrow lamentation pain, grief and despair are dukkha, association with what one dislikes is dukkha, separation from what one likes is dukkha, not to get what one

THE THREE UNIVERSAL MARKS OF EXISTENCE

The three basic features or marks of existence in Buddhist philosophy are *dukkha*, *anicca* (impermanence) and *anatta* (the absence of a permanent self or soul). It is delusion – the inability to see, understand and accept these truths – that Buddhism sees as the root cause of suffering.

wants is dukkha, the five groups of grasping which make up a person are dukkha.' Samyutta Nikaya

2 The second of the four noble truths claims that craving, attachment or desire (*tanha* – literally 'thirst') is the cause of suffering. It is seen as craving for pleasure, for being or for non-being. 'Being' refers to attachment to and hopes for immortality and eternal life, 'non-being' to a nihilisic rejection of any meaning or purpose of existence. In this, Buddhism offers the interesting psychological insight that the deliberate rejection of what appears to be good, can be a form of greed.

This second truth is expressed in a more extended teaching called paticca-samuppada (or dependent origination), which illustrates how present circumstances are due to past acts according to the law of kamma. Starting with ignorance, there follows an inexorable process of being driven by craving and attachment in the cycle of samsara.

It may be presented in the form of the nidanas, 12 links in a chain of causality:

1 Ignorance gives rise to
2 Activities, which gives rise to
3 Discriminating awareness, which gives rise to
4 Mind and body, which gives rise to
5 The six sense bases, which gives rise to
6 Sensory stimulation, which gives rise to
7 Feeling, which gives rise to
8 Craving, which gives rise to
9 Grasping, which gives rise to
10 Existence, which gives rise to
11 Birth, which gives rise to
12 Ageing, death, sorrow, lamentation, despair and grief.

According to the Buddha's teaching, all beings (except enlightened ones) are subject to 'renewal of being in the future

Even within its monastic traditions, the fact that Buddhist philosophy starts with the reality of suffering does not require unrelieved seriousness. Its goal is happiness and relief from suffering, and Buddhists are generally far from solemn.

rebirth'. This does not mean the transmigration of an eternal self or soul into another body, but the continuation of a process in which the various elements of present consciousness provide a basic pattern, which go to determine the nature and environment of another being in the future.

In other words, what we think of as the 'self' is a constantly changing bundle of elements, and that process of change happens both throughout this life and beyond it, into other lives.

3   The third 'noble truth' claims that a cure is possible through the cessation of craving, leading to a state called *nibbana* (or *nirvana*).

4   The fourth of the noble truths states that the way to ultimate freedom from suffering is the noble eight-fold path, which consists of:

1   Right Understanding
2   Right View
3   Right Action
4   Right Speech
5   Right Livelihood
6   Right Effort
7   Right Mindfulness
8   Right Concentration.

Of these, the first two steps concern wisdom – the perception of life in accordance with the Buddha's teaching and a commitment to exploring it. The next three steps define the basics of Buddhist ethics and lifestyle. And the final three steps describe the spiritual discipline that underlies the Middle Way. Namely, a constant effort to reinforce positive thoughts and eliminate negative ones, an attempt to be aware of present reality, and finally the practice of meditation.

It is called the Middle Way as it lies between the extremes of self-indulgence in sensual pleasure on the one hand, and asceticism, or self-denial, on the other. This reflects the life story to Siddharta Gotama, who experienced both indulgence in his life as a prince, and also asceticism in his spiritual quest before achieving enlightenment.

But there is another sense in which the Buddhist path is a 'middle way', namely that it provides a balance between eternalism and nihilism – neither denying the reality of things, nor seeking to ascribe to them permanent or inherent existence.

The concept of suffering, or the general unsatisfactoriness of life as we experience it, is therefore central to Buddhism, not in the sense that the Buddhist path welcomes suffering or accepts it as inevitable, but in that it represents a systematic attempt to face up to the reality of human limitations, and to overcome the suffering that they bring. In particular, it sees the illusion of a separate self, independent of the rest of the world, as the cause of those attitude that trap an individual into a cycle of craving, grasping and suffering.

BUDDHISM AND BELIEF IN GOD

It is commonly assumed in the West that Buddhism is atheistic, in that there is no belief in an ultimate and transcendent reality or supreme being. Theravada Buddhism certainly teaches that there is no reality corresponding to the Western concept of God, that can be relied upon for salvation, but accepts a belief in devas, or divine and celestial beings, who may dwell in a kind of heavenly realm, but who (like human beings) are still subject to the cyclic process of rebirth. Thus, although Buddhist scriptures may refer to 'gods and men', the term does not have the same meaning or significance as 'God' in the theistic religions.

In the Buddha's day there were 'forest dwellers' who stood apart from society in order to follow the spiritual life. Today, Buddhists may still go into 'retreat', setting themselves apart for a set period of time, in order to practice solitary meditation.

The Jains take their name from the term *jina* which means 'conqueror'. It is an honorific title given to twenty-four great religious teachers (called Tirthankaras — 'crossing-maker' or 'Fordmaker', because their teaching provides the ford or crossing by which people can cross over to salvation).

Mahavira, considered to be the 24th and final 'Fordmaker', lived and preached in the Ganges Valley in the fifth century BCE, at about the same time as the Buddha. All the earlier 'Fordmakers' are mythical.

Thus, although Jainism can be considered to have existed for 2500 years, Jains themselves consider their teachings to be eternal.

Mahavira's teachings were to some extent a reaction to practices and beliefs of the time, most notably (in common with the Buddha) to the belief that spiritual progress depended on correct performance of caste duties, status and brahminical rituals.

Jains see the universe as eternal and uncreated, and (like Hindus) conceive of time in terms of vast cycles. A full cycle consists of two main periods of some 600 million years each. One of these is a time of ascent, in which conditions will improve, the other is as time of descent, in which knowledge, behaviour and human stature decline. Twenty-four *jinas*, are believed to appear within each cycle.

GOD AND THE DESTINY OF THE SOUL IN JAIN THOUGHT

There is no supreme or creator God within Jainism. The *jinas* are not gods, but are worshipped as if they are divine beings. Jains talk of God as the sum of the *jinas* and other liberated souls, which blend together into a single soul.

The destiny of the soul is based on the Jain understanding of karma, and the nature of the *jiva* (the essential self or soul) within all living beings. In its pure state the *jiva* is pure knowledge and bliss, but in living beings, this is tainted by the effects of karma. The jiva is the real personality of the individual. It leaves the body at death and finds another body. The Jains believe that every living thing, from a single cell creature to a human being, is basically a *jiva*.

Since Jains believe that they have passed through many different forms, and in countless lives to come will pass through many more, they place great emphasis on *ahimsa*, or non-violence.

Jains believe in the law of karma, whereby present action affects future conditions. Unlike Hindus and Buddhists, however, they do not think of karma as an immaterial force, but as tiny material particles, which permeate the whole of the universe and flow into the *jiva*, or soul of the individual, a process known as *asrava* or inflow. Just as a virus may enters the body and cause illness, so karma particles cause an illness of the soul.

The aim of the Jain spiritual path is to stop this inflow and to shed particles already accumulated. The key to this is to get rid of all passion, anger, pride deceit and greed.

The *jiva* is believed to have the ability to comprehend all knowledge and to experience total tranquillity. This total knowledge (*kevala jnana*) is limitless in scope, and unrestricted by space or time, a complete and simultaneous understanding of the universe. The individual who attains this state while living in the world is known as an *arahant* who, on leaving this body, enters the ultimate state of *moksha*.

THE PROBLEM OF SUFFERING AND EVIL

Jains believe that unfortunate conditions in this life are due to misdeeds in a previous existence, and that the way to get rid of the harmful effects of karma is to live a pure life based on:

- Right faith
- Right knowledge
- Right conduct

Right conduct requires the practice of the five virtues:

1 ahimsa (non violence)
2 truth speaking
3 non-stealing
4 chastity or restraint in sex
5 non-attachment to material possessions.

To Jains, non-violence is the supreme ethical principle (*ahimsa paramo dharmah*) and a rule of life. A Jain layman, **Rajchandra Metha 1867-1901** was an important influence on **Gandhi**. It was through him that Gandhi became dedicated to the Jain principle of non-violence.

The aim of *ahimsa* is to avoid harm or suffering to the tiniest living being. This has many practical implications for the Jain way of life, in regard to their livelihood and diet. They are strict vegetarians and avoid eggs, alcohol (due to active agents in fermentation process) and root vegetables (because they contain tiny microscopic life).

Lay Jains (as opposed to those in the monastic orders) may practice self-discipline in a variety of ways, through daily rituals and meditation. For example, the supplementary vows a lay person may take include vowing to reduce attachment to material things by giving up certain foods or other objects of use for a fixed period of time, or to practice meditation two or three times a day, or to fast on certain days of the month.

The Jain understanding of the universe involves different levels of life, and these give some insight into the more desirable destinies for the soul after the end of this life, and also those that are likely to be encountered as the result of misdeeds.

The swastika, which is an ancient Indian symbol, is used to indicate the four levels of life into which a being can be reincarnated. They are:

1 Underworld (*adha loka*) – the abode of hell creatures.

2 Earthly or terrestrial world (*madhya loka*) – for humans, animals and plants.

3 Celestial realm (*urdhva loka*), the abode of heavenly beings (but not, of course, an all-powerful God, as in Western traditions).

4 The abode of liberated souls (*siddha loka*).

FOR FURTHER INFORMATION ON JAIN ETHICS, SEE PAGE 71

The Parasnath Jain temple in Calcutta. Although there is no creator God within Jainism, devotion is paid to the Jinas, and their images – which, in their simplicity and serenity, are similar to those of the Buddha in the early (Theravada) tradition – are housed in temples, whose elaborate architecture may contrast with the simplicity of the images found in them.

The main teachings of this philosophy are derived from a variety of scholars and philosophers from the sixth century to the second century BCE. **Tsou Yen** was the first to formulate the Chinese scientific view if the universe, based on the two universal energies of *Yin* (dark, female etc.) and *Yang* (light, male, etc.). His ideas inspired later Taoists such as Lao Tzu (sixth and fifth centuries BCE) and Chuang Tzu, whose writings are the fundamental mystical and theoretical sources for religious Taoism.

CHINESE PHILOSOPHY AND RELIGION

Among the many schools of philosophy that developed within China, three traditions are central to the Chinese philosophy of religion: Confucianism, Taoism (with its two strands of mystical philosophy and religious ritual and practice) and Buddhism.

Although distinctive in matters of belief and practice, these three systems of thought blend together within Chinese religion and culture. Taoism and Confucianism are fundamental and complementary within Chinese culture. A Confucian would ask 'What should I do?' whereas a Taoist would ask 'What kind of person should I be?'.

Thus, Confucianism is primarily concerned with social etiquette, cultivating humanity and following the rites that can embody truly humane qualities. Taoism is more concerned with the personal, religious and mystical aspects of the individual. Indeed, there is an element of non-conformity within Taoism which is unthinkable in the Confucian tradition.

The naturalness and simplicity of the Taoist ideal fitted well with the spirituality of the Buddhist tradition, when it arrived in China. Since none of the three spiritual and philosophical traditions demands exclusive allegiance, the Chinese have been contend to practice them alongside one another. All three – each with its own particular emphasis – has fed into China's ongoing cultural and artistic tradition.

BELIEF IN GOD/GODS

Taoism does not postulate the existence of an all-powerful god or deities, but regards the Tao as the fundamental source of life and order, and the guarantor of stability. To live in accord with Tao is to realize this order, nature and stability in one's own life.

In the *Tao-te-Ching* the classic 'Book of Tao and Te', 'the dark gate of the female' is the origin of all things. This is an allusion to an ancient belief in the earth or water goddess who gives birth to all things and takes them back after death.

That from which all being originated was therefore 'not being', and the conclusion was reached that all beings must finally revert back to the earth. The ancient goddess was replaced with a conception of a silent, unmoving energy, from which all movement and existence originates and then returns. So the notion of the goddess as the progenitor of all things is replaced by the philosophical term Tao.

*'Something mysteriously formed
Before heaven and earth.
In the silence and the void,
Standing alone and unchanging,
Ever present and in motion.
Perhaps it is the mother of ten thousand things.
I do not know its name.
Call it Tao .
For want of a better word, I call it great...
Man follows the earth.
Earth follows heaven.
Heaven follows the Tao.
Tao follows what is natural.*
Tao te Ching

HUMAN DESTINY AND SALVATION

The *Tao-te-Ching* suggests a non acquisitive, natural and harmonious life, through which the sage (a keyword in Chinese philosophy) may help create a stable, harmonious world. The book (only 5000 words long) can lead to deepest mysticism but is can also be seen as a practical guide to survival in times of trouble.

Religious Taoism, which grew out of the original, rather minimalist philosophy, developed rituals with seasonal liturgies and temples to the innumerable Chinese gods. Taoist monasteries and nunneries sprang up, due to later influences of Buddhism.

The notion of *ch'i* (vital energy) is fundamental to the magical/scientific side of Taoist thought and practice. In Chinese medical terms it is classified according to yin and yang qualities, the interdependence of which are illustrated by the *t'ai chi* symbol (see page 82).

The yin-yang theory governs the rituals of Taoism. The Chinese conception of the universe implies the yang realm of light in the heavens, and the yin realm of darkness and underworld.

Much magical Taoism is concerned with increasing one's *ch'i* to maintain or improve health, to live longer and even, in some schools, to attain physical immortality. Various types of yoga, including sexual yoga, were practised to these ends.

The life of simplicity is a spiritual ideal in Taoism, but is equally promoted by other religious and philosophical systems. Perhaps, the life of simplicity, suggests a mountain hut and pasture high in the Alps; a place of silence, with time to reflect and measure the ever-changing seasons. Perhaps some other place, remote from the pace of urban life, is percived as a spiritual haven. Yet it is not external circumstances, but inner peace, that is a mark of being at one with the Tao.

Although there are plenty of Taoist legends and fairytales about afterworlds – including a paradise in the far west and a hell underground – Taoism, like Confucianism, concentrated on this life rather than on the next.

The more mystical tradition of Taoism is expressed in the Taoist ascetic tradition as the practice of 'heart-fasting' and 'sitting in forgetfulness'. The method of emptying the mind of all judgements and concepts, and the heart of all desires, is a prerequisite for realizing the presence of the transcendent Tao.

The *Tao-te-Ching* attempts to describe the experience of union with the transcendent Tao in terms of nature using the symbols of water and wind:

Water is best of all.
Without contention,
It does good for all things,
It goes to the lowest place, that others avoid.
Because of this it is closest to Tao.

'To win the world, one must renounce all.
If one still has private ends to serve,
One will never be able to win the world.' *Tao te Ching,* **chapter 48**

Although many Taoists did withdraw from society to remote mountains or forests to meditate, the true mystic does not have to become a recluse but can help and heal others. True goodness is measured by the bringing of interior peace and blessing to all who come into contact with the Tao.

'Be like Tao…
Make little things important
Make the few many
Requite anger with goodness…
Polite and thoughtful, when invited as a guest,
Sensitive as ice beginning to melt;
Simple as an uncarved block of wood,
Unspoiled as a wild valley meadow,
Cleared of mud and silt like a placid pond.
One can only keep this kind of Tao
By not getting too full,
Staying new and fresh like sprouting grass.'

Confucian teachings and values have had a profound effect on the moral, social, religious and political life of traditional societies in the Far East. Confucianism is almost synonymous with loyalty, moral integrity, ritual correctness, self-restraint and respect for elders, ancestors and teachers.

Confucius is the Western version of the name of the Chinese sage **K'ung Fu Tzu (551-479) BCE**. Confucianism is not a religion, but the traditional view of life and code of manners of the Chinese gentry (i.e. scholarly bureaucrats and rulers) for more than 2000 years before the communist revolution of 1911 swept away the old regime.

The common Chinese term for followers of these traditional values is *ju* (or *ru*), meaning 'scholar', and educated followers of the Confucian school are called *ju-chia*. The writings of Confucius and other scholars who upheld these values are referred to as the **Confucian Classics**. They provide a system of government and rules of behaviour for members of the governing classes.

HUMAN DESTINY AND SALVATION

This way of life assumes that the natural world is a reflection of the ideal society. All that happens on earth is due to the decree of heaven and all things have a regular course to follow the Way of heaven: the succession of day and night; the sequence of the four seasons; the harmonious conduct of father and son, ruler and minister, husband and wife, friend and friend. 'All under heaven' (meaning the world as it appeared to them, consisting of China and its neighbours) is under the Emperor, the 'son of heaven' who owes his power to the decree of Heaven. If this harmony is maintained, the moral power of the emperor, and of his rituals, have

immediate and magical effects on the natural and social orders.

It is assumed that as long as the imperial government follows the way of heaven, as long as proper sacrifices are performed by the Emperor to Heaven and earth, by his magistrates to the mountains and rivers, and by families to their ancestors, there will be peace within the empire and natural conditions will be favourable.

But bad omens, flood, famine, and rebellion are indications of heavenly disapproval, and the heavenly mandate to the emperor may be withdrawn. Thus dynasties can be overthrown. The purpose of human conduct is therefore to develop and improve moral qualities.

Mencius (fourth century BCE), the second most important Confucian teacher, had an optimistic view of life, claiming that all human beings had an innate capacity for goodness. He argued that Heaven (*t'ien*) produces in human beings four potentials that define human nature: benevolence, propriety, practical wisdom and proper behaviour.

He developed the notion of vital energy (*ch'i*), as a fundamental factor in moral cultivation. The purpose of learning is to recover the lost mind/heart (*hsin*). Ch'i can be nurtured and accumulated by the sustained performance of moral actions. Once it is discovered, it becomes a means of moral reflection and a means of stilling the mind and focusing the will.

As for Confucian attitudes to survival after death, their standard view is that humans have no business except with the living, and should not concern themselves with what happens after death. Sacrifices to ones ancestors ensures their survival, but should be regarded as an expression of respect rather than a magical act.

BELIEF IN GOD OR GODS

Ideas of divinity are almost irrelevant to Confucianism. For Confucius, moral

principles were elevated to the highest level. His central doctrine was that of *jen*, variously translated as goodness, benevolence and humanity. He believed *jen* to be a universal virtue, and that human nature could be perfected through the cultivation of this quality. Although he did not teach about god, he believed that his own teachings came from the divine Mandate of Heaven. Confucian sages are revered for their wisdom but not deified, and temples in China and Japan are dedicated to Confucius' memory.

'Heaven is the author of the virtue that is me.'

Analects **7.23**

The nearest Chinese notion to spiritual reality is *shen*, the Chinese word for spirit. In ancient China this referred to the spirit of an ancestor, which enjoys an afterlife because of the continuing and periodical sacrifices offered to it from members of his or her family. *Shen* is not immortal, because it is contingent upon continuing offerings. In Confucianism, gods are not only imaginary, but irrelevant. The moral code is fundamental and does not need the support of an appeal to religious sanctions. The way of heaven is taken for granted as part of the natural order:

Chi-lu asked about the service of the spirits. The master said 'Until you can serve men, how can you serve spirits?' When he said, 'I should like to ask about death', the Master replied 'Until you understand life, how can you understand death?'

Analects xi,11

Confucian values and philosophy have had an indelible impression on Chinese culture, surviving the challenge of the Cultural Revolution in the 1960s. The work ethic, family loyalty and respect for social superiors are all part of the legacy of Confucianism to the contemporary Chinese world.

When asked for a definition of wisdom, Confucius said:

'Devotion to ones' duties as a subject, and respect for the spirits while keeping them at a distance, may be called wisdom.'

Analects vi, 20

FOR CONFUCIAN THINKING ON:	
ETHICS	SEE PAGE 84-85
EDUCATION	SEE PAGE 236
ART	SEE PAGE 275
HISTORY	SEE PAGE 281
POLITICS/LAW	SEE PAGE 297

Formality, a sense of the right ordering of society and the promotion of stability and family life; these Confucian values dominated Chinese society until the early years of the 20th century, and are still immensely influential.

LOGIC

Logic is concerned with the principles of valid inference; in other words, it seeks to distinguish good arguments from bad.

Traditional logic begins, like so much else, with Aristotle, and more or less ends in the 20th century with Russell, Whitehead and Godel.

LOGIC IN ANCIENT TIMES

Aristotle, in the works known as *Organon*, distinguished between two types of arguments, namely, demonstrative and dialectical arguments.

In demonstration we start with true premises and arrive with necessity at a true conclusion. In dialectical argument the premises are not known to be true, and so there is no necessity that the conclusion be true. Proofs of theorems in geometry formulated by the Pythagoreans and **Euclid (c.330-260BCE)** are some of the earliest examples of such logical demonstration.

The *Organon, Interpretations* and *Prior Analytics* contain Aristotle's most important work on logic. One of his important contributions in *Prior Analytics* is the introduction of variables into logical discourse.

Aristotle's logical system is known as 'syllogistic', from the prominence it gives to syllogisms. He defines a syllogism as a discourse in which, from certain propositions that are laid down, something other than what is stated follows from necessity.

For example, the syllogism that in traditional logic is called the Barbara syllogism, takes the form:

All B is A;
All C is B;
Therefore, all C is A.

By setting out such syllogisms, Aristotle wanted to show the form that a valid argument could take. Once the form is understood, using variables, it is a straightforward step to apply it to actual arguments.

To give an example, one can argue (following the Barbara syllogism) as follows:
All humans are mortal
All Greeks are human
Therefore all Greeks are mortal.
He classified the syllogisms (he called them figures) based on the position of the middle term. He then gave a proof that two of the syllogisms (Barbara and Celarent) implied all the other syllogisms.

Aristotle's last contribution to logic was modal syllogistic. This is the study of syllogisms that examine the way we reason concerning things that are either possibly the case, or necessarily the case.

It is crucial in logical argument to know whether the conclusions follow of necessity from the premises, or are only a possible consequence of them, and so modal logic looks at the different claims that can be made about the necessity of conclusions.

Aristotle's work was continued and extended by his pupil **Theophrastes**, who contributed to modal syllogistic and developed the theory of hypothetical syllogisms, which anticipated the work of Megarian and Stoic logicians on the logic of propositions.

MEGARIANS AND STOICS

The Megarian school was founded by **Euclides of Megara**, a former pupil of Socrates. **Diodorus Cronus** of this school developed modal concepts involving past, present and future. **Philo of Megara (4th-3rd centuries BCE)** formulated the truth-functional definition of implication. He argued that an implication is true in three ways and false in one way. It is false if its antecedent is true and the consequent is false.

As distinct from the Aristotelian logic of terms, that of the Stoics was a two-valued logic of propositions. They divided propositions into simple and non-simple, and propositions were either true or false. Denial was true if the denied proposition was false and false if the denied proposition was true.

(In other words, if I say something is wrong and it is indeed wrong, then I am right; but if it is right, then I am wrong.)

They followed the truth-functional definition of implication given by Philo. Logical connectives (such as conjunctions), which occur in various types of non-simple propositions, give rise to logical principles. The Stoics represented these by an inference schemata, which they called indemonstrables (their equivalent of Aristotle's syllogisms) from which other inference schemata could be derived.

For example, the first of the five inference schemata set out by **Chrysippus (280-207BCE)**, one of the Stoic philosophers, is this:

If the first then second; but first; therefore the second.

Galen, who lived more that two hundred years after Chrysippus, drew from the world of Aristotle as well as the Stoics to write his book *Introduction to Dialectic*.

INDIAN LOGIC

Indian grammarians were interested in making descriptions of spoken language. They developed a 'metalanguage' of grammatical instruction, and used metarules to delineate the domains of metalanguage and object language. **Patanjali** applied logical principles such as contradiction and contraposition in his analyses.

Mimansa philosophy systematized the interpretation of Vedic rules by metarules. They analysed various possible negations of prescriptions and delineated the validity of various logical laws such as the law of contradiction of the different cases.

FOR FURTHER INFORMATION ON
ARISTOTLE, SEE PAGE 27

The Old Nyaya School of logicians focused on classification of meanings of words, or things to which words refer, as well as perception and inference. Their basic form of inference was the syllogism consisting of five members, the standard example of which is:

1 The mountain possesses smoke;
2 Where there is smoke, there is fire, as in a kitchen;
3 (This mountain) is similar (that is, it possesses smoke)
4 Therefore, (it) is similar (that is, it possesses fire).

'Metalanguage' is language that describes the use of language. 'Metarules' are rules for using rules.

Many activities in life require logic, planning, and an assessment of possible outcomes. It is the ability to think logically that distinguishes between a good and a bad chess player. You make a move, thinking that your opponent's counter-move will follow from necessity. Your opponent considers whether what you intend is indeed a necessary outcome, or only a possible one, able to be deflected to provide other possible outcomes. You don't need to understand formal logic to play chess, but the mental operations you are performing during the game are of interest to the logician.

5 The mountain possesses fire.

Buddhist logicians considered perception and inference to be the only means of achieving valid knowledge. They used complex analyses of quantified conditional statements to understand the relation between the 'reason' and the 'thing to be inferred'. They made many contributions to formal logic, particularly in the areas of *reductio ad absurdum* and infinite regress.

The New Nyaya School extended and developed the earlier work on analysis of inference. Formal rules, whose validity depended only on the structure of the sentences used, were established.

BUDDHIST, MIMAMSA AND NYAYA LOGIC FOLLOW FROM THEIR BASIC VIEWS OF THE NATURE OF REALITY, SEE ABOVE PAGE 58.

CHINESE LOGIC

The central school in Chinese logic is that of the **Moists (3rd century BCE)**. In the Moist Canons they considered questions of the form

'Is it or is it not the case that...'

They further argued that it is self-contradictory to deny or affirm all propositions. Thus, the statement 'All statements are mistaken' implies that it itself is mistaken, but one cannot 'reject rejection' without refusing to reject one's own rejection. Hence:

'All statements are mistaken' is self-contradictory.

They divided names into three types, 'unrestricted', 'of kinds', and 'private'. Take an example of a dog 'Fido' – that applies to a single, private example of a kind (namely, 'dog') and also of a broader category ('animal').

For each type of name, therefore, its use sets the boundaries for what does or does not get included – it selects the way we divide up reality. Hence, the term 'dog' excludes cats, but the term 'animal' applies equally to both.

The Moist logicians (although they were working more with general linguistic theory than what would be regarded as logic in a Western context) saw philosophical disputes arising from differences in the way these different names were applied.

In general, they took a realist view of language. In other words, they saw distinctions in the terms used as reflecting real differences in the experienced world.

FOR INFORMATION ON **MOIST ETHICS**, SEE PAGE **85**.

'Suitable for vegetarians' Fine, but can there be further differentiation? Some foods (e.g. cheese and eggs) will be acceptable to some vegetarians but not to vegans, who eat no animal products at all. A selection of food can therefore be divided in various ways, and be categorized accordingly, perhaps by use, by food type – vegetables, pulses etc – by country of origin even. These divisions are essential for language and logic, since the way we choose to divide up reality will affect the truth or otherwise of the claims we make. But is reality actually divided in any of these ways? Is it not merely the way we choose to see things, for our own convenience? Chinese logic has been particularly concerned with the correct use of terms, and with what is and is not excluded from the category of things to which they refer.

Distinctions of this sort are far from pedantic. For example, one can claim to be vegetarian, but what does that imply? Does fish count as meat? What about animal products like milk and cheese? The statement that someone is or is not a vegetarian, will therefore depend not on some internal logic, but on the way in which that term divides up reality.

Hence the separate term 'vegan' is used to specify a category, within the more general term vegetarian, for those who eat no animal produce of any sort.

It may also be disputed whether those who eat fish should be able to call themselves 'vegetarian'. Thus the truth of a statement is closely linked with the precise way in which its terms divide up experienced reality.

A further development of these issues, debated between **Hui Shi** and **Zhuangzi** in the fourth century BCE, concerned whether reality itself displayed divisions, or whether reality was essentially one and undifferentiated (Hui Shi's position) and therefore any divisions reflect our use of words, but not the reality to which they point.

For example, one might debate whether a shrub can grow big enough to be considered a tree – does nature itself make any difference in kind between shrubs and trees, or is that simply a reflection of human linguistic distinctions?

MEDIEVAL LOGIC

During the Middle Ages a formal and linguistic approach to logic flourished and was developed by many logicians from France and England.

The Aristotelian logic of terms was reconstituted from Arab sources (especially Averroes) from the 13th century onwards, and the laws of inference and syllogism were grounded on a general theory of implication.

Modal logic was developed far beyond its Aristotelian origins, and various logical paradoxes involving semantic and syntactical problems of an advanced sort were investigated, with the liar's paradox receiving considerable attention. (In other words, the dilemma, outlined above, that

to say that everything one says is a lie, is self-contradictory.)

Some of the important logicians of this period were, **Peter Abelard, William of Sherwood**, **pseudo Scotus** (an unknown author), and **William of Ockham (1285-1347)**, the English friar nicknamed the 'More than Subtle Doctor'.

Ockham famously framed 'Ockham's Razor' which states:

'Entities are not to be multiplied unnecessarily.'

In other words, if there are a number of possible explanations for something, it is logical to opt for the simplest. If there are other factors to be taken into account, these can be brought in only if the simplest explanation proves to be inadequate.

It is difficult to overestimate the influence of Aristotle's logic for the philosophy of the medieval period. Scholars were required to study both grammar and logic, and the latter was based on Aristotle's syllogisms. Hence, his logic lies behind most medieval philosophy and theology, as we have already seen in the section on the Philosophy of Religion, where the Ontological Argument of Anselm and the Cosmological Arguments of Aquinas owe much to Aristotle.

It may be particularly interesting to consider Leibniz' contribution to logic in the context of his general view of the nature of reality and of human knowledge.
His 'decomposing' of composite concepts into ultimate simples, parallels his discussion of the 'monads' of which all are comprised.

MODERN LOGIC

The last three centuries have seen numerous and dramatic developments in logic. Here we outline some of the important contributions.

The earliest contribution to modern, or 'mathematical' logic, was that of **Gottfried Wilhelm Leibniz**. He developed a universal language and a calculus of logic, assuming that composite concepts can be decomposed into a number of ultimate simples, just as an integer is uniquely decomposable into its prime factors.

The other major early contributor was **Bernard Bolzano (1781-1848)**, the Bohemian mathematician who introduced many important metalogical notions such as compatibility, dependency, exclusiveness, and derivability with respect to a given class of terms.

Some of the important developments after this came from England. **Augustus De Morgan (1806-1871)** introduced the well-known rules for negation of conjugation, which are now known as the De Morgan's laws.

George Boole (1815-1864), the Irish mathematician, wrote the groundbreaking booklet *Mathematical Analysis of Logic*, in which he introduced the algebra of classes, with which he analysed syllogisms and showed that it could also be used to perform a calculus of propositions.

FOR LEIBNIZ, SEE ALSO PAGE **30**.

LOGIC AND MATHEMATICAL REASONING

The goal of **Gottlob Frege's (1848-1925)** early work was to codify the logical principles used in mathematical reasoning. He axiomized classical propositional calculus for this purpose. In this book *Die Grundlagen der Arithmetik* he cleared up many of the earlier misconceptions and confusions about the nature of numbers and the laws of arithmetic.

His later works dealt with, among other things, the theory of cardinal numbers. Frege wanted to show that all mathematics derived from logical premises, and therefore that Mathematics and Logic were overlapping disciplines. Frege also made it clear that logic was concerned with objective truths about the world, not simply about the way in which human minds think about it.

The Italian mathematician, **Guiseppe Peano (1858-1932)** argued that acceptability of mathematical propositions should not depend on its intuitive plausibility, but instead on its premises and definitions. He is best remembered for 'Peano's Postulates', characterizing 'natural numbers' (0 is a number which is not the successor of any number; no two numbers have the same successor). Peano is also known as the founder of symbolic logic.

In *Principia Mathematica*, **Bertrand Russell** and **Alfred North Whitehead** set out to establish the logicist view, by deriving all of pure mathematics from a very small number of logical concepts and principles. In this project they drew on the works of Frege, Peano and **Georg Cantor (1845-1918)**.

The intuitionist conception of mathematics was developed by **L E J Brouwer (1881-1966)**. In classical mathematics, to know the meaning of a statement, it is sufficient to know the conditions under which the statement may be true or false. For the Intuitionists, only when we recognize the proof do we know the meaning. This leads them to require constructability of proofs.

The German **David Hilbert (1862-1943)** was the leading exponent of the Formalist philosophy of mathematics and

Although Bertrand Russell (1872-1970) contributed to many areas of philosophy, his early work (undertaken with A N Whitehead) was to show that mathematics was based on a small number of logical concepts.

he pioneered a development of logic known as Proof Theory. He stressed the axiomatic approach, and worked towards establishing the consistency (freedom from contradiction) of mathematics.

His idea was that the consistency of some given formalization of mathematics can be established if it could be shown that no manipulation of symbols which represents a passage from axioms to theorems could result in an absurdity such as $0 = 1$.

In 1931, **Kurt Godel (1906-1978)** perhaps the greatest mathematical logi-

cian, proved his celebrated Incompleteness Theorem. He showed that it was impossible to establish the consistency of arithmetic by methods that could be formalized within the systems themselves.

In other words, the formal system on which arithmetic is based cannot be absolutely proved to be correct from within its own logic. This is not to imply that normal arithmetical formulas are not proved correct, but that the formal axioms, upon which the whole sytem of mathematics is based, are unable to be proved.

A NOTE ON LOGIC

Unlike other sections within this survey of philosophy, it is clear that the study of logic and mathematics requires a more detailed examination of the way in which arguments are presented, and in particular the way in which formal symbolic logic is written out, than is possible here.

It is far from easy for the general reader, or even the practising philosophers working in another branch of the subject, to appreciate the subtleties of symbolic logic.

It would therefore be neither sensible nor possible to explore either mathematics or symbolic logic within the compass of this section.

Nevertheless, is should be appreciated that logic underpins all other branches of philosophy, in the same way that mathematics underpins the sciences, and is a key feature in, for example, cosmology.

Those wanting to explore this aspect of philosophy further should refer to more detailed books on, and original works by, those thinkers mentioned in this section.

At this point in our survey of world philosophy, it may be worth pausing to reflect on the process of philosophizing, and the part that logic plays within it.

Logic and mathematics are worked out with precision, and pages of symbolic logic may be quite unreadable by the uninitiated. This may therefore seem far removed from the process of thinking about the key issues in life, which is how most people start to philosophize. But is it?

Descartes went into his stove-warmed room and was determined to find the one thing he could not doubt, the starting point for subsequent philosophy. Perhaps his situation is not too far removed from that of the man portrayed below, sitting reflectively before his stove.

Nevertheless, the process of thought, which is examined with such careful attention in symbolic logic, is not so different from the normal working out of problems, sitting in front of a stove – it merely expresses in formal terms what counts as a good argument or a valid reason.

It is possible, or course, to spend a lifetime of reading and thinking without any knowledge of formal logic – just as it is possible to be articulate and poetic without any knowledge of grammar, or to enjoy music with no knowledge of composition or musical notation.

A modern Descartes?

Language reflects thought, which itself is influenced and moulded by language. It is essential both for expressing and working out ideas.

Socrates used language as a game to trap his opponents in their arguments, while other philosophers may view language as more purely functional and straightforward.

Language alone makes abstract thought and concepts possible, so all philosophy, at one level, is essentially about language. Equally, philosophical questions, whether of epistemology, metaphysics or ethics, depend on the definition of terms, phrased as 'What do we mean by x?' or 'It depends whether x is taken to mean y or z'.

The relationship between thought and language may seem baffling, even pointless, in a chicken-and-egg sort of way, to non-philosophers, but it is central to Western philosophy. The East has had very different ideas about language.

HOW WE SAY WHAT WE SAY

An awareness of the problems of language goes back to the early Greek philosophers. **Parmenides** gave us the first example of an argument from language to the world, saying that if we speak of a thing it must exist, and so, since we speak of the same thing at various times, it must continue to exist in some particular form. But only recently has language itself come to be studied in a systematic way, with the development of modern Linguistics in the 1960s and the Philosophy of Language earlier in the 20th century. **Bertrand Russell** admitted that, until he was in his 40s, he did not think about language *per se*, but regarded it as 'transparent'.

We need to distinguish between Linguistics and the Philosophy of Language. Linguistics is the study of language on all levels: its function, its vast diversity – more than 4,500 separate lan-

guages have been discovered so far – its history, grammar, breakdown of sounds and words, meaning, social use, physical and psychological origin and development. What linguistics discovers may be applied to philosophy, sociology, psychology, anthropology or physiology, but as a discipline of study, it remains independent of them.

The Philosophy of Language, as defined by the contemporary thinker **John Searle** (see page 218), attempts to analyse and give illuminating descriptions of general aspects of language, such as reference (how words relate to reality), truth, meaning and logical necessity. It is con-

cerned only incidentally with particular elements in a particular language. By contrast, Linguistic Philosophy tries to solve philosophical problems by analysing the ordinary use, meaning and relations of words in a particular language.

The divisions between these disciplines are not always clear-cut, but Linguistic Philosophy is a method, while the Philosophy of Language is a subject area; the method, however, may often be used within the subject area.

Searle also says that language is crucial to understanding human experience. **Wittgenstein** illustrated the dependence of experience on language with a

drawing of a triangle labelled with the words 'base' and 'apex'. These, he pointed out, meant nothing until their meaning was known. Only then could they give a different idea and experience of the triangle.

Some philosophers limit the Philosophy of Language to concerns about concepts and categories, but there are many other levels at which philosophy and language meet and interact. Thoughts about language, as well as illuminating philosophical method, also reflect or influence philosophical views on reality in ways very different from beliefs about concepts and categories. They affect views of language's relation to experience and mind. These will be examined in the sections on 'Language and Thought', and 'Innateness'.

Willard Quine (1908-), one of the most important American philosophers since World War II, stresses the importance of a linguistic approach to philosophy. By discussing the system of the language we use to assert a proposition, we are able to stand back from that system and note the way in which its structure is inherent in our way of thinking. By being aware of the structure of language in this way, we prevent it from becoming a barrier to the clear expression of thought.

The study of the Philosophy of Language may be approached in different ways: considering the relationship between language and its speaker (as opposed to the relationship between language and the outer world); considering language's nature or structure; or dividing it up by periods, thinkers or themes.

In this chapter, many of the themes to be explored have been examined by thinkers over wide periods of time, and many of the issues are bound up with one another. Hence the material is examined thematically, rather than chronologically, and philosophers who appear together in a section may not necessarily be associated in other contexts.

Language is inescapable. We cannot think without language. But do we shape our language, or does our language shape us?

There is little doubt about what it being communicated here. A couple in love display the nature of their relationship by gestures, body language, the way they stand, or walk, or touch one another. We may disbelieve what they say, if it is contrary to what we observe. Gestures often count for more than words.

In situations of frustration and tension, the same applies. The expression makes the need for description redundant. Yet once we are aware of the communication, we start to conceptualize and respond to it, but as soon as we do so, language creeps back in.

Plato and Aristotle had their own distinct views on the origin of language. Plato viewed the names of objects as being intrinsic to them, just as – in the case of onomatopoeia – a word may be intrinsically connected to what it describes by its sound ('splash', 'shriek', 'whisper' etc).

This is the most extreme view of correspondence between a word and its referent (what it refers to). Naturally this view can cause confusion, such as that displayed in **Aldous Huxley's** novel *Chrome Yellow* by Old Rowley who remarks, while watching pigs wallowing piggishly in mud:

'Rightly is they called pigs.'

Here Rowley has paired the term 'pig' with the referent (the pigs) in a way that suggests that the pairing is chosen arbitrarily but well (i.e. that 'pigs' is an appropriate thing to call them), whereas, of course, the pairing is an analytic process (see the later section on 'Analytic and Synthetic Propositions'), since the term 'pig' is defined with reference to the animals. So, is 'piggishness' something inherent to pigs, or simply a matter of how we choose to describe them?

Plato's theory of the divine origin of language (termed 'naturalistic') is

expressed in the *Cratylus* thus:

It is not surprising that Plato, who propounded the idea of universal Forms from which particular things take their character, sees all names as pre-existing in a greater reality. Obviously, this causes problems translating from one language to another. Even if we extend Plato's idea to argue that the words of different languages are simply particular examples of one 'universal language', we may ask which actual language contains the name that actually corresponds to that universal? (Doubtless the Greeks would have cited Greek!)

John Locke, in his *Essay Concerning Human Understanding*, supported Aristotle's theory that words were signs for ideas, and described them further as substitutes. This leads to the danger that the word rather than the idea might be fastened on to, and the idea misunderstood.

Locke proposed that we substitute the idea for the word. He did not accept that it was possible for a word to describe something abstract, only particular words stand for particular things. This, of course, reflects his theory of knowledge, in which everything we know has its origin in sense experience.

Like Plato, Aristotle also believed in the correspondence theory of truth, but for different reasons. He held the 'conventionalist' view that the connection

between words and their referents is purely arbitrary, i.e. established by human convention or agreement.

This arbitrariness is the more widely accepted today, but there is a problem: it requires a pre-existent language within which to make these arbitrary agreements about words and meanings.

Both approaches denote a correspondence theory of meaning, where each reference has a referent (that to which it refers). This was the approach taken by **Ludwig Wittgenstein's** *Picture Theory of Meaning* (1889-1951) in his earlier period. It is the result of a view of language based on the subject-predicate form, (as in the sentence 'John is king', where John is subject and king is predicate.) Here existence requires substance (which for Aristotle is the essence of a thing), in the form of properties that are not only attributable to it, but also contained in the word that describes it.

The problem of the need for a pre-existent language, to establish the pairing of word and referent, is picked up again in the problem of ostensive definition – defining a word by pointing to it. How do we explain which aspect of the object to which we refer is the aspect we wish to pick out?

As we saw in our 'Rightly is they called pigs' example, a word may have many different predicates attributable to it, but that which do we mean when we use the word?

For example, if I point to a house to explain the word 'house', am I pointing to a shape, size, colour or position in relation to the road? What am I actually pointing to? To explain this, I must then use other words to refine my definition.

'there is a correctness of name existing by nature for everything: a name is not simply that which a number of people jointly agree to call a thing.'

FOR PLATO ON THE FORMS, SEE PAGE **24**.
FOR LOCKE'S THEORY OF KNOWLEDGE, SEE PAGE **34**.

But then how do we explain these other words?

Implied in the idea of ostensive definition is the identification of the word with the word's true proposition, and with the state of affairs it describes. But this only leads to a closed circle of ideas – that a proposition is true because it corresponds to a true proposition. The problems with ostensive definition were raised by Wittgenstein in his later years and are partly answered by theories about inference (see page 219).

The object to which we make reference may be defined by numerous different terms, as **J G Herder (1744-1803)** pointed out. How then can we justify direct, one-to-one correspondence – either of so many to one, or of one to so many? How also do we deal with situations where a term describes something non-existent or only possible? What about subjunctive or conditional utterances, which describe non-existent or possible states of affairs?

Plato's Forms are a problem here. Although he put them forward as an answer to this dilemma (in that anything we can speak of already exists as a Form) this implies a world very crowded with imaginary objects.

Words are used to describe, but also to define. What of slang terms? These may be conventional, but also very limited within a particular social and political context.

And ostensive definition raises questions that require a constant selection of what counts as relevant. Does 'pig' refer to the quality of having a curly tail? Or standing in rows to eat? Or being pink skinned and fat? Or wearing no clothes?

The nature of language reflects the nature of our perceptions, and these are far from straightforward.

FOR WITTGENSTEIN,
SEE ALSO PAGE 42,
AND LATER IN THIS CHAPTER, PAGES
215-217.

These piglets may indeed be greedy, but they are at least eating in a vaguely orderly fashion, and – since they all have their heads in the trough – one could not complain that the greed of one deprives others of needed food.

Perhaps it is a pity then that 'pigs' get a bad linguistic reputation here – expressing behaviour that is far removed from their natural desire for food!

Might it not be possible to change the implications of the word 'pig', by emphasizing that some pigs – as here – are hardly being treated as individuals, with the ability to select their food or other necessities, but have everything provided in a communal 'trough'. If so, consumers of mass-produced goods might be labelled 'pigs', as a term referring to their acceptance of the standard fare, rather than to any sense of greed.

Franz Brentano (1838-1917), an Aristotelian-inspired metaphysician and phenomenologist, developed a theory of *intentionality*: that every mental phenomenon has a relation of direction to its object, i.e. perceptions, desires, imagination etc. are related to what is perceived, desired or imagined.

This becomes a theory of meaning, in that the sounds of speech – as the images of art and the marks of writing – are given the ability to represent objects by our imposing intentionality on the object. Thus, when we assert that we see or believe something, we impose, by convention and intention, the conditions of satisfaction (i.e. that it is true if and only if it is the case) on the statement, and these conditions are not contained intrinsically in the sounds that make it up, but in our perception of and belief about the fact.

The problem with this theory is that either non-existent things have their being through our thinking and talking about them, or there is a very strange kind of relation between the existent mind and its non-existent object.

Gottlob Frege (1848-1925), one of the founders of modern mathematical logic, also looked at language. His work on sense and reference was important in making a distinction between the two, which correspondence theories did not.

The relation of a word to the object it denotes, Frege said, was not merely one of identity with that object as its referent – as seems apparent in a statement like 'The Evening Star is the Evening Star' – for how otherwise do we explain the statement 'The Evening Star is the Morning Star'? There is also a word's **sense** (its descriptive content) in virtue of which it has that relation to its referent. We can then see how a word or proposition may have more then one sense according to its context and thus it is one particular sense that bears the reference to its referent(s) for each occasion of use.

In other words, depending on context, a single word can refer to a range of different things, or a range of words can refer to a single thing. Thus, although there is no simple identity of word and referent, the essential feature of words is that they do have a sense that relates to a referent – there is still a linking of object and word.

Although Frege was a logician, the later scientific and logical approach of the Logical Positivists rejected this sense-reference distinction, because of the problem of words that describe non-existent objects, and therefore have no referent.

Bertrand Russell (1872-1970) developed a 'Theory of Descriptions' as an attempt to answer many of the problems we have mentioned. He suggested that we **can** speak meaningfully about non-existent or abstract objects without the necessary implication – as in correspondence theories – that they do exist.

His method was to reject the whole concept of reference and to introduce the notion that something need not have substance (in the Aristotelian sense) to exist, but may be regarded as a property being described. In other words, he saw language as predicative.

There are therefore two sorts of objects, physical and non-physical. This might be seen as a division between what we can conceive and what we can perceive. But even physical objects are not necessarily perceived as directly as we assume.

No problem with identity here. This is the planet Venus, as seen from the Pioneer-Venus orbiter in February 1979, at a distance of 44,000 miles from the planet's surface.
However, seen in the sky with the naked eye, Venus appears as a bright star in both the morning and the evening; hence the ambiguity of 'The Morning Star' and 'The Evening Star'. A description is not always about reality, but about the circumstances of our perception of reality.

However, some things have to be accepted as premises. **Wittgenstein** said in the *Tractatus* that

'doubt can only exist when there is a question; a question only where there is an answer, and this only when something can be said.'

(which incidentally may be seen as implying also a structuring of knowledge by language). This necessarily leads to his statement:

'Whereof one cannot speak, thereof one must be silent.'

Mental Image Theory of Meaning

In this, there is no direct link between words and things, but only through the mind, and for every word there is an associated concept.

Linguists **C K Ogden** and **I A Richards**' mental image theory of meaning (1923) was similar to Wittgenstein's picture theory, in trying to explain the relationship between words and things via a third element – the concept. This explanation, however, comes no nearer to dealing with definition, since we have still to define the concept, as we previously had to define the object. Also, this approach allows for the possible difference in concept held in the mind of speaker and hearer – a real problem, although not one intended by the theory.

Leonard Bloomfield's (1887-1949) behaviourist theory answers the problem by saying that we may only deduce the meaning from the observed situation in which an utterance is made

In Wittgenstein's early work, language has a picturing function. It stands for, and is verified with reference to, objects of sense experience. If your word has no sense experience to which it refers, it is meaningless. But there are problems with a simple correspondence theory of meaning. What of abstract or non-existent objects? Does the word shape the perception? Is there any way of deciding between alternative words to describe the same thing? What of different languages? What of cartoons or political caracatures?

and from the observed response to it.

However, this does not allow for non-physical and thus unseen situations, such as feelings and attitudes, and those unknown to the observer, such as preceding events and relationships, which would provide explanations for unexpected and unusual linguistic behaviour.

In other words, a person may shout because they are angry, but you cannot see that anger, only its physical expression. Equally, you cannot see the prior

event that has led to the anger and the utterance. This is therefore a limit to how much is revealed simply by observing a word and its context; there is often more that can be said.

Later theories, such as those of **Paul Grice** and of **Dan Sperber** and **Deirdre Wilson** (described in the section on 'Ordinary Language Philosophy') deal further with this and attempt economical explanations of how meaning is established in linguistic interaction.

Theories about words being innate (in the mind at birth) and being universal are closely linked to one another, as we shall see from the work of Plato and **Noam Chomsky (b.1928)**.

Plato posited the existence of *universals* over and above the *particulars* we see in the world, to explain how we may have a definite (objective) knowledge about something, rather than merely an opinion or belief about it. His (admittedly circular) argument goes:

- If we have genuine (objective) knowledge, it is of something that must exist, whereas opinion or belief may be mistaken, and must therefore refer to things that may or may not exist.
- So the objects of these two activities must be different in quality or essence: we have *knowledge* of universals, and *opinion or belief* about particulars.
- If we speak of something that does not exist, it simply means that we have not seen a particular example.

Like Parmenides, Plato argues that to speak of something means *that it exists, at least as a universal*.

Implicit in this idea is that these universals are pre-existent. Because we can know them, we must have pre-existent knowledge of them. This knowledge or apprehension is therefore innate and is, in fact, memory rather than knowledge.

Until the 1950s, behavioural psychology had favoured the idea that every development of the human being was controlled by environmental and social factors. Rather like the view of ostensive explanation of meaning, it implied that everything was learnt through training and association.

Chomsky saw that this could not possibly explain the acquisition of such a complex phenomenon as lan-

AVRAM NOAM CHOMSKY
(B.1928)

Jewish American linguist, philosopher, liberal, anti-war campaigner and critic of US domestic and foreign policy, was born in Philadelphia in 1928. He attended the University of Pennsylvania and Harvard, studying maths, philosophy and linguistics.

His own anti-behaviourist stance led to a cognitive view of language and books such as *Syntactic Structures* (1957), *Language* (1959), *Aspects of the Theory of Syntax* (1965) and *Reflections on Language* (1976), amongst others. He became Professor of Modern Languages and Linguistics at the Massachusetts Institute of Technology in 1976.

guage – which is not taught bit by bit or systematically to infants (as is a second language), yet it is successfully acquired by (almost) everybody. The difficulty many people find in learning a second language at all illustrates that it is a very different process from that experienced with the first language.

Chomsky suggested that the first language is not in fact *learned*, but rather *acquired*, and that it develops from a universal (the principle) through exposure to a particular language – an idea known as principles and parameters. It grows from something pre-existent, or innate – a grammatical competence for, and set of rules to operate, language (as a universal). Chomsky's innateness is biological, but the parallels with Plato's mental/spiritual innateness are clear.

Not only does Chomsky posit the mere *competence* (as he calls it) for language as innate and therefore universal and pre-existing, but he also saw the structure of language as universal, spanning the particulars that are different languages. All languages share the same basic structure, the 'deep structure', as Chomsky terms it, which may be expressed as surface structures through

PRINCIPLES AND PARAMETERS THEORY

The innate, universal programming for grammar (as an abstract entity), versus the acquired, specific tuning to the grammar of the language to which one is exposed.

a process called 'transformation'.

For example, 'I love the cat' may become passivized as 'the cat is loved by me' or we may say 'the person that is I loves the cat' or 'the cat is loved by someone who is I', or we may use a present continuous 'I am loving the cat'. All of these are different ways of saying essentially the same thing.

Equally, across languages, the deep structure has surface structures that use varying grammatical methods to express the same proposition (such as different inflections or word order, or different idioms).

Chomsky's theory enables us to assume a universal system of grammar, which may generate an infinite number of particular languages and an infinite number of particular sentences within a language. This explains how we may recognize or create sentences we have never encountered before, from a limited set of grammatical rules. This 'competence' is a notion very akin to Plato's knowledge or memory of innate universals. Chomsky's approach, however, is intended as a rational, scientific method, positing principles to explain a state of affairs.

As to innateness determining what may be known, Chomsky, in his contribution to a symposium on the

FOR FURTHER INFORMATION ON PLATO AND THE THEORY OF FORMS, SEE PAGE 24.

subject, quotes Descartes' example of a child seeing a drawing of a triangle, which is imperfect, yet recognizing in it the true triangle. He argued that this showed that the child already possesses the actual *concept* of a triangle, and sees this, rather than the imperfect drawing.

This links with Chomsky's observation that not only does the competence of universal grammar generate an infinite number of possible sentences from a limited set of rules, but also a child develops this competence despite often very unfavourable environments.

Chomsky's idea of *abstract competence* has been criticized for its idealized nature with no applicability to how humans actually use language – which he termed '*performance*', to distinguish it from 'competence'.

SOCIOLINGUISTICS

The discipline of sociolinguistics views competence as including language usage. The American sociolinguist **Dell Hymes** proposes the notion of communicative competence as an integration of the innate formal linguistic (i.e. grammatical) ability with the capacity for using language in a social and cultural context, while taking account of diversity.

The sociolinguistic approach is to 'explain the meaning of language in human life, and not in the abstract' and, by its study of cultures, to reason from the particular to the universal, rather than vice versa.

It is one thing to have an innate ability to use language, quite another to use it effectively in a social or business context – which is what sociolinguistics examines.

Truth is a vital concern of philosophy – both what truth is (its definition) and how we can find and establish it logically.

We have already looked at the relationship between a word or concept and a referent 'out there' as opposed to the relationship between words or concepts within a context. Another way of looking at truth is in terms of 'truths of reason' and 'truths of fact'.

- The former, expressed by analytic statements, are 'necessarily true' or 'true by definition' and are used in arguments illustrating the 'coherence theory of truth'.
- The latter, expressed by synthetic statements, are 'contingently true' or 'true as a matter of fact' and thus belong with the 'correspondence theory of truth'.

In his *Critique of Pure Reason*, published in 1781, Kant explained the mental processes that enable us to recognize of which kind a truth is. A sentence or proposition is *analytic*, if the connection between subject and predicate is known to be true or false without reference to the outside world, i.e. the concept that the predicate expresses is contained already by definition in the subject.

Thus, to take a straightforward example, 'A ewe is a female sheep' is an analytic statement, since 'a female sheep' is the definition of the term 'ewe' – and no amount of examining sheep is going to prove that true or false. On the other hand 'Sheep are herbivorous' can only be shown true or false by observing their eating habits, and it is therefore a *synthetic* proposition.

A famous example of an analytic statement is 'All bachelors are unmarried', where the very term 'bachelor' expresses the concept of being unmarried. It is important to avoid the (understandable!) mistake of thinking that this refers to the outside world, through our awareness that the meaning of 'bachelor' originates from observing affairs in that outer world.

The idea of analyticity is that we look only at the sense of the word as we now understand it, i.e. it is true due to the conventions by which we use it; we do not need to look to see if it is true in the world because, once we accept the meaning of 'bachelor' (originally from that world), then we have all we need in the sentence to decide on its truth.

Thus analyticity may be described as 'trivially true', adding nothing to the meaning of the subject.

But there are problems here, as not all constructions are straightforwardly subject-predicate in form. For instance, a passive sentence has a grammatical subject which is not, in fact, semantically the subject of the sentence. If I say 'The book is received to you', then you are actually the subject doing the – admittedly passive – action (receiving) to the book.

Thus the receiving-of-the-book is the predicate of the subject you. Equally the grammatically missing subject of an imperative such as 'Go away!' must be understood semantically as 'You (go away)'. Prior analysis of a proposition is necessary therefore, before applying Kant's theory.

Let us take:

'If I am a woman, then I am short'.

This is an analytic proposition, if the antecedent proposition 'I am a woman' *entails* the following proposition 'I am short'. Here it does not, any more than the unconditional form 'Women are short' could be said to be analytic.

A sentence or proposition is judged to be synthetic if the connection between subject and predicate is such that one may only judge the truth of the proposition with reference to the outside world, i.e. the concept that the predicate expresses is not contained already by definition in the subject.

An example of this type of proposition would be the sentence we have already discussed 'Women are short', where the predicate 'are short' is not nec-

essarily contained in the subject 'women'. Although it may be true of some, it is not true by definition; we must look to the world to see where it is true, i.e. the meaning contained in the word 'women' is not descriptive of the truth of this particular sentence.

A further point needs to be considered here. What happens when negation is present in an analytic or synthetic sentence? Of course, in an analytic sentence such as 'Bachelors are unmarried', negation would make nonsense of the proposition. The resulting negative proposition is therefore termed *contradictory*.

On the other hand, negation of the synthetic sentence e.g. 'Women are not short' still results in a synthetic sentence, since it does not contradict any meaning by definition, but simply produces yet another sentence, the truth of which we will only know if we are prepared to go to the outside world and take a look. Here we are not rescuing a lack of analyticity by denying the original proposition; we cannot say that the second proposition is any closer to containing the meaning by definition of 'women' than the first.

Another possible criticism of this approach springs from something inherent in the theory. You will recall the careful distinction to be made between the truth by definition and truth according to the world, and the possibility we noted of confusion here, because our original definitions are made from observation of the world. It follows then that

FOR FURTHER INFORMATION ON KANT, SEE ALSO 38-41 AND ELSEWHERE, SINCE HE HAS CONTRIBUTED SIGNIFICANTLY TO MOST OF THE BRANCHES OF PHILOSOPHY.

'Bachelors may marry, but are never married!' This is a classic example of an analytic proposition, since the term bachelor is defined as a man who is not married.

There is no need to check the accuracy of this statement – as one might if it were synthetic – by asking a number of married men if they are still bachelors. If they claim to be married and also a bachelor, this does not falsify the original statement, it merely shows that the person does not understand the correct use of the term 'bachelor', or pretends he doesn't for his own purposes!

we are on philosophically shaky ground in talking about truth by definition having nothing to do with that world. We are, in fact, presupposing what we are setting out to prove, and thus risking a circular argument!

In general, of course, the two types of statement get alongside one another reasonable well, and common sense tells us which is which. Thus, scientists making claims for a theory will cite the evidence they have accumulated. Their statements are clearly synthetic. On the other hand, in setting out the theory, the same scientist may use mathematics – a very specific form of logic – to show the way in which one formula or theory implies another. In this case, the terms being used and the ways in which they are being manipulated do not depend on external evidence. We do not need to check the facts to know that the maths is either right or wrong.

Having looked at analytic and synthetic propositions as propounded by Kant, we may now move on to Logical Positivism (or Logical Empiricism as it was later called) initiated by that group of philosophers known as the Vienna Circle in the 1920s, as a reaction against metaphysics and the romanticism of German philosophy, and see how they used Kant's linguistic theories (among others) to develop their approach.

Their philosophy developed out of an already growing respect in Viennese circles for new scientific approaches, firmly grounded in empiricism and logic. The first chairman of the Vienna Circle, **Moritz Schlick**, was actually a physicist.

Impressed by the work in logic of philosophers such as **Bertrand Russell**, **Alfred North Whitehead** and **Gottlob Frege**, they took the empiricist and ultra-logical approach, that whatever could not be 'verified' by sense experience, or expressed in formal logic, was effectively meaningless.

Notoriously, some Positivists put religious, ethical, aesthetic and metaphysical statements in this category.

These two criteria of meaning correspond to Kant's analytic and synthetic statements. Logic was seen as consisting of tautologies, since analytic statements consist merely of repetition in the predicate of the concept(s) contained in the subject. All other meaningful statements had to satisfy the empiricist verification principle, that it should be possible to verify their truth through sense experience.

Logical Positivism therefore dismissed any philosophy that was metaphysical or non-logical. It sought to define concepts more precisely and to investigate language for these purposes. Questions of definition came to be treated as questions about language, rather than about concepts, making issues of language central to philosophy.

A J Ayer, a noted English Positivist, justified the extreme preoccupation of Logical Positivism (and much modern philosophy) with language by pointing out that our experience of the world is reflected in how we use language to describe it, so philosophical investigation of that language will throw light on what we know of the world. His book *Language Truth and Logic* had a huge influence on traditional philosophy after the Second World War. Its emphasis on clarity and precision, on the correspondence of statements to physical facts, provable by its methods, was in Ayer's later words, 'liberating'.

'The fact that natural languages allow the formation of meaningless sequences of words without violating the rules of grammar indicates that grammatical syntax is, from the logical point of view, inadequate.'   Carnap

The Vienna Circle had difficulties in formulating philosophical problems, because of problems in their logical analysis of language. The issue was one of language, rather than the world, and their answer was to reformulate the philosophical problems in a language that was ideal for the task.

Rudolph Carnap (1891-1970) had proposed this ideal language for philosophical use, suggesting that natural language was lacking in conventions to define and guide correct usage. Thus, natural languages allow the formation of meaningless sequences of words without violating the rules of grammar, which indicates that their grammatical syntax is, from the logical point of view, inadequate.

Carnap felt that natural language failed because of the gulf between grammar and logic. Metaphysical statements were seen as permissible and possible only because of this linguistically disastrous state of affairs.

He aimed to develop a language of logical syntax, and in his *The Logical Syntax of Language* he put forward a theory about its ideal nature based on mathematical systems. This involved a system of symbols and syntactic categories, which might be analysed quite separately from any interpretation they might be given.

Proof was according to the logic of the syntax only. The problem here is that any flaws within this artificial system will be undetectable. Proof was an internal affair, a sequence of well-formed formulae. There was no reference to consistency with anything we might actually know, but only logical consistency within the system.

When a problem arose, the theory had to weaken and allow semantics (concerning meaning in language) to help solve the problem. For example, the idea that a concept must be identical with the word used to express it fails, as there is often a vital difference between the two. 'We talked about our friends' does not, after all, mean we discussed the syntactic construction 'our friends'. We may not even have used these two words, although we discussed the beings to which those words refer.

Wittgenstein, in his *Tractatus Logico-Philosophicus*, developed the picture theory of meaning, which related language to the world and to thought, by suggesting that propositions are pictures, both expressions of thought and what we think with. The relation between words in a sentence – its structure and logical form – corresponds to the relation between the things in the world they describe.

To the problem of lies or inaccurate propositions, he answered that a proposition depicts a possible state of affairs. If correct, it is true, if not, it is false. Moral judgements and similar forms of language are in fact not part of language proper, since language only deals with fact and no abstract use of it is possible.

Therefore, as mentioned on page 209, he ends the *Tractatus* with 'whereof we cannot speak, thereof we must remain silent'.

However, having assumed that he had solved all the problems of philosophy through his early approach to language, and after a break from academic life, Wittgenstein then returned with a philosophy of language that offered a completely different approach.

The early ideas of Logical Positivism were later modified. Carnap was one of those who later offered a theory that incorporated pragmatics, to allow for the psychological and sociological motives of speakers and hearers. This leads on to the more general idea that the meaning of a statement is related to how it is used, and the intention of the user.

Philosophers who moved in this direction, included Wittgenstein (in his later writings), Paul Grice and Carnap.

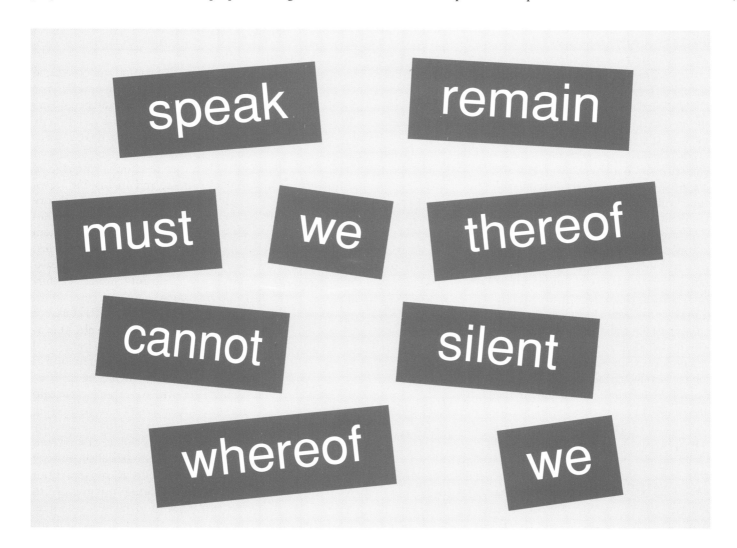

The idea of Logical Positivism was to give language a precision that its proponents so admired in the sciences. Every statement was required to be verified with reference to actual or potential evidence, or to be justified internally by the rules of logic, or by definition. Whatever did not fit this neat scheme was dismissed as meaningless.

But can we analyse language in this way, cutting words and sentences out of the flow of human communication and requiring them to justify themselves with reference to external evidence? Can a language live again, once it has been subjected to such surgery?

'The meaning of a word is its use in the language.'
Wittgenstein

Wittgenstein had inspired the Logical Positivists and supported the idea of an artificial language, but eventually saw its failure as due to applying an inappropriately scientific approach to an essentially non-scientific phenomenon. He also recognized the need to look more openly at how people actually use language. What is seen as chaotic, confusing and philosophically inadequate may in fact work very well.

Wittgenstein set out to illustrate how and why this is so with a theory known as family resemblances, which also offered a solution to the problems inherent in Plato's theory of Forms. It essentially demonstrated that we can apply a term to many different things which do not seem to share properties.

His argument ran that there cannot be a Form for Not-ness, or for a dead person, or non-existent thing, yet we can still refer to these things meaningfully. In addition, we may mean different things by the same word used in different contexts. From Plato, it would follow that we must have every instance of a thing in our mind, when we use the word for it, which obviously we do not.

Thus concepts must be open-ended; the use of words open-textured. There is no essence of a word.

Yet, if we look, we will discover properties that link the things described by that word, not all shared by all, but ranged along a continuum.

Take, as an example, the idea of a game.

- A game might be a card game, a ball game, a board game; all have different properties, yet are 'games'.
- Even within one of these categories, the games may not have many obvious things in common: football and ping-pong differ in that one is played with two teams, the other with two individuals, one on a pitch, the other over a table, one moves the ball with feet, the other with bats. But both remain ball games.
  - Are there properties that apply to all games? We might suggest that for all games, we play them to win? But then, what about Patience?
  - Yet some of all the activities to which we attach the term 'game' will share some of these features. The ones at the two extremities of the continuum may bear no resemblance to each other, but will be linked by their connection to those intermediate.
  - Thus there is no essence of the term game, but rather it has overlapping properties.

There are no boundaries, except those that we draw as we use a word. The meaning is in our own intention. For Wittgenstein, natural language was perfectly adequate and it was its misuse rather than its imperfection that created philosophical problems. We must always go back to how a word is used in its own language. The idea we have already discussed (in our friends example) of a word's meaning being identical with its referent is thus also ridiculed by Wittgenstein, partly because it encourages metaphysical ideas (the very thing its propounders were against) in that if we refer to something, we give it essence, and thus abstract ideas are given reality in a Platonic way.

According to Wittgenstein, a private language is impossible. You can only express yourself through words and meanings that are shared with others. Wittgenstein's 'private language argument' tried to prove that there could be no means, as the empiricists would have it, of expressing experience to oneself without reference to the external world

'Think of the tools in a toolbox; there is a hammer, pliers, a saw, a screwdriver, a rule, a glue-pot, glue, nails and screws. The functions of words are as diverse as the functions of these objects.'
Wittgenstein, Philosophical Investigations

or to others' usage of language. (He regarded their view as a mistake based on the idea that one defines a thing to oneself by naming it, quite arbitrarily and divorced from anything else, rather than by its general use.)

As for the danger of terms used being accepted without explanation, Wittgenstein would have argued that they were understandable in their context and thus could not be assigned to fixed categories. It is a case not of 'what must be the case for this to be true?' but 'under what conditions do we say this and what utility does it have for us?' To assign terms to fixed categories would have been to generalize. Most

ordinary language philosophers attempted to avoid this, despite insights about a system that might thereby be revealed and despite the resultant difficulty of using only limited examples to deal with universal problems.

The importance of Wittgenstein's later work to ideas of tolerance for other uses of language and other cultures, or variants within one's own culture, is obvious. It is in harmony with the egalitarian attitude of sociolinguistics that all language is adequate and none is inferior: there is no single criterion by which language can be judged.

The irony attached to this later work of Wittgenstein's was that, although it was

eagerly followed by the 'Ordinary Language Movement' at Oxford, he refused to describe his approach as a theoretical foundation, arguing that language use may not be controlled by philosophy, only described. It is not philosophy's place to provide a theoretical foundation, but rather it 'leaves everything as it is'. Where language is concerned, the philosopher's task is to observe and describe.

'Philosophy leaves everything as it is.'

Wittgenstein

No doubt about the nature of this game, but an appreciation of what happens in football requires a knowledge of the basic rules of the game. Imagine you had never seen or heard about a game of football. How obvious would it be what these players were trying to achieve?

If you are outside the circle of those who use a certain language, individual words within that language will mean little to you. As with a game, where each action is only understood in relationship to the game as a whole, each word is only to be understood in terms of the language game, or 'form of life', within which it is used.

JL Austin (1911-1960) attempted to formulate a theory of *performative* verbs, i.e. verbs that do, as they are uttered, the thing they describe, e.g. I name this ship, I forgive you, I promise.

John Searle pointed out that Logical Positivists had seen language as only about proposed truths and not about intentions. The structure of the language – not its use – had been central. Wittgenstein conversely had seen language as a tool, with which to do more than merely state facts. The exact meaning of a particular word lay with the speaker, not as an abstract relationship between elements of language (whether with referents in the world outside or simply with internal logical consistency). Austin illustrated a further use of language as forms of action, rather than statements of fact. These he called '*speech acts*'.

Originally, he made a distinction between *constative* utterances (statements and descriptions, involving truth propositions) and *performative* utterances (actions such as promises, bets or warnings), but later came to regard the former equally as speech acts, but of a different kind.

Austin classed these as *illocutionary*. In other words, the act is performed by virtue of the utterance being made. For by making a statement, we are by implication saying 'I state this' and thereby performing an act in the same way as with 'I promise that...' or 'I warn you

that...' These examples show that the focus is on the intentions of the speaker.

The *perlocutionary* force of an utterance, on the other hand, concerns the effect on a hearer of a person's uttering certain words.

An earlier advocate of this view of language was **Bishop Berkeley (1685-1753)**, who opposed Locke's view of words being mere substitutes for ideas, with the alternative possibility that words serve not only to mark and suggest distinct ideas, but to influence our conduct and actions, partly through their use in the formulation of rules, but mainly through the effect they have on our intellects or emotions.

John Searle, who was influential in formulating an economic classification of illocutionary acts, remarks of the relevance of Speech Act Theory to philosophy that it illustrates how language relates to the world through its effect on the world, via people's use. This impetus, which derives of course from Wittgenstein, focuses on language as behaviour, 'conferring intentionality'.

Searle says that by stating that it is raining, we state that we see it is and believe it is and thus we are imposing the same 'conditions of satisfaction' on the utterance that we do on the belief. In other words, the utterance is true if, and only if, it is in fact raining (see Brentano in Correspondence section for more on

this). Speech Act Theory, he remarks, also 'helps us understand syntax and how language evolved – because it shows us what humans use language to do.'

Although this analysis focuses on the intentions of the speaker, it is immediately obvious that, despite language use being – more often than not – successful, there are occasions when those intentions are not fulfilled and a different effect may be produced from that expected (see Inference).

JOHN R SEARLE

was born in 1932 in America. After becoming a Rhodes scholar at Oxford, where he was a pupil of J Austin in the 1950s, he taught there before returning to America. He is now Professor of Philosophy at the University of California at Berkeley. He is an anti-behaviourist, functional philosopher, interested in the philosophy of mind and of language, and particularly in 'intentionality' and continuing Austin's work on speech acts. His book *Speech Acts*, was published in 1969.

PRAGMATISM

Pragmatism is a philosophical approach that (in terms of language) examines the function and effectiveness of communication. Although it has ancient antecedents, it was developed in modern times by **Charles Peirce (1839-1914)**. Peirce's work fell within several areas, and he is particularly known for his mathematics and relational logic. He saw knowledge as coming about in a process of problem solving. Life throws us problems with which we need to deal, and we set about developing strategies and theories in order to do so. Words and ideas help us to make sense of our experience – that is why we use them, and why they are vital in communication. They can be judged by what they do. If a word makes no difference, then it has no meaning.

"Stop!"

an effective 'speech act'

'With this ring, I thee wed.' This is a classic example of a 'speech act'. It is not a description of something else that is happening; the action to which it refers is an action it performs. The declaration puts something into effect.

INFERENCE

Meaning may be derived not only from reference to the speaker's use but to the hearer's, by a process known as inference. Interpretation involves inference. This was the central element of the pragmatic theory introduced by the philosopher and linguist **Paul Grice (1913-1988)**, in an attempt to systematize (in an economical form reflecting the economy of the actual process) the rules of linguistic interaction that result in successful conversation.

The four rules are known in Linguistics as Grice's Maxims and revolve around the 'co-operative principle', i.e. that speakers communicate successfully by their (unconscious) will-ingness to observe these maxims and their assumption of the same willing-ness in others.

The maxims are of:

1 Quality, meaning truth (including not saying what you lack evidence for),
2 Quantity, meaning informativeness (saying no more nor less than required),
3 Relevance and
4 Manner, meaning clear and brief in format.

Assuming that these are being observed, listeners may infer from what has been said many other things, which have not; these additional things are known as *implicatures*.

An example can make this clear. If I say:

'My car has broken down.'

you may say:

'There's a phone around the corner.'

Now, on the face of it, your response appears irrelevant. The conversation is about cars, not about telephones. I will nevertheless derive your *implicature*, that I can call for help on such a phone. In this I have assumed your use of Grice's Maxims, in that you do not need to state explicitly how phones relate to cars.

Sperber and Wilson have developed **Relevance Theory** out of this. They seek to explain how everything can be accounted for by just the single maxim of relevance.

'the language habits of our community predispose certain choices of interpretation.' Edward Sapir

The section on 'Innateness' looked at Chomsky's ideas about our *competence*, in other words, our natural ability to use language. If such ideas about pre-programming, and the use of a very limited number of grammatical rules, suggest constraint or determinism, his theory also sets out to show that this competence is, in fact, a source of freedom, for it is the economy of a system which can nevertheless generate an almost infinite number of forms that produces creativity in language.

Despite Chomsky's assertion of this creativity, there are considerable implications for the relationship between language and thought. Chomsky sees the capacity for language as only one part of the mind, and therefore does not see language as enabling thinking, as do some other philosophers.

Nevertheless, his theory does have implications for what we can understand and communicate to others about the world, since it follows from it that anything that does not seem to be common to all language can therefore not be intelligible in any. Chomsky himself also makes the link with Plato, in talking of 'the insight of Platonist thinkers of today into the organizing principles of mind by which experiences are structured'.

John Searle makes the important point, in opposition to Plato's ideas and to correspondence theories generally, that:

'the world doesn't consist of a lot of entities to which we... then attach labels and names; but rather, the objects of experience don't exist separately from the concepts we have. In this way words enter into the very structure of our experience.'

However, he is quick to correct the view that might follow from this that language creates reality, but rather suggests that:

'what counts as reality... is a matter of the categories that we impose on the world; and those categories are for the most part linguistic.'

These categories, he believes, help to shape our experiences. We perceive something as an experience separate from another because of our system of repre-

sentation, and we divide these experiences up via language.

Thus, he says that an investigation of language is an investigation of the structure of experience, of ways of organizing the world and of being, a belief that informed the later Wittgenstein's description of language as a 'form of life'.

This can appear immediately applicable to the phenomenon of different idiomatic forms in different languages, and to the many instances of cross-cultural miscommunication that may occur. People speak of the 'mind-set' or attitude or identity of a race or nation, very often regarded as being bound up with their language.

The most extreme form of this relativist theory is known as the Sapir-Whorf Hypothesis, a somewhat misrepresentative name for a proposition actually synthesized from the work of **Edward Sapir (1884-1939)** and the development of the line of thought by his student, **Benjamin Lee Whorf (1897-1941)**. Sapir stated in his *The Status of Linguistics as a Science* in 1929 the statement given at the head of this page.

Whorf developed the idea through work with particular cultures. Of course, it might be argued that the language of our community has evolved thus as a reflection of that predisposition. The more accepted view currently is that this is a reciprocal process, with language and thought both reflecting and influencing each other. And of course, the individual is still to be accounted for – his experience, upbringing, education, self-awareness and confidence will all affect his language and his thought.

Certainly the Hypothesis explains the idioms in languages which cannot be translated from one language to another without losing their meaning – or expressing a different reality.

For example, the Gaelic language uses the idiom 'It is coming from under me' for 'I have thought of it' and has no word for 'have', with the possessive 'I have it' being expressed as 'It is at me'. The possibility that relativity is only applicable to vocabulary is disproved by these examples of a difference in syntax.

Whereas Sapir argued that our experience is influenced by the implicit expectations of our language, it was Whorf who developed the stronger hypothesis that language moulds thinking. The clichéd example of the many words for 'snow' in the Eskimo language and the one word used for cold, ice and snow in the Aztec language, is used to argue that the world must thus appear differently to users of the different vocabularies. However, **Paul Henle** in *Language Thought and Culture* in 1966 points out the other possible interpretation, that the world is perceived in the same way, but as distinctions are made, the language developed to express these then tends to reinforce them.

Prototype theory, which has immediate affinities with Wittgenstein's 'family resemblances', demonstrates this with the difference in use of terms cross-culturally. **E Rosch**, in her 1976 paper 'Classification of Real-World Objects', argues that the way language structures the world (by distinguishing meaning) depends on the way the world is structured and on the communicative needs of the speakers. Prototypes exist because of the way things are and through recognition of exceptions.

All languages share the same hierarchical structuring of concepts, with the basic level concept in the same position. For example, we have: food/pudding (or dessert)/pie/apple pie/hot apple pie. But there may be a difference in which concept a particular culture regards as the basic one.

Language is influenced by environment, physical and social. For many people, the Gaelic language reflects the wild beauty of the Scottish Highlands, or the Western Isles. The Gaelic language has distinctive idioms, and no word for 'have'. Meaning can be lost in literal translation.

A further connection between language and thought is seen in the standardization of language and its consequences for views of mental capacity. A standard language, such as 'Queen's English' or 'Hoch Deutsch' (High German) grew up because a particular part of the country (south-east England / north Germany) came to dominate, culturally as much as politically, the rest of the country concerned. Growing concentrations of power, wealth and prestige (especially in Britain) helped this particular dialect to become the 'standard' language.

However, once this occurs, there is a two-way connection between it and its speakers' attitudes to the language itself and to those who do not use it. It becomes an instrument of exclusion to the latter, but its proponents also find their attitude to it developing into a *prescriptivism*, which, in its extreme form, condemns users of older, non-standard forms as mentally deficient.

In English, this view of the prestige status of a linguistic variety has extended to what linguists regard as a confusion between the requirements of logic and of language – a 'confusion' which Logical Positivists would support and ordinary language philosophers would not.

The confusion is seen best by the grammatical prescriptivism, which developed in the 18th and 19th centuries through measuring English against Latin and through exposure to the logical thinking of the time. Dr Johnson's Dictionary, the first detailed attempt to standardize spelling, was published in 1755.

Such rules as not splitting infinitives or ending a sentence with a preposition, were forced onto a language to which they did not apply, since the rule for Latin merely reflects a state of affairs: the Latin infinitive is one word and cannot be split, but it can in English, and the ability to end with (or 'strand') a preposition was something introduced to English via Scandinavian languages, although not possible in Latin.

Equally, a double negative is common in many European languages and was so in Old and Middle English i.e. up to c.1500, but when logic was applied, the conclusion was that two negatives make a positive, and therefore the linguistic form made no logical sense.

The importance of these facts for philosophy lies both in the use of language for the manipulation of society, and in the expectations of its logical structure, which inform much of the thinking we examine elsewhere in this section.

THE CONSTRUCTIVIST THEORY

The Genevan psychologist **Jean Piaget (1896-1980)** developed a constructivist theory about the relationship between language and thought. This opposed Chomsky's view of the innate capacity for language, suggesting that the development of linguistic structures depends on the extent to which conceptual ability is established.

He proposed an order of acquisition of various skills and senses. For example, the sense of object permanence, which enables a child to search for something it no longer has in view, is necessary before a child can give these objects permanent linguistic status by naming them.

Notice how this contrasts with the view put forward earlier by Bertrand Russell, that the structure of language influences that of thought. He suggested, for example, that a possible cause of the whole Aristotelian idea of the existence of substances, is to be found in the subject-predicate logic. Thus he wrote:

> 'Substance is a metaphysical mistake, due to transference to the world-structure of the structure of sentences composed of a subject and predicate'.

The linguist **Richard Hudson**, in *Sociolinguistics*, suggests that some concepts are independent of language if they are learnt before language has developed, or if obviously developed without recourse to language.

There are instances where we have no word for a particular concept, even in our adult vocabulary, e.g. the collective name 'groceries' can be used for things bought at a grocer's, but there is no collective name for things bought at a newsagent's. But equally, some concepts are obviously dependent on language, where meaning is worked out after a concept is named.

Cultural relativism is evident here in the case of the meanings of frequently used words being learnt sooner and more accurately. For example, 'left' and 'right' are used in most cultures more than 'east' and 'west' to describe relative positions, and, in these societies, are familiar to children earlier than 'east' and 'west'. But some languages do use compass points for this purpose, and of these some are even without words for left and right.

So, concepts that are learnt through language will vary according to the language used, thus proving some influence of language on thought. But another argument against the strong version of the Sapir-Whorf hypothesis is that we not only have concepts we cannot express in language, as mentioned above, but we are also able to discuss the fact in that very language.

Another important consideration is the effect of language on its recipient. We have seen, in Austin's work on 'speech acts', that utterances may be seen as actions and in Grice's work that linguistic interaction may be seen as conforming to rules for meaning and understanding.

However, language is also used sarcastically, ironically, metaphorically, where

CONSTRUCTIVIST THEORY:

the idea that the order in which we develop linguistic structures, depends on the extent to which our conceptual ability is established.

Imagine the situation at a dance where you are not sure of the steps. How could you learn to dance without knowing your right from your left? The concepts of 'right' and 'left' are essential for communication about spatial movement, but do not correspond directly to anything perceived. Learning and using them correctly requires some sophistication. In moments of stress they may be confused – with resulting embarrassment, if you are trying to learn a dance, or even if you are on a military parade ground!

Try describing what 'right' means, without in some way pointing or showing its meaning. What is to your right might well be to my left. Hence the object referred to may have nothing physical that corresponds to either. On the other hand, a 'right' shoe is not the same as a 'left', such that a physical description will include that term. Sometimes, the confusion between these two different forms of description – that of inherent features of right and left, and that of relationship to the speaker – can be humorous, as with the old joke about a mug, designed with a handle that can clip onto either side, for right or left handed people!

what is said may in fact be the opposite of its superficially apparent meaning. There is often good reason for this – so that the hearer may intuit something else about the attitude of the speaker.

This use of language is accounted for in Sperber and Wilson's Relevance Theory, but is an interesting phenomenon to consider in a section on 'language and thought', as there is the double problem here: not only of how the process of utterance affects the thought of the hearer, but also of how the real meaning

of an apophatic statement, such as

'And of course, I didn't buy anything in the sales.'

may be understood to mean

'And of course I did'.

Similarly,

'No, no, please don't worry about doing that, of course you haven't got the time.'

may well be interpreted – and is intended to be interpreted – as meaning just the opposite!

Phenomenology, as a philosophical approach, was founded by **Edmund Husserl (1859-1938)**. It draws distinctions between perception and intuition, between indirect and direct knowledge, and between knowledge of aspects (or instances), and knowledge of essences (or universal properties).

This is clearly Platonic and idealist in approach, but it also has ties with Existentialism, since its method of reduction advocates direct experience of things without theoretical speculation. It suggests in fact a wholly fresh approach to philosophy, by systematically examining experience. It acquired its name because it treats everything as phenomena (see Kant, pages 38-41).

For phenomenologists, there is a '*Lebenswelt*' (lived-in world), which consists of the world as experienced and lived in by humans. Descriptions and explanations of this can have no objective basis, but are all coloured by our values, feelings and emotions. But instead of worrying about whether, when we look at, say, a chair, our awareness is of ourselves looking at the chair, and not of the chair itself, we should accept that the chair exists as an object of our consciousness, no matter what its status.

One of Phenomenology's chief proponents was **Maurice Merleau-Ponty (1907-1961)** who, along with the existentialist **Jean Paul Sartre (1905-1980)**, assimilated the structuralist ideas of **Ferdinand de Saussure (1857-1913)** in the 1940s and 50s.

However, Merleau-Ponty objected to Sartre's emphasis on subject and object relations, which he saw as still partly tainted by Cartesian Dualism (see page 132). He suggested that meaning comes from humanity, and personal meaning from oneself (an idea against which Wittgenstein set his 'private language' argument).

Merleau-Ponty asserted that lived experience was vital for understanding the nature of language. His aim was to go beyond Husserl's doubts about the 'givenness' of the world, by suggesting that the very fact of our bodily experiencing, which is at the root of phenomenology, ties us to a world which we are of, rather than in.

He effectively rephrased Descartes' famous dictum

'I think, therefore I am.'

with

'I belong to myself while I belong to the world.'

We should not objectify the world, ourselves, or the process by which we perceive the world.

The connection of this to a philosophy of language lay in his highlighting of two of Saussure's principles: that of the relation between signs in language, and that of the non-explicability of current usage or meaning from the study of the history of a language.

So, the emphasis in language use, as in perception, is on the person's lived relationship to the world. Language must be viewed as enacted, rather than as an abstract evolving entity.

Each use of language is a becoming aware of a living present.

Talk about language is equally enactment. Therefore, language may not be treated objectively, but only understood from the inside.

Merleau-Ponty's emphasis, however, is on only half of Saussure's theory. Saussure identified *langue* (the system of language, akin to Chomsky's 'competence') and *parole* (the actual enactment of language, akin to Chomsky's 'performance').

Merleau-Ponty necessarily could look only at the latter, for to take account of the former would be to allow objectification of language, by separating the speaker from what is spoken.

Saussure opposed the view that language mirrors thought, or any correspondence or intrinsic link between a name and its object. His emphasis was on the internal structure of language without reference to the outside world. Its meaning lay within that structure, viewed as a whole.

The relationship between word and object, is replaced by '*signifier*' (word) and '*signified*' (concept). Language is autonomous and not dependent on reality. Although it is a social institution, its changes are independent of its speakers' will, which has implications for the idea of language structuring thought.

Saussure emphasized the relation of sense to structure and use, regarding interpretation as misguided and subject to the errors of intuition. However, although language use was important, structuralism was not concerned with the human mind or social reality.

The idea that meaning it to be found in the speaker's intention was replaced by the idea of meaning inherent in a particular use – language was divorced both from the individual (its source) and from the idea of reference (its correspondence), but was accessible to others by virtue of their membership of the same language system.

Thus, language was seen as an entity in itself, used for communication, but not created by the user. It did not reflect reality, but created it.

This theory, unlike phenomenology, allowed for objectivity, but not for individuality, nor for context or situation.

FOR FURTHER INFORMATION ON HUSSERL, AND ON EXISTENTIALISM, SEE PAGES 44-45.

Post-structuralism has adapted the theory to allow for the system shifting in response to these factors.

The structuralist view of language, namely that it consists of a series of relations between elements, although opposed to the view of language as logical and rational, essentially follows from the scientific and logical analyt-ical methods of such thinkers as Frege and Russell, who developed a logic of relations as a tool for philosophical analysis.

These developments produce a view of language that is radically different from that of the Logical Positivists in the early part of the 20th century. Then, the aim was to analyse how language could convey correct and verifiable infor-mation about the world. Now, language is recognized as a means of communi-cation, which reflects the nature of the world as we experience it – not as science would seek to show it. Our lan-guage reflects that we are 'of' the world we experience, and not its external observers.

And we are 'of' the world as members of various groups, with shared inter-ests and forms of language. We are not isolated – and if we were, we could not use language to overcome that isola-tion, for langue is only created from within the group.

So language becomes both richly sug-gestive of emotions, hopes and so on,

In a phenomenological approach to language, descriptions do not have a completely objective basis, but are always coloured by values, feelings and emotions. We deal with the world as it is lived in and experienced.

In a structuralist approach, we use language that is an already existing part of, and expression of, our culture. It has a meaning that extends beyond our particular use of it, and is certainly richer than a simple analysis of what is encountered.

Hence, something like a travel advert suggests far more than the actual transport being offered – it includes style, the hint of a certain life that is possible for those who travel in this way. Advertisers know that they need to do more than simply describe their product, or even explain its benefits. They need to suggest a whole range of ideas and values that will appeal to the consumer, and may – with greater or lesser degrees of probability – be linked to the pur-chase of their product.

Words are always open to misinterpretation. Those we avoid are as important as those we use. Even silence speaks.

'Silence is an essential possibility of discourse.' Heidegger

EASTERN APPROACHES TO
THE PHILOSOPHY OF LANGUAGE

If there is one theme that runs through much, if not all, Eastern thought, it is a deep-seated suspicion about the relationship between language and reality.

Despite this, Eastern approaches to the philosophy of language have been as varied and as numerous as their Western counterparts. However, unlike in the West where philosophy of language only became of central philosophical concern in the last hundred years or so, Asian thinking about the nature of language is extremely ancient, with many of the theories, particularly in India and China, predating the beginning of the Christian era.

To put it quite simply, many Eastern thinkers doubt whether language has any ability to connect, or adequately describe, the real world.

Given the deep-rooted nature of this suspicion, this leads many of them to speak about a 'non-conceptual reality' that is untainted by the imprint of words. What the nature of such a reality would be, and how we could ever 'know' it, is extremely problematic. Nevertheless the assertion that there is such a kind of reality is linked to the various *soteriologies* (theories of liberation) that underpin much of Eastern theorization.

Thus the differing approaches to language to be found in the philosophies of India, China, and Japan present us with a tight knot of theories concerning language, knowledge, and metaphysics, which are in turn linked to soteriologies.

INDIA

Indian philosophers, unlike their Western counterparts, never developed an interest in formal logic. The attention they gave to issues of language and logic was almost always motivated by epistemological considerations (i.e. those concerned with the theory of knowledge).

Indian thinkers developed models of reasoning that were never purely deductive i.e., arguing from premises to a conclusion. As such, Indian logic seems to have been a search for a suitable model that would account for both deductive and inductive inferences.

Given that the interest of Indian thinkers was primarily epistemological, they were especially concerned with the nature of our cognitive acts (by which we come to know something) and in particular the constructive side of those acts. This inevitably led to a concern with language or speech and the role, or non-role, that it might play in perception, which was considered as representative of such acts.

To offer a glimpse into the complex kinds of theorization about language to be found in the philosophies of the Indian sub-continent we will take the Dinnaga-Dharmakirti school of Buddhism, and the Nyaya school of Hinduism.

THE DINNAGA-DHARMAKIRTI SCHOOL

Dinnaga and Dharmakirti were Buddhist philosophers who flourished in the fifth and sixth centuries CE respectively. Both Dinnaga and Dharmakirti claim that perception, which has been mediated through the distorting lens of language, can never show us reality.

Their argument for this claim runs in the following manner: the elements that make up language are all universals (*samanya*) and as such are at best imaginative or conceptual constructions (*vikalpa* or *kalpana* – words which mean 'imagination' in ordinary Sanskrit) and, at worst, 'fictions'.

If the whole of language is composed of universals then it cannot adequately describe reality, which consists of unique and unrepeatable particulars (*svalaksana*). Dinnaga's philosophy of language is expressed in an epigram:

DINNAGA AND DHARMAKIRTI

Much of the information that we have in regard to Eastern thinkers is purely mythological in character. Eastern philosophy has never attempted to preserve accurate biographies of its major thinkers, on the grounds that the message is more important than the individual thinker.

Dinnaga was born in South India at about the beginning of the fifth century CE. Traditional sources tell us that he studied with the great Indian thinker Vasubandhu at the monastic university of Nalanda, in present day Bihar.

His major work on logic and epistemology, the *Pramanasamuccaya* (Synthesis of Validating Cognitions), was completed whilst he was living in Orissa. After he completed the work he travelled around much of Orissa, debating with, and ultimately converting, Brahmins and eventually gained the patronage of the King of Orissa.

Dharmakirti was born in Tamilnadu in South India in about 580 CE. Initially he was trained in the Brahmanical tradition but was attracted to Buddhism at any early age.

Traditional sources tell us that he was so attracted to Buddhism that he began dressing as a Buddhist, thereby gaining the displeasure of his fellow Brahmins, which eventually led to him being driven away.

Like Dinnaga before him, Dharmakirti joined the monastic university of Nalanda, and studied with a monk who was a direct disciple of Dinnaga.

Dharmakirti's major work the *Pramanavarttika* is ostensibly a commentary on Dinnaga's work. However, this work probably stands as one of the greatest works in the Indian philosophical tradition on logic and epistemology. Dharmakirti wrote six other major works and even some erotic poetry.

'Speech is born out of conceptual construction and conceptual construction is born out of speech.'

In Dinnaga and Dharmakirti's view it is always the particular, and not the universal, which has any claim to truth. What this means is that when I use a term such as 'cow' (this is after all India!) I am using a generality, which homogenizes all differences between this particular cow and another particular cow. What their theory represents is a complete reversal of the kind of doctrine espoused by Plato, wherein it is the universal that has the claim to reality and never the particular instance.

Given Dinnaga's and Dharmakirti's position, the question arises as to whether words ever refer to unique particulars and, if so, how? Their answer to this question is found in the doctrine of apoha or 'word meaning as exclusion'. The implication of this is that, rather than referring to unique particulars directly, words or concepts eliminate or exclude other concepts. So the word 'cow' negates all other concepts such as 'table', 'chair', 'house', etc.

Thus words are purely arbitrary, having no positive content (essence) and no direct connection with what is named. Each word simply divides the world into those things to which it can be applied and to those to which it cannot.

If this initially sounds implausible, a good way of illustrating such a conception would be the learning of colour words within a foreign language. To learn what things the word 'noir' applied to we would have to be able to contrast it with another colour such as 'rouge'. Thus, each word 'excludes' the object from the class of those objects to which cannot be applied.

The kind of model of language with which both Dinnaga and Dharmakirti work is one of naming. Language is seen to consist of five different kinds of names. These are known as the five designators, qualifiers (*visesana*), or predicate constructions. The five designators are as follows: Proper names; class names; quality names; action names; substance names. Each name 'qualifies' or differentiates what is being named.

What Dinnaga and Dharmakirti are doing is focusing our attention on the quality aspect of meaning. In doing this they show that the qualifiers distinguish their objects simply by being mere names, without in any way implying the existence of 'real entities.' As such, all five kinds of names are devoid of what Dinnaga and Dharmakirti call 'implied sense' (*artha sunya*).

> This view has gained a certain currency in the West via the work of the Swiss linguist Ferdinand de Saussure, at the beginning of the 20th century, and has been enormously influential on the development of French structuralist thought. See also page 224.

Eastern thought is concerned primarily with the 'real'. The key question is whether language is capable of connecting with it.

NYAYA

The Nyaya school – one of the six orthodox schools of Hinduism – take as the view that genuine proper names such as personal names e.g., 'David', implies a universal concept of the thing which is qualified by this name.

This quite simply means that the name names a universal, or essence, which underlies all change. In the case of the name 'David' it names the essence or 'David-ness' of the individual. This essentialist view of language attempts to show that behind the ever-changing mental and physical states of the individual named 'David' there is a substratum, or essence, which remains constant.

Therefore, unlike the Buddhist views of Dinnaga and Dharmakirti, language does imply real entities. As a corollary to this view, the Nyaya philosophers believed that the objects of the external world are real only insofar as they are expressed in language.

Once again we can discern the primarily epistemological concerns of the Nyaya thinkers, in that genuine perception can only take place via the medium of language.

CHINA

In China, there can be seen to be two major trains of thought operative which can be broadly categorized as Taoist and Confucian – the Ch'an or Zen Buddhist approach I will deal with in the section on Japan.

Confucianism

Confucianism, as a primarily socio-ethical philosophy, concentrates its attention on the communicative aspect of language.

For Confucius, what is important is what occurs as result of particular utterances. What this implies is that the 'meaning' or *locutionary* aspect of propositions can never be divorced from the context in which they are delivered.

Thus, for Confucius, the 'truth' of an utterance resides in the kinds of effects it produces on the communicants.

The whole Confucian approach to language is somewhat similar to the kind of 'speech act' theory outlined by the British philosopher J Austin in the 1950s. This can be seen particulary in Austin's analysis of what he terms the *perloctionary* (what is effected in others by saying something) and *illocutionary* (what is done in saying something) force of utterances.

Taoism

In the Taoist approach to language there can once again be discerned the kind of scepticism referred to above. Both the *Tao te Ching*, and the other classic work of Taoism, the book of *Chuang Tzu*, make it clear that the Tao (the Way) that can be named is not the real Way, or true Tao. The *Tao te Ching* begins with the classic line:

> 'The way that can be told is not the constant way.'

Taoists seem to be sceptical about ever saying anything. The Chinese thinker Chuang Tzu makes clear in his work an important epistemological distinction, one portion of which is extremely useful in helping us to understand the Taoist position on language. Chuang Tzu quite clearly makes a distinction between 'knowing how' and 'knowing that'.

For Chuang Tzu, knowing that is purely conceptual or intellectual knowledge, and is radically separated from real knowledge which is entirely practical.

Given this position we find in the *Chuang Tzu* many stories in which contempt is expressed for all kind of book learning. Real knowledge for the Taoist can never be expressed in words!

FOR J L AUSTIN AND JOHN SEARLE ON 'SPEECH ACTS' SEE PAGE 218.

> 'My words are very easy to understand, and very easy to practice.
>
> But the world cannot understand them, nor practice them.
>
> My words have an Ancestor.
>
> My deeds have a Lord.
>
> The people have no knowledge of this.
>
> Therefore they have no knowledge of me.
>
> The fewer persons know me,
>
> The nobler are they that follow me.
>
> Therefore, the Sage wears coarse clothes,
>
> While keeping the jade in his bosom.'
>
> *Tao te Ching, 70*

JAPAN

Zen Buddhism has it origins in the form of Chinese Buddhism known as Ch'an – both *Ch'an* and *Zen* are translations of the Sanskrit term *dhyana*, which can be rendered as 'meditation'. The founding legend of Ch'an is indicative of both Ch'an and Zen Buddhism's general approach to language. In this legend, the Buddha, wishing to convey the 'essence of the true Dharma', holds up a flower to an assembly of monks. No-one understands the gesture accept Mahakassyapa, who smiles, and as a consequence is declared to be the Buddha's true successor.

What is represented by this approach is a *via negativa*, with the Zen masters of Japan stressing the power of silence and gesture. However, the Rinzai form of Zen continues to use language in the form of *koan* to induce particular effects. The *koan* is a kind of irrational riddle, which is designed to induce in the practitioner a kind of psychological stasis. As such koans can be seen as perfomatory uses of language having particular illoctionary and perlocutionary force.

One interesting development in the Japanese approach to language was the elevation of poetry to the position of 'skilfull means' (*kyogen kigo*). What this meant was that poetry was conceived to be a unique form of language, which was capable of expressing or speaking the truth of Being.

This was a position the German philosopher **Martin Heidegger** took in the latter part of his career. It is perhaps not coincidental that Heidegger had many Japanese students in the 1930s and was extremely interested in Chinese thought.

'Autumn –
even the birds
and clouds look old.'

A Haiku by Basho

The Confucian view, like the 'speech act' theory, assesses language in terms of its practical effectiveness.

Perhaps this links with the other great Chinese philosophical tradition, for Taoism is concerned with the practical application of language, not with mere book learning.

FOR HEIDEGGER ON:

KNOWLEDGE SEE PAGE 45

MIND SEE PAGE 145.

The Philosophy of Education is concerned both with the nature and purpose of education, and with its content, and while few philosophers have written extensively on education, most would accept its crucial importance both for creating the just society (however defined) and for the intellectual development of individuals.

Issues in education link to many other areas of philosophy:

- The way in which a language is learned is considered under the Philosophy of Language.

PHILOSOPHY AND THE CURRICULUM

Today, the Philosophy of Education is largely concerned with the nature and delivery of the school curriculum. A notable figure for the development of this in the 1960s and '70s was **P H Hirst** (see his *Knowledge and the Curriculum* Routledge and Kegan Paul, 1975) who looked at the curriculum in terms of the different 'forms of knowledge' each with its own concepts and norms.

Issues of current debate include an examination of the actual process of learning, the self-determination of the student, indoctrination, and the social and political constraints on curriculum content and on the funding and development of education, as well as the broad issue about the value and justification of education as a whole, the place of vocational education, and education for citizenship and as a preparation for adult life.

Much work in the Philosophy of Education is an analysis of the actual process of teaching and learning, and as such it is bound up with the practice of these things in school. Clearly, it would be quite impossible to get an adequate view of such issues in the few pages available in this book, so instead we have focused on some broad but relevant issues that are fundamental to the whole process of education.

- Both Ethics and Politics are relevant to the purpose and conduct of the educational process.
- Logic, the philosophy of science, of art, of history and of religion, are all – directly or indirectly – part of an educational curriculum.
- The theory of knowledge is crucial to understanding the way in which knowledge may be transmitted, and to distinguish objective knowledge from subjective opinions.
- Education is concerned with individuals and with the nature of mind and selfhood; such questions are explored within the Philosophy of Mind.

All philosophy is therefore relevant to education. Equally, education (in the broadest sense) is essential to philosophy, since, without it, ideas die with the individual who has them.

This chapter will examine the key questions for the Philosophy of Education, which are:

- **What is education for?**
- **By what process do we learn?**
- **What should determine the content of education?**

There are many ways to approach education. It may be seen as the process by which what is best in a culture is transmitted from one generation to the next, an idea that is the basis of a traditional liberal approach to education.

Equally, its function may be seen as utilitarian, equipping individuals for their expected role in society. It may be seen as an end in itself, or as a vehicle for cultivating personal qualities that will be of value to society.

This chapter will explore the key question though looking at the views of a limited number of philosophers who contributed widely on other issues. The intention here is to show how education relates to, and grows out of, other areas of philosophy. Of those considered:

- Plato has been selected because he relates education to clear political goals.

- Buddha relates what is learned to the process of critical reflection and internalization, which is an important feature of the process of learning.
- Hobbes sees education as based on sense experience, rejecting an uncritical acceptance of tradition.
- Rousseau seeks to develop the natural goodness of individuals, freeing them from the corruption of imposed tradition.
- Dewey, representing the pragmatic tradition in philosophy, sees education as best through the process of acting and problem solving.
- And finally we look at Confucius and Russell, who from utterly different backgrounds explore the function of education in cultivating personal qualities needed to improve society.

LEARNING FOR SOCIETY: PLATO

The Republic is probably the greatest book ever written about the Philosophy of Education. In considering of the nature of the state and of its rulers, Plato examines what sort of education is needed to produce leaders truly fit to govern, and in doing so came up with radical ideas.

In one sense therefore, education is not an end in itself, but a tool of social engineering. However, that is far from the whole truth, for Plato holds that those best suited to rule are philosophers who are able to see reality, rather than the passing shadows of sense experience (see the Analogy of the Cave, page 25). Hence it can equally be argued that Plato's scheme of education is aimed at an appreciation of the 'Form of the Good' (see page 24).

Plato wanted to educate people in a way that would be certain, he thought, to produce the just society. Having no interest in liberal ideals of individuals being encouraged to follow their own interests and tastes, he saw education as anything but child-centred. Children were quite unable to attain wisdom by themselves, although of course they have within them its seeds. Instead, they must be moulded to serve the ideal State. Plato took care to select only the most able and well-equipped pupils from the start. He seeks those who display all the virtues.

'If we can find, for this long course of training and study, men who are at all points sound of limb and sound of mind, then Justice herself will have no fault to find with us and we shall ensure the safety of our commonwealth and its institutions. We should only ruin it by choosing pupils of a different stamp...'

The Republic chapter 28

Notice the assumptions that lie behind this: that personal qualities are a natural endowment and not the result of education (selection happens before education, not after it); that aspirants to Plato's course of study are male; that the justification of the whole enterprise is the safety of the commonwealth and its institutions.

He seeks communalistic education for the elite who would form the top two classes of his Republic: Guardians and Soldiers. After selection, students would be brought up together in camps, holding almost everything in common, including wives and children (his scheme of education lasted well into adult life). The ideal of education as the quest for the real is therefore set within the social context of his day.

Plato's education is a long process, only considered complete after a considerable number of years being tested out in practical and military situations:

'Then, when they are fifty, those who have come safely through and proved the best at all points in action and in study must be brought at last to the goal. They must lift up the eye of the soul to gaze on that which sheds light on all things; and when they have seen the Good itself, take it as a pattern for the right ordering of the state and of the individual, themselves included. For the rest of their lives, most of their time will be spent in study; but they will all take their turn at the troublesome duties of public life and act as Rulers for their country's sake, not regarding it as a distinction, but as an unavoidable task.'

The Republic chapter 18

The running of society is thus seen as a chore for those whose ability to rule is unquestioned, but who would rather dwell on higher things. Plato saw the creation of such an elite as the aim of education. As we shall see, other philosophers have different views.

His enterprise raises issues, which continue with the world of education:

- To what extent should education be dependent on selection by ability?
- To what extent should education be aimed to equip students for particular tasks within society? In other words, should society set the curriculum?
- Given the changed social background, and the need for universal education in an industrialized society, should there be very different forms of education for people of different classes?

Plato argues for a broadly based education, developing individuals fit to rule. Graduation marks the point at which a student is deemed to have achieved the required understanding of his or her chosen subject. But should more degrees be vocational? Should the supply of graduates be determined by the needs of society, or by the ebb and flow of interest in particular subjects? Issues raised in *The Republic* continue to be relevant to those concerned with education.

The Buddha's philosophy was based on the investigation of mental states. The *Satipatthana Sutta* records his teachings on the 'four foundations of mindfulness', which are awareness of body, of feelings, of mental states and of the objects of thought. He regarded awareness of these four things as the means of overcoming suffering and attaining the state of Nirvana.

The key feature of all Buddhist education therefore is awareness: an analytical introspection of physical, emotional and intellectual processes.

Two key features of the Buddha's philosophy of education are that:
- knowledge comes from reflection upon experience.
- the purpose of such knowledge is practical, namely the overcoming of suffering.

The implications of these are:
- that personal experience takes priority over received tradition.
- that, where there are received formulae (e.g. the Sutta lists the 'Four Noble Truths' and other basic principles of Buddhist philosophy), such 'mind objects' are to be examined critically in order to become established as personal convictions.

Hence, there are three levels of knowledge, or wisdom:

shrutamayi prajna – wisdom that comes from listening or reading, in other words, engaging with an established tradition.

chintamayi prajna – wisdom developed as a result of personal reflection and thought.

bhavamayi prajna – wisdom that arises as a result of spiritual practice (bhavana), in other words, wisdom that arises when ideas are fully integrated into a person's overall view of life.

Thus, within Buddhist philosophy, education is a matter of examining and internalizing received tradition and of integrating it with a reflective awareness of personal experience.

Buddhist philosophy is, in a sense, both secular and religious (the distinction between these being largely a Western phenomenon), but in terms of the process of education in what might be called Buddhist spirituality, there are two other important features to keep in mind:

Particularly in the Zen tradition, there is the sense that moments of insight arise spontaneously, and that this happens under the guidance of a teacher but without the need for a study of written scriptures.

Great importance is placed on the relationship between pupil and teacher, although critical analysis is still paramount, it is considered that guidance is needed in order for a person to make personal progress. Much is made of the lineage of particular teachers, and thus of the particular tradition within which they stand.

> '*A fool who thinks he is wise goes through life with himself as his enemy...*'
>
> **Buddha (from the *Dhammapada*)**

Notice the contrast with Plato's view. Here the process of education is analytical, individual and potentially universal. It does not aim to create people of a certain character or social function, but to enable individuals to develop and integrate their own awareness. This is not seen as selfish, however, since Buddhist philosophy sees selfishness as a sign of ignorance, and universal compassion a sign of enlightenment. Hence, individual self awareness is itself socially valuable.

FOR FURTHER INFORMATION ON THE BUDDHA SEE PAGES 55 AND 187.

A novice monk in his room in a temple in Bangkok. Critical reflection on teachings, and an awareness of experience at every level, are central features of the Buddhist view of education. The Buddha himself framed his teachings in the form of lists, so that they could be memorized easily – a useful educational technique.

John Locke (1632-1704) is best known for his work on the theory of knowledge. He is generally considered to be the founding father of **Empiricism**, which regards all knowledge as coming by way of the senses (see page 34). His political works (see page 310) also had a profound influence on the establishment of the basic principles of modern democracy in Britain and the United States.

These major features of his work have implications for education, and he wrote specifically on the subject in *Some Thoughts Concerning Education* (1693), where he made suggestions about the methods used in education (e.g. that children should not be forced to learn things by rote, and should develop language skills through practice rather than solely by studying grammars).

These would seem unexceptional today, but they were a radical attempt to break away from a view of education based on the handing down of information, ideas and sayings from the ancient Greeks and Romans, taught in an authoritarian, often brutal way. Westminster School, which Locke attended, was notorious for its savage beatings.

The key feature of Locke's theory of knowledge is that people start with minds like blank sheets of paper (*tabula rasa*) and acquire all knowledge though sense experience. Unlike Plato, he held that we have no innate ideas. Thus, we only know what is means to use the word 'dog' because we have experienced a number of individual dogs and recognize them as examples of a particular kind of animal. If we had never experienced a dog (directly or indirectly), we would have no concept of one.

This view is in contrast to Plato's idea of 'dogginess', given as an example of his Theory of Forms, on page 24.

So we all start on an equal footing, and gradually build up our awareness of the world through sense impressions. Thus all knowledge depends on education (in the broadest sense of that term), and education becomes a vehicle for self-improvement, no matter what social background a person comes from.

Unlike Plato, Locke opposed the idea of selecting and educating only the most gifted, but argued that all should be offered the possibility of education, so that all could have an opportunity to improve themselves. This does not imply that everyone will prove to be equally gifted, but it does suggest that there should be equality of opportunity, since all start life with an equally blank sheet.

In fact, Locke was probably thinking more of the education of the gentry, of which he was a member, but adding a democratic, rather puritanical, common-sensical note to their education.

There is a further feature of Locke's thought in general, a feature he shared particularly with Francis Bacon (in the area of scientific investigation) and which was to be taken up also by Hume (in his general approach to reason and experience), and which had also been key to the Buddha's view; the insistence that one should not follow tradition unthinkingly, but that everything should be assessed against evidence.

Locke was against...

'entertaining any proposition with greater assurance than the proofs it is built upon will warrant.'

The implication for education was clear; everything should be examined in the light of reason and experience. But it also implied that one's own conclusions should be presented to others on a similar basis, accepting that they will be critically examined. Thus the whole process of education becomes less dogmatic and authoritarian.

> '*A characteristic of Locke, which descended from him to the whole Liberal movement, is lack of dogmatism.*'
>
> Bertrand Russell

For both Bacon and Locke, education needed to be reformed, undogmatic and to encourage the development of critical faculties. As such it could become a vehicle of social reform, and its curriculum and method better suited to bring about a greater measure of equality and to ensure liberty.

FOR GENERAL INFORMATION ON: LOCKE, SEE PAGE 33.

LEARNING TO BE NATURAL

No philosopher before **Jean-Jacques Rousseau (1712-1778)** and few since have had such a dramatic, if delayed, impact on education.

Rousseau is best known for his political philosophy, and in particular his idea of the Social Contract. He believed that people were born free and noble, but were enchained and corrupted by society. He sought to promote liberty, equality and fraternity, and so was one of the chief intellectual forces behind the French Revolution. How far his philosophy was responsible for the (often bloody) things done in its name is a matter of continuing debate, but his radical rejection of civilization, as he knew it, was to prove enormously influential.

Rousseau's radical views are clearly expressed in his treatise on education – *Emile* (1762). This book takes the form of a novel, where a child is brought up and educated in isolation from other children, but it is used by Rousseau primarily as a vehicle for setting out his views on natural education. He argued that social conditioning led to a competitive spirit rather than one that reflected co-operation. We are born natural, but trained to be unnatural. We are born good, but trained to be evil. If we could be free from social constraints, all would be well.

His view of education, therefore, is one that allows for a free expression of the natural qualities and inquisitiveness of the child. He was the first to proclaim that children were not simply unformed adults, waiting for their social conditioning, but individuals, each able to explore and learn in a natural way.

Thus Rousseau's main contribution to the philosophy of education is the recognition of the need for education to be child-centred. It should not be a process of transmitting tradition, but of allowing the individual child to develop his or her own natural ability to learn.

Child-centred approaches to education have been refined through the development of educational psychology, which examines the way in which people learn at different ages and seeks to develop appropriate education methods. Early work on this was done by a German philosopher **Friedrich Herbart (1776-1841)**.

Rousseau wanted each child to develop naturally, in total isolation from society, under the guidance of a personal tutor. In practice, of course, this would never have been possible for the majority of children, and so his view is elitist, even if he did not intend it to be so.

On the other hand, Rousseau's general principal of wanting education to be a facilitating of a child's natural inquisitiveness, has had a lasting impression.

'God made all things good, man meddles with them and they become evil.'

J-J Rousseau

Rousseau's philosophy influenced the work of two pioneering educationalists: **J H Pestalozzi (1746-1827)** put Rousseau's view, that children should learn through experience, into practice at his school in Yverdon in Switzerland, and **F W A Froebel (1782-1852)** was a German educationalist, who believed that young children should be allowed to learn, to express themselves, and to develop simple social skills through play. He established the first Kindergarten, for children between the ages of 4 and 6, in 1837.

LEARNING BY DOING

John Dewey (1859-1952) was an American thinker who made an immense contribution to many areas of philosophy. He developed 'pragmatism', a view (which had already been argued by **C S Peirce** and **William James**) that the meaning of a statement could best be seen in terms of its practical application. A pragmatist asks (of a claim to knowledge, or an ethical proposition, for example) if it is adequate for the purpose to which we intend to put it, and whether it works.

The model for much of Dewey's philosophical work was the sciences, and he applied the scientific method of testing hypotheses to other areas. He held that no claim to knowledge could ever be absolutely certain, since everything was in principle fallible, but that did not stop such fallible knowledge being of service.

His approach to the issue of education (as with the acquisition of all knowledge) was primarily to see it as a process of problem solving, an approach which is generally termed '**instrumentalism**' – which one might characterize as the process of turning a muddle into something that can be handled.

Dewey was much involved in politics and with education, and was particularly concerned to develop new approaches to schooling in the United States, based on 'learning by doing'.

The main features of his approach to education are found in *The School and Society* (1899).

Dewey argued that, following the success of the sciences, the key to intellectual enquiry was the process of problem solving. As far as education was concerned, children are likely to learn most effectively by activity that involve formulating and solving problem, not by being fed with information that they cannot naturally assimilate.

SEE ROUSSEAU – ON POLITICS
SEE PAGE 312

He also held that all education was a social activity. The full meaning of the educational process is revealed in the conduct and personal qualities of the child, as they are revealed in his or her needs and aims as an individual. But these, of course, are socially based.

Therefore, in contrast with traditional education, which Dewey regarded as elitist and socially divisive, he sees the ideal as a process by which people learn together through communal projects.

This approach is reflected in classroom activities where a teacher does not directly prescribe what should be done, but acts as a facilitator, encouraging group exploration and problem solving.

There is one clear limitation to the curriculum suggested by Dewey's approach, since there are areas of study (History, for example) that are not readily available as the basis for a problem-solving activity – unless, of course, there is an archaeological site to hand.

Dewey's approach may therefore be challenged by one that sees education as offering to the student all that is best in human culture, irrespective of the limitations of his or her own personal experience and situation.

There remain fundamental questions about education as the transmission of knowledge. Can it really be enough (as Dewey and Rousseau suggest) to allow education to be a matter of personal exploration? Is there not a basic need to pass on experience from one generation to the next, and is this not a distinctive characteristic of the human species, by which our knowledge and experience has been accumulated with each successive generation?

MARIA MONTESSORI
(1870-1952)
She developed a system of pre-school teaching, which is known as the Montessori Method. Children are given equipment and materials through which they can learn with the minimum of external adult help. It is a method designed to encourage individual initiative. They learn through doing.

Learning by doing – a key feature of modern educational method.

An important aspect of education is developing personal qualities which will be of value to the individual who possesses them and also to society as a whole. We shall look at two thinkers who examine this from very different perspectives and cultures: Confucius and Bertrand Russell.

CONFUCIUS

For Confucius, the process of thinking could not to be separated from the cultural and social matrix within which it took place.

Education, for him, meant the study of the classics of the early Chou dynasty (1100-255BCE), including the Book of Songs, the Book of Rites and the Spring and Autumn Annals. To be educated meant to be aware of your place within society, to know the appropriate thing to do in any situation and to develop those qualities that made for harmonious living.

His own teaching on moral and social matters is found in the Analects (Lun-yu). Although it is ascribed to Confucius, this work is a compilation of teachings produced over a period of time, some possibly pre-dating Confucius and others by his disciples.

Confucius argued that education was necessary in order to achieve balance and restraint, without which even positive qualities could have negative consequences. Thus, for example, a love of learning can lead to unorthodoxy, without the restraint of learning (in that ideas will not be set within tradition), similarly, straightforwardness is in danger of becoming rudeness, courage in danger of becoming rebelliousness, and strength in danger of becoming violence. Qualities must therefore not only be developed, but placed within a social and traditional framework – and education is the means of providing that framework.

Much of Confucius' social teaching takes the form of brief comments, often contrasting the 'gentleman' with the small man':

'The gentleman is dignified but not arrogant. The small man is arrogant but not dignified.' *Analects* 13.26

In education, Confucius was also concerned also with the proper definition of terms. He considered that if concepts were misunderstood, then it would always be unclear what action should be taken, and as a result of this, social principles would not be followed and the result would be chaos.

So the task of philosophy is to clarify concepts, and the task of education is to ensure that a correct understanding of concepts and of culture is transmitted from one generation to the next.

Without a sense of culture, society disintegrates; without education, culture is not transmitted. This is the central thrust of Confucius' view of the significance of education.

Notice however, that Confucius does not simply use education to enforce blind obedience to established norms. Rather he seeks to use it to shape the personal qualities of individuals, as a result of which they will become culturally refined and restrained.

In general, then, tradition holds the key to harmonious life, and the handing on of tradition is the essential function of education.

Education can be used as the vehicle for transmitting cultural, social and political norms. These are acquired, in the course of education, through the ethos of a school and the social background of those with whom one studies, and well as through the subjects studied. The traditional image of an English boys' public school conveys far more than statistics about educational achievement; it is about learning how to live in a way that reflects tradition.

SEE ALSO THE PLACE OF RITUAL IN CONFUCIAN ETHICS, SEE PAGE 84.

RUSSELL

'The main causes of unhappiness at present are: ill health, poverty and an unsatisfactory sex life.' **Russell** *On Education*

On Education (1926) is a sharp and at times witty exposition of Bertrand Russell's view of the place of education. He argues that education should be evaluated from a utilitarian point of view, namely that education serves an end, in terms of the happiness of the individual, and of society as a whole.

One may perhaps smile at Russell's prescriptions for happiness, but his thinking as to the place of education is clear. Education – aided by the new technologies available to humanity, which would overcome all ill health and poverty – is about fostering those qualities that will be valuable in later life. Russell, in his own way, saw education as being as vitally important as Plato and Rousseau had done.

Russell argued that society could only be changed by a generation of children educated to be free and courageous.

'The education we desire for our children must depend upon our ideals of human character, and our hopes as to the part they are to play in the community.' *On Education*

As a humanist, Russell was convinced that human nature was essentially good, frustrated only by the mistreatment that young children receive, both as infants and through schooling. Therefore he saw education as the key to a New World.

In some respects, the presuppositions with which Russell worked were shared by Rousseau, since both saw human potential being thwarted by poor education. On the other hand, one of Russell's criticisms of both Locke and Rousseau is that their theories presuppose an elitist view of education, since they require a personal tutor who can give a child a great deal of individual attention. The very nature of the education they propose excludes all but the most wealthy.

Russell is more concerned with education for all, and therefore with what is possible for everyone to put into practice, either through the personal mother-child relationship or later through the school system.

Russell makes some controversial comments on the relevant importance of what is to be taught if education is to fulfil his dream of creating a world where poverty, illness and psychological unhappiness are overcome:

'In such an education, applied science will have to be the chief ingredient. Without physics and physiology and psychology we cannot build the new world. We can build it without Latin and Greek, without Dante and Shakespeare, without Bach and Mozart. That is the great argument in favour of utilitarian education.' *On Education*

He was particularly concerned with the effects of a classical education:

'A classical education is almost entirely critical: a boy learns to avoid mistakes and to despise those who commit them. This tends to produce a kind of cold correctness, in which originality is replaced by respect for authority.'

Contrast this with Confucius' approach. Confucius saw the ideal society in a past golden age; therefore he needs to maintain cultural continuity. Russell sees the past and present as flawed; therefore he wants new criteria for the educational project.

Education is therefore about fostering qualities that will contribute positively to the future. We must therefore decide what qualities are needed for an ideal society. Russell saw them as vitality, courage, sensitivity and intelligence. Only by creating individuals with the right characteristics, can society improve.

PRACTICAL ASPECTS OF THE PHILOSOPHY OF EDUCATION

Much of the philosophy of education is concerned with the application of general principles to the practice of teaching, the conceptual abilities of students at various stages of their development, and the way in which educational establishments should be organized.

This section has sought to highlight the fundamental purposes of education, as they have been seen from very different philosophical perspectives. A key question is the extent to which education should be seen as:

– transmitting a social and cultural tradition
– encouraging the spirit of critical enquiry
– allowing natural qualities and interests to develop
– manipulating the content of education in order to develop what are seen as desirable personal qualities.

THE PHILOSOPHY OF ART
THEMES IN MODERN ANALYTIC DEBATES

This chapter is divided into three parts. The first deals with themes concerned with art and aesthetics in the modern 'analytic' tradition, followed by a section on 'art and understanding'. The second looks at some major European traditions in aesthetics and in particular the idea of 'modernism'. The third considers the Eastern approaches to the philosophy of art.

AESTHETICS AND ANALYTIC PHILOSOPHY

Most of us have very general puzzles about art and its understanding, partly because it is frequently the function of challenging works of art to stimulate such questions. However, relating them clearly and systematically to philosophical questions we may meet with elsewhere is a far more difficult matter. For this reason the best work in this field is that which has not become isolated from the main body of philosophical enquiry.

A difficulty for the study of aesthetics is that, despite the existence of serious discussion of some of the central issues within Greek philosophy – Aristotle's influence here as elsewhere being pervasive – the systematic study of the problems of aesthetics was recognized rather late in the history of European philosophy, and still tends to be somewhat marginalized from its mainstream.

The German philosopher **Baumgarten (1714-1762)** coined of the term 'aesthetics' for the category of a specific area of judgement and experience. The older concept of aesthetic, meaning more or less un-interpreted sensory experience still survives in modern English 'anaesthetic'.

It might well come as a shock to people if they were told that the administration of an anaesthetic would deprive them of a capacity to respond to the arts or to natural beauty!

In a comparable manner, but over a much longer period, certainly reaching back to Medieval European philosophical debate, the common word 'taste', or its equivalent, also travelled up-market to the idea of Taste as a category of judgement as applied to the arts or to natural beauty or ugliness.

The strongly reductivist traditions of radical empiricism that underlay the early developments of analytic philosophy, together with analytic philosophy's central concern with linguistic meaning and reference, also tended to the view that the limits of serious aesthetics, and philosophy of art, would be an analysis of the critical language we may use in describing art or (just possibly) making direct judgements of preference concerning the natural world.

Hence, for example a well-known collection of essays edited by **W Elton** in mid-century was entitled *Aesthetics and Language*.

AESTHETICS AND LANGUAGE

More recently, the idea that it is possible to locate, within the arts themselves, forms of thought and communication that need to be taken seriously in their own right, has begun to provide a growth area within the subject.

Perhaps the crucial events in this process, as far as mid-century 'Anglo-Saxon' philosophy is concerned, was the publication of **E H Gombrich**'s *Art and Illusion* in 1960 and **Richard Wollheim**'s inaugural lecture 'On Drawing an Object' (1964) followed by his *Art and its Objects* (first edition 1968, second edition 1980) and the publication of **Nelson Goodman**'s *Languages of Art* (1968). Many of the core debates concerning the place of aesthetic understanding within its wider context still centre round the issue raised in these works.

Significantly, Gombrich placed his account of pictorial recognition in art within the context of the psychology of perception, Wollheim made connections with philosophical issues connected with a wider psychoanalytic tradition, and Goodman's key questions connect with those raised in his parallel and earlier work in the philosophy of science.

An underlying question here is whether there are forms of communication and understanding that are not simply reducible to literal description, and (if so) how such forms may connect with other domains of thought.

These questions certainly haunted earlier English language philosophy in the 20th century, most importantly perhaps **R G Collingwood**'s still influential *Principles of Art* (1925), but Collingwood conscientiously related his ideas to the idealist tradition of **Croce** (see page 259), and was a rebel against the early phases of analytic philosophy (see page 42 for the background to this).

It is therefore possible to think of the topics of aesthetics from two different points of view. One has to do with a problem about experience and values, whether concerned with the arts or not.

To many it is unquestionable that aesthetic responses are subjective: both David Hume and Immanuel Kant begin from the position of acknowledging that it is proverbial that 'there is no disputing matters of taste.'

Yet we are sometimes able to establish common agreement about such things, and it has even been thought that principles of harmony (whether in music or in the spatial ordering of architecture) may be rationally demonstrated or objectively perceived.

So we ask:

– How do we find or justify common agreement in judgement?
– Then, if we can, how might we weigh one kind of value directly against another?

Both questions are central to the mainstream of so-called Anglo-Saxon philosophy.

The second kind of issue is concerned with concepts of understanding, and the variety of claims that different arts make on our thought and feeling, perhaps better thought of as topics in the philosophy of art, rather than 'aesthetics'.

EXPERIENCE AND VALUE

Are aesthetic judgements entirely 'subjective', merely an expression of our individual feelings or preferences, making no demand on the rightness or wrongness of the feelings or preferences of others?

The idea of the 'subjective' here is more slippery than we might suppose. A few further questions may begin to indicate just how slippery.

We describe things as ungainly, graceful, ugly, beautiful, delightful or disgusting much as if we were referring to their actual qualities. We may be too depressed to notice the beauty of a landscape, or too attracted by the subject matter of a picture to notice how clumsy its composition and execution may be.

Perhaps we should not suppose that such so-called 'qualities' are part of the objective world, in which how things really are is independent of any observer's beliefs or preferences.

But then very much the same might be said of moral judgements, yet many tend to take it for granted that somehow aesthetic judgements are more manifestly subjective than that. Indeed one common objection to 'subjectivism' in ethics is that it 'reduces' moral judgement to the status of aesthetic preference.

Although some Renaissance thinkers (certainly, **Kepler**) saw aesthetic judgement, as it concerned the assessment of harmony and proportion in the world, as an objective matter, for many, perhaps most, people's matters of taste remain subjective.

L'Aubade, 1942, by Pablo Picasso
If you say that this work of art is beautiful, do you imply that it has some objective quality of beauty, or is the comment simply an expression of your own taste. What counts as great art?

HUME AND KANT

David Hume's essay 'On the standard of taste' (1757) and Immanuel Kant's *Critique of Aesthetic Judgement* (1790) still provide the best introduction to contemporary disputes in this area, especially as they may be related to the context of 20th century analytic philosophy.

Hume sees judgements of taste deriving not from 'matters of fact' but from 'sentiment'. He acknowledges that, if we take it that all preferences expressed are an individual's response to an experience, then there necessarily could be no question of a rational disagreement between such individuals.

Consider two people who insist that, while they know nothing about art, they do know what they like: in effect they have simply and systematically agreed to differ. But suppose these two people say the same thing about wine. Even if we allow them their (vacuous) authority in taste, we might still insist that one may be far less educated in wine tasting than the other, and moreover that, as they continue with their education-in-experience, they may each come to notice aspects and subtleties in flavour that the other has overlooked. They may therefore converge, both in their attention to the aspects of the subtler qualities of the wine and, more importantly, to what it may be that underlies the preferences that actually have.

What Hume terms the great similarity between bodily and mental tastes forms the basis for an analogy with the more sophisticated area of critical judgement of the arts.

The premise of Hume's account is that if we assume (or inductively establish) a broadly similar physiology and psychology of reaction among humans, the differences may be explained and largely negotiated by individual differences in trained experience and by different cultural predilections.

Despite his rejection of this idea in his more general discussion of Locke's theory of perception, this is very close to an assimilation of aesthetic qualities to secondary qualities, the outcome of a causal

Discerning the subtleties of taste...
This photograph, taken in 1954, is of the then head of Gonzales Byass, examining sherry in a blending and testing room in Jerez, the world's capital of sherry-making.

interaction between us and the world around us.

Kant nowhere explicitly refers to Hume, but he does refer disparagingly to 'Canary Wine judgements' and to the sort of judgements that we may make in attempting to please disparate groups of people at dinner parties: there, he acknowledges, we do rely on a kind of induction about what may please others (what he calls an 'anthropology' of taste).

Kant's account is often taken as one that dramatically separates aesthetic value from moral value. Certainly, this reading fits a great deal of what he has to say, and has had the most significant influence on subsequent thought, but it is a misleading over simplification.

The main bulk of his analysis, that con-

cerned with our judgements concerning the beautiful, elaborates four doctrines or '*moments*' that taken together have the effect of locating a special status for his category, neither reducible to the 'agreeable' (as we might find wine, food or what we merely enjoy as charming) nor to the 'good' (the object of moral approval). It is central to his conception that beauty 'has significance only to humans... at once animal and rational' as opposed, that is, to pure rational intelligence on the one hand or mere animals on the other (or humans as they might restrict themselves to one or other of these roles).

This makes huge claims for the philosophical account of aesthetics, in terms of our understanding of what it is to be human.

Kant's first claim is that aesthetic judgements are 'disinterested'. This was a commonplace before him, and his own account of it is difficult, but the nub of it is that in a judgement of this sort what matters is our 'representation' of the object not primarily its 'real existence'.

The force of what he has to say might be brought out in the distinction we may ourselves wish to make between delighting in something aesthetically (a nude, say) and seeing it as an object of desire. Perhaps we normally have both sorts of feelings at once, but there is still a difference between desiring something and delighting in how we think of it, or in how it is represented, or depicted in art.

In such cases our aesthetic delight is not dependant of what appetites we, as opposed to others, may happen to have.

This fact enables his second claim to face in two ways. First, that aesthetic judgements are indeed subjective – means that they are not dependant on concepts. We cannot be 'argued into' aesthetic agreement by the application of general principles, as we might in the case of moral considerations. In every case we need to be presented with a particular case, which (whatever our prior conceptions) may always triumph over our expectations.

However subjective, serious aesthetic judgements are never content to rest with individual preference, but by their nature seek (though can neither require not predict) universal assent.

It is as if we say not 'Well, I like that' but rather 'Isn't that lovely!'

The third step in his account deals with the content of aesthetic value. It is this which seems to warrant the view that Kant anticipates modern 'aesthetic formalism', namely the view that it is the internal design of what we admire, whether a work of art or a natural object, rather than what it may represent that is crucial.

A way of explaining it might go something like this. One of the delights we may get from (say) contemplating a beautiful machine, such as a watch, may be to grasp how it is that the movement of each part contributes to the working of the whole. What each part is 'doing' is only intelligible in terms of how the

whole thing works. Normally we conceive of this in terms of what the watch is for – telling the time. But this is not essential to this sense of organized form: disregarding the 'end' or purpose, we might simply see it as a marvellous work of moving sculpture, or regard it as we might a piece of abstract music.

In this case, the source of our delight is – as Kant puts it – a harmony of imagination and understanding; it derives from how we may make imaginative sense of what we see.

The final 'moment' is more speculative.

The nub of it is that, in making such aesthetic judgements, Kant argues that we commit ourselves to a hope in a common core of human capacity for understanding and imagination – what, in very traditional terms, he calls a concept of a 'common sense.'

This, above all, pays a compliment to the central role of aesthetic thinking – that we thereby celebrate our sense of a common humanity, and thus provide the grounding for morality.

For Kant our aesthetic capacity is to be able to:

'communicate universally without recourse to concepts.'

If, for Kant, our judgements concerning the beautiful centre primarily on our responses to natural beauty, his account of the idea of the sublime (one which was central to late 18th century and romantic thought, even though it has now become out-dated) was essentially a moral category.

Kant distinguishes between what he calls the mathematical sublime (where our conception of vast scale out-runs our capacity to imagine what we may conceive) from the dynamically sublime where our sense of what we might achieve or of what we may fear goes beyond how we may conceive how we could overcome our limitations. In each case the sublime, as it may be found either in the imaginative impact of contemplation of the tragic or of the vastness

of nature faces us directly with the limitations of our moral capacities and our need to overcome them.

Incorporated within art, this makes sense only in terms of moral feeling. On Kant's account therefore, aesthetic judgement is in different ways both the imaginative ground for, and grounded in, the moral enterprise.

'It appears then that amidst all the variety and caprice of taste, there are certain principles of approbation or blame, whose influence a careful eye may trace in all the operations of the mind. Some particular forms or qualities are calculated to please. And others to displease; and if they fail in their effect in any particular instance it is from some apparent defect or imperfection in the organ.'

David Hume,
Of the Standard of Taste

'Agreeableness is a significant factor even with irrational animals; beauty has purport and significance only for human beings, i.e. for beings at once animal and rational (but not merely for them as rational-intelligent beings – but only for them as at one animal and rational); whereas the good is good for every rational being in general.'

Immanuel Kant,
The Critique of Judgement

AESTHETICS, ART AND MORALITY

The accounts of Hume and of Kant may provide one starting point for questions concerning aesthetics, art and morality. Few people would deny that positive aesthetic experience or art has value. A large problem arises, however, when we attempt to say clearly how such value stands to other values we may have.

Might we simply suppose that since aesthetically good things, or art we value, is something we prefer to have, then it must simply be part of what we value overall, as an aspect of how people should live in a morally better world?

In a more complex manner, we might suppose that the values of art, of great drama, literature or the visual arts are perhaps best fitted for conveying moral content, or in educating us in the necessary moral virtues of imaginative sensitivity or breadth of understanding. In effect, this is to regard the values of art as morally instrumental.

If so, what should we say if presented with art which is aesthetically or imaginatively powerful yet deplorable from a certain moral point of view? Which might 'trump' which?

An alternative view might be to say that the values we find expressed in art are – or should be – independent of moral values, even that art and morality are autonomous areas.

Kant's account may seems to warrant this, and has been so interpreted by, for example, **Mary Mothersill**, whose *Beauty Restored* is an analytic reconstruction of what she takes to be Kant's theory of beauty. Different interpretations, from this point of view, may be found in **Paul Guyer**'s *Aesthetics and the Claims of Taste* or in **Paul Crowther**'s *The Kantian Sublime*.

Big autonomy theories can be found in **Schopenhauer, Hegel, Schiller**, and in the tradition of 'aesthetic formalism' dominant in certain aspect of early 20th century modernism, in England in for example in the writings of **Clive Bell**.

One question that may be asked is whether it would, in principle, make sense to take such a general view as covering the claims of all art, ranging from highly abstract painting to the great tragedies, comedies or novels. Even so, the question of just how we might negotiate between different kinds of values would still remain.

The Nude Maja, 1805, by Goya.
Should art be required to deliver moral content? Clearly, Plato thought it should. Should it reflect values? Clearly, the best art does indeed challenge and encourage sensitivity. Yet art frequently depicts the most sensual of subjects. Should it be allowed to stimulate desire? Kant made the point that aesthetic judgements are 'disinterested', in other words, the delight is in the artistic representation itself, not necessarily in the desire one might have for that which is depicted. Goya's painting was originally criticized for its overtly erotic content.

Why should it matter so much that we say what we know is not true, either because if is fictional or because, since metaphorical, it cannot be literally true? How does fiction logically relate to truth and falsity, and how does the metaphorical relate to the literal?

FICTION

The old dispute between Plato and Aristotle concerning the function of fiction is still a live issue within contemporary analytic philosophy. Why should we tell stories which we know to be false?

Aristotle's defence of tragic dramatic poetry in the *Poetics*, firmly asserts that fictional stories, even if highly improbable, may be more 'philosophical' than plain factual history. The reason is that what we may be free to fictionally suppose, can enable us to consider the consequences and ramifications of possible situations for ourselves. We imagine situations in ways that range far beyond what we have actually experienced ourselves.

The Aristotelian doctrine, that by tragic drama we are purged of pity and terror, invites us to question how our reactions to what we know to be fictional, compare with the responses we have to real life. The horror we must feel as part of any informed response to a dramatic tragedy, is not the same as the horror we would feel towards the same events in real life.

As **Edward Bullough** pointed out in 1912, our emotional response has a 'psychical distance' that seems to map onto a distinction we recognize between fact and fiction.

One way of tracing that relation is first to recognize the subtle connections between emotion and beliefs. This places the initial analytic burden on how the recognition of fiction engages our beliefs.

It might even be thought that the topic of fiction as such belongs most naturally within the domain of 'philosophical logic', or the 'philosophy of language', rather than within aesthetics, and it is often the case that theorists in these different areas pay less attention to one another than they should.

One way of posing the problem here is to ask what might be the most illuminating way of tunnelling between an account of 'fiction', as a general logical, or metaphysical category, and an understanding of the philosophical issues raised by the arts of Fiction.

It is worth bearing in mind that the distinction between that fictional play which is non-deceptive pretending (say children playing at being bears) as opposed to (say) deceptively pretending to be hurt, is one that children, perhaps unlike other young playful animals, seem to grasp (and to find entertaining) at a very early stage of cognitive development.

Recognizing that a narrative is 'only a story' is an aspect of this.

So what is it that is recognized? One answer might be that it is simply the ability to distinguish between merely supposing that something might be so and thinking that it really is. But this too does not take us far. In many contemporary discussions, subsequent to the work of such philosophers as **David Lewis** and **Saul Kripke** it has become normal to think of the fictional thought or narrative of what might be (such as the existence of Holmes and Watson in late Victorian London) as the proposal of a '*possible world*', different from this actual one but sharing overlapping features with it (such as London, the English weather and so on). **Nicholas Wolterstorff** uses this discourse in his book *Works and Worlds of Art*, and even commits himself to the view that storytellers thus create not only possible worlds but impossible ones too (such as that created by the composition of the world of *Alice in Wonderland*).

In some ways, this it attractive. It seems to fit not only our natural ways of thinking that there 'really are' certain possibilities, which we need to take seriously as part of the way things are, and also that authors create more than linguistic texts (or, we might add, pictures) but 'worlds,' to which they refer and which we may even imaginatively 'enter' as we respond to their work.

For all that both these metaphysical strategies, and the simpler thought that fiction is merely speculation concerning what might be but is not, fail to capture a further feature of reading and engaging with fiction whether in language pictures, drama or film. This is, that it is essential to our informed response, that the plausibility, even the intelligibility of a fiction, depends on the inter-relation of two types of judgement concerning the content and presentation of the fiction, to which we now turn.

'…the essential difference [between history and poetry] is that the one tells us what happened and the other the sort of thing that would happen. That is why poetry is more like philosophy and more worthwhile than history…'

Aristotle, *Poetics*, 1451b

FICTION AND NON-FICTIONAL BELIEFS

The first of these amounts to the logical fact that not all of an intelligible fiction could be fictional; in our understanding of a story, we draw on facts that we and the story-teller both know, concerning how things normally are. For example whether, trivially, rain makes people wet and cold, whether it be us, Lear on the heath, or Holmes on Dartmoor, or far less trivially, how we really do think that people would respond under the stress of events.

If the fiction fails to fit this we may either criticize it for artistic faults, such as sentimentality or lack or verisimilitude or, alternatively, grant that these variations too are part of the fictional component of the story.

The second type of judgement depends on the fact that even the most unlikely stories can be made plausible so long as we tell the story 'sparsely' enough, so for example time travel, giants with seven league boots, or matter-transmission, make perfect sense so long as we know what questions not to ask, what non-fictional beliefs not to access.

If fiction is to invoke possible worlds they must be remarkably sketchy if they are to be imaginable, let alone conceivable. Different genera of fiction – the realist novel, fantasy, fairy-tales, science fiction – may be distinguished from one another by the often quite systematic ways in which we suspend such questions.

Alternatively, ironic 'games' with our genera expectations of what we may have to do to track intelligibility, such as *magic realism*, may shock us as readers into confronting just what strategies of plausibility we do in fact adopt.

This clearly makes a connection with Coleridge's famous aphorism concerning the reader's 'willing suspension of disbelief', but it also confronts a central issue concerning philosophical method. It is often assumed by philosophers that we may test 'conceptual possibility' by investigating what we may tell convincing stories about.

But if part of what constitutes finding a fiction intelligible can be to suspend judgement concerning the ramifications of its consequences, nothing of the sort follows. Thus **Deryk Parfitt**'s investigation of the problems of personal identity in *Reasons and Persons* which makes use of such fictional ideas (such as the science fiction idea of matter transmission) is criticized by **Cathy Wilkes,** in her book *Real People: Personal Identity without thought experiments*, for making just this assumption. Thought experiments in science may similarly require what is envisaged be thought of sparsely; hence the idealization of such counter-factual reflections.

Hence both science and the apparently quite different domain of literature, may sometimes require reflective simplification.

The English novelist and poet, Robert Graves, writing at his home, in December 1941.
To what extent does simplification make fiction more imaginable?
Does fiction serve to highlight non-fictional beliefs about the world shared by both writer and reader? But particularly, a philosopher might want to explore the nature of that creative process by which the writer shapes a text, in order to convey meaning through fiction. What is the difference between writing fiction and non-fiction? Do both require the manipulation of facts?

METAPHOR AND IMAGERY

The body of analytic philosophical literature on metaphor is vast, much of it highly technical, but within the discussion it is possible to locate some persistent themes.

Perhaps the oldest and most persistent question is whether metaphor is *cognitively necessary*. In other words, whether metaphor, figures of speech, tropes and imagery, serve an essentially decorative, or sometimes 'pragmatic', function (so that the core sense of what is said could well be expressed in less elegant but literal terms) or whether such use of language corresponds to a form of thinking that *needs* to be respected in its own right.

One, perhaps combative, way of posing the questions is *to ask whether metaphor has cognitive content*. A tradition that goes back to Aristotle effectively sees metaphor as rhetorically disguised simile.

We could put it that, since our language inevitably contains far fewer words to discriminate features of the world that we may attend to, we may construct new descriptive terms by way of comparisons.

On this account departure from the literal is merely departure from standard language, by the creation of new words. Familiar examples might be colour words: violet, orange and puce (the colour of a squashed flea), are names of shades that derive from tacit comparisons of one thing with another. Once established, none are metaphorical.

Similarly, on this account, the foot of a bed, a hill or a page, tacitly compares all such things with the lowest part of a limb. There is, on this interpretation, no special force to the (literally absurd) thought that the lowest part of a hill may after all somehow be as animate as a part of a possibly living body. Yet for many theorists it is this departure from literal sense that is the nub of the issue.

So-called 'interaction theories', such as **Max Black**'s in his greatly influential *Models and Metaphors* or **Goodman**'s description of metaphor as 'deliberate category mistakes'. (This term had central currency at the time, largely due to **Gilbert Ryle's** use of it in *The Concept of Mind*, where for example to suppose that thoughts are in our heads, as opposed to being somewhere else, is to apply a predicate to a subject which can neither accept nor reject it.) So Goodman's description is then itself a metaphor: it is an oxymoron for a mistake to be deliberate.

All pay tribute to what **William Empson** in the 1930s described in *Seven Types of Ambiguity*, and later in *The Structure of Complex Words* as an irreducible conceptual ambiguity within the metaphorical phrase. The essential point then is that 'right understanding' on the part of the reader cannot imply a demand to resolve such ambiguities.

> 'Briefly, a metaphor is an affair between a predicate with a past and an object that yields while protesting.'
>
> Nelson Goodman, *Languages of Art*

The question then remains what kind of a function this may have within our thought and imagination. A narrow conception of meaning that holds that the meaning of an expression is grasped in terms of (imaginable) truth conditions, for its application would have to hold that metaphor has no meaning since necessarily there could not be such truth conditions. But an extended conception of meaning would accept the metaphor as an expression of our attempt to communicate beyond our own conceptual limits. We then may be able to adjust such limits, by internally driven processes of conceptual change.

Many philosophers have recognized such conceptual change as central to the history of science, and this role of metaphor may be more recognized by philosophers of science than by philosophers of art. One reason for this is that within poetry there is very little pressure for a later resolution into new concepts.

The use of live metaphor in poetry and imaginative prose is an essential resource of art that enables us both to recognize and thus fictionally speculate beyond the bounds of what we take to be in principle possible.

The concept of 'imagery' in poetic language should perhaps be contrasted with such accounts of metaphor. An 'imagist' use of language – one which enables the reader as directly as possible to concretely imagine – 'bring to the mind's eye' – what the words refer to has received far less attention from philosophers of language than from theorists of literature.

In the latter there is a tradition of 'Imagism' as a poetic and critical movement, which explains its contrast between 'concrete' and 'abstract' use of words. This central theme among literary thinkers of the time had little parallel in analytic philosophy, since it arose during a period when the two disciplines were, sadly, not on speaking terms with one another.

There are a number of reasons for this, not least the influence in mid-century analytic philosophy of the later Wittgenstein, who rejected the idea that the meaning of a word could be a private inner experience.

This added to a wider scepticism, concerning the value of conceptions of imagination that rest on the vividness of such inner experience. On this view the concept of vivid imagery (which certainly need not be metaphorical) belongs, not to the category of meaning, but to an account of the causal effects that language may then have on a reader.

What is it to recognize painted or otherwise marked surfaces, as pictures of what they represent?

Since being a picture of 'x' seems to compare directly with being a sentence about 'x', for both are in very general terms more or less straightforward concepts of denoting, the question seems to arise how like or unlike linguistic representation should we take this to be? How does this connect with the problems of understanding visual art?

How we answer the first two of these questions may largely determine our approach to the third.

We might begin by insisting on a sharp distinction between linguistic and pictorial communication. At the root of it is the thought that, whereas language is a set of essentially arbitrary signs that derive their meaning from learnt codes and rules, pictorial signs are dramatically different.

The sentence 'the cat sat on the mat' only represents what it does, insofar as we apply learnt interpretative rules that enable us to understand it. By contrast a picture of a cat on a mat (however crudely or skilfully drawn) communicates what it does as a direct consequence of our capacity for recognizing actual cats.

Hence however puzzling strange or hard to recognize pictures may be, this cannot be because pictures require translation in the way that languages might.

Our capacity to directly recognize the pictures of ancient European rock art seems to testify to the dramatic extent to which pictorial signs are not arbitrary. What we cannot recognize, perhaps never will, is the wider purposes in the depiction of such animals.

There will inevitably be borderline cases: pictures may also be used in quasi-linguistic ways. A drawn halo, for example, is best regarded as a conventional sign that the depicted person is holy. The viewed placing of a figure within a composition, choice of subject matter, all have 'iconographic' significance that does need to be learnt and decoded by specific cultural knowledge.

As such theorists as **Panofsky** have insisted much of the interpretative work of art historians must consist in providing methods for such interpretation, where, however visual, the medium of communication goes well beyond merely pictorial representation.

A way of putting this may be that any capacity we have for recognizing cats (or ancient bison) not only extends to a capacity for imagining unseen cats (or even unreal winged cats) but also carries with it a capacity for recognizing pictures of cats.

It seems to be a general truth, that our capacity for recognizing familiar visual objects extends also to our capacity for recognizing pictures of them. This is, for instance, how we use pictures to test whether witnesses recognize what they claim to have seen.

However, we seem to retain that capacity, even when pictures of things (thought of as surfaces marked in a certain way) are at the same time manifestly visually very unlike what they represent, not merely by being flat but, for example, by being very sketchy monochrome line drawings.

Pictures may represent kinds of things far less specific than the particular items in the world we actually see. We can do this for an astonishingly wide variety of depictive styles.

However mere recognition of visual likeness between pictures and what they depict seems, to be inadequate to explain how we grasp depictive significance. (Famously, **Nelson Goodman** has denied that such resemblance could ever provide the key to the matter: even visual resemblance is neither a necessary no sufficient condition of pictorial success).

Our grasp of successful depiction seems to carry with it a capacity to distinguish in the picture what is to count as relevant likeness, as opposed to irrelevant unlikeness. We are moreover, perfectly content to accept pictures as of recognizable objects even though, because of their lack of specificity, there is no particular object we suppose them to resemble.

Moreover, when we respond to pictures in visual art, it is these varieties of ways of depicting, as well as the recognition of what is depicted, that plays a central role in our understanding.

E H Gombrich, for whom our capacity to construct schema pictorial representation is continuous with our general capacities to recognize items in the visual world (though the two may on particular occasions diverge dramatically), holds that if the 'illusion' of the picture is not to be dispelled, our attention to the qualities of the marked surface itself excludes attention to what it depicts.

Richard Wollheim, on the other hand, insists that a 'twofold' response to both aspects of our experience of a picture is essential to our understanding of visual art. For Wollheim our recognition of pictures springs from a capacity for imaginative projection; a form of 'seeing in' (as we see figures in clouds, or landscapes) that goes beyond mere recognition. But in the case of pictures, we do this with criteria of correct pictorial understanding.

The question remains what concepts of understanding we are dealing with here. But even to ask the question is to make the unavoidable assumption that we need to recognize pictorial forms of thought.

We recognize a familiar face, even after the changes brought about through age or illness, or in spite on an unusual expression. We do this by selecting a limited number of significant features, and eliminating others. We 'read' someone's face, too, by selecting and interpreting elements of what we see – we judge their mood and their personality at a glance. Art images and photographs are treated in the same way. Even though represented on a flat surface, we read the face, interpret the gesture, or imaginatively enter into the scene or the action depicted.

Sometimes particular images become icons, representing a particular quality or feature of life with almost archetypal force. Look at the friendly man with neat hair and moustache, speaking on the telephone. The shape of the telephone and cut of his jacket immediately signify the age of the photograph, but otherwise he could be anyone's friendly uncle!

Now look at the image inset on the left. The smile has gone, but otherwise the face remains the same. But, detached from its surroundings and set against a black background, the effect is quite different. This is not simply a non-smiling uncle; it is an image that we 'read' as an icon of brutality and hate. The face does not just illustrate the man, it expresses all that happened in the Third Reich, with the Holocaust and other horrors.

But, in a lighter vein, the same thing happens with pop stars, film idols and so on. The attractive person who might well live next door, is moulded to represent all that we might desire – an image of sexiness, or toughness, or intelligence, or rebellion. Yet these things are merely hinted at in the image, and we are invited to 'read in' the rest.

Some philosophers, most notably Collingwood, have taken expression to be central to the very idea of art, even to be its defining characteristic. Others have been equally anxious to thrust the whole concept to one side.

'Expression' is in itself a drastically slippery concept. In many contexts the idea of what something expresses can be virtually synonymous with 'meaning'. On the other hand when we refer to such things as a facial expression we may mean little more than that we are presented with a symptom of a state of mind.

A popular view of emotional expression through art may be parodied as the idea that somehow feelings and emotions may be held within a person, 'pent up', and in need of removal by being healthily expressed outside.

Aristotle's account of the art of tragedy, as being a catharsis or purge of inner pity or terror, indicates clearly enough how ancient this idea is.

Any difficulty we may have with the idea of emotion as a kind of bottled up material that requires ejection, belongs to a wider context in the philosophy of mind, but it is within the theory of art that such ideas may cause the most trouble.

To many philosophers (and to many artists) such concepts of expression have given the very idea of expressiveness a bad name. It is also important to distinguish the idea of expressiveness as a category of certain styles of art, where the handling of the medium becomes a dominant content of the work, from a universal concept that may be applied to all art.

What, however, links the ideas of thinkers such as Aristotle and Collingwood, is the far more serious thought that it is a major function of serious art to present emotional states, and situations which must inevitably be charged with emotion for our imaginatively engaged reflection. **That expression may thus make what we take to be personal and private into something that is, in a significant sense, public.**

Part of the problem is how far we should take the idea of something's being 'expressive' as meaning that it expresses an emotion or feeling, either in the person who produces it or as the beholder may perhaps imagine feeling it?

Such views may seem most attractive when we think of certain sorts of music as having, or 'expressing', certain specific emotional qualities, such as being sad, or cheerful, even nervous or relaxed.

Much the same may be said about visual art. A picture may be said in this vein to be sad or cheerful and we may even – illuminatingly – say similar things concerning a passage of painting of drawing within the picture. A drawn line may be nervous, hesitant relaxed, or charged with energy. Much the same may be said about a passage of writing whether in poetry or prose.

The problem is that while it would be manifestly foolish to deny that such ways of talking have a place, and are in fact indispensable for any significant account of the style of a work of art, it is equally difficult to see just what they amount to. The relaxed quality of a drawn line or the nervous quality of a line of music can hardly be a symptom of the line's, or the sound's, inner emotional states.

Hence either such descriptions are metaphorical (the appropriateness of which itself needs explaining) or are elliptical ways of claiming that the states of mind of the makers of such things, are induced by them in their hearers or beholders.

But this latter claim seems obviously false. Recognizing the emotional expressiveness of a work, requires neither that the composer or artist, nor the audience, reader or beholder of the work should feel such emotions. Good performers can give an emotional quality to a passage of music or dance a quality of feeling which they certainly need not feel themselves at the time of the performance, and paintings may exhibit a quality of lyrical, and joyous calm that we may know to be very different from the actual state of mind of the painter at the time.

Indeed the capacity to achieve this separation between the immediate feelings of a performer of an artist and the feelings that may be presented by the work, would seem to constitute the characteristic skill of serious art.

In the same way, anyone able to give proper attention to a work must be able to recognize, even in the most trivial cases, that a song may be sad or cheerful even though it may produce no such state of mind in its hearers. **What is required, is that such qualities should be directly recognizable 'in' the work itself.**

One way of understanding this is to think of how actors may behave in a way that makes it appear that they are expe-

The relaxed quality of a drawn line or the nervous quality of a line of music can hardly be a symptom of the line's, or the sound's, inner emotional states.

riencing an emotion, or a state of feeling: they may thus exhibit the appropriate state of mind for our reflective and imaginative response.

Behaviour, which may otherwise be merely symptomatic of feeling, may thus become detached from that origin, so that forms of behaviour, or the outcome of ways of making works, such as the qualities of the handling of materials, 'expressively' come to belong to them in their own right.

Thus, the so-called 'expressive' qualities of works may be ascribed to them neither metaphorically nor elliptically, but in terms of the way in which they are produced, as their causal story.

This thought may enable us to reintegrate the concept of expressiveness as a particular style of art into the wider story. For from this point of view there must be a concept of style that applies to any work of art that can do much of the work of the most general ideas of expression. Goodman in 'The status of style' reprinted in his *Ways of Worldmaking* distinguishes between 'style as signature' – where the way a work is made may both be distinguished from what is made and then provides clues concerning who made it – from 'style as content' where it makes no sense to suppose that the same thing could have been 'done another way'.

If style is content, then the ways of making a picture or a sculpture, or a way of performing a piece of music, have to be attended to as part of a properly informed response to the work. The restricted sense of 'expressiveness' as a style, then becomes just one of many ways in which this may the achieved.

But art in general makes these demands on our dual attention in ways that non-artistic products and activities do not. **Richard Wollheim's** concept of an essential 'twofold' response to painterly depiction pays one tribute to this, the value we place, when responding to imaginative literature, on ways of writing which we are reluctant to segment from 'content'.

'Good performers can give an emotional quality to a passage of music…' Part of the delight of opera is the imaginative identification with emotions expressed in the music and actions of the singers.

But is this expressiveness 'style' or 'content'. In any performance, these two things come together. There cannot be performed content without style – however minimalist that style may be, and the communication of feeling is integral to the arts, even those less overtly expressive of emotion than opera.

MEANING, INTENTION AND INTERPRETATION

The concept of a work of art, if contrasted with the simple idea of an aesthetically valued natural object, carries the suggestion that it is essential to a proper response to it that we suppose that, via the work, we must respond to the mind of its maker

This is because, so long as we take art to be the outcome of human activity (making, composing, selecting or performing) the very idea of a work must commit us to a minimal account of the mind of the artist, or artists meeting the minds of a work's beholders. The problem then is how we are to give content to that response.

The natural thing to say is that we should regard the work as the outcome of its maker's intentions, and indeed much of the proper understanding of critical historians of any of the arts does indeed need to assume that. Does this mean that the correct interpretation of a work must rest on an identification of its author's intentions? This view has been castigated as 'the intentional fallacy', on the grounds that many of the intentions of an author may either not be realized in the work or be quite beyond our knowledge.

Certainly in many cases we may have no knowledge of who a work's maker was, and even if we did have such knowledge, it would be irrelevant: what we need to respond to is the work itself, not the intentions behind it. The concept of an 'intentional fallacy', to be avoided by sensible readers and critics, thus ran in tandem with a strong insistence on the identity of the text, or the work as something which had an autonomous identity quite independent of external historical background or any biographical facts concerning the author.

The slogan of the 'New Critics' of the 1950s (associated in English literary studies with writing in the periodical *Scrutiny* and with the influence of **F R Leavis**) was that what the reader needed to attend to was simply and purely 'the words on the page'.

But can this distinction be maintained?

In most contexts outside the arts, we identify an action (and often the intended outcome of an action) by our understanding of the agent's intention, and relevant background knowledge and beliefs.

To take an example from **Elizabeth Anscombe**'s seminal monograph *Intention*, a person moving his arm in a certain way, while standing in the cellar of a house and holding a wooden handle, is doing something quite different depending on whether he knows he is working a half rotary hand pump, knows and is content with the knowledge that the water is poisoned, or, further knows that the house is about to be used by the inner circle of the Nazi Party. Depending on all this he is either performing a morally neutral action, a wicked or a brave one.

It would be odd if the same kind of principle did not apply to works of art as well. The idea that it is in principle possible to segregate the meaning of words, thus of texts, from either their speaker's or author's intentions or the historical context of the language to which they belong seems equally untenable. Indeed it is the parallel between these two considerations that links the idea's of an agent's intention and (in relevant contexts) what the user of a language, or other form of communication may 'mean', which connects these issues with main stream topics within 20th century analytic philosophy.

Within recent analytic philosophy it is important, for example, to distinguish the idea of 'intention' meaning purpose from the technical term 'intentionality', which has to do with the content of a thought or communication. This is important because only then may we trace subtle and complex connections between the two.

One device here might be to seek to distinguish those intentions whose identification must be essential to any informed description of the work, from 'external' intentions which, while they may explain the existence of the work, need not play any part in our grasp of what the work is. Hence, while it may be quite irrelevant to the understanding or evaluation of a literary work that it

was composed with the intention of paying the author's bills, it may be quite central to that understanding that it had a moral or political purpose, the outcome of which may be apparent within the work.

The central question then becomes how such interpretations may be justified. At this point philosophical analysis needs to join hands with informed historical method as, for example in the art historian **Michael Baxendall**'s *Patterns of Intention*. Extreme scepticism might hold that the correct tactic would be to ignore the role of the author or the historical context altogether, allowing virtually any 'reading' of a text or interpretation of a work of art.

ORIGINALITY, AUTHENTICITY AND CREATIVITY

We place a high value on the virtues of originality and creativity in art. One reason for thinking that fakes and forgeries are a bad thing is not merely that they subvert the art market but that they may subvert our understanding of art.

What counts as a fake, and how works should be preserved or restored, testifies to the significance we attach to the causal history of works of art, when we make claims about the identity of particular works.

Theorists such as **Strawson, Wollheim** or **Wolterstorff**, have chosen to adopt and adapt, **C S Peirce**'s distinction between type objects and their tokens. Consider how we may count words in different, but complementary, ways. The sentence 'Our dog bit their dog' has 5 words in it if words are counted as tokens, 4 if counted as types. The crucial point here is that we may say of the type-word (or of any comparable object) that it occurs more than once. A type object is one that may be instantiated in a variety of different material instances. We say that two people possess the same photograph, each having different prints of the same work, while we do not say (or think) this of drawings or paintings. In the former case, but not in the latter, if two objects are visually indistinguishable we normally conclude that at least one is either a 'mere' reproduction or a fake or forgery.

Nelson Goodman in *Languages of Art* distinguished between '*autographic*' works, such as paintings, which are as it were identical with their own manuscripts and of which typically there may be forgeries, and, '*allographic*', typically performance works, such as plays, works of music or dance, which derive their identity from their performance. While the subject of pastiche and imitation, these cannot be forged.

For Goodman, the core problem of a work's identity does not centre on the distinction between single and multiple works (it is possible to have multiple autographs) but on whether the conditions of a work's continuity rest on an individual agent's intentions or rather on those intentions mediated by score-like instructions for further performance compliance. The weakness of Goodman's account may be thought to be the relatively small place this permits for the independent artistic and interpretative role of a performer's judgement.

A comparable difficulty may be seen in an un-adapted Peircien account of type-identity: Peirce conceived of type objects on the model of a typewriter's keys, which produce multiple token signs. But, in the context of art, to be guided by type considerations is, rather, to be guided by a grasp of what is essential or inessential to the preservation or continuity of a work. This question of what should count as relevant is central both to the authenticity of performance and, in non performance art, of preservation and restoration. The question is then how far such distinctions may be found within an understanding of an artist's, author's or composer's intentions.

We need to recognize that in many art forms (in music, drama, dance, most manifestly in film, and more subtly in the visual arts and in architecture) the idea that a work is the outcome of the thought of one author is absurd. Most often the relevant process of thought is a very specifically structured engagement of a group of makers working as a team within a creative process, the understanding of which locates our sense of what makes a particular work the work it is.

A deeper issue here is that the process of thought we need to understand via the work is most unlikely to be a simple matter of an agent setting a pre-set goal with which the work then has to comply. Characteristically, an artist or composer will come to understand the work only within the process of making it. A performer's understanding of the work similarly emerges within a process of engagement. The insistence that such agents can only come to 'know what they want' in the process of achieving it, was thought (e.g. by Collingwood) to be characteristic of emotional expression. There is no good reason for supposing that this has essentially – or often much – to do with emotion, every reason to suppose that such forms of understanding are characteristic of intellectual creativity, whether within the arts or in any other context.

Creativity and interpretation are essential to the work of an artist. What the sculpter produces is not merely a three dimensional reproduction of the photographs he uses for reference, but a personal interpretation of the subject.

It is tempting to think of the question 'What counts as art?' as the natural stating point for any philosophy of art, for how otherwise could we know what our subject is concerned with?

Perhaps, however, it is best approached, if at all, only after an enquiry had already been well under way, not least because it is a serious question whether (apart, perhaps, from concern with tax laws) we do in fact require such an overall concept at all.

Many big theories of art seek an essential core for the concept: art has been defined for example in terms of *pure representation* (within much of the theories of art associated with the modernism of Cézanne) of *expression* (as for **Croce** and **Collingwood**) or (in a tradition that is often seen to run from Kant via such thinkers as **Clive Bell** to, more recently, **Clement Greenberg**) to the presentation of *pure aesthetic form*.

Counter examples tend to crop up immediately, as if indeed it had become the business of serious art to challenge such theoretical programmes.

The very idea of definition in this area is troublesome: perhaps we need to recognize that we are dealing with what has to be accepted as a loose or open concept. Yet it seems to be one we cannot do without.

The idea that there must be such open concept, which cannot be pinned down by a set of necessary and sufficient conditions, may be strongly encouraged by Wittgenstein's metaphor of family resemblances, where – to use his example – there are many different forms of 'game', with little by way of particular qualities or forms of activity in common.

Are the various forms of art to be as disparate as the various activities to which the term 'game' can rightly be applied?

The history of art seems itself to incorporate that puzzle. All sorts of things that we now think of as art from the past (such as religious sculpture) were almost certainly not regarded as art at all by their makers. Indeed many societies seem not to have had a clear concept of art as a separate area of human endeavour at all.

Perhaps such societies were simply mistaken about what they were doing, or perhaps the very idea of art is a fragile concept that might have no place in our own future?

Either way, it seems proper to ask what may give anyone the right to apply the term 'art'. In the 20th century many works seem to make the issue part of their subject matter.

A brisk way of dealing with this question might be simply to grant that whatever is allowed to be art by the 'institutions' of art (by galleries, dealers, concert promoters theatres, and so on) should be generally considered to be art.

This somewhat reductivist 'Institutional theory of art', which certainly has the virtue of a healthy scepticism concerning the value of a priori philosophical theory, may be associated with the writings of **George Dickie**.

The immediate question it gives rise to is, as Richard Wollheim has pointed out, whether such institutions might conceivably make mistakes about this, and – if so – what would make for such mistakes?

To reply that the very idea of mistakes here would make no sense, would have the consequence that the relevant institutions exercise an irrational power. In other words, it would suggest that the only criterion for something being considered 'art' is that it should be presented within that cultural and economic system:

if an art dealer can sell it, then it must be art.

Clearly, the question about whether it is reasonable to grant such power would not be a question within the philosophy of art, but at best one solely within the philosophy of politics, sociology or economics.

A more subtle view might be that the very idea of art evolves or changes, as it were, from within its own practice; that new works or new types of art, may sometimes, but not always, have the function of altering our conception of art itself.

For **Arthur Danto** – who is also called an institutional theorist – continuous questioning of the very idea of art has become part of the subject matter of art itself, during the modern period. If so, we might perhaps need to take care that we do not foreclose on this process by seeking to define the concept of art in advance.

Danto's idea of an 'institution', in this context, seems subtler and wider than Dickie's; in effect it embraces all those aspects of our culture that need to find space for those exercises of imaginative celebration that cannot be reduced to other cultural categories.

There seems to be, however, a tension within his account that is in some ways typical of many recent discussions of this issue. He endorses an up-dated version of a Hegelian idea that, just as other cultures have had no conception of art, so we might see in our own a corresponding 'death of art', with art being absorbed into a new kind of philosophy.

But he also thinks of the cultural institutions of art as being essentially located in forms of understanding, involving concepts of style, the recognition of intention and of metaphorical ambiguity of reference, which would then seem to be genuine characteristics of art that an uninformed society might (mistakenly) fail to recognize.

So, even if absorbed into the context of other cognitive enquiries, the question

Les Grandes Baigneuses by Paul Cézanne
Can you define art as pure representation? Issues of the separateness and interrelationships between visible objects, are a major feature of the interpretation of the work of Cézanne. Prior to the freedom of 20th century art to take apart and re-fashion the world in creative ways, Cézanne and other post-impressionists were already moving in that direction, and away from the straight representation of the visible world, by the boldness and emotional power of their art.

still remains whether 'we', or other societies, could be wrong about what art really is or is not?

How far can we find, within the processes of art's re-definition or cultural context, a philosophical justification for categories of 'significance', 'imagination' and 'communication' that cannot be reduced to those dominant in other domains of thought and experience?

To the extent that such questions are live ones, the central philosophical enquiries need to continue, both within, and as a challenge to, the continuing debates of analytic philosophy.

FOR GREENBERG ON AESTHETICS SEE ALSO PAGE **266** AND FOR HIS ASSOCIATION WITH KANT SEE PAGE **254**

'I identify Modernism with the intensification, almost the exacerbation, of this self-critical tendency that began with the philosopher Kant. Because he was the first to criticize the means itself of criticism, I conceive of Kant as, the first real Modernist.'

American art critic Clement Greenberg (1909-1994)

PURE REASON AND AESTHETIC LOGIC

Kant's philosophy is an attempt to secure an understanding of how our cognitive (practical) and pre-cognitive (theoretical) faculties allow us to form things like knowledge and opinions. His (notoriously difficult) *The Critique of Pure Reason* repositions the mind in relation to the world and to our ideas about reality. Instead of our ideas about reality being a mere consequence of reality-itself, that is instead of the mind being like a blank sheet of paper on to which the world paints a picture (as John Locke described it) the mind itself figures as a pre-determining factor in our ideas about the world.

In order to consider the mind as an effective agent in our understanding, Kant focuses his attention on the a priori faculties (an a priori fact can be established without reference to experience and provides 'pure knowledge'). This suggests that the individual is given at the point of creation (birth) certain powers of reason, and the ability to apply these powers in the attempt to understand the world.

A priori knowledge includes concepts such as time, space and causality; the building blocks of experience and the basis of all knowledge. As such it provides only the 'pure schema of possible experience' and so is aesthetic, not logical; it can yield only 'pure concepts' and is knowledge in the purest of forms: *aesthetic knowledge*.

KANT'S DEFINITION OF ART

Kant's definition of art comes in *The Critique of Judgement*, 1790, which is not about art as such, but the manner in which the mind forms relative assessments of value via the senses. For that reason it has proved amenable to the discussion of artistic value.

The artist is regarded by Kant as possessing a particular form of reason that yields creative vision, and so has the unique ability to see and translate the world into what we call art. This vision he calls genius, an inherent quality of mind that is informed by nature itself. In this way the genius has the unique capacity to be truly creative.

Kant claims that art should be distinguished from:

● **nature** (in that art must be immediately recognizable as being a product of intentional human labour);

● **science** (in that the moment of creation of art must intuitive, and not the result of a set of theoretical determinations); and from

● **handicraft** (in that handicrafts aim at some kind of pre-determined end result which provide what Kant refers to as 'the pay').

Kant then goes on to distinguish art proper from what he calls '*mechanical art*'. By this he probably means works that apply procedural rules to achieve a given effect, for example perspective drawing, which relies heavily on mathematically calculated schemes. What pleases us in mechanical art are the rules and devised effects; but such pleasure cannot be thought of as pure, since we are not merely pleased by the work itself but by its supporting rules.

The pleasure, then, is not an aesthetic one, since it is linked to a set of conscious determinations. By contrast, an aesthetic attitude takes pleasure in something for its own sake; it is a pure form of engagement, that asks nothing of the object beyond its formal appearance; this is known as '*disinterested delight*'. As soon as a pleasure becomes 'interested' in what the object can potentially provide us with, a practical benefit, then the pleasure is no longer purely aesthetic.

In contrast to mechanical art, *fine art*, like nature, is 'intrinsically final' in that it has no discernable rules or structure and pleases us on its own account.

Presumably what concerns Kant about mechanical art is the evident display of devices – such as the structure of single point perspective – since he later claims that fine art must adopt 'the aspect of nature, although we recognize it to be art' without the 'academic form betraying itself'.

Art proper, or fine art, becomes the superlative form of all creative activity, and when it is applied to lower forms of art, the name is retained only by 'analogy'. Kant doesn't deny that mechanical art can be enjoyable, but implies that it cannot be properly aesthetic. He thus draws the distinction between agreeable and fine art. Art proper is a fine balance between human labour and natural endowment, and can only be achieved by the genius, since

> genius is 'a talent for producing that for which no definite rule can be given.'

IMMANUEL KANT
(1724-1804)

Undoubtedly one of the most important figures in the field of philosophical aesthetics. Without Kant the dominant forms of art critical debate in the modern period would be inconceivable. Moreover, it might be claimed that Kant marks a significant point in the development of modernism generally.

Kantian aesthetics, then, plays a central role in the theory of artistic-modernism generally and when postmodernism threatens the stability of modernist aesthetics it is against this Kantian derived scheme, with the art critic Clement Greenberg at its centre, that it is largely opposed. This section will examine some of these themes and attempt to schematically plot the line just indicated.

Kant was critical of 'mechanical art', a term he used for art that depended upon rules (e.g. those of perspective) to produce a chosen effect.

Crivelli and other Renaissance artists used rules of perspective to give a sense of depth to their works. But particularly in the work of Crivelli, there is the sense that he is almost more concerned to give the illusion of depth and space, than to depict the dramatic events that the painting portrays. His technical ability to portray details in architecture is stunning, and one may almost be deflected onto them, rather than remaining focused on the central figures. It would seem that it is this shift of focus (or the danger of it) that Kant wants to criticize.

Is our delight in such work derived from the technique, or from the subject matter, or from the quality of artistic execution? Perhaps from all three.

For general information on Kant and his theory of knowledge, see page 38

For Kant on Ethics, see page 89

For Kant on Religion, see page 168

'The true content of romantic art is absolute inwardness.'

'The pure appearnce of art has the advantage that it points through and beyond itself, and itself hints at something spiritual of which it is to give us an idea.' Hegel *Aesthetics*

Like Kant, **Hegel (1770-1831)** assumes there is such a thing as reality-in-itself; that behind our fleeting experiences lies a stable, ultimate truth. This he calls **the Absolute**, which lies in the supra-sensuous world. It is the task of the *Geist* (translated either as Mind or Spirit, the German word meaning both), to penetrate that world by developing an ever-increasing conscious state of knowledge.

Each stage of the development represents a higher level of achievement and gets closer to the Absolute. In this way, history is seen as a rational, purposeful and directional process, which has an aim and end in view. This is known as Hegel's '*historical dialectic*'. (This notion of an historical process includes the rejection of the past and a vision towards the future and will become central to ideas about modernism – a revolt against tradition and the embracing of the new.)

Hegel wrote that his was:

'a birth-time and a period of transition to a new era... Spirit is indeed never at rest but always engaged in moving forward.'
Phenomenology of Spirit

Kant and Hegel differed, however, about the human capacity to understand this absolute truth.

For Kant, our ideas about reality are hemmed in by the limitations of the human faculties and, therefore, reality-in-itself will always be unintelligible for us. This is because he thought that all knowledge relied on the a priori faculties which can only cope with formal knowledge and not reality-in-itself.

For Hegel, the advancing endeavours of the Spirit, whose aim is absolute knowledge through self-consciousness, are manifest in all aspects of life. Artistic developments are seen to represent this advancing state of consciousness.

Hegel's history of art is therefore a history of the Spirit in visual terms.

Again, like Kant, Hegel distinguishes between higher and lower forms of art. The lower forms 'serve the ends of pleasure and entertainment' and as such are 'not independent, not free, but ancillary'.

He regarded imitation, for example, which adds nothing to the form of reality already known, with the same kind of contempt as in Plato. Simple copying is seen as a debased form of repetition; it presents what we already have before us 'in our gardens or our own houses'.

True art must abandon this immobile state of repetition and become part of the creative move towards Absolute knowledge. In order to fulfil this, art must free itself from the finite ends of the immediate world.

Insofar as art is a product of the intellect, fine art is seen as a middle ground between the immediate, finite world and the supra-sensuous world and so claims that its beauty/truth stands higher than that of nature itself.

'For the beauty of art is the beauty that is born of the spirit.'

In short, fine art, which is free and has reached beyond the immediate world, is imbued with the forms of a higher reality. For Hegel, the mere forms of immediate reality are not what constitutes the form of Absolute reality; the Absolute and the supra-sensuous are beyond the immediate and formal aspects of knowledge. This is the advantage that art has, for art 'points beyond itself' and refers to 'something spiritual'.

In his 'Lectures on Fine Art', Hegel considers three styles in respect of the history of Spirit: the symbolic, the classical and the romantic. He proposes that each period marks a development towards an ideal state where the work and its meaning become one.

Symbolic art fails this test, since the symbolic is 'understood not simply as it confronts us immediately on its own account' but rather as 'the meaning' and 'the expression thereof'. There remains, then, a duality that leaves the works 'incompatible with their meaning'. Egyptian hieroglyphics are seen as attempts to externalize and present an inner-truth.

Classical art has the advantage that it overcomes this duality and presents a unification of form and inner meaning. Hegel seems to regard this as possible, in part, because the Greeks conceived of their Gods in 'the bodily shape of man'.

Romantic art, however, rejects this unity to become 'absolute inwardness', and obtains a status of 'oneness' with the work concerned.

The increased perfection of thought in romanticism allowed for a perfection of form in the work so that there is an 'inter-penetration of meaning and shape'. Thus the form is inessential since its role is to 'point back to the inner'.

Painting is particularly well suited to such presentations since, unlike sculpture, it is 'free from the complete sensuous spatiality of material things by being restricted to the dimensions of the plane surface'.

However, it is poetry that presents the highest form of romantic art, since the form of poetry presents 'a sign of the idea which has become concrete in itself' and so:

> 'poetry is the universal art of spirit which has become free in itself and which is not tied down for its realization to the external sensuous material; instead it launches out exclusively in the inner space and the inner time of ideas and feelings.'

Romanticism thus allows art to fulfil its true vocation; an adequate presentation of Spirit. In this sense Hegel is often read as presenting the 'end of artistic progress'.

Apollo; a marble copy of the Greek original.

'...the classical form of art-form is the first to afford the production and vision of the completed Ideal and to present it as actualized in fact.'

FOR FURTHER INFORMATION ON: HEGEL'S PHILOSOPHY, ESPECIALLY AS RELATED TO RELIGION, SEE PAGE 170.

ARTHUR SCHOPENHAUER

Kant thought of the aesthetic realm as one including a free and contemplative attitude – an attitude unconnected with, and unfettered by, the immediacy of the (real) world. In **Schopenhauer (1788-1860)** this realm becomes of central importance, since for him it provides not only an opportunity for contemplative exercise but allows the individual mind to escape from the mundane. This produces a 'state of pure knowledge' which 'comprehends things free from their relation to will' and so 'without interest, without subjectivity'.

Schopenhauer, drawing on the Kantian model, divides the world into two aspects. On one side is the 'world as representation' where *'everything that exists for knowledge, and hence the whole of this world, is only object in relation to the subject, perception of the perceiver, in a word, representation.'*

There is no distinction to be made between our perception and the object of our perception. (Contrast this with Berkeley, who stated that all reality exits only in the form of ideas.)

On the other side of this world-model is the 'world as Will'. It is through the stimulus provided by the will (to eat, reproduce, possess and so on) that the body is motivated. The body, for Schopenhauer, is nothing but objectified Will (but note that Schopenhauer only conceives of one will in the world and not a series of individual wills).

Although Schopenhauer distinguishes these two aspects, he wants to claim that they are inseparable, since it is the Will that stimulates and promotes active engagement (in terms of both action and knowledge) with the world. The world is an inseparable mix of representation and Will, in which knowledge of objects is always knowledge of objects for a willed-subject.

Upon this Kantian basis, Schopenhauer adds a deeply pessimistic vision of existence. The only escape is provided by the aesthetic realm which, whether produced by works of art or nature, provides solace from the relentless will:

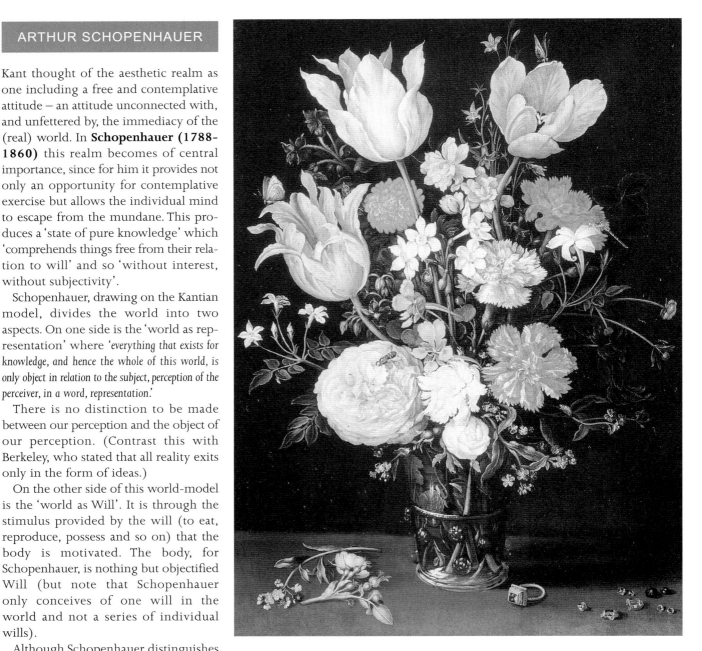

Vase of Flowers by Brueghel.
For Schopenhauer, pure phenomenal existence was achieved by...
'those admirable Dutchmen who directed such purely objective perception to the most insignificant objects, and set up a lasting monument of their objectivity and spiritual peace in paintings of still life.'

All conscious existence, because it is determined and governed by the active will, is in a constant state of attempting to maintain, for example, levels of comfort and well-being. The result is a state of continual striving and this is worsened, according to Schopenhauer, by the fact that all acts of will ultimately result in a state of dissatisfaction which he calls 'pain'. Our response is to attempt an escape from this mundanity of painful existence, by responding to the Will's impulse to obtain pleasure. But pleasure, even when it is obtained is short lived and the mind is plunged back into dissatisfaction. Moreover, the sense of pleasure is restricted, because for every 'wish that is fulfilled there remain at least ten that are denied' and so the 'sense of final satisfaction is only apparent'.

Schopenhauer's negative and pessimistic image of the world seems to present a 'no win' situation. Indeed this is Schopenhauer's warning: if we live by the demands of the will, our lives will continually fluctuate between relative pleasure and pain, but pain will always pre-dominate. The only way to escape is to avoid any confrontation with the will since it is the will that causes our desires.

'the fine arts work at bottom towards the solution of the problem of existence'.

The World as Will and Representation

What aesthetics allows for, is knowledge which is unfettered by the demands of will – that is, pure knowledge, apart from and independent of contingent mundane relations. In this state, according to Schopenhauer 'happiness and unhappiness have vanished'. We engage with the world as pure phenomenal existence without any practical potential.

This, according to Schopenhauer, is achieved by 'those admirable Dutchmen who directed such purely objective perception to the most insignificant objects, and set up a lasting monument of their objectivity and spiritual peace in paintings of still life'. This state is a triumph of representation over will, a state of giving oneself up 'entirely to knowledge'. Art is particularly successful in these terms because it itself presents representations that the artist has separated out from the will and so from all practical utilities. It is a sheer presentation of representation.

At the beginning of his *Lectures on Fine Art*, Hegel noted that the term aesthetics was not 'wholly satisfactory' to describe the task ahead of him since aesthetics, properly defined, relates to the 'science of sensation, of feeling' and describes 'the spacious realm of the beautiful'.

Hegel appears to mean that aesthetics is too general a science for a consideration of the value of art. Certainly Kant's definition of aesthetics has more to do with particular kinds of (innate) understanding and knowledge, which, while involving judgements of taste, does not describe anything about the material-object itself.

Art, being in part decorative, becomes a subject of aesthetic consideration; aesthetics becomes the primary methodology for organizing an understanding of the meaning, value and definition of art. This has often led philosophers to that claim that art can not be identified with the work qua material object.

For example, the Italian philosopher **Benedetto Croce (1866-1952)**, in his *Guide to Aesthetics*, 1913, discusses the 'error of materializing art'. Basing his argument on a metaphysical understanding about the nature of reality, he claims that art is not a 'physical fact' but 'is supremely real' (in much the same sense as Plato's forms). Adopting a Kantian-like approach, reality is understood as 'a construction of our intellect for the purposes of science'. Reality-itself is 'beyond experience.'

The short answer to the question, 'What is art?', is given in the response

'art is vision or intuition.'

For Croce this intuition involves seeing 'beyond' the immediate, towards this supreme reality.

The art-object (the actual canvas or stone, say) is not what we pay attention to in contemplating art. Indeed, these physical facts divert our attention from the aesthetic effect which is obtained through the intuition.

This attitude towards the material was to become one of the central themes in American Formalist criticism. In 1967, the American art critic **Michael Fried** wrote of 'modernist painting's self-imposed imperative that it defeat or suspend its own objecthood'. (*Art and Objecthood*, p153)

In *The Principles of Art*, 1938, **R G Collingwood (1889-1943)** claimed that:

art proper '...need not be what we should call a real thing.'

This is because, for Collingwood, art-proper is a matter of imaginative-expression and not of physical properties. **This shows that he is concerned to oppose art-proper to the products of a craft.**

Here Collingwood echoes Kant, who had opposed art to science and handicraft; art over science is a case of ability over knowledge (*Critique of Judgement*, p163). According to him, science permits you to achieve something 'if you know how', but this knowledge, in itself, does not necessarily enable someone to make something of it, a certain 'human skill' is often required.

Kant illustrates this by saying that someone who 'describes very exactly how the best shoe must be made' may not be 'able to turn one out himself'. (Of course, the 'best shoe' would not be art for Kant either, nevertheless, the point he makes stands.)

In Collingwood, craft is distinguished from art by a consideration of means and ends. For a craft, the end is determined first; for example, the decision to build a bridge. The means by which it will be made are worked out by considering the practicalities involved. The making involves the implementation of those means which have been designed to facilitate the desired end. But art-proper cannot aim at a predetermined end, since it does not involve knowing beforehand the nature of what is to be made.

This rests on Collingwood's theory of expression; an expression engenders a discovery, for the person expressing it, as much as for anyone else.

For art-proper:

'the end is not something foreseen and preconceived.'

Expression, then, allows someone to get to know the nature of their own feelings.

EXPRESSION AND DISCOVERY

We saw that, for Collingwood, the actual production of art was a process of discovery for the artist. Until something is expressed, so goes the theory, it is not really known – only felt.

Collingwood thinks that this is as true for 'expressions of anger' as it is for creative expressions. In the case of art-proper, then, even the artist doesn't know exactly what the work is to be until it has been made/expressed; unlike the bridge engineer who knows to the last bolt what it will be before building even starts. In this sense, art-proper cannot be worked out or formulated prior to the act itself.

However, Collingwood goes further by suggesting that even when the work has been made and presented, the form of the presentation is not the art-work-proper. This is the second aspect of his theory. Art, he claims, is essentially *an imaginative activity*. Its modes of expression, which take shape in the form of the work qua object, are only the means of transferring the artist's original imaginative form into the audience's imagination:

'The work of art proper is not something seen or heard, but something imagined.'

'"forms" are nothing but the perceived structures of bodily "works of art."'

This attitude puts Collingwood's theory at odds with the Formalist theory of art, which is discussed below.

Henri Matisse at work in his studio, May 1913.
Was he, following Collingwood's view, discovering the work of art in the process of painting it? Or did he have the finished work ready conceived before he took up his brushes and mounted his step-ladder?

In 1936 **Alfred H Barr Jr.**, then director of the Museum of Modern Art in New York, published a diagram depicting the development of abstract art. It displays the idea that the development of art results from internal debates about style. Modern art, and particularly abstraction, is not seen as a response to its environment, political or social. Instead, artistic development is thought of as being self-perpetuating and as developing out of itself. Accordingly art is about style, form and nothing else. **Hence the term Formalism.**

Barr's explanation centres on two basic notions. Firstly, that works-of-art, quite apart from presenting the viewer with images, present formal arrangements. Abstract works desist from producing analogies of natural forms, and instead present works which 'confines the attention to its immediate, sensuous, physical surface' (Cubism and Abstract Art). Secondly, Barr's theory is based on the notion that the pictorial conquest of the visual world had been completed to such a degree that

the 'more adventurous and original artist had grown bored with painting facts.'

Understood in this way each style is a developmental process emanating from the previous style.

No attempt is made to ground the work within a wider historical or social setting. This dissociation from the socio-political background leaves such accounts open to being accused of engendering an incomplete understanding of the implications of art. As we will see, this is something that **Greenberg** seems to have understood in 1939 but forgotten by the mid-1940s, thus leaving his own accounts open to this accusation.

The British critics **Roger Fry** and **Clive Bell** were amongst the earliest critics to start thinking about art in this way.

'It is only when an object exists in our lives for no other purpose than to be seen that we really look at it.' Roger Fry

For this reason the work of art, as a visual spectacle, allows Fry to describe a formal vision that is difficult to achieve in day-to-day life. Artists like Cezanne and Monet are no longer admired for producing optical equivalents of reality; Fry sees them not as 'imitating form by illusion... but at creating form'. In Picasso, he saw the artist giving up the attempt to copy the world and creating instead a 'purely abstract language of form, a visual music'.

Even works that contain recognizable images it is 'the equivalence, not a likeness of nature that is sought'. In this way the work-itself, as a visual presentation, becomes endowed with self-contained meaning and value. It is not a replicated form of reality but a form of reality in its own right; it is its own means and end.

'To appreciate a work of art we need bring with us nothing but a sense of form and colour and a knowledge of three-dimensional space.' Clive Bell

The theory of aesthetic sensibility often involves more than a simple appreciation of beauty; Kant claimed that it was a 'mark of a good soul'. Clive Bell, in *The Aesthetic Hypothesis*, wrote: 'people who respond immediately and surely to works of art are in my judgement more enviable than men of massive intellect but slight sensibility'. Bell also claims that if the term art has any meaning at all then there must be a common element otherwise 'when we speak of works of art we gibber'.

In order to identify the ingredient of art, Bell refered to 'symbolic form' which he claimed, is 'the one quality common to all visual art'. It is the presence of symbolic form that, in his words, 'stirs our aesthetic emotions'. Aesthetic emotion must be related to the formal experience and nothing else.

To appreciate such qualities in art, Bell claimed; 'we need bring with us nothing but a sense of form and colour and a knowledge of three-dimensional space'.

As such art is to be understood as operating at an intuitive level. In the same way that Kant linked knowledge of time and space to the a priori, responses to 'symbolic form' must now be regarded as innate. The work becomes a source of pure optical experience of form, detached from practical knowledge.

Representational works were not necessarily dismissed, but neither would a work be celebrated because it was representational. Bell uses Luke Fildes' *The Doctor* (1891) as an example of a work lacking symbolic form.

In fact Bell claimed that 'The Doctor is not a work of art'. His problem with this kind of work seems to be that it is not an end in itself; it is not an object-of-emotion but an object that aims to arouse our moral sentiments; art should be 'above morals.'

It is not the representational content in itself that detracts from the work for Bell, which, while not necessarily being harmful, is 'always irrelevant'. Rather, Bell's complaint about *The Doctor* is that it is linked to the arousal of sentiment and therefore not of aesthetic value. *The Doctor* has too much content and not enough significant form.

THE EARLY GREENBERG AND THEODOR W. ADORNO

In 1939 **Clement Greenberg** presented himself as a defender of cultural standards. Citing a crisis in culture, he blamed the break down of bourgeois society and the subsequent breaking up of 'the accepted notions upon which artists and writers must depend in large part for communication with their audiences'.

In other words society, the church and state, no longer provided serious art with its basis (subject matter or money). This break down of patronage left art in danger of becoming a mere market product.

The response to this would be a new kind of culture. Born from 'a superior consciousness of history' which provided a 'new kind of criticism of society.' Greenberg introduces the **avant-garde**. This driving force of historical, and in the arts, stylistic change in the modern period, is burdened with securing a future for art.

Greenberg's 'superior consciousness of history' is, of course, Marxism. His cultural avant-garde belonged to that 'bold development of scientific and revolutionary thought' in that it succeeded in retreating from the 'markets of capitalism' and so saving art from becoming a market product.

In short, the task of the artists unwilling to see their work 'thrown' into the market place, was to secure a sustainable environment for high art. Art responded by turning itself into an ideological space that remained separated from the restrictions of socio-political forces. The aim then was to establish art as being 'valid solely on its own terms'. This was a call for 'pure art'.

At this point Greenberg also identified a form of low art called **kitsch**; commercial art, magazine covers and Hollywood movies.

According to Greenberg, kitsch had been introduced in order to satisfy the cultural needs of the lower classes, who had arrived in the cities from the country-side as part of Western industrialization in the 19th century.

This is the side view of a statue in Moscow of a male worker and a woman, united beneath a hammer and sickle, designed by Vera Mukhina, in c.1937.

Art can play an important role in reinforcing political ideology. But is it thereby corrupted by its political message? Does not all art reflect the ethos and values of the society that produces it? It is possible for art to be completely divorced from the political and economic structures within which it is produced?

CLEMENT GREENBERG
(1909-1994)

One of the most important figures in 20th century art criticism. Largely regarded as the spokesman of American Modernism, he has been accorded a papal-like position in the art-world.

Broadly speaking, Greenberg's writings are a well balanced mix of Marxist ideology (his analysis of cultural elitism – the division between high and low art), Hegelian dialectics (the historical development of artistic styles) and Kantian aesthetics (his insistence upon the notion of disinterestedness as the only way to judge the true quality of art).

His most important works are: *Avant-Garde and Kitsch*, 1939, and *Towards a Newer Laocoon*, 1940. *Modernist Painting*, 1960, is generally considered to be his seminal essay.

Separated not just from their background (the countryside) but also from their cultural identity (Greenberg's term for this identity is 'folk art') the newly urbanized citizen was without a cultural form of leisure.

Moving in to the capitalist market as work-labour, thus becoming the working class, meant also that they were largely uneducated. Their limited leisure time effectively cut them off from bourgeois high-culture which demanded educated understanding and, therefore, time. Low art, ersatz culture or kitsch, Greenberg thought, was a product of this situation.

Introduced into this cultural vacuum, kitsch answered the needs of a class unversed in bourgeois tastes since it required no level of literacy or educated understanding; it promised 'universal literacy'.

Kitsch could be consumed without effort and within the limited time available to the working classes; it 'pretends to demand nothing of its consumers except their money – not even their time.'

Hence the bourgeoisie's dwindling attention to serious art; kitsch was a marketable, and profitable product that satisfied the masses. More dangerously,

kitsch, because it presents 'self evident meanings', rather than meanings only available to the educated sensibility, could easily be injected with propagandist content that the uneducated eye could easily accept as a picture of truth.

Hence Greenberg's warning:

'Kitsch keeps a dictator in closer contact with the 'soul' of the people.'

Greenberg's concern is that kitsch is as a form of cultural repression, which acts to satisfy desire without stimulating an appetite for more 'advanced' forms of culture.

Theodor Adorno (1903-1969) had a theory of the 'culture industry' with much in common with Greenberg's early analysis. The 'culture industry' manufactures low forms of art for the masses. Consequently, Adorno distinguishes between folk-art made by the masses and mass-art produced by the market and directed at the masses: 'the masses are not primary, but secondary, they are the object of calculation'. (see *The Culture Industry* edited by J M Bernstein). Primary for the culture industry is calculated profit (hence the name industry) as opposed to 'specific content and harmonious formation'.

The industry is able to calculate because it operates 'according to plan'. The film industry, for example, has created standardized forms, e.g. the Western, with the effect that the movie-goer, due to the rationalization of narrative style and genre, is familiar with the form of the film before seeing it. This standardization also has the effect of creating an appetite for more of the same (see Kant's attack on mechanical art, page 254).

Insofar as the products of the culture industry are tailor-made to produce

particular effects, Adorno describes them as 'pre-digested' (Greenberg uses the same term).

In other words, the culture industry treats the consumer like a baby by making works which demand little or no effort; consumers are assumed unable or incapable of digesting for themselves.

The effect of low forms of pre-digested culture in capitalist society upon the consumers' imaginative capacity impedes development since culture is no longer providing a space within which the imaginative dimension can be exercised.

The culture industry is 'a means for fettering consciousness'.

The imaginative dimension is important to Adorno, since it provides an ideological space, which remains free from the market-place of consumer capitalism – the culture industry has effectively taken the consumers' responsibility of schematizing and judging for him or herself.

Thus Adorno's regard for high art – it provides a space outside of the constraints and restraints of capitalism, and as such it keeps alive our (imaginative) sense of freedom and autonomy as a symbolic gesture.

'the masses… are the object of calculation.'

Theodor Adorno, on the 'Culture Industry'

WALTER BENJAMIN

Walter Benjamin's 'The Work of Art in the Age of Mechanical Reproduction' (in *Illuminations*, H Arendt ed., pp211-44) can be read as a counter position to Greenberg's. Unlike Greenberg, Benjamin sees the integration of art into social and political settings as part of historical progress. Art in its traditional form has two defining characteristics, according to Benjamin: an aura and a cultic or ritualistic setting. Aura is Benjamin's way of describing aesthetic presence and uniqueness in 'categories of space and time perception'. (Benjamin was both an admirer of Bertolt Brecht's revolutionary theatre and fascinated by Surrealism and kabbalistic Judaism – seemingly contradictory influences that underly his views.)

Uniqueness is crucial to Benjamin's views, since the artwork, as part of its ritualistic setting, must be seen to impart something special. The idea of aura is further qualified by the introduction of 'distance': the 'phenomenon of a distance, however close it may be.' 'Distance' implies a kind of formal detachment from the object appropriate to an attitude of reverence – 'mere contemplation' is an underlying sentiment here. To illustrate 'distance' Benjamin cites religious sculptures in cathedrals, which 'are invisible to the spectator on ground level'. The importance is the 'presence' as a device of ritual. In this instance the cathedral also marks the ritualistic setting; 'the location of its original use value'.

The mass reproduction of art works wrenches art out of its ritualistic setting and destroys its unique sense of aura. But far from describing this as a loss, Benjamin describes the work as 'emancipated... from its parasitical dependence on ritual'. Faced with this 'decay of aura' he says that 'art reacted with the doctrine

WALTER BENJAMIN

Born in Berlin in 1892 to a Jewish family, Benjamin's early schooling was in philosophy and literature. With the increasing threat of Nazi rule, he moved to Paris in 1933. At the beginning of the Second World War Benjamin tried to flee Europe and gain entrance to America but he was turned away at the Spanish border. Faced with the prospect of being sent back to Germany and becoming prisoner of the Nazis, on September 26th 1940, he committed suicide.

l'art pour l'art' (art for art's sake), which he regards as an attempt to retain an aesthetic and ritual-type formulation.

Art for art's sake

But this is seen as a 'negative theology', a pointless attempt to implement a form of ' "pure" art, which not only denied any social function of art but also any categorizing by subject matter'.

In the same way that Greenberg links kitsch to the development of the working class, Benjamin sees mass art as 'related to the increasing significance of the masses in contemporary life'. Here the decay of aura and the advent of the mass image signals a move by the masses 'to bring things "closer" spatially'. This, of course, is opposed to the inherent distance of auratic art.

Mass reproducibility 'can put the copy of the original into situations which would be out of reach for the original itself'. Photography and sound-recording are obvious examples here. Such reproductions will not 'touch the actual work of art, yet the quality of its presence is always depreciated'. More importantly, what this loss of unique aura potentially means is that 'instead of being based on ritual, it (art) begins to be based on another practice – politics'. In other words, art enters into the material relations and developments of social life. (It should be added, with reference to Greenberg, that in an Epilogue, Benjamin issues a warning about the use of mass art by fascist orders.)

Mass production wrenches art out of its ritual setting, but does it thereby destroy its aura, or emancipate it?

Having established the importance of the avant-garde, Greenberg abandoned his Marxist rhetoric in favour of a Kantian-derived strategy more suitable to the task of justifying the inherent value of high art. Now the principle aim becomes pure art for its own sake. This implication was already afoot in 1939 but was framed as a response to Fascism and Stalinism.

Art had to be seen to provide an experience 'not to be obtained from any other kind of activity'. This required art to defeat what Greenberg called a 'denial of medium'. Medium (canvass, oil, stone etc.) had always been a 'regretful if necessary physical obstacle', something that resisted the artist's intentions. The ability to manipulate the material, and thereby restrict its evident presence in the final work, had once been linked to the artist's skill.

Greenberg reads this skill as the use of 'art to conceal art'; the task of the avant-garde is to retrieve art from this 'confusion'. Skill becomes associated with the specifics of medium and using 'art to call attention to art'.

The underlying assumption is that there is something irreducibly essential called the work-of-art-itself; it is the itself-of-art, pure and uncluttered, that Greenberg now seeks to present as an essential definition of art.

(It needs stressing, however, that Greenberg's account of Modernist art is not simply a materialist one. This is already evident in his attempt to distance art from the material interests of politicized culture and in wanting to see art as an end in itself; works are 'looked at for their own sake'. This is a Kantian claim for an a priori pleasure established without reference to anything beyond the direct experience itself.)

The painting or sculpture, instead of pointing the viewers attention to a subject or content, now 'exhausts itself in the visual sensation it provides'. In other words, there is no longer an anterior narrative structure, or indeed any form of narrative, that allows for a contemplation beyond what the work is – an aesthetic presence of art-itself.

In Greenberg's view, painting was quick to respond to this situation, and **Gustave Courbet (1819-77)** became

'the first real avant-garde painter... by painting only what the eye could see as a machine unaided by the mind.'

He was followed by **Edouard Manet (1832-83)**, whose paintings

'declared the flat surfaces on which they were painted'.

Such developments are seen as sacrifices, for they reject the illusionism of Western academic painting in the attempt to secure a position for art in the modern period. Supposedly, the moment of viewing should only contain a formal presentation of aesthetic presence. This is central to late Formalist aesthetics; the work becomes absolutely present as a manifestation of its own status qua art.

In 1959, Greenberg suggested that abstraction was emerging as compensation for the Western 'obsession with material production and purposeful activity', and becomes central to this quest.

More specifically the role of Modernism involved the individual arts being 'hunted back to their mediums' where they were to be 'isolated, concentrated and defined'. The result: 'The arts lie safe now, each within its "legitimate" boundaries'.

This is part of modernisms 'task of self-criticism' which sought to 'eliminate from the specific effects of each art any and every effect that might conceivably be borrowed from or by the medium of any other art'.

As Courbet and Manet began to demonstrate, the specific effects of painting proved to be 'the ineluctable flatness of the surface'. (Sculpture had its own limiting conditions.) Thus the aim of advanced painting was to articulate that condition as part of paintings aesthetic content. This required a heightened awareness of the 'integrity of the picture plane'.

Greenberg is best known for his championing of American Modernist Abstraction (particularly the work of **Jackson Pollock (1912-1956)**), the readings for which are based in this logic. For example, Greenberg wrote:

'Pollock has gone beyond the stage where he needs to make his poetry explicit in ideographs. What he invents instead has perhaps, in its very abstractness and absence of assignable definition, a more reverberating meaning'.

This calls to mind Hegel's aesthetics of 'adequate form'. The reverberating meaning is seen to lie in the 're-created flatness of the surface'; re-created because the painting doesn't simply present the sheer physicality of flatness (a blank canvas, say). Instead, the painting presents flatness as an aesthetic component of the painting. In other words, the flatness Greenberg refers to is something that the painting, through the manipulation of medium, stresses.

THE BEGINNING OF THE END OF TRANSCENDENTAL AESTHETICS

Formalism presented an idealized notion of the 'work-of-art-itself' towards which the successful work should tend. Within these parameters, Greenberg sought to demonstrate that the history of painting, for example, defined itself by the marking out of surface with paint – this had to be acknowledged as part of an aesthetic response to the work.

MINIMALIST ART: PRACTICE AND THEORY

Following on from that, Minimalism (which emerged first in the late 1950s, partly as a reaction to the emotiveness of Abstract Expression, and so is not identical with current fashions) can be understood as the attempt to mark out the phenomenological perceptions of three-dimensional space.

Presented as the apogee of late Formalist theorizing, Minimalism is often read as going one logical step further than Greenbergian criticism had permitted. However, in taking this step, Minimalism also marks something of a break with the Modernist aesthetic.

It is this completing of, and breaking with, the Modernist aesthetic that describes the unique position of Minimalism.

One way to understand Minimalism is to consider it as a shifting of the narrative-space from an interior formal (visual) arrangement of medium to an externalized arrangement of objectified (tactical) material qua mass. Part of the concern that motivated this move, was to overcome the kind of 'illusionism' inherent in all types of painting.

This is a key point in **Donald Judd**'s essay 'Specific Objects', 1965, which became a kind of Minimalist manifesto. Judd's aim was to make art works 'less containers, more defined' – specific objects in fact. His answer to this was to move art into three-dimensions, thereby getting 'rid of the problem' of illusion-

ism. In practice, this meant making box-like shapes cantilevered to a wall, often tailored to the gallery where they would be exhibited. Judd thought that certain possibilities, particularly in painting, had been exhausted as a result of following the road advocated by Modernism.

The appearance of Minimalist art usually consists of simple, often geometric, shapes and forms presented in the gallery space. This is where Minimalism is seen to complete the Modernist dialectic; it presents a form of 'sculpture' so reduced that it seems to take Greenberg at his word when he says that art should do away with its 'expendable conventions' and leave only what is essential to that medium.

In this sense Minimalism would mark a *reductio ad absurdum*. Leaving the absolute minimum and essential element, sculpture as medium; physical mass in space. (In painting it was the blank or monochrome canvas.)

But this is also the precise point at which Minimalism breaks with that aesthetic tradition, because in so doing it involves a rejection of the transcendentalism of Modernist aesthetics. Part of that aesthetic relies on the work being viewed as an a priori, formal arrangement.

This concept of the work necessitates that the moment of viewing is unconnected to anything beyond the formal appearnce. Greenberg described this state in 1959:

Modernist aesthetics causes a sense of selflessness, as Schopenhauer thought, then Minimalism puts the self back into the viewing experience.

This is its phenomenology. The presence, no longer an aesthetic transcendental presence but an objectified ordinary presence, allows for a mediation between object, space and viewer that secures the moment of viewing within relation to the specific consciousness of time and place.

Not surprisingly, Formalist critics reacted strongly to Minimalism. **Michael Fried**, a disciple of Greenberg, in an essay attacking Minimalism, described it as a state of 'theatre' and theatre as 'the negation of art'. This observation is rooted in the belief that aesthetic excellence involves a transcendence 'of the actual circumstances in which the beholder encounters the … work'. Minimalism, in its overt presence (Fried's preferred term for Minimalism is 'literalist art') denies the beholder this opportunity.

In this sense the Formalists saw everything that they had argued for being destroyed by Minimalism's phenomenology of the art object.

Paradoxically, however, Fried's essay, despite his obvious hostility, turns out to be one of the best descriptions of Minimal Art available. This has something to do with the fact that, in the attempt to present a defence of Modernist aesthetic sensibilities, he was required, more so than most, to 'appreciate'

'You become selfless… entirely identified with the object of your attention.'

He called this state 'at-onceness'. Outside of space/time relations it describes a purity of formal perception unconnected to supporting ideas. If

the significance of the Minimalist ethos. His clear understanding of Minimalism is a direct result of his antithetical position.

ARTHUR C DANTO: THE END OF ART AND MODERNISM

Like Greenberg, **Danto (b.1924)** regards the history of Modernism in a Hegelian light, as an unfolding of specific historical tasks, whose aim it is to achieve ultimate and definitive conclusions. Unlike Greenberg, however, they are regarded in strictly ontological terms; they are a matter for knowledge not taste.

So Danto sees the history of art as a philosophical endeavour to secure its own meaning. Modernism is the historical phenomenon that describes the development of that identity. The aim is to present, in as philosophical a form as possible, these questions in the form of works of art. Like most models of Modernism this history is represented by the development of style – but style framed in strict ontological terms, not in relation to an aesthetics of taste.

These questions become fully elaborated for Danto when **Andy Warhol** presented his 'Brillo Boxes' in 1964. These, Danto claims, end the historical narrative of Modernism. What Warhol achieved in 1964 was a work that bought the question of art's identity to the fore. The Boxes may not resolve that question, in the same way that Greenberg thought that art itself could resolve its own essence, but they can crystallize it. The question raised is:

Why are Warhol's Brillo Boxes art, when ordinary Brillo boxes are not ?

Danto sees these questions as unavoidable because for the first time a work of art had become indistinguishable from a mere object despite having a different ontological status. Of course, this requires a faith that they are art. Greenberg may have been happy to rely on an aesthetic intuition for his faith, but Danto's faith relies on 'theory', which he refers to as the 'Artworld'. For Danto, Brillo Boxes are to be understood as works of art because they are located in the 'Artworld' – the context provided by other artists and critics.

There are obviously self-referential dangers to this belief but, unlike an aesthetic faith, Danto's theory of art was 'something the eye can not decry'. The status of art turns out to be a matter of philosophical knowledge for Danto. Arts identity, as part of a theoretical determination – as opposed to an aesthetic one – is also linked to its historical determination.

Brillo Boxes appeared at a time when they were relevant to the development of Modernism, which is partly why Danto did not doubt their status. They are part of the narrative of art history; Brillo Boxes could not have been presented as art, or involved this kind of philosophical determinism, at any earlier time.

Not only do the Brillo Boxes mark the end of Modernism but also the end of art, since its history had been an attempt to investigate the question of its own status. With that question now fully elaborated, art's historical relevance is over. But when art history ends it doesn't mean that art will stop. What it does mean is that art produced in what Danto refers to as the post-historical phase (other theories refer to postmodernism) is free to do what it likes, it is no longer obliged to advance in any particular direction, since art no longer has a direction.

For some commentators, Greenberg included, the idea of postmodernism is abhorrent, since it is taken to mean that art is now valueless. However, Danto's strict Hegelianism means that the end of Modernism is an historical inevitably.

> # 'A great deal of art has been made since the end of art.'
>
> Danto, *After the End of Art*

In the Asian tradition, philosophy and theology are effectively interchangeable, for the concept of philosophy does not exists as it does in Western civilization. However there are parallels in Asian logic, analysis and scholarly debate, and there are collections of writing and schools of thought. An intense curiosity about the human condition and its relationship to the transcendental, has produced an array of ideas of great depth, breadth and complexity, fully equal to the efforts of Western philosophy. These are reflected at all levels of cultural activity and art.

While there are obviously variations in the interpretation and expression of Hindu and Buddhist beliefs across the continent, they inform the theological framework for much of Asia. There are a number of basic concepts that underpin the notion of how and why people are and the purpose of human life. Strongly interwoven with religious belief, they derive from the oldest tenents of Indian thinking.

The law of *karma* states that every action mental or physical, good or evil has consequences in the life of the individual. This means that present conditions have been determined by past actions, and future conditions determined by present actions. This idea is closely connected to beliefs about rebirth, wherein time after time we experience birth and death, until through spiritual realization we attain *moksha*, or release from *samsara*. Samsara refers to the world with its endless manifestations of karma and cycles of time.

In Hinduism there is stress on *maya* (the illusional aspect of what we know); because of our ignorance (*avidya*) we are unable to penetrate the Absolute Reality that transcends everything and is omnipresent and infinite, called *Brahman*. The manifestation of Brahman in the human self is called Atman. The divine pervades the self and world, and the spiritual task is to realize Atman and Brahman are the same ultimate Reality.

Buddhism, deriving from an atheistic Indian tradition, revised and extended these ideas. Whilst Hinduism remained confined to India, Buddhism spread south to the cultures of Sri Lanka and the region now including Burma, Thailand, Laos and Kampuchea. This great area, which was deeply influenced by all aspects of Hindu culture, adopted the Theravada form of Buddhism. By contrast, the Buddhism that spread north to Nepal, Tibet, China, Mongolia, Korea and Japan, was of the other school, the more colourful, diverse and dynamic Mahayana. It continues to colour the Asian world-view to the present day.

In 325BCE, Alexander the Great of Macedon conquered much of northwest India, bringing with him classical Greek culture. His successors soon abandoned Indian conquests, but the Greek artistic impact proved far more pervasive and enduring. In subsequent centuries, the Greek concentration of depicting gods in idealized human form, influenced the art of the first Buddhist empire, that of Asoka. Long after Asoka's death (in 236BCE), indeed long after Buddhism itself had died out in India, the serenely smiling statues of the Buddha continued to reflect this mingling of East and West, from Afghanistan all the way to Japan.

It provided the images needed for the Mahayan cult of the Bodhisattva, adapted to local cultures.

When we look at a Tibetan Buddhist *thangka* (a wall hanging), its rich red, black, gold and green colours depicting the strange, wrathful form of Mahakala, a *dharmapala*, or protector of the Dharma, we are given little hint that it symbolizes the removal of all that obscures our progress towards Enlightenment, and is really a manifestation of Avalokiteshvara, the Bodhisattva of Compassion.

Equally, it is not just to be admired as an image, it is to be meditated on. Images such as this are used to help the meditator visualize the qualities they hope to develop in themselves. On the mundane level, what may appear as a terrifying form, in meditation appears as an aspect of Wisdom and Compassion.

In a Chinese landscape painting from the Sung Dynasty (c.960-1260CE), the subtle greys that describe the atmosphere, space and mountains, seem to flow into each other, the mountains turning to mist, and the mist turning into the far distance. There is no time of day indicated by the position of the sun, only a timeless season. Each brush stroke is used with spontaneity and control, embodying the balance of opposites; we see the world as the Taoist sage sees it, in sympathy with the Tao. This is the fruit of the other great Asian tradition, that of China.

The islands of rock amongst the carefully raked gravel in the Zen garden of the Ryoan-ji Temple in Kyoto seem primordial. Stripped to bare essentials, the essential is still impossible to locate; without insight, they stubbornly remain rock and sand. Yet, if by contemplating them, we are able to drop all concepts, all duality, we can transform our awareness, we can gain Enlightenment.

There is no need to know the creator of these art works, though of course skill and expressiveness in art are highly valued. What is important is the state of mind they produce. The Hindu devotee journeys to the temple in hope of receiving *dharsan*, desiring to be blessed by the gaze of the deity. The relationship is deeply personal, the devotee feeling that they have communicated with the divine. Dharsan, the Sanskrit word meaning 'to see' or the act of looking, is customarily translated as world-view, philosophy or vision.

Aesthetic awareness can be instrumental, even crucial. Notions of art and beauty are determined by the mood they induce, rather than in relationship to a specific canon or tradition of art. That is to say, the beauty they allude to is firstly a spiritual beauty.

This huge temple guardian towers over visitors who come to see the Daibutsu (Big Buddha) at Nara, Japan.

Hinduism itself is very ancient, and has evolved into a complex web of religious practice and social policy. Its ability to contain diverse beliefs and to absorb challengers, whilst providing a cohesive framework in which to live, has ensured its survival.

Hinduism has created a rich culture where most if not all art is devotional. As the model for art is provided by the spiritual, the human form and symbols are used to describe the transcendental, giving material substance to the formless Absolute.

The basic tenants of Hinduism are found in a vast body of literature. The oldest writings are the *Vedas*, dating from 1500BCE, which belong to a long line of sacred texts. Part epic, part philosophy, these texts embody the core of spiritual belief and social theory. They record the prime concern of Indian thought; the relationship between the human and the divine and also provide a wealth of narrative and image to enrich imagination and spirituality, and therefore find expression within Hindu art.

By 100 BCE, three principal divinities emerge from the multiplicity of religious practice that was found in India:
- **Vishnu**, the preserver;
- **Shiva**, the destroyer, and
- **Devi** or **Shake,** the Great Goddess.

These divinities derive from very ancient roots, and they represent both abstract concepts and human qualities. A deity can have several aspects, and are portrayed as having multiple limbs and heads, a pictorial device enabling different attributes to be expressed in one image. Deities can also be presented in symbolic form.

Shiva, for example is usually shown as the *lingum*, a phallic pillar, representing the aspect of formless energy and creative potential. Often the *lingum* is depicted as rising up from a yoni, a vulva shaped dish, which symbolizes female power and energy, or *shake*.

Shiva is commonly depicted as a meditating ascetic, surrounded by beasts, but also as Nataraja, the cosmic dancer, the Lord of Beginnings and Ends, who creates and destroys, beating a rhythm through the universe with a drum as he dances in a circle of flame.

An unorthodox and mysterious figure, he inhabits the poles of experience, and contains and resolves all opposites.

In contrast to Shiva with his wild and knotted hair, **Vishnu** is depicted wearing a crown. He carries a club, a discus, a conch shell and a lotus flower. The crown tells us Vishnu represents social order, its preservation and stability.

Vishnu is associated with emotion, especially love, and he is adored through his most famous incarnations, **Krishna** and **Rama**.

The notion that gods could manifest in human form, or *avatars*, first appears in the most popular part of the Mahabharata epic, the *Bhagavad-Gita*. As *avatars*, they express and return the love that is offered to them. *Bhakti* – or love directed at a deity – became increasingly central to religious practice, often acted out through *Puja*, the worship of a deity, its image or symbols.

Mystical love for a divine figure stems from the tradition of poets and saints called Altars, devotees of Vishnu, and Nayanars, devotees of Shiva.

Ramanuja (1050-1113) a renowned teacher and scholar, and a follower of Vishnu, was instrumental in establishing the importance of ritual and devotion in religious practice.

The upsurge in devotion stimulated the need for images and instructions as to how to describe the divine form of the gods and construct temples began to appear in the first century CE.

Temples where built to reflect a cosmological structure or Mandala, with the deity housed in a central inner chamber, situated beneath a tower or *shikhara*, symbolic of the Himalayas, the home of the gods.

Externally they are decorated with ornate panels and sculpture, often illustrating themes from the deities' life. Internally, they are designed to make the journey towards the deity one of mounting reverence and devotion. As the devotee draws towards the deity they encounter images of increasing significance. When the devotee reaches the image, he or she hopes to receive *dharsan* through the deities gaze.

Temple images are shown has having large eyes, out of proportion to the rest of the body, substantiating this act of connection with, and recognition by the deity. Offerings made by the devotees are returned as *prasad*, sanctioned and blessed by the divine.

Hinduism contains a number of spiritual disciplines that do not function as organized religions.

In **Yoga** there is no god or priesthood, yet it does provide a system of self-knowledge. The Yoga Sutras, written by **Patanjali** in the second century BCE elucidate this profound tradition that offers a means of cultivating the highest form of consciousness or awareness of Self, or *purusha*, through mental and physical training.

Tantra also has no centralized institutions, its literature going back to the Vedas. Tantric practices were aided by the development of visual material, especially symbols, diagrams and illustrations. These practices have a strong magical element aimed at harnessing opposites and transforming all levels of energy in ones self, cumulating in spiritual realization. Artistic creativity therefore had a place in terms of the expression of emotion, linked to fundamental Tantric beliefs.

Both these systems have contributed to the density of Indian thought and spiritual practice, supporting the notion of the truth seeker, whose personal effort, reaches the highest goal.

Shiva Nataraja – Lord of the Dance.
The god Shiva is here depicted dancing within a circle of flames, which represents the universe. He maintains a balance, being both creative and destructive, death and re-birth leading on one after another. In his upper right arm he holds a drum, representing the sound of creation, and his upper left is the flame of destruction. In his dance, he treads on the demon of ignorance.

Buddhist art, which spreads across Asia from the great sandstone figures of the Buddha at Bamian, Afghanistan (now destroyed by fundamentalist Muslims) to Japan, is one of the great religious arts of the world. Behind its varied manifestations lies a very distinct philosophy.

The title 'Buddha' means 'one who is awake' or Enlightened. It is used to describe the spiritual achievements of **Siddhartha Gautama**, who was born in India in 566 BCE. Enlightenment, a state beyond all description, is sometimes called Nirvana, signifying the extinction of all attachment.

After his attainment, he taught a system based on ethics, meditation and insight that would eventually lead to release from the suffering of *samsara* into the Enlightened state.

Though challenged by the religious orthodoxy of the day mainly because of his opposition to the caste system, he attracted many followers, who organized themselves into the *Sangha* to practice the *Dharma*, his teaching.

The earliest form of Buddhism, later referred to as Hinayana, is represented today by the Theravada tradition. Members of the Sangha saw the Buddha as a human, a teacher who had perfected his own teaching, rather than as a divine figure.

Originally his teachings where passed on orally, and not written down until four hundred years after his death. Over a period of time divergent interpretations of his teaching arose, forming the basis for eighteen schools, the two most influential being the Theravadins and the Sarvastivardins.

The Buddha's teaching was now arranged into three collections, known as the *Tripitaka*. The *Abhidharma* collection records the attempt of these schools to classify the teachings and define basic concepts.

The Sarvastivardins believing that wisdom could be obtained by analytical process categorized the world into seventy-five 'dharmas', or irreducible elements of existence. As competing schools produced different lists, the Abhidharma became increasingly unwieldy until the monk Buddhaghosa, an outstanding scholar of the fifth century, organized and commentated on the Abhidharma, clarifying its content.

Visual images portraying events in the Buddha's life appear before the writing down of texts. Initially his presence was suggested by symbols; the moment of his Enlightenment indicated by a tree, later called a Bodhi tree, under which he meditated.

The first teaching of the Dharma at Sarnath, is represented as a Wheel (following its description as the first turning of the Wheel of the Dharma), and his death is represented by a *stupa* or funeral monument.

The Jakata tales – stories concerning the previous lives of the Buddha – also proved popular subjects for artists. Examples of all of these can be seen decorating the Great Stupa at Sanchi, in Central India, and at Amaravati, in South East India.

The first human images of the Buddha appear at a juncture in Buddhist thinking with the emergence of Mahayana Buddhism. The Mahayanists, though they valued monastic life, made less distinction between laity and the ordained community recognizing the value of all spiritual practice.

A growing devotional mood stimulated an upsurge in image making. Indeed the production and the commissioning of images was itself seen as meritorious.

Early images depicted the Buddha as a monk seated in the Lotus or meditation posture, derived from the Yoga tradition. This image of the meditating Buddha was quickly adopted throughout the Buddhist world.

Influenced by the *Prajnaparamita* or the Perfection of Wisdom texts, which posited an Ultimate Reality of non-duality beyond all concepts, the Mahayanists revised the earlier theory of *dharmas*, by proposing that ultimately all phenomena are empty of any real self. They called this state *shunyata*, translated as Emptiness, and this was brilliantly argued by **Nagarjuna**, (200CE) who established the **Madhyamaka** school.

In reaction to the emphasis on the wisdom aspect of Enlightenment, the **Yogacara** school developed a philosophy created through knowledge gained in meditation practice, and called *citta-matra*, or 'mind only'. The Yogacara tradition is associated with a number of thinkers, amongst them **Asanga** and **Vasubandhu** of the fourth century CE, who took the central ideas from various teachings, sutras and commentaries to support the Absolute Mind as the only Reality. They also proposed that the entity of the Buddha could have three forms, each being an aspect of the Enlightened state.

The Mahayana took the Buddha of the Jakata tales (which depict a sequence of lives, some human and others in animal form, each developing qualities that will come to maturity in the Buddha) as the model for the Bodhisattva who – lifetime after lifetime – works for the salvation of others.

Bodhisattvas personify the perfection of selfless ethical action, displaying such qualities as fearlessness, kindness, energy, patience and particularly cultivating Wisdom and Compassion – the hallmark of an Enlightened person.

Given the possibility of depicting different Buddhas and Bodhisattvas, Buddhist art flowered. Two main styles emerge. The first style named after **Gandhara** region, located in the foothills of the Himalayas, which came into contact with Hellenic culture. Depiction's of the Buddha from the Gandhara region show him dressed in toga type garments, his face given the clean symmetry of the Hellenic ideal.

By contrast, the Buddha images from

the **Mathura** region are more in keeping with Indian aesthetics. The images retain their sensuous forms, dressed in veil like garments that cover an ethereal body rather than an earthly one.

A variety of hand postures, *mudras*, and attributes, *lakshanas*, where employed to deepen the meaning of the images. Halos, flowers and thrones appear. The Bodhisattva, in contrast to the renunciate Buddha, are rendered as royal figures, wearing ornate clothing and jewellery, carrying emblems that identify their virtues.

With the demands of the Mahayana, the Buddha became increasingly associated with the heavenly and the transcendental, the role of the historic Buddha diminishing in importance.

Here is the reaction of one author on seeing a Buddha image in Sri Lanka:

'Among the ruins of Anuradhapura, the ancient capital of Sri Lanka, there rests alone on a pedestal above the grass a seated image of the Buddha in stone, slightly larger than life. The statue is conventional, probably more than a thousand years old, of a type found throughout Buddhist Asia. The legs are folded in meditation, the hands laid one upon the other in the lap. Buddhists hold that it was in this posture, seated beneath a tree more than 2500 years ago, that the Buddha was awakened, attaining decisive knowledge of the human condition and the unshakable certainty that he was released from its suffering.

'In its excellence, however, the Anuradhapura image is far from conventional. The back and head are disciplined and upright; but the arms are relaxed and the face reposes in tranquillity. The figure seems intelligent and serene, wed perfectly to the unmoving granite.'

from M Carrithers, *The Buddha*

> FOR FURTHER INFORMATION ON:
> EARLY BUDDHISM, SEE PAGE 54F
> FOR BUDDHIST PHILOSOPHY OF
> RELIGION, SEE PAGES 187-191
> FOR NAGARJUNA AND MADHYAMAKA
> PHILOSOPHY, SEE PAGE 59.

Buddha images in Thailand. These reflect the simplicity of the Theravada, in contrast to the more elaborate images of Buddhas and Bodhisattvas found in the Mahayana tradition.

ART AND EASTERN PHILOSOPHY

According to tradition, Padmasambhava, a semi-mythical, semi-historical figure, brought Buddhism to Tibet in the seventh century CE. A Tantric adept from India, he encountered the indigenous Bon-Po, which was principally concerned with occult practice, the control of spirits, burial rites and prophecy of the future, but was without any core theory or practice of its own.

From the beginning, the Tibetans saw themselves as the preservers of the Indian tradition, referring to the Yogacara and the Madhyamaka schools for their inspiration. They also borrowed from Indian Tantra, to form the basis of the Vajrayana practice.

Vajrayana Buddhism aims to develop the primordial qualities of the Enlightened Mind, Compassion and Wisdom, as quickly as possible, and rituals and practice are designed to harness all our energies in this direction.

The school adopted the vajra as an emblem. Associated with Indra, an ancient Indian god, it is an object that is capable of cutting through all illusion, to get to the heart of Reality.

Everything, even our most base desires, can be transformed towards the ultimate goal of liberation.

Tibetan Buddhism is full of ritual objects, images and texts. Notable are the *thangkas*, thought to have originated from decorated Indian manuscripts, which are used to embellish the walls of shrines and temples. The subject matter of thangkas are figures, both real and imagined: teachers, philosophers lamas and saints, as well as the historical Buddha Shakyamuni and the Five Transcendent Buddhas (Vairochana, Ratnasambhava, Amoghasiddhi, Amitabha and Akshobhya), the wrathful aspects, and Bodhisattvas.

All appear in brilliant colour, and are used for inspiration, instruction, and as meditation objects, in which the qualities that these figures embody are contemplated on in the hope that the meditator may develop them.

Chinese civilization was already more than 2000 years old when Buddhism was introduced to the 'Middle Kingdom' by the Indian sage **Bodhidharma** in 520 CE. There was already a strong tradition of philosophical thought, out of which two distinct schools emerged, Confucianism and Taoism.

Confucius (551-479CE) developed philosophy concerned with social values, government, benevolence and correct behaviour. Whilst it did not contribute to art from the point of view of commentary on its content, or the relationship between art and spiritual matters, it did contribute to a stable society in which significance was given to ancestor worship and the court, and which did provide patronage of the arts. It tended to favour images that reflected these values.

Confucian tenents where antithetical to the concerns of Buddhism and Taoism, disapproving of sages who withdrew from society to further personal rather than social aims. Confucius did not always approve of an intimate relationship with the divine either:

'To revere the gods, and keep at a due distance from them, may be called knowledge.'

Analects: chapter 6

Taosim grew out of the speculation of the sage **Lao Tzu**, and is based on his famous *Tao te Jing*, 'Classic of the Way'. Like followers of Hinduism, they believed in an underlying reality in all phenomena, which they called the Tao, or the Way.

They conceived of a dynamic universe, whose rhythms and patterns could be discerned, the goal being to harmonize oneself with these forces of constantly changing and alternating opposites, seen as being inherent in all things. Change was viewed as the prime feature of nature.

According to the Taoist system, when the people follow the flow of nature without resistance, then order and happiness follow.

There is a strong relationship between Taoist philosophy and aesthetics, to the extent that its visual work and poetry are almost an embodiment of the spirit of Tao.

Their observations of nature produced schools of landscape painting, that flourished under the patronage of the Northern Sung Court (960-1127CE).

Geographical features such as mountains, clouds, pines, water, mist and rivers, where imbued with inner meaning. A valley for example, represented stillness, and water. Perhaps the paintings illustrate so well the Tao approach.

The images are not rendered in terms of photographic representation, as truthfulness to nature was not a requirement as they often included objects and views that would not be able to be seen together. Instead, it was important to display the grandeur and scale of the world, evoking a great mass of space and land. Light was described by tonal change rather than colour and the ability to create atmosphere with the utmost economy of brushstrokes, was greatly prized. Mountains were especially revered, being the place where Taoist sages retreated to experience Tao.

The fortunes of Buddhism rose and fell with the political and imperial history of China. It had much in common with Taoism, and they borrowed each others ideas.

Buddhism itself, developed three

different trends. The Ch'an Schools favoured meditation and looked to the inspiration of the Yogacara school, the Tantric schools took their influence from esoteric practices and Vajrayana Buddhism, and the Pure Land schools, which revered the Buddha Amitabha became primarily devotional in character.

Both Taoism and Buddhism expressed great reverence for the teacher and the strongly imbibed Confucian notions of heritage and ancestor worship encouraged the production of some of the most moving figurative work in the depiction of the *luohan*, or philosopher sage.

A Chinese Taoist work of art, showing the sage Mei Fu. Geographical features take on inner meaning within Taoist art. The intention with the Taoist depiction of nature is not to be realistic, but to display its sense of grandeur and scale.

ART AND EASTERN PHILOSOPHY

Buddhism reached Japan, via China, in the fifth century CE. It was part of the so-called Great Borrowing – the period when Japan imported so many aspects of Chinese culture, from its alphabet to its arts and government, that for a while Japanese art became indistinguishable from Chinese.

The Buddhism that reached Japan was fully Mahayana in character. To begin with, Buddhism encountered the indigenous religion of Shinto, concerned with burial rites and the appeasement of ancestor spirits. Buddhism eventually integrated itself well with Shinto, but was reliant on the support of the imperial courts for its survival.

Forms of Buddhism that had evolved in China continued to flourish in Japan, and the founding of the Shingon School by **Kodo Daishi (774-835)** and the Tendia School by **Saicho (767-822)** signalled a growing sense of cultural and religious confidence.

Pure Land Buddhism also continued to prosper, with major figures **Honen Shonin (1133-1212)** and his pupil **Shinran Shonin (1173-1262)** founding the Pure Land School and the True Pure Land School respectively. Based on faith and devotion, reciting the name of Buddha Amida (Amitabha) was considered enough to ensure rebirth in Sukhavati, his heavenly Western Realm. Though meditation and study where viewed as unimportant, Pure Land Buddhism claimed **Nagarjuna** and **Vasubandhu** as notable forebears.

The strongly devotional element encouraged the creation of Amida images, depiction's of his heavenly realm, and scenes of Amida descending from Sukhavati to welcome the dying believer, where especially popular. This belief in the surety of salvation arose in the context of a growing cultural mood called moon no aware, a melancholy sharpened by the awareness of the transitory nature of life.

Zen Buddhism developed in the 11th century and is unique in its emphasis on the Enlightenment experience or *satori*. It was generally agreed that the experience of *satori* was beyond concepts, and Zen practice avoided any theory. However knowledge of *satori* could be passed from teacher to pupil. This importance of the Master/pupil relationship echoes that between the Buddha and his disciples, and is responsible for the production of portraits of Masters, rather than the production of Buddha images.

Two schools came into being. Soto Zen, established by **Dogen (1200-1253CE)**, emphasized 'Just Sitting' meditation, and encouraged an accumulative route to *satori* and the realization of ones own Buddha nature. The second the Rinzia School was established by **Myoan Eisai (1141-1215CE)**. Rinzia Zen favoured the use of the *koan* in meditation. The *koan* is a kind puzzle to which there is no solution on the plane of dualistic thinking, instead

Girls engaged in domestic duties, by Koriusai.

its purpose is to over throw all conceptual thought, releasing the mind.

In contrast to the ornate Pure Land imagery, Zen inspired a composed and economical aesthetic, producing some of the most beautiful works of art especially in the late Kamakura (1185-1392) and Muromachi (1392-1568) periods. Here aesthetics and the process leading to Enlightenment were brought together, often in the creative activities of the artist monk.

Like followers of Tao, the Japanese desired to create as harmoniously and spontaneously as nature. This is especially exemplified in the design of temple gardens. The garden at Byodo-in Temple west of Kyoto, was originally conceived to reflect the beauty of Sukhavati, providing pleasure and evoking devotion. Employing moss, stones, trees, rocks and water, the designers created a sense of scale in a small area, emulating the spatial arrangement of landscape painting. The mood evoked through Zen gardens, like the famous dry garden at Ryoan-ji was contemplative, providing the opportunity for insight.

Zen ideals extended into secular life, and following the example of Taoism, a number of 'Ways' became popularised. Archery, the martial arts and flower arranging, activities associated with the every day became potential *satori* experiences. However in order to gain insight these activities had to be approach with complete mindfulness or presence of being, requiring many years of training.

The notable calligrapher **Ikkyu Sojun (1394-1481)** was also a Zen Master as was the highly accomplished painter and writer **Hakuin (1685-1769)**, attributed with reviving the Zen tradition. Traditional subjects of brush and ink painting were portraits of Daruma (Bodhidharma), the natural world and landscape. However, Zen monk **Segai Gibon (1750-1837)** produced enigmatic and profound images, using geometric forms, which are utterly void of any content but themselves. Like the gravel and rock gardens of Ryoan-ji in order to know them, we must change our way of seeing.

Tea drinking, originally designed to

In visual art, the relationship between calligraphy and painting is particularly close, each using the same equipment; ink brushes and a support of paper or silk. The medium leaves little room for revision once the brush mark has been made and the process requires discipline and spontaneity, aptly suited to the Zen sensibility.

The perfection of calligraphy is found in the authenticity of the brushstroke. The greater the union between intent gesture and result, the more spiritually meaningful the activity.

relieve long periods of meditation, developed into cha no yo, or the Tea Ceremony. The Tea Ceremony became a total experience, involving the roles of Tea Master and guest, the appreciation of poetry, painting, ones surroundings and the tea-making objects for which a

new ceramic ware, Raku, was created. The quiet joy and satisfaction to be found in this Ceremony requires attention at all levels of being and with all the senses.

FOR ZEN ON LANGUAGE, SEE PAGE 229

WHAT IS HISTORY?

We could start exploring the philosophy of history by asking a fundamental question 'What is history?'

It cannot be an account of all that has happened in the past. That will not do, for theoretically an infinite number of events have happened in the past, and even if they were all remembered and recorded, it would take an infinite amount of time to write up an account of them – events would unfold faster than history could be recorded.

History is therefore selective about what it records; most things are ignored, either because there is no evidence for them, or because they appear to be of no interest, or because an examination of them would require too vast an enterprise and would therefore smother any attempt to get an overall view of what happened.

This last factor is significant, for all history involves an interpretation of events, and that interpretation depends on the ideas and assumptions of the historian or philosopher concerned.

Issues in the Philosophy of History parallel those in other areas of philosophy. Much work in this field during the 20th century is 'critical' or 'analytic'. The issues debated are not first order ones (what actually happened) but second order ones (how can we validate and interpret statements about events). Concern has shifted to the possibilities and processes of writing history, seen most clearly in the Postmodernist debate outlined below.

The other approach to the philosophy of history is speculative. It seeks to examine the historical records in search of ideas about how one event influences another, in the hope of formulating general laws or principles to explain the process of human history

This approach, too, has a long history, sometimes as a means of understanding and transmitting culture (as in Confucius), or for religious purposes (for Jews and Christians), or as a way of assessing the mechanisms of social change (for Hegelians and Marxists).

Probably the most important question for this second approach is: Does studying historical events reveal more than a chaotic flux, lacking all direction and meaning, or can an overarching pattern be discerned, such as God's will manifesting itself in human affairs?

From the ancient Jews on to Hegel and later, Western theologians and philosophers have returned to these questions. One difference between, say, ancient Greeks and Hindus on the one hand, and those from the Judaeo-Christian tradition on the other, concerns beliefs about the nature of historical time.

For most Indians and Greeks, history is essentially cyclical, like the seasons of the year, and is not going anywhere. So, for example, most Hindu philosophy entertains the idea of vast cosmic cycles, accounting for the apparent progress of change, but these cycles repeat themselves.

Similarly, Mahayana Buddhism, tends to describe the 'eternal' significance of things in terms of endless world-systems. There is progression of a sort, since buddhas appear in each of the systems, leading to more and more developed teaching of the Dharma, but nevertheless the overall feeling of the material – as, for example, in the Lotus Sutra – is of the present world-system being set in a context of an overwhelming succession of worlds.

For Jews and Christians, however, time follows a linear course, running arrow-like from the Creation to the end of time, according to a diving plan. **Augustine** expressed this in Christian terms in *The City of God*.

In the 20th century, **Arnold Toynbee** made a famous contribution to speculative history in *A Study of History* (1934-1954). The furious attacks this provoked, however, have diminished enthusiasm for speculative history for the present.

The Philosophy of History can therefore never be an entirely objective account of facts. It is an interpretative tale, told by someone interested in the significance of particular features of the past. More than one layer of interpretation may be involved. Thus, for example, a modern historian, examining ancient texts, is bringing to his examination his or her own views, but equally, those of the original authors of those texts, who were also interpreting the events that they recorded. In terms of the analysis of this process, history becomes historiography, the study of historical writing.

'Herodotus of Halicarnassus, his Researches are here set down to preserve the memory of the past by putting on record the astonishing achievements both of our own and of other peoples…'

Herodotus, *Histories*

But should Herodotus be considered a historian? Is he setting out to record the facts, or telling a tale to entertain and inform? The question of what constitutes history, and how fact and interpretation are balanced, are central issues for the Philosophy of History.

POSTMODERNISM AND FACTS

Much of the debate about the nature of historical writing reflects broader philosophical considerations. Postmodernist thinkers (e.g. **Jacques Derrida** – see page 49) would argue that texts are simply based on other texts (the process called '*intertextuality*'), rather than on external 'facts'. The truth of what is given in an historical text therefore stems primarily from the authority of the circles that have established it, not to events it claims to describe.

The American philosopher of history, **Hayden White**, in his book *Metahistory* (1973) put forward the postmodernist view that the historian is actually producing a creative literary invention, rather than dealing in bare facts. Of course, some of the information with which the historian deals may be factual, but it only

becomes 'history' once it becomes part of a story, set in a structured narrative. An historian works at creating a narrative, and that narrative enables the evidence used to become part of what is presented as history.

For White, there is a distinction to be made between 'events' and 'facts'. The former are what took place, the latter are simply linguistic forms that claim to describe the event. It is the objectivity of such 'facts' that postmodernism challenges.

Within postmodernism, it is impossible to get beyond language to a fundamental reality to which the words can be shown to point. Rather we have to be content with the story itself – and that story is a *metanarrative*, a framework that is used to interpret the past. Each person is free to construct his or her own version of history.

This postmodernist approach raises absolutely crucial issues for historians.

For a clear introduction to and evaluation of the postmodernist view of the Philosophy of History, see *The Past and its Presenters* (Hodder & Stoughton, 1998) by John Warren, upon which the above comments are based.

If we cannot claim to be presenting 'facts' about events that took place in the past, then the implication is that **any interpretation of the past is as good as any other.**

Now, it is clear that no historian would pretend to claim that his or her account of an event is *totally* objective, since the very selection of events to be examined represents a personal choice and therefore a bias in some sense. But, on the other hand, once evidence is gathered and assessed, it is important to be able to say – within limits – what happened.

A crucial example here is the holocaust. Historians who examine evidence for the exterminations, both written records and physical remains, see it as essential to record as 'facts' that such events took place. An extreme postmodernist view would be that such 'facts' are just one way of looking at the evidence. Hence, for example, some neo-Nazi attempts to claim that the holocaust did not take place. In order to refute such a claim, it is essential to be able to say what constitutes an historical 'fact'.

On the speculative approach to history:

History is coloured by the selection of events. Some history, for example, may reflect a male bias. Some may ignore the working classes. Different accounts of events can be given from different perspectives. But which events and perspectives are worth recording?
Many occasions are described as 'historical' when they involve decisions taken by those in power. Leaders of nations take decisions that influence the lives of millions, and hence those decisions and those leaders, become part of 'history', simply by virtue of the scale of their impact on the world around them. But are the lives of ordinary people any less historical? Should historians be concerned with meetings of world leaders, or should they concentrate on recording the lives of ordinary people?

'The history of the world is none other than the progress of the consciousness of freedom.'

Hegel *The Philosophy of History*

FOR FURTHER INFORMATION ON:

AUGUSTINE, SEE PAGE   154

HEGEL, SEE PAGE   256.

In the 'historical' books of the Jewish scriptures – for example II *Kings*, which gives an account of the Kings of Israel and Judah – we have material that recounts historical events, but it also shows that the authors were fundamentally interested only in assessing the obedience to religious principles. (The issues are complicated through an analysis of the sources found within those books, but that is an issue beyond our concern here.) Events are recorded in order to illustrate a theological point of view.

'The Israelites persisted in all the sins of Jeroboam and did not turn away from them until the Lord removed them from his presence, as he had warned through all his servants the prophets. So the people of Israel were taken from their homeland into exile in Assyria, and they are still there.'   II *Kings*, 17: 22, 23

Here the author of II *Kings* gives a theological reason for the social and political event of the exile to Assyria of the leaders of Israel. The intention here is quite different from that of a modern historian looking at the Assyrian policy towards the nations it conquered.

The purpose of the Biblical narrative is not to record facts per se, but to show religious significance. In this, it is an overt and exaggerated form of the selective interpretation of the past that is a feature of all history.

The same can be said for the Jewish Scriptures overall. They are an account of the dealings of God with mankind, and specifically with his chosen people, the Jews.

The Christian scriptures of the New Testament also present an overall pattern of interpretation of history, from the creation and the Garden of Eden to the Second Coming of Christ and the end of time.

Thus, for both the Jewish and Christian traditions, historical events are significant, but only because they are set within an overall framework that is determined by religion. In other words, what we have here is sacred history.

This does not prejudge questions about whether particular events did or did not happen as described. It is simply to point out that such issues (which would be considered critical in modern secular history) are relatively unimportant compared with the overall purpose of the written account. It is the story that conveys meaning, and the link with events in the past provides the context for the present experience of faith.

A nineteenth-century attempt to give natural explanations for the miraculous elements in the story, as for example in **D F Strauss'** *Life of Jesus, a Critical Treatment* (1836) simply illustrates a confusion about the nature of sacred history. Modern attempts to prove or disprove biblical events equally miss the mark if they assume that the outcome of critical research will be religiously significant.

Some religious material becomes particularly significant when seen against its historical background. For example, when **Augustine** wrote *The City of God* between 413 and 426, he was responding to the catastrophe of the sacking of Rome in 410. His purpose was clearly theological, for he was concerned to make an absolute distinction between the 'City of God' as a spiritual reality and any earthly institution, even one as central to the political awareness of the time as Rome.

His argument is that earthly events cannot simply be equated with the divine purpose, but that there is an overall divine plan, within which God's justice is to be revealed. In this, the division he makes between the real and the transient, earthly phenomena, shows his philosophical debt to Plato.

The writer of sacred history sees the significance of past events insofar as they set a context for, or illustrate in some other

THE APPEAL OF LOCAL HISTORY

Local or family history not only satisfies people's curiosity, it also gives a sense of identity and continuity, within a family or within a community. On a broader canvass, sacred history offers the same thing to the members of a faith community. History and identity are closely intertwined; for good or ill, those with a keen sense of history tend to understand themselves in terms of their past. Communities divided along sectarian lines may justify their present situation in terms of past grievances. On the other hand, a sense of loyalty may be engendered by awareness of the number of generations of one's family who have lived in a particular, country, place or even a particular house. There is a world of difference between a house that is regarded as a family home, and one that is simply a temporary dwelling, to be bought or sold depending on market conditions or the increasing desirability of some other neighbourhood.

way, religious beliefs. Like creation stories, or family histories, their purpose is to give a sense of identity. The criteria by which it is reasonable to judge such religious narratives are therefore very different from those used by historians in order to assess factual accuracy in recording events.

SOME EASTERN PERSPECTIVES

The **Vedanta** tradition of interpreting the Hindu scriptures is based on the conviction that all scripture is of eternal validity and significance. Historical facts, however, are merely contingent, incidents in an ever-changing world. How then can accounts of them be regarded as scripture?

Vedanta's answer to this dilemma is to regard all such accounts as of significance only insofar as they can be interpreted in terms of an insight or command relevant to the present time.

This is perhaps an extreme form of the point that was made on the previous page about sacred history in general. Events in the past are only significant to the extent that they can be prescriptive, and thus made the basis for present religious life.

Thus, the great Hindu epics, the *Ramayana* and the *Mahabharata*, although superficially appearing to be historical narratives, are treated as vehicles for eternal, spiritual truths, not as accounts of events in the past. Thus you have the interplay between gods and men, as when the god Krishna appears as the charioteer of Prince Arjuna in the most famous part of the *Mahabharata*, the *Bhagavad Gita*. What we have here is a story intended to establish meaning and identity.

The Buddhist similarly places no great significance on historical fact *per se*. Buddhist literature is full of stories about events that took place in previous lives, showing their interaction with the present. It is also notable – for example in the *Lotus Sutra*, a key document for Mahayana Buddhism – that the life of the historical Buddha, Shakyamuni, is given its significance by being set within a vista which embraces many other world-systems.

In other words, events have to be given an eternal significance – and that is done through creating what appears to be a fantastic historical and cosmological framework for them. The material is read as a spiritual text, not as an historical document. Nobody is fooled by the descriptions of fantastic realms into thinking that this is objective information about past states; the relevant question is not 'Did it happen?' but 'What is the significance of this story?'

The sense of historical continuity, respect for ancestors, and deference to idealized political and cultural systems of the past, is an important feature of Confucian philosophy.

Indeed, **K'ung Fu-Tsu** (Confucius) saw the early Chou dynasty, which started in 1027 BCE, as in some way a golden age

FOR FURTHER INFORMATION ON: CONFUCIUS, SEE PAGE 196.

compared with the relative turbulence of his own time (sixth century BCE). Thus he saw the study of *The Book of Documents* – which contains mainly the archives of Western Chou – as an important source of wisdom, in his attempt to reclaim the stability and culture of the past.   Thus he is using overtly historical material as a resource for cultural and moral

The Master said: 'I transmit but do not create. Being fond of truth, I am an admirer of antiquity...'

The Analects, 7.1

This depicts a scene from the Ramayana. The various characters who appear in the great Hindu epics, the Mahabharata and the Ramayana, represent spiritual qualities to be developed, or vices to be avoided. The identification of the reader with issues that give rise to the battles of good and evil, as portrayed in the epics, provide an opportunity to explore the moral and spiritual dimensions of life through historical narrative.

DOGEN AND HISTORY

Dogen (1200-1253) was founder of the Japanese Soto Zen Buddhist tradition. He emphasized the idea of a Buddha-nature within everything, and of enlightenment as something to be recognized through the process of sitting meditation.

Following the general Mahayana view, he saw the worlds of *samsara* (impermanence) and *nirvana* as being one and the same. For Dogen, Buddha-nature is not something separate from the world of experience. It is found in and through the experience of impermanence, not by escaping from it.

Impermanence (*mujo*) is thus the fundamental feature of Dogen's view of reality, and this leads him to an interesting description of time; a description that is relevant to the Philosophy of History.

In *Shobogenzo*, his principal work, Dogen claimed that being is time and time is being. In other words, he challenged the conventional view of time as a kind of container or framework within which events take place.

Phenomena, he argued, do not exist 'within' time, they are time.

His argument may be presented thus:
- Time itself cannot be something that goes past, something that happens.
- If it were, it could only be known if it had gaps within it. In other words, to see the passing of time, one would have to isolate one moment, separate it from the next, and then show the way in which time formed a link between the one and the other.
- But in reality, it is impossible to slice up experience in that way. There is no passage between one event and the next, no gap created by something external called 'time'.
- Time is therefore the 'passageless passage' as one state flows without break into the next.
- Time is therefore the name we give to the ever-flowing nature of being.

Thus there are not two separate things – being and time – but a single, changing reality. There is no separate 'eternal' realm to which individual things can relate. Every moment is eternal, because every moment reveals the '*passageless passage*' of time.

Dogen's view of the '*passageless passage*' suggests that time and space are mental constructs through which we seek to organize our understanding of the world of changing phenomena. To say that one event causes another presupposes our ability to treat things as separate entities, rather than as parts of a single whole.

This has important implication for the process of writing history. We mentally set out a range of events before us and select those we think are significantly linked. From these we construct an historical narrative. But we never know all the events that interlock in the on-going process of change.

Dogen goes one step further – the very process, by which we identify 'events', is itself artificial. The historian is putting together fragments of that which, through the eye of wisdom, would never have been seen as fragmented in the first place.

In other words, you only create an 'event' by artificially separating off certain things and putting them together. But if all things are interconnected (which is a very basic Buddhist view of reality), then the world is a single event, not a succession of separate ones.

THE MECHANISMS OF CHANGE

Is it possible to see the course of history as the outworking of mechanisms that can be examined and applied like scientific laws?

One might associate such a question with the post-Renaissance period (since at that time there was a general tendency to seek laws or principles governing every area of enquiry, using the physical sciences as a model). However, the issue was explored first in the 14th century, by the Muslim philosopher **Ibn Khaldun**.

His approach was descriptive and analytic. He examined the basis for human society, and considered that it arose from

Projecting a film gives the illusion of movement as one frame follows another. Should we see history in the same way, as a sequence of separate events linked by a structure called 'time'? Dogen would disagree. The film is an artificial process for reconstructing the appearance of movement; whereas the original movement itself is a single organic process.

the weakness of individuals and their consequent need to associate together in order to survive. He argued that society was influenced by climate, and by the abundance or otherwise of food and natural resources.

His is therefore probably the first thinker to attempt to give a scientific account of human culture, and of the environmental and economic factors that produce social change. His view of history starts with evidence, not theology, and he is clearly concerned with issues of historical accuracy.

However, Christian historiography remained under the influence of Augustine for more than 1000 years, until the scientific revolution of the 17th century demanded a new approach. **Giambattista Vico (1668-1744)**, a Neapolitan thinker, propounded in his *New Science* of 1726 that human societies, far from being identical and changeless, pass through different stages of development, each marked by different rituals, art, outlooks etc.

To understand the past, he argued, we must enter into it imaginatively, via its archaeology, literature or myths. Although difficult, this is possible, because human societies, unlike the natural world, which he saw as created by God, are made by human beings. It therefore becomes

---

**IBN KHALDUN
(1332-1406)**

A Muslim statesman, philosopher and historian. He set out to explore history as a natural science, and society as a phenomenon, rather than the more usual way of approaching events at the time, which was to see their significance in terms of law, politics or religion.
His principal work is entitled *The Prolegomena*.

---

possible to examine those human creations that influence and affect social change.

Vico's radicalism lay in this realization that human societies change over time.

HEGEL

Vico's thought had little direct influence, but the German philosopher **J G Herder**, perhaps unknowingly, repeated his key ideas in *Philosophy of the History of Mankind* of 1784, where he stressed the importance of the cultural milieu of each age.

A very different approach to the past emerged in the philosophy of **G W F Hegel (1770-1831)**. Hegel thought that is was possible to discern a particular 'spirit' or *Geist*, unfolding in the historical process in an 'ascent to an ever higher concept of itself'. He saw spirit as moving through the process described as his dialectic, a term taken from Plato.

Thus each age has its particular feature (its 'thesis'), which then produces a reaction ('antithesis'), which is then resolved (in a 'synthesis'), only to find that this process then repeats itself. In practice, Hegel seems to have considered the Prussian state in which he lived as the most perfect embodiment of Geist so far.

FOR FURTHER INFORMATION ON:

DOGEN AND AN EXPOSITION OF HIS CONCEPT OF TIME AS A CONTRIBUTION TO THE UNDERSTANDING OF KNOWLEDGE AND REALITY, SEE PAGES **60F.**

SEE ALSO KANT PAGE **41** FOR ANOTHER APPROACH TO THE SAME ISSUE – NAMELY THAT SPACE, TIME AND CAUSALITY ARE PART OF OUR MENTAL APPARATUS, AND A NECESSARY FEATURE OF OUR WAY OF ORGANISING WHAT WE EXPERIENCE. ONE COULD ALSO EXPLORE PARALLELS WITH THE WORK OF HEIDEGGER, SEE PAGE **45**.

FOR FURTHER INFORMATION ON:
HEGEL, SEE PAGES **170** AND **256**

'Men make their own history, but they do not make it just as they please; they do not make it under circumstances chosen by themselves, but under circumstances directly encountered, given, and transmitted from the past. The tradition of all the dead generations weighs like a nightmare on the brain of the living.'

Karl Marx, *The Eighteenth Brumaire of Louis Bonaparte*

MARX

Karl Marx (1818-1883) started as a Hegelian, but went on to use Hegelian dialectic to very different ends. What Marx did was to take Hegel's philosophy and apply it to the material and economic base of society.

In doing so, he claimed to have found an overall rational theory (since Hegel stood within the European idealist tradition) that could be applied to all history.

Marx argued that economic structures formed the basis of society, and that social existence determined consciousness. Therefore (in what is termed 'historical materialism') history (along with all political, social and religious ideologies) is driven by the economic conditions upon which a given society is based.

The most significant relations in terms of social change are the 'relations of production' (e.g. between the workers and the capitalists who employ them), and all aspects of society are shaped by them.

From the standpoint of the Philosophy of History, therefore, Marx is arguing for **economic determinism**.

Even this brief and superficial outline of Marx' thinking, makes his significance for the Philosophy of History clear. The historian is required to interpret actual events in terms of their underlying economic structures.

There is a vast literature on Marx and his interpretation of history. One significant area of debate is the extent to which economics is the only driving force in the process of change, or whether there is scope for political ideals and commitments.

It may be argued that Marx's own commitment to the communist cause and the rise of the proletariat, which he clearly hoped would be effective, was not in itself the product of an economic process. Indeed, one possible consequence of seeing history as simply an outworking of economics is that there is no need for political commitment of any sort – since the inevitable outworking of the economic system will bring about change without the need for political activism.

'The mode of production in material life determines the general character of the social, political, and spiritual processes of life. It is not the consciousness of men that determines their existence, but, on the contrary, their social existence determines their consciousness.'

from *A Contribution to the Critique of Political Economy*, 1859

'The history of all society up to now is the history of class struggles.' The Communist Manifesto

American soldiers in the Saudi desert, 1990. Should warfare by seen primarily in terms of the underlying economics, or as fought for matters of principle? The answer you give to this question will colour your interpretation of history.

FOR INFORMATION ON MARX AND RELIGION, SEE PAGE 172, AND ON ETHICS, SEE PAGE 92.

Early secular historians seem to have been concerned to record significant deeds and to see them as events from which people in the present can learn. But in doing so, they increasingly show the need for a critical approach to their material.

Thus, whereas **Heroditus (484-430)** in his *Histories* (about the Persian invasions of Greece) offers a mixed collection of tales, some intended to inspire, other perhaps mainly to entertain, **Thucydides (c.460-400)** traced the events of the Peloponnesian War, with the stated intention of allowing people to learn from them as a guide to the future, and did so with the serious intention of establishing the truth of what took place.

Clearly, whenever a historian comes to approach a complex situation, he or she will bring to it his or her own perspective and agenda. That in turn influences both the selection of facts, the assessment of their relevance, and their interpretation. To think that it could be otherwise is naive.

Thus the historian with a religious purpose (e.g. Eusebius or Augustine) will select and focus on issues that appear to support the religious perspective. Equally, historians of the 18th century – e.g. **Hume (1711-1776)** or **Gibbon (1737-1794)**, author of *The Decline and Fall of the Roman Empire*, look on earlier periods with a critical eye, and from the perspective of a Enlightenment sense that reason had now replaced superstition. History could also be a way of commenting obliquely on the issues of their own day. Significantly, neither of these two men was Christian.

But a mark of the professionalism of the historian is to stand back from his or her own time and prejudices and allow the material evidence to speak for itself. The historian who contributed most to the development of this approach was **Leopold von Ranke (1795-1886)**. He did not claim to be judging the past, simply to show how things happened,

without ignoring evidence simply because it was unattractive.

In approaching and assessing material, there are two general approaches that may be taken:

1 To consider events insofar as they fit within an overall principle or law – this is the '*covering law model*'. In other words, you take a single event and see it as an example of a number of different factors and principles. Until an event has been so interpreted, it cannot become part of history.

2 To consider an event in terms of the experience of those who took part and whose decisions were crucial to its outcome. **R G Collingwood**, much influenced by the Italian historian **Benedetto Croce (1866-1952)**, argued that the way to understand historical events was to enter imaginatively into the position of those involved, to see the nature of the decisions that had to be made.

One might caricature those two approaches by saying that the first sees events being pushed forward by historical influences, while the second sees them as being pulled forward by the hopes and intentions of those taking part.

The first approach sees events as caused by something, the second as aiming at something.

One might relate this to issues of freedom and determinism (see page 66), and Kant's view of everything as phenomenally determined but noumenally free (page 38ff).

Once an event is analysed and set within an historical continuum, it appears the inevitable outcome of on-going historical trends and pressures. This follows the 'covering law model'. From the standpoint of the person involved, however, a choice is made based on hopes for a suitable outcome.

R G Collingwood
(1889-1943)

Collingwood was an Oxford philosopher and historian. A key feature of his thought was the importance of the imagination. In the field of art, he considered it important to enter imaginatively into the mind of the artist or composer. In history he similarly saw the need to enter imaginatively into the minds of those being studied.

His major works are: *The Idea of History* (1936) and *The Principles of Art* (1938).

> 'It is necessary that the historian keeps his eyes open for the general. He will not have preconceived ideas as does the philosopher, but rather while he observes the particular, the course which the development of the world in general has taken will be revealed to him…'
>
> Leopold von Ranke

SEE ALSO COLLINGWOOD ON: ART, SEE PAGE 259.

Until relatively recently, the selection of topics for research by most historians was quite narrow. Ranke, for example, was concerned with nationality and with the great political and diplomatic events that shaped nation states.

It was only in the second half of the 20th century that history started to focus more on the lives of ordinary people. A particularly popular example of this was **Emmanuel Le Roy Ladurie**'s book *Montaillou* (1975), which explored life in the village of Montaillou in South West France. It featured the court records of villagers in the 14th century who were investigated as part of an attempt to stamp out the Cathar 'heresy'. In the course of giving their evidence, fascinating details of mundane life appear.

Today archaeologists are fascinated by the remains of ordinary working people, building up a picture of just a few of those 'events' in the past that would probably not have been considered significant by historians of an earlier age.

The importance of this, for the Philosophy of History, is that it indicates that the quest for overarching theories about political and social change, has partly given way to a more general sense that it is possible to enter imaginatively into the lives of ordinary people from past ages. But in this, the selection of the ordinary as being of interest is itself a reflection of social and political values in the present.

Nietzsche distinguished three uses for history (in his book *Untimely Meditation, On the Use and Disadvantage of History*, 1874):

1 **Antiquarian**. This approach simply seeks to preserve the past.
2 **Monumental**. This approach gives to events in the past a role and significance that transcends their actual time and space. They become suprahistorical ideals to be emulated, their values regarded as eternal. (In some ways this finds parallel in the Eastern approach taken by the Vedanta.)
3 **Critical**. This approach seeks to liberate the present from any claims that the past might try to make upon it.

History is not limited to the interpretation of great events of the past. There is a growing interest in how ordinary people lived. This follows a shift in the perception of the significance of history. We might want to consider how the poor coped with their poverty and the prospect of early death in the 19th century, for example, entering imaginatively into their situation.

These, particularly the third, reflect Nietzsche's general concern for the freedom and autonomy of the present, and the need to set one's own goals, freed from restraints imposed by past authorities. Nevertheless, it would seem that much of the Philosophy of History has moved to and fro between the first two.

On the one hand, whether from political or religious motives, many have sought inspiration from the past on the assumption that there are eternal truths exemplified in it. On the other, there is the sense that the professional historian is there to let the past speak for itself, and that the imaginative attempt to enter into past events is in itself a valuable human enterprise.

But the third of Nietzsche's uses remains important. One has only to reflect on the situation in the Middle East, with the tensions between Israel and the Palestinians, or consider the tensions between groups within the former Yugoslavia, to see the way in which the past – often distorted for partisan purposes – can shackle the lives of people in the present. There are also those who are determined to overcome such long-term historical legacies, as we see in the continuing progress towards reconciliation in Northern Ireland.

To be aware of one's roots is an important aspect of human well-being, to be free from their legacy may be equally essential.

FOR FURTHER INFORMATION ON:
NIETZSCHE SEE PAGES **93** AND **174.**

What can we learn from ancient civilizations? Perhaps, more than anything else, that the world is a place of constant change, and that the elaborate schemes of today will be the archaeological site of tomorrow. What were the hopes and fears of the people who lived here? We can attempt to reconstruct their lives; can learn from them; can selectively build up a picture of the historical process of change through which they lived. Hopefully, we can also learn from their mistakes.

In philosophy, the study of the moral foundations of politics and law has a prominent place. This is not surprising, given that the primary focus of political philosophy is the institutions, laws and norms by which the rights and obligations of life are determined and justified.

Although political philosophy has often been viewed in the 20th century as secondary to what are assumed to be the more fundamental concerns of epistemology, this was not always the case. In Ancient Greece, philosophers often understood only too clearly that an inquiry into the political was primary because it was the political circumstances that provided, or limited, the conditions under which other philosophical inquiries might – or, in the case of Socrates, might not – be pursued.

The realm of the political includes, particularly, the institution of the state: its arrangements, or modes of organization, and the rules that the state enforces, namely the laws and regulations concerning human action and interaction.

Political philosophy does not, however, describe or explain such affairs, even though description and explanation are important in political philosophies. Rather, political philosophy is fundamentally **normative – it seeks to specify what should or should not be done in the political realm**.

- Should there be a state?
- What should the state do?

Although political philosophy is normative it is more than a mere attempt to prescribe affairs.

Unlike political ideologies, political philosophy seeks to justify its claims, and this enterprise of justification may involve explications of important political concepts (such as freedom, equality, justice, or rights) and it may even argue about the value of such concepts, whether they should be put into practice, and what their consequences are.

Political philosophy, then, poses fundamental questions about the political realm and seeks answers using reason, insight, and analysis.

But there is no standard method of political philosophy; political philosophers do not all pose the same question or provide the same answer. Indeed, political philosophy has a varied and glorious history in which topics, ideas, and themes are developed in distinct ways and with divergent emphases and implications.

Throughout all of these philosophies runs the underlying question: how human beings should live together and order their living arrangements into obligations, prohibitions, and permissions.

'Man is by nature a political animal.'

Aristotle Politics, I, 2.9

Thus, political philosophy is intimately tied to philosophical questions concerning law and society. For example, one's understanding of society (and of humanity, that social animal) influences one's views about political institutions; on the other hand, political institutions themselves obviously affect society profoundly.

Clearly, we can understand a society and the way it works by examining its laws, and how they control what people do and particularly how they relate to one another. We are therefore led to ask the basic questions:

- What is the nature of a law?
- How does it differ from a rule or norm?

While political philosophy focuses on accounts and justifications of political entities (such as states and governments), social theory or social philosophy concerns the processes and elements of social interaction (and whether there are rules or norms by which that interaction may occur or produce certain effects). But, clearly, these two aspects of life cannot be kept separate, for politics influences society, just as society in turn can present issues that shape politics.

Several salient questions or assumptions are often considered when thinking philosophically about politics:

- What is human nature? And what sort of society is compatible with human nature?
- Is there a difference between a state and a society?
- What is the proper goal or aim of a state? Or should a state have no substantive goal but opt instead to provide the conditions by which its members may pursue their own (various) goals?
- What are the proper grounds of state action (or inaction)? Are these grounds found in human nature, human goodness, rights, liberty or equality? Or are political norms, like all moral norms, merely conventions? Do they merely express the goals of one group, class, or society?
- What is the nature of liberty? And how valuable is it?
- What is the nature of equality? Which types of equality are valuable?

At any one time, within the History of Philosophy, one or more of these questions will come to the fore, but all have their place within an overall consideration of law and politics.

As so often, all philosophy's roads lead back to Ancient Greece, for it is in that period that we find discussion of political entities that remain relevant for us today, raising fundamental questions about the nature of the just society.

It is therefore with Socrates, Plato and Aristotle that our examination of the Philosophy of Politics and Law will need to start.

FOR GENERAL INFORMATION ON:

PLATO, SEE PAGE 23

ARISTOTLE, SEE PAGE 26

Socrates is one of the most fascinating figures in all philosophy. His trial and death moulded Plato's views on justice and society.

In the Western world, political philosophy begins in classical Athens with Socrates, and especially with his pupil Plato. Plato, little though he may have liked it, lived in a democracy. Athenian democracy was not an occasional affair like a modern representative democracy with elections every few years, but a direct one, demanding the active attention of its citizens, voting every issue almost daily in the Assembly.

For Socrates, Plato, and even Aristotle, the city-state or *polis*, (from which of course the word 'political' derives) was the formative and only conceivable basis of individual life.

Even though not all Athenians could participate – women, slaves and *metics* (resident aliens) being among those excluded – the citizens of an ancient Greek city were expected to identify their individual good with that of the whole community to a degree unthinkable in a modern democracy.

So one of the most pressing questions for the Greeks was identifying the best form of government in which human beings could realize the human good. Socrates experienced in his own person the limitations of government when he was put to death on what was at least partly a trumped-up charge. But the vital question of government involved a prior question:

● What is a human being?

Athenian democracy suffered numerous travails in the last quarter of the fifth-century BCE. Finally it was defeated by Sparta and its democracy replaced with a short-lived fascistic junta in 404BCE before democracy was restored.

It was against this backdrop of political turmoil that Socrates, teacher of Plato and a paradigm of the practicing philosopher, was brought to trial on charges of 'corrupting the young and of not believing in the gods in whom the city believes, but in other new spiritual things'.

In the course of his trial, as recounted

What of the nature and importance of liberty? This is just one of the key questions for the Philosophy of Politics and Law. It reflects one of humankind's deepest concerns, to be free from restraint, to be able to live life and follow one's own projects. But how is it to be achieved and safeguarded? How does my liberty affect the liberty of others?

SOCRATES' DANGEROUS FRIENDS

Among Plato's dialogues is the *Critias*, named after a real man: Critias, leader of the 'Thirty Tyrants', the junta which seized power in 404 and for ten months exercised a reign of terror in Athens. Critias was a friend and ex-pupil of Socrates, as Athenians could remember.

Socrates in fact refused to support the junta and lived to tell the tale – a sign of favouritism, perhaps.

After the junta's overthrow and the amnesty, Socrates was unpopular among many in Athens for his friends and ex-pupils.

in Plato's *Apology* (not of course a wholly impartial source), Socrates adumbrated a view of philosophy that emphasized reason, morality, and loyalty to one's polis.

Socrates' philosophy was developed by his dialectic method, arguing against other philosophers, known as **Sophists** (see page 23), itinerant teachers who taught rhetoric to the sons of the wealthy. Aiming for political and social success rather than the pursuit of truth, many Sophists were moral relativists; others suggested, more nihilistically, that you should heed only self-interest because conventional morality simply masks the aims of those already in power.

Arraying himself against the Sophists (with whom he was at times wrongfully confused), Socrates contends that the most important thing for a human being is the care of the soul. To take care of one's soul is to be concerned with virtue and virtue is to be sought in knowledge. Against the Sophists' relativist or nihilist claims, Socrates affirmed the importance of virtue and morality.

SOCRATES' DIALECTIC

Having heard from the Delphic Oracle that 'no one is wiser than he', Socrates embarked on a quest in which he hoped to show that the Oracle was mistaken, and that others were wiser than he was. However, in the course of his quest, Socrates came to the realization that those who claim to know often do not know what they claim; as a result, Socrates recognized that his own wisdom began as an awareness of what one doesn't know.

Socrates' original quest becomes a calling, in which he urged the Athenians to subject all their beliefs to examination; in this way the Athenians might come to some awareness of what can be known and what cannot.

As Socrates set out to cross-examine Athenians about their beliefs, using his typical gadfly technique of *dialectic*, he annoyed many citizens, who believed that Socrates himself had some sort of special, perhaps ungodly knowledge. This finally led to his trial (any citizen could start such a trial) with Socrates accused of corrupting young people, introducing new deities into the city (a strange charge in normally tolerant, polytheistic Athens, but they were abnormal times) and not worshipping the traditional city gods.

In the course of the trial, Socrates refuted many misconceptions about him, reminded the jury of the origin of his philosophical questioning, and denied all the charges.

Because he considered examining one's beliefs to be of paramount importance, Socrates made an appeal to the jury in which he asked himself hypothetically whether he would give up the practice of philosophy if he were to be acquitted.

He gave the following reply to this momentous question:

'Gentlemen of the jury, I am grateful and I am your friend, but I will obey the god rather than you, and as long as I draw breath and am able,

I shall not cease to practise philosophy, to exhort you and in my usual way to point out to any one of you whom I happen to meet: Good Sir, you are an Athenian, a citizen of the greatest city with the greatest reputation for both wisdom and power; are you not ashamed of your eagerness to possess as much wealth, reputation and honours as possible, while you do not care for nor give thought to wisdom or truth, or the best possible state of your soul?' **from the *Apology***

Socrates then argues that, if the person he encounters claims to be so concerned with his soul, he will probe and question him, to see if he has indeed gained the claimed goodness.

In particular, Socrates makes the point that he will challenge the person concerned about the value he places on some things rather than others. In other words,

from the start, his philosophy is concerned with values and norms – and that there are revealed only through questioning the meaning of words, and the implications of the concepts people use.

Though he had urged the Athenians to seek knowledge and truth, Socrates was found guilty and condemned to death. He willingly suffered this penalty, on the grounds that he accepted the very legal system that found him guilty. He may also have reckoned that his death was likely to reflect badly on the city, but well on himself. And anyway, he guessed that he could not hope to live much longer.

In Plato's Crito, Socrates is portrayed in prison, arguing against those who offered a means of escape, that such would be a violation of his duty to Athens: Socrates had agreed to live in Athens and abide by its laws (including those laws which allowed for his indictment, trial, and punishment) and so, it would be wrong for Socrates to seek to escape, for that would be a violation of his own agreement and duty.

Socrates considered his obligation to the city of Athens and its laws. Nobody should be forced to stay within the state, but for those who choose to do so, he argues on behalf of the rulers:

'... whoever of you remains, when he sees how we conduct our trials and manage the city in other ways, has in fact come to an agreement with us to obey our instructions. We say that the one who disobeys does wrong in three ways, first because in us he disobeys his parents, also those who brought him up, and because in spite of his agreement, he neither obeys us nor, if we do something wrong, does he try to persuade us to do better.'

Incarnate in Socrates is the pervasive Western belief that reason itself can unite morality and power, so that the law may legitimately oblige someone to perform an act (or refrain from some act) that requires personal sacrifice.

The reconciliation of morality and power is the single most important problem for the political philosopher, and it receives a systematic elaboration in Plato's works. His *Republic* is a dialogue – about 'justice' (the standard translation for *dikaiosune*, the Greek word for the moral or the right). Through the character of Socrates, Plato poses the question:

● Why should one be just?
  In other words:
● Is there an intrinsic value in justice?

Plato was interested in the question of why an individual should be just (especially when there are strong selfish reasons for being unjust). He was also concerned about the practical political questions of a just polis and how a just state's social arrangements should be justified. In addition, he was concerned about the issues of private interest versus public good:

● How can public affairs be managed in the public interest rather than the private interest?

Plato's concerns were partly a response to two Sophistic claims:

1 that there is no absolute knowledge about right and wrong;
2 that one should seek only to fulfil one's desires.

In addition, Plato was attempting to rebut a popular belief about the nature of the laws (and right and wrong more generally), namely, that they have no intrinsic value but are mere instruments which prevent us from suffering at the hands of others. This popular viewpoint ran as follows:

'They say that to do injustice is naturally good, and to suffer injustice bad, but that the badness of suffering it so far exceeds the goodness of doing it, that those who have done and suffered injustice and tasted both, but who lack the power to do it and avoid suffering it, decide that it is profitable to come to an agreement with each other neither to do injustice nor to suffer it. As a result, they begin to make laws and covenants, and what the law commands they call lawful and just. This, they say, is

the origin and essence of justice... People value it not as a good but because they are too weak to do injustice with impunity.' Republic, 359ab

To consider whether justice has some intrinsic, as well as extrinsic, value, and to respond to the relativism and immoralism of some Sophists, Plato offered a characterization of justice 'writ large': justice on the social scale, justice in the *polis*.

In so doing, Plato hopes to show how the best regime is a just society and that the justice of that society is grounded in a standard that is universal and rational, a standard accessible to all regardless of historical, personal, or social perspective.

THE JUST CITY

Plato's just city originates in his observations of human nature: that no one is self-sufficient; that each of us may be better at some tasks than at others; that we need others to help us to accomplish our ends and must live together in a polis.

Dividing the city into three classes, the guardians (rulers), and soldiers, and producers, Plato defined the role of justice:

● the guardians demonstrate their wisdom as they exercise good judgement on behalf of the city as a whole;
● the soldiers show their courage by which they protect the wise polis established by the rulers;
● moderation is especially important for the producers, but is required for all classes. It involves a willing acceptance by rulers and subjects alike that those who are rule do so as of right.

Justice is determined as each class performing its proper role (and recognizing how that role contributes to the common good).

THE JUST INDIVIDUAL

Although Plato looked chiefly to the next world for perfection, he laid down a blueprint for the ideal state in this which has little appeal for modern democrats.

With this account of justice in the city, Plato then turned to the individual, noted how the individual soul is composed of rational, spirited, and appetitive aspects, and then explained that a person is wise when the rational aspect rules, courageous when spirit acts on behalf of reason, and moderate when the rule of reason is accepted by each part of the soul.

A just person is one in whom each aspect of the soul is performing its proper role.

By providing this characterization, Plato believes that he has shown that justice is good itself. Moreover, as he proceeds to show in later books of the *Republic*, he believes that justice is not only intrinsically valuable but also serves as a condition for achieving goods extrinsic to justice; indeed, the unjust person would not only lead an intrinsically bad life, but a life in which he could not obtain extrinsic goods.

However, even as Plato offered a reply to the Sophists' relativism and nihilism, he developed an account of the human which shows that the human being is to be understood in terms of reason rather than appetite or desire: a good life for a person and a good *polis* are both guided by reason and knowledge.

In addressing the primary question of the Republic ('Why should I be moral?') Plato not only showed that justice has intrinsic value, but that there is a political form of justice which transcends the ebb and flux of historical institutions. Of course, one might reasonably ask whether Plato really thought that his model could ever be realized, even approximately.

FOR PLATO, SEE ALSO PAGES 23-25
FOR HIS ETHICS,
SEE PAGES 74 AND 75
FOR HIS RELIGIOUS THINKING,
PAGE 151.

Plato posed this sort of question at the end of Book IX:

'But perhaps, I said, there is a model of it in heaven, for anyone who wants to look at it and to make himself its citizen on the strength of what he sees. It makes no difference whether it is or ever will be somewhere, for he would take part in the practical affairs of that city and no other.'

Republic, 592b

Plato may be returning to the original motivation of the *Republic*, that of whether an individual should be moral, and he may be also be asserting that he is indifferent to the realization of political justice in the earthly city. Rather, the model of political justice is simply a model to which one is to conform one's individual behaviour.

Hence, the real political question is not the large-scale question of how to organize a city, but the (seemingly smaller) question of the individual soul: political justice requires that the individual make himself a just citizen, and this may only be possible of 'a model in heaven.'

The circle of wagons is a classic defensive arrangement, offering protection to those within the enclosed space. Should the state be viewed similarly, as a protective arrangement to defend its citizens against attack from those outside? What is the function of society? What are its obligations to those within its closed circle? Does it have obligations to those on the outside that circle, or should the autonomy of the sovereign state be paramount and inviolable?

A TOTALITARIAN STATE?

Plato was serious about his political proposals, and may have believed that they could indeed be instituted on earth (which would not be so unthinkable at this time, for sages were sometimes called on to frame laws and constitutions for Greek cities, as Solon had been in Athens two centuries earlier). But his image of the 'good' state would be totally unacceptable to almost all contemporary political thinkers.

Plato's ideal state is geared towards one particular ethical end – what he considers the highest good of human beings – and only those few with specialized knowledge or wisdom may take part in its governance. This vision resembles in a way the Marxist concept of the 'dictatorship of the proletariat', whereby a self-appointed elite rules the masses for their own good.

By contrast, most modern thinkers believe that the state should be neutral towards personal values and desires. In their view the state should not prefer one moral end over another.

They support this view by appealing to scepticism regarding our knowledge of the human good, the value of experimentation, appeals to autonomy, and peaceful coexistence among people with divergent conceptions of the good.

ARISTOTLE DISAGREES – AGAIN!

This modern view was not shared by Plato's student, **Aristotle (384–322BCE)**, little though he agreed with Plato either. Aristotle opens his *Politics* with these words:

'Observation shows us, first, that every polis (or state) is a species of association, and secondly, that all associations are instituted for the purpose of attaining some good.'

Politics, 1252a1

Politics and ethics are practical (rather than theoretical) inquiries, seeking how we can become good, whether individually or collectively.

He therefore considered ethics to be a part of political science, for both branches of philosophy consider what is 'good' for the human being. And such inquiry must, for Aristotle, unlike Plato, duly observe actual political institutions and public opinion.

In this way, Aristotle seems to adopt a common-sense empiricism Plato would have rejected. For example, arguing against Plato's theory of communal property (as elaborated in the Republic), Aristotle contends:

'There is another matter, which must not be ignored – the teaching of actual experience. We are bound to pay some regard to the long past and the passage of the years, in which these things [advocated by Plato as new discoveries] would not have gone unnoticed if they had been really good. Almost everything has been discovered already; though some of the things discovered have not been co-ordinated, and some, though known, are not put into practice.'

Politics, 1264a1-8

As noted above, Aristotle assumed that a state exists so that people can achieve their ends; moreover, the state – which he does not distinguish from society generally – should provide the optimal conditions for our human ends. However, these ends are natural ends, in the sense that they are determined by the biological (or natural) character of the human being.

In other words, the aim of the state is to create the best conditions for individuals to realize those characteristics,

which they possess naturally as human beings, but which might, under the wrong conditions, remain unrealized.

Aristotle, having described how the *polis* is composed of smaller associations (such as the household of husband, wife, and children, as well as the association of families into villages, what Burke later called 'the little battalions'), explains that the state exists by nature.

'Because it is the completion of associations existing by nature, every polis exists by nature, having itself the same quality as the earlier associations from which it grew. It is the end or consummation to which those associations move, and the "nature" of things consists in their end or consummation; for what each thing is when its growth is completed we call the nature of that thing, whether it be a man or a horse or a family.'

Politics, 1252b27-30

What is the highest good of the human being? Aristotle dealt with this question in his *Nicomachean Ethics* where he wrote that our highest good is happiness.

Happiness, or living well, is not to be reduced to mere pleasure, honour, or money-making but is to be understood in terms of what is characteristic or unique about humanity.

In the *Nicomachean Ethics*, Aristotle wants to establish what should be considered the highest good, by considering the proper function of humanity.

First he asks if its function is simply to go on living. But he concludes that humanity shares that even with plants, whilst he is looking for something that is peculiar to humans. Similarly, the process of feeding and growing is also excluded, since it is shared with the animals. The same thing applies to sense perception, for this, too, humankind has in common with the horse, the ox, and every animal.

He therefore concludes that it is the rational aspect that constitutes the distinctive function of man:

'There remains then the active life of reason. This rational element has two parts: one is rational in that it obeys the rule of reason, the other in that it possesses and conceives rational rules. Since the expression 'life of the rational element' also can be used in two senses, we must make it clear that we mean a life determined by the activity, as opposed to the mere possession, of the rational element. For the activity, it seems has a greater claim to be the function of man.'

A life of rational activity must be seem as rational activity performed exceedingly well and the excellent performance of this function requires, for Aristotle, that the performance be an effect of excellence or virtue (the Greek word *arete* translates as either). Aristotle concludes that:

'the good of humanity is an activity of the soul in conformity with excellence/virtue, and if there are several virtues, in conformity with the best and most complete.'
Nicomachean Ethics, **Book I, chapter 7**

Virtue, then, is defined in four aspects: it is a state or characteristic (a long-standing tendency or disposition) which involves choosing an action, or having an emotion, that expresses **a mean or middle way between two extremes**, a mean which is itself determined by reason.

'We may conclude that virtue/excellence is a characteristic involving choice, and that it consists in observing the mean relative to us, a mean which is defined by a rational principle, such as a person of practical wisdom would use to determine it. It is the mean by reference to two vices: the one of excess and the other of deficiency. It is, moreover, a mean because some vices exceed and others fall short of what is required in emotion and in action, whereas virtue finds and chooses the median'.
Nicomachean Ethics

FOR ARISTOTLE ON ETHICS, SEE ALSO PAGE 76.

THE GOOD LIFE

Among the virtues that constitute a life lived well are courage, self-control, generosity, and justice.

Justice can be understood in two ways: a just person could be a law-abiding person and, as such, the just person is one who obeys the laws of the city. However, and more broadly, justice can also be considered as the fair or equal division of good things. In *Nicomachean Ethics*, Aristotle says:

'The laws make pronouncements on every sphere of life, and their aim is to secure either the common good of all or of the best, or the good of those who hold power either because of their excellence or on some other basis of this sort. Accordingly, in one sense we call those things "just" which produce and preserve happiness for the social and political community.'

In other words, laws are there to enable virtue to be of benefit to the whole of society.

The laws of a city could be good or bad; and they should be judged in relation to the general sense of justice as a comprehensive virtue.

To sum up Aristotle's view:

The highest end, complete justice, can be reached only through just political association, for it is only there that one's nature can be realized. The state is the mechanism by which human individuals can realize their full humanity, in a life where every manner of activity reflects the rational elements characteristic of human beings.

Although Aristotle recognizes that there is a highest end of political association, he saw clearly the difficulties inherent in constructing any form of ideal *polis*. If a citizen is one who shares in the deliberative and judicial offices of the state, then the duties of citizenship will differ according to the type of rule.

Surprisingly, Aristotle believes that in most cases the good citizen and the good man will diverge. In the *Politics* he notes that if we are ever to discover which constitution is best for realizing the good life, then we should examine actual and ideal constitutions. Having done so, Aristotle then notes that there have been a variety of political constitutions. He categorizes these according to two variables: the number of persons who are ruling and the *de facto* aim of that rule:

Kingship	–	Tyranny
Aristocracy	–	Oligarchy
Constitutional Government	–	Democracy

The forms of political organization listed above are states that may be considered just, in that they not only aim at the common good, but tend to do so with an eye to natural justice.

This is most obvious in the case of kingship and aristocracy. Although kingship is a conceivable ideal it is generally irrelevant to the typical conditions of political life in Greece of his time.

Although Aristotle sometimes speaks as if the natural good could best be realized by an aristocracy, he also defends, on both pragmatic grounds and on grounds of wisdom, any constitutional government as good.

'People came to the city to live, they stayed to live the good life.'

'Our account of this science [politics] will be adequate if it achieves such clarity as the subject matter allows; for the same degree of precision is not to be expected in all discussions, any more than in all the products of handicraft. Instances of morally fine and just conduct — which is what politics investigates — involve so much difference and variety that they are widely believed to be such only by convention and not by nature.'

Aristotle, *Nicomachean Ethics*, Book I, chapter 1
from the translation by J A K Thomson

For Aristotle, the basis of a just society should be one that allows individuals to achieve their own happiness and highest good.
But what image do we have of happiness? Is it something that can be described in rational terms?

Chinese philosophy has often surprisingly similar concerns about law and justice to the Greeks, if phrased rather differently. But the ideas of their greatest social philosopher, Confucius, became part of the imperial ethos, in a way not even Stoicism could match in the West.

Although not as systematic as Aristotle or Plato, the philosophers of ancient China articulated many similar ideas over the millennia. The most important of these thinkers was **K'ung Fu Tzu, or Confucius (551–479BCE)**, whose *Analects* provide the backbone of Confucian doctrine.

Like Socrates, Confucius was interested in morality and a human-centred approach, but from the Chinese viewpoint. Like Aristotle, Confucius focused on the idea of virtue, especially insofar as virtue expresses itself as a mean between two extremes.

However, Confucius also emphasizes traditional social rules (later referred to as li). Against the movement of the legalists, who rejected any link between morality and state power (even as they emphasized the public and universal application of law), Confucious incorporates virtue into the practice of law. The legalists' views are analogous to the view of some of the Greek sophists, who held that justice is nothing but the interest of the stronger.

In seeking to unify law and morality, Confucius noted that one of the first tasks of a proper government is that of the *'rectification of names'* whereby rank, duty, and action appropriately correspond. Hence, thought and the right use of language provide a basis for all else in the state.

'Lead the people with governmental measures and regulate them by law and punishment, and they will avoid wrongdoing but will have no sense of honor and shame. Lead them with virtue and regulate them by the rules of propriety (li), and they will have a sense of shame and, moreover, set themselves right.'   **Analects, 2.3**

'The superior man regards righteousness as the substance of everything. He practices it according to the principles of propriety. He brings it forth in modesty. And he carries it to its conclusion with faithfulness. He is indeed a superior man!'   Analects, 15; 17

Confucious also indicated that a government has proper duties and limits beyond which it should not stray. One of his disciples, **Meng Tzu, or Mencius (c.371–c.289BCE)**, explicitly believed in the goodness of human nature and pronounced a claim about revolution. An unrighteous ruler loses the 'mandate of heaven' (the right to rule).

'The King said, "Is it all right for a minister to murder his king?" Mencius said, "He who injures humanity is a bandit. He who injures righteousness is a destructive person. Such a person is a mere thus. I have heard of killing a mere thus... but I have not heard of murdering the ruler."'   **The Book of Mencius, 1B:8**

Such a doctrine will find not dissimilar expression in some Western philosophers, including the medieval philosopher, St Thomas Aquinas, as well as the seventeenth-century English thinker, John Locke.

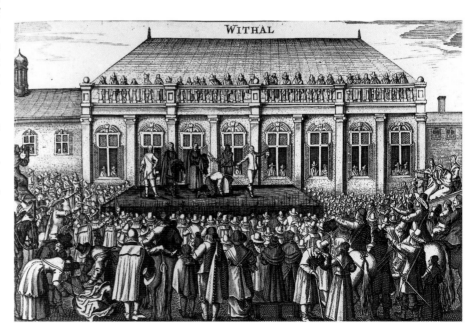

There are times when political structure change, literally, at a stroke – as here with the execution of Charles I. In China, Mencius believed that a bad ruler loses the 'mandate of heaven' and can be removed from office.

'Governing a large state is like boiling a small fish (i.e. very difficult).'

Chuang Tzu

Against the Confucian emphasis on virtue and continuity with tradition, the theory of **Mo Tzu (c.470–c.391 BCE)** argued that virtue or virtuous action is good only because of its consequences. Whereas the Confucians believed that morality is born of particular attachments and duties, the doctrines of Mo Tzu (found in the book that is names after him) emphasized universal love or benevolence:

'What the man of humanity devotes himself to, surely lies in the promotion of benefits for the world and the removal of harm from the world.

from the *Mo Tzu*

He offered the following prescription for universal love:

'What is the way of universal love and mutual benefit? Mo Tzu said: It is to regard other people's countries as one's own. Regard other people's families as one's own. Regard other people's person as one's own.

The semi-mythical Taoist philosopher **Lao Tzu (sixth century BCE)** offered profound insights into society and government. These challenged the Confucian views that the ruler should encourage conformity to tradition above everything.

FOR CONFUCIUS AND LANGUAGE, SEE ALSO PAGE 228.

Known by Confucius, Lao Tzu's *Tao te Ching* is a classic work whose small size is inversely proportional to its immense power. Lao Tzu offered the way of the One, the ideal for a natural and spontaneous life, whether of the individual or the government.

'Heaven obtained the One and became clear. Earth obtained the One and became tranquil. The spiritual beings obtained the One and became divine. The valley obtained the One and became full. The myriad things obtained the One and lived and grew. Kings and barons obtained the One and became rulers of the empire. What made them so is the One.' Tao te Ching, 39

The paradox of the Tao is that weakness provides strength, that in following nature one is akin to water:

'The highest good is to be like water. Water is good; it benefits all things and does not compete with them. It dwells in (low) places that all usually disdain. This is why it is so near to Tao.'

In the realm of government, Lao Tzu advocated an idealized anarchy in which the less that is done by the state the greater the opportunity for natural social processes to emerge and reach excellence:

The best (rulers) are those whose existence is (merely) known by the people.

The next best are those who are loved and praised.

The next are those who are feared. And the next are those who are despised.

Tao te Ching, 17

However, he takes the view that excessive political and legal regulations only breed more trouble:

The more taboos and prohibitions there are in the world,
The poorer the people will be.
The more sharp weapons the people have,
The more troubled the state will be.
The more cunning and skill man possesses,
The more vicious things will appear.
The more laws and orders are made prominent,
The more thieves and robbers there will be.

He therefore promotes the idea that the ruler should take only minimal and natural action, allowing the people to become tranquil and their lives simpler:

'I take no action and the people of themselves are transformed. I love tranquillity and the people of themselves become correct. I engage in no activity and the people of themselves become prosperous. I have no desires and the people of themselves become simple. Tao te Ching, 57

More than two and a half thousand years later, Lao Tzu's views may still be heard in debates on the free-market economy, the dangers of too much legislation, or what may be seen as excessive government interference in people's lives.

The Hellenistic era lasted from the death of Alexander the Great (323BCE) to the establishment of the Roman Empire in 31BCE, but the Roman period merely continued the Hellenistic intellectual trends, just as in many ways it continued it politically. The self-governing polis or city-state was now overshadowed by huge intercontinental empires, which dwarfed individuals. This wide new world required new ethical and political theories: Epicureanism, Scepticism and Stoicism.

THE GARDEN PHILOSOPHER

Epicurus (341-270BCE), unlike Plato and Aristotle, rejected any teleological view of the universe (in other words, that it had an implicit purpose), arguing instead that the cosmos is constructed solely from atoms colliding in the void.

Epicurus contends that good and evil are simply matters of sensation, and that the end or goal of life is pleasure and peace of mind. This doctrine, sometimes called *hedonism*, does not mean mindlessly pursuing any and every pleasure, however.

'When we say that pleasure is the goal we do not mean the pleasures of the profligate or the pleasures of over-consumption, as some believe, either from ignorance and disagreement or from deliberate misinterpretation, but rather the lack of pain in the body and agitation in the soul.'
Letter to Menoeceus

Unlike Plato, the Epicureans consider justice to be an instrument. The result of our desires not to suffer at the hands of others:

'There is no such thing as justice in the abstract; it is merely a compact between men in their various relations with each other, in whatever circumstances they may be, that they will neither injure nor be injured.'
Principle Doctrines, XXXIII

As the Epicureans aimed, above all, to avoid pain and secure peace of mind, they advocated a life of prudence, virtue, and the shunning of fame, and especially political renown.

Revealingly, Epicurus' school was in a secluded garden. They were noted, often unfavourably, for accepting women on equal terms. The chief Roman Epicurean was the poet **Lucretius (95-52BCE)**, whose long poem *De Rerum Natura* (About the nature of things) is the most lyrical expression of philosophy in Western tradition.

'The purest security is that which comes from a quite life and withdrawal from the crowd, although a certain degree of security from other men does come by... the power to repel and by prosperity.'
Epicurus Principal Doctrines

A RATIONAL UNIVERSE

The political and ethical doctrines of the Stoics were totally different, and proved far more influential than those of the Epicureans, for they encouraged active participation in political life. **Zeno of Citium (334-262BCE)** first propounded Stoic doctrines in Athens, and his ideas were followed up by **Chrysippus (c.280-207BCE)**. Romans such **Seneca (5 BCE-65AD)**, a wealthy senator, **Epictetus (50-130BCE)**, a one-time slave, and even an Emperor, **Marcus Aurelius (121-180CE)** were among its noted adherents. In political and legal matters the most notable Roman Stoic was **Cicero**.

The heart of Stoicism lies in its conception of the universe. Stoics consider the cosmos a rational whole, in which God pervades matter so completely that the workings of the universe reflect a divinely rational order. The orderly workings of the universe reflect rational laws, and whatever happens is the effect of a rational unfolding of cause and effect throughout the universe.

The Stoics suggested seeking to understand this rational order, and to conform our desires, attitudes, emotions, and actions to it. The supremely rational unfolding of the universe is beyond our control; what is up to our control is our attitude towards it.

In their emphasis on the reason common to all humans, the Stoics developed a cosmopolitan idea of humanity, ignoring differences of class, race and religion. In his *Discourses*, Epictetus urges us to recognize our commonality. In his *Meditations*, Marcus Aurelius asserts:

'I am by nature a reasonable and social creature; my city and fatherland...is Rome, (but), as a human being it is the universe.'

This cosmopolitan outlook (literally so, since the term 'cosmopolitan' comes from this Stoic claim that one's *polis* is the *cosmos*) derived from a belief in universal laws that transcend the particular and the circumstantial.

THE STOIC AS LAWGIVER

The Roman Stoic **Marcus Tullius Cicero (106-43BCE)**, politician, writer and lawyer, made a particular contribution by synthesizing earlier Greek thought into a conception of a transcendent and natural law.

Although Cicero sometimes sounded a sceptical note, his overtly political works, *De republica* and *De legibus*, written (following the style set by Plato) as dialogues, offer a portrait of the ideal regime and a stoical account of law as natural law.

Concerned about the Epicurean disparagement of all political participation, Cicero maintained in *The Republic* that political activity is a duty, while admitting that its rewards may not compare with the life of philosophical contemplation.

Following Aristotle, Cicero categorized possible states as kingships, aristocracies, or democracies, each of which has its corollary perversion. Kingship is indisputably the best, for it combines wisdom with political power.

However, a regime which incorporates elements of kingship, aristocracy, and democracy might be best in most circumstances, because it allowed not only for the application of wisdom in ruling but also for democratic liberty. Such a mixed regime would embody the rule of law, the essential elements of which are expressed in the *Laws*, the sequel to the *Republic*, which reveals Cicero's Stoic inclinations.

For Cicero, there is a distinction between a *mere* law and a *true* law: true law is an expression of reason and itself natural to humanity, a natural expression of a rationally ordered universe. In this sense Cicero, like Plato, seeks to defeat any relativist notion of law and justice.

Law is the highest reason, implanted in Nature, which commands what ought to be done and forbids the opposite. This reason, when firmly fixed and fully developed in the human mind, is Law. And so they believe that Law is intelligence, whose natural function it is to command right conduct and forbid wrongdoing. Now if this is correct, as I think it to be in general, then the origin of Justice is to be found in Law, for Law is a natural force; it is the mind and reason of the intelligent man, the standard by which Justice and Injustice are measured.

The Laws, I, vi

True Law, then, is a natural expression of reason, and sets an unchanging standard for Justice. The human and the divine share a common reason, a reason that is part of the ordered cosmos. In this sense, all humans share a recognition of natural law. This does not mean,

however, that every particular human law can or will reflect adequately what is truly rational. However, any human law that is a true law will bear some resemblance to the universal and natural law:

From this point of view it can be readily understood that those who formulated wicked and unjust statutes for nations, thereby breaking their promises and agreements, put into effect anything but 'laws.' It may thus be clear that, in the very definition of the term 'law' there inheres the idea and principle of choosing what is just and true.'

The Laws, II, v

In adumbrating his account of law, Cicero synthesized the classical tradition of Plato, Aristotle, and later Hellenistic philosophers, developing an account that connects law with reason and nature. In so doing, he offers an account of natural law that would reappear in the medieval philosophy of St Thomas Aquinas and in the work of the seventeenth-century philosopher, John Locke.

For Stoics, the justice implied in the idea of true law was absolute and natural, reflecting the rational structure of the universe. This implies that, to live well, one will also live in a way that reflects the entire life and form of the cosmos. This places ethics and politics within a context of cosmology and fundamental beliefs and values. 'Mere' laws may come and go, as is expedient, but 'true' law is fundamental and touches the deepest levels of humankind, namely its origins and place within the whole of reality.

'In the very definition of the word "law" there inheres the idea and principle of choosing what is just and true.'

Cicero, *De Legibus*

FOR EPICUREAN AND STOIC ETHICS, SEE ALSO PAGE 77

Augustine wrote *The City of God* after the sack of Rome, the 'eternal city'. In it, he sought to refute pagan views, and outline the nature of a society based on the divine order.

Among the main provinces of the declining Roman Empire was North Africa, where **Augustine (354-430)** grew up. Unlike the classical authors of Greece or Rome, Augustine was not deeply interested in concepts of the best regime for the state, or in asserting that the very ends of life required participation in the life of the city (*polis*). Indeed, Augustine's work, which provides the basis for much later medieval Christian philosophy and theology alike, was relatively unconcerned with politics:

'Concerning this life of mortals, which is lived and ended in a few days, what difference does it make whose governance a man who is about to die lives under, so long as those who rule do not compel him to impiety and sin?'

The City of God, V.17

Written just after the traumatic sack of Rome by the Goths in 410CE, *The City of God* is not a systematic political treatise but focuses on questions about how the Christian can reconcile the duties of faith with those of citizenship.

Augustine offers an account of all human history, back to the creation of the world (which he placed firmly about 6000 years before), the city of Rome's very long moral decline, and the failures of pagan religion. For Augustine, Rome was sinful from its very foundation.

He then considered respectively the heavenly and earthly cities. While the fall of Rome came to be accounted for by its ever-greater moral degeneration (rather than by its recent conversion to Christianity, as pagans often claimed), it was also the moral restraint of natural human impulses that provided the conditions for Rome's success.

By explaining the contingencies of failure and success, Augustine points out that the permanent things are in a heavenly rather than an earthly realm. In this he repeats Plato, whom he much admired.

Augustine saw the political order not as an agreement concerning justice but as an association united in reference to some set of desires or loves, whether or not these be inhumane, perverse, or counter to Christianity:

If, for example it is said that a people is 'a fellowship of a multitude of rational beings united through sharing in an agreement about what it loves', then truly, in order to see the character of a people, what it loves must be considered.

If it is not a fellowship of a multitude of beasts, but of rational creatures, and is united through sharing in an agreement about what it loves, then, no matter what it loves, it is not unreasonable to call it 'a people.' It is a better people if it agrees in loving better things; a worse one if it agrees in loving worse things. According to this definition, the Roman people did indeed form 'a people', and its affair is without doubt a republic. However, history gives witness to what that people loved originally and subsequently, and by what morals it

arrived at the bloodiest revolutions and then at social and civil wars, utterly shattering and annihilating concord itself, which is, in a certain sense, the well-being of a people.

The City of God, XIX, 24

Augustine attacked those in power (and it was a chaotic time) whose state-licensed action so often differed little if all from those of mere brigands:

Without justice, what are kingdoms but great robber bands? What are robber bands but small kingdoms? The band is itself made up of men, is ruled by the command of a leader, and is held together by a social pact. Plunder is divided in accordance with an agreed-upon law. If this evil increases by the inclusion of dissolute men to the extent that it takes over territory, establishes headquarters, occupies cities, and subdues peoples it publicly assumes the title of kingdom! This title is manifestly conferred on it, not because greed has been removed, but because impunity has been added. A fitting and true response was once given to Alexander the Great by an apprehended pirate. When asked by the king what he thought he was doing by infesting the sea, he replied with noble insolence, 'What do you think you are doing by infesting the whole world? Because I do it with one puny boat, I am called a pirate; because you do it with a great fleet, you are called an emperor.'

The City of God, IV, 4

'Without justice, what are kingdoms but great robber bands?'

For Augustine, politics serves as a means to limit the selfish impulses of a fallen creature. The earthly city has its loves and those who reside within it live 'according to the flesh,' as opposed to the heavenly city which lives 'according to the spirit' (XIV.4).

At the heart of Augustine's account of politics is the division between the two fundamental loves or yearnings, which characterize a society: a love of God and a love of self:

The two contrasting cities, were therefore created by two different loves:
the earthly city by love of oneself (even to the point at which it leads to contempt for God);
the heavenly city by the love of God (even to the point at which it leads to contempt for oneself).
The first glories in itself, the second in the Lord. The first seeks glory from human beings; God, who is the witness of the conscience, is the greatest glory of the other... The first, its princes and the nations that it subjugates, is dominated by the lust to dominate; in the second, all mutually serve one another in charity, the leaders through their counsel and the subjects through their obedience.'

The City of God, XI, 28

The two loves, and the two cities, are distinguishable in theory, but in actuality they are mixed and this entails that individuals may have ambiguous commitments, and that some individuals and some societies will be in greater need of transforming their loves and desires.

Nonetheless, there is an ideal Christian ruler whose success and happiness derives not from the duration of rule, empire, or legacy. Rather, the Christian emperors:

'are happy if they rule justly and if, instead of being exalted by the praises of those who pay them the highest honors and by the groveling of those who salute them with excessive humility, they remember instead that
they are human beings.'   V.24

Thus true justice will involve a recognition of Christianity:

What sort of justice is it, then, that takes a man away from the true God and subjects him to unclean demons? Is this to distribute to each his due? Or, is he who takes the ground purchased by someone and gives it to another who has not right to it unjust, but he who takes himself away from the dominion of the God who made him and enslaves himself to malicious spirits just?   XIX.21

Just as Augustine represents a Platonist outlook, other medieval philosophers sought to reconcile the thought of classical thinkers with their own religious perspectives. **al-Farabi, 870–950**, sought to unite Islam with the idea of a 'virtuous regime' in which individuals could best achieve human excellence.

The most famous medieval Jewish philosopher, **Maimonides (Moses ben Maimon, 1135–1204)**, was born in Cordoba, the capital of Moorish Spain. Influenced by al-Farabi. He tried to reconcile the revealed Law of Moses with the thought of Aristotle in his *Guide for the Perplexed*.

Might these gentlemen depict Augustine's view of kingdoms that lack justice?

St Thomas Aquinas (1225-1274), who came from an aristocratic family in Naples, achieved a remarkable synthesis of Aristotelian and Christian principles, which had previously seemed to be impossible.

Like Aristotle, but unlike Augustine, Aquinas holds that the state is natural in that it provides the conditions under which the human can achieve a distinctively human potential.

That potential, understood as something more than human happiness, involves the comprehension of God.

Wishing to maintain the authority of the Catholic Church, Aquinas contends that the law of the state should be in conformity with a higher or natural law which is itself a reflection of a divine law.

Thus insofar as he defends monarchy he also stipulates that the people have a right to depose any monarch who violates natural law.

For Aquinas moral knowledge is not only possible, but infallible. This is knowledge of natural law, a law or measure that is available to each individual's reason.

Notice that it is the natural law that serves as the standard by which true and just human laws are to be made and justified. In this way, politics and law are to be linked to the fundamental (and for Aquinas, God-given) principles of design and purpose within the universe.

The norms that are so knowable, are norms that are appropriate to our nature and provide the constraints and permissions by which we can function well as human beings.

These general principles are first known through a process called **synderesis**, a natural disposition of reason by which we are able to grasp or apprehend the most basic and general principles of natural law.

Although Aquinas held that our grasp of such first general principles may be infallible, the application of these general principles to particular circumstances will inevitably involve us in fallible, human reasoning.

'Accordingly, we conclude that just as, in the speculative reason, from naturally known indemonstrable principles we draw the conclusions of the various sciences, the knowledge of which is not imparted to us by nature but acquired by the efforts of reason, so too it is from the precepts of the natural law, as from general and indemonstrable principles, that the human reason needs to proceed to certain particular determinations of the laws. These particular determinations, devised by human reason, are called human laws...'

Summa Theologiae, **Question 91, Third article**

The first concept of the natural law is that 'good is to be done and pursued, and evil is to be avoided.' (Question 94, Second article).

The precepts of the natural law provide a general framework for reasoning about those things which are necessary for human flourishing, including the preservation of human life and the avoidance of harm, love, family, knowledge, and friendship. From these general and self-evident

FOR AQUINAS:

ON RELIGION, SEE PAGE **161F**

ON ETHICS, SEE PAGE **79.**

precepts the more particular laws of societies are to be derived:

'Now, in human affairs a thing is said to be just from being right according to the rule of reason. But the first rule of reason is the law of nature, as is clear from what has been stated above. Consequently, every human law has just so much of the nature of law as it is derived from the law of nature. But if, in any point, it deflects from the law of nature, it is no longer a law but a perversion of law.'

Summa Theologiae, **Question 95, Second article**

What are the characteristics of law? Aquinas summarizes the essence of law by emphasizing four conditions:

Law is a 'certain ordinance of reason for the common good, made by him who has care of the community, and promulgated.' *Summa Theologiae*, Question 90, Fourth article.

Law is rationally commanded, and it directs human beings to the ends that are proper. Now, the final end of the human being is happiness. Therefore, the law should direct the individuals, as members of a community, so that each individual may appropriately relate to the community in which his end can be realized.

Law, as the command of reason, should be issued, either by the people themselves, or by a sovereign who has authority to act on behalf of the people.

Finally, for the law to be binding, it has to be known. Therefore the law must be promulgated. However, in the case of natural law, Aquinas considered that God had instilled the knowledge of such law directly in men's hearts. (Question 90, Fourth article).

The human law is derived from the natural in either of two ways:

1 a human law is demonstrated when it is logically derived from a general precept (for example, the precept that one should not harm others, entails that one should not kill);

2 a human law is determined when a general precept is applied to some particular circumstances.

A demonstrated law is derived directly from the natural law and is therefore a true law; a determined law is a true law insofar as it is compatible with the general precepts of the natural law.

Aquinas' own application of his doctrine led him to hold that one is bound to obey the human law and human sovereigns, except when the sovereign has usurped power, or has commanded that which violates the natural law (and is, therefore, unjust).

In addition, Aquinas applies his views to war and killing, articulating the central tenets of the just war theory.

In order for a war to be just, three things are necessary:

● Firstly, the authority of the ruler, by whose command the war is to be waged.

● Secondly, a just cause is required, namely that those who are attacked, should be attacked because they deserve it on account of some fault.

● Thirdly, it is necessary that the belligerents should have a rightful intention, so that they intend the advancement of good or the avoidance of evil.

These are given in *Summa Theologiae*, Question 40, First article.

Aquinas adds that even though an act proceeds from a good intention, the act may become unjust if it brings about consequences which outweigh the good intention.

In developing his account of natural law as the basis for positive human law, Aquinas articulates, in the most systematic way, a doctrine whose power still resonates today. It would not be until the modern era of the 17th century that the doctrine of Aquinas would receive its most forceful challenge in the work of Thomas Hobbes.

Hiroshima after the Bomb.
Aquinas set down principles to establish whether or not a war could be considered just. This is known as the 'just war' theory, and has been extended to cover a consideration of the methods used in warfare. In other words, justice applies both to the way a war is fought, and to the reason why a war should be fought. The latter should not automatically be taken to justify the former.

For the Greeks such as Plato and Aristotle, the aim of government was not to protect individuals' spheres of liberty, but to provide the political framework and social conditions for citizens to become good.

In their view, the role of the state is not to prevent conflicts among and between individuals, whose goals in life may vary and whose conceptions of the good life may differ, but to point individuals towards a defined 'good'.

If, for the Greeks, political philosophy aimed at the state making us good individuals and good citizens, then political theorizing must begin with some account of what is 'good'.

What is good, in relation to humans, is determined by the very nature of the human being. Human nature is determined not by inquiring into what most humans *actually* do, but by inquiring into *the best that humans could possibly be.*

The state could, therefore, be described as natural, in the sense that the good state expresses the best in human nature. Within this good state, 'freedom' is best understood as the ability to do the right thing, to be the best sort of human being, whether that is understood in terms of the just person (Plato) or in terms of the citizen who rules and can be ruled in turn (Aristotle).

Influenced by both Plato and Aristotle, the medieval and (in England) Tudor conception of the person and society was one in which both individuals and social orders were oriented towards a defined end.

Society was thought to reflect a transcendent order, in which each human beings had a designated place, somewhere between the angels and the animals, and in which the elements of the universe formed a harmonic order.

'Take but degree away, untune that string, and hark what discord follows.'

said **Shakespeare** in *Troilus and Cressida*, voicing a common sentiment.

Society was properly hierarchical and stable, because such an order reflected and expressed God's purpose. The order of society was understood to be natural and inalterable. Change, whether at the individual or social level, was discouraged. Indeed, since each person had a place in society that reflected a permanent order, established by God, change was unnatural.

Sir Thomas Moore (1478-1535), lawyer, statesman, writer and (to Catholics) a martyr, was deeply influenced by Renaissance thought. His *Utopia* of 1516, the first book about an ideal society, reveals his debt to Plato as well as some almost modern sympathies (for example, cruelty to animals is abhorred by Utopians).

But his overall social and religious outlook was still deeply medieval, as his other writings and his actions reveal. And he died for a concept – that of the universal Catholic church – already old-fashioned in an England breaking away from Rome.

But the Renaissance rediscovery of Greek texts and Greco-Roman art, fostered new attitudes. In Italy, where thriving city-states had long ago rejected the Holy Roman Empire's authority, political circumstances in many ways recalled those of the Greek *polis*, where conditions fostered independence of mind and spirit.

MACHIAVELLI – THE FIRST MODERN THINKER

Often considered one of the first to articulate a modern sensibility, **Niccolo Machiavelli (1469-1527)** came from a legal Florentine family. He served as an advisor to the Republican government of Florence, but lost his post in 1512 after the overthrow of the government. After his dismissal, he wrote his classic work *The Prince* (1513), which he dedicated to the new Medici rulers in the (vain) hope of winning their favour, and *The Discourses on Livy* (1517). The Discourses perhaps represent his real view, but the cold-blooded advice in *The Prince* made him notorious.

Drawing on his wide knowledge of ancient history and current Italian politics – he knew Cesare Bogia, the most ruthless tyrant of the age – while ignoring the Middle Ages almost completely, Machiavelli expounded in *The Prince* the lessons that he thought vital for ruling and retaining power. He did so especially in the context of the ruler of a new regime, who is subject to competition from other rulers, and potentially threatened by ambitious advisors and subjects.

'The prince must read histories and in them study the deeds of great men; he must see how they conducted themselves in wars; he must examine the reasons for their victories and for their defeats in order to avoid the latter and to imitate the former.'

The Prince, XIV

Machiavelli takes what many considered a realistic account of statecraft, in which individuals are self-interested, ambitious, and acquisitive:

'The desire to acquire is truly a very natural and normal thing; and when men who can do so, they will always be praised and not condemned.'

The Prince, III

In describing how rulers should govern, Machiavelli severed the ancient and medieval links between power and morality by offering realistic advice, unconstrained by ethical qualms, about how rulers could retain power.

'... since my intention is to write something useful for anyone who understands it, it seemed more suitable to me to search after the effectual truth of the matter rather than its imagined one. And many writers have imagined for themselves republics and principalities that have never been seen nor known to exist in reality; for there is such a gap between how one lives and how one ought to live that anyone who abandons what is done for what ought to be done learns his ruin rather than his preservation: for a man who wishes to make a vocation of being good at all times will come to ruin among so many who are not good. Hence it is necessary for a prince who wishes to maintain his position to learn how not to be good, and to use this knowledge or not to use it according to necessity.'

The Prince, XV

By providing realistic advice, Machiavelli hoped to give rulers the knowledge to prevail against *fortuna*, the uncontrolled and unforeseen contingencies of life that create instability and uncertainty. The greater one's exposure to *fortuna* the more important is one's *virtu*, combining skill, ingenuity, and strength that allows one to confront and overcome the unpredictability of change.

Although *virtu* is not virtue, it may require the application of morality just as it may require the use of vice and amoral methods.

THE BORGIA EXAMPLE

Machiavelli recounted a story about Cesare Borgia, who took over the Romagna, in central Italy, and found that the population was 'full of thefts, fights, and of every other kind of insolence...'

To deal with this situation, Cesare Borgia appointed Remirro de Orco, who was known to be both cruel and able, to take command, and gave him complete authority. After a period of very harsh rule, the province was pacified. Once that was achieved, in order that he himself should appear reasonable, Borgia set up a civil court, with a distinguished president, and appointed a counsellor from each city. Having thus shown that the former cruelty was the responsibility of Remirro de Orco, rather than himself, he arranged for him to be killed and displayed his body in the piazza at Cesena, cut in two and separated by a block of wood.

Machiavelli records that:

'The ferocity of such a spectacle left those people satisfied and amazed at the same time.'

In his *Discourses on Livy*, Machiavelli turned from a consideration of how to maintain power, to a consideration of how to ensure that citizens act for the public rather than the private good. Here he showed how much he admired the Ancient Roman republic, but still revealed a generally negative view of human nature.

'As is demonstrated by all who discuss civic life (and as history is full of such examples), it is necessary for anyone who organizes a republic and institutes laws to take for granted that all men are evil and that they will always express the wickedness of their spirit whenever they have the opportunity...'

Discourses on Livy

Machiavelli then described how the Republican institutions of Ancient Rome, institutions which were the unintended outcomes of conflicts between patricians and plebeians, provided a mixed government. By allowing for various different factions to rule, this proved favorable to liberty, for it allowed for personal ambition, the expression of opinion, and for participation in governing.

By creating institutions and social conditions in which no single faction would govern for prolonged periods - which might have led to them governing only in self-interest — the government of ancient Rome provided a basis, and a model, by which individuals could govern and be governed in turn, thereby becoming more rather than less public-spirited.

Even more than Machiavelli, **Thomas Hobbes (1588-1679)** is the prototype of a modern political philosopher. Although he had had a classical education in Latin and Greek, and wrote his first books in Latin, Hobbes self-consciously later broke away from traditional forms of politics and of political philosophy.

In so doing, he not only develops such important concepts as the state of nature and the social contract, but he develops important conceptions of liberalism and law.

Hobbes rightly saw himself as diverging from the ancients. He considers freedom as the absence of any external impediment to the realization of one's desires, a liberty that can be guaranteed only through the institution of a sovereign state. He did not speak of freedom in terms of the ability to become virtuous.

For Hobbes, one should not begin political theorizing by postulating a final end or goodness. Rather, Hobbes believed that one must begin with an account of human nature, but an account that is true and scientific, unlike (as he believed) that of the ancient Greeks.

THE MAN-MADE SOCIETY

For Hobbes, society is no longer a reflection of some divinely transcendent plan, nor is the order within society to be understood as natural; rather, social and political orders are artificial in the sense that they are the artifices of human beings.

Thus, in the introduction to his treatise, The Leviathan (1651), Hobbes draws the distinction between nature and artifice and asserts that the Leviathan, the sovereign state, is a result of human artifice. It is this artifice that brings about order within society; indeed, it is this artifice that effectively creates a stable society!

'Nature, the art whereby God hath made and governs the world, is by the art of man, as in many other things, so in this also imitated, that it can make an artificial animal. For seeing life is but a motion of limbs, the beginning whereof is in some principal part within; why may we not say, that all automata (engines that move themselves by springs and wheels as doth a watch) have an artificial life? For what is the heart but a spring; and the nerves, but so many strings; and the joints, but so many wheels, giving motion to the whole body, such as was intended by the artificer? Art goes yet further, imitating that rational and most excellent work of nature, man. For by art is created that great LEVIATHAN called a COMMONWEALTH, or STATE, in Latin CIVITAS, which is but an artificial man; though of greater stature and strength than the natural, for whose protection and defence it was intended; and in which the sovereignty is an artificial soul, as giving life and motaion to the whole body...'

Leviathan, **from the Introduction**

That life is but a 'motion of limbs' and that the state gives motion to all those who live within it, reveals how developments in recent science influenced Hobbes. **Galileo (1564-1642)** had broken with Aristotelian tradition by proposing a universe in which motion is natural, (whereas, for Aristotle, the natural state is one of rest). Under the influence of Galileo, whom he had visited when in Italy, Hobbes thought of human beings as matter in motion.

However, Galileo had another significant influence on Hobbes, regarding scientific methodology. Galileo's procedure for understanding some natural phenomenon was that of resolution and composition: an understanding of some whole can be achieved only if one breaks (or resolves) that whole into its relevant components, understands these components in terms of their relevant qualities, and then rebuilds (composes) the whole from its components.

Hobbes links the method of resolution and composition to the demonstrative method of geometry, whereby one defines certain terms and then proceeds to deduce, from these definitions, new theorems. Hobbes tries to reason from the properties of the state to the generation of the state. In other words, he broke the state down into its properties (or components), defined these, and then reconstructed (or generated) the state from these very properties.

For Hobbes, the relevant components of the state are individuals, who can be further understood, or resolved, into relevant properties. Hobbes characterizes individuals as creatures of internal motions. These generate appetites and aversions (passions), which determine what the individuals love or hate, and therefore what they call good or evil. Hobbes argued that nothing is in itself good or evil, but is only judged so by common agreement (see also page 88).

As creatures of passions, we seek a happiness, which is, for Hobbes, nothing but the continual satisfaction of desires. Power is nothing more than the means to attain those things that we desire. As Hobbes puts it:

For there is no such finis ultimus, utmost aim, nor summum bonum, greatest good, as is spoken of in the books of the old moral philosophers... Felicity is a continual progress of the desire, from one object to another; the attaining of the former, being still but the way to the latter... So that in the first place, I put for a general inclination of all mankind, a perpetual and restless desire of power after power, that ceaseth only in death.

Leviathan, **chapter 11**

In a 'state of nature', in which there is no single power, and no sovereign state, there will be no agreement as to a standard of good or evil. As Hobbes assumes that individuals are more or less equal in their capacities to satisfy their desires, then the state of nature devolves into a state of conflict or war.

Of this state of nature, Hobbes offers a telling description:

'Whatsoever therefore is consequent to a time of war, where every man is enemy to every man; the same is consequent to the time, wherein men live without other security, than what their own strength, and their own invention shall furnish them withal. In such condition, there is no place for industry; because the fruit thereof is uncertain: and consequently no culture of the earth; no navigation, nor use of the commodities that may be imported by sea; no commodious building; no instruments of moving and removing, such things as require much force; no knowledge of the face of the earth; no account of time; no arts; no letters; no society; and which is worst of all, continual fear, and danger of violent death; and the life of man, solitary, poor, nasty, brutish, and short.'

Leviathan, chapter 13

In such a situation, we come to fear death, the ultimate loss of the power to satisfy our desires. The fear of death – or, conversely, the desire to live – inclines us to desire a state of order. By using our reason, we discern rules, which Hobbes refers to as 'laws of nature', which would, if generally implemented, secure order and peace.

These rules are not only the basis for peaceful living but also provide some of the inherent formal characteristics of any law, such as *impartiality*, *equal treatment*, and *non-particularity*. Unlike the medieval conception of natural law, however, Hobbes does not identify his natural laws with some transcendent norm; rather, Hobbes is contending only that these natural laws would be sufficient for peace.

Happiness is… '…a continual progress of desire, from one object to another.'

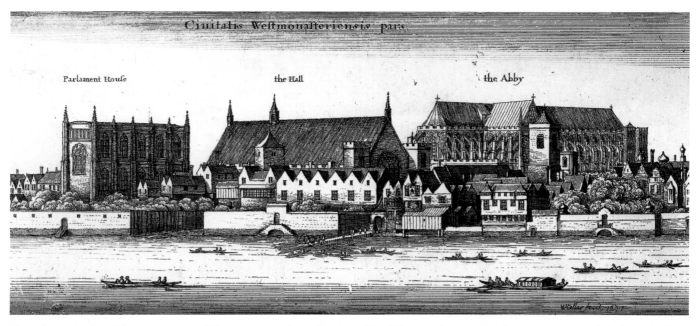

Westminster in the 17th century; one of the major cogs in Hobbes' machine. The state is an artificial construct, not a divinely established order.

NATURAL CHAOS V. SOCIAL CONTRACT

In the state of nature, however, individuals cannot be sure that, if they follow the rules, others will too. However, if they obey rules when others do not, then they are at a severe disadvantage. Since everyone in the state of nature is faced with the same uncertainty ('How can I be assured that others will follow the laws of nature?'), no one adheres to the rules, and the result is general chaos and conflict. The problem, therefore, is how to ensure that everyone will adhere to the laws of nature, the very rules that will ensure peace.

Hobbes' answer is that the individuals within the state of nature will contract amongst themselves to set up a ruler with absolute power. Once this sovereign is instituted, be it a monarchy, aristocracy, or democracy, then the sovereign can institute civil laws and enforce the laws of nature, bringing about a realm of peace in which individuals will be free to pursue their desires.

The only way to erect such a common power, as may be able to defend them from the invasion of foreigners, and the injuries of one another, and thereby to secure them in such sort, as that by their own industry, and by the fruits of the earth, they may nourish themselves and live contentedly; is, to confer all their power and strength upon one man, or upon one assembly of men, that may reduce all their wills, by plurality of voices, unto one will: which is as much as to say, to appoint one man, or assembly of men, to bear their person; and every one to own, and acknowledge himself to be author or whatsoever he that so beareth their person, shall act, or cause to be acted, in those things which concern the common peace and safety; and therein to submit their wills, every one to his will, and their judgments, to his judgment. This is more than consent, or concord; it is a real unity of them all, in one and the same person, made by convenant of every man with every man, in such manner, as if every man should say to every man, I authorize and give up my right of governing myself, to this man, or to this assembly of men, on this condition, that thou give up thy right to him, and authorize all his action in like manner. This done the multitude so united in one person, is called a commonwealth, in Latin civitas.

Leviathan, chapter 17

THE ABSOLUTE STATE

A sovereign or absolute government is therefore established, and this sovereign is (with tiny restrictions) granted absolute power. For Hobbes, it is unimportant whether the sovereignty is of any particular type: monarchy, aristocracy, or democracy. Only when a reliable sovereign is instituted can people hope to enjoy freedom.

Hobbes suggested a state whose power is absolute, but whose purpose is freedom. The state is neutral, but with enough power to ensure that individuals with differing desires and interests can live together peacefully.

Just as Hobbesian reason is an instrument of the passions, so the state is an instrument or artifice designed to control and adjudicate the conflicting passions and interests of (equal) individuals. In this way, the state ensures that each can seek to satisfy his or her own concept of what is good. **Hobbes' conception of the state is the first of the modern liberal conceptions of political power.**

Having erected a state, Hobbes considered how the sovereign should achieve peace. Natural law contains the 'formal' qualities by which peace is to be attained, qualities realized through the sovereign's laws.

Hobbes' offers a command theory of law:

'Civil law, is to every subject, those rules, which the commonwealth hath commanded him, by word, writing, or other sufficient sign of the will, to make use of, for the distinction of right and wrong; that is to say, of what is contrary, and what is not contrary to the rule.'

Leviathan, chapter 26

For Hobbes, the very authority of law is found, not in how it is justified by some transcendent standard (as for Aquinas), but in the sovereign's commands (a view very acceptable to King Charles II when he was restored to the British throne in 1660!). The Law attains its authority because it is a command of the Sovereign, and everyone is obligated to obey the law because they contracted to establish such a Sovereign.

Everyone must obey the law, even if it is not a good law. However, the law, which is established by the Sovereign, will – if it is to be a law – contain the formal characteristics of the natural laws which should, if implemented, allow people to own property, exchange goods, and to otherwise act freely without the threat of interference from others:

Hobbes resolved the state, or commonwealth, into its relevant component parts and then recomposed it from them. By drawing out the consequences of human nature, he attempted to show that, in a state without authority, there would be endless wars and anarchy. In order to bring about order, peace, and security, a coercive apparatus is required: a common power capable of enforcing the laws of nature, and of establishing and enforcing a civil law that – as a command of the sovereign – establishes liberty.

'*A good law is that, which is needful, for the good of the people, and withal perspicuous...For the use of laws, which are but rules authorized, is not to bind the people from all voluntary actions; but to direct and keep them in such a motion, as not to hurt themselves by their own impetuous desires, rashness or indiscretion; as hedges are set, not to stop travellers, but to keep them in their way.*'

Leviathan, chapter 30

Hobbes argues that the role of the state is to allow each individual to pursue his or her own desires, free from the fear that haunts any state of lawlessness or anarchy. It allows for the free exchange of goods, a key feature of life in a time of peace. Business dealings are possible because, although each has his or her own ends in mind, all operate within an overall structure – there are established ways of trading, which enable fair exchanges to be contracted. Hobbes sees laws, not as a form of restraint, but as a means to guide people and enable them to achieve their chosen ends.

Writing some thirty years after the publication of the *Leviathan*, **John Locke (1632-1704)** was the second modern political theorist to use the terms 'state of nature' and 'social contract' as a means of understanding and justifying the institution of a liberal state. In this sense, Locke's work resembles Hobbes.

However, the differences between Locke and Hobbes are so fundamental that they generally eclipse their similarities.

Although Locke had the standard classical education (see page 33), he also studied medicine and worked as a scientist. He wrote *A Letter Concerning Toleration* (1667), a defence of religious toleration, but his most famous work, at least in the 17th and 18th centuries, was *An Essay Concerning Human Understanding*, written over the course of some fifteen years, and published in 1689. It was followed by the *Second Treatise of Government*, which might be considered a response to Hobbes.

However, Locke's immediate target was not Hobbes, but **Sir Robert Filmer**, a minor thinker who, like Hobbes, had defended absolutist government, specifically, the doctrine of the 'Divine Right of Kings'.

Along with attacking Sir Robert Filmer, the preface to the *Treatise* makes clear that he also saw it as an attempt to provide the theoretical foundation 'sufficient to establish the throne of our great restorer, our present King William'.

FOR FURTHER INFORMATION ON:
LOCKE, SEE PAGE 32.

LOCKE'S STATE OF NATURE

Locke's political theory begins in a state of nature in which there is no government or overarching power. A state of freedom and juridical equality, the Lockean state of nature lacks any political institutions but it is, unlike Hobbes' state of nature, still a state with some sort of moral order.

According to Locke there are fundamental moral norms, or natural laws, which are recognizable to natural reason, and whose enforcement does not depend solely on there being an institution (such as a government) to enforce them.

The state of nature has a law of nature to govern it, which obliges every one: and reason, which is that law, teaches all mankind, who will but consult it, that being all equal and independent, no one ought to harm another in his life, health, liberty, or possessions: for men being all the workmanship of one omnipotent, and infinitely wise maker... and being furnished with like faculties, sharing all in one community of nature, there cannot be supposed any such subordination among us, that may authorize us to destroy one another as if we were made for one another's uses, as the inferior ranks of creatures are for our's. Everyone, as he is bound to preserve himself, and not to quit his station wilfully, so by the like reason, when his own preservation comes not in competition, ought he, as much as he can, to preserve the rest of mankind, and may not, unless it be to do justice on an offender, take away, or impair the life, or what tends to the preservation of the life, the liberty, health, limb, or goods of another.

Second Treatise, chapter II, para.6

'Men living together according to reason, without a common superior on earth...is properly the state of nature.'

LAND AND LAW

Within this state of nature conflicts may arise but not open war; indeed, given the assumptions of freedom, equality, and an overarching moral law, individuals may acquire land and resources, attaining a natural, pre-political, rights to property.

Locke's account of the natural right to ownership is justifiably famous, though not uncontroversial: An individual acquires a property right in some land or resource, when the individual, whom Locke assumes is self-owning (in the sense that the person is free and equal) mixes his labour with some previously unowned piece of land or resource:

'Though the earth, and all inferior creatures, be common to all men, yet every man has a property in his own person: this no body has any right to but himself. The labour of his body, and the work of his hands, we may say, are properly his. Whatsoever then he removes out of the state that nature hath provided, and left it in, he hath mixed his labour with, and joined to it something that is his own, and thereby makes it his property.'

Second Treatise, chapter V

When disputes arise, individuals leave the state of nature in order to establish a common power to adjudicate those disputes and protect their rights.

First a political society is formed as a result of universal consent. Once formed, the majority of individuals choose some form of government, whose power is not absolute. That a political society begins only from an act of consent, reveals our natural liberty.

The very aim of a government is to protect our natural rights and liberties, including the right to acquire property. These accrue to a human being simply by virtue of his humanity.

Just as moral norms of liberty and property transcend the political sphere, they also provide the definitions and limits of the political.

The political realm is limited in such a way that the public good is primarily considered in terms of the protection of freedom, a negative freedom to live and enjoy property.

The laws that are established by the legislature must not be arbitrary or partial:

They are to govern by promulgated established laws, not to be varied in particular cases, but to have one rule for rich and poor, for the favourite at court, and the country man at plough.

Second Treatise, chapter 12

Moreover, the legislative body must not transfer its power of law-making, nor raise taxes on property, without the consent of the people.

When the state transgresses its limits consistently, and violates natural rights, and when there is no opportunity for a peaceful reform, then the people may revolt, argued Locke. The right of revolution follows from the fact that an individual has entrusted the government to protect his or her natural rights; **if the government fails to live up to that trust, that government has effectively rebelled against the conditions of consent, and has thereby set up a state of war against its citizens.**

So, for Locke, the very reason why people enter into agreements, and form society, is that they may protect their own possessions and property. Each is entitled to life and liberty.

He then argues that, if a government fails in its basic duty, it can be replaced:

'Whensoever therefore the legislative shall transgress this fundamental rule of society; and either by ambition, fear, folly or corruption, endeavour to grasp themselves, or put into the hands of any other, an absolute power over the lives, liberties, and estates of the people; by this breach of trust they forfeit the power the people had put into their hands for quite contrary ends, and it devolves to the people, who have a right to resume their original liberty, and, by the establishment of a new legislative, (such as they shall think fit) provide for their own safety and security, which is the end for which they are in society.'

Second Treatise, chapter 19

Can I claim as mine any piece of land with which I have 'mixed my labour'? What rights does anyone have over land that is at the moment free from the attentions of humanity? Many practical issues follow from this, from the enclosure of common land, to the exploitation of natural resources. If I take something that belongs to everybody or nobody, and then do something with it, does it thereby become my own property?

Some have argued that Lock's conception of the state and society neglects vital aspects of the human good. From the often muddled but always impassioned texts of **Jean-Jacques Rousseau (1712-1778)** came two critical questions.

The first is egalitarian:

● Do Locke's views allow for an inequality of wealth or resources that is itself unjust?

The second concerns the value of freedom:

● Is freedom valuable in itself? Or is it valuable only insofar as we freely do the right thing?

Rousseau was born in Geneva but moved to France in 1742 where, some years later, he saw an advertisement for an essay contest. Sponsored by the Academy of Dijon, the contest posed this question: 'Has the restoration of the Arts and Sciences Tended to Purify Morals?' Rousseau's prize-winning essay gave a totally negative and so highly original response to this. For Rousseau, in contradiction to other intellectuals of his day, civilization was corrupt, encouraging hypocrisy and undermining real religion and morality.

This essay made him famous, the next made him notorious. In his *Discourse on the Origin of Inequality* (1755), Rousseau not only described how individuals have, through social evolution, come to have certain qualities and dispositions, but he tried to show how material inequality emerged. Rousseau's aim was not, however, merely descriptive: he wanted to show how this evolution, from natural man to modern man, has corrupted us and created an inequality that alienates us from ourselves and from one another.

THE VILLAGE STATE

At the heart of Rousseau's philosophy, there lies a nostalgia for small-scale city-states, which to modern eyes would seem hardly larger than villages. Geneva, the self-governing city where he was born, then had a population of only 20,000, and he shared Plato's distaste for large cosmopolitan cities. Instead he looked back and forward to a (supposedly) simpler and better life more in accord with nature. This arcadian colouring to most of his work partly explains his wide appeal.

Hobbes had believed that the natural qualities of human beings were effectively those of ambitious egocentric moderns. But Rousseau believes that, unlike his philosophical predecessors, he has stripped the human of all social artifacts and, by so doing, has shown how 18th Century society encouraged egoism, at the expense of fellow-feeling or pity, exacerbating our innate inequalities.

NATURAL MAN

To describe the origin of inequality, Rousseau had to begin with a description of a (truly) natural human being. To understand the natural human, one must strip away from one's conception of humanity, all attributes and qualities that are artefacts of society: **Reason, Language, Morality, and Politics**.

Only by arriving at a conception of the natural human, can one begin to understand how a certain social condition, such as inequality, could have arisen.

The resulting narrative, argues Rousseau, need not be understood to be a strict history, but a device by which we can better understand who we are. Thus, Rousseau is articulating a certain profoundly modern set of questions: Who am I? Who is the real me?

According to Rousseau, the natural human has but two innate principles: self-preservation and compassion.

Like other animals, the human seeks to preserve and care for itself. This however, is not selfishness, for with this natural tendency there is another, a compassion for the suffering of our fellow human beings. However, the human is distinct from other animals in that we have free will (as most Christian philosophers have argued) and, far more dramatically, the capacity for perfectibility in this life. Of course, this capacity for perfectibility is, in a real sense, also a capacity for corruptibility. As Rousseau hopes to show, the natural qualities of the human being have been so corrupted that our self-love has been converted into selfishness, and our compassion has been diminished by reason.

'Reason engenders egocentrism, and reflection strengthens it. Reason is what turns man in upon himself. Reason is what separates him from all that troubles him and afflicts him. Philosophy is what isolates him and what moves him to say in secret, at the sight of a suffering man, "Perish if you will; I am safe and sound." No longer can anything but danger to the entire society trouble the tranquil slumber of the philosopher and yank him from his bed. His fellow man can be killed with impunity underneath his window. He has merely to place his hands over his ears and argue with himself a little in order to prevent nature, which rebels within him, from identifying him with the man being assassinated. Savage man

does not have this admirable talent, and for lack of wisdom and reason he is always seen thoughtlessly giving in to the first sentiment of humanity.'

Discourse on the Origin of Inequality, **Part One**

NOBLE SAVAGE

From the most primitive state, in which humans roam the untilled land freely, without reason or language, Rousseau described how males and females formed families, and from families, more permanent associations.

At this stage of evolution, there was no civil society. Precisely because of this lack, it was humanity's happiest stage, according to Rousseau. With the inventions of agriculture and metalworking – both of which he deplored – there came division of labour, and with this division the institution of ownership, the most important element in the evolving corruption of the human species:

The first person who, having enclosed a plot of land, took it into his head to say this is mine and found people simple enough to believe him, was the true founder of civil society. What crimes, wars, murders, what miseries and horrors would the human race have been spared, had someone pulled up the stakes or filled in the ditch and cried out to his fellow men: 'Do not listen to this imposter.

You are lost if you forget that the fruits of the earth belong to all and the earth to no one!' But it is quite likely that by then things had already reached the point where they could no longer continue as they were.

Discourse on the Origin of Inequality, **Part Two**

'Rousseau was the first militant lowbrow.'

Isaiah Berlin, 1952 (from an article in *The Observer***)**

Rousseau had a somewhat romantic ideal of the primitive person being naturally kind and noble, uncorrupted by society. But all primitive societies have their rules and forms of government. Is a tribe very different from any other form of social organization?

THE SOCIAL CONTRACT

With the advent of ownership, inequality increases, bringing increased corruption of our behaviour. The society which emerges after the institution of property is one which quickly develops into a society of war; in such a violent situation, the rich will persuade the poor to join in establishing a government, and as Rousseau writes:

> ## 'They all ran to chain themselves, in the belief that they secured their liberty.'
>
> *Discourse on the Origin of Inequality*, Part Two

The *Second Discourse* provides a diagnosis of society's ills, but Rousseau does not believe that the prescription calls for our returning to a primitive state of nature. Rather, a society should be created which will not deform our natural propensities but seek to unite self-interest with the common good. This is the society that Rousseau elucidates in *The Social Contract* (1762).

Rousseau begins *The Social Contract* by exclaiming that he will consider 'men as they are and laws as they might be', in order to develop 'some legitimate and sure rule of administration'. In other words, Rousseau does not wish to take us back to the state of nature; rather, he wishes to construct a social order in which our natural self-love (not egoism) can be united with our propensity to compassion; thus, Rousseau writes:

> *'I will always try in this inquiry to bring together what right permits with what interest prescribes, so that justice and utility do not find themselves at odds with one another.'*

Such a social order must be founded on a contract that is fully voluntary. Once one has entered into such a contract then an 'association' is founded. Such an association Rousseau contends must be one that:

> *'... defends and protects with all common forces the person and goods of each associate, and by means of which each one, while uniting with all, nevertheless obeys only himself and remains as free as before.'*
>
> **Book I, chapter VI**

Within this association, reason will deliberate for the common good, thereby serving as a civilized extension of natural compassion. And as each citizen legislates within the association, so is the individual legislating for himself as a subject.

THE GENERAL WILL

How can one obey oneself while nonetheless being a subject of an illiberal government? To solve this problem Rousseau invented the concept of the 'general will', a concept since used to justify some of the worst excesses or dictators, from Robespierre, during the French Revolution, to Hitler and Pol Pot more recently. How far this is Rousseau's fault is still debated.

Rousseau drew a distinction between active and passive participation:

- As active members of a political association, we are citizens; subject to the norms and standards of that association, we are passive subjects.
- As citizens we can deliberate and vote on the form of government; that government, in turn, forces us to act in certain ways.

In Rousseau's view, the votes of the citizenry constitute the 'will of all'. Of course, the will of all may not always be correct. However, there is an ideal to which the will of all should approximate, and that ideal is the **General Will**.

> *'The General Will is always right and always tends toward the public utility. However, it does not follow that the deliberations of the people always have the same rectitude. We always want what is good for us, but we do not always see what it is…There is often a great deal of difference between the will of all and the general will. The latter considers only the general interest, whereas the former considers private interest and is merely the sum of private wills.*
>
> *Social Contract* **book II, chapter III**

So the actual will of the people is distinct from the General Will. Rousseau hoped the two would converge if individuals had sufficient information. In this way, each individual will make up his own mind and will not be a partisan of any particular group or faction.

Although this sounds simple enough – perhaps too simple – there remained the question of exactly what the General Will really was. In the Discourse, Rousseau contended that:

> ## 'the sublime maxim of reasoned justice, (is) Do unto others as you would have them do unto you.'
>
> *Discourse*, Part One

Such a maxim describes, he believes, the behaviour of the natural individual.

In the *Social Contract*, Rousseau contends that individuals should deliberate without regard to private interest but thinking only of how each measure would affect others. A law that is wrought through such deliberations would, Rousseau believed, approximate to the General Will, and in so doing it would support the common good.

It is significant that the state Rousseau most admired was ancient Sparta, not Athens, where the voters could only acclaim the decisions of their rulers by shouting together.

In terms of the form of law, Rousseau contends that:

'the law considers subjects as a body and actions in the abstract, never a man as an individual or a particular action.'

The Social Contract, book II, chapter VI

'Liberty is precious so precious it must be rationed.'

Lenin (1870-1924)

A problem with Rousseau's theory is to know what should be considered 'The General Will'. Agreement among people does not guarantee that something is right, or ultimately to the benefit of all.

Rousseau argued that the government that is set up, whether it be a democracy, aristocracy, or monarchy, should be subject to the sovereign, by which he meant the collective power of the state, rather than an actual individual.

Rousseau also proposed that a tribunal be set up to 'preserve morality' and to encourage and lead the citizens to embrace their civic duties wholeheartedly.

In its chillingly totalitarian picture of the good society, Rousseau was undoubtedly inspired not only by Plato's ideal Republic but also by his fellow-Genevan, the religious reformer **John Calvin**, under whose grim regime in Geneva two centuries earlier, almost everything enjoyable had been forbidden: theatre, art, wine, (most) sex, elegant clothes and so on.

Without religion as the basis of morality and civic duty, he nevertheless looks to some sort of faith:

'There is, therefore, a purely civil profession of faith, the articles of which it belongs to the sovereign to establish, not exactly as dogmas of religion, but as sentiments of sociability, without which it is impossible to be a good citizen or a faithful subject.'

The French Revolutionary, Robespierre, later duly established a 'cult of the Supreme Being' to replace religion. He organized special ceremonies to take the place of Christianity, which had been banned by the new republic. The cult soon died, along with Robespierre.

THE CONTRACT CHALLENGED

The idea common to Hobbes, Locke and Rousseau is the social contract, although they meant utterly different things by it. But this idea was challenged in the 18th century by the great Scottish philosopher **David Hume (1711-1776)** – a personal friend of Rousseau, and one who tolerated the increasingly paranoid behaviour of the apostle of natural man with immense patience.

For Hume the very idea of a state of nature is something of a fiction. Society began, thought Hume, not with isolated individuals meeting up in forests but with families.

Rules of justice emerge over time as conventions, not as the results of explicitly declared contracts. Most governments have been established by other means, and to these we owe our allegiance not out of some abstract promise, but out of contingent considerations of custom and the general interests of society.

Indeed, a contract, in itself, does not explain why we are so bound, a point made explicit by Hume:

'We are bound to obey our sovereign, it is said; because we have given a tacit promise to that purpose. But why are we bound to observe our promise? It must here be asserted, that the commerce and intercourse of mankind, which are of such mighty advantage, can have no security where men pay no regard to their engagements. In like manner, may it be said, that men could not live at all in society, at least in a civilized society, without laws and magistrates and judges, to prevent the encroachments of the strong upon the weak, of the violent upon the just and equitable. The obligation to allegiance being of like force and authority with the obligation to fidelity, we gain nothing by resolving the one into the other. The general interests or necessities of society are sufficient to establish both.'

'Of the Original Contract', in *Essays Moral, Political, and Literary*

'Custom ...is the great guide of human life.'

Hume, *Inquiry concerning Human Understanding*

KANT'S MAXIM

Though more famous for his metaphysical, epistemoligical, and moral writings, **Immanuel Kant (1724-1804)** believed in a social contract, not as an historical fact but as an ideal.

In spite of Hume's appeal to the contingencies of circumstance, Kant believed that moral and political right must be grounded in a priori reason.

FOR **HUME**, SEE ALSO PAGES **36F**

ON **ETHICS**   SEE PAGE **88**

ON **RELIGION**   SEE PAGE **166**

ON **ART**   SEE PAGE **240**.

In the moral realm one is to exercise a good will, and a good will acts from a motive of duty, a duty which is determined by appeal to a law of universal reason:

'Act only according to that maxim whereby you can at the same time will that it should become a universal law.'

Grounding for the Metaphysics of Morals (1785).

Since each person is a free and rational human being, capable of acting in accordance with the moral law, the law should ensure that each person's external actions are compatible with an equal freedom for others.

Thus the universal law of right is as follows: let your external actions be such that the free application of your will can co-exist with the freedom of everyone in accordance with a universal law. And although this law imposes an obligation on me, it does not mean that I am in any way expected, far less required, to restrict my freedom myself to these conditions purely for the sake of this obligation. On the contrary, reason merely says that individual freedom is restricted in this way by virtue of the idea behind it, and that it may also be actively restricted by others; and it states this as a postulate, which does not admit of any further proof.

The Metaphysical Elements of the Theory of Right (1797), Section C

How might we know that a law is compatible with universal right? We can assume, Kant contends, that:

'so long as it is not self-contradictory to say that an entire people could agree to such a law, however painful it might seem, then the law is in harmony with right.'

The Guillotine, originally devised as a more humane form of execution, has become synonymous with the terrors of the French Revolution. Rousseau held that people had the right to change their form of government, hence justifying revolutionary overthrow of the established order. He also held that people could agree together on how they should live and legislate. He looked back to the time of the noble savage – but the question remains whether humankind, freed from social restraint in times of crises, tends towards the 'noble' or the 'savage'.

FOR FURTHER INFORMATION

ON KANT,

SEE PAGES 38-41.

Burke was the great opponent of Rousseau and the French Revolution, although he supported the American Revolution.

Like Hume and against Rousseau, the Irish-born **Edmund Burke (1729-1797)** argued against the idea of a social contract in his very first work *A Vindication of natural Society*, 1756. Rebuffing Rousseau, as Hume had done, Burke scorned the invocation of any a priori justification of political or moral principles. But whereas Hume's appeal to custom and circumstance is decidedly sceptical, Burke became very much a traditionalist, for whom custom was vitally important. A practicing politician, Burke did not have the time to write many more systemic works on the nature of society.

Burke worked as a writer and political advisor until he found himself elected to Parliament, where he championed the causes of Irish emancipations of the American Revolution.

The French Revolution, however, struck him as something very different, and his *Reflections on the Revolution in France* (1790) attacked the bloodshed, atheism and disregard for property and freedom he saw emerging.

For Burke the French Revolution marked a dramatic and terrible rejection of all of the social, moral, and political standards of the past. He saw not just a change in government but an attack on civilized society and life:

'All circumstances taken together, the French Revolution is the most astonishing that has hitherto happened in the world.'

Reflections on the Revolution in France

Burke considered Rousseau the intellectual father of the Revolution – with good reason. Rousseau had argued that society was totally corrupt and that its salvation should be found in the expression of popular sovereignty.

The Old Regime of France – an absolutist monarchy, based on local distinctions among the classes – collapsed with the storming of the Bastille (the prison in Paris) on July 14th, 1789. The Revolution that followed abolished aristocratic privileges in favour of a (theoretical) universal equality.

In *The Declaration of the Rights of Man and Citizen* are several phrases clearly derived from Rousseau:

Article 1: 'Men are born and remain free and equal in rights. Social distinctions can be based only upon public utility.'

Article 3: 'The source of all sovereignty is essentially in the nation....'

Article 6: 'Law is the expression of the general will. All citizens have the right to take part personally or by their representatives in its formation.'

'People will not look forward to prosperity who never looked back to their ancestors.'

Reflections on the Revolution in France

Although Burke was writing before the revolution had taken its bloodiest turn, he had seen enough to diagnose that this revolution was unlike others; it sought to overturn not just a government but an entire society and culture.

Burke holds that individual reason is limited, and it is the mark of the reasonable person to recognize these limits. In a notebook from the 1750s, Burke wrote:

'A man who considers his nature rightly will be diffident of any reasonings that carry him out of the ordinary roads of life; Custom is to be regarded with great deference especially if it be an universal Custom; even popular notions are not always to be laughed at. There is some general principle operating to produce Customs, that is a more sure guide than our Theories...

A man is never in greater danger of being wholly wrong than when he advances far in the road of refinement... Great subtleties and refinements of reasoning are like spirits which disorder the brain and are much less useful than ordinary liquors of a grosser nature...'

One should be wary about wholesale social or political changes. That does not mean that no change should be allowed; Reform is valued but it 'is not a change in the substance or in the primary modification of the object, but a direct application of a remedy to the grievance complained of'.

Burke's point is not simply that reason is limited but that there is something else about the human species that is morally, socially, and politically important – feelings and sentiment. Feelings constitute the fuel of society and they cannot be dismissed as irrational or irrelevant.

Burke wrote of the rationalist claims of the French revolutionaries:

'All the decent drapery of life is to be rudely torn off. All the superadded ideas, furnished from the wardrobe of a moral imagination, which the heart owns and the understanding ratifies, as necessary to cover the defects of our naked, shivering nature, and to raise it to dignity in our own estimation, are to be exploded, as a ridiculous, absurd, and antiquated fashion.'

Reflections on the Revolution in France

Any philosophy that eschews the emotions and affections, that treats circumstances which do not accord with reason as irrational, will find that it cannot command our hearts. In the political sphere the consequences can be devastating:

'In the groves of their academy, at the end of every vista, you see nothing but the gallows.'

Reflections on the Revolution in France

Closely related to his distrust of mere rationalism, was Burke's growing liking for tradition. History is an undesigned process, in which the cumulated experience of many anonymous individuals becomes embodied in specific rules and institutions, indeed, whole cultures.

Taking history and tradition as one's guide, one need not look to any systematic philosophy or metaphysics for guides to action. Burke criticized the legislators of the new French Republic because:

'Nothing in the Revolution, no not to a phrase or a gesture, not to the fashion of a hat or a shoe, was left to accident. All has been the result of design; all has been the matter of institution.'

Reflections on the Revolution in France

And as to the states of Europe, Burke favourably notes:

'Not one of them has been formed upon a regular plan or with any unity of design. As their constitutions are not systematical, they have not been directed to any peculiar end, eminently distinguished, and superseding every other. The objects which they embrace are of the greatest possible variety...'

Reflections on the Revolution in France

In addition, the very idea of a social contract, as it has been typically used, implies a certain mistaken view of the state: 'the state ought not to be considered as nothing better than a partnership agreement in a trade of pepper and coffee, calico, or tobacco, or some other such low concern.' Dismissing social contracts, Burke is willing to grant that human beings have rights. These rights, however, must not be considered in abstraction from social and historical circumstance.

In such complex circumstances, the governors of a nation should exercise 'prudence'. The correct political decision or the best law cannot always be decided by appealing to principles or theories. Any principles to which one might appeal must be carefully fitted to actual circumstance.

As Burke writes:

'The lines of morality are not like the ideal lines of mathematics'

Rules are not exact; they may require compromise; and they demand attention to particular circumstances. This cannot be acquired by theory, only by practical experience. Elected representatives should exercise such prudential judgment. They should do so rather than merely voting for whatever their constituents desire.

It was Burke's view that a new age and culture, inferior to its predecessors, was emerging:

'But the age of chivalry is gone. That of sophisters, economists, and calculators has succeeded; and the glory of Europe is extinguished forever.'

Reflections on the Revolution in France

That the age of chivalry was gone, or at least receding, was not to be doubted, and that an age of economists, or political economists, was rising was also true. One of the great economists, and a friend of Burke, was **Adam Smith (1723-1790)**, whose account of political economy offers the classic social and economic justification for the doctrine of liberalism.

Smith hoped to show that a classical liberal state was a plausible notion, by articulating a defence of the market. In a society framed by laws of 'natural liberty' a division of labour emerges out of a human disposition to trade and interact; as each person is drawn to that activity which he performs best, then so does the overall division of labour serve to increase productivity and wealth of the entire society.

The trade that gives rise to the division of labour allows us to overcome our limited benevolence as well as our limited knowledge:

But man has almost constant occasion for the help of his brethren, and it is in vain for him to expect it from their benevolence only. He will be more likely to prevail if he can interest their self-love in his favour, and shew them that it is for their own advantage to do for him what he requires of them. Whoever offers to another a bargain of any kind, proposes to do this. Give me that which I want, and you shall have this which you want, is the meaning of every such offer; and it is in this manner that we obtain from one another the far greater part of those good offices which we stand in need of.

The Wealth of Nations, I, ii

A year after Smith articulates his economic theory, the **Constitutional Convention of the United States** was held. From October of 1787 until May 1788, there appear in the newspapers of New York a series of articles designed to persuade the citizens of that state that the Constitution should be ratified.

Written by Alexander Hamilton, James Madison, and John Jay, these papers were published under the pseudonym of 'Publius', and comprise The Federalist Papers. Arguing that the Articles of Confederation, under which the American states were then organized, did not establish a central government sufficiently strong to levy taxes, deal with foreign powers, or avoid internal conflict. The authors contend that any stable government must discourage special interests or factions:

'By a faction, I understand a number of citizens , whether amounting to a majority of the whole, who are united and actuated by some common impulse of passion, or of interest, adverse to the rights of other citizens, or to the permanent and aggregate interests of the community.'

The Federalist Papers

The prime cause of faction are conflicting economic interests, and these are not easily controlled.

The remedy for them in a representative democracy, or a republic, is to take representatives drawn from an extensive population, either directly elected (as in the House of Representatives) or indirectly elected (as in the case of the Senate). Through this constitutional structure, representatives must take into account a greater number of views and

> 'It is not from the benevolence of the butcher, the brewer, or the baker, that we expect our dinner, but from their regard to their own interest. We address ourselves, not to their humanity but to their self-love, and never talk to them of our own necessities but of their advantages.'
>
> Adam Smith

interests and will, thereby, be inclined to work for a greater public good.

The importance of modern commerce was also stressed by **Benjamin Constant (1767-1830)**, a Frenchman, born in Switzerland. He was influenced by, among others, the political economy of Smith and the practical emphases of Hume.

Constant recognized that modern government, unlike that of the ancients (see Constant's essay, 'The Liberty of the Ancients Compared with that of the Moderns'), must have a structure suited to modern commerce, and the demands that material productivity would place on large societies.

Rejecting Bentham's Utilitarianism (see page 322) as well as any doctrine of a natural right to liberty, Constant articulated a defence of liberty, based on a view that liberty, as individual autonomy and freedom of action, was the only practical means by which to realize the goods of the modern age.

Constant argued that property existed only through society and that society had found that the best way of allowing everyone to enjoy the goods that were common to all (or which had been generally disputed, prior to the setting up of the society) was to give everyone a share.

On the other hand, Constant recognized that such shares need not be equal, but that people should be allowed to retain benefits that they had formerly enjoyed, and that inequality might anyway result because some worked harder than others.

In claiming that property is 'merely a social convention' Constant commented:

Is property merely social convention? If so, what follows? It there anything in a particular piece of land that determines who should own it? What if I consider the distribution of property to be unfair? What if, at some time in the past, land was appropriated? Am I now entitled to take it back? What if the land was divided as a result of warfare and invasion? Should invaders be allowed to benefit permanently from the spoils of war? What of colonial properties? Should indigenous people have the right to claim back their land, where it has been taken from them many generations ago? A 'Private Keep Out' sign carries with it a whole philosophy of rights and the justice of distribution, as well as a history of the way in which property has been passed from one generation to the next.

'But if we recognize it as such, it does not follow from this that we consider it as less sacred, less inviolable, less necessary, than those writers who subscribe to a different system....

'But property is intimately bound up with other aspects of human existence, some of which are in no way subjected to collective jurisdiction, while others are subjected to it only to a limited extent. Consequently society must restrain its action over property because it could hardly exercise this to its full extent without encroaching upon objects which are by no means subordinate to it.

'Arbitrary power over property is soon followed by arbitrary power over people; first, because arbitrary power is contagious; secondly, because violation of property necessarily provokes resistance.'

Principles of Politics
Applicable to all Representative
Governments, **chapter 15**

Unhappy with the doctrine of natural rights, which he called 'nonsense upon stilts', **Jeremy Bentham (1748-1832)** wanted to develop a doctrine which would serve to reform laws and norms accepted more out of tradition than reason, a doctrine which would provide a clear and empirical method by which to make moral and political decisions.

A lawyer by training, though not by practice, Bentham's most influential work was An Introduction to the Principles of Morals and Legislation (1789). In it he defends the principle of utility as 'but the property or tendency of a thing to prevent some evil or to procure some good'.

'Morality in general is the art of directing the actions of men in such a way as to produce the greatest possible sum of good. Legislation ought to have precisely the same object.'

Principles of Legislation, chapter XII

Utilitarianism's normative theory is: **an act is morally right if and only if the act maximizes utility (or accords with a rule which, if generally followed, would maximize utility).**

Stated in this manner the doctrine of utilitarianism includes both a theory of right action and a theory of value: The former states that rightness entails maximizing utility, the latter contends that those things which have 'utility,' or some intrinsic value, are certain types of states (such as pleasure or the satisfaction of preferences).

UTILITARIANISM, LIBERTY, AND THE LAW

That utilitarianism should be taken to be a liberating doctrine of reform and progress, was emphasized by Bentham's disciple, **John Stuart Mill (1806-1873)**, whose account of utilitarianism also forms the basis for his doctrine of liberty.

In chapter two of his work, Utilitarianism (1861), Mill offers a summary statement of his doctrine:

'the Greatest Happiness Principle, holds that actions are right in proportion as they tend to promote happiness, wrong as they tend to produce the reverse of happiness. By happiness is intended pleasure, and the absence of pain.'

Subsequent to this statement, Mill discusses more fully how his account of value differs from that of his predecessor, Jeremy Bentham.

Unlike Bentham, who did not distinguish qualities of pleasure, Mill believes that pleasure has a higher and a lower form:

'Of two pleasures, if there be one to which all or almost all who have experience of both give a decided preference, irrespective of any feeling of moral obligation to prefer it, that is the more desirable pleasure. If one of the two is, by those who are competently acquainted with both, placed so far above the other that they prefer it, even though knowing it to be attended with a greater amount of discontent, and would not resign it for any quantity of the other pleasure which their nature is capable of, we are justified in ascribing to the preferred enjoyment a superiority in quality so far outweighing quantity as to render it, in comparison, of small account.'

Utilitarianism, chapter 2

After developing his account of the higher and lower pleasures, Mill proceeds to consider some objections to the general doctrine of utilitarianism, finally pointing out how utilitarianism is compatible with rules of justice.

That utilitarianism might provide a basis for liberty, is developed in On Liberty (1859). There, Mill seeks to defend a principle of liberty:

'... the only purpose for which power can be rightfully exercised over any member of a civilized community, against his will, is to prevent harm to others. His own good, either physical or moral, is not a sufficient warrant. He cannot rightfully be compelled to do or forbear because it will be better for him to do so, because it will make him happier, because, in the *opinions of others, to do so would be wise or even right. These are good reasons for remonstrating with him, or reasoning with him, or persuading him, or entreating him, but not for compelling him or visiting him with any evil in case he do otherwise. To justify that, the conduct from which it is desired to deter him must be calculated to produce evil to someone else. The only part of the conduct of anyone for which he is amenable to society is that which concerns others. In the part which merely concerns himself, his independence is, of right, absolute. Over himself, over his own body and mind, the individual is sovereign.'*

On Liberty, **chapter I**

'The greatest happiness of the greatest number is the foundation of morals and legislation.'

Bentham, *The Commonplace Book*

THE NECESSITY OF FREEDOM

Liberty, for Mill, concerns one's 'tastes and pursuits' as well as liberty of thought and opinion. A particular concern of Mill is liberty of thought and opinion which he justifies by appeal to how the freedom to speak, think, and deliberate, provides a process by which truth is discovered.

Mill considers, in addition, the way in which such liberty is essential to an individual's self-development. (Similarly, Mill attempts pointed out how different experiments in living allow us to discern what should be kept and what should be relinquished.) The only things that would be prohibited, by Mill's own principle, would be 'harm to others'. What is left unclear is what is meant by this phrase:

'The fact of living in society renders it indispensable that each should be bound to observe a certain line of conduct toward the rest. This conduct consists, first, in not injuring the interest of one another, or rather certain interests which, either by express legal provision or by tacit understanding, ought to be considered as rights; and secondly, in each person's bearing his share (to be fixed on some equitable principle) of the labours and sacrifices incurred for defending the society or its members from injury and molestation.'

On Liberty, **chapter IV**

A neighbour and disciple of Bentham, **John Austin (1790-1859)** developed a theory of law in which he distinguished the conceptual aspect of law from its normative value. In developing his theory, Austin inaugurates a tradition of analytical jurisprudence that continues to this day.

This approach seeks to understand the law apart from its historical, moral, or economic dimensions, and provides a neutral account of important legal concepts. Following Bentham and Hobbes, Austin developed a conceptual account of law in which a 'law' is a command of the sovereign. To understand 'law,' one must analyse 'command' and 'sovereign'.

'A command is an expression of desire, which generates an obligation. But a command is distinguished from other significations of desire by this peculiarity: that the party to whom it is directed, is liable to evil from the other, in case he comply not with the desire.

'Being liable to evil from you if I comply not with a wish which you signify, I am bound or obliged by your command, or I lie under a duty to obey it.'

The Province of Jurisprudence Determined, **Lecture I**

The idea of 'sovereignty' is defined in terms of a 'habit of obedience': a political sovereign is that person or institution to which the 'bulk of the given society are in a habit of obedience or submission to a determinate and common superior' which itself has no determinate human superior.

Province of Jurisprudence Determined, **Lecture VI**

Austin's efforts to provide a neutral conception of law are subject to a variety of criticisms (the most prominent of which was developed by the twentieth-century philosopher of law, H L A Hart – see page 326), for the very idea of law as a command omits the idea that a law can be a rule of behaviour, rather than a prediction about a possible penalty that will befall a person who fails to comply.

FOR FURTHER INFORMATION ON: THE UTILITARIANISM OF BENTHAM AND MILL, SEE PAGE 86.

One of the chief criticisms of 19th century liberalism is that it merely served to support a ruling class, and to thwart the good of those without power or money. Although there were a variety of socialist movements and theoreticians who made such claims, it was Karl Marx's theories – purportedly scientific and non-utopian – which were to have an enormous influence on political movements in the 20th century.

The story of Marxism begins, however, with the German philosopher **Georg Wilhelm Friedrich Hegel (1770-1831)**.

For Hegel, what we take to be the material world of nature, things and events is but the activity of spirit (*Geist*) producing for itself an object, through which its own self is made conscious. The force behind history is the activity of spirit, as it brings forth an objective world; the spiritual is primary and the material is but the objectification of the spirit.

This objectification occurs through history, and the ultimate development of history is realized in freedom:

'Universal history – as already demonstrated – shows the development of the consciousness of Freedom on the part of Spirit, and of the consequent realization of that Freedom.'

Lectures on the Philosophy of History

The realization of this freedom, or self-consciousness, comes about through civil society, but also through the state itself. This realization entails an embodiment of freedom in a community. There are three forms of community: family, civil society, and state. The family is centred on particular feeling. Civil society, following from Adam Smith's account in *The Wealth of Nations*, is the locus of exchange among and between individuals with particular needs. However, it is in the state that the partial expression of family and civil society are overcome in through a more

organic constitution; within the state, the self-consciousness of Spirit is realized, insofar as a universal rationality is rendered concrete and situated in institutions and practices.

Whereas Hegel had seen history as a development of spirit or mind, **Karl Marx (1818-1883)** viewed history as the development of a material substructure of economic systems, generating ideas and ideologies.

For Marx, it is not the spiritual that is primary, but the material; and it is through labour, under conditions of production, that we come to manifest a certain consciousness. **The development of history is a history of classes in conflict, and this struggle will end when one class, the proletariat, comes to embody the consciousness of all humanity, when the proletariat becomes a universal class.**

Marx saw human beings as inseparable from their labour. In *The Economic and Philosophical Manuscripts of 1844* Marx takes as fact that workers sink further into poverty as production increases. As this happens, workers become alienated from their world. This *alienation* takes four forms:

- The worker's product is seen as a loss, as something that is taken from him and which acquires a power of its own;
- The very activity of labour seems *external* to the worker and involuntary;
- Human beings are alienated from each other.
- Finally, the worker is alienated from his 'species-being' – that conception of self which links us, as rational and free beings, to other rational and free beings, as the objects of our activity.

Alienation is an effect of private property and capitalism, but:

'Communism is the positive abolition of private property, of human self-alienation, and thus the real appropriation of human nature

through and for man. It is, therefore, the return of man himself as a social, i.e. really human, being, a complete and conscious return which assimilates all the wealth of previous development. Communism as a fully-developed naturalism is humanism and as a fully-developed humanism is naturalism. It is the definitive resolution of the antagonism between man and nature.'

The Economic and Philosophical Manuscripts of 1844

That idea that human consciousness is developed out of his economic relations of production is developed more fully in *The German Ideology* (1845-1846), a collaborative effort of Marx and **Frederick Engels (1820-1895)**.

The Hegelian doctrine of an independent Mind or Spirit was turned upside down, as Marx and Engels develop a *materialist* conception of history:

'In direct contrast to German philosophy, which descends from heaven to earth, here we ascend from earth to heaven. That is to say, we do not set out from what men say, imagine, conceive, nor from men as narrated, thought of, imagined, conceived, in order to arrive at men in the flesh. We set out from real, active men, and on the basis of their real life process we demonstrate the development of the ideological reflexes and echoes of this life process... Morality, religion, metaphysics, all the rest of ideology and their corresponding forms of consciousness, thus no longer retain the semblance of

FOR FURTHER INFORMATION ON:
HEGEL, SEE ALSO PAGES 256.
FOR MARX ON
ETHICS   SEE PAGE 92
RELIGION   SEE PAGE 172.

independence. They have no history, no development; but men, developing their material production and their material intercourse, alter, along with this, their real existence, their thinking, and the products of their thinking. Life is not determined by consciousness, but consciousness by life.'
                          The German Ideology

Although the exact relation between material substructure and the super-structure of ideas is not made clear by Marx or Engels, what is clear, at least from *The Communist Manifesto* (1848), is that they believed that the development of history occurs as modes of economic production undergo change; these modes of production generate classes, which exist in antagonistic relations to one another.

Under modern commercial development, however, the class relationships have simplified into two distinct groups, the bourgeoisie and the proletariat. Although the proletariat arises alongside the bourgeoisie, the proletariat must sell its labour power to the bourgeoisie. As the bourgeoisie increase productivity, the ranks of the proletariat increase, wages grow lower and capital is increasingly concentrated in the hands of fewer and fewer capitalists.

The proletariat turns into a revolutionary force, which, in seeking its own liberation, will liberate all of humanity. Once in power, the proletariat will centralize production in the state; during this period there is a '*dictatorship of the proletariat*' intended to be but a temporary stage about which Marx proclaims:

'We shall have an association, in which the free development of each is the condition for the free development of all.'   *The Communist Manifesto*

'Workers of the world unite! You have nothing to lose but your chains!'

Karl Marx, *The Communist Manifesto*, 1848

The reading room at the British Museum – where Marx worked for many years, and where he wrote *Das Kapital*, the great work that dominated the latter years of his life.

Although the 20th Century has witnessed numerous political movements and ideologies, some of which have been very bloody, throughout the first two-thirds of the century political philosophy was surprisingly quiet.

THE TWENTIETH CENTURY: POLITICAL PHILOSOPHY AND PHILOSOPHY OF LAW

The political ideologies that most disastrously marked the 20th Century were communism and fascism. One interpreter of Marx, **Leszek Kolakowski**, contended that it was logical to derive from Marxism the doctrines of 20th Century communism:

'... there was nothing flagrantly illogical in deducing from this (Marxism) that the expropriation of the bourgeoisie and the nationalization of industry and agriculture would bring about the general emancipation of mankind. In the event it turned out that, having nationalized the means of production, it was possible to erect on this foundation a monstrous edifice of lies, exploitation, and oppression.'

Main Currents of Marxism, vol 3

Fascist ideology, which itself borrowed much from Lenin's totalitarian Communism, was, like Communism, anti-democratic and anti-liberal. Unlike communism however, fascism – including its racist and anti-semitic species, Nazism – was nationalist in appeal rather than internationalist. Whereas Communism appealed, in theory, to ideas of rationality and science, fascism appealed to more romantic notions of the realization, in the state, of the spiritual unity of a people.

Oddly, at the same time as the ideological movements of communism and fascism were arising, political philosophy is on the wane. Much of this is due to larger developments in philosophy, including the rise (in the thirties) of Logical Positivism, a movement that held that the only meaningful statements of discourse were either empirical statements of science or tautologies.

This meant that entire spheres of thought, including those of ethics, politics, and aesthetics, were meaningless. Although this view prevailed only briefly, its influence affected philosophy for several decades, leading many philosophers to satisfy themselves with the analysis of political concepts, rather than the postulation and justification of political principles.

The Positivists' exclusive attention to language had some important effects. In the area of the philosophy of law, for example, it produced an increased attention to the positivistic theory of law, originated by **John Austin** in the 19th Century.

One of the earliest to resuscitate the positivist conception of law was **Hans Kelsen (1881-1973)**, who, in his Introduction to the Problems of Legal Theory (1934), argued that law is a command whose authority derives, ultimately, from an un-derived, but higher norm of legality. Clearly, however, the most important legal philosopher has been **H L A Hart (1907-1992)** whose work reflects, most clearly, the influence of 20th Century analytic philosophy. Hart argued that the primary difficulty in John Austin's account of the law is that it omits the idea of a rule, and in so doing leaves no account of legal obligation.

The law, argues Hart, is comprised of primary and secondary rules. A primary rule specifies when or how we are to abstain from some action or perform some action; these are duty-imposing rules. However, there are also secondary rules, which specify or grant the power to introduce, alter, or change a primary rule, and the basic foundation for legal validity is found in a secondary rule of recognition.

Such a rule, or set of rules, will delineate, if only by implicit practice, the criteria by which a primary rule is to be identified.

The sense in which the rule of recognition is the ultimate rule of a system, is best understood if we pursue a very familiar chain of legal reasoning. If the question is raised whether some suggested rule is legally valid, we must, in order to answer the question, use a criterion of validity provided by some other rule.

For example, we may ask

'Is this purported by-law of Oxfordshire County Council valid? Yes: because it was made in exercise of the powers conferred, and in accordance with the procedure specified, by a statutory order made by the Minister of Health.'

The Concept of Law, 1961

Hart hoped that his account would provide a positive (or non-normative) account of the normative rules that make up the law. The American legal philosopher, **Lon Fuller (1902-1978)** doubted, however, whether the positivist programme could succeed. Fuller believed that, since the law attempts to order our practical and moral concerns, it must exhibit an 'internal morality'. In his work The Morality of Law (1964), Fuller tells the mythical story of a King Rex who tries, in a bumbling fashion, to construct a code of law but fails to do so because his code does not contain the internal criteria of law: **generality, publicity, non-retroactivity, comprehensibility, consistency, practicability, predictability, and consistent execution and administration.**

Within the past 25 years, the philosophy of law has attracted increasing attention. A more recent critic of Hart has been **Ronald Dworkin (1931-)**, a Professor at New York University and Oxford, who, in *Taking Rights Seriously* (1977), contends that Hart's account of law as a system of rules fails to consider how the courts, in adjudicating 'hard cases', do not rely merely on a set of rules but invoke moral principles.

THE PARTIAL LAW?

More recently, the Critical Legal Studies movement has attacked the positivist claim that the law is neutral and independent of politics. The law, they contend, is often used to express and reinforce the interests of the powerful (whether that power is economic, ethnic, racial, or sexual), and perpetuate inequalities.

That there is some relation between the law and economic effects has also been the concern of another group, loosely referred to as the 'law and economics' movement. Employing the tools of economic theory, these philosophers and economists argue that the law is, and should be, understood as an effort of a society to engage in wealth maximization.

'In coming to decisions on "hard cases", the courts do not merely rely on the application of rules, but also invoke moral principles.' Hence, giving a judicial summary of a situation is far from a mechanical or routine task – it requires the careful application of all the relevant aspects of law, but also the awareness of the moral principles which the law seeks to uphold, which may influence the way in which the law is applied, where there is scope for varieties of interpretation.

That philosophy of law has grown increasingly rich and varied, does not mean that there have not been deep and interesting developments in 20th Century political philosophy. Many of these developments have focused on important concepts of political and social thought (for example, the nature of justice, liberty, equality), exploring political possibilities, including varieties of socialism, such as 'market socialism'. After the Second World War, however, there emerged several political philosophers whose work resonates with deep insight.

One of the most original was **Michael Oakeshott (1901-1990)**. A historian by training, a Hobbesian liberal on matters of the state, and a Hegelian in his account of the moral life, Oakeshott's work is elegant and subtle.

Arguing that the human being is not an abstract rational self (such as a Kantian might claim) but a particular being, situated in a concrete tradition, Oakeshott holds that political philosophy itself always draws from a tradition of practices, abstracting one point or theme.

The major problem of the modern mind, argues Oakeshott, is that we are too often rationalists who fail to realize that our thoughts are but abridgements of particular practices. Political activity, however, is not to be understood as the activity of following some set of principles or guidelines, however much we might believe it to be so, for an ideology is but an abstraction from something more primordial:

'a concrete manner of attending to the arrangements of a society.'

'Political Education', in
*Rationalism in Politics and
Other Essays*

Informed by his insights in economics, **F A Hayek (1899-1993)**, an economist and social philosopher, argued that the principle problem of societies is not the allocation of resources but their coordination among disparate individuals with divergent ends and local, sometimes inarticulable knowledge.

From his concern with this economic problem – a problem that has convinced many socialists to opt for a version of 'market socialism' that relies on market prices – Hayek turned to social and political philosophy, contending that most of the rules and institutions of society are the unintended outcomes of evolution over time.

The best political order, he argues, is a classical liberal one, whose 'purpose-independent' laws allow individuals to use their own knowledge for their own ends.

'It is because it was not dependent on organization, but grew up as a spontaneous order, that the structure of modern society has attained that degree of complexity which it possesses and which far exceeds any that could have been achieved by deliberate organization… To maintain that we must deliberately plan modern society because it has become so complex is therefore paradoxical, and the result of a complete misunderstanding of these circumstances. The fact is, rather, that we can preserve an order of such complexity not by the method of directing the members, but only indirectly by enforcing and improving the rules conducive to the formation of a spontaneous order.'

Law, Legislation, and Liberty, vol 1.

Hayek offered a highly influential version of 20th Century liberalism – the British Prime Minister Margaret Thatcher was an admirer of his ideas – in which a liberal state is justified as the instrument by which a social order will emerge. This will allow individuals to satisfy their various and emergent desires.

EGALITARIAN LIBERALISM

Intellectually, perhaps the most influential of the political philosophers of the last 40 years, has been another, far more egalitarian, exponent of liberalism, the American philosopher **John Rawls (1921-)**. Rawls revived political philosophy by employing a contractarian device, as well as a Kantian conception of the person, to justify two principles of justice. Rawls' interest is not so much in the justification of the state, or the exploration of political authority, but in the very content of justice.

In Rawls' view, the way to arrive at an understanding of the fundamental principles of justice is to consider what principles would be chosen (unanimously) by rational actors who, having set aside morally irrelevant considerations, deliberate together in some hypothetical bargaining situation.

Rawls believes that it is the very *fairness* of this hypothetical situation, a situation in which individuals shed their particularities and deliberate as rational agents, that allows one to claim that the principles which the individuals would agree to in this original bargaining situation are the appropriate principles of justice by which a real society should be ordered.

The essence of Rawls' position is this: If you want to know which principles of justice should determine a society's basic institutions, then you should imagine yourself as an individual in a hypothetical situation. This situation is, in

Rawls' view, circumscribed by certain principles of fairness: When imagining yourself in this hypothetical situation, deliberate as a free and rational person who is seeking to advance his own interests. However, you must deliberate behind a 'veil of ignorance': deliberate about the principles of justice without taking into account your status in society, class, educational level, intelligence, strength, or psychological dispositions. The purpose of this 'veil of ignorance' is to ensure that when deliberating about the principles of justice, you do not seek to construct principles that would favour your particular interests, aptitudes, or status.

Two Principles of Justice

From this fair and hypothetical bargaining position, Rawls believes that individuals would choose two principles of justice:

Each person is to have an equal right to the most extensive total system of equal basic liberties compatible with a similar system of liberty for all.

Social and economic inequalities are to be arranged so that they are both:
(a) to the greatest benefit of the least advantaged...and
(b) attached to positions and offices open to all under conditions of fair equality of opportunity.

A Theory of Justice, section 46

Although the first of these principles has a priority over the second, they are both related to a more general principle, an egalitarian principle that places the burden of justification on any departure from equality, and seeks to ameliorate the inequalities that arise from the contingencies of history and circumstance:

Is it possible to set aside an awareness of one's own position in society? If not, can one ever legislate in the way that Rawls suggests?

'All social values — liberty and opportunity, income and wealth, and the bases of self-respect — are to be distributed equally unless an unequal distribution of any, or all, of these values is to everyone's advantage.' *A Theory of Justice*

Another type of liberalism is that of the natural rights perspective. In 1974, **Robert Nozick (1938-2002)**, a philosopher at Harvard, published *Anarchy, State, and Utopia*, a book which commenced with this sentence:

> '*Individuals have rights, and there are things no person or group may do to them (without violating their rights).*'

According to Nozick, a just state must be limited to protecting individual rights of life, liberty, and property. Only a state so limited can be considered a just state.

Assuming, but not arguing for, a Lockean conception of rights, Nozick labels his theory of justice '*the entitlement theory.*' For Nozick, a state of affairs is to be determined by whether or not a person is entitled to his 'holdings' (or property).

The entitlement theory must contain three parts:

1 **Original acquisition:** There must be some principles which explain how any person could acquire a holding (or property) out of some unowned state.

2 **Transfer:** There must be some explanation of the principles by which holdings can be transferred from one person to another.

3 **Rectification:** There must be some principles which explain how any violation of principles 1 and 2 are to be rectified.

An entitlement theory of justice is an historical theory. To determine whether some state of affairs is just, one must consider how that state of affairs came about. It is also what Noziek calls an 'unpatterned' theory of justice. For Nozick, there is no specific ordering (or pattern) of rewards and penalties, to which our holdings must conform.

Other political theorists have been concerned that such patterns may mask forms of domination and power. For example, **Jurgen Habermas (1929-)**, is a German philosopher whose thought emerged from the tradition of Critical Theory, a form of Marxist social thought embraced by the Frankfurt Institute for Social Research.

Perhaps the most prominent of the Frankfurt School thinkers was **Max Horkheimer (1895-1973)**, whose *Dialectic of Enlightenment* (1947), co-authored with **Theodore Adorno (1903-1969)**, argues that the progressive rationalism born of the European Enlightenment was destructive of humanity and human community.

For Habermas, however, there is an ideal mode of communication, free of domination, which points to a ideal form of social life, itself evolving out of an unconstrained discourse, which he considers in *Communication and the Evolution of Society* (1976).

The involvement of women in politics is a recent phenomenon. Many of the philosophers surveyed in this chapter do not take women, or issues of specific concern to them, into account. Feminist political philosophy developed mainly during the final quarter of the 20th century, along with the increased involvement of women in political and legislative spheres.

The feminist criticism, which comes in several varieties, is sometimes a critical claim about how women and women's perspectives have been omitted from the thought of major political thinkers; in other respects, feminist political philosophy expresses the points of political philosophy proper.

One of the first and major texts of feminist political philosophy comes from **Simone de Beauvoir (1908-1986),** whose book *The Second Sex* (1949) provides an analysis of the historical and social status of women.

In the last quarter of the 20th century, feminist political philosophy has been developed along liberal, socialist, and radical lines, with each considering whether the status of women is a matter of law and equal opportunity (liberal), or an effect of economic structures (socialist and Marxist), or is rooted in a deeper system of domination and enforced heterosexuality (radical).

Dictionary definitions of feminism always stress the key issue of equality. The concise Oxford Dictionary defines feminism as 'advocacy of women's rights on the grounds of equality of the sexes'. Webster's calls it 'the doctrine which declares that social, political and economic rights for women be the same as men'.

In ethics, this has implications for both utilitarian and rights-based approaches, but it is just as vitally important for assessing political and legal theory.

Feminism generally takes a dual-track approach to political theory:

● On the one hand it seeks to present an historical critique of the social injustices suffered by women generally, suggesting that gender bias is institutional as well as individual.

● On the other hand, it offers a broader consideration of the relationship between the sexes, the distinctive role of woman, and the ethical implications of gender, all of which can operate on an individual and political level.

GENDER-BIAS IN LAW

Some feminists argue that laws in Western societies are in fact 'gender-biased' and so play a major role in reinforcing ideologies – such as those dividing the public and private spheres – which maintain women's subordination.

Thus the law, far from being neutral, generally reflects and supports male viewpoints and interests, rather than those of women. The law, they argue, inevitably reflects the attitudes of those who established it and administer it.

Some feminists even envisage a wholly separate feminist jurisprudence, which could avoid the bias of conventional law and could offer real legal equality and 'gender justice', as opposed to legal neutrality.

Discussion of women and women's issues is remarkably uncommon in Western philosophy. And where there are issues concerning families and children (for example. in John Locke's *Two Treatises of Government*) it often focuses on the issue of parental rights and authority.

It is only with the application of utilitarian principles to the political sphere, particularly with John Stuart Mill in the mid-nineteenth century, that ethical theory and political philosophy come together to promote a practical feminist issue – in this case, the issue of women having the right to vote.

FOR SOME ETHICAL ASPECTS OF THE FEMINIST PERSPECTIVE, SEE PAGE **98**

'One is not born a woman: one becomes a woman. No biological, psychological or economic destiny can determine how the human female will appear in society.'

The Second Sex

PLATO'S VIEW OF WOMEN

Plato argued that people should do the work for which nature best fitted them. Having made the point that those of different natures should do different work, he went on to say:

'… we never meant every and any sort of sameness and difference in nature, but the sort that was relevant to the occupation in question. We meant, for instance, that a man and a woman have the same nature if both have a talent for medicine; whereas women have different natures if one is a born physician, the other is a born carpenter.

'To conclude then, there is no occupation concerned with the management of social affairs which belongs either to women or to men, as such. Natural gifts are to be found here and there in both creatures alike; and every occupation is open to both, so far as their natures are concerned, though woman is for all purposes the weaker.'

The Republic **v.454, 455**

However, having established gender equality among the Guardians (the rulers of the ideal state), Plato advocated that they should hold wives and children in common, and that breeding should be done to suit society's needs, rather than individuals' personal choice.

This was to be most strictly enforced, and those whose unions are not approved, would have to practice abortion or infanticide.

Although Plato offered a rare equality of opportunity, his views of society still showed a pronounced gender bias, since he placed social expediency and manipulation (traditionally, though hardly exclusively, male characteristics) above the feminine qualities of nurture.

It is probably fair to say that Plato did no more than allow women to become honorary men. Thus, they were required to exercise naked along with men, and to take a 'masculine' view of society and the process of bringing up children!

Here again, Plato found a prototype in Sparta, that closed society he so admired but never actually saw, where girls suffered the same gruelling regime as boys, and family life was almost non-existent.

'If then, we find that either the male sex or the female is specifically qualified for any particular form of occupation, then that occupation, we shall say, ought to be assigned to one sex or the other. But if the only difference appears to be that the male begets and the female brings forth, we shall conclude that no difference between men and women has yet been produced that is relevant to our purpose.'

The Republic **v.454**

The Epicureans alone genuinely accepted women – and slaves – on terms of complete equality, but they were always a tiny minority in the ancient world. The position of women – both in practical life and as regarded by philosophers – indisputably worsened with the triumph in the fourth century by a Christianity much influenced by St Paul's views, whatever the original intentions of its founder.

However, the acceptance of gender equality, and the recognition of parallel talents does not in itself imply any single political or social solution to gender issues. Thus **Mary Wollstonecraft**'s *A Vindication of the Rights of Women* (1792) argued for equality on the ground of intellect, but she was happy to see women and men play very different roles in society. She saw women as primarily contributing from within the home.

One of the continuing issues for feminism, therefore, is whether an emphasis on absolute social equality fails to take into account the distinctive contribution or biological functions of women.

Thus, to have a form of legal equality which does not take into account that women have a different psychological make-up from men, could be to deny women the right to assert their equality as women.

A TAOIST VIEW

Taoism, perhaps uniquely among the philosophies we have been considering, always recognized the essential balance of masculine and feminine, Yin and Yang.

In fact, the Feminine is seen as the most fundamental of forces, both subtle and yet inexhaustible:

The Spirit of the Fountain dies not.

It is called the Mysterious Feminine.

The Doorway of the Mysterious Feminine

Is called the Root of Heaven-and-Earth.

Lingering like gossamer, it has only a hint of existence;

And yet when you draw upon it, it is inexhaustible.

Tao te Ching, 6

Significantly, the Taoists translated this metaphysical view of the feminine into their attitude to the practical issues of women and their place in society. In the first century BCE, the Taoists were notably (and almost alone in China at the time) opposed to the spread of the custom of footbinding, a form of female oppression which was to last as long as imperial

We take it for granted today that women and men can work alongside one another in a whole range of roles and occupations. Physiological differences are increasingly irrelevant for the performance of most tasks, but how does the changed situation affect our view of society, or the family, or psychology? Philosophy considers issues thrown up by society, examines principles that have lasting significance. The issue of gender, here considered as a separate topic, is more likely to infiltrate the whole of serious thought, as its social implications become accepted. Gender differences will then only be considered – as Plato suggested – if there is some reason why they might be significant to the questions being considered.

The most important books in philosophy, the original works by the philosophers included in this book, are generally cited in the text itself. The books listed here are suggestions, provided by the contributors, for 'further reading' in each of the sections.

They are not listed in any particular order, but are loosely grouped together according to their subject matter. The titles included here should certainly not be taken as exhaustive, since new books are constantly appearing, and they represent no more than a personal selection.

There are, of course, a good number of books that introduce the thought of individual philosophers, but in general these do not appear in this list, since it has been compiled in terms of the branches of philosophy, rather than by particular thinker of period.

GENERAL

Of the many introductions to and histories of philosophy, see for example:

Ninian Smart, *World Philosophies*, London and New York, Routledge, 1999.

Bryan Magee, *The Story of Philosophy*, London, Dorling Kindersley, 1998.

Ted Honderich, (ed.), *The Oxford Companion to Philosophy*, Oxford and New York, Oxford University Press, 1995.

There are also some very fine older histories of Western philosophy. See, for example the single volume *History of Western Philosophy* by Bertrand Russell published originally in 1946, or the multi-volume *A History of Philosophy* by Frederick Copleston, published in 1959.

For general reference purposes, one could try:
The Concise Routledge Encyclopedia of Philosophy, Routledge, 2000
But for a feeling of what it is like to be enthusiastic about philosophy, and to be drawn into the study of it, try:
Bryan Magee *Confessions of a Philosopher*, Phoenix paperback, 1998.

KNOWLEDGE AND REALITY – WESTERN APPROACHES

J Moravcsik, *Plato and Platonism*, Cambridge, MA, Blackwell, 1992.

Jonathan Barnes, (ed.), *The Cambridge Companion to Aristotle*, Cambridge University Press.

David Appelbaum, *The Vision of Kant*, Vega Books, 2002 (Spirit of Philosophy Series).

John Dunn, J C Urmson, Alfred J Ayer, J O Urmshon, *The British Empiricists: Locke, Berkeley, Hume*, Oxford University Press, 1992.

Christopher Wart, Andrzej Klimowshi, Richard Appighanes, *Introducing Kant*, Totem Books, 1977.

John Cottingham, (ed.), *Descartes* (Oxford Readings in Philosophy), Oxford and New York, Oxford University Press, 1998.

A C Grayling, *Wittgenstein* (Past Masters Series), Oxford and New York, Oxford University Press, 1988.

Jim Powell, Joe Lee, *Postmodernism for Beginners*, Writers and Readers, 1988.

INDIAN PHILOSOPHY

The Rig Veda, translated by Wendy Doniger O'Flaherty, Penguin Classics, 1981.

Upanisads, Translated by Patrick Olivelle, Oxford World's Classics, 1996.

Rupert Gethin, *The Foundations of Buddhism*, Oxford University Press, 1998.

Bimal Krishna Matilal, *Perception: An Essay on Classical Indian Theories of Knowledge*, Oxford University Press, 1986.

Edward Conze, (ed.), *Buddhist Scriptures*, Penguin Classics, 1959.

Sarvepalli Radhakrishnan and Charles A Moore, (eds.), *A Sourcebook in Indian Philosophy*, Princeton University Press, 1989.

Heinrich Zimmer, edited by Joseph Campbell, *Philosophies of India*, Princeto University Press, 1974.

F T Stcherbatsky, *Buddhist Logic* (Two Volumes), Dover Publications.

Pulinbihari Chakravarti, Munishiram Manoharlal, *Origin and Development of the Samkhya System of Thought*, 1975.

Klaus K Klostermaier, *A Survey of Hinduism*, State University of New York, 1994.

CHINESE THOUGHT

Tao te Ching, translated by John C H Wu, Shambala, 1989.

A C Graham, *Chuang Tzu The Inner Chapters: A Classic of Taoism*, Mandala, 1991.

Confucius, *The Analects*, translated with an introduction by D C Lau, Penguin Classics, 1979.

A Sourcebook in Chinese Philosophy translated and compiled by Wing-Tsit Chan, Princeton University Press, 1973.

David L Hall and Roger T Ames, *Thinking Through Confucius*, State University of New York, 1987.

JAPANESE THOUGHT

Moon in a Dewdrop Writings of Zen Master Dogen, edited by Kazuaki Tanahashi, Element Books, 1985.

Steven Heine, *Existential and Ontological Dimensions of Time in Heidegger and Dogen*, State University of New York, 1985.

Bernard Faure, *The Rhetoric of Immediacy: A Cultural Critique of Chan/Zen Buddhism*, Princeton University Press, 1991.

Bernard Faure, *Chan Insights and Oversights: An Epistemological Critique of the Chan Tradition*, Princeton University Press, 1993.

THE PHILOSOPHY OF SCIENCE

Introductory books covering a range of topics in the philosophy of science:

Losee, *An Historical Introduction to the Philosophy of Science* (3rd edition, Oxford University Press, 1993).

D Chalmers, *What is this Thing Called Science?* (2nd edition, Open University Press, 1982).

A O'Hear, *An Introduction to the Philosophy of Science*, Oxford University Press, 1989.

A Bird, *Philosophy of Science*, UCL Press, 1998.

More advanced books on this subject include:

Newton-Smith, *The Rationality of Science*, Routledge and Kegan Paul, 1981.

Hacking, *Representing and Intervening*, Cambridge University Press, 1983.

Popper's most famous work in which he introduces falsificationism is *The Logic of Scientific Discovery*, Hutchinson, 1980.

Hempel's view on confirmation can be found in his *Philosophy of Natural Science*, Prentice-Hall, 1966, which is an excellent introduction to many aspects of the philosophy of science.

Abductivism is advocated in Lipton's *Inference to the Best Explanation*, Routledge, 1993.

Van Fraassen advocates his version of anti-realism in *The Scientific Image*, Clarendon Press, 1980.

Kuhn introduces scientific revolutions in *The Structure of Scientific Revolutions*, Chicago University Press, 1970.

Feyerabend's views are advocated in *Against Method*, Verso, 1978.

Lakatos presents his account of progress in *The Methodology of Scientific Research Programmes, Philosophical Papers*, vol.1, Cambridge University Press, 1980.

A good introduction to the philosophy of physics is Powers *Philosophy and the New Physics*, Methuen, 1982.

A more demanding text on this is Sklar, *Philosophy of Physics*, Oxford University Press, 1992.

There are some superb recent collections of essays in the philosophy of biology, notably:

E Sober, *Conceptual Issues in Evolutionary Biology*, MIT Press (Volume 2), 1994.

D Hull and M Ruse, *The Philosophy of Biology*, Oxford University Press, 1998.

For Collections of essays on function and adaptation:

C Allen, M Bekoff and C Lauder *Nature's Purposes*, MIT Press, 1998.

D Buller, *Function and Design*, SUNY Press, 2000.

Evolutionary ethics is discussed in:

M Ridley, *The Origins of Virtue*, Viking, 1996.

E Sober and D S Wilson *Unto Others*, Harvard University Press, 1998.

General texts in philosophy of biology include:

E Sober, *The Philosophy of Biology*, 1994.

For the definitive statement of gene selectionism:

Richard Dawkins, *The Selfish Gene*, Oxford University Press, 1976.

THE PHILOSOPHY OF MIND

Robert Aitken, *The Gateless Barrier*, New York: Farrar Straus/NorthPoint, 1990.

James Austin, *Zen and the Brain*, Cambridge, MA: MIT Press, 1998.

John Blofeld, *The Zen Teachings of Huang Po*, Boston: Shambhala, 1994.

Paul Churchland, *The Engine of Reason, the Seat of the Soul*, Cambridge, MA: MIT Press, 1996.

Daniel Dennett, *Consciousness Explained*, Boston: Little, Brown, 1991.

Douglas Hofstadter and Daniel Dennett, (eds.), *The Mind's Eye*, New York: Bantam, 1981.

Ray Kurzweil, *The Age of Spiritual Machines*, New York: Viking, 1999.

William Lyons, (ed.), *Modern Philosophy of Mind*, Penguin Everyman Classics, 1995.

Isshu Miura and Ruth Fuller Sasaki, *The Zen Koan*, New York: Harcourt Brace, 1965.

David Rosenthal, (ed.), *The Nature of Mind*, Oxford: Oxford University Press, 1991.

John Searle, *The Rediscovery of the Mind*, Cambridge, MA: MIT Press, 1994.

ETHICS

Peter Singer, (ed.), *A Companion to Ethics*, Blackwell 1991.

Helga Kuhse and Peter Singer, (ed.), *A Companion to Bioethics*, Blackwell, 1998.

J P Sterba, (ed.), *Ethics: the big questions*, Blackwell, 1998.

Mary Warnock, *An Intelligent Person's Guide to Ethics*, Duckworth, 1998.

Andrew Belsey and Ruth Chadwick, (eds.), *Ethical Issues in Journalism and the Media*, Routledge, 1992.

Peter Singer, *How are we to live?*, Mandarin Paperbacks, 1994.

Philosophy and Practice of Medical Ethics published by the British Medical Association in 1988 (summary of main ethical statements).

Peter Singer, (ed.), *Applied Ethics*, OUP, 1986.

Colin Brown, *Crash Course in Christian Ethics*, Hodder & Stoughton, 1998.

O A Johnson, *Ethics: Selections from Classical and Contemporary Writers*, (7th edition) Harcourt Brace, 1994.

A Maclean, *The Elimination of Morality: reflections on Utilitarianism and Bioethics* Routledge, 1993.

Iris Murdoch, *Metaphysics as a Guide to Morals*, OUP, 1992.

Iris Murdoch, *The Sovereignty of Good*, Routledge, original version 1970, Ark Paperback, 1985.

On the Genealogy of Morals, F Nietzsche 1887, OUP, Oxford and New York; (trans.) D Smith 1996, World Classics series.

Lloyd Gerson, *God and Greek Philosophy: Studies in the Early History of Natural Theology*, Routledge, 1990.

Christopher Stead, *Philosophy in Christian Antiquity*, Cambridge University Press, 1994.

Oliver Leamen, *An Introduction to Medieval Islamic Philosophy*, Cambridge University Press, 1985.

Colette Sirat, *A History of Jewish Philosophy in the Middle Ages*, Cambridge University Press, 1985.

G R Evans, *Philosophy and Theology in the Middle Ages*, Routledge, 1993.

D S Luscombe, *Medieval Thought*, Oxford University Press, 1997.

Brian Copenhaver and Charles Schmitt, *Renaissance Philosophy*, Oxford University Press, 1994.

B Davies, (ed.), *Philosophy of Religion, A Guide to the Subject*, Cassell, 1998.

S Davis, *God, Reason and Theistic Proofs*, Edinburgh University Press, 1997.

C S Evans, *Faith Beyond Reason*, Edinburgh University Press, 1998.

P Helm, (ed.), *Faith and Reason*, Oxford University Press, 1999.

P Helm, *Faith and Understanding*, Edinburgh University Press, 1997.

P Helm, *Faith with Reason*, Oxford University Press, 2000.

R Le Poidevin, *Arguing for Atheism*, Routledge, 1997.

P L Quinn and C Taliaferro, (eds.), *A Companion to the Philosophy of Religion*, Blackwell, 1997.

Martin Stone, 'Philosophy of Religion' in *Philosophy*, (2nd edition), A C Grayling, Oxford University Press, 1998.

R Swinburne, *Faith and Reason*, Clarendon Press, 1981.

C Taliaferro, *Contemporary Philosophy of Religion*, Blackwell, 1998.

EASTERN PHILOSOPHY OF RELIGION

J Bowker, (ed.), *The Oxford Dictionary of World Religions*, Oxford University Press, 1997.

J Hinnells, (ed.), *A New Handbook of Living Religions*, Blackwell, 1997.

R C Zaehner, (ed.), *A Concise Encyclopaedia of Living Faiths*, (3rd edition), Hutchinson, 1977.

M and J Stutley, *A Dictionary of Hinduism,* *Its mythology, folklore and development 1500B.C. – A.D.1500*, Routledge and Kegan Paul, 1977.

S Radhakrishnan and C Moore, (eds.), *A Sourcebook in Indian Philosophy*, Princeton University Press, 1957.

W D O'Flaherty, *Textual Sources for the study of Hinduism*, Manchester University Press, 1988.

G Flood, *An Introduction to Hinduism*, Cambridge University Press, 1996.

D Goodhall, (ed.), *Hindu Scriptures*, Pheonix, 1996.

P Bowen, *Themes and Issues in Hinduism*, Cassell, 1998.

J Lipner, *Hindus: Their Beliefs and Practices*, Routledge, 1994.

Paul Deussen, *The Philosophy of the Upanishads*, Dover Publications, 1966.

P Harvey, *An Introduction to Buddhism*, Cambridge University Press, 1990.

R Gethin, *The Foundations of Buddhism*, Oxford University Press, 1998.

H Brechert and R Gombrich, (eds.), *The World of Buddhism: Buddhist monks and nuns in Society and Culture*, Thames and Hudson, 1984.

E Conze, *Buddhist Scriptures*, Penguin Books, 1978.

Denise Cush, *Buddhism*, Hodder and Stoughton, 1990.

H Saddhatissa, *The Buddha's Way*, Allen and Unwin, 1985.

W Rahula, *What the Buddha Taught*, Grove Press, 2nd edition, 1984.

T Ling, (ed.), *The Buddha's Philosophy of Man*, Dent Everyman, 1993.

Bhikku Nanmioli (Trans.), *Visddhimagga: The Path of Purification*, Kandy, The Buddhist Publication Society, 1991.

Bhikku Nanmoli and Bhikkhu Bohdi *The Middle Length Discourses of the Buddha*, Wisdom Publications, 1995.

M Walshe, (trans.) Digha Nikaya. *The Long Discourses of the Buddha*, Wisdom Publications, 1995.

P Williams, *Mahayana Buddhism: The Doctrinal Foundations*, Routledge, 1991.

R Gombrich, *Theravada Buddhism: A Social History from Ancient Benares to Modern Columbo*, Routledge, 1990.

M Carrithers and C Humphrey, (eds.), *The assembly of listeners: Jains in society*, Cambridge University Press, 1991.

P Dundas, *The Jains*, Routledge, 1992.

J Laidlaw, *Riches and Renunciation: Religion Economy and Society among the Jains*, Clarendon Press, 1995.

P S Jaini, *The Jaina Path of Purification*, University of California Press, 1979.

R Wilhelm, *Confucius and Confucianism*, Harcourt Brace Jovanovich, 1931.

Donald S Lopez, *Religions of China in Practice*, Princeton University Press, 1996.

Arthur Waley, *The Way and its Power*, Unwin Hyman, 1987.

Gilbert Rozman, (ed.), *The East Asia Region, Confucian Heritage And Its Modern Adaptation*, Princeton University Press, 1991.

L Thompson, *Chinese Religion: An Introduction*, Wadsworth, 1979.

Livia, Kohn, (eds.), *The Taoist Experience: An Anthology*, University of New York Press, 1993.

Gia-Fu Feng and Jane English, (trans.), *Tao te Ching*, Wildwood House, 1980.

LOGIC

B Carr and I Mahalingam, *The Companion Encyclopedia of Asian Philosophy*, Routledge, 1997.

Joseph Needham, *Science and Civilization in China*, Cambridge University Press, 1959.

B Russel, *Introduction to Mathematical Philosophy*, London, 1938.

A Church, *Introduction to Mathematical Logic*, Princeton, 1956.

E Nagel, and J R Newman, *Godel's Proof*, New York University Press, 1958.

THE PHILOSOPHY OF LANGUAGE

Bryan Magee, *Men of Ideas*, Viking, 1979.

David Crystal, *Cambridge Illustrated Encyclopaedia of Language*.

John Searle, *Speech Acts*, Cambridge University Press, 1969.

Ludwig Wittgenstein, *Philosophical Investigations*, Blackwell, 1967.

Dan Sperber and Deirdre Wilson, *Relevance*, Blackwell, 1995

Noam Chomsky, *Reflections on Language*, 1976.

John Lucy, *Selected Writings of Edward Sapir in language, culture and personality Language Diversity and Thought*, Cambridge University Press, 1992.

Richard Hudson, *Sociolinguistics*, Cambridge University Press, 1996.

PHILOSOPHY OF EDUCATION

R Barrow and R Woods, *An Introduction to Philosophy of Education*, (3rd edition), Routledge, 1988.

C M Hamm, *Philosophical Issues in Education*, Falmer Press, 1989.

J Dewey, *Experience and Education* (1938), Simon & Schuster (Touchstone edition), 1997.

John Locke, (ed.), R W Grant and W Tarcov, *Some Thoughts Concerning Education*, Hackett Publishing Co., 1996.

Bertrand Russell, *On Education* (1926), Unwin Paperbacks, 1985.

THE PHILOSOPHY OF ART

D Cooper, (ed.), *A Companion to Aesthetics* (currently the most available encylopedia of aesthetics), Blackwell, 1995.

M C Beardsley, *Aesthetics from Classical Greece to the Present*, University of Alabama Press, 1976.

Paul Guyer, *The Claims of Taste*, Cambridge University Press, 1997.

Paul Crowther, *The Kantian Sublime*, Clarendon Press, 1991.

U Eco, *Art and Beauty in the Middle Ages*, (trans.) H Bredin, Yale Nota Bene, 2002.

N Goodman, *Languages of Art*, Hackett, 1997.

A Harrison, *Philosophy and the Arts, seeing and believing*, Thoemmes Press, 1997.

Richard Wollheim, *Art and Its Objects*, (2nd edition), Cambridge University Press, 1980.

F Schier, *Deeper into Pictures*, Cambridge University Press, 1986.

R Scruton, *The Aesthetics of Music*, Clarendon Press, 1999.

Berel Lang, (ed.), *The Concept of Style*, Cornell University Press, 1993.

David Hume, 'The Standard of Taste' in *Essays Moral, Political, Literary*, Oxford.

Kant, *Critique of Pure Reason*, (trans.) N Kemp Smith, Macmillan.

Kant, *Critique of Judgement*, (trans.) J C Meredith, Oxford University Press.

Hegel, *Phenomonology of Spirit*, (trans.) A V Miller, Oxford University Press.

Hegel, *Aesthetics: Lectures on Fine Art*, Vols I-II, (trans.) T M Knox, Oxford University Press.

Schopenhauer, *The World as Will and Representation*, Vols.1-2, (trans.) E J Payne, Dover Publications.

Schopenhauer, *Essays and Aphorisms*, (trans.) R J Hollingdale, Penguin.

B Croce, *Guide to Aesthetics*, (trans.) P Romanell, Hackett Publishing.

R G Collingwood, *The Principles of Art*, Oxford University Press, 1968.

Clement Greenberg, *The Collected Essays and Criticism*, Vols.1-4, (ed.), J O'Brian, Chicago University Press.

T W Adorno, *Culture Industry Selected Essays on Mass Culture*, (ed.), Bernstien, Routledge.

W Benjamin, *Illuminations*, (trans.) H Zohn, Fontana Press.

G Battcock, (ed.), *Minimal Art: A Critical Anthology*, University of California Press.

Michael Fried, *Art and Objecthood*, 1967 in *Essays and Reviews*, University of Chicago Press.

Arthur Danto, *The Transfiguration of the Commonplace*, Harvard University Press.

Arthur Danto, *After the End of Art*, Princeton University Press.

EASTERN ART

R E Fisher, *Buddhist Art and Architecture*, Thames & Husdon, 1993.

Vidya Dehejia, *Indian Art*, Phaidon, 1997.

T Blurton, *Hindu Art*, British Museum Press, 1992.

Vessantara, *Meeting the Buddhas*, Windhorse Publications, 1998.

THE PHILOSOPHY OF HISTORY

Routledge Companion to Historiography, Routledge, 1997.

John Cannon, (ed.), *The Blackwell Dictionary of Historians*, Oxford, 1988.

The Past and its Presenters, John Warren Hodder & Stoughton, 1998, (this book includes an extensive bibliography for those wanting further information).

See also the classic texts giving particular interpretations of history e.g. Augustine *The City of God*, or Karl Marx in Marx and Engels *Basic Writings on Politics and Philosophy*, (ed.), Lewis S Feuer, Fontana, 1969, and particularly *The Communist Manifesto*.

THE PHILOSOPHY OF LAW AND POLITICS

Joel Feinberg, *Social Philosophy*, Prentice-Hall, 1973.

Murray Forsyth and Maurice Keens-Soper, (eds.), *The Political Classics: A Guide to the Essential Texts from Plato to Rousseau*, Oxford University Press, 1988.

Murray Forsyth and Maurice Keens-Soper, (eds.), *The Political Classics: Green to Dworkin*, Oxford University Press, 1996.

Martin Golding, *Philosophy of Law*, Prentice-Hall, 1975.

Gerald MacCallum, *Political Philosophy*, Prentice-Hall, 1987.

Kenneth Minogue, *Politics: A Very Short Introduction*, Oxford University Press, 1995.

John Plamenatz, *Man and Society*, 2 volumes, McGraw-Hill, 1963.

Anthony Quinton, 'Political Philosophy' in *The Oxford History of Western Philosophy*, (ed.), Anthony Kenny, Oxford University Press, 1994.

Leo Strauss and Joseph Cropsey, (eds.), *History of Political Philosophy*, (3rd edition), Chicago: The University of Chicago Press, 1987.

Jonathan Wolff, *An Introduction to Political Philosophy*, Oxford University Press, 1996.

A priori – thought or knowledge which is derived from a concept or principle known prior to experience.

Abdution – reasoning from evidence to the truth of the hypothesis which best explains that evidence; also known as *inference to the best explanation*.

Abhidharma – literally 'about the Dharma'; the name given to the collection of analytical writing that makes up one of the three collections of the Buddhist Tripitaka. Each school produced its own Abhidharma, though the concerns are the same: the examination of the dharmas and the relationship between them. The Abhidharma continued to influence Indian Buddhist thought until the decline of Buddhism in India after the 10th century.

Aesthetics – the study of taste and judgement in experience; used more generally for the philosophical examination of art and questions about the nature of beauty.

Ahimsa – the principle of non-violence; used in Jain, Buddhist and Hindu philosophy.

Analytic – the proposition can be analysed by the structure alone, i.e. can be said to be true by definition – the definition is understood by convention to apply to what it defines.

Anatta – Buddhist teaching that individual things lack inherent or independent existence, and thus that there is no permanent self or soul.

Anicca – the Pali term for 'impermanence' and the transitoriness of everything. It is one of the three universal marks of existence, central to all Buddhist teaching and practice.

Anti-realism (scientific) – the rejection of scientific realism (see below).

Arahant – used in both Buddhist and Jain philosophy for one who has attained complete insight. In Theravada Buddhist is particularly used of one who is bound to attain nibbana.

Asrava – inflow of karmic particles, in Jain philosophy.

Asvara – hindrances or impediments to liberation in Buddhist philosophy.

Atman – Sanskrit term for the soul or self.

Avatar – the descent of a god from heaven to earth, used particularly of the earthly forms taken by the Hindu deity Vishnu.

Avidya – This describes our ignorance, our distorted view of the world, which causes us suffering.

Axiological ethics – the study of the values and aims that underpin moral choices.

Behaviourism – the view that mind is a way of describing bodily action (see particularly the work of Gilbert Ryle).

Bhakti – the adoration and devotion of a personal deity, often manifesting itself in cults surrounding particular figures, for example Krishna. Devotional celebration and worship has been responsible for the bulk of literature, visual art and music in celebration of the chosen deity. *Bhakti-yoga* is the term for the path of liberation through devotion.

Bodhi – awakening or enlightenment.

Bodhisattva – literally, 'Enlightened Being'; evolving within Mahayana

Buddhism, a Bodhisattva is a figure who has, through aeons of spiritual effort reached liberation by practising generosity, ethics, patience, energy, meditation and insight. Bodhisattvas epitomise altruistic activity; remaining in cyclic existence in order to save others from the suffering.

Cartesian dualism – the absolute distinction between mind and matter, resulting from Descartes' systematic doubt, through which he concluded 'I think, therefore I am'.

Categorical imperative – an absolute obligation, independent of anticipated results, that forms the basis of moral action. Expounded particularly by Kant.

Ch'i – vital energy, a key term within Taoist philosophy. It denotes air, breath and also strength.

Cittamatra – translated as 'mind only', it describes the belief of the Yogacara School, that all experience derives from within the mind, implying that the perceived world is, in fact, a mental impression.

Complementarity – the idea in quantum physics that precise measurement of both of a pair of complementary properties is impossible.

Confirmation – the support lent by positive evidence to a hypothesis.

Deconstructualism – a method of describing and analysing reality which aims to show the arbitrariness and bias in all human understanding of the world as it is.

Deism – the belief in a rational and natural religion, based on the idea of a God known primarily through evidence of design in the universe.

Demarcation – differentiating science from non-science.

Dharma – a Sanskrit word that can mean simply 'thing' or 'reality'. It can also refer to 'truth' in the sense of the way in which the world is ordered, and by extension the teaching which reveals such truth. In Buddhism it is also used to describe the Buddha's teaching. In Ethics, it means right or appropriate action or duty.

Dharmapala – literally 'Guardian of the Dharma'; a Buddhist deity responsible for guarding the secrets of the Vajrayana and those who sincerely practice it beliefs. They are portrayed in wrathful, sometimes frightening forms and their major role is to protect the four doors of the mandala, repelling deep negative forces both internally and externally.

Dharsan – in Hinduism, dharsan refers to what is felt or experienced when in contact with the presence of a deity, usually though viewing the image. Dharsan can also be received when in the presence of a religious teacher or guru. In Buddhism, dharsan is also taken to mean inspirational vision.

Difference – this is a word Derrida created as a play on the meaning of the two French words, 'difference' (difference; diversity) and 'differer' (to postpone, or defer). In doing this Derrida combines both meanings. So, difference, in pointing to the difference between things, calls for meaning to be deferred and held in question.

Dukkha – Buddhist term for the unsatisfactoriness of all conditioned life, sometimes loosely translated as 'suffering' but with a broader, existential sense of the frustrations associated with the limitations of human existence.

Emotivism – ethical theory that identifies moral assertions with the expression of emotions. i.e. to say that something is wrong is merely to say that you dislike it.

Empiricism – a philosophical movement promoting the idea that nothing can be known without using the five human senses.

Epistemology – the branch of philosophy concerned with the nature and limits of human knowledge.

Existentialism – a philosophy concerned with the individual and the problems of human existence.

Falsificationism – Popper's doctrine that science proceeds by attempting to refute hypotheses.

Forms, theory of – used of Plato's view of the existence of universals, in which particular instances participate.

Hadith – records of the example of the Prophet Muhammad, used as a moral guide in Muslim ethics.

Hedonism – the moral view that the quest for one's own happiness is a valid criterion for the assessment of action, and an adequate goal for human life.

Historiography – the study of historical writing.

Humanism – a cultural movement, stemming from the rediscovery of the classical works of Greek philosophy and widely influential from the 15th to 17th centuries, emphasising the dignity of humankind and the centrality of human reason as opposed to the unquestioning acceptance of tradition. Humanism in the 20th century was particulary associated with the rejection of the traditional religious beliefs.

Hypothesis – a claim whose truth can only be known by inference from evidence.

Idealism – the view that knowledge starts with ideas rather than experience.

Ideology – the structure of ideas that forms the basis for a political or economic system.

Illocutionary – speech act is performed by virtue of the utterance being made, e.g. promising, threatening.

Incommensurability – a property shown by a pair of theories when they cannot be compared because there are no common standards of comparison, or because they are couched in languages which cannot be mutually translated.

Induction – reasoning from particular cases to some general claim.

Inference and Implicature – the process by which we derive meaning, even if not directly stated, from utterances or sentences versus the meanings or implications which can be drawn thereby.

Instrumentalism – the anti-realist view that scientific theories are to be regarded as instruments for generating accurate predictions.

Intuitionism – ethical theory that 'good' cannot be further defined, but is known by intuition.

Jen (or Ren) – Confucian term for 'humaneness', the central virtue incorporating humanity, love and benevolence.

Jina – literally 'conqueror', an honorific title given to the 24 Jain religious teachers (Tirankaras), and from which the term 'Jain' is derived.

Jiva – in Hindu thought this refers to the living soul within a body. In Jain thought is is one of the two categories into which everything must fall: the living soul, pure and eternal, which dwells in all living beings.

Ju (Japanese) – a term for praise or eulogy.

Just sitting meditation – the form of meditation predominant in the Soto Zen School. The meditation practice requires stilling the mind of all activity, in order to experience the innate Buddha quality already present.

Karma – the idea that actions (good or bad) produce effects for the person who performs them in this or future lives, found in slightly different forms in Hinduism, Buddhism and Jainism. The literal meaning of karma is 'action', but it is loosely used of the effects of action. *Karma yoga*: the way of liberation based on selfless action.

Kevala jnana – a state of total knowledge, in Jain philosophy. Denotes also freedom from all impurities of mind and body, and from karmic influences.

Koan – in Rinzai Zen, a paradox in the form of a question or statement given by the Master to the student to use in meditation. In the process of trying to grasp the koan the student has no choice but to let go of all conceptualizations and logical understanding if the koan is to bring about increasing levels of awareness.

Lakshana – characteristic or attribute, real and fanciful, that indicates spiritual status. (e.g. It was thought that the Buddha displayed thirty-two, including the protuberance on his crown, which is depicted as a topknot of hair, and webbed fingers.)

Langue and *Parole* – Ferdinand de Saussure's terms for the system of a language, akin to Chomsky's 'competence', versus the actual situated utterance of an individual speaker, akin to Chomsky's 'performance'.

Li – Confucial term for social etiquette.

Linga – a symbolic form of Shiva representing fertility and creative energy in the shape of a phallic pillar. The energy the pillar symbolizes is a spiritual quality, rather than sexual in the accepted sense, and to suggest as much, would be to impoverish its meaning. Symbolically, sexual imagery can mean the union and the

transcendence of opposites and Shiva himself is often portrayed as being half male and half female, united in one body.

Logical Positivism – the view, taken by the Vienna Circle and others, that the meaning of statements (other than analytic statements) is given with reference to sense experience.

Logos – Greek term, literally 'word' used by the Stoics to indicate the fundamental rational nature of the universe. Used also within Christian thought as the word of creation, identified with Christ.

Mandala – a mandala can be made in two or three dimension, and are common throughout the Buddhist world. They can be highly complex, involving layers of meaning and represent the universe internally and externally.

Maya – in Hinduism, the word maya is used to describe the insubstantial, illusionary nature of the world in contrast to the Absolute Reality.

Meta-ethics – the study of the nature and justification of ethical language.

Metanarrative – an overall framework used to interpret the past (used within the Philosophy of History).

Metaphysics – the human search beyond the world of the senses to discover why the world is as it is.

Methodology – the study of scientific method; a theory about scientific method.

moksha – liberation or release from suffering and rebirth (used within Indian religious philosophy).

Monism – the view that everything that is, is part of a united whole.

Mono no aware – phrase used to describe a cultural mood that evolved in Japan

in the 10th century and which continues to inform the Japanese psyche to the present day. The Buddhist awareness of change combined with the notion of 'Mappo', a belief that civilization will eventually disintegrate, created a mood of reflective melancholy in response to the beauty of the passing moment and the transience of life.

Mudra – hand gestures used in ritual and depicted in images, they may for example indicate giving, meditation or teaching.

Murti – Indian term for a statue or image of a god or goddess.

Natural Law – the rational interpretation of the structures of existence as a guide to moral and political thought.

Nirvana (*nibbana* in Pali) – translated as 'extinction', it refers to the liberation from negative states of craving, hatred and delusion, leaving the experience of Enlightenment.

Ontology/Ontological – the study of the nature of being itself.

Ostensive Definition – defining by showing or pointing. Presupposes idea of direct correspondence between item and its definition.

Panentheism – the idea (associated, for example, with Spinoza) that God is within all things.

Paradigm – in Kuhn's philosophy of science a framework which guides and constrains scientific research, consisting of a central theory, great texts, standard techniques and problem solutions.

Paticca-samuppada – conditioned co-production, or interconnectedness; fundamental term for the Buddhist view of conditioned reality.

Perlocutionary Force – speech act is defined by reference to the effect it has on the hearer, e.g. beliefs, fears.

Phenomenology – the philosophical view that sees the human task of interpreting the world as phenomenal (i.e. as objects of perception rather than as facts or occurrences that exist independently).

Positivism – an empiricist philosophy which rejects as meaningless metaphysical views and hypotheses about the unobservable.

Postmodernism – the modern philosophy that concentrates on cultural and social phenomena that shows that no global explanation of conduct or meaning is credible in an age in which rationality is so problematic.

Prajnaparamita – literally 'Perfection of Wisdom'; the name given to thirty-five Mahayanan texts, the production of which span a number of centuries from 100BCE onwards. They concern transcendental wisdom, that is, knowledge of things as they really and ultimately are, beyond duality of subject and object.

Prasad – in Hinduism, offerings, usually money, food, flowers and incense, made to a deity. After being offered they are used to decorate the shrine and being blessed by the deity, they are then returned as prasad.

Prescriptivism – theory that equates an ethical assertion with the prescribing of a course of action.

Puja – used both in Hinduism and Buddhism to donate the practice of paying respect and reverence to a chosen deity or the Buddha.

Purusha – in the Yoga system, the word is used to mean person or self. In Samkhya it is used alongside Prakriti, the latter being the object that is known, and purusha the knowing subject, together forming the basis of Samkhya's view of reality. Purusha also has the sense of being the unchanging principle of intelligence behind the universe.

Rationalism – the appeal to reason rather than experience as the source of all knowledge.

Realism (scientific) – the view that science aims at uncovering truths about unobservable entities, processes and laws – and that science to some extent succeeds in this.

Rebirth – the notion that one life-time follows the next in a cycle of rebirth and death, the direction of past, present and future lives being determined by karma. Both Buddhism and Hinduism uphold rebirth but differ over exactly who or what is reborn.

Reductionism – a philosophical approach which regards complex entities as 'no more than' their constituent parts.

Relativism (ethical relativism) – the view that, in both social and ethical terms, there are no absolutes, but all is dependent upon the wishes of particular individuals or societies.

Relativism – the view that there is no absolute truth but that what is true is relative to some community or tradition.

Research programme – a sequence of theories which share a common theoretical core.

Sac'c'itananda – Vedantic term describing liberation, comprising sat (being), c'it (mind) and ananda (bliss).

Samsara – Indian term for the experienced world, of which the key feature is impermanence, and its ceaseless cycles of birth and death.

Samvara – cessation of the inflow of karmic particles, in Jain philosophy.

Sanatana dharma – Sanskrit term meaning 'eternal teaching', taken to embody the eternal principles of goodness, honesty and purity in personal, social and religious matters.

Sangha – refers to those who follow the Buddhist path in general and those who are members of a monastic community in particular.

Satori – Satori is the word used to describe a sudden awareness or realization, leading to the state of enlightenment. Satori can be progressive, leading to ever deepening states of realization.

Satya – Sanskrit term for 'truth', in the Rig Veda this can indicate the ultimate nature of reality, or eternal truth.

Scepticism – a view which doubts any claims to knowledge and certainty.

Scholasticism – a theological and philosophical method taught in the schools of medieval Europe (especially 12th-14th centuries) which tried to integrate orthodox Christian teaching with Aristotelian and Platonic philosophy.

Shakti – a term used to describe the female energy in the universe and is a generic term for the archetypal goddess. Also thought of as Divine Mother or Devi, Shakti has many names. As Parvati, she is Shiva's consort, and is worshipped with him at Maduria, as Minakshi, probably as a vestige of a more ancient goddess cult. She also appears in a benign form as Sarasvati, a goddess associated with music and speech, and Kali, a wrathful form associated with death and destruction.

Shakyamuni – This is the name given to the historical Buddha who was born into the Shakya clan, it means 'Sage of the Shakyas'.

Shunyata – commonly translated as 'emptiness' or 'voidness', though these two words can be misleading. It is the core teaching of the Prajnaparamita texts; a complex and profound concept, based on the notion of an absence of inherent existence or a real 'self' in anything. This extends to ideas themselves, in that anything we can conceive of is inevitably limited.

Structuralism – an approach to the study of language and the social sciences seeking to uncover underlying structures and organizing principles within language and society.

Stupa – a solid, earthen burial mound. Early ones contained the ashes of the Buddha. Subsequent ones were built to hold the relics of notable Buddhist figures or even religious texts. They became the subject of veneration, symbolizing the Buddha's death or Parinarvana. Variations on the original form appear across the Buddhist world, notably the pagoda in China and Japan, and the chorten in Tibet.

Sutra – the word sutra means 'thread'. A sutra is a discourse given by the Buddha.

Synthetic – the truth of the proposition may only be sought with reference to the outside world, i.e. the way things are.

Tanha – Buddhist term (literally 'thirst') for craving, attachment or desire.

Tao – 'the way', key term of Taoist philosophy; has the sense of fundamental source of life and also a sense of order and stability within the universe of experience.

Te – Confucian term for energy or power, as manifested in that which is at one with the *Tao*.

Thangka – the name given to painted images used in Tibetan Buddhism for devotional and meditational purposes. Painted on cloth, the images vary in size and are easy to roll up and transport. The images derive from the vast store of Tibetan Buddhist iconography and are considered sacred, as, once the deity has been painted, it is thought its presence resides in the thangka.

Tripitaka – the Buddha's teachings were eventually formed into three groups, collectively called the Tripitaka. The Tripitaka is made up of the Vinaya Pitaka, concerned with monastic rules and discipline, the Sutra Pitaka, concerned with discourses, and the Abhidharma Pitaka, concerned with the analytical examination of the Dharma.

Utilitarianism – ethical theory in which actions are justified in terms of the anticipated benefit they offer, commonly expressed in the phrase 'the greatest good to the greatest number'.

Varna – literally 'colour', it refers to the major caste divisions in Indian society.

Verisimilitude – nearness or approximation to the truth.

Virtue ethics – moral theory based on the cultivation of those qualities and virtues thought to embody the good life, rather than on absolute rules or the anticipated results of action.

Wu Wei – literally 'no action' it is used within Taoist philosophy to denote action that is natural and spontaneous.

Yoga – Indian term for a discipline or method of self cultivation.

Yoni – the female counterpart of the *linga*, a stylized representation of a vulva in the form of a dish-shaped object on which the linga stands. As such it is the non-representational form of the archetypal goddess or Devi, and is synonymous with the female aspect of Shiva.

INDEX

ACKNOWLEDGEMENTS

The publishers would like to thank the following for supplying copyright images for inclusion in this book:

Anglo Australian Telescope Board: 153;
The Art Archive: 239, 242, 253, 255, 257, 258, 275, 290;
Ashmolean Museum: 297;
Associated Press: 102, 284;
BFI film stills, posters and designs: 247 right;
British Museum: 188, 307;
Colour Library International: 11, 16, 227;
Corbis: 41, 43, 45, 67, 70, 72, 82, 113, 143, 235, 249, 251, 262, 292, 299, 309, 313, 325, 327, 329, 333;
Finlay Holiday Films: 116, 177;
Flora London Marathon: 85;
Fox Photos: 59;
Gary parfill Archives: 301;
Heather Angel: 111;
Hella Bachs, Cairo: 97;
Horniman Museum: 271;
Hulton Archive: 25, 69, 172, 173, 174, 193, 197, 202, 207, 232, 240, 244, 260, 267;
Imperial War Museum: 179, 247 left, 303, 315;
John & Penny Hubley (via B T Batsford): 184;
The Kobal Collection: 282;
Llewellyn-Jones, M: 231;
Methodist Archive: 178;
Mrs Armitage, Manchester: 162;
NASA: title verso, 9, 93, 115, 170;
National Portrait Gallery: 118;
Photo Buloz, Paris: 19;
Photographic Bureau, S P G (1960): 272;
Reuters: 74, 279, 330;
R M Adam, Royal Botanical Gardens, Edinburgh: 221;
Royal Observatory, Edinburgh: 109;
Science Photo Library: 125;
The Photo Source: 164;
The Weinar Library: 95;
Thompson, J D: 186;
Thompson, M: 3, 10, 22, 31, 34, 36, 46, 57, 94, 131, 132, 137, 138, 155, 156, 169, 185, 195, 236, 287, 311;
Thompson, R J: half title, 12, 21, 24, 29, 47, 48, 59, 60, 147, 161, 175, 199, 264, 269, 321 and all Chinese and Japanese calligraphy.
US Navy Observatory: 77, 121;
United Kingdom Atomic Energy Authority: 107;
Victoria & Albert Museum: 189, 281;
Welcome Institute: 33;

The following images were taken from the photographic archive held by Chrysalis Group plc, the publisher: 14, 17, 18, 20, 27, 39, 50, 52, 53, 54, 58, 62, 79, 80, 87, 99, 105, 110, 119, 123, 129, 151, 158, 163, 167, 176, 180, 183, 187, 190, 191, 200, 203, 208, 209, 217, 225, 273, 286, 289, 296, 317.

The remaining images have been taken from sources that are free of copyright.